Microsoft® Excel 2000 Formulas

Microsoft® Excel 2000 Formulas

John Walkenbach

M&T Books
An imprint of IDG Books Worldwide, Inc.

Foster City, CA ◆ Chicago, IL ◆ Indianapolis, IN ◆ New York, NY

Microsoft® Excel 2000 Formulas

Published by
M&T Books
An imprint of IDG Books Worldwide, Inc.
919 E. Hillsdale Blvd., Suite 400
Foster City, CA 94404
www.idgbooks.com (IDG Books Worldwide Web site)

Copyright © 1999 IDG Books Worldwide, Inc. All rights reserved. No part of this book, including interior design, cover design, and icons, may be reproduced or transmitted in any form, by any means (electronic, photocopying, recording, or otherwise) without the prior written permission of the publisher.

ISBN: 0-7645-4609-0

Printed in the United States of America

10 9 8 7 6 5 4 3 2 1

1B/RV/RQ/ZZ/FC

Distributed in the United States by IDG Books Worldwide, Inc.

Distributed by CDG Books Canada Inc. for Canada; by Transworld Publishers Limited in the United Kingdom; by IDG Norge Books for Norway; by IDG Sweden Books for Sweden; by IDG Books Australia Publishing Corporation Pty. Ltd. for Australia and New Zealand; by TransQuest Publishers Pte Ltd. for Singapore, Malaysia, Thailand, Indonesia, and Hong Kong; by Gotop Information Inc. for Taiwan; by ICG Muse, Inc. for Japan; by Intersoft for South Africa; by Eyrolles for France; by International Thomson Publishing for Germany, Austria and Switzerland; by Distribuidora Cuspide for Argentina; by LR International for Brazil; by Galileo Libros for Chile; by Ediciones ZETA S.C.R. Ltda. for Peru; by WS Computer Publishing Corporation, Inc., for the Philippines; by Contemporanea de Ediciones for Venezuela; by Express Computer Distributors for the Caribbean and West Indies; by Micronesia Media Distributor, Inc. for Micronesia; by Chips Computadoras S.A. de C.V. for Mexico; by Editorial Norma de Panama S.A. for Panama; by American Bookshops for Finland.

For general information on IDG Books Worldwide's books in the U.S., please call our Consumer Customer Service department at 800-762-2974. For reseller information, including discounts and premium sales, please call our Reseller Customer Service department at 800-434-3422.

For information on where to purchase IDG Books Worldwide's books outside the U.S., please contact our International Sales department at 317-596-5530 or fax 317-596-5692.

For consumer information on foreign language translations, please contact our Customer Service department at 800-434-3422, fax 317-596-5692, or e-mail rights@idgbooks.com.

For information on licensing foreign or domestic rights, please phone +1-650-655-3109.

For sales inquiries and special prices for bulk quantities, please contact our Sales department at 650-655-3200 or write to the address above.

For information on using IDG Books Worldwide's books in the classroom or for ordering examination copies, please contact our Educational Sales department at 800-434-2086 or fax 317-596-5499.

For press review copies, author interviews, or other publicity information, please contact our Public Relations department at 650-655-3000 or fax 650-655-3299.

For authorization to photocopy items for corporate, personal, or educational use, please contact Copyright Clearance Center, 222 Rosewood Drive, Danvers, MA 01923, or fax 978-750-4470.

Library of Congress Cataloging-in-Publication Data

Walkenback, John
    Microsoft Excel 2000 formulas / John Walkenback
        p.   cm.
    Includes index.
    ISBN 0-7645-4609-0 (alk. paper)
    1. Microsoft Excel for Windows.   2. Business--Computer programs.   3. Electronic spreadsheets.
    I. Title.
HF5548.4.M523W3458   1999
005.369--dc21   99-38070
                                                       CIP

Trademarks: All brand names and product names used in this book are trade names, service marks, trademarks, or registered trademarks of their respective owners. IDG Books Worldwide is not associated with any product or vendor mentioned in this book.

®is a registered trademark or trademark under exclusive license to IDG Books Worldwide, Inc. from International Data Group, Inc. in the United States and/or other countries.

is a trademark of IDG Books Worldwide, Inc.

ABOUT IDG BOOKS WORLDWIDE

Welcome to the world of IDG Books Worldwide.

IDG Books Worldwide, Inc., is a subsidiary of International Data Group, the world's largest publisher of computer-related information and the leading global provider of information services on information technology. IDG was founded more than 30 years ago by Patrick J. McGovern and now employs more than 9,000 people worldwide. IDG publishes more than 290 computer publications in over 75 countries. More than 90 million people read one or more IDG publications each month.

Launched in 1990, IDG Books Worldwide is today the #1 publisher of best-selling computer books in the United States. We are proud to have received eight awards from the Computer Press Association in recognition of editorial excellence and three from Computer Currents' First Annual Readers' Choice Awards. Our best-selling ...*For Dummies*® series has more than 50 million copies in print with translations in 31 languages. IDG Books Worldwide, through a joint venture with IDG's Hi-Tech Beijing, became the first U.S. publisher to publish a computer book in the People's Republic of China. In record time, IDG Books Worldwide has become the first choice for millions of readers around the world who want to learn how to better manage their businesses.

Our mission is simple: Every one of our books is designed to bring extra value and skill-building instructions to the reader. Our books are written by experts who understand and care about our readers. The knowledge base of our editorial staff comes from years of experience in publishing, education, and journalism — experience we use to produce books to carry us into the new millennium. In short, we care about books, so we attract the best people. We devote special attention to details such as audience, interior design, use of icons, and illustrations. And because we use an efficient process of authoring, editing, and desktop publishing our books electronically, we can spend more time ensuring superior content and less time on the technicalities of making books.

You can count on our commitment to deliver high-quality books at competitive prices on topics you want to read about. At IDG Books Worldwide, we continue in the IDG tradition of delivering quality for more than 30 years. You'll find no better book on a subject than one from IDG Books Worldwide.

John Kilcullen
Chairman and CEO
IDG Books Worldwide, Inc.

Steven Berkowitz
President and Publisher
IDG Books Worldwide, Inc.

Eighth Annual Computer Press Awards ≥ 1992

Ninth Annual Computer Press Awards ≥ 1993

Tenth Annual Computer Press Awards ≥ 1994

Eleventh Annual Computer Press Awards ≥ 1995

IDG is the world's leading IT media, research and exposition company. Founded in 1964, IDG had 1997 revenues of $2.05 billion and has more than 9,000 employees worldwide. IDG offers the widest range of media options that reach IT buyers in 75 countries representing 95% of worldwide IT spending. IDG's diverse product and services portfolio spans six key areas including print publishing, online publishing, expositions and conferences, market research, education and training, and global marketing services. More than 90 million people read one or more of IDG's 290 magazines and newspapers, including IDG's leading global brands — Computerworld, PC World, Network World, Macworld and the Channel World family of publications. IDG Books Worldwide is one of the fastest-growing computer book publishers in the world, with more than 700 titles in 36 languages. The "...For Dummies®" series alone has more than 50 million copies in print. IDG offers online users the largest network of technology-specific Web sites around the world through IDG.net (http://www.idg.net), which comprises more than 225 targeted Web sites in 55 countries worldwide. International Data Corporation (IDC) is the world's largest provider of information technology data, analysis and consulting, with research centers in over 41 countries and more than 400 research analysts worldwide. IDG World Expo is a leading producer of more than 168 globally branded conferences and expositions in 35 countries including E3 (Electronic Entertainment Expo), Macworld Expo, ComNet, Windows World Expo, ICE (Internet Commerce Expo), Agenda, DEMO, and Spotlight. IDG's training subsidiary, ExecuTrain, is the world's largest computer training company, with more than 230 locations worldwide and 785 training courses. IDG Marketing Services helps industry-leading IT companies build international brand recognition by developing global integrated marketing programs via IDG's print, online and exposition products worldwide. Further information about the company can be found at www.idg.com.   1/24/99

Credits

ACQUISITIONS EDITOR
Greg Croy

DEVELOPMENT EDITOR
Terry O'Donnell
Terri Varveris

TECHNICAL EDITOR
Greg Guntle

COPY EDITOR
Victoria Lee

PROJECT COORDINATORS
Linda Marousek
Tom Debolski

PRODUCTION
Mario Amador
Stephanie Hollier
Jude Levinson
Ramses Ramiriz

QUALITY CONTROL SPECIALIST
Chris Weisbart

PROOFREADING AND INDEXING
York Production Services

BOOK DESIGNER
Jim Donohue

COVER IMAGE
© TSM/Lightscapes Inc. 1999

About the Author

John Walkenbach is a leading authority on spreadsheet software, and principal of JWalk and Associates Inc. — a Southern California-based consulting firm that specializes in spreadsheet application development. John is the author of about 30 spreadsheet books, and has written more than 300 articles and reviews for a variety of publications, including *PC World, InfoWorld, PC Magazine, Windows*, and *PC/Computing*. Currently, he's contributing editor for *PC World*, and writes the magazine's monthly "Here's How" spreadsheet tips column. He also maintains a popular Internet Web site (*The Spreadsheet Page,* www.j-walk.com/ss), and is the developer of the Power Utility Pak, an award-winning add-in for Microsoft Excel. John graduated from the University of Missouri, and earned a masters degree and a Ph.D. degree from the University of Montana.

John's other interests include guitar, MIDI music, novels, digital photography, and gardening.

This one's for Michelle.

Preface

Greetings, computer book consumer...

You're either standing around in a bookstore trying to decide which Excel book to buy, or (better yet) you've already made your choice and you're leafing through your purchase to assure yourself that you made a good decision. If the former, just buy it and stop loitering. If you're at all interested in developing killer formulas in Excel, this book is as good as it will get. If you already own the book, thanks. I'm confident that you'll agree that you invested your money wisely.

Why I Wrote This Book

I approached this project with one goal in mind: To write the ultimate Excel book that would appeal to a broad base of users. That's a pretty ambitious goal, but I think I've accomplished it.

I spend a lot of time participating in the Excel newsgroups on the Internet, and I also write the monthly "Here's How" spreadsheet tips column for *PC World* magazine. Consequently, I think I have an excellent perspective on what people actually do with spreadsheets. I'm familiar with the types of questions that come up time and time again. Much of the material in this book was inspired by questions on the Excel newsgroups, and this book provides the answers to those questions.

As you probably know, most bookstores offer dozens of Excel books - some good, some bad, and some downright ugly. The vast majority of these books are general-purpose user guides that explain how to use the features available in Excel. A few others focus on advanced issues such as macro programming or scientific applications. None (that's right, none!) hone in on the one fundamental component of Excel that is critically important to every user: formulas. Think about it. Have you ever developed a spreadsheet that *didn't* use formulas? Fact is, formulas are what make a spreadsheet a spreadsheet. The more you know about formulas, the better your spreadsheets will be. It's that simple.

Excel is the spreadsheet market leader, by a long shot. This is the case not only because of Microsoft's enormous marketing clout, but because it is truly the best spreadsheet available. One area in which Excel's superiority is most apparent is formulas. Excel has some special tricks up its sleeve in the formulas department. As you'll see, Excel enables you to do things with formulas that are impossible with other spreadsheets.

It's a safe bet that only about 10 percent of Excel users really understand how to get the most out of worksheet formulas. In this book, I attempt to nudge you into that elite group. Are you up to it?

What You Should Know

This is *not* a book for beginning Excel users. If you have absolutely no experience with Excel, this may not be the best book for you - unless you're one of a rare breed who can learn a new software product almost instantaneously.

To get the most out of this book, you should have some background using Excel. Specifically, this book assumes that you know how to:

- ◆ Create workbooks, insert sheets, save files, and other basic tasks

- ◆ Navigate through a workbook

- ◆ Use Excel's menus, toolbars, and dialog boxes

- ◆ Use basic Windows features, such as file management and copy and paste techniques.

If you're an experienced spreadsheet user, but you are new to Excel, Chapter 1 presents a concise overview of what this product has to offer.

What You Should Have

To make the best use of this book, you need a copy of Microsoft Excel. When I wrote this book, I used both Excel 97 and Excel 2000 for Windows. With very few exceptions (noted in the text), the material in this book also applies to all earlier versions of Excel that are still in use.

To use the examples on the companion CD-ROM, you need a CD-ROM drive. Duh! The examples on the CD-ROM are discussed further in the "About the Companion CD-ROM" section later in this preface.

 I use Excel for Windows, and do not own a Macintosh. Therefore, I can't guarantee that all of the examples will work with Excel for Macintosh. Excel's cross-platform compatibility is pretty good, but it's definitely not perfect.

As far as hardware goes, the faster the better. And, of course, the more memory in your system, the happier you'll be.

Conventions in This Book

Take a minute to skim this section and learn some of the typographic conventions used throughout this book.

Keyboard conventions

You need to use the keyboard to enter formulas. In addition, you can work with menus and dialog boxes directly from the keyboard — a method you may find easier if your hands already are positioned over the keys.

FORMULA LISTINGS

Formulas usually appear on a separate line in `monospace font`. For example, I may list the following formula:

```
=VLOOKUP(StockNumber,PriceList,2,False)
```

Excel supports a special type of formula known as an array formula. When you enter an array formula, press Ctrl+Shift+Enter (not just Enter). Excel encloses an array formula in brackets in order to remind you that it's an array formula. When I list an array formula, I include the brackets to make it clear that it is, in fact, an array formula. For example:

```
{=SUM(LEN(A1:A10))}
```

 Do not type the brackets for an array formula. Excel puts them in automatically.

VBA CODE LISTINGS

This book contains examples of VBA code. Each listing appears in a `monospace font`; each line of code occupies a separate line. To make the code easier to read, I usually use one or more tabs to create indentations. Indentation is optional, but it does help to delineate statements that go together.

If a line of code doesn't fit on a single line in this book, I use the standard VBA line continuation sequence: a space followed by an underscore character. This indicates that the line of code extends to the next line. For example, the following two lines comprise a single VBA statement:

```
If Right(cell.Value, 1) = "!" Then cell.Value _
    = Left(cell.Value, Len(cell.Value) - 1)
```

You can enter this code either exactly as shown on two lines, or on a single line without the trailing underscore character.

KEY NAMES

Names of keys on the keyboard appear in normal type. When you press two keys simultaneously, the keys are connected with a plus sign: "Press Ctrl+G to display the Go To dialog box." Here's a list of the key names used throughout the book:

Alt	Down arrow	Num Lock	Right arrow
Backspace	End	Scroll Lock	Shift
Caps Lock	Home	PgDn	Tab
Ctrl	Insert	PgUp	
Del	Left arrow	Up arrow	

FUNCTIONS, PROCEDURES, AND NAMED RANGES

Excel's worksheet functions appear in all uppercase, like so: "Enter a SUM formula in cell C20." Macro and procedure names appear in normal type: "Execute the InsertTotals procedure." I often use mixed upper- and lowercase to make these names easier to read. Named ranges appear in italic: "Select the *InputArea* range."

Unless you're dealing with text inside of quotation marks, Excel is not sensitive to case. In other words, both of the following formulas produce the same result:

```
=SUM(A1:A50)
=sum(a1:a50)
```

Excel, however, converts the characters in the second formula to uppercase.

Mouse Conventions

The mouse terminology in this book is all standard fare: "pointing," "clicking," "right-clicking," "dragging," and so on. You know the drill.

What the Icons Mean

Throughout the book, *icons* are used to call your attention to particularly important points.

 This icon indicates a new feature in Excel and in what versions this feature is available or unavailable.

I use Note icons to tell you that something is important — perhaps a concept that may help you master the task at hand or something fundamental for understanding subsequent material.

Tip icons indicate a more efficient way of doing something, or a technique that may not be obvious. These often impress your officemates.

These icons indicate that an example file is on the companion CD-ROM. (See the following "About the Companion CD-ROM" section.)

I use Caution icons when the operation that I'm describing can cause problems if you're not careful.

I use the Cross Reference icon to refer you to other chapters that have more to say on a particular topic.

How This Book Is Organized

There are hundreds of ways to organize this material, but I settled on a scheme that divides the book into five main parts. In addition, I've included a few appendixes that provide supplemental information that you may find helpful.

Part I: Basic Information

This part is introductory in nature, and consists of Chapters 1 through 3. Chapter 1 sets the stage with a quick and dirty overview of Excel designed for readers who are new to Excel but have used other spreadsheet products. In Chapter 2, I cover the basics of formulas - this is absolutely essential reading in order to get the most out of this book. Chapter 3 deals with names. If you thought names were just for cells and ranges, you're missing out on quite a bit!

Part II: Using Functions in Your Formulas

This part consists of Chapters 4 through 11. Chapter 4 covers the basics of using worksheet functions in your formulas. I get more specific in subsequent chapters. Chapter 5 deals with manipulating text; Chapter 6 covers dates and times; and Chapter 7 explores various counting techniques. In Chapter 8, *we* discuss various types of lookup formulas. Other chapters in this part deal with databases and lists, financial calculations, and miscellaneous calculations such as unit conversions and rounding.

Part III: Array Formulas

This part consists of Chapters 12 and 13. The majority of Excel users know little or nothing about array formulas - a topic that happens to be dear to me. Therefore, I devote an entire part to this little-used, yet extremely powerful, feature.

Part IV: Miscellaneous Formula Techniques

This part consists of Chapters 14 through 19. They cover a variety of topics — some of which, on the surface, may appear to have nothing to do with formulas. Chapter 14 demonstrates that a circular reference can be a good thing. In Chapter 15, you'll see why formulas can be important when you work with charts. Chapter 16 covers formulas as they relate to pivot tables. Chapter 17 contains some very interesting (and useful) formulas that you can use in conjunction with Excel's conditional formatting and data validation features. Chapter 18 covers a topic that I call "megaformulas." A megaformula is a huge formula that takes the place of several intermediary formulas. And what do you do when your formulas don't work correctly? Consult Chapter 19 for some debugging techniques.

Part V: Developing Custom Worksheet Functions

This part consists of Chapters 20 through 23. This part explores Visual Basic for Applications (VBA) — the key to creating custom worksheet functions. Chapter 20 introduces VBA and the VB Editor, and Chapter 21 provides some necessary background on custom worksheet functions. Chapter 22 covers programming concepts, and Chapter 23 provides a slew of worksheet function examples that you can use as-is, or customize for your own needs.

Appendixes

What's a computer book without appendixes? This book has five appendixes. In the appendixes, you'll find secrets about importing 1-2-3 files, a reference guide to Excel's worksheet functions, tips on using custom number formats, and a handy guide to Excel resources on the Internet. The final appendix describes all of the files on the CD-ROM.

How to Use This Book

You can use this book any way you please. If you choose to read it cover to cover while lounging on a sunny beach in Maui, that's fine with me. More likely, you'll want to keep it within arm's reach while you toil away in your dimly lit cubicle.

Due to the nature of the subject matter, the chapter order is often immaterial. Most readers probably will skip around, picking up useful tidbits here and there. The material contains many examples, designed to help you identify a relevant formula quickly. When faced with a challenging task, you may want to check the index first to see whether the book specifically addresses your problem.

About the Companion CD-ROM

The inside back cover of this book contains a CD-ROM that consists of three basic elements:

♦ Example workbooks that demonstrate concepts presented in the text

♦ A trial copy of my Power Utility Pak 2000 – a popular Excel add-in

♦ A demo copy of my Sound-Proof add-in. Sound-Proof is a handy auditing tool that uses a synthesized voice to read the contents of cells.

The files on the companion CD-ROM are not compressed, so you can access them directly from the CD-ROM (installation not required). The exception is Power Utility Pak and Sound-Proof, both of which require installation. Refer to Appendix E for details.

About the Power Utility Pak Offer

Toward the back of the book, you'll find a coupon that you can redeem for a discounted copy of my award-winning Power Utility Pak – a collection of useful Excel utilities, plus many new worksheet functions. I developed this package using VBA exclusively.

You also can use this coupon to purchase the complete VBA source code for a nominal fee. Studying the code is an excellent way to pick up some useful programming techniques. You can take the product for a test drive by installing the shareware version from the companion CD-ROM.

 The trial version of Power Utility Pak requires Excel 97 for Windows or later.

Reach Out

After you have had a chance to become familiar with this book, take a moment to register this book on the `http://my2cents.idgbooks.com` Web site. (Details are listed in the my2cents page in the back of this book.) Be honest with your evaluation. I can take it. If you thought a particular chapter didn't tell you enough, let me know. If you picked up a formula that saved you a few hours time, let me know about that as well. And if you have suggestions for future editions, please send them my way.

Unfortunately, I'm not able to reply to specific questions. The Excel newsgroups on the Internet are, by far, the best source for such assistance. See Appendix D for specifics.

Also, when you're out surfing the Web, don't overlook my Web site ("The Spreadsheet Page"):

`http://www.j-walk.com/ss/`

Now, without further ado, it's time to turn the page and expand your horizons.

Acknowledgments

Many of the ideas for the topics in this book came from postings to the Excel Internet newsgroups and mailing lists. Thanks to all who frequent these services. Your problems and questions inspired many of the examples I present in this book. Special thanks are due to the following people, who contribute to my daily dose of Excel information: Dermot Balson, Colin Banfield, Alan Beban, Aaron Blood, Rob Bovey, Dave Boylan, David Braden, Stephen Bullen, Shane Devonshire, Jonathan Falk, Terry Fitzpatrick, John Green, David Hager, Nick Hodge, Myrna Larson, Dave Lewinski, Laurent Longre, Ture Magnusson, Bill Manville, Colin McNair, David McRitchie, Dick Moffat, Kenneth Moulton (and the Graphics Programming Department), Graeme Muat, Brian Murphy, Dan Newman, Thomas Ogilvy, Chip Pearson, Jim Rech, David Ringston, Larry P. Shreve, Harold Staff, Rick Teale, Tim Tow, Bob Ulmas — and many others whom I haven't mentioned.

This book would not be in your hands if it weren't for the talented people at IDG Books. Special thanks to Greg Croy, who okayed my original proposal for this book and provided continued encouragement along the way. Thanks also are due to my Development Editors, Terri Varveris and Terry O'Donnell. Despite the challenges inherent in working with two editors with sound-alike names, we managed to pull it off without missing a deadline. I'm also indebted to Greg Guntle, the technical editor, who identified quite a few errors on my part.

John Walkenbach
La Jolla, California

Contents at a Glance

Contents

Part II   **Using Functions in Your Formulas**

Part V   Developing Custom Worksheet Functions

Appendixes

Part I

Basic Information

Chapter 1

Excel in a Nutshell

IN THIS CHAPTER

- ◆ A brief history of Excel

- ◆ The object model concept in Excel

- ◆ The workings of workbooks

- ◆ The user interface in Excel

- ◆ The two types of cell formatting in Excel

- ◆ Worksheet formulas and functions

- ◆ Objects on the worksheet's invisible drawer layer

- ◆ Macros, toolbars, and add-ins for Excel customization

- ◆ Analysis tools in Excel

- ◆ Protection options offered in Excel

MICROSOFT EXCEL HAS BEEN CALLED the best application ever written for Windows. You may or may not agree with that statement, but you cannot deny that it's one of the *oldest* Windows products, and has undergone many reincarnations and face-lifts over the years. Cosmetically, the current version – Excel 2000 – barely even resembles the original version (which, by the way, was written for the Macintosh). However, many of its key elements have remained intact over the years – with significant enhancements, of course.

This chapter presents a concise overview of the features available in the more recent versions of Excel, with specific emphasis on Excel 2000. It sets the stage for the subsequent chapters and provides a transition for those who have used other spreadsheet products and are moving up to Excel. Hard-core Lotus 1-2-3 users, for example, usually need some help to start thinking in Excel's terms.

 If you're an old-hand at Excel, you might want to ignore this chapter or just skim through it quickly.

The History of Excel

This section presents a brief history of Excel. You probably weren't expecting a history lesson when you bought this book, but you may find this information interesting. At the very least, this section provides fodder for the next office trivia match.

Spreadsheets comprise a huge business, but most of us tend to take this software for granted. In fact, you may find it difficult to fathom, but there really existed a time when spreadsheets were not available. Rather, people relied on clumsy mainframes or calculators and spent hours doing what now takes minutes.

It started with VisiCalc

Dan Bricklin and Bob Frankston conjured up VisiCalc, the world's first electronic spreadsheet, back in the late 1970s when personal computers were unheard of in the office environment. They wrote VisiCalc for the Apple II computer – an interesting, little machine that seems like a toy by today's standards. VisiCalc caught on quickly, and many forward-looking companies purchased the Apple II for the sole purpose of developing their budgets with VisiCalc. Consequently, VisiCalc is often credited for much of the Apple II's initial success.

Then there was Lotus

When the IBM PC arrived on the scene in 1982, legitimizing personal computers, VisiCorp wasted no time porting VisiCalc to this new hardware environment. Envious of VisiCalc's success, a small group of computer geeks at a start-up company in Cambridge, Massachusetts, refined the spreadsheet concept. Headed by Mitch Kapor and Jonathon Sachs, the company designed a new product and launched the software industry's first full-fledged marketing blitz. Released in January 1983, Lotus Development Corporation's 1-2-3 was an instant success. Despite its $495 price tag (yes, people really paid that much for software), it quickly outsold VisiCalc and rocketed to the top of the sales charts, where it remained for many years. It was, perhaps, the most popular application ever.

Microsoft enters the picture

Most people don't realize that Microsoft's experience with spreadsheets extends back to the early 1980s. In 1982, Microsoft released its first spreadsheet, MultiPlan. Designed for computers running the CP/M operating system, the product was subsequently ported to several other platforms, including Apple II, Apple III, XENIX, and MS-DOS. MultiPlan essentially ignored existing software user-interface standards. Difficult to learn and use, it never earned much of a following in the United States. Not surprisingly, Lotus 1-2-3 pretty much left MultiPlan in the dust.

Excel partly evolved from MultiPlan, first surfacing in 1985 on the Macintosh. Like all Mac applications, Excel was a graphics-based program (unlike the character-based MultiPlan). In November 1987, Microsoft released the first version of Excel for Windows (labeled Excel 2 to correspond with the Macintosh version). It took a while for Excel to catch on, but as Windows gained popularity so did Excel. Lotus eventually released a Windows version of 1-2-3, and Excel had additional competition from Quattro Pro - originally a DOS program developed by Borland International, then sold to Novell, and then sold again to Corel (its current owner).

Excel versions

Excel 2000 is actually Excel 9 in disguise. You might think that this represents the ninth version of Excel. Think again. Microsoft may be a successful company, but their version-naming techniques are quite confusing. As you'll see, Excel 2000 actually represents the seventh Windows version of Excel. In the following sections, I briefly describe the major Windows versions of Excel.

EXCEL 2

The original version of Excel for Windows, Excel 2, first appeared in late 1987. It was labeled Version 2 to correspond to the Macintosh version (the original Excel). Because Windows wasn't in widespread use at the time, this version included a *run-time* version of Windows — a special version with just enough features to run Excel and nothing else. This version is quite crude by today's standards, as shown in Figure 1-1.

EXCEL 3

At the end of 1990, Microsoft released Excel 3 for Windows. This offered a significant improvement in both appearance and features. It included toolbars, drawing capabilities, worksheet outlining, add-in support, 3-D charts, workgroup editing, and lots more.

EXCEL 4

Excel 4 hit the streets in the spring of 1992. This version made quite an impact in the marketplace as Windows increased in popularity. It boasted lots of new features and "usability" enhancements that made it easier for beginners to get up to speed quickly.

EXCEL 5

In early 1994, Excel 5 appeared on the scene. This version introduced tons of new features, including multisheet workbooks and the new Visual Basic for Applications (VBA) macro language. Like its predecessor, Excel 5 took top honors in just about every spreadsheet comparison published in the trade magazines.

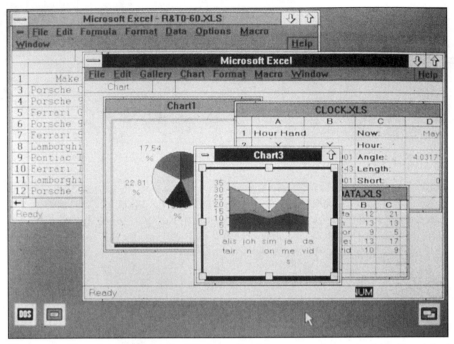

Figure 1-1: The original Excel 2 for Windows. Excel has come a long way since its original version. (Photo courtesy of Microsoft Corporation)

EXCEL 95

Excel 95 (also known as Excel 7) shipped in the summer of 1995. On the surface, it resembled Excel 5 (there were only a few major new features). But Excel 95 was significant because it was the first version to use more advanced 32-bit code. Excel 95 and Excel 5 use the same file format.

EXCEL 97

Excel 97 (also known as Excel 8) probably offered the most significant upgrade ever. The toolbars and menus took on a great new look, online help moved a dramatic step forward, and the number of rows available in a worksheet quadrupled. And if you're a macro developer, you might have noticed that Excel's programming language (VBA) moved up several notches on the scale. Excel 97 also introduced a new file format.

EXCEL 2000

Excel 2000 (also known as Excel 9) was released in June 1999. Excel 2000 has quite a few minor enhancements, but the most significant advance enables you to use HTML as an alternative file format. It still supports the standard binary file format, of course, which is compatible with Excel 97.

Many of these versions of Excel also include *subversions*. For example, Microsoft released two service releases (SR-1 and SR-2) for Excel 97. These service releases correct various problems with the software.

The Object Model Concept

If you've dealt with computers for any length of time, you've undoubtedly heard the term *object-oriented programming*. An object essentially represents a software element that a programmer can manipulate. When using Excel, you might find it useful to think in terms of objects, even if you have no intention of becoming a programmer. An object-oriented approach can often help you keep the various elements in perspective.

Excel objects include the following:

- ◆ Excel itself
- ◆ An Excel workbook
- ◆ A worksheet in a workbook
- ◆ A range in a worksheet
- ◆ A button on a worksheet
- ◆ A ListBox control on a UserForm (a custom dialog box)
- ◆ A chart sheet
- ◆ A chart on a chart sheet
- ◆ A chart series in a chart

Notice that something of an *object hierarchy* exists here: The Excel object contains workbook objects, which contain worksheet objects, which contain range objects. This hierarchy is called Excel's *object model*. Other Microsoft Office 2000 products have their own object model. The object model concept is vitally important when developing VBA macros.

The Workings of Workbooks

One of the most common Excel objects is a *workbook*. Everything you do in Excel takes place in a workbook, which stores in a file with an .xls extension.

Where Are the VBA Module Sheets?

In Excel 5 and Excel 95, a VBA module appeared in a workbook as a separate sheet. A VBA module, as you may know, holds VBA code. In Excel 97 and Excel 2000, VBA modules still store with a workbook, but they no longer show up as a separate sheet. Rather, you work with VBA modules in the Visual Basic Editor (VB Editor). To view or edit a VBA module, activate the VB Editor by pressing Alt+F11. See Part V of this book for more information about VBA.

 Beginning with Excel 2000, you can also use HTML as a "native" file format for Excel. Unless you have a real need to save your work in HTML by using this feature, you should use the normal .xls file format.

An Excel workbook can hold any number of sheets (limited only by memory). There are four types of sheets:

◆ Worksheets

◆ Chart sheets

◆ XLM macro sheets (obsolete, but still supported)

◆ Dialog sheets (obsolete, but still supported)

You can open as many workbooks as you like (each in its own window), but at any given time, only one workbook is the *active workbook*. Similarly, only one sheet in a workbook is the *active sheet*. To activate a different sheet, click its corresponding tab at the bottom of the window, or press Ctrl+PgUp (for the next sheet) or Ctrl+PgDn (for the previous sheet). To change a sheet's name, double-click its Sheet tab and enter the new text for the name. Right-clicking a tab brings up a shortcut menu with some additional sheet-manipulation options.

You can also hide the window that contains a workbook by using the Window → Hide command. A hidden workbook window remains open, but not visible. A single workbook can display in multiple windows (select Window → New Window). Each window can display a different sheet.

Worksheets

The most common type of sheet is a worksheet – which you normally think of when you think of a spreadsheet. Every Excel worksheet has 256 columns and 65,536 rows. And, to answer a common question, the number of rows and columns is permanently fixed; you cannot change it. You can hide unneeded rows and columns to keep them out of view, but you cannot increase the number of rows or columns.

The current number of rows is a new feature. Versions prior to Excel 97 contained only 16,384 rows.

The real value of using multiple worksheets in a workbook is not access to more cells. Rather, multiple worksheets enable you to organize your work better. Back in the old days, when a spreadsheet file consisted of a single worksheet, developers wasted a lot of time trying to organize the worksheet to hold their information efficiently. Now, you can store information on any number of worksheets and still access it instantly.

You have complete control over the column widths and row heights, and you can even hide rows and columns (as well as entire worksheets). You can display the contents of a cell vertically (or at an angle) and even wrap around to occupy multiple lines.

How Big Is a Worksheet?

It's interesting to stop and think about the actual size of a worksheet. Do the arithmetic (256 × 65,536), and you'll see that a worksheet has 16,777,216 cells. Remember: this is in just one worksheet. A single workbook can hold more than one worksheet.

If you're using the standard VGA video mode with the default row heights and column widths, you can see nine columns and 18 rows (or 162 cells) at a time. This works out to less than 0.001 percent of the entire worksheet. In other words, nearly 104,000 VGA screens of information reside inside a single worksheet.

If you entered a single digit into each cell at a relatively rapid clip of one cell per second, it would take you about 194 days, nonstop, to fill up a worksheet. To print the results of your efforts would require more than 36,000 sheets of paper – a stack about six feet tall.

By default, every new workbook starts out with three worksheets. You can easily add a new sheet when needed, so there's really no reason to start with three sheets. You might want to change this default to a single sheet. To change this option, use the Tools → Options command, click the General tab, and change the setting for Sheets in new workbook.

Chart sheets

A chart sheet normally holds a single chart. Many users ignore chart sheets, preferring to use "embedded charts," stored on the worksheet's draw layer. Using chart sheets is optional, but they make it a bit easier to print a chart on a page by itself, and they are especially useful for presentations. I discuss embedded charts (or floating charts on a worksheet) later in this chapter.

XLM macro sheets

An XLM macro sheet (also known as an MS Excel 4 macro sheet) is essentially a worksheet, but it has some different defaults. More specifically, an XLM macro sheet displays formulas rather than the results of formulas. Also, the default column width runs larger than in a normal worksheet.

As the name suggests, an XLM macro sheet is designed to hold XLM macros. As you may know, the XLM macro system consists of a holdover from previous versions (version 4.0 or earlier) of Excel. However, Excel 2000 continues to support XLM macros for compatibility reasons, although it no longer provides the option of recording an XLM macro. This book does not cover the XLM macro system; instead, it focuses on the more powerful VBA macro system.

Dialog sheets

In Excel 5 and Excel 95, you can create a custom dialog box by inserting a special dialog sheet. When you open a workbook that contains an Excel 5/95 dialog sheet, the dialog sheet appears as a sheet in the workbook. Excel 97 and Excel 2000 still support these dialog sheets, but they provide a much better alternative: UserForms. You can work with UserForms in the VB Editor.

 If, for compatibility purposes, you need to insert an Excel 5/95 dialog sheet in later versions of Excel, you won't find the command to do so on the Insert menu. You can only add an Excel 5/95 dialog sheet by right-clicking on any Sheet tab and selecting Insert from the shortcut menu. Then, in the Insert dialog box, click the MS Excel 5.0 Dialog icon, as shown in Figure 1-2.

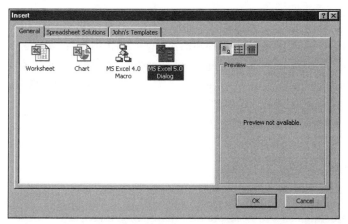

Figure 1-2: Right-click a Sheet tab and then select Insert to display the Insert dialog box.

Excel's User Interface

A *user interface* (UI) is the means by which an end user communicates with a computer program. A UI includes elements such as menus, dialog boxes, toolbars, keystroke combinations, as well as features such as drag-and-drop. For the most part, Excel uses the standard Windows UI to accept commands.

Menus

Beginning with Excel 97, Excel's UI deviates from the standard Windows UI by providing non-standard Windows menus. The menus in Excel 2000 and Excel 97 are actually toolbars in disguise. A dead give-away lies in the icons that accompany some menu items.

Excel's menu system is relatively straightforward. Two different menu bars exist (one for an active worksheet and the other for an active chart sheet or embedded chart). Consistent with Windows conventions, inappropriate menu commands are dimmed ("grayed out") and commands that open a dialog box are followed by an ellipsis (three dots). Where appropriate, the menus list any available shortcut key combinations (for example, the Edit menu lists Ctrl+Z as the shortcut key for Edit → Undo).

Several menu items are *cascading menus* and, as such, lead to submenus that have additional commands (e.g., Edit → Fill represents a cascading menu). A small arrow on the right of the menu item text indicates a cascading menu.

Excel also features context-sensitive shortcut menus. They appear when the user right-clicks after selecting one or more objects.

A new feature of Excel enables an end user or developer to customize the entire menu system. To do so, choose the View → Toolbars → Customize command. You must understand that menu changes made by using this technique are "permanent." In other words, the menu changes will remain in effect even if you close Excel and restart it. This differs greatly from the Menu Editor found in Excel 5 and Excel 95, which is no longer available in Excel 97 and later versions.

Dialog boxes

Most of the menu commands in Excel display a dialog box, in which you can clarify your intentions. These dialog boxes are quite consistent in terms of how they operate. Some of Excel's dialog boxes use a notebook tab metaphor, which makes a single dialog box function as several different dialog boxes. Tabbed dialog boxes provide access to many options without overwhelming you. The Options dialog box (choose Tools → Options) is an example of a tabbed dialog box (see Figure 1-3).

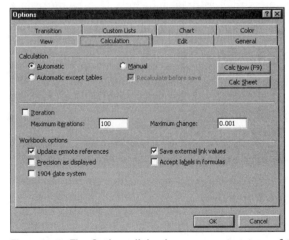

Figure 1-3: The Options dialog box represents a type of tabbed dialog box.

Toolbars

Excel 2000 ships with 43 predefined toolbars (including the two toolbars that function as menus). These toolbars typically appear automatically, when appropriate. For example, if you activate a chart, the Chart toolbar is displayed.

You can *dock* toolbars (position them along any edge of the screen) or make them *float*. By default, Excel displays the Standard and Formatting toolbars directly below the menu bar.

Drag-and-drop

Excel's drag-and-drop UI feature enables you to freely drag objects that reside on the draw layer to change their position. Pressing Ctrl while dragging duplicates the selected objects.

Excel also permits drag-and-drop actions on cells and ranges. You can easily drag a cell or range to a different position. And pressing Ctrl while dragging copies the selected range.

Cell drag-and-drop is optional; you can disable it in the Edit tab of the Options dialog box.

Keyboard shortcuts

Excel has many keyboard shortcuts. For example, you can press Ctrl+C to copy a selection. If you're a newcomer to Excel – or you just want to improve your efficiency – do yourself a favor and check out the online help (search for *Keyboard Shortcuts*). The help file contains tables that summarize useful keyboard commands and shortcuts.

Customized on-screen display

Excel offers a great deal of flexibility regarding on-screen display (status bar, formula bar, toolbars, and so on). For example, by choosing View → Full Screen, you can get rid of everything except the menu bar, thereby maximizing the amount of information visible. In addition, by using the View tab in the Options dialog box, you can customize what displays in a worksheet window (for example, hide scroll bars and grid lines).

Data entry

Data entry in Excel is quite straightforward. Excel interprets each cell entry as one of the following:

◆ A value (including a date or a time)

◆ Text

◆ A Boolean value (TRUE or FALSE)

◆ A formula

Data-Entry Tips

The following list of data-entry tips can help those who move up to Excel from another spreadsheet.

◆ To end a cell entry and move to the next cell in the selected range, select a range of cells before entering data. Then press Enter. Similarly, to move up, use Shift+Enter; to move to the right, use Tab; and to move to the left, use Shift+Tab.

◆ To enter data without pressing the arrow keys, enable the Move selection after entering an option in the Edit tab of the Options dialog box (which you access from the Tools → Options command). You can also choose the direction that you want to go.

◆ To enter the same data in all cells within a range, select the range, enter the information in the upper left cell, and then press Ctrl+Enter.

◆ To copy the contents of the active cell to all other cells in a selected range, press F2 and then Ctrl+Enter.

◆ To fill a range with increments of a single value, press Ctrl while you drag the fill handle at the corner of the selection.

◆ To create a custom AutoFill list, use the Custom Lists tab of the Options dialog box.

◆ To copy a cell without incrementing, drag the fill handle at the corner of the selection, or press Ctrl+D to copy down or Ctrl+R to copy to the right.

◆ To make text easier to read, you can enter tabs and carriage returns in a cell. To enter a tab, press Ctrl+Alt+Tab. To enter a carriage return, press Alt+Enter. Carriage returns cause a cell's contents to wrap within the cell.

◆ To enter a fraction, press 0, a space, and then the fraction (using a slash). Excel formats the cell using the Fraction number format.

◆ To automatically format a cell with the currency format, type a dollar sign before the value.

◆ To enter a value in percent format, type a percent sign after the value. You can also include commas to separate thousands (for example, 123,434).

◆ To insert the current date, Press Ctrl+semicolon. To enter the current time into a cell, press Ctrl+Shift+semicolon.

◆ To set up a cell or range so it only accepts entries of a certain type (or within a certain value range), use the Data → Validation command.

Formulas always begin with an equal sign (=). Excel accommodates habitual 1-2-3 users, however, and accepts an ampersand (@), a plus sign (@pl), or a minus sign (@ms) as the first character in a formula. It automatically adjusts the entry after you press Enter.

Object and cell selecting

Generally, selecting objects in Excel conforms to standard Windows practices. You can select a range of cells by using the keyboard (the Shift key along with the arrow keys) or clicking and dragging the mouse. To select a large range, click a cell at any corner of the range, scroll to the opposite corner of the range, and press Shift while you click the opposite corner cell.

Clicking an object placed on the draw layer selects the object. To select multiple objects or noncontiguous cells, press Ctrl while you select the objects or cells.

In versions prior to Excel 97, you clicked an embedded chart to select the chart. In Excel 97 and later, clicking a chart actually selects a specific object within the chart. To select the chart object itself, press Ctrl while you click the chart

Cell Formatting

Excel provides two types of cell formatting. The two types are numeric formatting and "stylistic" formatting.

Numeric formatting

Numeric formatting refers to how a value appears in the cell. In addition to choosing from an extensive list of predefined formats, you can create your own number formats in the Number tab of the Format Cells dialog box (choose Format → Cells).

Excel applies some numeric formatting automatically, based on the entry. For example, if you precede a value with a dollar sign, Excel applies Currency number formatting.

Refer to Appendix C for additional information about creating custom number formats.

The number format does not affect the actual value stored in the cell. For example, assume a cell contains the value 3.14159. If you apply a format to display two decimal places, the number appears as 3.14. When you use the cell in a formula, however, the actual value (3.14159), not the displayed value, is used.

Stylistic formatting

Stylistic formatting refers to the cosmetic formatting (colors, shading, fonts, borders, and so on) that you apply in order to make your work look good. The Format Cells dialog box (see Figure 1-4) is your one-stop-shopping place for formatting cells and ranges.

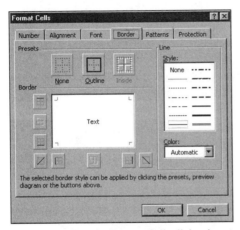

Figure 1–4: Use the Format Cells dialog box to apply stylistic formatting.

Many toolbar buttons offer direct access to common formatting options, regardless of whether you work with cells, drawn objects, or charts. For example, you can use the Fill Color toolbar button to change the background color of a cell, change the fill color of a drawn text box, or change the color of a bar in a chart. But, you'll want to access the Format dialog box for the full range of formatting options.

Each type of object has its own Format dialog box. You can easily get to the correct dialog box and format an object by selecting the object, right-clicking, and then choosing Format *xxx* (where *xxx* is the selected object) from the shortcut menu. This action leads to a tabbed dialog box that holds all the formatting options for the selected object.

Beginning with Excel 97, you can take advantage of the conditional formatting feature. This handy tool enables you to specify formatting that appears only when certain conditions are met. For example, you can make the cell's interior red if the cell contains a negative number. Chapter 17 describes how to create conditional formatting formulas that greatly enhance this feature.

Worksheet Formulas and Functions

Formulas, of course, are what make a spreadsheet a spreadsheet. Excel's formula building capability is as good as it gets. You will discover this as you explore subsequent chapters in this book.

Worksheet functions enable you to perform calculations or operations that would otherwise be impossible. Excel provides a huge number of built-in functions, and you can access even more functions (many of them quite esoteric) by attaching the Analysis ToolPak add-in.

See Chapter 4 for more information about worksheet functions.

All spreadsheets enable you to use names for cells and ranges, but Excel handles names in some unique ways. A *name* represents an identifier that enables you to refer to a cell, range, value, formula, or graphic object. Formulas that use names are much easier to read than formulas using cell references; and you can easily create formulas that use named references.

I devote Chapter 3 entirely to names.

Objects on the Draw Layer

As I mentioned earlier in this chapter, each worksheet has an invisible draw layer, which holds shapes, charts, maps, pictures, and UserForm controls. I discuss some of these items below.

Shapes

You can insert AutoShapes from the Drawing toolbar. You can choose from a huge assortment of shapes. Once placed on your worksheet, you can modify the shape by selecting it and dragging its handles. In addition, you can apply drop shadows, text, or 3-D effects to the shape. Also, you can group multiple drawing objects into a single drawing object, which you'll find easier to size or position.

Linked picture objects

For some reason, the designers of Excel make the *linked picture object* rather difficult to generate. To use this object, copy a range and then press Shift and select the Edit → Paste Picture Link command (which appears on the Edit menu only when you press Shift). The Paste Picture Link command originally accommodated users who wanted to print a noncontiguous selection of ranges. Users could "take pictures" of the ranges and then paste the pictures together in a single area, which they could then print.

Dialog box controls

Many of the controls used in custom dialog boxes can be placed directly on the drawer layer of a worksheet. Doing so can greatly enhance the usability of some worksheets and eliminate the need to create custom dialog boxes. Figure 1-5 shows a worksheet with some dialog box controls added to the draw layer.

 Dialog box controls could come from two sources: The Forms toolbar or the Control Toolbox toolbar. Controls from the Control Toolbox toolbar consist of ActiveX controls and are available only in Excel 97 or later.

Charts

Excel, of course, has excellent charting capabilities. As mentioned earlier in this chapter, you can store charts on a chart sheet or float them on a worksheet.

Excel offers extensive chart customization options. If a chart is free-floating, just click a chart element to select it (or double-click it to display its formatting dialog box). Right-clicking a chart element displays a shortcut menu.

You can easily create a free-floating chart by selecting the data to be charted and then use the Chart Wizard (you can choose the corresponding button on the Standard toolbar). The Chart Wizard walks you through the steps to create a chart that meets your needs, as shown in Figure 1-6.

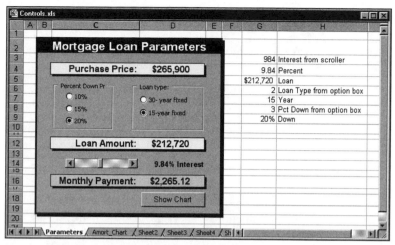

Figure 1-5: Excel enables you to add many controls directly to the drawer layer of a worksheet.

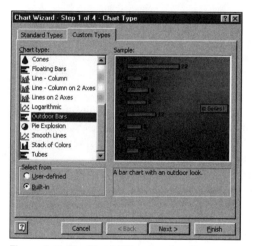

Figure 1-6: The Chart Wizard makes it easy to create charts for worksheet data.

Chapter 15 contains additional information about charts.

Customization in Excel

This section describes various features that enable you to customize Excel. They include macros, toolbars, and add-in programs.

Macros

Excel's VBA programming language provides a powerful tool that can make Excel perform otherwise impossible feats. You can classify the procedures that you create with VBA into two general types:

- Macros that automate various aspects of Excel

- Macros that serve as custom functions that you can use in worksheet formulas

Part V of this book describes how to use and create custom worksheet functions using VBA.

Toolbars

As I noted earlier, Excel includes many toolbars. You can, if so inclined, create new toolbars that contains existing toolbar buttons, or new buttons that execute macros.

Use the View → Toolbars → Customize command to customize toolbars or create new ones. You can also write VBA code to manipulate toolbars.

Add-in programs

An *add-in* is a program attached to Excel that gives it additional functionality. For example, you can store custom worksheet functions in an add-in. To attach an add-in, use the Tools → Add-Ins command.

Excel ships with quite a few add-ins (which include the Analysis ToolPak). In addition to the add-ins, you can purchase or download many third-party add-ins from online services. My Power Utility Pak represents an example of an add-in. You can access a trial version on the companion CD-ROM.

Chapter 21 describes how to create your own add-ins that contain custom worksheet functions.

Analysis Tools

Excel is certainly no slouch when it comes to analysis. After all, that's what most people use a spreadsheet for. Many analysis tasks can be handled with formulas, but Excel offers many other options, which are discussed in the following sections.

Database access

Over the years, most spreadsheets have enabled users to work with simple flat database tables (even the original version of 1-2-3 contained this feature). Excel's database features fall into two main categories:

♦ **Worksheet databases.** The entire database stores in a worksheet, limiting the size of the database. In Excel, a worksheet database can have no more than 65,535 records (since there are 65,536 rows; the top row holds the field names) and 256 fields (since there are 256 columns).

♦ **External databases.** The data stores in one or more disk files and you can access it as needed.

Generally, when the cell pointer resides within a worksheet database, Excel recognizes it and displays the field names whenever possible. For example, if you move the cell pointer within a worksheet database and choose the Data → Sort command, Excel enables you to select the sort keys by choosing field names from a drop-down list.

A particularly useful feature, Excel's AutoFilter, enables you to display only the records that you want to see. When AutoFilter mode is on, you can filter the data by selecting values from pull-down lists (which appear in place of the field names when you choose the Data → Filter → AutoFilter command). Rows that don't qualify are temporarily hidden. See Figure 1-7 for an example.

If you prefer, you can use the traditional spreadsheet database techniques that involve criteria ranges. To do so, choose the Data → Filter → Advanced Filter command.

Chapter 9 provides additional details regarding worksheet lists and databases.

Excel can automatically insert (or remove) subtotal formulas in a table set up as a database. It also creates an outline from the data so that you can view only the subtotals, or any level of detail you desire. Figure 1-8 shows some automatic subtotals and the accompanying outline.

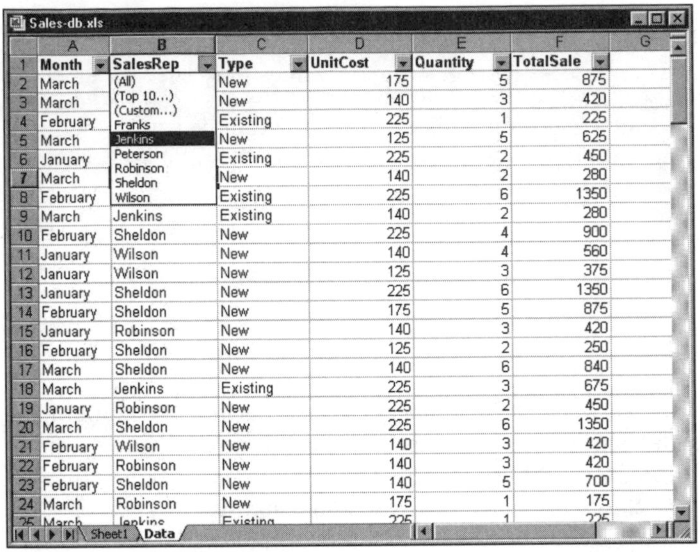

	Month	SalesRep	Type	UnitCost	Quantity	TotalSale
2	March		New	175	5	875
3	March		New	140	3	420
4	February		Existing	225	1	225
5	March		New	125	5	625
6	January		Existing	225	2	450
7	March		New	140	2	280
8	February		Existing	225	6	1350
9	March	Jenkins	Existing	140	2	280
10	February	Sheldon	New	225	4	900
11	January	Wilson	New	140	4	560
12	January	Wilson	New	125	3	375
13	January	Sheldon	New	225	6	1350
14	February	Sheldon	New	175	5	875
15	January	Robinson	New	140	3	420
16	February	Sheldon	New	125	2	250
17	March	Sheldon	New	140	6	840
18	March	Jenkins	Existing	225	3	675
19	January	Robinson	New	225	2	450
20	March	Sheldon	New	225	6	1350
21	February	Wilson	New	140	3	420
22	February	Robinson	New	140	3	420
23	February	Sheldon	New	140	5	700
24	March	Robinson	New	175	1	175
25	March	Jenkins	Existing	225	1	225

Figure 1-7: Excel's AutoFilter feature makes it easy to view only database records that meet your criteria.

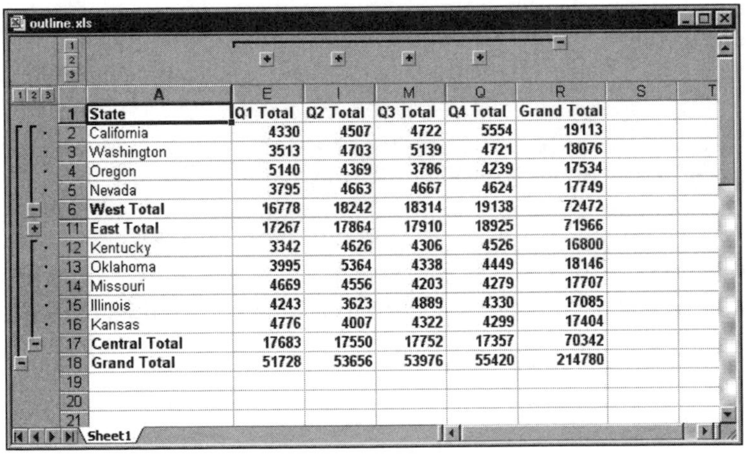

	State	Q1 Total	Q2 Total	Q3 Total	Q4 Total	Grand Total
2	California	4330	4507	4722	5554	19113
3	Washington	3513	4703	5139	4721	18076
4	Oregon	5140	4369	3786	4239	17534
5	Nevada	3795	4663	4667	4624	17749
6	**West Total**	16778	18242	18314	19138	72472
11	**East Total**	17267	17864	17910	18925	71966
12	Kentucky	3342	4626	4306	4526	16800
13	Oklahoma	3995	5364	4338	4449	18146
14	Missouri	4669	4556	4203	4279	17707
15	Illinois	4243	3623	4889	4330	17085
16	Kansas	4776	4007	4322	4299	17404
17	**Central Total**	17683	17550	17752	17357	70342
18	**Grand Total**	51728	53656	53976	55420	214780

Figure 1-8: Excel can automatically insert subtotal formulas and create outlines.

Outlines

A worksheet outline often serves as an excellent way to work with hierarchical data, such as budgets. Excel can create an outline automatically by examining the formulas in your worksheet. When outlining is in effect, you can collapse or expand an outline to display various levels of details.

Scenario management

Scenario management is the process of storing input values that drive a model. For example, if you have a sales forecast, you may create scenarios such as best case, worst case, and most likely case.

If you seek the ultimate in scenario-management features, 1-2-3's Version Manager is probably your best bet. Unlike Version Manager, Excel's Scenario Manager can only handle simple scenario-management tasks. However, it definitely is easier than trying to keep track of different scenarios manually.

Analysis ToolPak

The Analysis ToolPak add-in provides 19 special-purpose analysis tools (primarily statistical in nature) and many specialized worksheet functions. These tools make Excel suitable for small- to medium-scale statistical analysis.

Pivot tables

Pivot tables are one of Excel's most powerful tools. A *pivot table* enables you to display summarized data in just about any possible way. Data for a pivot table comes from a worksheet database or an external database and stores in a special cache, which enables Excel to recalculate data rapidly after a pivot table is altered.

Chapter 16 contains additional information about pivot tables.

Excel 2000 also supports the pivot chart feature. Pivot charts enable you to link a chart to a pivot table.

Auditing capabilities

Excel also offers useful auditing capabilities that help you identify errors or track the logic in an unfamiliar spreadsheet. To access this feature, select Tools → Auditing.

Chapter 19 covers Excel auditing features in detail.

Solver add-in

For specialized linear and nonlinear problems, Excel's Solver add-in calculates solutions to what-if scenarios based on adjustable cells, constraint cells, and, optionally, cells that must be maximized or minimized. Excel's Solver closely resembles the feature found in 1-2-3 for Windows and Quattro Pro for Windows. (This similarity is not surprising when you know that a single company, Frontline Systems, was largely responsible for the feature in all three products.)

Protection Options

Excel offers a number of different protection options. For example, you can protect formulas from being overwritten or modified, protect a workbook's structure, and protect your VBA code.

Protecting formulas from being overwritten

In many cases, you may want to protect your formulas from being overwritten or modified. To do so, perform the following steps:

1. Select the cells that *may* be overwritten.

2. Select Format → Cells, and click the Protection tab of the Format Cells dialog box.

3. In the Protections tab, remove the checkmark from the Locked checkbox.

4. Click OK to close the Format Cells dialog box.

5. Select Tools → Protection → Protect Sheet to display the Protect Sheet dialog box shown in Figure 1-9.

6. In the Protect Sheet dialog box, specify a password if desired, and click OK.

 By default, all cells are Locked. This has no effect, however, unless you have a protected worksheet.

Figure 1-9: The Protect Sheet dialog box

You can also hide your formulas so they won't appear in Excel's formula bar when the cell is activated. To do so, select the formula cells and make sure the Hidden checkbox is checked in the Protection tab of the Format Cells dialog box.

Protecting a workbook's structure

When you protect a workbook's structure, you cannot add or delete sheets. Use the Tools → Protection → Protect Workbook command to display the Protect Workbook dialog box, as shown in Figure 1-10. Make sure you check the Structure checkbox. If you also check the Windows checkbox, the window cannot be moved or resized.

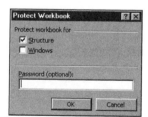

Figure 1-10: The Protect Workbook dialog box

It's important to keep in mind that Excel is not really a secure application. The protection features, even when used with a password, are intended to prevent casual users from accessing various components of your workbook. Anyone who really wants to defeat your protection can probably do so using readily available password-cracking utilities.

Summary

This chapter provided a general overview of the features available in Excel and is primarily intended for newcomers to Excel. The next chapter gets into the meat of the book and provides an introduction to Excel formulas.

Chapter 2

Basic Facts About Formulas

IN THIS CHAPTER

◆ How to enter, edit, and paste names into formulas

◆ The various operators used in formulas

◆ How Excel calculates formulas

◆ Cell and range references used in formulas

◆ How to make an exact copy of a formula

◆ How to convert formulas to values

◆ How to prevent formulas from being viewed

◆ The types of formula errors

◆ Circular reference messages and correction techniques

◆ Excel's goal-seeking feature

THIS CHAPTER SERVES AS A basic introduction to using formulas in Excel. Although I direct its focus on newcomers to Excel, even veteran Excel users may find some new information here.

Entering and Editing Formulas

This section describes the basic elements of a formula. It also explains various ways of entering and editing your formulas.

Formula elements

A formula entered into a cell can consist of five element types. The five element types are any of the following:

◆ Operators. These include symbols such as + (for addition) and * (for multiplication).

◆ Cell references (including named cells and ranges). They can refer to cells in the current sheet, cells in another sheet in the same workbook, or even cells in a sheet in another workbook.

◆ Literal values or strings (such as 7.5, or *Year-End Results*).

◆ Worksheet functions (such as SUM or AVERAGE) and their arguments.

◆ Parentheses to control the order in which expressions within a formula are evaluated.

Entering a formula

When you type an equal sign into an empty cell, Excel assumes that you are entering a formula (a formula always begins with an equal sign). Excel's accommodating nature also permits you to begin your formula with a minus sign or a plus sign. However, Excel will always insert the leading equal sign after you enter the formula.

As a concession to former 1-2-3 users, Excel also enables you to use an ampersand (@) to begin a formula that starts with a function. For example, Excel accepts either of the following formulas:

```
=SUM(A1:A200)
@SUM(A1:A200)
```

However, after you enter the second formula, Excel replaces the ampersand with an equal sign. You can enter a formula into a cell in one of two ways: enter it manually, or enter it by pointing to cell references. I discuss each of these methods in the following sections.

ENTERING FORMULAS MANUALLY

Entering a formula manually involves, well, entering a formula manually. You simply activate a cell and type an equal sign (=) followed by the formula. As you type, the characters appear in the cell as well as in the formula bar. You can, of course, use all the normal editing keys when entering a formula. Once you insert the formula, press Enter.

If you enter an array formula, press Ctrl+Shift+Enter rather than just Enter. I discuss array formulas in Part III.

After you press Enter, the cell displays the result of the formula. The formula, it-self, appears in the formula bar when the cell is activated.

ENTERING FORMULAS BY POINTING

The other method of entering a formula still involves some manual typing, but you can simply point to the cell references instead of entering them manually. For ex-ample, to enter the formula =A1+A2 into cell A3, follow these steps:

1. Move the cell pointer to cell A3.

2. Type an equal sign (=) to begin the formula. Notice that Excel displays *Enter* in the status bar.

3. Press the up arrow twice. As you press this key, notice that Excel displays a faint moving border around the cell and that the cell reference (A1) appears in cell A3 and in the formula bar. Also notice that Excel displays *Point* in the status bar.

4. Type a plus sign (+). The faint border disappears and *Enter* reappears in the status bar.

5. Press the up arrow one more time. A2 is added to the formula.

6. Press Enter to end the formula. As with entering the formula manually, the cell displays the result of the formula, and the formula appears in the formula bar when the cell is activated.

Pointing to cell addresses rather than entering them manually is usually more accurate and less tedious.

When you create a formula that refers to other cells, the cell that contains the formula has the same number format as the first cell to which it refers. The only exception is when the first cell reference is formatted as a percentage.

Excel 97 and later includes the Formula Palette feature that you can use when entering or editing formulas. To access the Formula Palette, click on the Edit Formula button in the edit line (it has an image of an equal sign). The Formula Palette enables you to enter formulas manually or use the pointing techniques de-scribed previously, as shown in Figure 2-1.

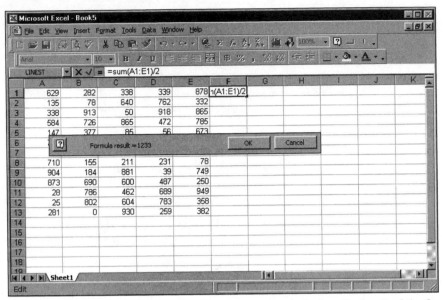

Figure 2-1: The Formula Palette — introduced in Excel 97 — displays the result of the formula as you enter it.

Pasting names

As I discuss in Chapter 3, you can assign a name to a cell or range. If your formula uses named cells or ranges, you can type the name in place of the address or choose the name from a list and have Excel insert the name for you automatically.

To insert a name into a formula, select the Insert → Name → Paste command (or Press F3) to display the Paste Name dialog box. Excel displays its Paste Name dialog box with all the names listed, as shown in Figure 2-2. Select the name and click OK. Or, you can double-click the name, which inserts the name into the formula and closes the dialog box.

Figure 2-2: The Paste Name dialog box lets you insert a name into a formula.

Spaces and line breaks

Normally, you enter a formula without using any spaces. However, you can use spaces (and even line breaks) within your formulas. Doing so has no effect on the formula's result, but may make the formula easier to read. To enter a line break in a formula, press Alt+Enter. Figure 2-3 shows a formula that contains spaces and line breaks.

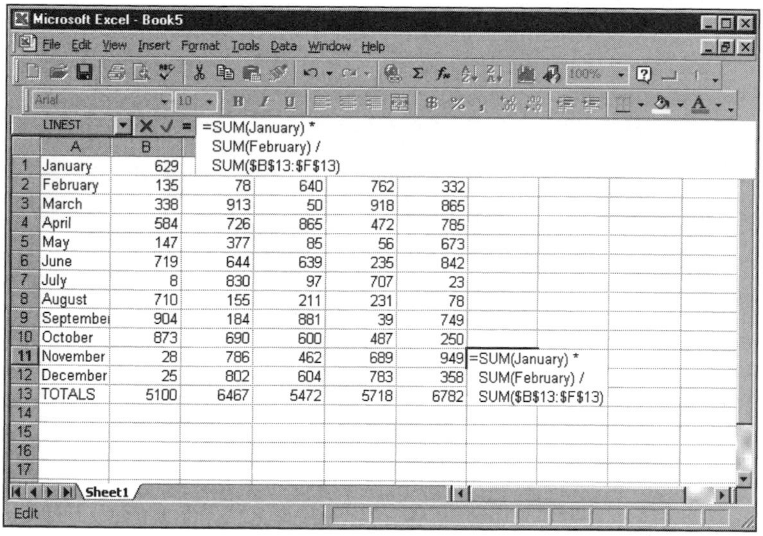

	A	B	C	D	E	F	G
1	January	629					
2	February	135	78	640	762	332	
3	March	338	913	50	918	865	
4	April	584	726	865	472	785	
5	May	147	377	85	56	673	
6	June	719	644	639	235	842	
7	July	8	830	97	707	23	
8	August	710	155	211	231	78	
9	Septembe	904	184	881	39	749	
10	October	873	690	600	487	250	
11	November	28	786	462	689	949	=SUM(January) *
12	December	25	802	604	783	358	SUM(February) /
13	TOTALS	5100	6467	5472	5718	6782	SUM($B$13:$F$13)

Figure 2-3: This formula contains spaces and line breaks.

Formula limits

A formula can consist of up to 1,024 characters. If you need to create a formula that exceeds this limit, you must break the formula up into multiple formulas. You also can opt to create a custom function (using VBA).

Part IV focuses on creating custom functions.

Sample formulas

If you follow the above instructions for entering formulas, you can create a variety of formulas. This section provides a look at some sample formulas.

◆ The following formula multiplies 150 times .01, and returns 1.5. This formula uses only literal values, so it is not all that useful. (You can simply enter the value 1.5 instead of the formula.)

`=150*.01`

◆ The following formula adds the values in cells A1 and A2:

`=A1+A2`

◆ The next formula subtracts the value in the cell named *Expenses* from the value in the cell named *Income:*

`=Income-Expenses`

◆ The following formula uses the SUM function to add the values in the range A1:A12:

`=SUM(A1:A12)`

◆ The next formula compares cell A1 with cell C12 by using the = operator. If the two cells are identical, the formula returns TRUE; otherwise it returns FALSE.

`=A1=C12`

◆ This final formula subtracts the value in cell B3 from the value in cell B2, then multiplies the result by the value in cell B4:

`=(B2-B3)*B4`

Editing formulas

You may need to edit a formula if you make some changes to your worksheet requiring you to adjust the formula to accommodate them. Or, the formula may return one of the error values described later in this chapter and you will need to edit the formula to correct the error. You can edit your formulas just like you edit any other cell.

There are four ways to get into cell edit mode:

1. Double-click the cell. This lets you edit the cell contents directly in the cell.

2. Press F2. This enables you to edit the cell contents directly in the cell.

3. Activate the cell that you want to edit, and then click in the formula bar. This enables you to edit the cell contents in the formula bar.

4. Click the Edit Formula button (it has an equal sign icon) in the edit line to access the Formula Palette.

Using the Formula Bar as a Calculator

If you simply need to perform a calculation, you can use the formula bar as a calculator. For example, enter the following formula but don't press Enter:

```
=(145*1.05)/12
```

If you press Enter, Excel enters the formula into the cell. But because this formula always returns the same result, you might prefer to store the formula's result rather than the formula. To do so, press F9 followed by Enter. Excel stores the formula's result (12.6875), rather than the formula. This also works if the formula uses cell references.

This technique is most useful when you use worksheet functions. For example, to enter the square root of 221 into a cell, enter =SQRT(221), press F9, and press Enter. Excel enters the result: 14.8660687473185. You also can use this technique to evaluate just part of a formula. Consider this formula:

```
=(145*1.05)/A1
```

If you want to convert just the part in the parentheses to a value, get into edit mode and drag the mouse over the part that you want to evaluate (in other words, select 145*1.05). Then, press F9 followed by Enter. Excel converts the formula to the following:

```
=152.25/A1
```

When you edit a formula, you can select multiple characters by dragging the mouse over them or by holding down Shift while you use the direction keys.

 Suppose you have a lengthy formula that contains an error, and Excel won't let you enter it because of the error. In this case, you can convert the formula to text and tackle it again later. To convert a formula to text, just remove the initial equal sign (=). To try the formula again, insert the initial equals sign to convert the cell contents back to a formula.

Using Operators in Formulas

As previously discussed, an operator is one of a formula's basic elements. An *operator* is a symbol that represents an operation. Excel supports the following operators:

+	Addition
-	Subtraction
/	Division
*	Multiplication
%	Percent
&	Text concatenation
^	Exponentiation
=	Logical comparison (equal to)
>	Logical comparison (greater than)
<	Logical comparison (less than)
>=	Logical comparison (greater than or equal to)
<=	Logical comparison (less than or equal to)
<>	Logical comparison (not equal to)

You can, of course, use as many operators as you need. Formulas can be quite complex.

Reference operators

Excel supports another class of operators known as *reference operators*. Reference operators, which are listed below, work with cell references.

: (colon)	Range operator. Produces one reference to all the cells between two references.
, (comma)	Union operator. This combines multiple cell or range references into one reference.
(single space)	Intersection operator. This produces one reference to cells common to two references.

Sample formulas that use operators

The following examples of formulas use various operators:

♦ The following formula joins *(concatenates)* the two literal text strings to produce a new text string: *Part-23A:*

```
="Part-"&"23A"
```

- The next formula concatenates the contents of cell A1 with cell A2:

  `=A1&A2`

  Usually, concatenation is used with text, but concatenation works with values as well. For example, if cell A1 contains 123 and cell A2 contains 456, the preceding formula would return the value 123456.

- The following formula uses the exponentiation operator to raise 6 to the third power — to produce a result of 216:

  `=6^3`

- A more useful form of the above formula uses a cell reference instead of the literal value. The following example raises the value in cell A1 to the third power:

  `=A1^3`

- The following formula returns the cube root of 216 (which is 6):

  `=216^(1/3)`

- The next formula returns TRUE if the value in cell A1 is less than the value in cell A2. Otherwise, it returns FALSE.

  `=A1<A2`

  Logical comparison operators also work with text. If A1 contains *Bill* and A2 contains *Monica,* the formula returns TRUE because Bill comes before Monica in alphabetical order.

- The following formula returns TRUE if the value in cell A1 is less than or equal to the value in cell A2. Otherwise, it returns FALSE.

  `=A1<=A2`

- The next formula returns TRUE if the value in cell A1 does not equal the value in cell A2. Otherwise, it returns FALSE.

  `=A1<>A2`

- Unlike some other spreadsheets (such as 1-2-3), Excel doesn't have logical AND or OR operators. Rather, you use functions to specify these types of logical operators. For example, the following formula returns TRUE if cell A1 contains either 100 or 1000:

  `=OR(A1=100,A1=1000)`

  This last formula returns TRUE only if both cell A1 and cell A2 contain values less than 100:

  `=AND(A1<100,A2=100)`

Operator precedence

You can (and should) use parentheses in your formulas to control the order in which the calculations occur. As an example, consider the following formula that uses references to named cells:

```
=Income-Expenses*TaxRate
```

If you enter the above formula, you discover that Excel computes the wrong answer. The goal is to subtract expenses from income, and then multiply the result by the tax rate. Rather, the formula multiplies expenses by the tax range, and then subtracts the result from the income. The formula *should* appear as:

```
=(Income-Expenses)*TaxRate
```

To understand this, you need to understand a concept called *operator precedence* – the set of rules that Excel uses to perform its calculations. Table 2-1 lists Excel's operator precedence. Operations with a lower precedence number are performed before operations with a higher precedence number.

Use parentheses to override Excel's built-in order of precedence. Returning to the previous example, the formula without parentheses is evaluated using Excel's standard operator precedence. Because multiplication has a higher precedence, the *Expense* cell multiplies by the *TaxRate* cell. Then, this result is subtracted from *Income* – producing an incorrect calculation.

The correct formula uses parentheses to control the order of operations. Expressions within parentheses always get evaluated first. In this case, *Expenses* is subtracted from *Income*, and the result is multiplied by *TaxRate*.

TABLE 2-1 OPERATOR PRECEDENCE IN EXCEL FORMULAS

Symbol	Operator	Precedence
-	Negation	1
%		2
^	Exponentiation	3
* and /	Multiplication and division	4
+ and -	Addition and subtraction	5
&	Text concatenation	6
=, <, >, and <>	Comparison	7

Nest parentheses

You also can *nest* parentheses in formulas. Nesting means putting parentheses inside of parentheses. If you do so, Excel evaluates the most deeply nested expressions first and works its way out. The following is an example of a formula that uses nested parentheses:

```
=((B2*C2)+(B3*C3)+(B4*C4))*B6
```

This formula has four sets of parentheses. Three sets are nested inside the fourth set. Excel evaluates each nested set of parentheses and then adds up the three results. This sum is then multiplied by the value in B6.

It's a good idea to make liberal use of parentheses in your formulas, even when they aren't necessary. Using parentheses clarifies the order of operations and makes the formula easier to read. For example, if you want to add 1 to the product of two cells, the following formula does this:

```
=A1*A2+1
```

You may find it much clearer, however, to use the following formula (with superfluous parentheses):

```
=(A1*A2)+1
```

Every left parenthesis, of course, must have a matching right parenthesis. If you have many levels of nested parentheses, you might find it difficult to keep them straight. If the parentheses don't match, Excel pops up a message telling you and won't permit you to enter the formula. Fortunately, Excel lends a hand in helping you match parentheses. When you enter or edit a formula that has parentheses, pay attention to the text. When the cursor moves over a parenthesis, Excel momentarily makes it and its matching parenthesis bold. This lasts for less than a second, so watch carefully.

In some cases, if your formula contains mismatched parentheses, Excel may propose a correction to your formula (Excel 97 introduced this Formula AutoCorrect feature.) Figure 2-4 shows an example of Excel's AutoCorrect feature in action.

It seems tempting to simply accept the correction proposed in the dialog box, but be careful. In many cases, the proposed formula, although syntactically correct, isn't the formula that you want!

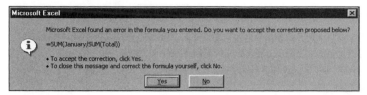

Figure 2-4: Excel's Formula AutoCorrect feature often suggests a correction to an erroneous formula.

Calculating Formulas

You've probably noticed that the formulas in your worksheet get calculated immediately. If you change any cells that the formula uses, the formula displays a new result with no effort on your part. This occurs when Excel's Calculation mode is set to Automatic. In this mode (the default mode), Excel follows certain rules when calculating your worksheet:

◆ When you make a change – enter or edit data or formulas, for example – Excel calculates immediately those formulas that depend on new or edited data.

◆ If working on a lengthy calculation, Excel temporarily suspends calculation when you need to perform other worksheet tasks; it resumes when you finish.

◆ Formulas are evaluated in a natural sequence. Essentially, if a formula in cell D12 depends on the result of a formula in cell D11, cell D11 is calculated before D12.

Don't Hard-Code Values

When you create a formula, think twice before using a literal value in the formula. For example, if your formula calculates 7.5 percent sales tax, you may be tempted to enter a formula such as:

```
+A1*.075
```

A better approach is to insert the sales tax rate into a cell and use the cell reference in place of the literal value. This makes it easier to modify and maintain your worksheet. For example, if the sales tax range changes to 7.75 percent, you need to modify every formula that uses the old value. If the tax rate is stored in a cell, you simply change one cell and all the formulas automatically get updated.

Excel's Calculation Bugs

You may have heard about some calculation bugs that affect Excel 97. Microsoft has acknowledged that these bugs exist. Basically, the bugs involve a failure to recalculate some formulas under certain conditions. The bugs do not affect most people, but knowing that they exist can definitely cause you to lose confidence in your software.

If you use Excel 97, make sure that you install SR-2 - the most recent service release. Better yet, check with Microsoft's Web site (www.microsoft.com) for the latest word on calculation bugs.

Sometimes, however, you may want to control when Excel calculates formulas. For example, if you create a worksheet with thousands of complex formulas, you'll find that things can slow to a snail's pace while Excel does its thing. In this case, you can set Excel's calculation mode to Manual. Do this in the Calculation panel of the Options dialog box. (Select Tools → Options to display this dialog box.)

When you work in Manual calculation mode, Excel displays *Calculate* in the status bar when you have any uncalculated formulas. You can use the following shortcut keys to recalculate the formulas:

- ◆ **F9:** Calculates the formulas in all open workbooks.

- ◆ **Shift+F9:** Calculates only the formulas in the active worksheet. It does not calculate other worksheets in the same workbook.

- ◆ **Ctrl+Shift+F9:** Forces a recalculation of everything. This represents an undocumented key sequence. Use it if Excel (for some reason) doesn't seem to return correct calculations.

 Excel's Calculation mode isn't specific to a particular worksheet. When you change Excel's Calculation mode, it affects all open workbooks - not just the active workbook.

Cell and Range References

Most formulas reference one or more cells by using the cell or range address or name (if it has one). Cell references come in four styles; the dollar sign differentiates them:

- ◆ **Relative.** The reference is fully relative. When the formula is copied, the cell reference adjusts to its new location. Example: A1

◆ **Absolute.** The reference is fully absolute. When the formula is copied, the cell reference does not change. Example: $A$1

◆ **Row Absolute.** The reference is partially absolute. When the formula is copied, the column part adjusts, but the row part does not change. Example: A$1

◆ **Column Absolute.** The reference is partially absolute. When the formula is copied, the row part adjusts, but the column part does not change. Example: $A1

Creating an absolute reference

When you create a formula by pointing to cells, all cell and range references are relative. To change a reference to an absolute reference, you must do so manually by adding the dollar signs. Or, you can use the F4 key to cycle among all possible reference modes.

If you think about it, you may realize that the only reason you would ever need to change a reference is if you plan to copy the formula. Figure 2-5 demonstrates this. Note the formula in cell C4:

```
=C$3*$B4
```

This formula calculates the area for various widths (listed in column B) and lengths (listed in Row 3). Once you enter the formula, it can then be copied down and across. Because the formula uses absolute references to row 3 and column B, each copied formula produces the correct result. If the formula uses relative references, copying the formula causes the references to adjust and produce the wrong results.

	A	B	C	D	E	F	G	H	I	J	K	L
1												
2												
3			1.00	1.50	2.00	2.50	3.00	3.50	4.00	4.50	5.00	
4		1.00	1.00	1.50	2.00	2.50	3.00	3.50	4.00	4.50	5.00	
5		1.50	1.50	2.25	3.00	3.75	4.50	5.25	6.00	6.75	7.50	
6		2.00	2.00	3.00	4.00	5.00	6.00	7.00	8.00	9.00	10.00	
7		2.50	2.50	3.75	5.00	6.25	7.50	8.75	10.00	11.25	12.50	
8		3.00	3.00	4.50	6.00	7.50	9.00	10.50	12.00	13.50	15.00	
9		3.50	3.50	5.25	7.00	8.75	10.50	12.25	14.00	15.75	17.50	
10		4.00	4.00	6.00	8.00	10.00	12.00	14.00	16.00	18.00	20.00	
11		4.50	4.50	6.75	9.00	11.25	13.50	15.75	18.00	20.25	22.50	
12		5.00	5.00	7.50	10.00	12.50	15.00	17.50	20.00	22.50	25.00	
13												

Figure 2-5: An example of using non-relative references in a formula

A1 vs. R1C1 Notation

Normally, Excel uses an A1 notation. Each cell address consists of a column letter and a row number. However, Excel also supports R1C1 notation. In this system, cell A1 is referred to as cell R1C1, cell A2 as R2C1, and so on.

To change to R1C1 notation, select Tools → Options to get the Options dialog box, click the General tab, and place a checkmark next to R1C1 reference style. Now, notice that the column letters all change to numbers. And, all of the cell and range references in your formulas also adjust.

Look at the following examples of formulas using standard notation and R1C1 notation. The formula is assumed to be in cell B1 (also known as R1C2).

```
Standard              R1C1
=A1+1                 =RC[-1]+1
=$A$1+1               =R1C1+1
=$A1+1                =RC1+1
=A$1+1                =R1C[-1]+1
=SUM(A1:A10)          =SUM(RC[-1]:R[9]C[-1])
=SUM($A$1:$A$10)      =SUM(R1C1:R10C1)
```

If you find R1C1 notation confusing, you're not alone. R1C1 notation is not too bad when you are dealing with absolute references. But when relative references are involved, the brackets can drive you nuts.

The numbers in brackets refer to the relative position of the references. For example, R[-5]C[-3] specifies the cell that appears five rows above and three columns to the left. Conversely, R[5]C[3] references the cell that appears five rows below and three columns to the right. If you omit the brackets, it specifies the same row or column. For example, R[5]C refers to the cell five rows below in the same column.

Although you probably won't use R1C1 notation as your standard system, it *does* have at least one good use. R1C1 notation makes it very easy to spot an erroneous formula. When you copy a formula, every copied formula is exactly the same in R1C1 notation. This remains true regardless of the types of cell references you use (relative, absolute, or mixed). Therefore, you can switch to R1C1 notation and check your copied formulas. If one looks different from its surrounding formulas, it's probably incorrect.

Referencing other sheets or workbooks

References to cells and ranges do not need to appear in the same sheet as the formula. To refer to a cell in a different worksheet, precede the cell reference with the sheet name followed by an exclamation point. Here is an example of a formula that uses a cell reference in a different worksheet (Sheet2):

```
=Sheet2!A1+1
```

You can also create link formulas that refer to a cell in a different workbook. To do so, precede the cell reference with the workbook name (in square brackets), the worksheet name, and an exclamation point like this:

```
=[Budget.xls]Sheet1!A1+1
```

If the workbook name in the reference includes one or more spaces, you must enclose it (and the sheet name) in single quotation marks. For example:

```
='[Budget Analysis.xls]Sheet1'!A1+A1
```

If the linked workbook is closed, you must add the complete path to the workbook reference. For example:

```
='C:\MSOffice\Excel\[Budget Analysis.xls]Sheet1'!A1+A1
```

Although you can enter link formulas directly, you also can create the reference by using normal pointing methods discussed earlier. To do so, make sure you have an open source file. Normally, you can create a formula by pointing to results in relative cell references. But, when you create a reference to a workbook by pointing, Excel creates *absolute* cell references. (If you plan to copy the formula to other cells, you must make the references relative.)

 Working with links can prove tricky. For example, if you use the File→Save As command to make a backup copy of the source workbook, you automatically change the link formulas to refer to the new file (not usually what you want). You also can mess up your links by renaming the source workbook file.

Using Links to Recover Data in a Corrupt File

At some point, you may find one of your Excel workbooks damaged, or corrupt. If you cannot load a corrupt workbook, you can write a link formula to recover all or part of the data (but not the formulas). You can do this because you do not need to have the source file in a link formula open. If your corrupt file is named Badfile.xls, for example, open a blank workbook and enter the following formula into cell A1 to attempt to recover the data from Sheet1:

```
=[Badfile.xls]Sheet1!A1
```

Copy this formula down and to the right to recover as much information as you can. As a better approach, however, you can maintain a backup of your important files.

Making an Exact Copy of a Formula

When you copy a formula, Excel adjusts the formula's cell references when you paste it to a different location. This is usually exactly what you want. Sometimes, however, you may want to make an exact copy of the formula. You can do this by converting the cell references to absolute values, as discussed earlier - but this isn't always desirable.

A better approach enables you to select the formula while in edit mode and then copy it to the Clipboard as text. There are several ways to do this. Here I present a step-by-step example of how to make an exact copy of the formula in A1 and copy it to A2:

1. Double-click cell A1 to activate the edit mode.

2. Drag the mouse to select the entire formula. You can drag from left to right or right to left.

3. Click the Copy button on the Standard toolbar. This copies the selected text to the Clipboard.

4. Press Enter to end the edit mode.

5. Activate cell A2.

6. Click the Paste button on the Standard toolbar to paste the text into cell A2.

You also can use this technique to copy just *part* of a formula to use in another formula. Just select the part of the formula that you want to copy by dragging the mouse; then use any of the available techniques to copy the selection to the Clipboard. You can then paste the text to another cell.

Formulas (or parts of formulas) copied in this manner won't have their cell references adjusted when you paste them to a new cell. This is because you copy the formulas as text, not as actual formulas.

Converting Formulas to Values

If you have a range of formulas that always produce the same result (i.e., dead formulas), you may want to convert them to values. You can use the Edit → Paste Special command to do this.

Suppose that range A1:A20 contains formulas that calculate a result and that never change. To convert these formulas to values:

1. Select A1:A20.

2. Click the Copy button on the Standard toolbar.

3. Select the Edit → Paste Special command. Excel displays its Paste Special dialog box.

4. Select the Values option button and then click OK.

5. Press Enter or Esc to cancel paste mode.

This technique is very useful when you use formulas as a means to convert cells. For example, assume you have a list of names (in uppercase) in column A. You want to convert these names to proper case. In order to do so, you need to create formulas in a separate column, then convert the formulas to values and replace the original values in column A. The following steps illustrate how to do this.

1. Insert a new column after column A.

2. Insert the following formula into cell B1:

   `=PROPER(A1)`

3. Copy the formula down column B to accommodate the number of entries in column A. Column B then displays the values in column A, but in proper case.

4. Select all of the names in column B.

5. Click the Copy button on the Standard toolbar.

6. Select cell A1.

7. Select the Edit → Paste Special command. Excel displays its Paste Special dialog box.

8. Select the Values option button and then click OK.

9. Press Enter or Esc to cancel paste mode.

10. Delete column B.

Hiding Formulas

In some cases, you may not want others to see your formulas. For example, you may have a special formula you developed that performs a calculation proprietary to your company. You can use the Format Cells dialog box to hide cells.

To prevent one or more formulas from being viewed

1. Select the formula or formulas.

2. Choose Format → Cells. In the Format Cells dialog box, click the Protection tab.

3. Place a checkmark next to the Hidden checkbox, as shown in Figure 2-6.

4. Use the Tools → Protection → Protect Sheet command to protect the worksheet. To prevent others from unprotecting the sheet, make sure you specify a password in the Protect Sheet dialog box.

By default, all cells are "locked." Protecting a sheet prevents any locked cells from being changed. Therefore, you should unlock the input cells before protecting your sheet.

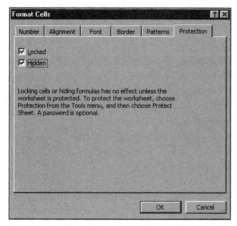

Figure 2-6: Use the Format Cells dialog box to change the Hidden status of a cell.

Errors in Formulas

It's not uncommon to enter a formula only to find that the formula returns an error. Table 2-2 lists the types of error values that may appear in a cell that has a formula.

Formulas may return an error value if a cell that they refer to has an error value. This is known as the ripple effect — a single error value can make its way to lots of other cells that contain formulas that depend on that cell.

When to Use AutoFill Rather Than Formulas

Excel's AutoFill feature provides a quick way to copy a cell to adjacent cells. AutoFill also has some other uses that may even substitute for formulas in some cases. I'm surprised to find that many experienced Excel users don't take advantage of the AutoFill feature, which can save a lot of time.

Besides serving as a shortcut to copy cells, AutoFill can quickly create a series of incremental values. For example, if you need a list of values from 1 to 100 to appear in A1:A100, you can do it with formulas. You enter 1 in cell A1, the formula =A1+1 into cell A2, and then copy the formula to the 98 cells below.

You also can use AutoFill to create the series for you without using a formula. To do so, enter 1 into cell A1 and 2 into cell A2. Select A1:A2 and drag the fill handle down to cell A100. (The fill handle is the small square at the lower-right corner of the active cell.) When you use AutoFill in this manner, Excel analyzes the selected cells and uses this information to complete the series. If cell A1 contains 1 and cell A2 contains 3, Excel recognizes this pattern and fills in 5, 7, 9, and so on. This also works with decreasing series (10, 9, 8, and so on) and dates. If there is no discernible pattern in the selected cells, Excel performs a linear regression and fills in values on the calculated trend line.

Excel also recognizes common series names such as months and days of the week. If you enter Monday into a cell and then drag its fill handle, Excel fills in the successive days of the week. You also can create custom AutoFill lists using the Custom Lists panel of the Options dialog box. Finally, if you drag the fill handle with the right mouse button, Excel displays a shortcut menu to enable you to select an AutoFill option.

TABLE 2-2 EXCEL ERROR VALUES

Error Value	Explanation
#DIV/0!	The formula attempts to divide by zero (an operation not allowed on this planet). This also occurs when the formula attempts to divide by an empty cell.
#NAME?	The formula uses a name that Excel doesn't recognize. This can happen if you delete a name used in the formula or if you have unmatched quotes in your text.
#N/A	The formula refers (directly or indirectly) to a cell that uses the NA functions to signal unavailable data.

Error Value	Explanation
#NULL!	The formula uses an intersection of two ranges that don't intersect. (I describe this concept later in the chapter.)
#NUM!	A problem occurs with a value; for example, you specify a negative number where a positive number is expected.
#REF!	The formula refers to an invalid cell. This happens if the cell has been deleted from the worksheet.
#VALUE!	The formula includes an argument or operand of the wrong type. An *operand* refers to a value or cell reference that a formula uses to calculate a result.

If the entire cell fills with pound characters, this usually means that the column isn't wide enough to display the value. You can either widen the column or change the number format of the cell. The cell will also fill with pound characters if it contains a formula that returns an invalid date or time.

Dealing with Circular References

When you enter formulas, you may occasionally see a message from Excel like the one shown in Figure 2-7. This indicates that the formula you just entered will result in a *circular reference*.

A circular reference occurs when a formula refers to its own value – either directly or indirectly. For example, if you enter =A1+A2+A3 into cell A3, this produces a circular reference because the formula in cell A3 refers to cell A3. Every time the formula in A3 is calculated, it must be calculated again because A3 has changed. The calculation would go on forever. In other words, the answer never gets resolved.

Figure 2-7: Excel's way of telling you that your formula contains a circular reference

When you get the circular reference message after entering a formula, Excel gives you two options:

◆ Click OK to attempt to locate the circular reference.

◆ Click Cancel to enter the formula as is.

Normally, you'll want to correct any circular references, so you should choose OK. When you do so, Excel displays its Circular Reference toolbar (see Figure 2-8). On the Circular Reference toolbar, click the first cell in the Navigate Circular Reference drop-down list box, and then examine the cell's formula. If you cannot determine whether the cell is the cause of the circular reference, click the next cell in the Navigate Circular Reference drop-down list box. Continue to review the formulas until the status bar no longer displays *Circular*.

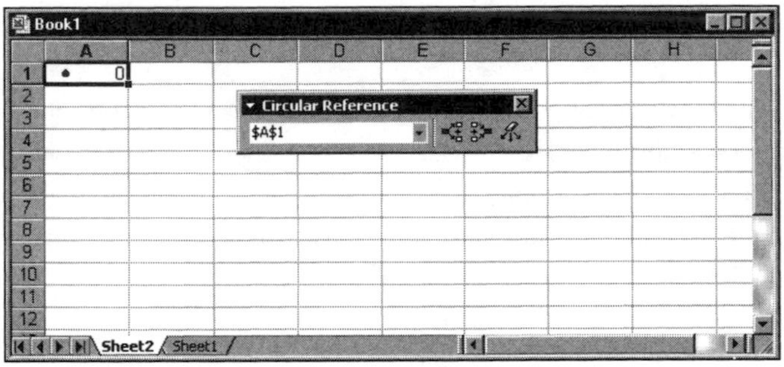

Figure 2-8: The Circular Reference toolbar

Some situations warrant you to use a circular reference intentionally. Refer to Chapter 14 for some examples.

If you ignore the circular reference message (by clicking Cancel), Excel enables you to enter the formula and displays a message in the status bar reminding you that a circular reference exists. In this case, the message reads *Circular: A3*. If you activate a different workbook, the message simply displays *Circular* (without the cell reference).

Excel won't warn you about a circular reference if you have the Iteration setting on. You can check this in the Options dialog box (in the Calculation panel). If Iteration is on, Excel performs the circular calculation the number of times specified in the Maximum iterations field (or until the value changes by less than .001, or whatever other value appears in the Maximum change field). You should, however, keep the Iteration setting off so that you'll be warned of circular references. Generally, a circular reference indicates an error that you must correct.

Usually, the cause of a circular reference is quite obvious and is therefore easy to identify and correct. Sometimes, however, you will encounter indirect circular references. In other words, a formula may refer to a formula that refers to a formula that refers back to the original formula. In some cases, it may require you to do a bit of detective work to reach the problem.

Use the tools on the Circular Reference toolbar or the Auditing toolbar for assistance in identifying a formula's dependents and precedents. See Chapter 19 for more information.

Goal Seeking

Many spreadsheets contain formulas that enable you to ask questions, such as, "What is the total profit if sales increase by 20 percent?" If you set up your worksheet properly, you can change the value in one cell to see what happens to the profit cell.

Goal seeking serves as a useful feature that works in conjunction with your formulas. If you know what a formula result *should* be, Excel can tell you which values of one or more input cells you need to produce that result. In other words, you can ask a question such as, "What sales increase is needed to produce a profit of $1.2 million?"

Single-cell goal seeking (also known as *backsolving*) represents a rather simple concept. Excel determines what value in an input cell produces a desired result in a formula cell. You can best understand how this works by walking through an example.

A goal-seeking example

Figure 2-9 shows a mortgage loan worksheet that has four input cells (C4:C7) and four formula cells (C10:C13). The formulas calculate various values using the input cell. The formulas are:

C10: =(1-C5)*C4

C11: =PMT(C7/12,C6,-C10)

C12: =C11*C6

C13: =C12-C10

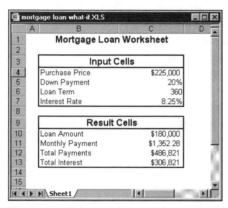

Figure 2-9: This worksheet presents a good demonstration of goal seeking.

Imagine that you're in the market for a new home and you know that you can afford $1,200 per month in mortgage payments. You also know that a lender can issue a fixed-rate mortgage loan for 8.25 percent, based on an 80 percent loan-to-value (a 20 percent down payment). The question is, "What is the maximum purchase price you can handle?" In other words, what value in cell C4 causes the formula in cell C11 to result in $1,200? You can plug values into cell C4 until C11 displays $1,200. A more efficient approach lets Excel determine the answer.

To answer this question, select Tools → Goal Seek. Excel responds with the Goal Seek dialog box shown in Figure 2-10. Completing this dialog box resembles forming a sentence. Set cell C11 to 1200 by changing cell C4. Enter this information in the dialog box by either typing the cell references or by pointing with the mouse. Click OK to begin the goal-seeking process.

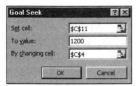

Figure 2-10: The Goal Seek dialog box

Almost immediately, Excel announces that it has found the solution and displays the Goal Seek Status box. This box tells you the target value and what Excel came up with. In this case, Excel found an exact value. The worksheet now displays the found value in cell C4 ($199,663). As a result of this value, the monthly payment amount is $1,200. Now, you have two options:

◆ Click OK to replace the original value with the found value.

◆ Click Cancel to restore your worksheet to its original form before you chose Tools → Goal Seek.

More about goal seeking

If you think about it, you may realize that Excel can't always find a value that produces the result you're looking for – sometimes a solution doesn't exist. In such a case, the Goal Seek Status box informs you of that fact (see Figure 2-11). Other times, however, Excel may report that it can't find a solution, even though you believe one exists. In this case, you can adjust the current value of the changing cell to a value closer to the solution, and then reissue the command. If that fails, double-check your logic, and make sure that the formula cell does indeed depend on the specified changing cell.

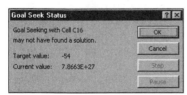

Figure 2-11: The Goal Seek Status box tells you if Excel can't find a solution to your goal-seeking problem.

Like all computer programs, Excel has limited precision. To demonstrate this, enter =A1^2 into cell A1. Then, select Tools → Goal Seek to find the value in cell A1 that causes the formula to return 16. Excel returns a value of 4.00002269 – close to the square root of 16, but certainly not exact. You can adjust the precision in the Calculation panel of the Options dialog box (make the Maximum change value smaller).

In some cases, multiple values of the input cell produce the same desired result. For example, the formula =A1^2 returns 16 if cell A1 contains either –4 or +4. If you use goal seeking when two solutions exist, Excel gives you the solution that has the same sign as the current value in the cell.

Perhaps the main limitation of the Tools → Goal Seek command is that it can find the value for only one input cell. For example, it can't tell you what purchase price *and* what down payment percent result in a particular monthly payment. If you want to change more than one variable at a time, use Solver.

Summary

This chapter provided an introduction to Excel formulas and covered the various elements that comprise a formula. The chapter also discussed related topics such as relative and absolute references, converting formulas to values, formula errors, and circular references.

The next chapter covers how to work with names in Excel.

Chapter 3

Using Names

IN THIS CHAPTER

- ◆ An overview and the advantages of using names in Excel
- ◆ Various ways to create cell and range names
- ◆ How to create names that extend across multiple worksheets
- ◆ The difference between workbook- and worksheet-level names
- ◆ How to perform common operations with range and cell names
- ◆ How Excel maintains cell and range names
- ◆ Potential problems that may crop up when you use names
- ◆ The secret behind names and examples of named constants and named formulas
- ◆ Examples of advanced techniques that use names

MOST EXPERIENCED USERS of Excel are familiar with the concept of named cells or ranges. Naming cells and ranges is an excellent practice and offers several important advantages. As you'll see in this chapter, Excel supports other types of names — and the power of this concept may surprise you.

What's in a Name?

You can think of a *name* as an identifier for something in a workbook. This "something" can consist of a cell, a range, a chart, a shape, and so on. If you provide a name for a range, you can then use that name in your formulas. For example, suppose your worksheet contains daily sales information stored in the range B2:B200. Further, assume that cell C1 contains a sales commission rate. The following formula returns the sum of the sales, multiplied by the commission rate:

```
=SUM(B2:B200)*C1
```

This formula works fine, but its purpose is not at all clear. To help clarify the formula, you can define a descriptive name for the daily sales range and another descriptive name for cell C1. For example, assume that the range B2:B200 is named *DailySales* and cell C1 is named *CommissionRate*. You can then rewrite the formula to use the names instead of the actual range addresses:

```
=SUM(DailySales)*CommissionRate
```

As you can see, using names instead of cell references makes the formula "self-documenting," and much easier to understand.

Using named cells and ranges offers a number of advantages:

◆ Names make your formulas more understandable and easier to use —
especially for people who didn't create the worksheet. Obviously, a
formula such as =Income-Taxes is more intuitive than =D20-D40.

◆ When entering formulas, a descriptive range name (such as *Total_Income*)
is easier to remember than a cell address (such as AC21). And, typing a
name is less error-prone than entering a cell or range address.

◆ You can quickly move to areas of your worksheet either by using the
Name box, located at the left side of the formula bar (click the arrow for a
drop-down list of defined names), or by choosing Edit → Go To (or F5) and
specifying the range name.

◆ When you select a named cell or range, its name (if it has one) appears in
the Name box.

◆ You may find creating formulas easier. You can paste a cell or range name
into a formula by using the Insert → Name → Paste command (or F3).

◆ Macros are easier to create and maintain when you use range names
rather than cell addresses.

Methods for Creating Cell and Range Names

Excel provides several ways to create names for cells and ranges. I discuss these methods in this section, along with other relevant information that pertains to names.

Creating names using the Define Name dialog box

To create a name for a cell or range, start by selecting the cell or range that you want to name. Then, select Insert→Name→Define (or press Ctrl+F3). Excel displays the Define Name dialog box, shown in Figure 3-1.

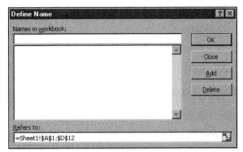

Figure 3-1: Use the Define Name Dialog box to create names for cells or ranges.

Type a name in the field labeled Names in your workbook (or use the name that Excel proposes, if any). The selected cell or range address appears in the Refers to field. Verify that the address listed is correct, click OK to add the name to your worksheet, and close the dialog box. Or, click the Add button to continue adding names to your worksheet. If you do this, you must specify the Refers to range either by typing an address (make sure to begin with an equal sign) or by pointing to it in the worksheet.

 A single cell or range can have any number of names. I can't think of a good reason to do so, but Excel does permit it. If a cell or range has multiple names, the Name box always displays the first name when you select the cell or range.

A name also can refer to a noncontiguous range of cells. You can select a noncontiguous range by pressing the Ctrl key while you select various cells or ranges with the mouse.

 If you try to edit the contents of the Refers to field manually, you'll find that this field is in "point" mode. You can't use keys such as End and Home to edit the field contents. To switch from point mode to normal edit mode, press F2. Then, you can use the standard editing keys when the Refers to field is activated.

Rules for Naming Names

Although Excel is quite flexible about the names that you can define, it does have some rules:

1. Names can't contain any spaces. You may want to use an underscore or a period character to simulate a space (such as *Annual_Total* or *Annual.Total*).

2. You can use any combination of letters and numbers, but the name must begin with a letter or underscore. A name can't begin with a number (such as *3rdQuarter*) or look like a cell reference (such as *Q3*).

3. You cannot use symbols, except for underscores and periods. Although not documented, I've found that Excel also permits a backslash (\) and question mark (?) as long as they don't appear as the first character in a name.

4. Names are limited to 255 characters. Trust me — you should not use a name anywhere near this length. In fact, it defeats the purpose of naming ranges.

5. You can use single letters (except for R or C), but generally I do not recommend this because it also defeats the purpose of using meaningful names.

6. Names are not case sensitive. The name *AnnualTotal* is the same as *annualtotal*.Excel stores the name exactly as you type it when you define it, but it doesn't matter how you capitalize the name when you use it in a formula.

Excel also uses a few names internally for its own use. Although you can create names that override Excel's internal names, you should avoid doing so unless you know what you're doing. Generally, avoid using the following names: *Print_Area*, *Print_Titles*, *Consolidate_Area*, *Database*, *FilterDatabase*, and *Sheet_Title*.

Creating names using the Name box

A faster way to create a name involves the Name box. The Name box is the drop-down box to the left of the formula bar. Select the cell or range to name and then click the Name box and type the name. Press Enter to create the name. If a name already exists, you can't use the Name box to change the range to which that name refers. Attempting to do so simply selects the original range. You must use the Define Name dialog box to change the reference for a name.

When you type a name in the Name box, you *must* press Enter to actually record the name. If you type a name and then click in the worksheet, Excel won't create the name.

The Name box serves double-duty by also providing a quick way to activate a named cell or range, as shown in Figure 3-2. To select a named cell or range, click the Name box and choose the name. This selects the named cell or range. Oddly, the Name box does not have a keyboard shortcut. In other words, you can't access the Name box by using the keyboard; you must use a mouse. After you click the Name box, however, you can use the direction keys and Enter to choose a name.

Figure 3-2: The Name box provides a quick way to activate a named cell or range.

Creating names automatically

You may have a worksheet that contains text that you want to use for names of adjacent cells or ranges. Figure 3-3 shows an example of such a worksheet. In this case, you might want to use the text in column A to create names for the corresponding values in column B. Excel makes this very easy to do.

To create names by using adjacent text, start by selecting the name text and the cells that you want to name (these can consist of individual cells or ranges of cells). The names must be adjacent to the cells that you're naming (a multiple selection is allowed). Then, choose Insert → Name → Create (or Ctrl+Shift+F3). Excel displays the Create Names dialog box, shown in Figure 3-4.

	A	B	C	D	E
1		**Total Sales**			
2	January	26,663.0			
3	February	56,593.0			
4	March	14,486.0			
5	April	31,376.0			
6	May	11,651.0			
7	June	35,685.0			
8	July	26,435.0			
9	August	30,549.0			
10	September	36,191.0			
11	October	89,874.0			
12	November	43,877.0			
13	December	27,442.0			
14					
15					
16					

Figure 3-3: Excel makes it easy to create names by using text in adjacent cells.

The check marks in this dialog box are based on Excel's analysis of the selected range. For example, if Excel finds text in the first row of the selection, it proposes that you create names based on the top row. If Excel doesn't guess correctly, you can change the checkboxes. Click OK and Excel then creates the names. Note that when Excel creates names using text in cells, it does not include those text cells in the named range.

Figure 3-4: The Create Names dialog box

If the text in a cell results in an invalid name, Excel modifies the name to make it valid. For example, if a cell contains the text *Net Income* (invalid for a name because it contains a space), Excel converts the space to an underscore character. If Excel encounters a value or a formula instead of text, however, it doesn't convert it to a valid name. It simply doesn't create a name.

Naming entire rows and columns

Sometimes it makes sense to name an entire row or column. Often, a worksheet is used to store information that you enter over a period of time. The sheet in Figure 3-6 is an example of such a worksheet. If you create a name for the data in column B, you need to modify the name's reference each day you add new data. The solution is to name the entire column.

	A	B	C	D	E	
1	**Products**	Quantity	Price			
2	Pencils	433	0.29			
3	Paper	109	3.89			
4	Erasers	33	0.89			
5	Pens	112	1.49			
6	Paperclips	92	2.89			
7						
8						

Book3 — Sheet1

Figure 3-5: Creating names from the data in this table may produce unexpected results.

Double-check the names that Excel creates. Sometimes the Insert→ Name→Create command works counter-intuitively. Figure 3-5 shows a small table of text and values. If you select the entire table, choose InsertName→Create, and accept Excel's suggestions (Top row and Left column options). You'll find that the name *Products* doesn't refer to A2:A6, as you may expect, but instead refers to B2:C6. If the upper-left cell of the selection contains text and you choose the Top row and Left column options, Excel uses that text for the name of the entire data — excluding the top row and left column. So, before you accept the names that Excel creates, take a minute to make sure that they refer to the correct ranges.

	A	B	C	D	E	F	
1	1-Jan	13					
2	2-Jan	89					
3	3-Jan	93					
4	4-Jan	113					
5	5-Jan	321					
6	6-Jan	299					
7	7-Jan	301					
8	8-Jan	188					
9	9-Jan						
10	10-Jan						
11	11-Jan						
12	12-Jan						
13	13-Jan						
14	14-Jan						
15	15-Jan						

Book3 — Sheet1

Figure 3-6: This worksheet, which tracks daily sales, uses a named range that consists of an entire column.

For example, you might name column B *DailySales*. Its reference appears like this:

```
=Sheet1!$B:$B
```

Hidden Names

Some Excel macros and add-ins create hidden names. These names exist in a workbook, but don't appear in the Define Name dialog box or the Name box. For example, the Solver add-in creates a number of hidden names. Normally, you can just ignore these hidden names. However, sometimes these hidden names create problems. If you copy a sheet to another workbook, the hidden names are also copied, and they may create a link that is very difficult to track down.

Excel doesn't make it very easy to work with names. For example, you have no way of viewing a *complete* list of names defined in a workbook. When you use the Define Name dialog box, it lists only the worksheet-level names in the active worksheet. And, it never displays hidden names.

If you'd like a better tool to help you work with names, you can use the Name Lister utility, which is part of the Power Utility Pak. This utility displays a list of all names, and you can filter the list in a number of ways — for example, show only sheet-level names, or show only linked names. The utility is also useful for identifying and deleting "bad" names — names that refer to an invalid range. I include a trial version of the Power Utility Pak on the companion CD-ROM.

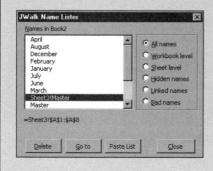

Names created by Excel

Excel creates some names on its own. For example, if you set a print area for a sheet, Excel creates the name *Print_Area*. If you set repeating rows or columns for printing, you also have a worksheet-level named *Print_Titles*. When you execute a query that returns data to a worksheet, Excel assigns the data that returns. Also, many of the add-ins that ship with Excel create hidden names (see the following "Hidden Names" sidebar).

You can modify the reference for any of the names that Excel creates automatically, but make sure that you understand the consequences.

Creating Multisheet Names

Names can extend into the third dimension; in other words, they can extend across multiple worksheets in a workbook. You can't simply select the multisheet range and enter a name in the Name box, however. You must use the Define Name dialog box to create a multisheet name. (The Name box won't work for this.) The format for a multisheet reference looks like this:

```
FirstSheet:LastSheet!RangeReference
```

In Figure 3-7, a multisheet name (*DataCube*), defined for A1:C3, extends across Sheet1, Sheet2, and Sheet3.

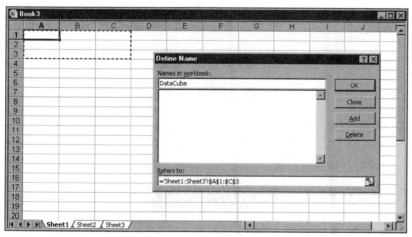

Figure 3-7: Creating a multisheet name

You can, of course, simply type the multisheet range reference into the Refers to field. But if you want to create the name by pointing to the range, you'll find it a bit tricky. Even if you begin by selecting a multisheet range, Excel does not use this selected range address in the Define Name dialog box.

Follow this step-by-step procedure to create a name called *DataCube* that refers to the range A1:C3 across three worksheets (Sheet1, Sheet2, and Sheet3):

1. Activate Sheet1.

2. Choose Insert → Name → Define (or press Ctrl+F3) to display the Define Name dialog box.

3. Type **DataCube** in the Names in workbook field.

4. Activate the Refers to field, and press Del to delete the range reference.

5. Select the range A1:C3 in Sheet1. The following appears in the Refers to field:

```
=Sheet1!$A$1:$C$3
```

6. Press Shift and then click the Sheet tab for Sheet3. You'll find that Excel inexplicably changes the range reference to a single cell. At this point, the following appears in the Refers to field:

```
='Sheet1:Sheet3'!$A$1
```

7. Reselect the range A1:C3 in Sheet1. The following appears in the Refers to field:

```
='Sheet1:Sheet3'!$A$1:$C$3
```

8. Since the Refers to field now has the correct multisheet range address, click OK to close the Define Name dialog box.

After you define the name, you can use it in your formulas. For example, the following formula returns the sum of the values in the range named *DataCube:*

```
=SUM(DataCube)
```

 Multisheet names do not appear in the Name box or in the Go To dialog box (which appears when you select Edit → Go To). In other words, Excel enables you to define the name, but it doesn't give you a way to select automatically the cells to which the name refers.

If you insert a new worksheet into a workbook that uses multisheet names, the multisheet names will include the new worksheet — as long as the sheet resides between the first and last sheet in the name's definition. In the preceding example, a worksheet inserted between Sheet1 and Sheet2 will be included in the *DataCube* range. But a worksheet inserted before Sheet1 or after Sheet 3 will not be included.

If you delete the first or last sheet included in a multisheet name, Excel changes the name's range in the Refers to field automatically. In the preceding example, deleting Sheet1 causes the Refers to range of *DataCube* to change to:

```
='Sheet2:Sheet3'!$A$1:$C$3
```

A Name's Scope

Normally, when you name a cell or range, you can use that name in all worksheets in the workbook. For example, if you create a name called *RegionTotal* that refers to the cell A1 on Sheet1, you can use this name in any formula in any worksheet. This is referred to as a workbook-level name (or a global name). By default, all cell and range names are workbook-level names.

Creating worksheet-level names

What if you have several worksheets in a workbook and you want to use the same name (such as *RegionTotal*) on each sheet? In this case, you need to create worksheet-level names (sometimes referred to as local names).

To define a worksheet-level name *RegionTotal*, activate the worksheet in which you want to define the name and choose Insert → Name → Define. The Define Name dialog box then appears. In the Names in workbook field, precede the worksheet-level name with the worksheet name, followed by an exclamation point. For example, to define the name *RegionTotal* on Sheet2, activate Sheet2 and enter the following in the Names in workbook field of the Define Name dialog box:

```
Sheet2!RegionTotal
```

If the worksheet name contains at least one space, enclose the worksheet name in single quotation marks, like this:

```
'Marketing Dept'!RegionTotal
```

You can also create a worksheet-level name by using the Name box. Select the cell or range you want named, click in the Name box, and type the name. Precede the worksheet-level name with the sheet's name and an exclamation point (as shown above). Press Enter to create the name.

When you write a formula that uses a worksheet-level name on the sheet in which you defined it, you don't need to include the worksheet name in the range name (the Name box won't display the worksheet name either). If you use the name in a formula on a *different* worksheet, however, you must use the entire name (sheet name, exclamation point, and name).

Only the worksheet-level names on the current sheet appear in the Name box. Similarly, only worksheet-level names in the current sheet appear in the list when you open the Paste Name or Define Name dialog boxes.

Combining worksheet- and workbook-level names

Using worksheet-level names can be a bit confusing because Excel lets you define worksheet-level names even if the workbook contains the same name as a workbook-level name. In such a case, the worksheet-level name takes precedence over the workbook-level name, but only in the worksheet in which you defined the sheet-level name.

For example, you may define a workbook-level name of *Total* for a cell on Sheet1. You also can define a worksheet-level name of *Sheet2!Total*. When Sheet2 is active, *Total* refers to the worksheet-level name. When any other sheet is active, *Total* refers to the workbook-level name. Confusing? Probably. To make your life easier, I recommend that you simply avoid using the same name at the workbook level and worksheet level.

Referencing names from another workbook

Chapter 2 described how to use links to reference cells or ranges in other workbooks. The same rules apply when using names defined in another workbook.

For example, the following formula uses a range named *MonthlySales*, defined in a workbook named Budget.xls (which is assumed to be open).

```
=AVERAGE(Budget.xls!MonthlySales)
```

Working with Range and Cell Names

Once you create range or cell names, you can work with them in a variety of ways. This section describes how to perform common operations with range and cell names.

Creating a list of names

If you create a large number of names, you may need to know the ranges that each name refers to, particularly if you're trying to track down errors or document your work.

Excel lets you create a list of all names (and their corresponding addresses) in the workbook. To create a list of names, first move the cell pointer to an empty area of your worksheet (the two-column name list, created at the active cell position, overwrites any information at that location). Use the Insert→Name→Paste command (or press F3). Excel displays the Paste Name dialog box (see Figure 3-8) that lists all the defined names. To paste a list of names, click the Paste List button.

Figure 3-8: The Paste Name dialog box

 The list of names does not include worksheet-level names that appear in sheets other than the active sheet.

The list of names pasted to your worksheet occupies two columns. The first column contains the names, and the second column contains the corresponding range addresses. The range addresses in the second column consist of text strings that look like formulas. You can convert such a string to an actual formula by editing the cell (press F2, then press Enter). The string then converts to a formula. If the name refers to a single cell, the formula displays the cell's current value. If the name refers to a range, the formula returns a #VALUE! error.

Using names in formulas

After you define a name for a cell or range, you can use it in a formula. If the name is a workbook-level name (the default type), you can use the name in any sheet in the workbook. Just enter the name in place of the cell reference. For example, the following formula calculates the sum of the values in the range named *UnitsSold:*

```
=SUM(UnitsSold)
```

When you write a formula that uses a worksheet-level name on the sheet in which it's defined, you don't need to include the worksheet name in the range name. If you use the name in a formula on a different worksheet, however, you must use the entire name (sheet name, exclamation point, and name). For example, if the name *UnitsSold* represents a worksheet-level name defined on Sheet1, the following formula (on a sheet other than Sheet1) calculates the total of the *UnitsSold* range:

```
=SUM(Sheet1!UnitsSold)
```

Natural Language Formulas? Just Say No!

Beginning with Excel 97, you can use worksheet labels in your formulas, even if you haven't officially defined the names. Microsoft calls this "natural language formulas." For example, the workbook, shown in the accompanying figure, contains no defined names.

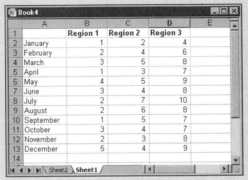

Excel, however, can interpret the row and column labels. For example, the following formula returns 7 - the sum of the values in the row labeled January:

```
=SUM(January)
```

You can also make use of the column labels. The following formula, for instance, returns 29 - the sum of the values for Region 1:

```
=SUM(Region 1)
```

You can even use multiple labels in a formula. This next formula returns 4 - the value at the intersection of February and Region 2:

```
=February Region 2
```

Using natural language formulas may seem like an easy way to get the benefits of names without going through the trouble of defining names. However, this feature sometimes does not work as advertised. Formulas that use these "pseudonames" sometimes do not get calculated when the data changes. Even worse, two identical formulas may return different results! Another problem is that, unlike a real named range, you really have no way of determining how Excel interprets a particular label. Finally, Excel imposes a limit of 32,764 natural language formulas; try to use more and Excel will probably crash.

I strongly recommend that you simply ignore this feature and use real names instead. To disable natural language formulas, select Tools → Options. In the Options dialog box that appears, click the Calculation tab, and uncheck the Accept labels in formulas option. This setting is stored with each workbook, so if you open a file that uses natural languages formulas, you need to turn it off for that file. When you turn this feature off, Excel scans your formula and converts any labels to actual cell references.

As you type a formula, you can select Insert → Name → Paste (or simply press F3) to display the Paste Name dialog box. Select a name from the list, click OK, and Excel inserts that name into your formula. As I previously mentioned, the Paste Name dialog box lists all workbook-level names, plus worksheet-level names for the active sheet only.

If you use a nonexistent name in a formula, Excel displays a #NAME? error, indicating that it cannot find the name you are trying to use. Often, this means that you misspelled the name.

Using the intersection operators with names

Excel's range intersection operator is a single space character. The following formula, for example, displays the sum of the cells at the intersection of two ranges: B1:C20 and A8:D8:

```
=SUM(B1:C20 A8:D8)
```

The intersection of these two ranges consists of two cells: B8 and C8.

The intersection operator also works with named ranges. Figure 3-9 shows a worksheet containing named ranges that correspond to the row and column labels. For example, the name *January* refers to B2:D2 and the name *Region_1* refers to B2:B13. The following formula returns the contents of the cell at the intersection of the *January* range and the *Region_1* range:

```
=January Region_1
```

	A	B	C	D	E	F
1		Region 1	Region 2	Region 3		
2	January	3,750	2,591	4,885		
3	February	2,431	5,591	3,252		
4	March	2,584	1,494	5,324		
5	April	4,117	2,301	3,339		
6	May	3,218	5,573	2,679		
7	June	1,108	3,535	5,275		
8	July	3,509	1,323	3,343		
9	August	3,482	2,120	4,140		
10	September	1,366	3,585	2,709		
11	October	2,891	3,790	2,458		
12	November	4,210	4,490	5,282		
13	December	4,687	5,725	2,412		
14						
15						

Figure 3-9: This worksheet contains named ranges that correspond to row and column labels.

Using a space character to separate two range references or names is known as *explicit intersection* because you explicitly tell Excel to determine the intersection of the ranges. Excel, however, also can perform *implicit intersections*. An implicit intersection occurs when Excel chooses a value from a multicell range based on the row or column of the formula that contains the reference. An example should clear this up. Figure 3-10 shows a worksheet that contains a range (B4:B20) named *MyData*. Cell D6 contains the simple formula shown here:

```
=MyData
```

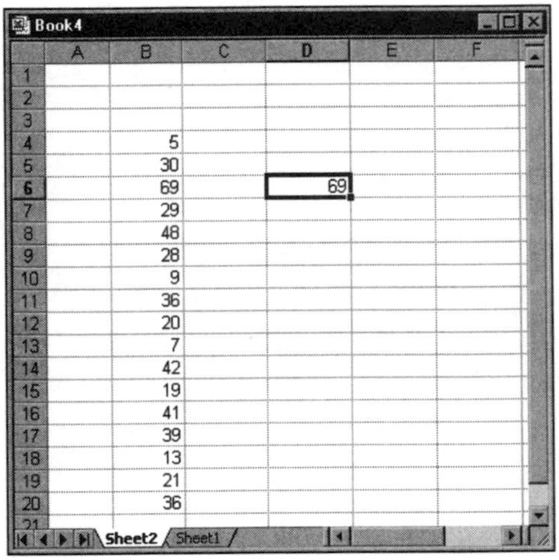

Figure 3-10: Range B4:B20 in this worksheet is named MyData.

Notice that cell D6 displays the value from *MyData* that corresponds to the formula's row. Similarly, if you enter the same formula into any other cell in rows 4 through 20, the formula displays the corresponding value from *MyData*. Excel performs an implicit intersection using the *MyData* range and the row that contains the formula. It's as if the following formula is being evaluated:

```
=MyData 6:6
```

If you enter the formula in a row not occupied by *MyData*, the formula returns an error because the implicit intersection returns nothing.

By the way, implicit intersection is not limited to named ranges. In the preceding example, you get the same result if cell D6 contains the following formula (which doesn't use a named range):

```
=$B$4:$B$20
```

Using the range operator with names

You also can use the range operator—a colon (:)—to work with named ranges. Refer back to Figure 3-9. For example, this formula returns the sum of the values for Region 1 through Region 2 for January through March (six cells):

```
=SUM((Region_1 January):(Region_2 March))
```

Referencing a single cell in a multicell named range

You can use Excel's INDEX function to return a single value from a multicell range. Assume that range A1:A50 is named *DataRange*. The following formula displays the second value (the value in A2) in *DataRange*:

```
=INDEX(DataRange,2)
```

The second and third arguments for INDEX function are optional, although at least one of them must always be specified. The second argument (used in the preceding formula) is used to specify the row offset within the *DataRange* range.

If *DataRange* consists of multiple cells in a single row, use a formula like the following one. This formula omits the second argument for the INDEX function, but uses the third argument that specifies the column offset with the *DataRange* range:

```
=INDEX(DataRange,,2)
```

If the range consists of multiple rows and columns, use both the second and third arguments for the INDEX function. For example, this formula returns the value in the fourth row and fifth column of a range named *DataRange*:

```
=INDEX(DataRange,4,5)
```

Applying names to existing formulas

When you create a name for a cell or range, Excel does not scan your formulas automatically and replace the cell references with your new name. You can, however, tell Excel to "apply" names to a range of formulas.

Select the range that contains the formulas that you want to convert. Then, choose Insert → Name → Apply. The Apply Names dialog box will appear, as shown in Figure 3-11. In the Apply Names dialog box, select which names you want applied to the formulas. Only those names that you select will be applied to the formulas.

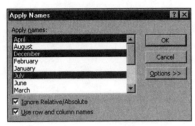

Figure 3-11: The Apply Names dialog box

 To apply names to all the formulas in the worksheet, select a single cell before you choose Insert → Name → Apply.

The Ignore Relative/Absolute checkbox controls how Excel substitutes the range name for the actual address. A cell or range name is usually defined as an absolute reference. If the Ignore Relative/Absolute checkbox is checked, Excel applies the name only if the reference in the formula matches exactly. In most cases, you will want to ignore the type of cell reference when applying names.

If the Use row and column names checkbox is checked, Excel takes advantage of the intersection operator when applying names. Excel uses the names of row and column ranges that refer to the cells if it cannot find the exact names for the cells. Excel uses the intersection operator to join the names. Clicking the Options button displays some additional options available only when you have the Use row and column names checkbox checked.

Applying names automatically when creating a formula

When you insert a cell or range reference into a formula by pointing, Excel automatically substitutes the cell or range name if it has one.

 This behavior occurs only in Excel 97 and later.

In some cases, this is a good thing. In other cases, you may prefer to use an actual cell or range reference instead of the name. Unfortunately, you cannot turn off this feature. If you prefer to use a regular cell or range address, you need to type the cell or range reference manually (don't use the pointing technique).

Unapplying names

Excel does not provide a direct method for unapplying names. In other words, you cannot replace a name in a formula with the name's actual cell reference automatically. However, you can take advantage of a trick described here. You need to change Excel's Transition formula entry option so it emulates 1-2-3. Select Tools → Options, and click the Transition tab in the Options dialog box. Place a checkmark next to Transition formula entry, and click OK.

Next, press F2 to edit a formula that contains one or more cell or range names. The formula displays the actual range references instead of the names. (The formula bar, however, continues to show the range names.) Press Enter to end cell editing. Next, go back to the Options dialog box and remove the checkmark from the Transition formula entry checkbox. You'll find that the edited cell no longer uses names.

The Power Utility Pak includes a utility that enables you to unapply names in selected formulas. The companion CD-ROM contains a trial version of the Power Utility Pak.

Deleting names

If you no longer need a defined name, you can delete it. Deleting a range name deletes the name only. It *does not* delete the contents of the range. Choose Insert → Name → Define to display the Define Name dialog box. Choose the name that you want to delete from the list and then click the Delete button.

Be extra careful when deleting names. If the name is used in a formula, deleting the name causes the formula to become invalid (it will display #NAME?). It would be very helpful if Excel simply replaced all references to the name with the actual cell or range reference of the deleted name — but it doesn't. However, you can undo the act of deleting a name, so if you find that formulas return #NAME?, after you delete a name, select Edit → Undo to get the name back.

Deleting named cells or ranges

If you delete the rows or columns that contain named cells or ranges, the names will not be deleted (as you might expect). Rather, each name will contain an invalid reference. For example, if cell A1 on Sheet1 is named *Interest* and you delete row 1 or column A, *Interest* then refers to =Sheet1!#REF! (i.e., an erroneous reference). If you use *Interest* in a formula, the formula displays #REF.

Redefining names

After you define a name, you may want to change the cell or range to which it refers. Select Insert → Name → Define to display the Define Name dialog box. Select the name that you want to change, and then edit the cell or range address in the Refers to field. If you prefer, you can click the Refers to field and select a new cell or range by pointing in the worksheet.

Changing names

Excel doesn't provide a simple way to change a name once you create the name. If you create a name and then realize that you prefer a different name — or, perhaps, that you spelled it incorrectly — you must create the new name and then delete the old name. In the Define Name dialog box, select the old name in the list of names, change the text in the Names in workbook field to the new name, and click the Add button. Then, select the old name again and click the Delete button.

When you change a name, Excel does not adjust formulas that use the name automatically. You can, however, use the Edit → Replace command to find and replace occurrences of the old name with the new name.

Viewing named ranges

When you zoom a worksheet to 39 percent or lower, you see a border around the named ranges with the name displayed in blue letters, as shown in Figure 3-12. The border and name do not print; they simply help you visualize the named ranges on your sheet.

This feature is available in Excel 97 or later.

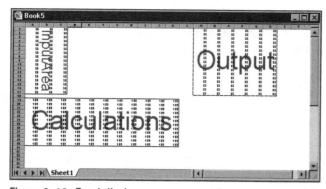

Figure 3-12: Excel displays range names when you zoom a sheet to 39 percent or less.

Using names in charts

When you create a chart, each data series has an associated SERIES formula. The SERIES formula contains references to the ranges used in the chart. If you have a defined range name, you can edit a SERIES formula and replace the range reference with the name.

Refer to Chapter 15 for additional information about charts.

How Excel Maintains Cell and Range Names

Once you create a name for a cell or range, Excel automatically maintains the name as you edit or modify the worksheet. The following examples assume that Sheet1 contains a workbook-level name (*MyRange*) that refers to =Sheet1!$C$3:$E$5 (a nine-cell range).

Inserting a row or column

When you insert a row above the named range or insert a column to the left of the named range, Excel changes the range reference to reflect its new address. For example, if you insert a new row 1, *MyRange* then refers to =Sheet1!$C$4:$E$6.

If you insert a new row or column within the named range, the named range expands to include the new row or column. For example, if you insert a new column to the left of column E, *MyRange* then refers to =Sheet1!$C$3:$F$5.

Deleting a row or column

When you delete a row above the named range or delete a column to the left of the named range, Excel adjusts the range reference to reflect its new address. For example, if you delete row 1, *MyRange* refers to =Sheet1!$B$3:$D$5.

If you delete a row or column within the named range, the name range adjusts accordingly. For example, if you delete column D, *MyRange* then refers to =Sheet1!$C$3:$D$5.

If you delete all rows or all columns that make up a named range, the named range continues to exist, but it contains an error reference. For example, if you delete columns C, D, and E, *MyRange* then refers to =Sheet1!#REF!. Any formulas that use the name also return errors.

Cutting and pasting

When you cut and paste an entire named range, Excel changes the reference accordingly. For example, if you move *MyRange* to a new location beginning at cell A2, *MyRange* then refers to =Sheet1!$A$1:$C$3. Cutting and pasting only a part of a named range does not affect the name's reference.

Potential Problems with Names

Names are great, but they can also cause some problems. This section contains information that you should remember when you use names in a workbook.

Name problems when copying sheets

Excel, as you know, lets you copy a worksheet within the same workbook, or to a different workbook. Let's focus first on copying a sheet within the same workbook. If the copied sheet contains worksheet-level names, those names will also be present on the copy of the sheet, adjusted to use the new sheet name. Usually, this is exactly what you want to happen. But if the workbook contains a workbook-level name that refers to a cell or range on the sheet that's copied, that name will also be present on the copied sheet. However, it will be converted to a worksheet-level name! That is usually *not* what you want to happen.

Consider a workbook that contains one sheet (Sheet1). This workbook has a workbook-level name (called *BookName*) for cell A1, and a worksheet-level name (called *Sheet1!LocalName*) for cell A2. If you make a copy of Sheet1 within the workbook, the new sheet is named Sheet1 (2). You'll find that, after copying the sheet, the workbook contains four names, listed and described in Table 3-1.

TABLE 3-1 NAMES IN A WORKBOOK AFTER COPYING A SHEET

Name	Refers To	Type
BookName	=Sheet1!$A$1	Workbook-level
Sheet1!LocalName	=Sheet1!$A$2	Worksheet-level
Sheet1 (2)'!BookName	='Sheet1 (2)'!$A$1	Worksheet-level
Sheet1 (2)'!LocalName	='Sheet1 (2)'!$A$2	Worksheet-level

This proliferation of names when copying a sheet is confusing and can result in errors that can be very difficult to identify. In this case, typing the following formula on the copied sheet displays the contents of cell A1 in the copied sheet:

```
=BookName
```

In other words, the newly created worksheet-level name (not the original workbook-level name) is being used.

When you copy the worksheet from a workbook that contains a name that refers to a multisheet range, you also copy this name. A #REF! error appears in its Refers to definition.

When you copy a sheet to a new workbook, all of the names in the original workbook that refer to cells on the copied sheet are also copied to the new workbook. This includes both workbook-level and worksheet-level names.

 Copying and pasting cells from one sheet to another does not copy names, even if the copied range contains named cells.

Bottom line? You must use caution when copying sheets from a workbook that uses names. After copying the sheet, check the names and delete those that you didn't intend to be copied.

Name problems when deleting sheets

When you delete a worksheet that contains cells used in a workbook-level name, you'll find that the name is not deleted. The name remains with the workbook, but it contains an erroneous reference in its Refers to definition.

Figure 3-13 shows the Define Name dialog box that displays an erroneous name. The workbook originally contained a sheet named Sheet1, which had a named range (a workbook-level name, *MyRange*) for A1:F12. After deleting Sheet1, the name *MyRange* still exists in the workbook, but the Refers to field in the Define Name dialog box displays the following:

```
=#REF!$A$1:$F$12
```

As far as I can tell, keeping erroneous names in a workbook doesn't cause any harm, but it's a good practice to delete all names that contain an erroneous reference.

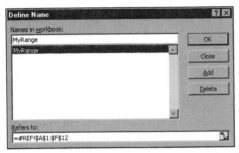

Figure 3-13: Deleting the sheet that contains the cell for MyRange causes an erroneous reference.

Naming Charts and Objects

When you add a chart or any other type of object to a worksheet, the object has a default name. For example, the first chart on a worksheet is named *Chart 1*. When you add a drawing object (such as a Rectangle or TextBox), the name reflects the type of object (for example, *Rectangle 3*).

To change the name of an object, select it, type the new name in the Name box, and press Enter. Naming charts is an exception. To rename a chart, you must first select the entire chart object. To do so, press Ctrl while you click the chart.

Excel is a bit inconsistent with regard to the Name box. Although you can use the Name box to rename an object, you can't use it to select an object (only named ranges and cells appear in the Name box). Also, you'll find that the Define Name dialog box does not list the names of objects.

The Secret to Understanding Names

Excel users often refer to *named ranges* and *named cells*. In fact, I've used these terms frequently throughout this chapter. Actually, this terminology is not quite accurate.

Here's the secret to understanding names:

> When you create a name, you're actually creating a named formula – a formula that doesn't exist in a cell. Rather, these named formulas exist in Excel's memory.

This is not exactly an earth-shaking revelation. However, if you keep this "secret" in mind, it will help you to understand the advanced naming techniques that follow.

When you work with the Define Name dialog box, the Refers to field contains the formula, and the Names in workbook field contains the formula's name. You'll find that the contents of the Refers to field always begin with an equal sign, which makes it a formula.

As you can see in Figure 3-14, the workbook contains a name (*InterestRate*) for cell B1 on Sheet1. The Refers to field lists the following formula:

```
=Sheet1!$B$1
```

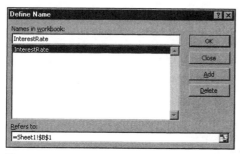

Figure 3-14: Technically, the name InterestRate is a named formula, not a named cell.

Whenever you use the name *InterestRate*, Excel actually evaluates the formula with that name and returns the result. For example, you might type this formula into a cell:

```
=InterestRate*1.05
```

When Excel evaluates this formula, it first evaluates the formula named *InterestRate* (which exists only in memory, not in a cell). It then multiplies the result of this named formula by 1.05 and displays the result. This cell formula, of course, is equivalent to the following formula, which uses the actual cell reference instead of the name:

```
=Sheet1!$B$1*1.05
```

At this point, you may be wondering if it's possible to create a named formula that doesn't contain any cell references. The answer comes in the next section.

Naming constants

Consider a worksheet that generates an invoice and calculates sales tax for a sales amount. The common approach is to insert the sales tax rate value into a cell, and then use this cell reference in your formulas. To make things easier, you probably would name this cell something like *SalesTax*.

You can do this another way. Figure 3-15 demonstrates the following steps:

1. Choose Insert → Name → Define (or press Ctrl+F3) to bring up the Define Name dialog box.

2. Enter the name (in this case, **SalesTax**) into the Names in workbook field.

3. Click the Refers to box, delete its contents, and replace it with a simple formula, such as **=.075**.

4. Click OK to close the dialog box.

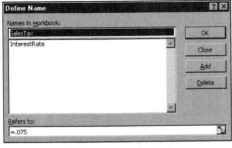

Figure 3-15: Defining a name that refers to a constant

The preceding steps create a named formula that doesn't use any cell references. To try it out, enter the following formula into any cell:

```
=SalesTax
```

This simple formula returns .075, the result of the formula named *SalesTax*. Since this named formula always returns the same result, you can think of it as a named constant. And, you can use this constant in a more complex formula such as:

```
=A1*SalesTax
```

SalesTax is a workbook-level name, so you can use it in any worksheet in the workbook.

Naming text constants

In the preceding example, the constant consisted of a numeric value. A constant also can consist of text. For example, you can define a constant for your company's name. If you work for Microsoft, you can use the Define Name dialog box to create the following formula named *MS*:

```
="Microsoft Corporation"
```

Then, you can use a cell formula such as:

```
="I work for "&MS
```

This formula returns the text *I work for Microsoft Corporation.*

 Names that do not refer to ranges do not appear in the Name box or in the Go To dialog box (which appears when you press F5). This makes sense, because these constants don't reside anywhere tangible. They *do* appear in the Paste Names dialog box, however, which *does* make sense, because you'll use these names in formulas.

As you might expect, you can change the value of the constant at any time by accessing the Define Name dialog box and simply changing the value in the Refers to box. When you close the dialog box, Excel uses the new value to recalculate the formulas that use this name.

Although this technique is useful in many situations, changing the value takes some time. Having a constant located in a cell makes it much easier to modify. If the value is truly a "constant," however, you won't need to change it.

Using worksheet functions in named formulas

Figure 3-16 shows another example of a named formula. In this case, the formula is named *ThisMonth*, and the actual formula is:

```
=MONTH(TODAY())
```

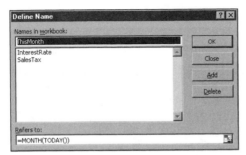

Figure 3-16: Defining a named formula that uses worksheet functions

The formula in Figure 3-16 uses two worksheet functions. The TODAY function returns the current date and the MONTH function returns the month number of its date argument. Therefore, you can enter a formula such as the following into a cell and it will return the number of the current month. For example, if the current month is April, the formula returns 4.

```
=ThisMonth
```

A more useful named formula would return the actual month name as text. To do so, create a formula named *MonthName*, defined as:

```
=TEXT(TODAY(),"mmmm")
```

Now, enter the following formula into a cell and it returns the current month name as text. In the month of April, the formula returns the text *April*.

```
=MonthName
```

Using cell and range references in named formulas

Figure 3-17 shows yet another example of creating a named formula, this time with a cell reference. This formula, named *FirstChar*, returns the first character of the contents of cell A1 on Sheet1. The named formula is:

```
=LEFT(Sheet1!$A$1,1)
```

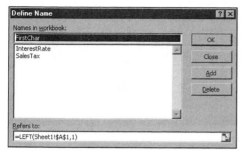

Figure 3-17: Defining a named formula that uses a cell reference

After creating this named formula, you can enter the following formula into a cell. The formula always returns the first character of cell A1 on Sheet1.

```
=FirstChar
```

The next example uses a range reference in a named formula. Figure 3-18 shows the Define Name dialog box when defining the following named formula (named *Total*).

```
=SUM(Sheet1!$A$1:$D$4)
```

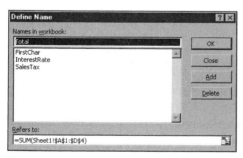

Figure 3-18: Defining a named formula that uses a range reference

After creating this named formula, you can enter the formula below into any cell on any sheet. The formula returns the sum of the values in A1:D4 on Sheet1.

```
=Total
```

Notice that the cell references in the two preceding named formulas are absolute references. By default, all cell and range references in named formulas use an absolute reference, with the worksheet qualifier. But, as you see in the next section, overriding this default behavior by using a relative cell reference can result in some very interesting named formulas!

Using named formulas with relative references

As I noted previously, when you use the Define Name dialog box to create a named formula that refers to cells or ranges, the Refers to field always uses absolute cell references and the references include the sheet name qualifier. In this section, I describe how to use relative cell and range references in named formulas.

USING A RELATIVE CELL REFERENCE

Let's begin with a simple example. Follow these steps to create a named formula that uses a relative reference:

1. Start with an empty worksheet.

2. Select cell A1. (This step is very important.)

3. Select Insert → Name → Define to bring up the Define Name dialog box.

4. Enter **CellToRight** in the Names in workbook field.

5. Delete the contents of the Refers to field, and type the following formula (don't point to the cell in the sheet).

   ```
   =Sheet1!B1
   ```

6. Click OK to close the Define Name dialog box.

7. Type something (anything) into cell B1.

8. Enter this formula into cell A1:

   ```
   =CellToRight
   ```

   You'll find that the formula in A1 simply returns the contents of cell B1.

Next, copy the formula in cell A1 down a few rows. Then, enter some values in column B. You'll find that the formula in column A returns the contents of the cell to the right. In other words, the named formula (*CellToRight*) acts in a relative manner.

You can use the *CellToRight* name in any cell (not just cells in column A). For example, if you enter **=CellToRight** into cell D12, it returns the contents of cell E12.

To demonstrate that the formula named *CellToRight* truly uses a relative cell reference, activate any cell other than cell A1 and display the Define Name dialog box (see Figure 3-19). Select the CellToRight item in the list box and examine the Refers to field. You'll see that the formula varies, depending on the active cell. For example, if cell E5 is selected when the Define Name dialog box is displayed, the formula for *CellToRight* appears as:

```
=Sheet1!F5
```

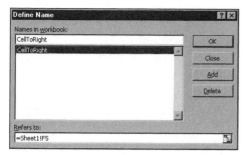

Figure 3-19: The CellToRight named formula varies, depending on the active cell.

If you use the *CellToRight* name on a different worksheet, you'll find that it continues to reference the cell to the right – but it's the cell with the same address on Sheet1. This happens because the named formula includes a sheet reference. To modify the named formula so it works on any sheet, do the following:

1. Activate cell A1 on Sheet1.

2. Select Insert → Name → Define to bring up the Define Name dialog box.

3. In the Define Name dialog box, click the CellToRight item in the list box.

4. Delete the contents of the Refers to field, and type this formula:

   `=!B1`

5. Click OK to close the Define Name dialog box.

After making this change, you'll find that the *CellToRight* named formula works correctly on any worksheet in the workbook.

The named formula does not work if you use it in a formula in column IV because the formula attempts to reference a nonexistent cell (there is no column to the right of column IV).

USING A RELATIVE RANGE REFERENCE

This example expands upon the previous example and demonstrates how to create a named formula that sums the values in 10 cells directly to the right of a particular cell. To create this named formula:

1. Activate cell A1.

2. Select Insert → Name → Define to bring up the Define Name dialog box.

3. Enter **Sum10Cells** into the Names in workbook field.

4. Enter this formula into the Refers to field:

```
=SUM(!B1:!K1)
```

After creating this named formula, you can insert the following formula into any cell in any sheet, and it will display the sum of the 10 cells directly to the right:

```
=Sum10Cells
```

For example, if you enter this formula into cell D12, it returns the sum of the values in the 10-cell range E12:N12.

Note that because cell A1 was the active cell when you defined the named formula, the relative references used in the formula definition are relative to cell A1. Also note that the sheet name was not used in the formula. Omitting the sheet name (but including the exclamation point) causes the named formula to work in any sheet.

If you select cell D12 and then bring up the Define Name dialog box, you'll see that the Refers to field for the *Sum10Cells* name displays the following:

```
=SUM(!E12:!N12)
```

The *Sum10Cells* named formula does not work if you use it in a cell that resides in a column beyond column IL. That's because the formula becomes invalid as it tries to reference a nonexistent cell beyond column IV.

USING A MIXED RANGE REFERENCE

As I discussed in Chapter 2, a cell reference can be absolute, relative, or mixed. A mixed cell reference consists of either:

◆ An absolute column reference and a relative row reference (for example, $A1)

◆ A relative column reference and an absolute row reference (for example, A$1)

As you might expect, a named formula can use mixed cell references. To demonstrate, activate cell B1. Use the Define Name dialog box to create a formula named *FirstInRow*, using this formula definition:

```
=!$A1
```

This formula uses an absolute column reference and a relative row reference. Therefore, it always returns a value in column A. The row depends on the row in which you use the formula. For example, if you enter the following formula into cell F12, it displays the contents of cell A12:

```
=FirstInRow
```

You cannot use the *FirstInRow* formula in column A because it generates a circular reference — a formula that refers to itself. Circular references are covered in Chapter 14.

Advanced Techniques That Use Names

This section presents several examples of advanced techniques that use names. The examples assume that you're familiar with the naming techniques described earlier in this chapter.

Using the INDIRECT function with a named range

Excel's INDIRECT function lets you specify a cell address indirectly. For example, if cell A1 contains the text *C45*, the following formula returns the contents of cell C45:

```
=INDIRECT(A1)
```

The INDIRECT function also works with named ranges. Figure 3-20 shows a worksheet with 12 range names that correspond to the month names. For example, *January* refers to the range B2:E2. Cell B16 contains the following formula:

```
=SUM(INDIRECT(A16))
```

This formula essentially returns the sum of the named range entered as text in cell A16.

Book7							
	A	B	C	D	E	F	G
1		North	South	West	East		
2	January	5,213	2,687	4,086	3,720		
3	February	4,417	4,410	2,399	4,927		
4	March	3,802	2,636	1,829	4,885		
5	April	4,394	1,195	3,569	4,279		
6	May	5,784	2,568	1,969	1,378		
7	June	1,122	4,913	5,315	5,545		
8	July	1,562	2,431	5,364	3,107		
9	August	1,722	4,060	1,693	1,578		
10	September	4,415	4,279	1,533	3,944		
11	October	4,124	2,613	1,200	4,391		
12	November	5,706	5,620	4,080	5,170		
13	December	3,174	4,640	4,874	1,239		
14							
15							
16	March	13,152					
17							
18							
19							

Figure 3-20: Using the INDIRECT function with a named range

 TIP   In Excel 97 or later, you can use the Data → Validation command to insert a drop-down box in cell A16 (use the List option in the Data Validation dialog box, and specify A2:A13 as the list source). This allows the user to select a month name from a list; the total for the selected month then displays in B16.

You can also reference worksheet-level names with the INDIRECT function. For example, suppose you have a number of worksheets named Region1, Region2, and so on. Each sheet contains a worksheet-level name called *TotalSales*. This formula retrieves the value from the appropriate sheet, using the sheet name typed in cell A1:

```
=INDIRECT(A1&"!TotalSales")
```

Using the INDIRECT function to create a named range with a fixed address

It's possible to create a name that always refers to a specific cell or range — even if you insert new rows or columns. For example, suppose you want a range named *UpperLeft* to always refer to the range A1. If you create the name using standard procedures, you'll find that if you insert a new row 1, the *UpperLeft* range changes to A2. Or, if you insert a new column, the *UpperLeft* range changes to B1. To create a named range that uses a fixed address that never changes, create a named formula using the following Refers to definition:

```
=INDIRECT("$A$1")
```

After creating this named formula, *UpperLeft* will always refer to cell A1, even if you insert new rows or columns. The INDIRECT function, in the preceding formula, lets you specify a cell address indirectly by using a text argument. Because the argument appears in quotation marks, it never changes.

 Because this named formula uses a function, it does not appear in the Go To dialog box or in the Name box.

Using arrays in named formulas

An array is a collection of items. You can visualize an array as a single-column vertical collection, a single-row horizontal collection, or a multirow and multicolumn collection.

 Part III of this book discusses arrays and array formulas, but this topic is also relevant when discussing names.

You specify an array by using brackets. A comma or semicolon separates each item in the array. Use a comma to separate items arranged horizontally and use a semicolon to separate items arranged vertically.

Use the Define Name dialog box to create a formula named *MonthNames* that consists of the following formula definition:

```
={"Jan","Feb","Mar","Apr","May","Jun","Jul","Aug","Sep","Oct","Nov",
"Dec"}
```

This formula defines a 12-item array of text strings, arranged horizontally.

After you define the MonthNames formula, you can use it in a formula. However, your formula needs to specify which array item to use. The INDEX function is perfect for this. For example, the following formula returns *Aug*:

```
=INDEX(MonthNames,8)
```

You can also display the entire 12-item array, but it requires 12 adjacent cells to do so. For example, to enter the 12 items of the array into A1:L1, follow these steps:

1. Use the Define Name dialog box to create the formula named *MonthNames*.

2. Select the range A1:L1.

3. Type **=MonthNames** in the formula bar.

4. Press Ctrl+Shift+Enter.

Using Ctrl+Shift+Enter tells Excel to insert an array formula into the selected cells. In this case, the single formula is entered into 12 adjacent cells in Figure 3-21. Excel places brackets around an array formula to remind you that it's a special type of formula. If you examine any cell in A1:L1, you'll see its formula listed as:

```
{=MonthNames}
```

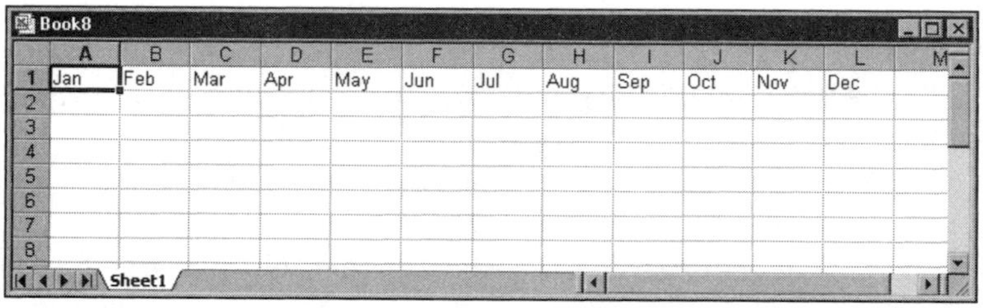

Figure 3-21: You can enter a named formula that contains a 12-item array into 12 adjacent cells.

Creating a dynamic named formula

A dynamic named formula is a named formula that refers to a range not fixed in size. You may find this concept difficult to grasp, so a quick example is in order.

Examine the worksheet shown in Figure 3-22. This sheet contains a listing of sales by month, through the month of April.

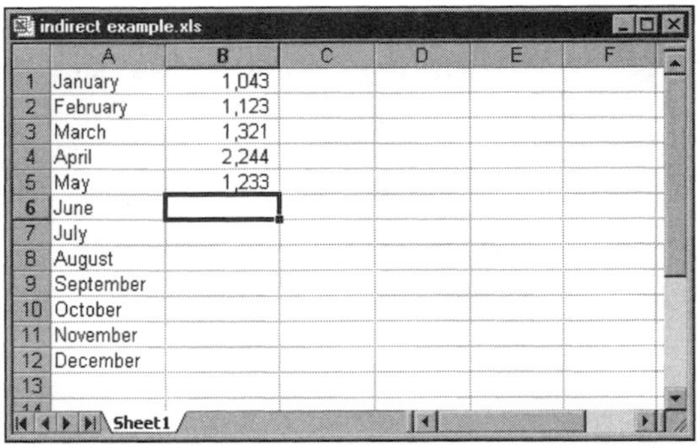

Figure 3-22: You can use a dynamic named formula to represent the sales data in column B.

Suppose you want to create a name (*SalesData*) for the data in column B, and you don't want this name to refer to empty cells. In other words, the reference for the *SalesData* range would change each month as you add a new sales figure. You could, of course, use the Define Name dialog box to change the range name definition each month. Or, you could create a dynamic named formula that changes automatically as you enter new data.

To create a dynamic named formula, start by recreating the worksheet shown in Figure 3-22. Then:

1. Bring up the Define Name dialog box.

2. Enter **SalesData** in the Names in workbook field.

3. Enter the following formula in the Refers to field:

   ```
   =OFFSET(Sheet1!$B$1,0,0,COUNTA(Sheet1!$B:$B),1)
   ```

4. Click OK to close the Define Name dialog box.

The preceding steps created a named formula that uses Excels OFFSET and COUNTA functions. To try out this formula, enter the following formula into any cell not in column B:

```
=SUM(SalesData)
```

This formula returns the sum of the values in column B. Note that *SalesData* does not display in the Name box and does not appear in the Go To dialog box.

At this point, you may be wondering about the value of this exercise. After all, a simple formula such as the following one does the same job, without the need to define a formula:

```
=SUM(B:B)
```

The value of using dynamic named formulas becomes apparent when creating a chart. You can use this technique to create a chart with a data series that adjusts automatically as you enter new data.

Refer to Chapter 15 for an example that uses this technique to create a dynamic chart.

Summary

This chapter introduced the concept of names. I described how to create and modify names, and compared workbook-level names with worksheet-level names. The chapter provided many examples of using names in your workbooks and also revealed the secret to understanding names – every name is actually a named formula.

Chapter 4 presents an introduction and overview of Excel's worksheet functions.

Part II

Using Functions in Your Formulas

Chapter 4

Introducing Worksheet Functions

IN THIS CHAPTER

♦ The advantages of using functions in your formulas

♦ The various types of arguments used by functions

♦ How to enter a function into a formula

♦ Excel's function categories

A THOROUGH KNOWLEDGE OF Excel's worksheet functions is essential for anyone who wants to master the art of formulas. This chapter provides an overview of the functions available for use in formulas.

What Is a Function?

A worksheet function is a built-in tool that you use in a formula. A typical function (such as SUM) takes one or more arguments, and then returns a result. The SUM function, for example, accepts a range argument and then returns the sum of the values in that range.

You'll find functions useful because they:

♦ Simplify your formulas

♦ Permit formulas to perform otherwise impossible calculations

♦ Speed up some editing tasks

♦ Allow "conditional" execution of formulas – giving them rudimentary decision-making capability

The examples in the sections that follow demonstrate each of these points.

Simplify formulas

Using a built-in function can simplify a formula significantly. For example, you might need to calculate the average of the values in 10 cells (A1:A10). Without the help of any functions, you need to construct a formula like this:

```
=(A1+A2+A3+A4+A5+A6+A7+A8+A9+A10)/10
```

Not very pretty, is it? Even worse, you need to edit this formula if you expand the range to be summed. You can replace this formula with a much simpler one that uses one of Excel's built-in worksheet functions. For example, the following formula uses Excel's AVERAGE function:

```
=AVERAGE(A1:A10)
```

Perform otherwise impossible calculations

Functions permit formulas to perform impossible calculations. Perhaps you need to determine the largest value in a range. A formula can't tell you the answer without using a function. This simple formula uses Excel's MAX function to return the largest value in the range A1:D100:

```
=MAX(A1:D100)
```

Speed up editing tasks

Functions can sometimes eliminate manual editing. Assume that you have a worksheet that contains 1,000 names in cells A1:A1000, and all the names appear in all uppercase letters. Your boss sees the listing and informs you that you need to mail merge the names with a form letter and that the use of all uppercase is not acceptable. For example, JOHN F. CRANE must appear as John F. Crane. You *could* spend the rest of the day reentering the list — or you could use a formula such as the following, which uses Excel's PROPER function to convert the text in cell A1 to proper case:

```
=PROPER(A1)
```

Enter this formula in cell B1 and then copy it down to the next 999 rows. Then, select B1:B1000 and use the Edit→Copy command to copy the range to the Clipboard. Next, activate cell A1 and use the Edit→Paste Special command (with the Values option) to convert the formulas to values. Delete column B, and you're finished. With the help of a function, you just accomplished several hours of work in less than a minute.

Provide decision-making capability

This last example demonstrated using conditions in formulas and should have convinced you of the power of functions. Suppose you have a worksheet that calculates sales commissions. If a salesperson sells more than $100,000 of product, the commission rate reaches 7.5 percent; otherwise, the commission rate remains at 5.0 percent. Without using a function, you would need to create two different formulas and make sure that you use the correct formula for each sales amount. Note this formula that uses the IF function to check the value in cell A1 and make the appropriate commission calculation:

```
=IF(A1<100000,A1*5%,A1*7.5%)
```

More about functions

All told, Excel includes more than 300 functions. And if that's not enough, you can purchase additional specialized functions from third-party suppliers, and even create your own custom functions (using VBA).

If you're ready to create your own custom functions, check out Part IV of this book.

The sheer number of available worksheet functions may overwhelm you, but you'll probably find that you use only a dozen or so of the functions on a regular basis. And as you'll see, Excel's Paste Function dialog box (described later in this chapter) makes it easy to locate and insert a function, even if you use it rarely.

Appendix B contains a complete listing of Excel's worksheet functions, with a brief description of each.

Function Argument Types

If you examine the preceding examples in this chapter, you'll notice that all of the functions used a set of parentheses. The information within the parentheses is called an *argument*. Functions vary in how they use arguments. A function may use:

◆ No arguments

◆ One argument

◆ A fixed number of arguments

◆ An indeterminate number of arguments

◆ Optional arguments

For example, the RAND function, which returns a random number between 0 and 1, doesn't use an argument. Even if a function doesn't require an argument, you must provide a set of empty parentheses, like this:

If a function uses more than one argument, then a comma separates each argument. For example, the LARGE function, which returns the "nth" largest value in a range, uses two arguments. The first argument represents the range; the second argument represents the value for n. The formula below returns the third-largest value in the range A1:A100:

```
=LARGE(A1:A100,3)
```

The character used to separate function arguments may be something other than a comma. For example, it could be a semicolon. This character is determined by your system's List separator setting, which is specified in the Regional Settings dialog box, accessible via the Control Panel.

The examples at the beginning of the chapter used cell or range references for arguments. Excel is quite flexible when it comes to function arguments, however. The following sections demonstrate additional argument types for functions.

Names as arguments

As you've seen, functions can use cell or range references for their arguments. When Excel calculates the formula, it simply uses the current contents of the cell or range to perform its calculations. The SUM function returns the sum of its argument(s). To calculate the sum of the values in A1:A20, you can use:

```
=SUM(A1:A20)
```

And, not surprisingly, if you've defined a name for A1:A20 (such as Sales), you can use the name in place of the reference:

```
=SUM(Sales)
```

Accommodating Former Lotus 1-2-3 Users

If you've ever used any of the 1-2-3 spreadsheets (or any version of Corel's Quattro Pro), you might recall that these products require you to type an "at" sign (@) before a function name. Excel is smart enough to distinguish functions without you having to flag them with a symbol.

Because old habits die hard, however, Excel accepts @ symbols when you type functions in your formulas — but it removes them as soon as you enter the formula.

These competing products also use two dots (..) as a range reference operator — for example, A1..A10. Excel also enables you to use this notation when you type formulas, but Excel replaces the notation with its own range reference operator, a colon (:).

This accommodation goes only so far, however. Excel still insists that you use the standard Excel function names, and it doesn't recognize or translate the function names used in other spreadsheets. For example, if you enter the 1-2-3 @AVG function, Excel flags it as an error. (Excel's name for this function is AVERAGE.) For more information about 1-2-3 compatibility, consult Appendix A.

For more information about defining and using names, refer to Chapter 3.

Full-column or full-row as arguments

In some cases, you may find it useful to use an entire column or row as an argument. For example, the formula that follows sums all values in column B:

```
=SUM(B:B)
```

Using full-column and full-row references is particularly useful if the range that you're summing changes (if you continually add new sales figures, for instance). If you do use an entire row or column, just make sure that the row or column doesn't contain extraneous information that you don't want included in the sum.

You might think that using such a large range (a column consists of 65,536 cells) might slow down calculation time. Not true. Excel's recalculation engine is quite efficient.

Literal values as arguments

A *literal argument* refers to a value or text string that you enter directly. For example, the SQRT function, which calculates the square root of a number, takes one argument. In the following example, the formula uses a literal value for the function's argument:

```
=SQRT(225)
```

Using a literal argument with a simple function like this one defeats the purpose of using a formula. This formula always returns the same value, so you could just as easily replace it with the value 15. Using literal arguments makes more sense with formulas that use more than one argument. For example, the LEFT function (which takes two arguments) returns characters from the beginning of its first argument; the second argument specifies the number of characters. If cell A1 contains the text "Budget", the following formula returns the first letter, or "B":

```
=LEFT(A1,1)
```

Expressions as arguments

Excel also enables you to use *expressions* as arguments. Think of an expression as a formula within a formula. When Excel encounters an expression as a function's argument, it evaluates the expression and then uses the result as the argument's value. Here's an example:

```
=SQRT((A1^2)+(A2^2))
```

This formula uses the SQRT function, and its single argument appears as the following expression:

```
(A1^2)+(A2^2)
```

When Excel evaluates the formula, it first evaluates the expression in the argument and then computes the square root of the result.

Other functions as arguments

Because Excel can evaluate expressions as arguments, it shouldn't surprise you that these expressions can include other functions. Writing formulas that have functions within functions is sometimes known as *nesting* functions. Excel starts by evaluating the most deeply nested expression and works its way out. Note this example of a nested function:

```
=SIN(RADIANS(B9))
```

The RADIANS function converts degrees to radians – the unit used by all of Excel's trigonometric functions. If cell B9 contains an angle in degrees, the RADIANS function converts it to radians, and then the SIN function computes the sine of the angle.

A formula can contain up to seven levels of nested functions. If you exceed this level, Excel pops up an error message. In the vast majority of cases, this limit poses no problem. Users often exceed this limitation when attempting to create a complex formula comprising nested IF functions.

Arrays as arguments

A function can also use an *array* as an argument. An array is a series of values separated by a comma and enclosed in brackets. The formula below uses the OR function with an array as an argument. The formula returns TRUE if cell A1 contains 1, 3, or 5.

```
=OR(A1={1,3,5})
```

See Part III of this book for more information about working with arrays.

Often, using arrays can help you simplify your formula. The formula below, for example, returns the same result but uses nested IF functions instead of an array.

```
=IF(A1=1,TRUE,IF(A1=3,TRUE,IF(A1=5,TRUE,FALSE)))
```

Ways to Enter a Function into a Formula

You can enter a function into a formula using either of two methods: (1) manually or (2) using the Paste Function dialog box.

Entering a function manually

If you're familiar with a particular function – you know how many arguments it takes and the types of arguments – you may choose simply to type the function and its arguments into your formula. Often, this method is the most efficient.

If you omit the closing parenthesis for a function, Excel adds it for you automatically. For example, if you type =SUM(A1:C12 and press Enter, Excel corrects the formula by adding the right parenthesis.

When you enter a function, Excel always converts the function's name to uppercase. Therefore, it's a good idea use lowercase when you type functions. If Excel doesn't convert your text to uppercase when you press Enter, then your entry isn't recognized as a function — which means that you spelled it incorrectly or the function isn't available (For example, it may be defined in an add-in not currently installed.)

Using the paste function dialog box to enter a function

The Paste Function dialog box assists you by providing a way to enter a function and its arguments in a semi-automated manner. Using the Paste Function dialog box ensures that you spelled the function correctly and it contains the proper number of arguments in the correct order.

To insert a function, select the function from the Paste Function dialog box, shown in Figure 4-1. You can access this dialog box by using any of one of the following three methods:

◆ Choose the Insert → Function command from the menu

◆ Click the Paste Function button on the Standard toolbar

◆ Press Shift+F3

The Paste Function dialog box shows the Function category list on the left side of the dialog box. When you select a category, the Function name list box displays the functions in the selected category.

The Most Recently Used category lists the functions that you've used most recently. The All category lists all the functions available across all categories. Access this category if you know a function's name, but not its category.

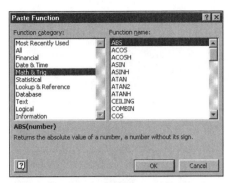

Figure 4-1: The Paste Function dialog box

TIP To select a function quickly in the Most Recently Used category, click the Edit Formula icon (which has an equal sign icon) in the formula bar and then select the function from the function list (which occupies the space usually used by the Name box).

When you select a function in the Function name list box, notice that Excel displays the function (and its argument names) in the dialog box, along with a brief description of what the function does.

When you locate the function that you want to use, click OK. Excel's Formula Palette appears, as in Figure 4-2, and the Name box changes to the Formula List box. Use the Formula Palette to specify the arguments for the function. You can easily specify a range argument by clicking the Collapse Dialog button (the icon at the right edge of each argument field in the Formula Palette). Excel temporarily collapses the Formula Palette to a thin box, so that you can select a range in the worksheet. When you want to redisplay the Formula Palette, click the Collapse Dialog button again.

NOTE The Formula Palette appears directly below the formula bar and often obscures the information you want to see. However, you can move it to any other location simply by dragging it.

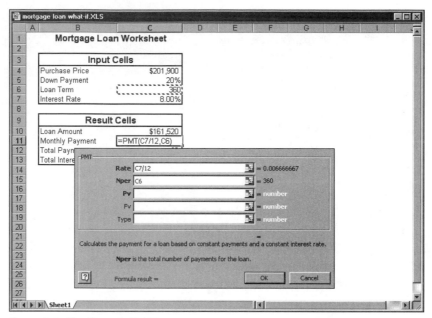

Figure 4-2: The Formula Palette

Let Excel Insert Functions for You

Most of the time, you're on your own when it comes to inserting functions. However, at least two situations arise in which Excel will enter functions for you automatically.

1. When you click the AutoSum button on the Standard toolbar, Excel does a quick check of the selected cells and the surrounding cells. It then proposes a formula that uses the SUM function. If Excel guessed your intentions, just press Enter (or click the AutoSum button a second time) to accept the proposed formula(s).

2. When you select the Data → Subtotals command, Excel displays a dialog box that enables you to specify some options. Then, it proceeds to insert rows and columns and enter some formulas automatically. These formulas use the SUBTOTAL function.

More tips for entering functions

The following lists some additional tips to keep in mind when you use the Paste Function dialog box and the Formula Palette to enter functions:

◆ Click the Help button (or press F1) at any time to get help about the function that you selected (see Figure 4-3).

◆ If you start a new formula, the Formula Palette automatically provides the initial equal sign for you.

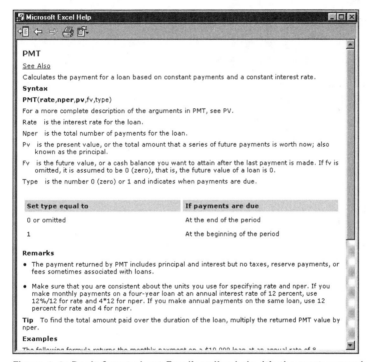

Figure 4-3: Don't forget about Excel's online help. It's the most comprehensive function reference source available.

◆ If the active cell already contains a formula, clicking the Paste Function button displays the Formula Palette.

♦ You can use the Paste Function dialog box to insert a function into an existing formula. Just edit the formula and move the insertion point to the location where you want to insert the function. Then, open the Paste Function dialog box and select the function.

♦ If you change your mind about entering a function, click the Cancel button.

♦ The number of arguments used by the function that you selected determines the number of boxes you see in the Formula Palette. If a function uses no arguments, you won't see any boxes. If the function uses a variable number of arguments (as with the AVERAGE function), Excel adds a new box every time that you enter an optional argument.

♦ On the right side of each box in the Formula Palette, you'll see the current value for each argument.

♦ A few functions, such as INDEX, have more than one form. If you choose such a function, Excel displays another dialog box that enables you to choose which form you want to use.

♦ If you only need help remembering a function's arguments, type an equal sign and the function's name, and then press Ctrl+Shift+A. Excel inserts the function with descriptive placeholders for the arguments, as shown in Figure 4-4. You need to replace these placeholders with actual arguments.

♦ To locate a function quickly in the Function name list that appears in the Paste Function dialog box, open the list box, type the first letter of the function name, and then scroll to the desired function. For example, if you select the All category and want to insert the SIN function, click anywhere on the Function name list box and press S. Excel selects the first function that begins with S. Keep pressing S until you reach the SIN function.

♦ If you use the Formula Palette and want to use a function as the argument for a function (a nested function), click in the box where you want the argument to appear. Then, open the function list and select the function. Excel inserts the nested function and prompts you for its arguments.

♦ If the active cell contains a formula that uses one or more functions, the Formula Palette enables you to edit each function. In the formula bar, click the function that you want to edit, then click the Edit Formula button (equal sign icon). Figure 4-5 shows a formula with multiple functions.

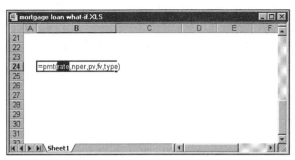

Figure 4-4: Press Ctrl+Shift+A to instruct Excel to display descriptive placeholders for a function.

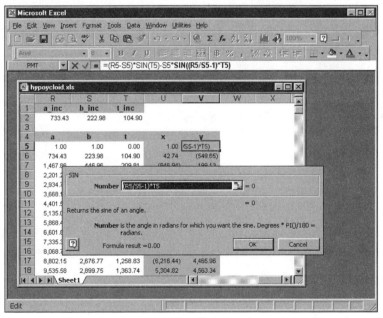

Figure 4-5: If the formula contains multiple functions, click the function in the formula bar to edit it.

Function Categories

I list and briefly describe Excel's function categories below. Refer to subsequent chapters for specific examples of using the functions.

Financial functions

The financial functions enable you to perform common business calculations that deal with money. For example, you can use the PMT function to calculate the monthly payment for a car loan. (You need to provide the loan amount, interest rate, and loan term as arguments.)

Date & Time functions

The functions in this category enable you to analyze and work with date and time values in formulas. For example, the TODAY function returns the current date (as stored in the system clock).

Math & Trig functions

This category contains a wide variety of functions that perform mathematical and trigonometric calculations.

 The trigonometric functions all assume radians for angles (not degrees). Use the RADIANS function to convert degrees to radians.

Statistical functions

The functions in this category perform statistical analysis on ranges of data. For example, you can calculate statistics such as mean, mode, standard deviation, and variance.

 Some of the functions in this category require you to install the Analysis ToolPak add-in.

Lookup and reference functions

Functions in this category are used to find (look up) values in lists or tables. A common example is a tax table. You can use the VLOOKUP function to determine a tax rate for a particular income level.

Database functions

Functions in this category are useful when you need to summarize data in a list (also known as a worksheet database) that meets specific criteria. For example, assume you have a list that contains monthly sales information. You can use the DCOUNT function to count the number of records that have a value greater than 10,000.

Text functions

The text functions enable you to manipulate text strings in formulas. For example, you can use the MID function to extract any number of characters beginning at any character position. Other functions enable you to change the case of text (convert to uppercase, for example).

Logical functions

This category consists of only six functions that enable you to test a condition (for logical TRUE or FALSE). You will find the IF function very useful, since it gives your formulas simple decision-making capability.

Information functions

The functions in this category help you determine the type of data stored within a cell. For example, the ISTEXT function returns TRUE if a cell reference contains text. Or, you can use the ISBLANK function to determine whether a cell is empty. The CELL function returns lots of potentially useful information about a particular cell.

Engineering functions

The functions in this category are useful for engineering applications. They enable you to work with complex numbers, and perform conversions between various numbering and measurement systems.

 To use the functions in the Engineering category, you must install the Analysis ToolPak add-in.

User-defined functions

Functions that appear in this category are custom worksheet functions created using VBA. These functions can operate just like Excel's built-in functions. One difference, however, is that custom functions do not display a description of each argument in the Paste Function dialog box and Formula Palette.

Other function categories

In addition to the function categories described above, Excel includes four other categories that may not appear in the Paste Function dialog box: Commands, Customizing, Macro Control, and DDE/External. These categories appear to be holdovers from older versions of Excel. If you create a custom function, you can assign it to one of these categories. In addition, you may see other function categories created by macros.

 Refer to Chapter 21 for information about assigning your custom functions to a function category.

Analysis ToolPak functions

When you feel comfortable with Excel's worksheet functions, you can explore other available functions when you load the Analysis ToolPak. This add-in provides you with dozens of additional worksheet functions.

When you load this add-in, the Paste Function dialog box displays a new category, Engineering. It also adds new functions to the following function categories: Financial, Date & Time, Math & Trig, and Information.

Volatile Functions

Some Excel functions belong to a special class of functions called *volatile*. Excel recalculates a volatile function whenever it recalculates the workbook — even if the formula that contains the function is not involved in the recalculation.

The RAND function represents an example of a volatile function because it generates a new random number every time Excel calculates the worksheet. Other volatile functions include:

AREAS	INDEX	OFFSET
CELL	INDIRECT	ROWS
COLUMNS	NOW	TODAY

As a side effect of using these volatile functions, Excel will always prompt you to save the workbook when you close it — even if you made no changes to it. For example, if you open a workbook that contains any of these volatile functions, scroll around a bit (but don't change anything), and then close the file, Excel will ask whether you want to save the workbook.

You can circumvent this behavior by using the Manual Recalculation mode, with the Recalculate before save option turned off.

Summary

This chapter provided an introduction to worksheet functions. Excel provides hundreds of functions that you can use in your formulas. In addition, you can use functions defined in add-ins. The remaining chapters in this book provide hundreds of examples of using functions in your formulas. The next chapter demonstrates many of the functions available in the Text category.

Chapter 5

Manipulating Text

IN THIS CHAPTER

- ◆ Information about how Excel handles text entered into cells
- ◆ Excel's worksheet functions that handle text
- ◆ Examples of advanced text formulas
- ◆ Custom VBA text functions

EXCEL, OF COURSE, IS BEST KNOWN for its uncanny ability to crunch numbers. However, it also proves its versatility when it comes to handling text. As you know, Excel enables you to enter text for things, such as row and column headings, customer names and addresses, part numbers, and just about anything else. And, as you might expect, you can use formulas to manipulate the text contained in cells.

This chapter contains many examples of formulas that use functions to manipulate text. Some of these formulas perform feats you may not have thought possible.

A Few Words About Text

When you enter data into a cell, Excel immediately goes to work and determines whether you're entering a formula, a number (including a date or time), or anything else. Anything else is considered text.

 You may hear the term *string* used instead of *text*. You can use these terms interchangeably. Sometimes, they even appear together, as in *text string*.

How many characters in a cell?

In Excel 5 and Excel 95, a single cell can hold up to 255 characters. Beginning with Excel 97, however, Microsoft upped the ante significantly. A single cell in Excel 97 can hold up to 32,000 characters. To put things into perspective, this chapter contains about 25,000 characters. I certainly don't recommend using a cell in lieu of a word processor, but if you use Excel 97 or later, you really don't have to lose much sleep worrying about filling up a cell with text.

 Although a cell can hold up to 32,000 characters, there is a limit on the number of characters that can actually display. And, as I describe later, some functions may not work properly for text strings greater than 255 characters.

Numbers as text

If you want to "force" a number to be considered as text, you can do one of the following:

♦ Apply the Text number format to the cell. Use Format → Cells, click the Number tab, and select Text from the category list. If you haven't applied other horizontal alignment formatting, the value will appear left-aligned in the cell (like normal text).

♦ Precede the number with an apostrophe. The apostrophe isn't displayed, but the cell entry will be treated as if it were text.

Even though the contents of a cell is formatted as Text (or has an apostrophe preceding it), you can still perform *some* mathematical operations on the cell if the entry *looks* like a number. For example, assume cell A1 contains a value preceded by an apostrophe. The formula that follows will display the value in A1, incremented by 1:

```
=A1+1
```

The formula that follows, however, will treat the contents of cell A1 as 0:

```
=SUM(A1:A10)
```

If switching from Lotus 1-2-3, you'll find this a significant change. Lotus 1-2-3 never treats text as values. In some cases, treating text as a number can be useful. In other cases, it can cause problems. Bottom line? Just be aware of Excel's inconsistency in how it treats a number formatted as text.

Text Functions

Excel has an excellent assortment of worksheet functions that can handle text. For your convenience, Excel's Paste Function dialog box places most of these functions in the Text category. A few other functions that are relevant to Text appear in other function categories. For example, the ISTEXT function is in the Information category in the Paste Function dialog box.

Refer to Appendix B for a listing of the functions in the Text category. Or, click the Paste Function toolbar button and scroll through the functions in the Text category.

Most of the text functions are not limited for use with text. In other words, these functions can also operate with cells that contain values. Unlike other spreadsheets (such as 1-2-3), Excel is very accommodating when it comes to treating numbers as text and text as numbers.

The examples discussed in this section demonstrate some common (and useful) things you can do with text. You may need to adapt some of these examples for your own use.

Determining if a cell contains text

In some situations, you may need a formula that determines the type of data contained in a particular cell. For example, you may use an IF function to return a result only if a cell contains text. Excel provides three functions to help you determine if a particular cell contains text:

◆ ISTEXT

◆ CELL

◆ TYPE

As you'll see, however, these functions are not always reliable.

The companion CD-ROM includes a workbook that demonstrates these functions (including their problems).

THE ISTEXT FUNCTION

The ISTEXT function takes a single argument, and returns TRUE if the argument contains text, and FALSE if it doesn't contain text. The formula that follows will return TRUE if A1 contains a string:

```
=ISTEXT(A1)
```

The ISTEXT function, although useful, is certainly not perfect. In fact, it will give you an incorrect result in some cases. Although Excel 97 and later can store a huge amount of text in a cell (up to 32,000 characters), the ISTEXT function doesn't seem to realize this fact. The ISTEXT function returns FALSE if its argument refers to a cell that contains more than 255 characters. Excel 2000 corrected this problem, so ISTEXT now works as expected regardless of the amount of text in the cell.

THE TYPE FUNCTION

The TYPE function takes a single argument and returns a value that indicates the type of data in a cell. If cell A1 contains a text string, the formula that follows will return 2 (the code number for text):

```
=TYPE(A1)
```

The TYPE function falls apart when a cell contains more than 255 characters: It returns 16 — the code number for an Error value.

THE CELL FUNCTION

Theoretically, the CELL function should help you determine if a particular cell uses the Text format, or has an apostrophe prefix. The CELL function's first argument can consist of any of 12 keywords, including *format*, *prefix*, or *type*.

None of these options work as advertised when a number is formatted as Text. For example, if you enter a number into cell A1 and then give it a number format of Text, the following formula returns *G* — which means Excel considers it formatted using the General format:

```
=CELL("format",A1)
```

Using *prefix* as the first argument for the CELL function returns an apostrophe if a value is preceded by an apostrophe, but it returns nothing if the cell contains a number and is formatted as Text. Using type as the first argument in the CELL function also yields inconsistent results. For example, if the cell contains more than 255 characters, the function returns *v* (for value).

Working with character codes

Every character that you see on your screen has an associated code number. For Windows systems, Excel uses the standard ANSI character set. The ANSI character set consists of 255 characters, numbered from 1 to 255.

Figure 5-1 shows an Excel worksheet that displays all of the 255 characters. This example uses the Arial font (other fonts may have different characters).

Font: Arial   **Size:** 10

Code	Char	Code	Char	Code	Char	Code	Char	Code	Char	Code	Char	Code	Char
1	□	39	'	77	M	115	s	153	™	191	¿	229	å
2	□	40	(	78	N	116	t	154	š	192	À	230	æ
3	□	41	)	79	O	117	u	155	›	193	Á	231	ç
4	□	42	*	80	P	118	v	156	œ	194	Â	232	è
5	□	43	+	81	Q	119	w	157	□	195	Ã	233	é
6	□	44	,	82	R	120	x	158	ž	196	Ä	234	ê
7	□	45	-	83	S	121	y	159	Ÿ	197	Å	235	ë
8	□	46	.	84	T	122	z	160		198	Æ	236	ì
9	□	47	/	85	U	123	{	161	¡	199	Ç	237	í
10	□	48	0	86	V	124	|	162	¢	200	È	238	î
11	□	49	1	87	W	125	}	163	£	201	É	239	ï
12	□	50	2	88	X	126	~	164	¤	202	Ê	240	ð
13	□	51	3	89	Y	127	□	165	¥	203	Ë	241	ñ
14	□	52	4	90	Z	128	€	166	¦	204	Ì	242	ò
15	□	53	5	91	[	129	□	167	§	205	Í	243	ó
16	□	54	6	92	\	130	‚	168	¨	206	Î	244	ô
17	□	55	7	93	]	131	ƒ	169	©	207	Ï	245	õ
18	□	56	8	94	^	132	„	170	ª	208	Ð	246	ö
19	□	57	9	95	_	133	…	171	«	209	Ñ	247	÷
20	□	58	:	96	`	134	†	172	¬	210	Ò	248	ø
21	□	59	;	97	a	135	‡	173	-	211	Ó	249	ù
22	□	60	<	98	b	136	^	174	®	212	Ô	250	ú
23	□	61	=	99	c	137	‰	175	¯	213	Õ	251	û
24	□	62	>	100	d	138	Š	176	°	214	Ö	252	ü
25	□	63	?	101	e	139	‹	177	±	215	×	253	ý
26	□	64	@	102	f	140	Œ	178	²	216	Ø	254	þ
27	□	65	A	103	g	141	□	179	³	217	Ù	255	ÿ
28	□	66	B	104	h	142	Ž	180	´	218	Ú		
29	□	67	C	105	i	143	□	181	µ	219	Û		
30	□	68	D	106	j	144	□	182	¶	220	Ü		
31	□	69	E	107	k	145	'	183	·	221	Ý		
32		70	F	108	l	146	'	184	¸	222	Þ		
33	!	71	G	109	m	147	"	185	¹	223	ß		
34	"	72	H	110	n	148	"	186	º	224	à		
35	#	73	I	111	o	149	•	187	»	225	á		
36	$	74	J	112	p	150	–	188	¼	226	â		
37	%	75	K	113	q	151	—	189	½	227	ã		
38	&	76	L	114	r	152	˜	190	¾	228	ä		

Sheet1

Figure 5-1: The ANSI character set (for the Arial font)

ON THE CD   The companion CD-ROM includes a copy of this workbook. It has some simple macros that enable you to display the character set for any font installed on your system. You must have Excel 97 or later.

Two functions come into play when dealing with character codes: CODE and CHAR. These functions aren't very useful by themselves. However, they can be quite useful in conjunction with other functions. I discuss these functions in the following sections.

THE CODE FUNCTION

Excel's CODE function returns the character code for its argument. The formula that follows, for example, returns 65 — the character code for uppercase *A:*

```
=CODE("A")
```

If the argument for CODE consists of more than one character, the function uses only the first character. Therefore, this formula also returns 65:

```
=CODE("Abbey Road")
```

THE CHAR FUNCTION

The CHAR function is essentially the opposite of the CODE function. Its argument should be a value between 1 and 255, and the function returns the corresponding character. The following formula, for example, returns the letter *A:*

```
=CHAR(65)
```

To demonstrate the opposing nature of the CODE and CHAR functions, try entering this formula:

```
=CHAR(CODE("A"))
```

This formula (illustrative rather than useful) returns the letter *A.* First, it converts the character to its code value (65), and then it converts this code back to the corresponding character.

Assume cell A1 contains the letter *A* (uppercase). The following formula returns the letter *a* (lowercase):

```
=CHAR(CODE(A1)+32)
```

This formula takes advantage of the fact that the alphabetic characters all appear in alphabetical order within the character set, and the lowercase letters follow the uppercase letters (with a few other characters tossed in between). Each lowercase letter lies exactly 32 character positions higher than its corresponding uppercase letter.

How to Find Special Characters

Windows includes a program called Character Map (charmap.exe) that is very useful for locating special characters. For example, you might (for some strange reason) want to include a smiley face character in your spreadsheet. It just so happens that the Wingdings font includes such a character — but you probably have no idea what character code it uses.

Launch the Character Map program and select the Wingdings font (see the accompanying figure). Examine the characters, and you'll find that the smiley face corresponds to the letter J (uppercase). Just type the letter J and format the character using the Wingdings font.

You'll find that some characters cannot be entered using standard keyboard keys. However, Character Map displays an Alt key combination in the lower-right corner. For example, when you select the last character in the Wingdings font (the Windows logo, or character code 255), Character Map displays Alt+0255. You can enter this character by holding down the Alt key and typing 0255 on the numeric keypad of your keyboard. Make sure you use the numeric keypad because the normal number keys will not generate the proper character.

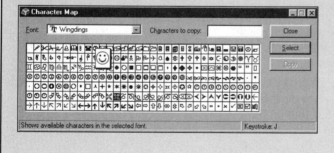

Determining if two strings are identical

You can set up a simple logical formula to determine if two cells contain the same entry. For example, use this formula to determine if cell A1 has the same contents as cell A2:

```
=A1=A2
```

Excel acts a bit lax in its comparisons when involving text. Consider the case in which A1 contains the word *January* (initial capitalization), and A2 contains *JANUARY* (all uppercase). You'll find that the formula above returns TRUE, even though the contents of the two cells are not really the same. In other words, the comparison is not case sensitive.

In many cases, you don't need to worry about the case of the text. But if you need to make an exact, case-sensitive comparison, you can use Excel's EXACT function. The formula that follows returns TRUE only if cells A1 and A2 contain *exactly* the same entry:

```
=EXACT(A1,A2)
```

This formula returns FALSE because the first string contains a trailing space:

```
=EXACT("zero ","zero")
```

Joining two or more cells

Excel uses an ampersand as its concatenation operator. *Concatenation* is simply a fancy term that describes what happens when you join the contents of two or more cells. For example, if cell A1 contains the text *San Diego*, and cell A2 contains the text *California*, the formula below will return *San Diego California*.

```
=A1&A2
```

Notice that the two strings are joined together without an intervening space. To add a space between the two entries (to get *San Diego California*), use a formula like this one:

```
=A1&" "&A2
```

Or, even better, use a comma and a space to produce *San Diego, California*:

```
=A1&", "&A2
```

To improve the legibility of the formula, you can eliminate the quote characters and use the CHAR function, with an appropriate argument. Note this example of using the CHAR function to represent a comma (44) and a space (32):

```
=A1&CHAR(44)&CHAR(32)&A2
```

If you'd like to force a "word wrap," concatenate the strings using CHAR (10) and make sure you apply the wrap text format to the cell. The following example joins the text in cell A1 and the text in cell B1, with a line break in between:

```
=A1&CHAR(10)&B1
```

Here's another example of the CHAR function. The formula below returns the string *Stop* by concatenating four characters returned by the CHAR function:

```
=CHAR(83)&CHAR(116)&CHAR(111)&CHAR(112)
```

Below you see a final example of using the & operator. In this case, the formula combines text with the result of an expression that returns the maximum value in Column C.

```
="The largest value in Column C is " &MAX(C:C)
```

 Excel also has a CONCATENATE function, which takes up to 30 arguments. This function simply combines the arguments into a single string. You can use this function if you like, but I prefer the & operator's efficiency.

Displaying formatted values as text

Excel's TEXT function enables you to display a value in a specific number format. Although this function may appear to have dubious value, it *does* serve some useful purposes as the examples in this section demonstrate. Figure 5-2 shows a simple worksheet. The formula in cell D1 is:

```
="The net profit is " & B3
```

	A	B	C	D	E
1	Gross	$155,690.84		The net profit is 104701.52	
2	Expenses	$ 50,989.32			
3	NET	$104,701.52			
4					
5					
6					
7					
8					
9					
10					
11					
12					

Figure 5-2: The formula in D1 doesn't display the formatted number.

This formula essentially combines a text string with the contents of cell B3 and displays the result. Note, however, that the contents of B3 are not formatted in any way. You might want to display B3's contents using a currency number format.

Contrary to what you might expect, applying a number format to the cell that contains the formula has no effect because the formula returns a string, not a value.

Note this revised formula that uses the TEXT function to apply formatting to the value in B3:

```
="The net profit is " & TEXT(B3,"$#,##0.00")
```

This formula displays the text along with a nicely formatted value: *The net profit is $47,219.79.*

The second argument for the TEXT function consists of a standard Excel number format string. You can enter any valid number format for this argument.

The preceding example uses a simple cell reference (B3). You can, of course, use an expression instead. Here's an example that combines text with a number resulting from a computation:

```
="Average Expenditure: " & TEXT(AVERAGE("A:A","$#,##0.00"))
```

Refer to Appendix C for details on Excel number formats.

Here's another example that uses the NOW function (which returns the current date and time). The TEXT function displays the date and time, nicely formatted.

```
="Report printed on "&TEXT(NOW(),"mmmm d, yyyy at h:mm AM/PM")
```

The formula might display the following: *Report printed on July 22, 1999 at 3:23 PM.*

Displaying formatted currency values as text

Excel's DOLLAR function converts a number to text using the currency format. It takes two arguments: the number to convert, and the number of decimal places to display. The DOLLAR function always uses the following number format:

```
$#,##0.00_);($#,##0.00).
```

You can sometimes use the DOLLAR function in place of the TEXT function. The TEXT function, however, is much more flexible since it doesn't limit you to a specific number format.

The formula below returns *Total: $1,287.37*. The second argument for the DOLLAR function specifies the number of decimal places.

```
="Total: "&DOLLAR(1287.367, 2)
```

Repeating a character or string

The REPT function repeats a text string (first argument) any number of times you specify (second argument). For example, the formula below returns *HoHoHo*.

```
=REPT("Ho",3)
```

You can also use this function to create crude vertical dividers between cells. This example displays a squiggly line, 20 characters in length:

```
=REPT("~",20)
```

Creating a text histogram

A clever use for the REPT function is to create a crude histogram directly in a worksheet (chart not required). Figure 5-3 shows an example of such a histogram. You'll find this type of graphical display especially useful when you need to visually summarize many values. In such a case, a standard chart may be unwieldy.

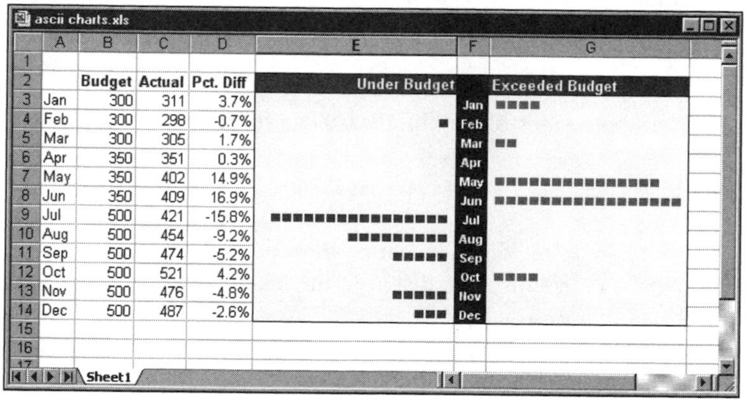

Figure 5-3: Using the REPT function to create a histogram in a worksheet range

The formulas in columns E and G graphically depict monthly budget variances by displaying a series of characters in the Wingdings font. A formula using the REPT function determines the number of characters displayed. Key formulas include:

```
E3: =IF(D3<0,REPT("n",-ROUND(D3*100,0)),"")
F3: =A2
G3: =IF(D3>0,REPT("n",-ROUND(D3*-100,0)),"")
```

Assign the Wingdings font to cells E3 and G3, and then copy the formulas down the columns to accommodate all the data. Right-align the text in column E, and adjust any other formatting. Depending on the numerical range of your data, you may need to change the scaling. Experiment by replacing the 100 value in the formulas. You can substitute any character you like for the n in the formulas to produce a different character in the chart.

 The workbook shown in Figure 5-3 also appears on the companion CD-ROM.

Padding a number

You're probably familiar with a common security measure (frequently used on printed checks) in which numbers are padded with asterisks on the right. The following formula displays the value in cell A1, along with enough asterisks to make 24 characters total:

```
=(A1 & REPT("*",24-LEN(A1)))
```

Or, if you'd prefer to pad the number with asterisks on the left, use this formula:

```
=REPT("*",24-LEN(A1))&A1
```

For asterisk padding on both sides of the number, use a formula such as this:

```
=REPT("*",12-LEN(A1))&A1&REPT("*",12-LEN(A1))
```

The preceding formulas are a bit deficient since they don't show any number formatting. Note this revised version that displays the value in A1 (formatted), along with the asterisk padding on the right:

```
=(TEXT(A1,"$#,##0.00")&REPT("*",24-LEN(TEXT(A1,"$#,##0.00"))))
```

Figure 5-4 shows this formula in action.

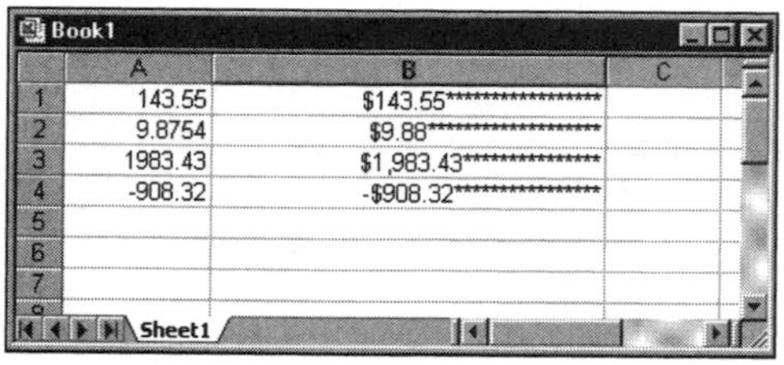

	A	B	C
1	143.55	$143.55*****************	
2	9.8754	$9.88*****************	
3	1983.43	$1,983.43*************	
4	-908.32	-$908.32**************	
5			
6			
7			

Figure 5-4: Using a formula to pad a number with asterisks

You can also pad a number by using a custom number format. To repeat the next character in the format to fill the column width, include an asterisk (*) in the custom number format code. For example, use this number format to pad the number with dashes:

$#,##0.00*-

To pad the number with asterisks, use two asterisks like this:

$#,##0.00**

> Refer to Appendix C for more information about custom number formats, including additional examples using the asterisk format code.

Removing excess spaces and nonprinting characters

Often, data imported into an Excel worksheet contains excess spaces or strange (often unprintable) characters. Excel provides you with two functions to help whip your data into shape: TRIM and CLEAN.

- ◆ TRIM: Removes all spaces from its text argument except for single spaces between words.

- ◆ CLEAN: Removes all nonprinting characters from a string. These "garbage" characters often appear when you import certain types of data. Of the 255 character codes, 39 of them comprise nonprinting characters. Specifically, the nonprinting character codes include 1-31, 128-129, 141-144, and 157-158.

The example below uses the TRIM function. The formula returns *Fourth Quarter Earnings* (with no excess spaces):

```
=TRIM("    Fourth    Quarter    Earnings    ")
```

Counting characters in a string

Excel's LEN function takes one argument, and returns the number of characters in the cell. For example, if cell A1 contains the string "September Sales," the following formula will return 15:

```
=LEN(A1)
```

Notice that space characters are included in the character count.

The following formula returns the total number of characters in the range A1:A3:

```
{=SUM(LEN(A1),LEN(A2),LEN(A3))}
```

 You will see example formulas that demonstrate how to count the number of specific characters within a string later in this chapter. Also, you may find relevant material in Chapter 7 on counting techniques and Chapter 13 on performing magic with array formulas.

Changing the case of text

Excel provides three handy functions to change the case of text:

- UPPER: converts the text to ALL UPPERCASE
- LOWER: converts the text to all lowercase
- PROPER: Converts the text to "proper" case (The First Letter In Each Word Is Capitalized)

These functions are quite straightforward. The formula that follows, for example, converts the text in cell A1 to proper case. If cell A1 contained the text *MR. JOHN Q. PUBLIC*, the formula would return *Mr. John Q. Public*.

```
=PROPER(A1)
```

These functions operate only on alphabetic characters; they simply ignore all other characters and return them unchanged.

Extracting characters from a string

Excel users often need to extract characters from a string. For example, you may have a list of employee names (first and last names) and need to extract the last name from each cell. Excel provides several useful functions for extracting characters:

◆ LEFT: Returns a specified number of characters from the beginning of a string

◆ RIGHT: Returns a specified number of characters from the end of a string

◆ MID: Returns a specified number of characters beginning at any position within a string

The formula that follows returns the last 10 characters from cell A1. If A1 contains fewer than 10 characters, the formula returns all of the text in the cell.

```
=RIGHT(A1,10)
```

This next formula uses the MID function to return five characters from cell A1, beginning at character position 2. In other words, it returns characters 2-6.

```
=MID(A1,2,5)
```

The following example returns the text in cell A1, with only the first letter in uppercase. It uses the LEFT function to extract the first character and convert it to uppercase. This then concatenates to another string that uses the RIGHT function to extract all but the first character (converted to lowercase).

```
=UPPER(LEFT(A1))&RIGHT(LOWER(A1),LEN(A1)-1)
```

If cell A1 contained the text *FIRST QUARTER*, the formula would return *First quarter.*

Replacing text with other text

In some situations, you may need to replace a part of a text string with some other text. For example, you may import data that contains asterisks, and you need to convert the asterisks to some other character. You could use Excel's Edit→Replace command to make the replacement. If you prefer a formula-based solution, you can take advantage of either of two functions:

◆ SUBSTITUTE: Replaces specific text in a string. Use this function when you know the character(s) to be replaced, but not the position.

◆ REPLACE: Replaces text that occurs in a specific location within a string. Use this function when you know the position of the text to be replaced, but not the actual text.

The following formula uses the SUBSTITUTE function to replace 1999 with 2000 in the string *1999 Budget*. The formula returns *2000 Budget*.

```
=SUBSTITUTE("1999 Budget","1999","2000")
```

The following formula uses the SUBSTITUTE function to remove all spaces from a string. In other words, it replaces all space characters with an empty string. The formula returns the title of an excellent Liz Phair CD: *Whitechocolatespaceegg*.

```
=SUBSTITUTE("White chocolate space egg"," ","")
```

The formula below uses the REPLACE function to replace one character beginning at position 5 with nothing. In other words, it removes the fifth character (a hyphen) and returns *Part544*.

```
=REPLACE("Part-544",5,1,"")
```

You can, of course, nest these functions to perform multiple replacements in a single formula. The formula that follows demonstrates the power of nested SUBSTITUTE functions. The formula essentially strips out any of the following seven characters in cell A1: space, hyphen, colon, asterisk, underscore, left parenthesis, and right parenthesis.

```
=SUBSTITUTE(SUBSTITUTE(SUBSTITUTE(SUBSTITUTE
(SUBSTITUTE(SUBSTITUTE(SUBSTITUTE(A1," ",""),"-",
""),":",""),"*",""),"_",""),"(",""),")","")
```

Therefore, if cell A1 contains the string *Part-2A-Z(4M1)_A**, the formula returns *Part2AZ4M1A*.

Finding and searching within a string

Excel's FIND and SEARCH functions enable you to locate the starting position of a particular substring within a string.

◆ FIND: Finds a substring within another text string and returns the starting position of the substring. You can specify the character position at which to begin searching. Use this function for non-case-sensitive text; you don't need to use wildcard characters.

◆ SEARCH: Finds a substring within another text string and returns the starting position of the substring. You can specify the character position at which to begin searching. Use this function for non-case-sensitive text or when you need to use wildcard characters.

The following formula uses the FIND function and returns 7 – the position of the first *m* in the string. Notice that this formula is case sensitive.

```
=FIND("m","Big Mamma Thornton",1)
```

The formula that follows, which uses the SEARCH function, returns 5 – the position of the first *m* (either uppercase or lowercase).

```
=SEARCH("m","Big Mamma Thornton",1)
```

You can use the following wildcard characters within the first argument for the SEARCH function:

◆ Question mark (?): Matches any single character

◆ Asterisk (*): Matches any sequence of characters

TIP If you want to find an actual question mark or asterisk character, type a tilde (~) before the question mark or asterisk.

The next formula examines the text in cell A1 and returns the position of the first three-character sequence that has a hyphen in the middle of it. In other words, it looks for any character followed by a hyphen and any other character. If cell A1 contains the text *Part-A90*, the formula returns 4.

```
=SEARCH("?-?",A1,1)
```

Searching and replacing within a string

You can use the REPLACE function in conjunction with the SEARCH function to replace part of a text string with another string. In effect, you use the SEARCH function to find the starting location used by the REPLACE function.

For example, assume cell A1 contains the text "Annual Profit Figures." The following formula searches for the word "Profit," and replaces it with the word "Loss":

```
=REPLACE(A1,SEARCH("Profit",A1),6,"Loss")
```

This next formula uses the SUBSTITUTE function to accomplish the same effect in a more efficient manner:

```
=SUBSTITUTE(A1,"Profit","Loss")
```

Advanced Text Formulas

The examples in this section appear more complex than the examples in the previous section. But, as you'll see, they can perform some very useful text manipulations.

 You can access all of the examples in this section on the companion CD-ROM.

Counting specific characters in a cell

This formula counts the number of Bs (uppercase only) in the string in cell A1:

```
=LEN(A1)-LEN(SUBSTITUTE(A1,"B",""))
```

This formula works by using the SUBSTITUTE function to create a new string (in memory) that has all of the Bs removed. Then, the length of this string is subtracted from the length of the original string. The result reveals the number of Bs in the original string.

The following formula is a bit more versatile. It counts the number of Bs — both upper- and lowercase — in the string in cell A1.

```
=LEN(A1)-LEN(SUBSTITUTE(SUBSTITUTE(A1,"B",""),"b",""))
```

Counting the occurrences of a substring in a cell

The formulas in the preceding section count the number of occurrences of a particular character in a string. The following formula works with more than one character. It returns the number of occurrences of a particular substring (contained in cell B1) within a string (contained in cell A1). The substring can consist of any number of characters.

```
=SUM(LEN(A1)-LEN(SUBSTITUTE(A1,B1,"")))/LEN(B1)
```

For example, if cell A1 contains the text *Blonde On Blonde* and B1 contains the text *Blonde*, the formula returns 2.

The comparison is case sensitive, so if B1 contains the text *blonde*, the formula returns 0. The following formula is a modified version that performs a case-insensitive comparison.

```
=SUM(LEN(A1)-LEN(SUBSTITUTE(UPPER(A1),UPPER(B1),"")))/LEN(B1)
```

Expressing a number as an ordinal

You may need to express a value as an ordinal number. For example, *Today is the 21st day of the month.* In this case, the number 21 converts to an ordinal number by appending the characters *st* to the number.

The characters appended to a number depend on the number. There is no clear pattern, making the construction of a formula more difficult. Most numbers will use the *th* suffix. Exceptions occur for numbers that end with 1, 2, or 3 – except if the preceding number is a 1 (numbers that end with 11, 12, or 13). These may seem like fairly complex rules, but you can translate them into an Excel formula.

The formula that follows converts the number in cell A1 (assumed to be an integer) to an ordinal number:

```
=A1&IF(OR(VALUE(RIGHT(A1,2))={11,12,13}),"th",IF(OR(VALUE(RIGHT(A1))
={1,2,3}),CHOOSE(RIGHT(A1),"st","nd","rd"),"th"))
```

This is a rather complicated formula, so it may help to examine its components. Basically, the formula works as follows:

1. If the last two digits of the number consist of 11, 12, or 13, then use *th*.

2. If Rule #1 does not apply, then check the last digit. If the last digit is 1, use *st*. If the last digit is 2, use *nd*. If the last digit is 3, use *rd*.

3. If neither Rule #1 nor Rule #2 apply, use *rd*.

 The formula uses two arrays, specified by brackets. Refer to Chapter 12 for more information about using arrays in formulas.

Figure 5-5 shows the formula in use.

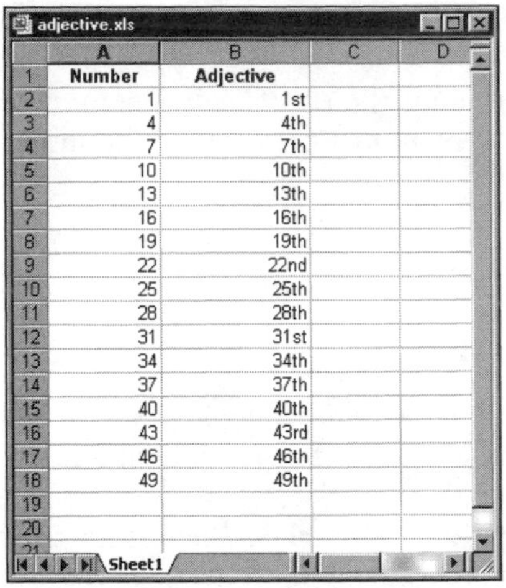

	A	B
1	Number	Adjective
2	1	1st
3	4	4th
4	7	7th
5	10	10th
6	13	13th
7	16	16th
8	19	19th
9	22	22nd
10	25	25th
11	28	28th
12	31	31st
13	34	34th
14	37	37th
15	40	40th
16	43	43rd
17	46	46th
18	49	49th

Figure 5-5: Using a formula to express a number as an ordinal

Determining a column letter for a column number

This next formula returns a worksheet column letter (ranging from A to IV) for the value contained in cell A1. For example, if A1 contains *29*, the formula returns *AC*.

```
=IF(A1>26,CHAR(CEILING(A1/26,1)+63),"")
&CHAR(IF(MOD(A1,26)=0,26,MOD(A1,26))+64)
```

Note that the formula doesn't check for a valid column number. In other words, if A1 contains a value less than 1 or greater than 256, the formula will still give an answer – albeit a meaningless one. The following modified version includes an IF function to ensure a valid column.

```
=IF(AND(A1>0,A1<257),IF(A1>26,CHAR(CEILING(A1/26,1)+63),"")
&CHAR(IF(MOD(A1,26)=0,26,MOD(A1,26))+64),"")
```

Extracting a file name from a path specification

The following formula returns the file name from a full path specification. For example, if cell A1 contains *c:\windows\desktop\myfile.xls*, the formula returns *myfile.xls:*

```
=MID(A1,FIND("*",SUBSTITUTE(A1,"\","*",LEN(A1)-
LEN(SUBSTITUTE(A1,"\",))))+1,LEN(A1))
```

This formula assumes that the system path separator consists of a backslash (\). It essentially returns all of the text following the last backslash character. If cell A1 doesn't contain a backslash character, the formula returns an error.

Extracting the first word of a string

To extract the first word of a string, a formula must locate the position of the first space character, and then use this information as an argument for the LEFT function. The following formula does just that.

```
=LEFT(A1,FIND(" ",A1)-1)
```

This formula returns all of the text prior to the first space in cell A1. However, the formula has a slight problem: It returns an error if cell A1 consists of a single word. A slightly more complex formula that checks for the error with an IF function solves that problem:

```
=IF(ISERR(LEFT(A1,FIND(" ",A1)-1)),A1,LEFT(A1,FIND(" ",A1)-1))
```

Extracting the last word of a string

Extracting the last word of a string is more complicated, since the FIND function only works from left to right. Therefore, the problem rests with locating the *last* space character. The formula that follows, however, solves this problem. It returns the last word of a string – all of the text following the last space character:

```
=RIGHT(A1,LEN(A1)-FIND("*",SUBSTITUTE(A1," ","*",LEN(A1)-
LEN(SUBSTITUTE(A1," ","")))))
```

This formula, however, has the same problem as the first formula in the preceding section: It fails if the string does not contain at least one space character. The following modified formula uses an IF function to count the number of spaces in cell A1. If it contains no spaces, the entire contents of cell A1 are returned. Otherwise, the formula listed above kicks in.

```
=IF(LEN(A1)-LEN(SUBSTITUTE(A1," ",""))=0,A1,RIGHT(A1,LEN(A1)-
FIND("*",SUBSTITUTE(A1," ","*",LEN(A1)-LEN(SUBSTITUTE(A1,"
","")))))
```

Extracting all but the first word of a string

The following formula returns the contents of cell A1, except for the first word:

```
=RIGHT(A1,LEN(A1)-FIND(" ",A1,1))
```

Extracting first names, middle names, and last names

Suppose you have a list consisting of people's names in a single column. You have to separate these names into three columns: one for the first name, one for the middle name or initial, and one for the last name. This task is more complicated than you may think, since not every name has a middle initial. However, you can still do it.

 The task becomes a *lot* more complicated if the list contains names with titles (such as Mr. or Dr.) or names followed by additional details (such as Jr. or III). In fact, the formulas below will *not* handle these complex cases. However, they still give you a significant head start if you're willing to do a bit of manual editing to handle the special cases.

The formulas that follow all assume that the name appears in cell A1. You can easily construct a formula to return the first name:

```
=LEFT(A1,FIND(" ",A1)-1)
```

Returning the middle name or initial is much more complicated, since not all names have a middle initial. This formula returns the middle name (if it exists). Otherwise, it returns nothing.

```
=IF(ISERR(MID(A1,FIND(" ",A1)+1,IF(ISERR(FIND(" ",A1,FIND
(" ",A1)+1)),FIND(" ",A1),FIND(" ",A1,FIND(" ",A1)+1))-
FIND(" ",A1)-1)),"",MID(A1,FIND(" ",A1)+1,IF(ISERR(FIND
(" ",A1,FIND(" ",A1)+1)),FIND(" ",A1),FIND(" ",A1,FIND
(" ",A1)+1))-FIND(" ",A1)-1))
```

Finally, this formula returns the last name:

```
=RIGHT(A1,LEN(A1)-FIND("*",SUBSTITUTE(A1," ","*",LEN(A1)-
LEN(SUBSTITUTE(A1," ","")))))
```

As you can see in Figure 5-6, the formulas work fairly well. There are a few problems, however; notably names that contain four "words." But, as I mention above, you can clean these cases up manually.

If you want to know how I created these complex formulas, refer to Chapter 18 for a discussion of megaformulas.

	A	B	C	D
1	Roger A. Smith	Roger	A.	Smith
2	Beth Robinson	Beth		Robinson
3	Ken Winkler	Ken		Winkler
4	Paula G. Franks	Paula	G.	Franks
5	Mr. James Olsen	Mr.	James	Olsen
6	J.P. Wilson	J.P.		Wilson
7	George Sanders Jr.	George	Sanders	Jr.
8	Patricia Landers	Patricia		Landers
9				
10				

first middle last names.xls — Sheet1

Figure 5-6: This worksheet uses formulas to extract the first name, middle name (or initial), and last name from a list of names in Column A.

Splitting Text Strings Without Formulas

In many cases, you can eliminate the use of formulas and use Excel's Data → Text to Columns command to parse strings into their component parts. Selecting this command displays Excel's Convert Text to Columns Wizard — a series of dialog boxes that walk you through the steps to convert a single column of data into multiple columns. Generally, you'll want to select the Delimited option (in Step 1) and use Space as the delimiter (in Step 2).

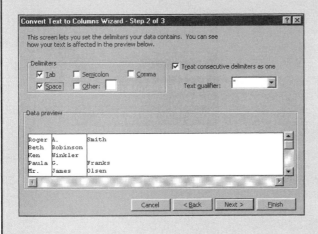

Removing titles from names

You can use the formula that follows to remove three common titles (Mr., Ms., and Mrs.) from a name. For example, if cell A1 contains *Mr. Fred Munster*, the formula would return *Fred Munster*.

```
=IF(OR(LEFT(A1,2)="Mr",LEFT(A1,3)="Mrs",LEFT(A1,2)="Ms"),
RIGHT(A1,LEN(A1) -FIND(" ",A1)),A1)
```

Counting the number of words in a cell

The following formula returns the number of words in cell A1:

```
=LEN(SUBSTITUTE(TRIM(A1),CHAR(32),CHAR(32)&CHAR(32)))-
LEN(TRIM(A1))+1
```

The formula works by creating a new string in memory that consists of the original string without any spaces. Then, you subtract the length of this new string from the original string to determine the number of spaces. A value of one is added to this result to arrive at the number of words. Notice that the TRIM function eliminates any multiple spaces between words.

Custom VBA Text Functions

Excel has many functions that work with text, but it's likely that you'll run into a situation in which the appropriate function just doesn't exist. In such a case, you can often create your own worksheet function using VBA.

Chapter 23 contains several additional text functions, written in VBA. I briefly describe these functions below.

- ◆ REVERSETEXT: Returns the text in a cell backwards. For example, using *Evian* as the argument returns *naivE*.

- ◆ ACRONYM: Returns the first letter of each word in its argument. For example, using *Power Utility Pak* as the argument returns *PUP*.

- ◆ SPELLDOLLARS: Returns a number "spelled out" in text — as on a check. For example, using *123.45* as the argument returns *One hundred twenty-three and 45/100 dollars*.

◆ SCRAMBLE: Returns the contents of its argument randomized. For example, using *Microsoft* as the argument may return *oficMorts* – or some other random permutation.

◆ ISLIKE: Returns TRUE if a string matches a pattern composed of text and wildcard characters.

◆ CELLHASTEXT: Returns TRUE if the cell argument contains text, or a value formatted as Text. This function overcomes the problems described at the beginning of this chapter (see "Determining If a Cell Contains Text").

◆ EXTRACTELEMENT: Extracts an element from a string based on a specified separator character (such as a hyphen).

Summary

This chapter provided some background on how Excel deals with text entered into cells. It also presented many useful examples that incorporate Excel's text functions.

The next chapter presents formulas that enable you to calculate dates, times, and other time-period values.

Chapter 6

Working with Dates and Times

Working with dates and times in Excel can be a frustrating experience – until you gain a solid understanding of how this feature works. This chapter provides the information you need to create powerful formulas that manipulate dates and times.

I formatted the dates in this chapter according to the United States English date format: month/day/year. For example, the date 3/1/1952 refers to March 1, 1952, not January 3, 1952.

How Excel Handles Dates and Times

This section presents a quick overview of how Excel deals with dates and times. We'll look at Excel's date and time serial number system and tips for entering and formatting dates and times.

Other chapters in this book contain additional date-related information. For example, refer to Chapter 7 for counting examples that use dates. Chapter 23 contains some VBA functions that work with dates.

Understanding date serial numbers

To Excel, a date is simply a number. More precisely, a date is a "serial number" that represents the number of days since January 0, 1900. A serial number of 1 corresponds to January 1, 1900; a serial number of 2 corresponds to January 2, 1900, and so on. This system makes it possible to deal with dates in formulas. For example, you can create a formula to calculate the number of days between two dates.

You may wonder about January 0, 1900. This "non-date" (which corresponds to date serial number 0) is actually used to represent times that are not associated with a particular day. See "How Excel Handles Times," later in this chapter.

To view a date serial number as a date, you must format the cell as a date. Use the Format Cells dialog box (Number tab) to apply a date format.

 Excel 97 and later versions support dates from January 1, 1900 through December 31, 9999 (serial number = 2,958,465). Previous versions of Excel support a much smaller range of dates: from January 1, 1900 through December 31, 2078 (serial number = 65,380).

Choose Your Date System: 1900 or 1904

Excel actually supports two date systems: the 1900 date system and the 1904 date system. Which system you use in a workbook determines what date serves as the basis for dates. The 1900 date system uses January 1, 1900 as the day assigned to date serial number 1. The 1904 date system uses January 1, 1904 as the base date. By default, Excel for Windows uses the 1900 date system, and Excel for Macintosh uses the 1904 date system. Excel for Windows supports the 1904 date system for compatibility with Macintosh files. You can choose the date system from the Options dialog box (select Tools → Options and select the Calculation tab). You cannot change the date system if you use Excel for Macintosh.

Generally, you should use the default 1900-date system. And, you should exercise precaution if you use two different date systems in workbooks that are linked together. For example, assume Book1 uses the 1904 date system and contains the date 1/15/1999 in cell A1. Assume Book2 uses the 1900 date system and contains a link to cell A1 in Book1. Book2 will display the date as 1/14/1995. Both workbooks will use the same date serial number (34713), but they will be interpreted differently.

One advantage in using the 1904 date system is that it enables you to display negative time values. With the 1900 date system, a calculation that results in a negative time (for example 4:00 p.m. – 5:30 p.m.) cannot be displayed. When using the 1904 date system, the negative time displays as -1:30 (that is, a difference of one hour and thirty minutes).

Entering dates

You can enter a date directly as a serial number (if you know it), but more often you'll enter a date using any of several recognized date formats. Excel automatically converts your entry into the corresponding date serial number (which it uses for calculations), and also applies the default date format to the cell so it displays as an actual date rather than a cryptic serial number.

For example, if you need to enter June 1, 2001, you can simply enter the date by typing **June 1, 2001** (or use any of several different date formats). Excel interprets your entry and stores the value 37043 – the date serial number for that date. It also applies the default date format, so the cell contents may not appear exactly as you typed them.

When you activate a cell that contains a date, the formula bar shows the cell contents formatted as a date. It does not display the date's serial number. If you need to find out the serial number for a particular date, format the cell using a non-date number format.

TIP To change the default date format, you need to change a system-wide setting. Access the Windows Control Panel, and select Regional Settings. In the Regional Settings dialog box, select the Date tab. The selected item for the Short date style determines the default date format used by Excel.

Table 6-1 shows a sampling of the date formats that Excel recognizes.

TABLE **6-1** DATE ENTRY FORMATS RECOGNIZED BY EXCEL

Entry	Excel's Interpretation
6-1-99	June 1, 1999
6-1-1999	June 1, 1999
6/1/99	June 1, 1999
6/1/1999	June 1, 1999
6-1/99	June 1, 1999
June 1, 1999	June 1, 1999
Jun 1	June 1 of the current year
June 1	June 1 of the current year
6/1	June 1 of the current year
6-1	June 1 of the current year

[Handwritten note:]

PROBLEM:
10/20/1962 FORMATTED AS TEXT

SOLUTION:
USE FIND AND REPLACE
FIND WHAT: /
REPLACE WITH: —

THEN CHANGE FORMAT
CELL TO DATE

As you can see in Table 6-1, Excel is rather smart when it comes to recognizing dates entered into a cell. It's not perfect, however. For example, Excel does *not* recognize any of the following entries as dates:

♦ June 1 1999

♦ Jun-1 1999

♦ Jun-1/1999

Rather, it interprets these entries as text. If you plan to use dates in formulas, make sure that Excel can recognize the date you enter as a date; otherwise, the formulas that refer to these dates will produce incorrect results.

If you attempt to enter a date that lies outside of the supported date range, Excel interprets it as text. If you attempt to format a serial number that lies outside of the supported range as a date, the value displays as a series of pound signs (########).

Understanding time serial numbers

When you need to work with time values, you simply extend Excel's date serial number system to include decimals. In other words, Excel works with times by using fractional days. For example, the date serial number for June 1, 2001 is 37043. Noon (halfway through the day) is represented internally as 37043.5.

The serial number equivalent of one minute is 0.0006944. The formula that follows calculates this number by multiplying 24 hours by 60 minutes, and dividing the result into 1. The denominator consists of the number of minutes in a day (1,440).

```
=1/(24*60)
```

Searching for Dates

If your worksheet uses many dates, you may need to search for a particular date by using Excel's Find dialog box (which you can access with the Edit → Find command, or Ctrl+F). You'll find that Excel is rather picky when it comes to finding dates. You must enter a full four-digit date into the Find what field in the Find dialog box. For example, if your worksheets contain a date displayed as 11/24/99, you must search for that date using 1/24/1999. If you try to locate 11/24/99 with a two-digit year, you won't find it.

Similarly, the serial number equivalent of one second is 0.0000115740740740741, obtained by the following formula (1 divided by 24 hours times 60 minutes times 60 seconds). In this case, the denominator represents the number of seconds in a day (86,400).

```
=1/(24*60*60)
```

In Excel, the smallest unit of time is one one-thousandth of a second. The time serial number shown here represents 23:59:59.999, or one one-thousandth of a second before midnight.

```
0.99999999
```

Table 6-2 shows various times of day, along with each associated time serial number.

TABLE 6-2 TIMES OF DAY AND THEIR CORRESPONDING SERIAL NUMBERS

Time of Day	Time Serial Number
12:00:00 AM (midnight)	0.00000000
1:30:00 AM	0.06250000
3:00:00 AM	0.12500000
4:30:00 AM	0.18750000
6:00:00 AM	0.25000000
7:30:00 AM	0.31250000
9:00:00 AM	0.37500000
10:30:00 AM	0.43750000
12:00:00 PM (noon)	0.50000000
1:30:00 PM	0.56250000
3:00:00 PM	0.62500000
4:30:00 PM	0.68750000
6:00:00 PM	0.75000000
7:30:00 PM	0.81250000
9:00:00 PM	0.87500000
10:30:00 PM	0.93750000

Entering times

As with entering dates, you normally don't have to worry about the actual time serial numbers. Just enter the time into a cell using a recognized format. Table 6-3 shows some examples of time formats that Excel recognizes.

TABLE 6-3 TIME ENTRY FORMATS RECOGNIZED BY EXCEL

Entry	Excel's Interpretation
11:30:00 am	11:30 a.m.
11:30:00 AM	11:30 a.m.
11:30 pm	11:30 p.m.
11:30	11:30 a.m.
13:30	1:30 p.m.

Because the preceding samples don't have a specific day associated with them, Excel (by default) uses a date serial number of 0, which corresponds to the non-day January 0, 1900. Often, you'll want to combine a date and time. Do so by using a recognized date entry format, followed by a space, and then a recognized time-entry format. For example, if you enter the text that follows in a cell, Excel interprets it as 11:30 a.m. on June 1, 2001. Its date/time serial number is 37043.4791666667.

```
6/1/2001 11:30
```

When you enter a time that exceeds 24 hours, the associated date for the time increments accordingly. For example, if you enter the following time into a cell, it is interpreted as 1:00 a.m. on January 1, 1900. The day part of the entry increments because the time exceeds 24 hours.

```
25:00:00
```

Similarly, if you enter a date *and* a time — and the time exceeds 24 hours — the date that you entered is adjusted. The entry below, for example, is interpreted as 9/2/1999 1:00:00 a.m.

```
9/1/1999 25:00:00
```

If you enter a time only (without an associated date), you'll find that the maximum time that you can enter into a cell is 9999:59:59 (just under 10,000 hours). Excel adds the appropriate number of days. In this case, 9999:59:59 is interpreted as 3:59:59 p.m. on 02/19/1901. If you enter a time that exceeds 10,000 hours, the time appears as a text string.

Formatting dates and times

You have a great deal of flexibility in formatting cells that contain dates and times. For example, you can format the cell to display the date part only, the time part only, or both the date and time parts.

You format dates and times by selecting the cells, and then using the Number tab of the Format Cells dialog box, shown in Figure 6-1. The Date category shows built-in date formats, and the Time category shows built-in time formats. Some of the formats include both date and time display. Just select the desired format from the Type list and click OK.

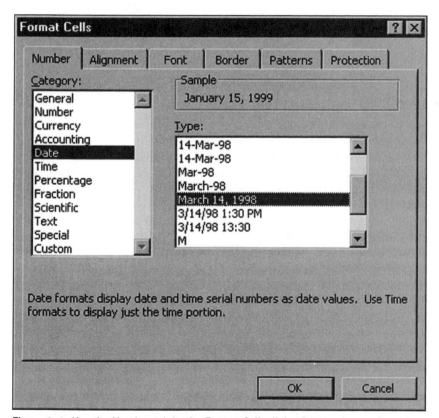

Figure 6-1: Use the Number tab in the Format Cells dialog box to change the appearance of dates and times.

When you create a formula that refers to a cell containing a date or a time, Excel automatically formats the formula cell as a date or a time. Sometimes, this is very helpful; other times it's completely inappropriate and downright annoying. Unfortunately, you cannot turn off this automatic date formatting. You can, however, use a shortcut key combination to remove all number formatting from the cell. Just select the cell and press Ctrl+Shift+~.

If none of the built-in formats meet your needs, you can create a custom number format. Select the Custom category, and then type the custom format codes into the Type box. (See Appendix C for information on creating custom number formats.)

A particularly useful custom number format for displaying times is:

`[h]:mm:ss`

Using square brackets around the hour part of the format string causes Excel to display hours beyond 24 hours. You will find this useful when adding times that exceed 24 hours. For an example, see "Summing Times That Exceed 24 Hours," later in this chapter.

Problems with dates

OK, I admit it: Excel has some problems when it comes to dates. Many of these problems stem from the fact that Excel was designed many years ago, before the acronym Y2K became a household term. And, as I describe, the Excel designers basically emulated Lotus 1-2-3's limited date and time features — which contain a nasty bug duplicated intentionally in Excel. Finally, versions of Excel show inconsistency in how they interpret a cell entry that has a two-digit year.

If Excel were being designed from scratch today, I'm sure it would be much more versatile in dealing with dates. Unfortunately, we're currently stuck with a product that leaves much to be desired in the area of dates.

EXCEL'S LEAP YEAR BUG

A leap year contains an additional day (February 29). Although the year 1900 was not a leap year, Excel treats it as such. In other words, when you type the following into a cell, Excel does not complain. It interprets this as a valid date and assigns a serial number of 60.

2/29/1900

If you type the following, Excel correctly interprets it as a mistake and *doesn't* convert it to a date. Rather, it simply makes the cell entry text:

`2/29/1901`

How can a product used daily by millions of people contain such an obvious bug? The answer is historical. The original version of Lotus 1-2-3 contained a bug that caused it to consider 1900 as a leap year. When Excel was released some time later, the designers knew of this bug, and chose to reproduce it in Excel to maintain compatibility with Lotus worksheet files.

Why does this bug still exist in later versions of Excel? Microsoft asserts that the disadvantages of correcting this bug outweigh the advantages. If the bug were eliminated, it would mess up hundreds of thousands of existing workbooks. In addition, correcting this problem would affect compatibility between Excel and other programs that use dates. As it stands, this bug really causes very few problems because most users do not use dates before March 1, 1900.

PRE-1900 DATES

The world, of course, didn't begin on January 1, 1900. People who work with historical information using Excel often need to work with dates before January 1, 1900. Unfortunately, the only way to work with pre-1900 dates is to enter the date into a cell as text. For example, you can enter the following into a cell and Excel won't complain:

`July 4, 1776`

You can't, however, perform any manipulation on dates recognized as text. For example, you can't change its numeric formatting, you can't determine which day of the week this date occurred on, and you can't calculate the date that occurs seven days later.

ON THE CD The companion CD-ROM contains an add-in that I developed called Extended Date Functions. When you install this add-in, you'll have access to eight new worksheet functions that enable you to work with any date in the years 0100 through 9999. Figure 6-2 shows a worksheet that uses these functions to calculate the number of days between various pre-1900 dates.

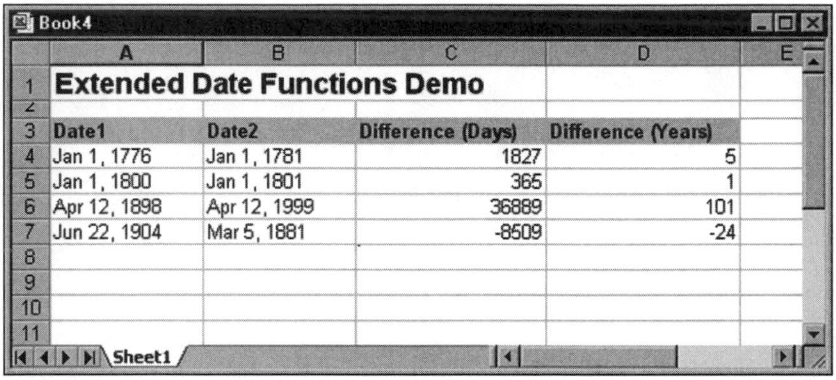

Figure 6-2: The Extended Date Functions add-in enables you to work with pre-1900 dates.

INCONSISTENT DATE ENTRIES

You need to exercise caution when entering dates by using two digits for the year. When you do so, Excel has some rules that kick in to determine which century to use. And those rules vary depending on the version of Excel that you use.

For Excel 97 and Excel 2000, two-digit years between 00 and 29 are interpreted as 21st century dates, and two-digit years between 30 and 99 are interpreted as 20th century dates. For example, if you enter 12/5/28, Excel interprets your entry as December 5, 2028. But if you enter 12/5/30, Excel sees it as December 5, 1930.

For previous versions of Excel (Excel 3 through Excel 95), two-digit years between 00 and 19 are interpreted as 21st century dates, and two-digit years between 20 and 99 are interpreted as 20th century dates. For example, if you enter 12/5/19, Excel interprets your entry as December 5, 2019. But if you enter 12/5/20, Excel sees it as December 5, 1920.

If for some unknown reason you still use Excel 2, when you enter a two-digit date, it is *always* interpreted as a 20th century date. Table 6-4 summarizes these differences for various versions of Excel.

TABLE 6-4 HOW TWO-DIGIT YEARS ARE INTERPRETED IN VARIOUS EXCEL
VERSIONS

Excel Version	20th Century Years	21st Century Years
2	00-78	N/A
3, 4, 5, 7 (95)	20-99	00-19
8 (97), 9 (2000)	30-99	00-29

To avoid any surprises, you should simply enter *all* years using all four digits for the year.

Date-Related Functions

Excel has quite a few functions that work with dates, and you can use these functions in your formulas. When you use the Paste Function dialog box, these functions appear in the Date & Time function category.

Table 6-5 summarizes the date-related functions available in Excel. Some of Excel's date functions require that you install the Analysis ToolPak.

TABLE 6-5 DATE-RELATED FUNCTIONS

Function	Description
DATE	Returns the serial number of a particular date
DATEDIF	Calculates the number of days, months, or years between two dates
DATEVALUE	Converts a date in the form of text to a serial number
DAY	Converts a serial number to a day of the month
DAYS360	Calculates the number of days between two dates based on a 360-day year
EDATE*	Returns the serial number of the date that represents the indicated number of months before or after the start date
EOMONTH*	Returns the serial number of the last day of the month before or after a specified number of months
MONTH	Converts a serial number to a month
NETWORKDAYS*	Returns the number of whole workdays between two dates
NOW	Returns the serial number of the current date and time
TODAY	Returns the serial number of today's date
WEEKDAY	Converts a serial number to a day of the week
WEEKNUM*	Returns the week number in the year
WORKDAY*	Returns the serial number of the date before or after a specified number of workdays
YEAR	Converts a serial number to a year
YEARFRAC*	Returns the year fraction representing the number of whole days between start_date and end_date

Function is available only when the Analysis ToolPak add-in is installed.

Displaying the current date

The following function displays the current date in a cell:

```
=TODAY()
```

You can also display the date, combined with text. The formula that follows, for example, displays text such as, "Today is Thursday, December 30, 1999."

```
="Today is "&TEXT(TODAY(),"dddd, mmmm d, yyyy")
```

It's important to understand that the TODAY function is updated whenever the worksheet is calculated. For example, if you enter either of the formulas into a worksheet, they will display the current date. But when you open the workbook tomorrow, they will display the current date – not the date when you entered the formula.

TIP

To enter a "date stamp" into a cell, press Ctrl+; (semicolon). This enters the date directly into the cell and does not use a formula. Therefore, the date will not change.

Displaying any date

As explained earlier in this chapter, you can easily enter a date into a cell by simply typing it, using any of the date formats that Excel recognizes. You can also create a date by using the DATE function. The following formula, for example, returns a date comprising the year in cell A1, the month in cell B1, and the day in cell C1.

```
=DATE(A1,B1,C1)
```
year-month-day

numerical argu

NOTE

The DATE function accepts invalid arguments and adjusts the result accordingly. For example, this next formula uses 13 as the month argument and returns January 1, 2000. The month argument is automatically translated as month 1 of the following year.

```
=DATE(1999,13,1)
```

Often, you'll use DATE function with other functions as arguments. For example, the formula that follows uses the YEAR and TODAY functions to return the date for Independence Day (July 4th) of the current year:

```
=DATE(YEAR(TODAY()),7,4)
```

The DATEVALUE function converts a text string that looks like a date into a date serial number. The following formula returns 36394, the date serial number for August 22, 1999:

```
=DATEVALUE("8/22/1999")
```

To view the result of this formula as a date, you need to apply a date number format to the cell.

Excel's NOW and TODAY functions retrieve their values from the system clock. If your system clock is not set correctly, these functions will not return correct results. Use the Windows Control Panel to adjust your system clock to the correct date and time.

Generating a series of dates

Often, you'll want to insert a series of dates into a worksheet. For example, in tracking weekly sales, you may want to enter a series of dates, each separated by seven days. These dates will serve to identify the sales figures.

The most efficient way to enter a series of dates doesn't require any formulas. Use Excel's AutoFill feature to insert a series of dates. Enter the first date, and drag the cell's fill handle while pressing the right mouse button. Release the mouse button and select an option from the shortcut menu (see Figure 6-3).

The advantage of using formulas to create a series of dates is that you can change the first date and the others will update automatically. You need to enter the starting date into a cell, and then use formulas (copied down the column) to generate the additional dates.

The following examples assume that you entered the first date of the series into cell A1, and the formula into cell A2. You can then copy this formula down the column as many times as needed.

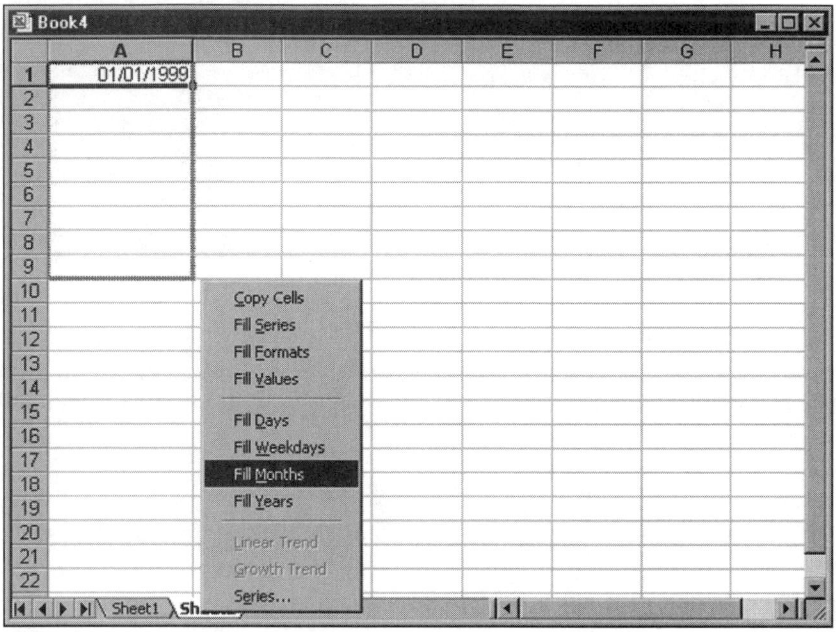

Figure 6-3: Using Excel's AutoFill feature to create a series of dates

To generate a series of dates separated by seven days, use this formula:

```
=A1+7
```

To generate a series of dates separated by one month, use this formula:

```
=DATE(YEAR(A1),MONTH(A1)+1,DAY(A1))
```

To generate a series of dates separated by one year, use this formula:

```
=DATE(YEAR(A1)+1,MONTH(A1),DAY(A1))
```

To generate a series of weekdays only (no Saturdays or Sundays), use the formula that follows. This formula assumes that the date in cell A1 is not a weekend.

```
=IF(WEEKDAY(A1)=6,A1+3,A1+1)
```

Converting a non-date string to a date

Often, you may import data that contains dates coded as text strings. For example, the following text represents August 21, 1999 (a four-digit year followed by a two-digit month, followed by a two-digit day):

```
19990821
```

To covert this string to an actual date, you can use a formula such as this one that assumes the coded data appears in cell A1:

```
=DATE(LEFT(A1,4),MID(A1,5,2),RIGHT(A1,2))
```

This formula uses text functions (LEFT, MID, and RIGHT) to extract the digits, and then uses these extracted digits as arguments for the DATE function.

Refer to Chapter 5 for information about manipulating text.

Calculating the number of days between two dates

A common type of date calculation determines the number of days between two dates. For example, you may have a financial worksheet that calculates interest earned on a deposit account. The interest earned depends on the number of days the account is open. If your sheet contains the open date and the close date for the account, you can calculate the number of days the account was open.

Because dates store as consecutive serial numbers, you can use simple subtraction to calculate the number of days between two dates. For example, if cells A1 and B1 both contain a date, the following formula returns the number of days between these dates:

```
=A1-B1
```

If cell B1 contains a more recent date than the date in cell A1, the result will be negative.

If this formula does not display the correct value, make sure that A1 and B1 both contain actual dates — not text that *looks* like a date.

Sometimes, calculating the difference between two days proves more difficult. To demonstrate, consider the common fence-post analogy. If somebody asks you how many units make up a fence, you can respond with either of two answers: the number of fence posts, or the number of gaps between the fence posts. The number of fence posts always remains one more than the number of gaps between the posts.

To bring this analogy into the realm of dates, suppose you start a sales promotion on February 1 and end the promotion on February 9. How many days was the promotion in effect? Subtracting February 1 from February 9 produces an answer of eight days. Actually, the promotion lasted nine days. In this case, the correct answer involves counting the fence posts, not the gaps. The formula to calculate the length of the promotion (assuming you have appropriately named cells) appears like this:

```
=EndDay-StartDay+1
```

Calculating the number of work days between two dates

Often, you may want to exclude weekends and holidays when calculating the difference between two dates. For example, you may need to know how many business days fall in the month of November. This calculation should exclude Saturdays, Sundays, and holidays. The NETWORKDAYS function can help out. (You can access this function only when you install the Analysis ToolPak.)

 The NETWORKDAYS function has nothing to do with networks or networking. Rather, it calculates the net workdays between two dates.

The NETWORKDAYS function calculates the difference between two dates, excluding weekend days (Saturdays and Sundays). As an option, you can specify a range of cells that contain the dates of holidays, which are also excluded. Excel has absolutely no way of determining which days are holidays, so you must provide this information in a range.

Figure 6-4 shows a worksheet that calculates the workdays between two dates. The range A2:A9 contains a list of holiday dates. The formulas in column C calculate the workdays between the dates in column A and column B. For example, the formula in cell C13 is:

```
=NETWORKDAYS(A13,B13,A2:A9)
```

This formula returns 4, which means that the seven-day period beginning with January 1 contains four workdays. In other words, the calculation excludes one holiday, one Saturday, and one Sunday.

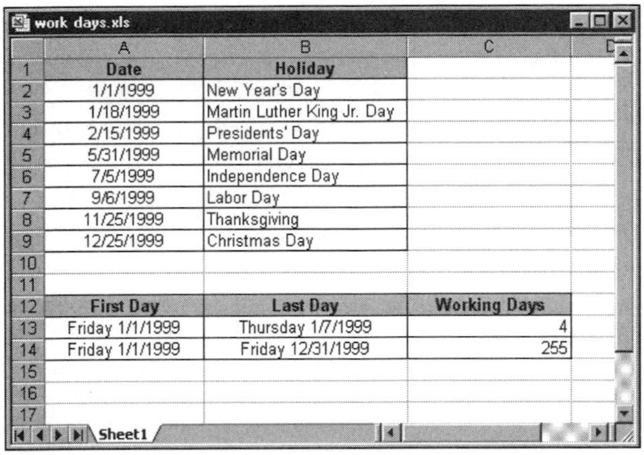

	A	B	C	D
	Date	Holiday		
1				
2	1/1/1999	New Year's Day		
3	1/18/1999	Martin Luther King Jr. Day		
4	2/15/1999	Presidents' Day		
5	5/31/1999	Memorial Day		
6	7/5/1999	Independence Day		
7	9/6/1999	Labor Day		
8	11/25/1999	Thanksgiving		
9	12/25/1999	Christmas Day		
10				
11				
12	First Day	Last Day	Working Days	
13	Friday 1/1/1999	Thursday 1/7/1999	4	
14	Friday 1/1/1999	Friday 12/31/1999	255	
15				
16				
17				

Figure 6-4: Using the NETWORKDAYS function to calculate the number of working days between two dates

Offsetting a date using only workdays

The WORKDAY function — available only when you install the Analysis ToolPak — presents the opposite of the NETWORKDAYS function. For example, if you start a project on January 4, and the project requires 10 working days to complete, the WORKDAY function can calculate the date you will finish the project.

The following formula uses the WORKDAY function to determine the date 10 working days from January 4, 1999. A working day consists of a weekday (Monday through Friday).

```
=WORKDAY("1/4/1999",10)
```

The formula returns January 18, 1999 (four weekend dates fall between January 4 and January 18).

The second argument for the WORKDAY function can be negative. And, as with the NETWORKDAYS function, the WORKDAY function accepts an optional third argument — a reference to a range that contains a list of holiday dates.

Calculating the number of years between two dates

The following formula calculates the number of years between two dates. This formula assumes that cells A1 and B1 both contain dates.

```
=YEAR(A1)-YEAR(B1)
```

This formula uses the YEAR function to extract the year from each date, and then subtracts one year from the other. If cell B1 contains a more recent date than the date in cell A1, the result will be negative.

Note that this function doesn't calculate *full* years. For example, if cell A1 contains 12/31/1999 and cell B1 contains 01/01/1998, the formula returns a difference of one year, even though the dates differ by only one day.

Calculating a person's age

A person's age indicates the number of full years that the person has been alive. The formula for calculating the number of years between two dates won't calculate this value correctly. You can use two other formulas, however, to calculate a person's age.

The following formula returns the age of the person whose date of birth you enter into cell A1. This formula uses the YEARFRAC function – available only when you install the Analysis ToolPak add-in.

```
=INT(YEARFRAC(TODAY(),A1,1))
```

The following formula, which doesn't rely on an Analysis ToolPak function, uses the DATEDIF function to calculate an age (see the sidebar, "Where's the DATEDIF Function?"):

```
=DATEDIF(A1,TODAY(),"Y")
```

Determining the day of the year

January 1 is the first day of the year, and December 31 is the last day. But what about all of the days in between? The following formula returns the day of the year for a date stored in cell A1:

```
=A1-DATE(YEAR(A1),1,0)
```

The   day   of the year is sometimes referred to as a *Julian date*.

The following formula returns the number of days remaining in the year from a particular date (assumed to be in cell A1):

```
=DATE(YEAR(A1),12,31)-A1
```

When you enter either of these formulas, Excel applies date formatting to the cell. You need to apply a non-date number format to view the result as a number.

Where's the DATEDIF Function?

In several places throughout this chapter, I refer to the DATEDIF function. You may notice that this function does not appear in the Paste Function dialog box. Therefore, when you use this function, you must always enter it manually.

The DATEDIF function has its origins in Lotus 1-2-3, and apparently Excel provides it for compatibility purposes. Versions prior to Excel 2000 failed to even mention the DATEDIF function in the online help.

DATEDIF is a handy function that calculates the number of days, months, or years between two dates. The function takes three arguments: start_date, end_date, and a code that represents the time unit of interest. The following table displays valid codes for the third argument (you must enclose the codes in quotation marks).

Unit Code	Returns
"y"	The number of complete years in the period.
"m"	The number of complete months in the period.
"d"	The number of days in the period.
"md"	The difference between the days in start_date and end_date. The months and years of the dates are ignored.
"ym"	The difference between the months in start_date and end_date. The days and years of the dates are ignored.
"yd"	The difference between the days of start_date and end_date. The years of the dates are ignored.

The start_date argument must be earlier than the end_date argument, or the function returns an error.

To convert a particular day of the year (for example, the 90th day of the year) to an actual date in a specified year, use the formula that follows. This formula assumes the year stores in cell A1, and the day of the year stores in cell B1.

```
=DATE(A1,1,B1)
```

PUP 2000 Date Utilities

My Power Utility Pak 2000 (which you can order using the coupon in the back of the book) includes several utilities that work with dates:

◆ Perpetual Calendar: Displays a calendar for any month, creates a graphic calendar image, and creates calendars in worksheets.

◆ Insert-A-Date: Simplifies date entries. You can insert a date into a cell by clicking a calendar and choosing from a list of common date formats.

◆ Reminder Alarm: Displays a reminder (with sound) at a specified time of day, or after a specified period of time has elapsed.

◆ Time Tracker: Tracks the amount of time spent working on up to six different projects.

◆ Date Report: Creates a useful report that describes all dates in a workbook. This utility is useful for spotting potential Y2K problems.

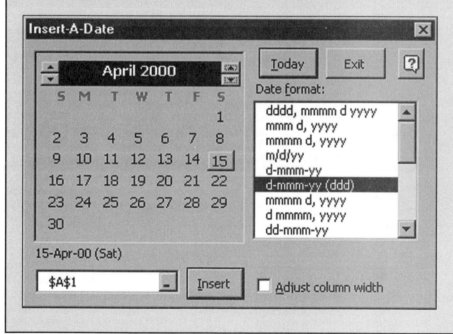

Determining the day of the week

The WEEKDAY function accepts a date argument and returns an integer between 1 and 7 that corresponds to the day of the week. The following formula, for example, returns 7 because the first day of the year 2000 falls on a Saturday:

```
=WEEKDAY(1/1/2000)
```

The WEEKDAY function uses an optional second argument that specifies the day numbering for the result. If you specify 2 as the second argument, the function returns 1 for Monday, 2 for Tuesday, and so on. If you specify 3 as the second argument, the function returns 0 for Monday, 1 for Tuesday, and so on.

You can also determine the day of the week for a cell that contains a date by applying a custom number format. A cell that uses the following custom number format displays the day of the week, spelled out:

dddd

Determining the date of the most recent Sunday

You can use the following formula to return the date for the previous Sunday. If the current day is a Sunday, the formula returns the current date:

```
=TODAY()-MOD(TODAY()-1,7)
```

To modify this formula to find the date of a day other than Sunday, change the 1 to a different number between 2 (for Monday) and 7 (for Saturday).

Determining the first day of the week after a date

This next formula returns the specified day of the week that occurs after a particular date. For example, use this formula to determine the date of the first Monday after June 3, 1999. The formula assumes that cell A1 contains a date, and cell A2 contains a number between 1 and 7 (1 for Sunday, 2 for Monday, etc.).

```
=A1+IF(A2<WEEKDAY(A1),7-WEEKDAY(A1)+A2,A2-WEEKDAY(A1))
```

If cell A1 contains June 3, 1999 and cell A2 contains 2 (for Monday), the formula returns June 7, 1999. This is the first Monday after June 3, 1999.

Determining the nth occurrence of a day of the week in a month

You may need a formula to determine the date for a particular occurrence of a weekday. For example, suppose your company payday falls on the second Friday of each month, and you need to determine the paydays for each month of the year. The following formula will make this type of calculation:

```
=DATE(A1,A2,1)+IF(A3<WEEKDAY(DATE(A1,A2,1)),7-WEEKDAY
(DATE(A1,A2,1))+A3,A3-WEEKDAY(DATE(A1,A2,1)))+((A4-1)*7)
```

The formula in this section assumes:

◆ Cell A1 contains a year

◆ Cell A2 contains a month

◆ Cell A3 contains a day number (1 for Sunday, 2 for Monday, etc.)

◆ Cell A4 contains the occurrence of interest (for example, 1 to select the first occurrence of the weekday specified in cell A3)

If you use this formula to determine the date of the first Friday in June 2000, it returns June 2, 2000.

 If the value in cell A4 exceeds the number of the specified day in the month, the formula returns a date from a subsequent month. For example, if you attempt to determine the date of the sixth Friday in June 2000 (there is no such date), the formula returns the first Friday in July.

Counting the occurrences of a day of the week

You can use the following formula to count the number of occurrences of a particular day of the week for a specified month. It assumes that cell A1 contains a date, and cell B1 contains a day number (1 for Sunday, 2 for Monday, etc.). The formula is an array formula, so you must enter it using Ctrl+Shift+Enter.

```
{=SUM((WEEKDAY(DATE(YEAR(A1),MONTH(A1),ROW(INDIRECT("1:"&
DAY(DATE(YEAR(A1),MONTH(A1)+1,0))))))=B1)*1)}
```

If cell A1 contains the date January 12, 1999, and cell A2 contains the value 2 (for Monday), the formula returns 4 — which reveals that January 1999 contains four Mondays.

The preceding array formula calculates the year and month by using the YEAR and MONTH functions. You can simplify the formula a bit if you store the year and month in separate cells. The following formula (also an array formula) assumes that the year appears in cell A1, the month in cell A2, and the day number in cell B1:

```
{=SUM((WEEKDAY(DATE(A1,A2,ROW(INDIRECT("1:"&
DAY(DATE(A1,A2+1,0))))))=B1)*1)}
```

Figure 6-5 shows this formula used in a worksheet. In this case, the formula uses mixed cell references so you can copy it. For example, the formula in cell C3 is:

```
{=SUM((WEEKDAY(DATE($B$2,$A3,ROW(INDIRECT("1:"&
DAY(DATE($B$2,$A3+1,0))))))=C$1)*1)}
```

	A	B	C	D	E	F	G	H	I	J
1			1	2	3	4	5	6	7	
2	YEAR ->	2000	Sun	Mon	Tue	Wed	Thu	Fri	Sat	Month
3	1	January	5	5	4	4	4	4	5	31
4	2	February	4	4	5	4	4	4	4	29
5	3	March	4	4	4	5	5	5	4	31
6	4	April	5	4	4	4	4	4	5	30
7	5	May	4	5	5	5	4	4	4	31
8	6	June	4	4	4	4	5	5	4	30
9	7	July	5	5	4	4	4	4	5	31
10	8	August	4	4	5	5	5	4	4	31
11	9	September	4	4	4	4	4	5	5	30
12	10	October	5	5	5	4	4	4	4	31
13	11	November	4	4	4	5	5	4	4	30
14	12	December	5	4	4	4	4	5	5	31
15		Total Days:	53	52	52	52	52	52	53	366

Figure 6-5: Calculating the number of each weekday in each month of a year

Additional formulas use the SUM function to calculate the number of days per month (column J) and the number of each weekday in the year (row 15).

ON THE CD   The workbook shown in Figure 6-5 also appears on the companion CD-ROM.

Expressing a date as an ordinal number

You may want to express a date as an ordinal number. For example, you can display 4/6/2000 as April 6th, 2000. The following formula expresses the date in cell A1 as an ordinal date. Note that the result is text, not an actual date.

```
=TEXT(A1,"mmmm ")&DAY(A1)&IF(INT(MOD(DAY(A1),100)/10)=1,
"th",IF(MOD(DAY(A1),10)=1,
"st",IF(MOD(DAY(A1),10)=2,"nd",IF(MOD(DAY(A1),10)=3,
"rd","th"))))&TEXT(A1,", yyyy")
```

The following formula shows a variation that expresses the date in cell A1 in day-month-year format. For example, 4/6/2000 would appear as 4th April, 2000. Again, the result of this formula represents text, not an actual date.

```
=DAY(A1)&IF(INT(MOD(DAY(A1),100)/10)=1, "th", IF(MOD(DAY(A1),10)=1,
"st",IF(MOD(DAY(A1),10)=2,"nd", IF(MOD(DAY(A1),10)=3, "rd","th"))))&
" " &TEXT(A1,"mmmm, yyyy")
```

 The companion CD-ROM contains a workbook that demonstrates the formulas for expressing dates as ordinal numbers.

Calculating dates of holidays

Determining the date for a particular holiday can be tricky. Some, such as New Year's Day and U.S. Independence Day are no-brainers, because they always occur on the same date. For these kinds of holidays, you can simply use the DATE function, which I covered earlier in this chapter. To enter New Year's Day – which always falls on January 1 – for a specific year in cell A1, you can enter this function:

```
=DATE(A1,1,1)
```

Other holidays are defined in terms of a particular occurrence of a particular weekday in a particular month. For example, Labor Day falls on the first Monday in September.

Figure 6-6 shows a workbook with formulas to calculate the date for 10 U.S. holidays. The formulas reference the year in cell A1. Notice that because New Year's Day, Independence Day, Veterans Day, and Christmas Day all fall on the same days of the year, the DATE function calculates their dates.

	A	B	C	D
1	2000	<-- Year		
2				
3	Holiday	Description	Date	
4	New Year's Day	1st Day in January	Saturday Jan-01-2000	
5	Martin Luther King Jr. Day	3rd Monday in January	Monday Jan-17-2000	
6	Presidents' Day	3rd Monday in February	Monday Feb-21-2000	
7	Memorial Day	Last Monday in May	Monday May-29-2000	
8	Independence Day	4th Day of July	Tuesday Jul-04-2000	
9	Labor Day	1st Monday in September	Monday Sep-04-2000	
10	Veterans Day	11th Day of November	Saturday Nov-11-2000	
11	Columbus Day	2nd Monday in October	Monday Oct-09-2000	
12	Thanksgiving Day	4thThursday in November	Thursday Nov-23-2000	
13	Christmas Day	25th Day of December	Monday Dec-25-2000	
14				
15				

Figure 6-6: Using formulas to determine the date for various holidays

The workbook shown in Figure 6-6 also appears on the companion CD-ROM.

MARTIN LUTHER KING JR. DAY

This holiday occurs on the third Monday in January. This formula calculates Martin Luther King Jr. Day for the year in cell A1:

```
=DATE(A1,1,1)+IF(2<WEEKDAY(DATE(A1,1,1)),7-WEEKDAY
(DATE(A1,1,1))+2,2-WEEKDAY(DATE(A1,1,1)))+((3-1)*7)
```

PRESIDENTS' DAY

Presidents' Day occurs on the third Monday in February. This formula calculates Presidents' Day for the year in cell A1:

```
=DATE(A1,2,1)+IF(2<WEEKDAY(DATE(A1,2,1)),7-WEEKDAY
(DATE(A1,2,1))+2,2-WEEKDAY(DATE(A1,2,1)))+((3-1)*7)
```

MEMORIAL DAY

The last Monday in May is Memorial Day. This formula calculates Memorial Day for the year in cell A1:

```
=DATE(A1,6,1)+IF(2<WEEKDAY(DATE(A1,6,1)),7-WEEKDAY
(DATE(A1,6,1))+2,2-WEEKDAY(DATE(A1,6,1)))+((1-1)*7)-7
```

Notice that this formula actually calculates the first Monday in June, and then subtracts 7 from the result to return the last Monday in May.

LABOR DAY

Labor Day occurs on the first Monday in September. This formula calculates Labor Day for the year in cell A1:

```
=DATE(A1,9,1)+IF(2<WEEKDAY(DATE(A1,9,1)),7-WEEKDAY
(DATE(A1,9,1))+2,2-WEEKDAY(DATE(A1,9,1)))+((1-1)*7)
```

COLUMBUS DAY

This holiday occurs on the second Monday in October. The formula below calculates Columbus Day for the year in cell A1:

```
=DATE(A1,10,1)+IF(2<WEEKDAY(DATE(A1,10,1)),7-WEEKDAY
(DATE(A1,10,1))+2,2-WEEKDAY(DATE(A1,10,1)))+((2-1)*7)
```

Calculating Easter

You'll notice that I omitted Easter from the previous section. Easter is an unusual holiday because its date is determined based on the phase of the moon and not by the calendar. Because of this, determining when Easter occurs proves a bit of a challenge.

Hans Herber, an Excel master in Germany, once sponsored an Easter formula contest at his Web site. The goal was to create the shortest formula possible that correctly determined the date of Easter for the years 1900 through 2078.

Twenty formulas were submitted, ranging in length from 44 characters up to 154 characters. Some of these formulas, however, work only with European date settings. The formula below, submitted by Thomas Jansen, is the shortest formula that works with any date setting. This formula returns the date for Easter, and assumes the year is stored in cell A1.

```
=DOLLAR(("4/"&A1)/7+MOD(19*MOD(A1,19)-7,30)*14%,)*7-6
```

Please don't ask me to explain this formula. I haven't a clue!

THANKSGIVING DAY

Thanksgiving Day is celebrated on the fourth Thursday in November. This formula calculates Thanksgiving Day for the year in cell A1:

```
=DATE(A1,11,1)+IF(5<WEEKDAY(DATE(A1,11,1)),7-WEEKDAY
(DATE(A1,11,1))+5,5-WEEKDAY(DATE(A1,11,1)))+((4-1)*7)
```

Determining the last day of a month

To determine the date that corresponds to the last day of a month, you can use the DATE function. However, you need to increment the month by 1, and use a day value of 0. In other words, the "0th" day of the next month is the last day of the current month.

The following formula assumes that a date is stored in cell A1. The formula returns the date that corresponds to the last day of the month.

```
=DATE(YEAR(A1),MONTH(A1)+1,0)
```

You can use a variation of this formula to determine how many days comprise a specified month. The formula that follows returns an integer that corresponds to the number of days in the month for the date in cell A1.

```
=DAY(DATE(YEAR(A1),MONTH(A1)+1,0))
```

When you enter this formula, Excel applies date formatting to the cell. Apply a non-date number format to view the result as a number.

Determining if a year is a leap year

To determine if a particular year is a leap year, you can write a formula that determines whether the 29th day of February occurs in February or March. You can take advantage of the fact that Excel's DATE function adjusts the result when you supply an invalid argument — for example, a day of 29 when February contains only 28 days.

The following formula returns TRUE if the year of the date in cell A1 is a leap year. Otherwise, it returns FALSE.

```
=IF(MONTH(DATE(YEAR(A1),2,29))=2,TRUE,FALSE)
```

 This function returns the wrong result (TRUE) if the year is 1900. See "Excel's Leap Year Bug," earlier in this chapter.

Determining a date's quarter

For financial reports, you might find it useful to present information in terms of quarters. The following formula returns an integer between 1 and 4 that corresponds to the calendar quarter for the date in cell A1:

```
=ROUNDUP(MONTH(A1)/3,0)
```

This formula divides the month number by 3, and then rounds up the result.

Converting a year to Roman numerals

Fans of old movies will like this one. The following formula converts the year 1945 to Roman numerals. It returns MCMXLV.

```
=ROMAN(1945)
```

You can access the ROMAN function once you install the Analysis ToolPak. This function returns a text string, so you can't perform any calculations using the result! Unfortunately, Excel doesn't provide a function to convert Roman numerals back to normal numbers.

Creating a calendar in a range

The example calendar you see in Figure 6-7 uses a single formula (an array formula) to display a calendar in a range of cells. The scroll bars are linked to cells that contain the month and year. The month is stored in cell B2 (named *m*) and the year is stored in cell D2 (named *y*). Enter the following array formula into the range B6:H11:

```
{=IF(MONTH(DATE(y,m,1))<>MONTH(DATE(y,m,1)-(WEEKDAY
(DATE(y,m,1))-1)+{0;1;2;3;4;5}*7+{1,2,3,4,5,6,7}-1),
"",DATE(y,m,1)-(WEEKDAY(DATE(y,m,1))-1)+{0;1;2;3;4;5}
*7+{1,2,3,4,5,6,7}-1)}
```

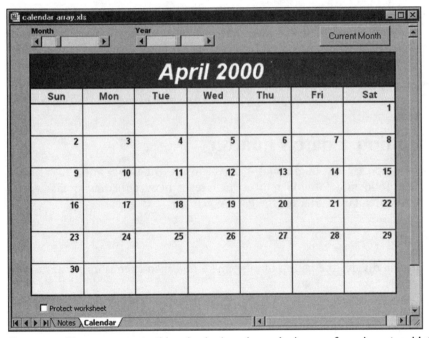

Figure 6-7: You can generate this calendar by using a single array formula, entered into 42 cells.

You can access the workbook shown in Figure 6-7 on the companion CD-ROM.

Time-Related Functions

Excel, as you might expect, also includes functions that enable you to work with time values in your formulas. This section contains examples that demonstrate the use of these functions.

Table 6-6 summarizes the time-related functions available in Excel. When you use the Paste Function dialog box, these functions appear in the Date & Time function category.

TABLE 6-6 TIME-RELATED FUNCTIONS

Function	Description
HOUR	Converts a serial number to an hour
MINUTE	Converts a serial number to a minute
MONTH	Converts a serial number to a month
NOW	Returns the serial number of the current date and time
SECOND	Converts a serial number to a second
TIME	Returns the serial number of a particular time
TIMEVALUE	Converts a time in the form of text to a serial number

Displaying the current time

This formula displays the current time as a time serial number (or, a serial number without an associated date):

```
=NOW()-TODAY()
```

 To enter a time stamp into a cell, press Ctrl+Shift+: (colon).

You need to format the cell with a time format to view the result as a recognizable time. For example, you can apply the following number format:

```
hh:mm AM/PM
```

You can also display the time, combined with text. The formula that follows displays the text "The current time is 6:28 PM."

```
="The current time is "&TEXT(NOW(),"h:mm AM/PM")
```

These formulas are updated only when the worksheet is calculated.

Displaying any time

Earlier in this chapter, I described how to enter a time value into a cell: Just type it into a cell, making sure that you include at least one colon (:). You can also create a time by using the TIME function. For example, the following formula returns a time comprising the hour in cell A1, the minute in cell B1, and the second in cell C1.

```
=TIME(A1,B1,C1)
```

Like the DATE function, the TIME function accepts invalid arguments and adjusts the result accordingly. For example, the following formula uses 80 as the minute argument and returns 10:20:15 AM. The 80 minutes are simply added to the hour, with 20 minutes remaining.

```
=TIME(9,80,15)
```

You can also use the DATE function along with the TIME function in a single cell. The formula that follows generates 36498.7708333333, the serial number that represents 6:30 p.m. on December 4, 1999.

```
=DATE(1999,12,4)+TIME(18,30,0)
```

The TIMEVALUE function converts a text string that looks like a time into a time serial number. The formula below returns 0.2395833333, the time serial number for 5:45 a.m.

```
=TIMEVALUE("5:45 am")
```

To view the result of this formula as a time, you need to apply number formatting to the cell. The TIMEVALUE function doesn't recognize all time formats. For example, the following formula returns an error because Excel doesn't like the periods in "a.m."

```
=TIMEVALUE("5:45 a.m.")
```

Summing times that exceed 24 hours

Many people are dismayed to discover that, when you sum a series of times that exceed 24 hours, Excel doesn't display the correct total. Figure 6-8 shows an example. The range B2:B8 contains times that represent the hours and minutes worked each day. The formula in cell B9 is:

```
=SUM(B2:B8)
```

As you can see, the formula returns an incorrect total (18 hours, 30 minutes). The total should read 42 hours, 30 minutes.

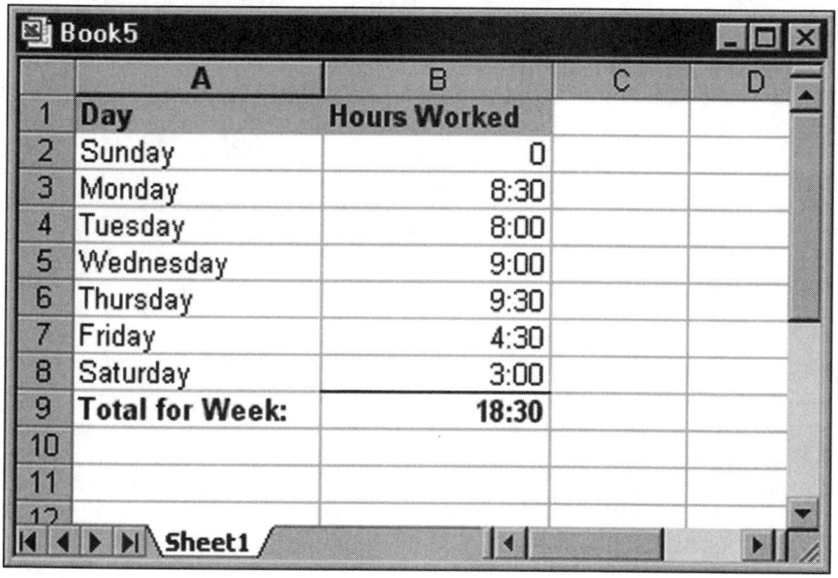

	A	B	C	D
1	Day	Hours Worked		
2	Sunday	0		
3	Monday	8:30		
4	Tuesday	8:00		
5	Wednesday	9:00		
6	Thursday	9:30		
7	Friday	4:30		
8	Saturday	3:00		
9	Total for Week:	18:30		
10				
11				
12				

Figure 6-8: Using the SUM function to add a series of times. The answer is incorrect because cell B9 has the wrong number format.

Unless told otherwise, Excel always displays times as if they comprise part of a day (in other words, limited to 24 hours). To view a time that exceeds 24 hours, you need to change the number format for the cell so square brackets surround the *hour* part of the format string. Applying the number format here to cell B9 displays the sum correctly:

```
[h]:mm
```

Figure 6-9 shows another example of a worksheet that manipulates times. This worksheet keeps track of hours worked during a week (regular hours and overtime hours).

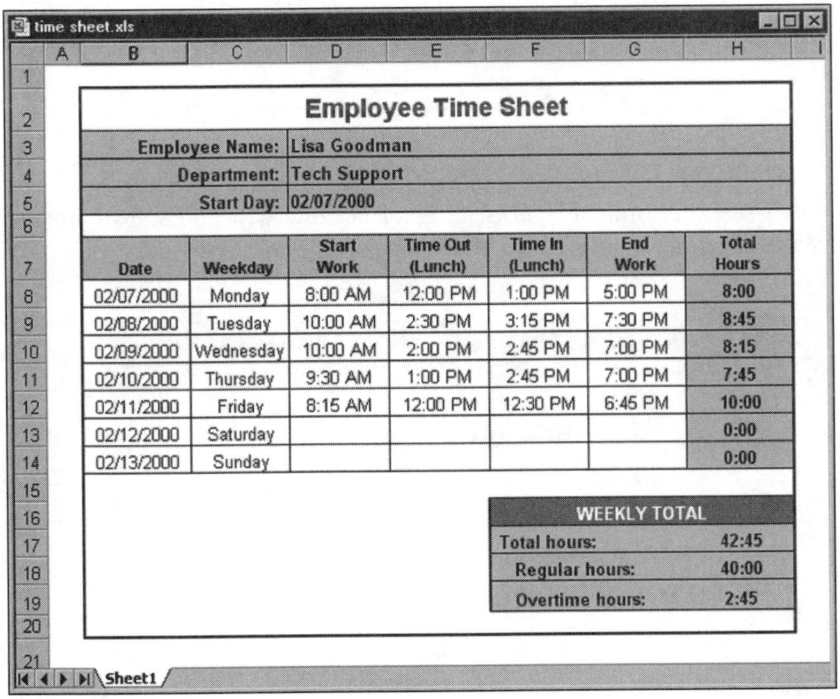

	Date	Weekday	Start Work	Time Out (Lunch)	Time In (Lunch)	End Work	Total Hours
				Employee Time Sheet			
	Employee Name:	Lisa Goodman					
	Department:	Tech Support					
	Start Day:	02/07/2000					
	02/07/2000	Monday	8:00 AM	12:00 PM	1:00 PM	5:00 PM	8:00
	02/08/2000	Tuesday	10:00 AM	2:30 PM	3:15 PM	7:30 PM	8:45
	02/09/2000	Wednesday	10:00 AM	2:00 PM	2:45 PM	7:00 PM	8:15
	02/10/2000	Thursday	9:30 AM	1:00 PM	2:45 PM	7:00 PM	7:45
	02/11/2000	Friday	8:15 AM	12:00 PM	12:30 PM	6:45 PM	10:00
	02/12/2000	Saturday					0:00
	02/13/2000	Sunday					0:00
					WEEKLY TOTAL		
					Total hours:		42:45
					Regular hours:		40:00
					Overtime hours:		2:45

Figure 6-9: An employee timesheet workbook

The week's starting date appears in cell D5, and the formulas in column B fill in the dates for the days of the week. Times appear in the range D8:G14, and formulas in column H calculate the number of hours worked each day. For example, the formula in cell H8 is:

```
=IF(E8<D8,E8+1-D8,E8-D8)+IF(G8<F8,G8+1-G8,G8-F8)
```

The first part of this formula subtracts the time in column D from the time in column E to get the total hours worked before lunch. The second part subtracts the time in column F from the time in column G to get the total hours worked after lunch. I use IF functions to accommodate graveyard shift cases that span midnight — for example, an employee may start work at 10:00 p.m. and begin lunch at 2:00 a.m. Without the IF function, the formula returns a negative result.

The following formula in cell H17 calculates the weekly total by summing the daily totals in column H:

```
=SUM(H8:H14)
```

The formula in cell H18 calculates regular hours (and assumes a 40-hour week). The formula returns the smaller of two values: the total hours, or 40 hours.

```
=MIN(H17,1+TIME(40,0,0))
```

The final formula in cell H19 simply subtracts the regular hours (cell H18) from the total hours (H16) to yield the overtime hours. If your standard workweek consists of something other than 40 hours, make the appropriate change to the formula in H18.

The times in H17:H19 likely will display time values that exceed 24 hours, so these cells use a custom number format:

```
[h]:mm
```

 The workbook shown in Figure 6-9 also appears on the companion CD-ROM.

Calculating the difference between two times

Because times are represented as serial numbers, you can subtract the earlier time from the later time to get the difference. For example, if cell A2 contains 5:30:00 and cell B2 contains 14:00:00, the following formula returns 08:30:00 (a difference of eight hours and 30 minutes).

```
=B2-A2
```

If the subtraction results in a negative value, however, it becomes an invalid time; Excel displays a series of pound signs (#######) because a time without a date has a date serial number of 0. A negative time results in a negative serial number, which is not permitted. This problem does not occur when you use a date along with the time.

If the direction of the time difference doesn't matter, you can use the ABS function to return the absolute value of the difference:

```
=ABS(B2-A2)
```

This "negative time" problem often occurs when calculating an elapsed time — for example, calculating the number of hours worked given a start time and an end time. This presents no problem if the two times fall in the same day. But if the work shift spans midnight, the result is an invalid negative time. For example, you may start work at 10:00 p.m. and end work at 6:00 a.m. the next day. Figure 6-10 shows a worksheet that calculates the hours worked. As you can see, the shift that spans midnight presents a problem.

	A	B	C	D
1	Start Shift	End Shift	Hours Worked	
2	8:00 AM	5:30 PM	9:30	
3	10:00 PM	6:00 AM	##################	
4				
5				
6				

Figure 6-10: Calculating the number of hours worked returns an error if the shift spans midnight.

Using the absolute value function (ABS) isn't an option in this case because it returns the wrong result (16 hours). The following formula, however, *does* work.

```
=(B2+(B2<A2)-A2)
```

Another, simpler, formula can do the job:

```
=MOD(B2-A2,1)
```

 TIP Negative times *are* permitted if the workbook uses the 1904 date system. To switch to the 1904 date system, select Tools → Options, and click the Calculation tab. Place a checkmark next to the 1904 date system option. But beware! When changing the workbook's date system, if the workbook uses dates, the dates will be off by four years.

Converting from military time

Military time is expressed as a four-digit number from 0000 to 2459. For example, 1:00 a.m. is expressed as 0100 hours, and 3:30 p.m. is expressed as 1530 hours. The following formula converts such a number (assumed to appear in cell A1) to a standard time:

```
=TIMEVALUE(LEFT(A1,2)&":"&RIGHT(A1,2))
```

The formula returns an incorrect result if the contents of cell A1 do not contain four digits. The following formula corrects the problem and returns a valid time for any military time value from 0 to 2459.

```
=TIMEVALUE(LEFT(TEXT(A1,"0000"),2)&":"&RIGHT(TEXT(A1,"0000"),2))
```

Converting decimal hours, minutes, or seconds to a time

To convert decimal hours to a time, divide the decimal hours by 24. For example, if cell A1 contains 9.25 (representing hours), this formula returns 09:15:00 (nine hours, 15 minutes):

```
=A1/24
```

To convert decimal minutes to a time, divide the decimal hours by 1,440 (the number of minutes in a day). For example, if cell A1 contains 500 (representing minutes), the following formula returns 08:20:00 (eight hours, 20 minutes):

```
=A1/1440
```

To convert decimal seconds to a time, divide the decimal hours by 86,400 (the number of seconds in a day). For example, if cell A1 contains 65,000 (representing seconds), the following formula returns 18:03:20 (18 hours, three minutes, and 20 seconds).

```
=A1/86400
```

Adding hours, minutes, or seconds to a time

You can use the TIME function to add any number of hours, minutes, or seconds to a time. For example, assume cell A1 contains a time. The following formula adds two hours and 30 minutes to that time and displays the result:

```
=A1+TIME(2,30,0)
```

You can use the TIME function to fill a range of cells with incremental times. Figure 6-11 shows a worksheet with a series of times in 10-minute increments. Cell A1 contains a time that was entered directly. Cell A2 contains the following formula, which copied down the column:

```
=A1+TIME(0,10,0)
```

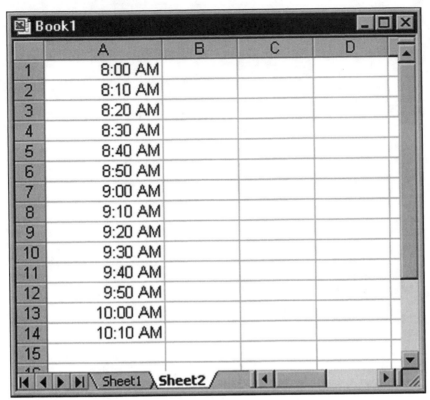

Figure 6-11: Using a formula to create a series of incremental times

Converting between time zones

You may receive a worksheet that contains dates and times in Greenwich Mean Time (GMT, sometimes referred to as Zulu time), and you need to convert these values to local time. To covert dates and times into local times, you need to determine the difference in hours between the two time zones. For example, to convert GMT times to U.S. Central Standard Time, the hour conversion factor is -6.

You can't use the TIME function with a negative argument, so you need to take a different approach. One hour equals 1/24 of a day, so you can divide the time conversion factor by 24, and then add it to the time.

Figure 6-12 shows a worksheet set up to convert dates and times (expressed in GMT) to local times. Cell B1 contains the hour conversion factor (-5 hours for U.S. Eastern Standard Time). The formula in B4, which copies down the column, is:

```
=A4+($B$1/24)
```

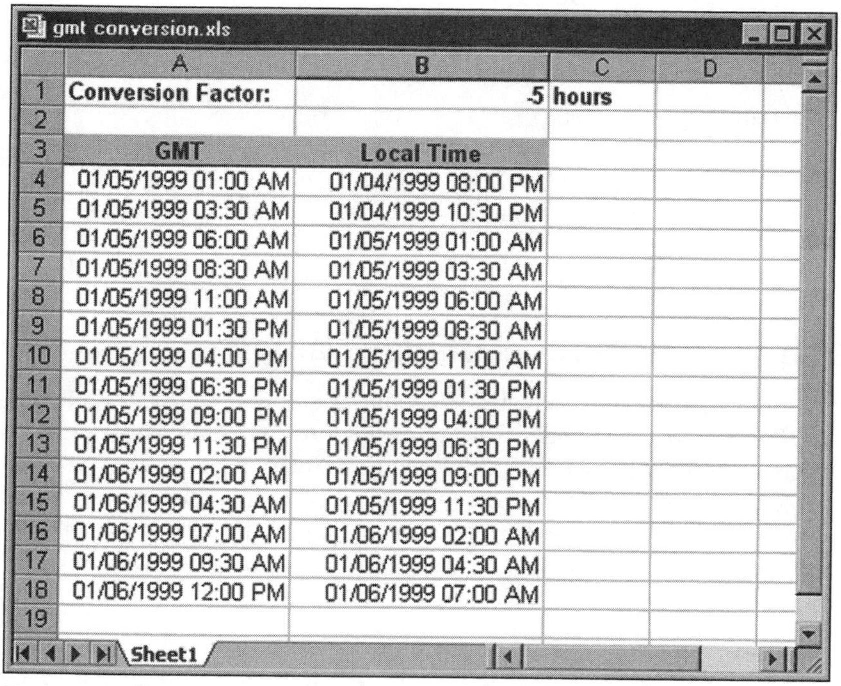

	A	B	C	D
1	Conversion Factor:	-5	hours	
2				
3	GMT	Local Time		
4	01/05/1999 01:00 AM	01/04/1999 08:00 PM		
5	01/05/1999 03:30 AM	01/04/1999 10:30 PM		
6	01/05/1999 06:00 AM	01/05/1999 01:00 AM		
7	01/05/1999 08:30 AM	01/05/1999 03:30 AM		
8	01/05/1999 11:00 AM	01/05/1999 06:00 AM		
9	01/05/1999 01:30 PM	01/05/1999 08:30 AM		
10	01/05/1999 04:00 PM	01/05/1999 11:00 AM		
11	01/05/1999 06:30 PM	01/05/1999 01:30 PM		
12	01/05/1999 09:00 PM	01/05/1999 04:00 PM		
13	01/05/1999 11:30 PM	01/05/1999 06:30 PM		
14	01/06/1999 02:00 AM	01/05/1999 09:00 PM		
15	01/06/1999 04:30 AM	01/05/1999 11:30 PM		
16	01/06/1999 07:00 AM	01/06/1999 02:00 AM		
17	01/06/1999 09:30 AM	01/06/1999 04:30 AM		
18	01/06/1999 12:00 PM	01/06/1999 07:00 AM		
19				

Figure 6-12: This worksheet converts dates and times between time zones.

This formula effectively adds *x* hours to the date and time in column A. If cell B1 contains a negative hour value, the value subtracts from the date and time in column A. Note that, in some cases, this also affects the date.

Rounding time values

You may need to create a formula that rounds a time to a particular value. For example, you may need to enter your company's time records rounded to the nearest 15 minutes. This section presents examples of various ways to round a time value.

The following formula rounds the time in cell A1 to the nearest minute:

```
=ROUND(A1*1440,0)/1440
```

The formula works by multiplying the time by 1440 (to get total minutes). This value is passed to the ROUND function; the result is divided by 1440. For example, if cell A1 contains 11:52:34, the formula returns 11:53:00.

The following formula resembles this example, except that it rounds the time in cell A1 to the nearest hour:

```
=ROUND(A1*24,0)/24
```

If cell A1 contains 5:21:31, the formula returns 5:00:00.

The following formula rounds the time in cell A1 to the nearest 15 minutes:

```
=ROUND(A1*24/0.25,0)*(0.25/24)
```

In this formula, 0.25 represents the fractional hour. To round a time to the nearest 30 minutes, change 0.25 to 0.5, as in the following formula:

```
=ROUND(A1*24/0.5,0)*(0.5/24)
```

Working with non-time-of-day values

Sometimes, you may want to work with time values that don't represent an actual time of day. For example, you might want to create a list of the finish times for a race, or record the time you spend jogging each day. Such times don't represent a time of day. Rather, a value represents the time for an event (in hours, minutes, and seconds). The time to complete a test, for instance, might take 35 minutes and 40 seconds. You can enter that value into a cell as:

```
00:35:45
```

Excel interprets such an entry as 12:35:45 AM — which works fine (just make sure that you format the cell so that it appears as you like). When you enter such times that do not have an hour component, you must include at least one zero for the hour. If you omit a leading zero for a missing hour, Excel interprets your entry as 35 hours and 45 minutes.

Figure 6-13 shows an example of a worksheet set up to keep track of someone's jogging activity. Column A contains simple dates. Column B contains the distance, in miles. Column C contains the time it took to run the distance. Column D contains formulas to calculate the speed, in miles per hour. For example, the formula in cell D2 is:

```
=B2/(C2*24)
```

Column E contains formulas to calculate the pace, in minutes per mile. For example, the formula in cell E2 is:

```
=(C2*60*24)/B2
```

Columns F and G contain formulas that calculate the year-to-date distance (using column B), and the cumulative time (using column C). The cells in column G are formatted using the following number format (which permits time displays that exceed 24 hours):

```
[hh]:mm:ss
```

	A	B	C	D	E	F	G	H
				Speed	Pace	YTD	Cumulative	
1	Date	Distance	Time	(mph)	(min/mile)	Distance	Time	
2	01/01/1999	1.50	00:18:45	4.80	12.50	1.50	00:18:45	
3	01/02/1999	1.50	00:17:40	5.09	11.78	3.00	00:36:25	
4	01/03/1999	2.00	00:21:30	5.58	10.75	5.00	00:57:55	
5	01/04/1999	1.50	00:15:20	5.87	10.22	6.50	01:13:15	
6	01/05/1999	2.40	00:25:05	5.74	10.45	8.90	01:38:20	
7	01/06/1999	3.00	00:31:06	5.79	10.37	11.90	02:09:26	
8	01/07/1999	3.80	00:41:06	5.55	10.82	15.70	02:50:32	
9	01/08/1999	5.00	01:09:00	4.35	13.80	20.70	03:59:32	
10	01/09/1999	4.00	00:45:10	5.31	11.29	24.70	04:44:42	
11	01/10/1999	3.00	00:29:06	6.19	9.70	27.70	05:13:48	
12	01/11/1999	5.50	01:08:30	4.82	12.45	33.20	06:22:18	
13								
14								

jogging log.xls — Sheet1

Figure 6-13: This worksheet uses times not associated with a time of day.

ON THE CD You can also access the workbook shown in Figure 6-13 on the companion CD-ROM.

Summary

This chapter explored the date- and time-related features of Excel. I provided an overview of Excel's serial number date and time system, and I described how to enter dates and times into cells. The chapter also listed many examples of formulas that use dates and times.

The next chapter presents various techniques to count data in a spreadsheet.

Chapter 7

Counting Techniques

IN THIS CHAPTER

- ◆ Information on counting and summing cells
- ◆ Information on counting and summing records in databases and pivot tables
- ◆ Basic counting formulas
- ◆ Advanced counting formulas
- ◆ Formulas for performing common summing tasks
- ◆ Conditional summing formulas using a single criterion
- ◆ Conditional summing formulas using multiple criteria
- ◆ The use of VBA to perform counting and summing tasks

MANY OF THE MOST FREQUENTLY asked spreadsheet questions involve counting and summing values and other worksheet elements. It seems that people are always looking for formulas to count or sum various items in a worksheet. If I've done my job, this chapter will answer the vast majority of such questions.

Counting and Summing Worksheet Cells

Generally, a counting formula returns the number of cells in a specified range that meet certain criteria. A summing formula returns the sum of the cells in a range that meet certain criteria. The range you want counted or summed may or may not consist of a worksheet database.

Table 7-1 lists Excel's worksheet functions that come into play when creating counting and summing formulas. If none of the functions in Table 7-1 can solve your problem, it's likely that an array formula can come to the rescue.

See Part V for detailed information and examples of array formulas used for counting and summing.

TABLE 7-1 EXCEL'S COUNTING AND SUMMING FUNCTIONS

Function	Description
COUNT	Returns the number of cells in a range that contain a numeric value
COUNTA	Returns the number of nonblank cells in a range
COUNTBLANK	Returns the number of blank cells in a range
COUNTIF*	Returns the number of cells in a range that meet a specified criterion
DCOUNT*	Counts the number of records in a worksheet database that meet specified criteria
DCOUNTA	Counts the number of nonblank records in a worksheet database that meet specified criteria
DEVSQ	Returns the sum of squares of deviations of data points from the sample mean; used primarily in statistical formulas
FREQUENCY	Calculates how often values occur within a range of values, and returns a vertical array of numbers; used only in a multicell array formula
SUBTOTAL	When used with a first argument of 2 or 3, returns a count of cells that comprise a subtotal; when used with a first argument of 9, returns the sum of cells that comprise a subtotal
SUM	Returns the sum of its arguments
SUMIF*	Returns the sum of cells in a range that meet a specified criterion
SUMPRODUCT	Multiplies corresponding cells in two or more ranges, and returns the sum of those products
SUMSQ	Returns the sum of the squares of its arguments; used primarily in statistical formulas
SUMX2PY2	Returns the sum of the sum of squares of corresponding values in two ranges; used primarily in statistical formulas
SUMXMY2	Returns the sum of squares of the differences of corresponding values in two ranges; used primarily in statistical formulas

Function	Description
SUMXMY2	Returns the sum of the difference of squares of corresponding values in two ranges; used primarily in statistical formulas.

Available in Excel 97 or later.

Getting a Quick Count or Sum

In Excel 97, Microsoft introduced a feature known as AutoCalculate. This feature displays — in the status bar — information about the selected range. Normally, the status bar displays the sum of the values in the selected range. You can, however, right-click the AutoCalculate display to bring up a menu with some other options.

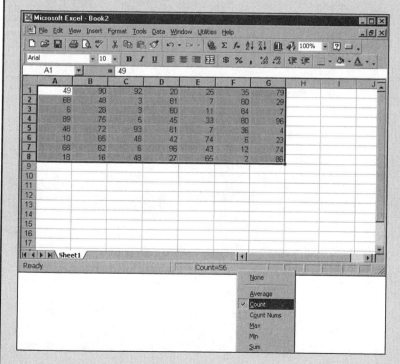

If you select Count, the status bar displays the number of non-empty cells in the selected range. If you select Count Nums, the status bar displays the number of numeric cells in the selected range.

Counting or Summing Records in Databases and Pivot Tables

Special database functions and the use of pivot tables provide additional ways to achieve counting and summing. Excel's DCOUNT and DSUM functions are database functions. They work in conjunction with a worksheet database and require a special criterion range that holds the counting or summing criteria.

Chapter 9 covers the database functions and provides information about counting and summing using a worksheet database.

Creating a pivot table is a great way to get a count or sum of items without using formulas. Like the database function, using a pivot table is appropriate when your data appears in the form of a database.

Refer to Chapter 16 for information about pivot tables.

Basic Counting Formulas

The basic counting formulas presented here are all straightforward and relatively simple. They demonstrate the ability of Excel's counting functions to count the number of cells in a range that meet specific criteria. Figure 7-1 shows a worksheet that uses formulas (in column E) to summarize the contents of range A1:B10 — a 20-cell range named *Data*.

You can access the workbook shown in Figure 7-1 on the companion CD-ROM.

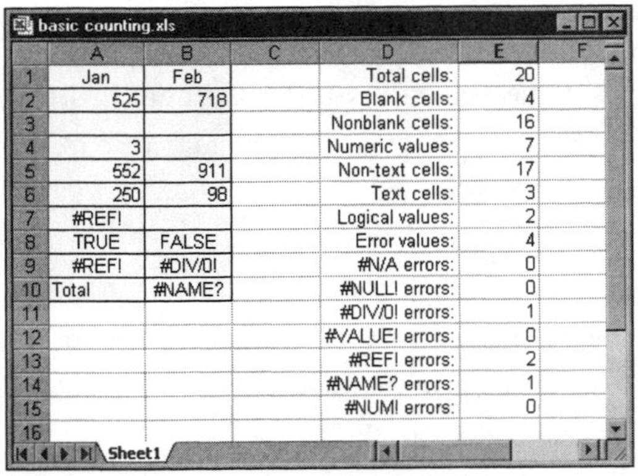

Figure 7-1: Formulas provide various counts of the data in A1:B10.

Counting the total number of cells

To get a count of the total number of cells in a range, use the following formula. This formula returns the number of cells in a range named *Data*. It simply multiplies the number of rows (returned by the ROWS function) by the number of columns (returned by the COLUMNS function).

```
=ROWS(Data)*COLUMNS(Data)
```

Counting blank cells

The following formula returns the number of blank (empty) cells in a range named *Data*:

```
=COUNTBLANK(Data)
```

About This Chapter's Examples

Many of the examples in this chapter consist of array formulas. An array formula, as explained in Chapter 12, is a special type of formula. You can spot an array formula because it is enclosed in brackets. For example:

```
{=Data*2}
```

When you enter an array formula, press Ctrl+Shift+Enter (not just Enter). And don't type the brackets. (Excel inserts the brackets for you.)

The COUNTBLANK function also counts cells containing a formula that returns an empty string. For example, the formula that follows returns an empty string if the value in cell A1 is greater than 5. If the cell meets this condition, then the COUNTBLANK function counts that cell.

```
=IF(A1>5,"",A1)
```

 The COUNTBLANK function does not count cells that contain a zero value, even if you uncheck the Zero values option in the Options dialog box (select Tools → Options, then click the View tab).

You can use the COUNTBLANK function with an argument that consists of entire rows or columns. For example, this next formula returns the number of blank cells in column A:

```
=COUNTBLANK(A:A)
```

The following formula returns the number of empty cells on the entire worksheet named Sheet1. You must enter this formula on a sheet other than Sheet1, or it will create a circular reference.

```
=COUNTBLANK(Sheet1!1:65536)
```

Counting nonblank cells

The following formula uses the COUNTA function to return the number of non-blank cells in a range named *Data*:

```
=COUNTA(Data)
```

The COUNTA function counts cells that contain values, text, or logical values (TRUE or FALSE).

Counting numeric cells

To count only the numeric cells in a range, use the following formula (which assumes the range is named *Data*):

```
=COUNT(Data)
```

Cells that contain a date or a time are considered to be numeric cells. Cells that contain a logical value (TRUE or FALSE) are not considered to be numeric cells.

Counting non-text cells

The following array formula uses Excel's ISNONTEXT function, which returns TRUE if its argument refers to any non-text cell (including a blank cell). This formula returns the count of the number of cells not containing text (including blank cells):

```
{=SUM(IF(ISNONTEXT(Data),1))}
```

Counting text cells

To count the number of text cells in a range, you need to use an array formula. The array formula that follows returns the number of text cells in a range named *Data*.

```
{=SUM(IF(ISTEXT(Data),1))}
```

Counting logical values

The following array formula returns the number of logical values (TRUE or FALSE) in a range named *Data*.

```
{=SUM(IF(ISLOGICAL(Data),1))}
```

Error values in a range

Excel has three functions that help you determine if a cell contains an error value:

- ◆ ISERROR: Returns TRUE if the cell contains any error value (#N/A, #VALUE!, #REF!, #DIV/0!, #NUM!, #NAME?, or #NULL!)

- ◆ ISERR: Returns TRUE if the cell contains any error value except #N/A

- ◆ ISNA: Returns TRUE if the cell contains the #N/A error value

You can use these functions in an array formula to count the number of error values in a range. The following array formula, for example, returns the total number of error values in a range named *Data*:

```
{=SUM(IF(ISERROR(data),1))}
```

Depending on your needs, you can use the ISERR or ISNA function in place of ISERROR.

If you would like to count specific types of errors, you can use the COUNTIF function. The following formula, for example, returns the number of #DIV/0! error values in the range named *Data*:

```
=COUNTIF(Data,"#DIV/0!")
```

Advanced Counting Formulas

Most of the basic examples I presented previously represent functions or formulas that perform conditional counting. The advanced counting formulas that I present here represent more complex examples for counting worksheet cells, based on various types of criteria.

Counting cells using the COUNTIF function

Excel's COUNTIF function is useful for single-criterion counting formulas. The COUNTIF function takes two arguments:

◆ *Range*: The range that contains the values that determine whether to include a particular cell in the count

◆ *Criteria*: The logical criteria that determine whether to include a particular cell in the count

Table 7-2 lists several examples of formulas that use the COUNTIF function. These formulas all work with a range named *Data*. As you can see, the *criteria* argument is quite flexible. You can use constants, expressions, functions, cell references, and even wildcard characters (* and ?).

TABLE 7-2 EXAMPLE FORMULAS THAT USE THE COUNTIF FUNCTION

Formula	What It Returns
=COUNTIF(Data,12)	The number of cells containing the value 12
=COUNTIF(Data,"<0")	The number of cells containing a negative value
=COUNTIF(Data,"<>0")	The number of cells not equal to 0
=COUNTIF(Data,">5")	The number of cells greater than 5
=COUNTIF(Data,A1)	The number of cells equal to the contents of cell A1
=COUNTIF(Data,">"&A1)	The number of cells greater than the value in cell A1
=COUNTIF(Data,"*")	The number of cells containing text
=COUNTIF(Data,"???")	The number of text cells containing exactly three characters

Formula	What It Returns
`=COUNTIF(Data,"budget")`	The number of cells containing the single word *budget* (not case sensitive)
`=COUNTIF(Data,"*budget*")`	The number of cells containing the text *budget* anywhere within the text
`=COUNTIF(Data,"A*")`	The number of cells containing text that begins with the letter A (not case sensitive)
`=COUNTIF(Data,TODAY())`	The number of cells containing the current date
`=COUNTIF(Data,">"&AVERAGE(Data))`	The number of cells with a value greater than the average
`=COUNTIF(Data,">"&STDEV(Data)*3)`	The number of values exceeding three standard deviations above the mean
`=COUNTIF(Data,3)+COUNTIF(Data,-3)`	The number of cells containing the value 3 or -3
`=COUNTIF(Data,TRUE)`	The number of cells containing logical TRUE
`=COUNTIF(Data,TRUE)+COUNTIF(Data,FALSE)`	The number of cells containing a logical value (TRUE or FALSE)
`=COUNTIF(Data,"#N/A")`	The number of cells containing the #N/A error value

Counting cells using multiple criteria

In many cases, your counting formula will need to count cells only if two or more criteria are met. These criteria can be based on the cells that are being counted, or based on a range of corresponding cells.

Figure 7-2 shows a simple worksheet that I use for the examples in this section. This sheet shows sales data categorized by Month, SalesRep, and Type. The worksheet contains named ranges that correspond to the labels in row 1.

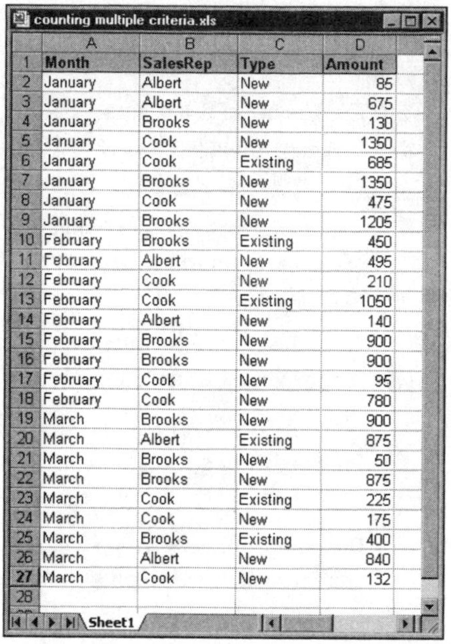

	A	B	C	D
1	Month	SalesRep	Type	Amount
2	January	Albert	New	85
3	January	Albert	New	675
4	January	Brooks	New	130
5	January	Cook	New	1350
6	January	Cook	Existing	685
7	January	Brooks	New	1350
8	January	Cook	New	475
9	January	Brooks	New	1205
10	February	Brooks	Existing	450
11	February	Albert	New	495
12	February	Cook	New	210
13	February	Cook	Existing	1050
14	February	Albert	New	140
15	February	Brooks	New	900
16	February	Brooks	New	900
17	February	Cook	New	95
18	February	Cook	New	780
19	March	Brooks	New	900
20	March	Albert	Existing	875
21	March	Brooks	New	50
22	March	Brooks	New	875
23	March	Cook	Existing	225
24	March	Cook	New	175
25	March	Brooks	Existing	400
26	March	Albert	New	840
27	March	Cook	New	132
28				

Figure 7-2: This worksheet demonstrates various counting techniques that use multiple criteria.

USING AND CRITERIA

An And criterion counts cells if all specified conditions are met. A common example is a formula that counts the number of values that fall within a numerical range. For example, you may want to count cells that contain a value greater than 0 *and* less than or equal to 12. Any cell that has a positive value less than or equal to 12 will be included in the count.

This sort of cell counting requires an array formula. The array formula that follows returns the count of the number of cells in a range named *Data* that are greater than 0 and less than or equal to 12:

```
{=SUM((Data>0)*(Data<=12))}
```

Sometimes, the counting criteria will be based on cells other than the cells being counted. You may, for example, want to count the number of sales that meet the following criteria:

- Month is January, *and*
- SalesRep is Brooks, *and*
- Amount is greater than 1000

The following array formula returns the number of items that meet all three criteria:

```
{=SUM((Month="January")*(SalesRep="Brooks")*(Amount>1000)))}
```

USING OR CRITERIA
To count using an Or criterion, you can sometimes simply use multiple COUNTIF functions. The following formula, for example, counts the number of 1s, 3s, and 5s in the range named *Data*:

```
=COUNTIF(Data,1)+COUNTIF(Data,3)+COUNTIF(Data,5)
```

You can also use the COUNTIF function in an array formula. The following array formula, for example, returns the same result as the previous formula:

```
{=SUM(COUNTIF(Data,{1,3,5}))}
```

But if you base your Or criteria on cells other than the cells being counted, the COUNTIF function won't work. Refer back to Figure 7-2. Suppose you want to count the number of sales that meet the following criteria:

◆ Month is January, *or*

◆ SalesRep is Brooks, *or*

◆ Amount is greater than 1000

The following array formula returns the correct count.

```
{=SUM(IF((Month="January")+(SalesRep="Brooks")+(Amount>1000),1))}
```

COMBINING AND AND OR CRITERIA
You can combine And and Or criteria when counting. For example, perhaps you want to count sales that meet the following criteria:

◆ Month is January, *and*

◆ SalesRep is Brooks, *or* SalesRep is Cook

This array formula returns the number of sales that meet the criteria.

```
{=SUM((Month="January")*IF((SalesRep="Brooks")+
(SalesRep="Cook"),1))}
```

Counting the most frequently occurring entry

Excel's MODE function returns the most frequently occurring value in a range. Figure 7-3 shows a worksheet with values in range A1:A10 (named *Data*). The formula that follows returns 10 because that value appears most frequently in the *Data* range:

```
=MODE(Data)
```

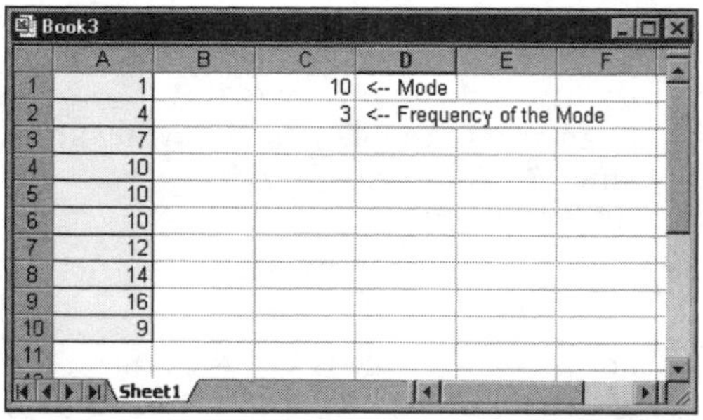

Figure 7-3: The MODE function returns the most frequently occurring value in a range.

To count the number of times the most frequently occurring value appears in the range (in other words, the frequency of the mode), use the following formula:

```
=COUNTIF(Data,MODE(Data))
```

This formula returns 3, because the modal value (10) appears three times in the *Data* range.

The MODE function works only for numeric values. It simply ignores cells that contain text. To find the most frequently occurring text entry in a range, you to need to use an array formula.

To count the number of times the most frequently occurring item (text or values) appears in a range named *Data*, use the following array formula:

```
{=MAX(COUNTIF(Data,Data))}
```

This next array formula operates like the MODE function, except that it works with both text and values.

```
{=INDEX(Data,MATCH(MAX(COUNTIF(Data,Data)),COUNTIF(Data,Data),0))}
```

Counting the occurrences of specific text

The examples in this section demonstrate various ways to count the occurrences of a character or text string in a range of cells. Figure 7-4 shows a worksheet used for these examples. Various text appears in the range A1:A10 (named *Data*); cell B1 is named *Text*.

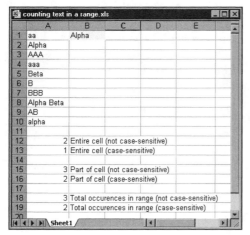

Figure 7-4: This worksheet demonstrates various ways to count characters in a range.

 The companion CD-ROM contains a workbook that demonstrates the formulas in this section.

ENTIRE CELL CONTENTS

To count the number of cells containing the contents of the *Text* cell (and nothing else), you can use the COUNTIF function. The following formula demonstrates:

```
=COUNTIF(Data,Text)
```

For example, if the *Text* cell contains the string "Alpha," the formula returns 2 because two cells in the *Data* range contain this text. This formula is not case-sensitive, so it counts both "Alpha" (cell A2) and "alpha" (cell A10). Note, however, that it does not count the cell that contains "Alpha Beta" (cell A8).

The following array formula is similar to the preceding formula, but this one is case-sensitive:

```
{=SUM(IF(EXACT(Data,Text),1))}
```

PARTIAL CELL CONTENTS

To count the number of cells that contain a string that includes the contents of the *Text* cell, use this formula:

```
=COUNTIF(data,"*"&Text&"*")
```

For example, if the *Text* cell contains the text "Alpha" the formula returns 3, because three cells in the *Data* range contain the text "alpha" (cells A2, A8, and A10). Note that the comparison is not case sensitive.

If you need a case-sensitive count, you can use the following array formula:

```
{=SUM(IF(LEN(Data)-LEN(SUBSTITUTE(Data,Text,""))>0,1))}
```

If the *Text* cells contain the text "Alpha," the preceding formula returns 2 because the string appears in two cells (A2 and A8).

TOTAL OCCURRENCES IN A RANGE

To count the total number of occurrences of a string within a range of cells, use the following array formula:

```
{=(SUM(LEN(Data))-SUM(LEN(SUBSTITUTE(Data,Text,""))))/
LEN(Text)}
```

If the *Text* cell contains the character "B," the formula returns 7 because the range contains seven instances of the string. This formula is case sensitive.

The following formula is a modified version that is not case sensitive.

```
=(SUM(LEN(Data))-SUM(LEN(SUBSTITUTE(UPPER(Data),
UPPER(Text),""))))/LEN(Text)
```

Counting the number of unique values

The following array formula returns the number of unique values in a range named *Data*:

```
{=SUM(1/COUNTIF(Data,Data))}
```

To understand how this formula works, you need a basic understanding of array formulas. (See Chapter 12 for an introduction to this topic.) In Figure 7-5, range A1:A12 is named *Data*. Range C1:C12 contains the following array formula (entered into all 12 cells in the range):

```
{=COUNTIF(Data,Data)}
```

count unique.xls

	A	B	C	D	E	F	G
1	100		3	0.333333			
2	100		3	0.333333			
3	100		3	0.333333			
4	200		2	0.5			
5	200		2	0.5			
6	300		1	1			
7	400		2	0.5			
8	400		2	0.5			
9	500		4	0.25			
10	500		4	0.25			
11	500		4	0.25			
12	500		4	0.25			
13				5	<-- Unique items in Column A		
14							

Sheet1

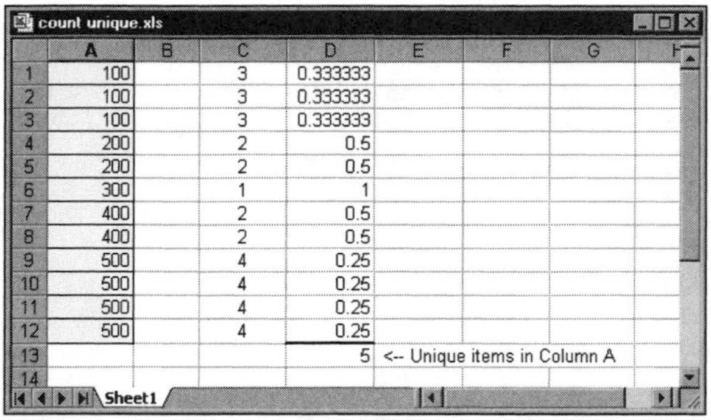

Figure 7-5: Using an array formula to count the number of unique values in a range

ON THE CD

You can access the workbook shown in Figure 7-5 on the companion CD-ROM.

The array in range C1:C12 consists of the count of each value in *Data*. For example, the number 100 appears three times, so each array element that corresponds to a value of 100 in the *Data* range has a value of 3.

Range D1:D12 contains the following array formula:

```
{=1/C1:C12}
```

This array consists of each value in the array in range C1:C12, divided into 1. For example, each cell in the original *Data* range that contains a 200 has a value of 0.5 in the corresponding cell in D1:D12.

Summing the range D1:D12 gives the number of unique items in *Data*. The array formula presented at the beginning of this section essentially creates the array that occupies D1:D12, and sums the values.

This formula has a serious limitation: If the range contains any blank cells, it returns an error. The following array formula solves this problem:

```
{=SUM(IF(COUNTIF(Data,Data)=0,"",1/COUNTIF(Data,Data)))}
```

XREF

To create an array formula that returns a list of unique items in a range, refer to Chapter 13.

Creating a frequency distribution

A frequency distribution basically comprises a summary table that shows the frequency of each value in a range. For example, an instructor may create a frequency distribution of test scores. The table would show the count of As, Bs, Cs, and so on. Excel provides a number of ways to create frequency distributions. You can:

◆ Use the FREQUENCY function

◆ Create your own formulas

◆ Use the Analysis ToolPak add-in

 A workbook that demonstrates these three techniques appears on the companion CD-ROM.

 If your data is in the form of a database, you can also use a pivot table to create a frequency distribution.

THE FREQUENCY FUNCTION

Using Excel's FREQUENCY function presents the easiest way to create a frequency distribution. This function always returns an array, so you must use it in an array formula entered into a multicell range.

Figure 7-6 shows some data in range A1:E20 (named *Data*). These values range from 1 to 500. The range G2:G11 contains the bins used for the frequency distribution. Each cell in this bin range contains the upper limit for the bin. In this case, the bins consist of 1-50, 51-100, 101-150, and so on. See the sidebar, "Creating Bins for a Frequency Distribution," to discover an easy way to create a bin range.

To create the frequency distribution, select a range of cells that correspond to the number of cells in the bin range. Then, enter the following array formula:

```
{=FREQUENCY(Data,G2:G11)}
```

The array formula enters the count of values in the *Data* range that fall into each bin. To create a frequency distribution that consists of percentages, use the following array formula:

```
{=FREQUENCY(Data,G2:G10)/COUNTA(Data)}
```

frequency distribution.xls

	A	B	C	D	E	F	G	H
1	55	316	223	185	124		Bins	
2	124	93	163	213	314		50	
3	211	41	231	241	212		100	
4	118	113	400	205	254		150	
5	262	1	201	172	101		200	
6	167	479	205	337	118		250	
7	489	15	89	362	148		300	
8	179	248	125	197	177		350	
9	456	153	269	49	127		400	
10	289	500	198	317	300		450	
11	126	114	303	314	270		500	
12	151	279	347	314	170			
13	250	175	93	209	61			
14	166	113	356	124	242			
15	152	384	157	233	99			
16	277	195	436	6	240			
17	147	80	173	211	244			
18	386	93	330	400	141			
19	332	173	129	323	188			
20	338	263	444	84	220			
21								

FREQUENCY Func

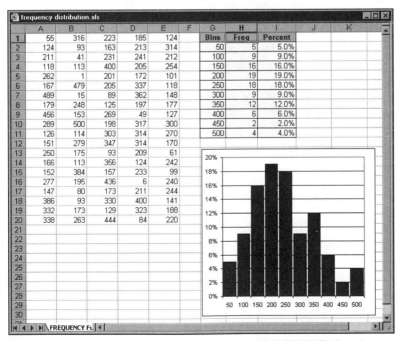

Figure 7-6: Creating a frequency distribution for the data in A1:E20

Figure 7-7 shows two frequency distributions – one in terms of counts, and one in terms of percentages. The figure also shows a chart (histogram) created from the frequency distribution.

frequency distribution.xls

	A	B	C	D	E	F	G	H	I
1	55	316	223	185	124		Bins	Freq	Percent
2	124	93	163	213	314		50	5	5.0%
3	211	41	231	241	212		100	9	9.0%
4	118	113	400	205	254		150	16	16.0%
5	262	1	201	172	101		200	19	19.0%
6	167	479	205	337	118		250	18	18.0%
7	489	15	89	362	148		300	9	9.0%
8	179	248	125	197	177		350	12	12.0%
9	456	153	269	49	127		400	6	6.0%
10	289	500	198	317	300		450	2	2.0%
11	126	114	303	314	270		500	4	4.0%
12	151	279	347	314	170				
13	250	175	93	209	61				
14	166	113	356	124	242				
15	152	384	157	233	99				
16	277	195	436	6	240				
17	147	80	173	211	244				
18	386	93	330	400	141				
19	332	173	129	323	188				
20	338	263	444	84	220				

FREQUENCY Fu

Figure 7-7: Frequency distributions created using the FREQUENCY function

Creating Bins for a Frequency Distribution

When creating a frequency distribution, you must first enter the values into the bin range. The number of bins determines the number of categories in the distribution. Most of the time, each of these bins will represent an equal range of values.

To create 10 evenly spaced bins for values in a range named *Data*, enter the following array formula into a range of 10 cells:

```
{=MIN(Data)+(ROW(INDIRECT("1:10"))*
(MAX(Data)-MIN(Data)+1)/10)-1}
```

This formula creates 10 bins, based on the values in the *Data* range. The upper bin will always equal the maximum value in the range.

To create more or fewer bins, use a value other than 10 and enter the array formula into a range that contains the same number of cells. For example, to create five bins, enter the following array formula into a five-cell range:

```
{=MIN(Data)+(ROW(INDIRECT("1:5"))*(MAX(Data)-MIN(Data)+1)/5)-1}
```

USING FORMULAS TO CREATE A FREQUENCY DISTRIBUTION

Figure 7-8 shows a worksheet that contains test scores for 50 students in column B (the range is named *Grades*). Formulas in columns G and H calculate a frequency distribution for letter grades. The minimum and maximum values for each letter grade appear in columns D and E. For example, a test score between 80 and 89 (inclusive) qualifies for a B.

The formula in cell G2 that follows is an array formula that counts the number of scores that qualify for an A:

```
{=SUM((Grades>=D2)*(Grades<=E2))}
```

You may recognize this formula from a previous section in this chapter (see "Counting Cells Using Multiple Criteria"). This formula was copied to the four cells below G2.

The formulas in column H calculate the percentage of scores for each letter grade. The formula in H2, which was copied to the four cells below H2, is:

```
=G2/SUM($G$2:$G$6)
```

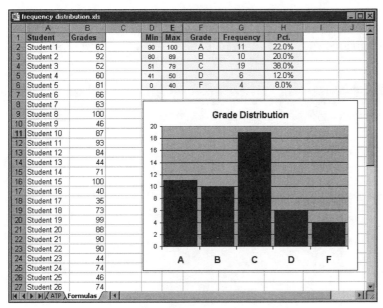

Figure 7-8: Creating a frequency distribution of test scores

USING THE ANALYSIS TOOLPAK TO CREATE A FREQUENCY DISTRIBUTION

Once you install the Analysis ToolPak add-in, you can use the Histogram option to create a frequency distribution. Start by entering your bin values in a range. Then, select Tools→Data Analysis to display the Data Analysis dialog box. Next, select Histogram and click OK. You should see the Histogram dialog box shown in Figure 7-9.

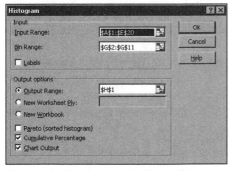

Figure 7-9: The Analysis ToolPak's Histogram dialog box

Specify the ranges for your data (Input Range), bins (Bin Range), and results (Output Range), and then select any options. Figure 7-10 shows a frequency distribution (and chart) created with the Histogram option.

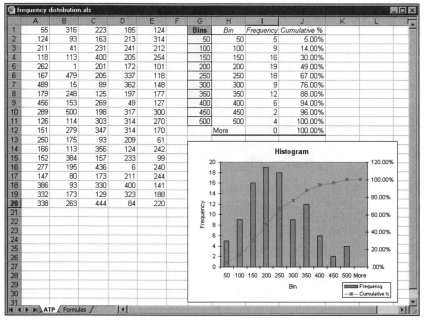

Figure 7-10: A frequency distribution and chart generated by the Analysis ToolPak's Histogram option

Note that the frequency distribution consists of values, not formulas. Therefore, if you make any changes to your input data, you need to re-run the Histogram procedure to update the results.

USING ADJUSTABLE BINS TO CREATE A HISTOGRAM

Figure 7-11 shows a worksheet with student grades listed in column B (67 students, total). Columns D and E contain formulas that calculate the upper and lower limits for bins, based on the entry in cell E1 (named *BinSize*). For example, if *BinSize* is 10, then each bin contains 10 scores (1-10, 11-20, and so on).

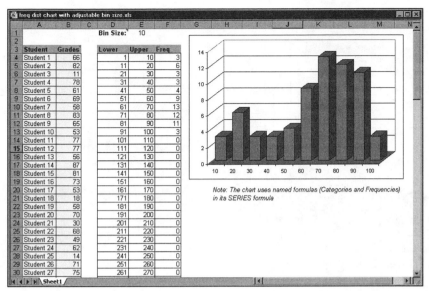

Figure 7-11: The chart displays a histogram; the contents of cell E1 determine the number of categories.

The chart uses two dynamic names in its SERIES formula. You can define the name *Categories* with the following formula:

```
=OFFSET(Sheet1!$E$4,0,0,ROUNDUP(100/BinSize,0))
```

You can define the name *Frequencies* with this formula:

```
=OFFSET(Sheet1!$F$4,0,0,ROUNDUP(100/BinSize,0))
```

See Chapter 15 for more about creating a chart that uses dynamic names in its SERIES formula.

The net effect is that the chart adjusts automatically when you change the *BinSize* cell. Figure 7-12, for example, shows the chart with a *BinSize* of 5.

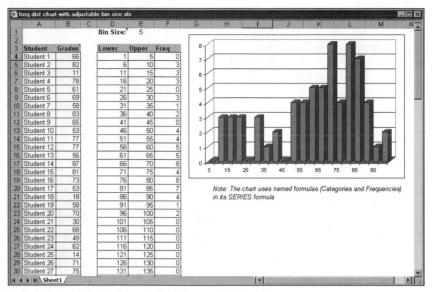

Figure 7-12: The previous chart with a smaller bin size

The workbook shown in Figure 7-12 also appears on the companion CD-ROM.

Summing Formulas

The examples in this section demonstrate how to perform common summing tasks using formulas. The formulas range from very simple to relatively complex array formulas that compute sums using multiple criteria.

Summing all cells in a range

It doesn't get much simpler than this. The following formula returns the sum of all values in a range named *Data*:

```
=SUM(Data)
```

The SUM function can take up to 32 arguments. The following formula, for example, returns the sum of the values in five noncontiguous ranges:

```
=SUM(A1:A9,C1:C9,E1:E9,G1:G9,I1:I9)
```

You can use complete rows or columns as an argument for the SUM function. The formula that follows, for example, returns the sum of all values in column A. If this formula appears in a cell in column A, it generates a circular reference error.

```
=SUM(A:A)
```

The following formula returns the sum of all values on Sheet1. This formula must appear on a sheet other than Sheet1.

```
=SUM(Sheet1!1:65536)
```

Computing a cumulative sum

Often, you may want to display a cumulative sum of values in a range – sometimes known as a "running total." Figure 7-13 illustrates a cumulative sum. Column B shows the monthly amounts, and column C displays the cumulative (year-to-date) totals.

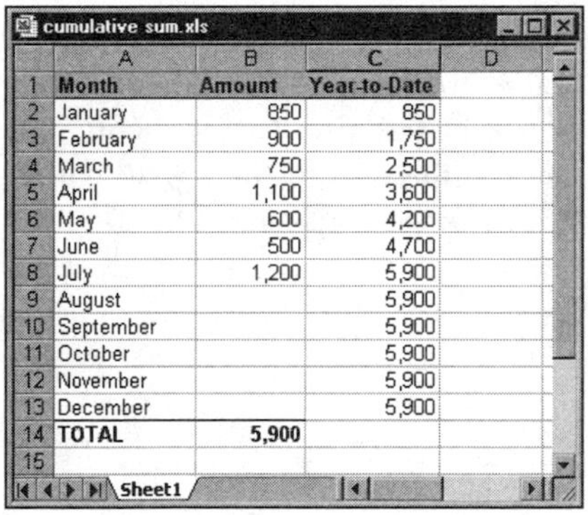

	A	B	C	D
1	Month	Amount	Year-to-Date	
2	January	850	850	
3	February	900	1,750	
4	March	750	2,500	
5	April	1,100	3,600	
6	May	600	4,200	
7	June	500	4,700	
8	July	1,200	5,900	
9	August		5,900	
10	September		5,900	
11	October		5,900	
12	November		5,900	
13	December		5,900	
14	TOTAL	5,900		
15				

Figure 7-13: Simple formulas in column C display a cumulative sum of the values in column B.

The formula in cell C2 is:

```
=SUM(B$2:B2)
```

Notice that this formula uses a *mixed reference*. The first cell in the range reference always refers to row 2. When this formula is copied down the column, the range argument adjusts such that the sum always starts with row 2 and ends with the current row. For example, after copying this formula down column C, the formula in cell D8 is:

```
=SUM(B$2:B8)
```

You can use an IF function to hide the cumulative sums for rows in which data hasn't been entered. The following formula, entered in cell C2 and copied down the column, is:

```
=IF(B2<>"",SUM(B$2:B2),"")
```

Summing the "top n" values

In some situations, you may need to sum the n largest values in a range – for example, the top 10 values. One approach is to sort the range in descending order, and then use the SUM function with an argument consisting of the first n values in the sorted range. An array formula such as this one accomplishes the task without sorting:

```
{=SUM(LARGE(Data,{1,2,3,4,5,6,7,8,9,10}))}
```

This formula sums the 10 largest values in a range named *Data*. To sum the 10 smallest values, use the SMALL function instead of the LARGE function:

```
{=SUM(SMALL(Data,{1,2,3,4,5,6,7,8,9,10}))}
```

These formulas use an array constant comprising the arguments for the LARGE or SMALL function. If the value of n for your top-n calculation is large, you may prefer to use the variation below. This formula returns the sum of the top 30 values in the *Data* range. You can, of course, substitute a different value for 30.

```
{=SUM(LARGE(Data,ROW(INDIRECT("1:30"))))}
```

Conditional Sums Using a Single Criterion

Often, you need to calculate a *conditional sum*. With a conditional sum, values in a range that meet one or more conditions are included in the sum. This section presents examples of conditional summing using a single criterion.

The SUMIF function is very useful for single-criterion sum formulas. The SUMIF function takes three arguments:

◆ *Range*: The range containing the values that determine whether to include a particular cell in the sum.

◆ *Criteria*: An expression that determines whether to include a particular cell in the sum.

◆ *sum_range*: Optional. The range that contains the cells you want to sum. If you omit this argument, the function uses the range specified in the first argument.

The examples that follow demonstrate the use of the SUMIF function. These formulas are based on the worksheet shown in Figure 7-14 — set up to track invoices. Column F contains a formula that subtracts the date in column E from the date in column D. A negative number in column F indicates payment. The worksheet uses named ranges that correspond to the labels in row 1.

	A	B	C	D	E	F	G
1	InvoiceNum	Office	Amount	DateDue	Today	Difference	
2	AG-0145	Oregon	$5,000.00	03-Apr	06-May	-33	
3	AG-0189	California	$450.00	21-Apr	06-May	-15	
4	AG-0220	Washington	$3,211.56	30-Apr	06-May	-6	
5	AG-0310	Oregon	$250.00	02-May	06-May	-4	
6	AG-0355	Washington	$125.50	06-May	06-May	0	
7	AG-0409	Washington	$3,000.00	12-May	06-May	6	
8	AG-0581	Oregon	$2,100.00	25-May	06-May	19	
9	AG-0600	Oregon	$335.39	25-May	06-May	19	
10	AG-0602	Washington	$65.00	30-May	06-May	24	
11	AG-0633	California	$250.00	01-Jun	06-May	26	
12	TOTAL		$14,787.45			36	
13							
14							

Figure 7-14: A negative value in column F indicates a past-due payment.

All of the examples in this section also appear on the companion CD-ROM.

Summing only negative values

The following formula returns the sum of the negative values in column F. In other words, it returns the total number of past-due days for all invoices. For this worksheet, the formula returns -58.

```
=SUMIF(Difference,"<0")
```

You can also use the following array formula to sum the negative values in the *Difference* range:

```
{=SUM(IF(Difference<0,Difference))}
```

Because you omit the third argument, the second argument (">0") applies to the values in the *Difference* range.

You do not need to hard-code the arguments for the SUMIF function into your formula. For example, you can create a formula such as the following, which gets the criteria argument from the contents of cell G2.

```
=SUMIF(Difference,G2)
```

This formula returns a new result if you change the criteria in cell G2.

Summing values based on a different range

The following formula returns the sum of the past-due invoice amounts (in column C):

```
=SUMIF(Difference,"<0",Amount)
```

This formula uses the values in the *Difference* range to determine if the corresponding values in the *Amount* range contribute to the sum.

Let a Wizard Create Your Formula

Beginning with Excel 97, Excel ships with an add-in called Conditional Sum Wizard. Once you install this add-in, you can invoke the Wizard by selecting Tools → Wizard → Conditional Sum.

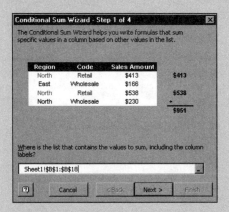

You can specify various conditions for your summing, and the add-in creates the formula for you (always an array formula). The Conditional Sum Wizard add-in, although a handy tool, is not all that versatile. For example, you can combine multiple criteria using an And condition, but not an Or condition.

You can also use the following array formula to return the sum of the values in the *Amount* range, where the corresponding value in the *Difference* range is negative.

`{=SUM(IF(Difference<0,Amount))}`

Summing values based on a text comparison

The following formula returns the total invoice amounts for the Oregon office:

`=SUMIF(Office,"=Oregon",Amount)`

Using the equal sign is optional. The following formula has the same result:

`=SUMIF(Office,"Oregon",Amount)`

To sum the invoice amounts for all offices *except* Oregon, use this formula:

`=SUMIF(Office,"<>Oregon",Amount)`

Summing values based on a date comparison

The following formula returns the total invoice amounts that have a due date beyond June 1, 1999.

`=SUMIF(DateDue,">=6/1/1999",Amount)`

The formula that follows returns the total invoice amounts that have a future due date (including today).

`=SUMIF(DateDue,">="&TODAY(),Amount)`

Notice that the second argument for the SUMIF function is an expression. The expression uses the TODAY function, which returns the current date. Also, the comparison operator, enclosed in quotes, is concatenated (using the & operator) with the result of the TODAY function.

Conditional Sums Using Multiple Criteria

The examples in the preceding section all used a single comparison criterion. The examples in this section involve summing cells based on multiple criteria. Because the SUMIF function does not work with multiple criteria, you need to resort to using an array formula. Figure 7-15 shows the sample worksheet again, for your reference.

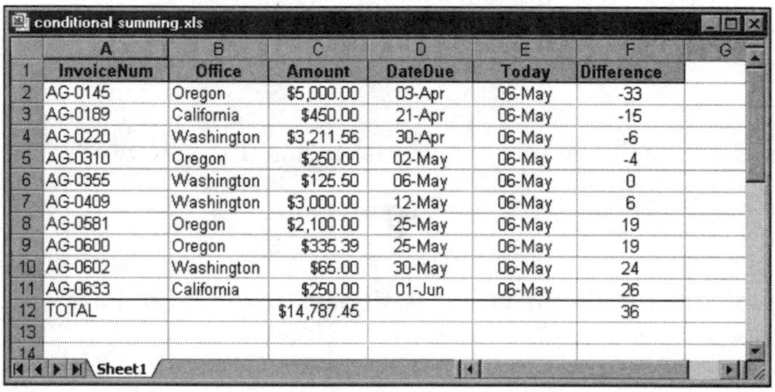

	A	B	C	D	E	F	G
1	InvoiceNum	Office	Amount	DateDue	Today	Difference	
2	AG-0145	Oregon	$5,000.00	03-Apr	06-May	-33	
3	AG-0189	California	$450.00	21-Apr	06-May	-15	
4	AG-0220	Washington	$3,211.56	30-Apr	06-May	-6	
5	AG-0310	Oregon	$250.00	02-May	06-May	-4	
6	AG-0355	Washington	$125.50	06-May	06-May	0	
7	AG-0409	Washington	$3,000.00	12-May	06-May	6	
8	AG-0581	Oregon	$2,100.00	25-May	06-May	19	
9	AG-0600	Oregon	$335.39	25-May	06-May	19	
10	AG-0602	Washington	$65.00	30-May	06-May	24	
11	AG-0633	California	$250.00	01-Jun	06-May	26	
12	TOTAL		$14,787.45			36	
13							
14							

Figure 7-15: This worksheet demonstrates summing based on multiple criteria.

Using And criteria

Suppose you want to get a sum of the invoice amounts that are past due, *and* associated with the Oregon office. In other words, the value in the *Amount* range will be summed only if both of the following criteria are met:

- The corresponding value in the *Difference* range is negative.
- The corresponding text in the *Office* range is "Oregon."

The following array formula does the job:

```
{=SUM((Difference<0)*(Office="Oregon")*Amount)}
```

This formula creates two new arrays (in memory):

- A Boolean array that consists of TRUE if the corresponding *Difference* value is less than zero; FALSE otherwise
- A Boolean array that consists of TRUE if the corresponding *Office* value equals "Oregon"; otherwise, it consists of FALSE

Multiplying Boolean values results in the following:

```
TRUE * TRUE = 1
TRUE * FALSE = 0
FALSE * FALSE = 0
```

Therefore, the corresponding *Amount* value returns non-zero only if the corresponding values in the memory arrays are both TRUE. The result produces a sum of the *Amount* values that meet the specified criteria.

You may think that you can rewrite the previous array function as follows, using the SUMPRODUCT function to perform the multiplication and addition:

`{=SUMPRODUCT((Difference<0),(Office="Oregon"),Amount)}`

For some reason, the SUMPRODUCT function does not handle Boolean values properly, so the formula does not work. This points out another example of inconsistency in Excel's functions.

Using Or criteria

Suppose you want to get a sum of past-due invoice amounts, *or* ones associated with the Oregon office. In other words, the value in the *Amount* range will be summed if either of the following criteria is met:

- ◆ The corresponding value in the *Difference* range is negative.
- ◆ The corresponding text in the *Office* range is "Oregon."

The following array formula does the job:

`{=IF((Office="Oregon")+(Difference<0),1,0)*Amount}`

A plus sign (+) joins the conditions; you can include more than two conditions.

Using And and Or criteria

As you might expect, things get a bit tricky when your criteria consists of both And and Or operations. For example, you might want to sum the values in the *Amount* range when the following conditions are met:

- ◆ The corresponding value in the *Difference* range is negative.
- ◆ The corresponding text in the *Office* range is "Oregon" or "California."

Notice that the second condition actually consists of two conditions, joined with Or. The following array formula does the trick:

```
{=SUM((Difference<0)*IF((Office="Oregon")+
(Office="California"),1)*Amount)}
```

Using VBA Functions to Count and Sum

Some types of counting and summing tasks are simply impossible using Excel's built-in functions, or even array formulas. Fortunately, Excel has a powerful tool that enables you to create custom functions. Excel's Visual Basic for Applications (VBA) language can usually come to the rescue when all else fails.

I devote Part V of this book to VBA. Chapter 23 contains several custom functions relevant to counting and summing. I briefly describe these functions below:

◆ COUNTBETWEEN: Returns the number of cells that contain a value between two specified values.

◆ COUNTVISIBLE: Returns the number of visible cells in a range.

◆ DATATYPE: Returns a string that describes the type of data in a cell. This function enables you to count cells that contain dates (something not normally possible).

◆ ISBOLD, ISITALIC, FILLCOLOR: These functions return TRUE if a specified cell has a particular type of formatting (bold, italic, or a specific color). You can use these functions to sum or count cells based on their formatting.

◆ NUMBERFORMAT: Returns the number format string for a cell. This function enables you to count or sum cells based on their number format.

◆ SUMVISIBLE: Returns the sum of the visible cells in a range.

Summary

This chapter provided many examples of functions and formulas that count or sum cells meeting certain criteria. Many of these formulas are array formulas.

The next chapter covers using formulas to look up specific information in tables or ranges of data.

Chapter 8

Lookups

IN THIS CHAPTER

◆ An introduction to formulas that look up values in a table

◆ An overview of the worksheet functions used to perform lookups

◆ Basic lookup formulas

◆ More sophisticated lookup formulas

THIS CHAPTER DISCUSSES VARIOUS techniques that you can use to look up a value in a table. Excel has three functions (LOOKUP, VLOOKUP, and HLOOKUP) designed for this task, but you may find that these functions don't quite cut it. This chapter provides many lookup examples, including alternative techniques that go well beyond Excel's normal lookup capabilities.

What Is a Lookup Formula?

A lookup formula essentially returns a value from a table (in a range) by looking up another value. A common telephone directory provides a good analogy. If you want to find a person's telephone number, you first locate the name (look it up), and then retrieve the corresponding number.

Figure 8-1 shows a simple worksheet that uses several lookup formulas. This worksheet contains a table of employee data (named *EmpData*), beginning in row 9. When you enter a name into cell C2, lookup formulas in D2:G2 retrieve the matching information from the table. The following lookup formulas use the VLOOKUP function.

D2	`=VLOOKUP(C2,EmpData,2,FALSE)`
E2	`=VLOOKUP(C2,EmpData,3,FALSE)`
F2	`=VLOOKUP(C2,EmpData,4,FALSE)`
G2	`=VLOOKUP(C2,EmpData,5,FALSE)`

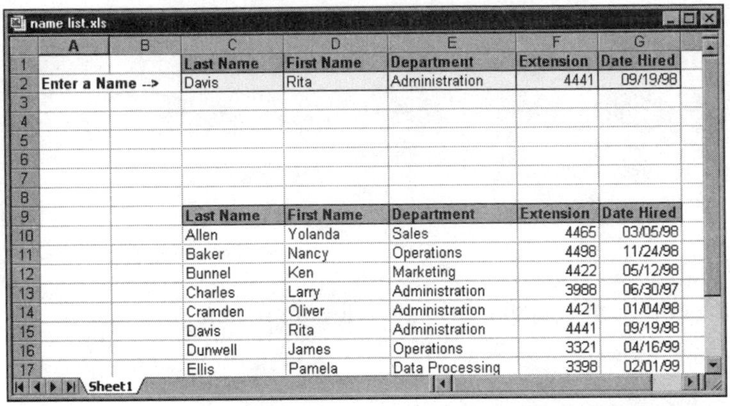
name list.xls

	A	B	C	D	E	F	G
1			Last Name	First Name	Department	Extension	Date Hired
2	Enter a Name -->		Davis	Rita	Administration	4441	09/19/98
3							
4							
5							
6							
7							
8							
9			Last Name	First Name	Department	Extension	Date Hired
10			Allen	Yolanda	Sales	4465	03/05/98
11			Baker	Nancy	Operations	4498	11/24/98
12			Bunnel	Ken	Marketing	4422	05/12/98
13			Charles	Larry	Administration	3988	06/30/97
14			Cramden	Oliver	Administration	4421	01/04/98
15			Davis	Rita	Administration	4441	09/19/98
16			Dunwell	James	Operations	3321	04/16/99
17			Ellis	Pamela	Data Processing	3398	02/01/99

Sheet1

Figure 8-1: Lookup formulas in row 2 look up the information for the employee name in cell C2.

This particular example uses four formulas to return information from the *EmpData* range. In many cases, you'll only want a single value from the table, so use only one formula.

Functions Relevant to Lookups

Several Excel functions are useful when writing formulas to look up information in a table. Table 8-1 lists and describes these functions.

The examples in this chapter use the functions listed in Table 8-1.

Basic Lookup Formulas

You can use Excel's basic lookup functions to search a column or row for a lookup value to return another value as a result. Excel provides three basic lookup functions: HLOOKUP, VLOOKUP, and LOOKUP. The MATCH and INDEX functions are often used together to return a cell or relative cell reference for a lookup value.

The VLOOKUP function

The VLOOKUP function looks up the value in the first column of the lookup table and returns the corresponding value in a specified table column. The lookup table is arranged vertically. The syntax for the VLOOKUP function is:

```
VLOOKUP(lookup_value,table_array,col_index_num,range_lookup)
```

TABLE 8-1 FUNCTIONS USED IN LOOKUP FORMULAS

Function	Description
CHOOSE	Returns a specific value from a list of values (up to 29) supplied as arguments
HLOOKUP	Horizontal lookup. Searches for a value in the top row of a table and returns a value in the same column from a row you specify in the table
INDEX	Returns a value (or the reference to a value) from within a table or range
LOOKUP	Returns a value either from a one-row or one-column range
MATCH	Returns the relative position of an item in a range that matches a specified value
OFFSET	Returns a reference to a range that is a specified number of rows and columns from a cell or range of cells
VLOOKUP	Vertical lookup. Searches for a value in the first column of a table and returns a value in the same row from a column you specify in the table

The VLOOKUP function's arguments are as follows:

- *lookup_value:* The value to be looked up in the first column of the lookup table.

- *table_array:* The range that contains the lookup table.

- *col_index_num:* The column number within the table from which the matching value is returned.

- *range_lookup:* Optional. If TRUE or omitted, an approximate match is returned (if an exact match is not found, the next largest value that is – less than *lookup_value* – is returned). If FALSE, VLOOKUP will find search for an exact match. If VLOOKUP cannot find an exact match, the function returns #N/A.

If the *range_lookup* argument is TRUE or omitted, the first column of the lookup table must be in ascending order. If *lookup_value* is smaller than the smallest value in the first column of *table_array*, VLOOKUP returns #N/A. If the *range_lookup* argument is FALSE, the first column of the lookup table need not be in ascending order. If an exact match is not found, the function returns #N/A.

The classic example of a lookup formula involves an income tax rate schedule (see Figure 8-2). The tax rate schedule shows the income tax rates for various income levels.

	A	B	C	D	E	F	G
				Income is Greater Than or Equal To...	But Less Than...	Tax Rate	
1							
2	Enter Income:	$21,566		$0	$2,650	15.00%	
3	The Tax Rate is:	28.00%		$2,651	$27,300	28.00%	
4				$27,301	$58,500	31.00%	
5				$58,501	$131,800	36.00%	
6				$131,801	$284,700	39.60%	
7				$284,701		45.25%	
8							

basic lookup examples.xls

vlookup / hlookup / lookup / match_Index / compare

Figure 8-2: Using VLOOKUP to look up a tax rate

ON THE CD You can access the workbook shown in Figure 8-2 on the companion CD-ROM.

The following formula returns the same result as the LOOKUP formula presented in the previous section:

```
=VLOOKUP(B2,D2:F7,3)
```

The lookup table resides in a range that consists of three columns (D2:F7). Because the last argument for the VLOOKUP function is 3, the formula returns the corresponding value in the third column of the lookup table.

Note that an exact match is not required. If an exact match is not found in the first column of the lookup table, the VLOOKUP function uses the next largest value that is less than the lookup value. In other words, the function uses the row in which the value you want to look up is greater than or equal to the row value, but less than the value in the next row.

The HLOOKUP function

The HLOOKUP function works just like the VLOOKUP function, except that the lookup table is arranged horizontally instead of vertically. The HLOOKUP function looks up the value in the first row of the lookup table and returns the corresponding value in a specified table row.

The syntax for the HLOOKUP function is:

```
HLOOKUP(lookup_value,table_array,col_index_num,range_lookup)
```

The HLOOKUP function's arguments are as follows:

◆ *lookup_value:* The value to be looked up in the first row of the lookup table.

◆ *table_array:* The range that contains the lookup table.

◆ *col_index_num:* The row number within the table from which the matching value is returned.

◆ *range_lookup:* Optional. If TRUE or omitted, an approximate match is returned (if an exact match is not found, the next largest value – less than *lookup_value* – is returned). If FALSE, VLOOKUP will search for an exact match. If VLOOKUP cannot find an exact match, the function returns #N/A.

Figure 8-3 shows the tax rate example with a horizontal lookup table (in the range D1:J3). The formula in cell B3 is:

```
=HLOOKUP(B2,D1:J3,3)
```

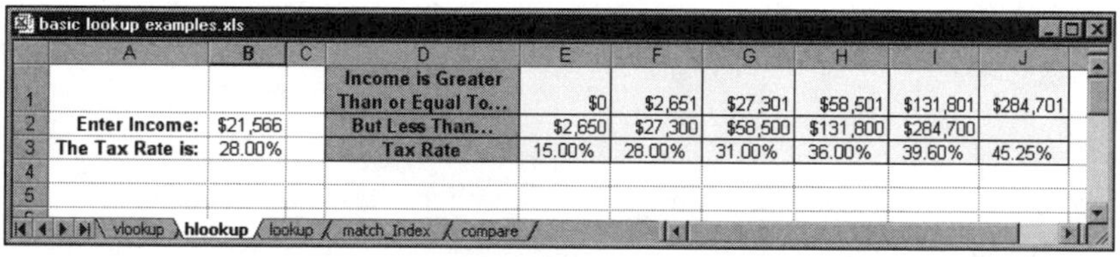

	A	B	C	D	E	F	G	H	I	J
1				Income is Greater Than or Equal To...	$0	$2,651	$27,301	$58,501	$131,801	$284,701
2	Enter Income:	$21,566		But Less Than...	$2,650	$27,300	$58,500	$131,800	$284,700	
3	The Tax Rate is:	28.00%		Tax Rate	15.00%	28.00%	31.00%	36.00%	39.60%	45.25%
4										
5										

Figure 8-3: Using HLOOKUP to look up a tax rate

The LOOKUP function

The LOOKUP function searches a single-column or single-row table. The syntax for the LOOKUP function is:

```
VLOOKUP(lookup_value,lookup_range,result_range)
```

The LOOKUP function's arguments are as follows:

◆ *lookup_value:* The value to be looked up in the *lookup_range*

◆ *lookup_range:* A single-column or single-row range that contains the values to be looked up

◆ *result_range:* The single-column or single-row range that contains the values to be returned

Values in the *lookup_range* must be in ascending order. If *lookup_value* is smaller than the smallest value in *lookup_range*, LOOKUP returns #N/A.

Figure 8-4 shows the tax table again. This time, the formula in cell B3 uses the LOOKUP function to return the corresponding tax rate. The formula in B3 is:

```
=LOOKUP(B2,D2:D7,F2:F7)
```

basic lookup examples.xls					
	A	B	C	D	E	F
1				Income is Greater Than or Equal To...	But Less Than...	Tax Rate
2	Enter Income:	$123,409		$0	$2,650	15.00%
3	The Tax Rate is:	36.00%		$2,651	$27,300	28.00%
4				$27,301	$58,500	31.00%
5				$58,501	$131,800	36.00%
6				$131,801	$284,700	39.60%
7				$284,701		45.25%
8						

vlookup / hlookup \ lookup / match_Index / compare

Figure 8-4: Using LOOKUP to look up a tax rate

If the values in the first column are not arranged in ascending order, the LOOKUP function may return an incorrect value.

Note that LOOKUP (as opposed to VLOOKUP) requires two range references (a range to be looked in, and a range that contains result values). VLOOKUP, on the other hand, uses a single range for the lookup table and the third argument determines which column to use for the result. This argument, of course, can consist of a cell reference.

Combining the MATCH and INDEX functions

The MATCH and INDEX functions are often used together to perform lookups. The MATCH function returns the relative position of a cell in a range that matches a specified value. The syntax for MATCH is:

```
MATCH(lookup_value,lookup_array,match_type)
```

The MATCH function's arguments are as follows:

◆ *lookup_value:* The value you want to match in *lookup_array*, which can include wildcard characters * and ?

◆ *lookup_array:* The range being searched

◆ *match_type:* An integer (-1, 0, or 1) that specifies how the match is determined

If *match_type* is 1, MATCH finds the largest value less than or equal to *lookup_value* (*lookup_array* must be in ascending order). If *match_type* is 0, MATCH finds the first value exactly equal to *lookup_value*. If *match_type* is -1, MATCH finds the smallest value greater than or equal to *lookup_value* (*lookup_array* must be in descending order). If you omit *match_type*, it is assumed to be 1.

The INDEX function returns a cell from a range. The syntax for the INDEX function is:

```
INDEX(array,row_num,column_num)
```

The INDEX function's arguments are as follows:

◆ *array:* A range

◆ *row_num:* A row number within *array*

◆ *col_num:* A column number within *array*

If *array* contains only one row or column, the corresponding *row_num* or *column_num* argument is optional.

Figure 8-5 shows a worksheet with dates, day names, and amounts in columns D, E, and F. When you enter a date in cell B1, the following formula (in cell B2) searches the dates in column D and returns the corresponding amount from column F. The formula in B2 is:

```
=INDEX(F2:F21,MATCH(B1,D2:D21,0))
```

	A	B	C	D	E	F	G
1	Date:	01/19/2000		Date	Weekday	Amount	
2	Amount:	163		01/03/2000	Monday	146	
3				01/04/2000	Tuesday	179	
4				01/05/2000	Wednesday	149	
5				01/06/2000	Thursday	196	
6				01/07/2000	Friday	131	
7				01/10/2000	Monday	179	
8				01/11/2000	Tuesday	134	
9				01/12/2000	Wednesday	179	
10				01/13/2000	Thursday	193	
11				01/14/2000	Friday	191	
12				01/17/2000	Monday	176	
13				01/18/2000	Tuesday	189	
14				01/19/2000	Wednesday	163	
15				01/20/2000	Thursday	121	
16				01/21/2000	Friday	100	
17				01/24/2000	Monday	109	
18				01/25/2000	Tuesday	151	
19				01/26/2000	Wednesday	138	
20				01/27/2000	Thursday	114	
21				01/28/2000	Friday	156	
22							

Figure 8-5: Using the INDEX and MATCH functions to perform a lookup

To understand how this works, start with the MATCH function. This function searches the range D2:D21 for the date in cell B1. It returns the relative row number where the date is found. This value is then used as the second argument for the INDEX function. The result is the corresponding value in F2:F21.

In many cases, it's advantageous to use MATCH and INDEX together rather than the LOOKUP or VLOOKUP functions. The MATCH function supports wildcard characters for approximate matches (VLOOKUP and LOOKUP don't support this). An asterisk (*) matches any characters, and a question mark (?) matches any single character. For example, the following formula looks up a string that begins with the letter "B" in *Range1*, and returns the corresponding value in *Range2*:

```
=INDEX(Range2,MATCH("b*",Range1,0))
```

Specialized Lookup Formulas

You can use some additional types of lookup formulas to perform more specialized lookups. For instance, you can look up an exact value, search in another column besides the first in a lookup table, perform a case-sensitive lookup, return a value from among multiple lookup tables, and perform other specialized and complex lookups.

When a Blank Is Not a Zero

Excel's lookup functions treat empty cells as zeros. The worksheet in the accompanying figure contains a two-column lookup table, and this formula looks up the name in cell B1 and returns the corresponding amount:

```
=VLOOKUP(B1,D2:E8,2)
```

Note that the Amount cell for Charlie is blank — but the formula returns a 0.

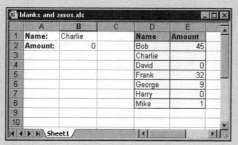

If you need to distinguish zeros from blank cells, you must modify the lookup formula by adding an IF function to check if the length of the returned value is 0. When the looked up value is blank, the length of the return value is 0. In all other cases, the length of the returned value is non-zero. The following formula displays an empty string (a blank) whenever the length of the looked-up value is zero, and the actual value whenever the length is anything but zero:

```
=IF(LEN(VLOOKUP(B1,D2:E8,2))=0,"",(VLOOKUP(B1,D2:E8,2)))
```

Looking up an exact value

As demonstrated in the previous examples, VLOOKUP and HLOOKUP don't necessarily require an exact match between the value to be looked up and the values in the lookup table. In some cases, you may require a perfect match. When the value to be looked up is a text string, you *always* require a perfect match.

To look up an exact value only, use the VLOOKUP (or HLOOKUP) function with the optional fourth argument set to FALSE.

Figure 8-6 shows a worksheet with a lookup table that contains employee numbers (column C) and employee names (column D). The lookup table is named *EmpList*. The formula in cell B2, which follows, looks up the employee number entered in cell B1 and returns the corresponding employee name:

```
=VLOOKUP(B1,EmpList,2,FALSE)
```

	A	B	C	D	
1	Employee No:	107035	**Employee Number**	**Employee Name**	
2	Employee Name:	#N/A	104566	Yolanda Allen	
3			204555	Nancy Baker	
4			227402	Ken Franklin	
5			331743	Larry Magadan	
6			211090	Oliver Nory	
7			107031	Rita Rudolph	
8			199732	James Storey	
9			123487	Pamela Victor	
10			201981	Ed Wilson	
11					
12					
13					

Sheet1

Figure 8-6: This lookup table requires an exact match.

Because the last argument for the VLOOKUP function is FALSE, the function returns a value only if an exact match is found. If the value is not found, the formula returns #N/A. This, of course, is exactly what you want to happen because returning an approximate match for an employee number makes no sense. Also, notice that the employee numbers in column C are not in ascending order. If the last argument for VLOOKUP is FALSE, the values need not be in ascending order.

If you prefer to see something other than #N/A when the employee number is not found, you can use an IF function to test for the #N/A result (using the ISNA function) and substitute a different string. The following formula displays the text "Not Found" rather than #N/A.

```
=IF(ISNA(VLOOKUP(B1,EmpList,2,FALSE)),"Not Found",
VLOOKUP(B1,EmpList,2,FALSE))
```

Looking up a value to the left

The VLOOKUP function always looks up a value in the first column of the lookup range. But what if you want to look up a value in a column other than the first column? It would be helpful if you could supply a negative value for the third argument for VLOOKUP — but you can't.

Figure 8-7 illustrates the problem. Suppose you want to look up the batting average (column B, in a range named *Averages*) of a player in column C (in a range named *Players*). The player you want data for appears in a cell named *LookupValue*. The VLOOKUP function won't work because the data is not arranged correctly. One option is to rearrange your data, but sometimes that's not possible.

	A	B	C	D	E	F	G	H
1	At Bats	Average	Player	Player to lookup:	Arias			
2	115	0.393	Gwynn					
3	47	0.349	Myers	Average	0.250	<-- LOOKUP		
4	88	0.288	Sanders	At Bats:	20	<-- LOOKUP		
5	58	0.288	Vander Wal					
6	38	0.263	Nevin	Average	0.250	<-- INDEX and MATCH		
7	77	0.260	Magadan	At Bats:	20	<-- INDEX and MATCH		
8	20	0.250	Arias					
9	92	0.244	Joyner					
10	73	0.229	Gomez					
11	70	0.227	Leyritz					
12	45	0.227	Owens					
13	65	0.180	Jackson					
14	80	0.177	Rivera					
15	96	0.169	Veras					
16								

Figure 8-7: The VLOOKUP function can't look up a value in column B, based on a value in column C.

One solution is to use the LOOKUP function, which requires two range arguments. The following formula returns the batting average from column B of the player name contained in the cell named *LookupValue*.

```
=LOOKUP(LookupValue,Players,Averages)
```

This formula suffers from a slight problem: If you enter a nonexistent player (in other words, the *LookupValue* cell contains a value not found in the *Players* range), the formula returns an erroneous result.

A better solution uses the INDEX and MATCH functions. The formula that follows works just like the previous one, except that it returns #N/A if the player is not found.

```
=INDEX(Averages,MATCH(LookupValue,Players,0))
```

 You can access a workbook that demonstrates both of the formulas in this section on the companion CD-ROM.

Performing a case-sensitive lookup

Excel's lookup functions (LOOKUP, VLOOKUP, and HLOOKUP) are not case sensitive. For example, if you write a lookup formula to look up the text *budget*, the formula considers any of the following a match: *BUDGET, Budget,* or *BuDgEt*.

Figure 8-8 shows a simple example. Range D2:D7 is named *Range1*, and range E2:E7 is named *Range2*. The word to be looked up appears in cell B1 (named *Value*).

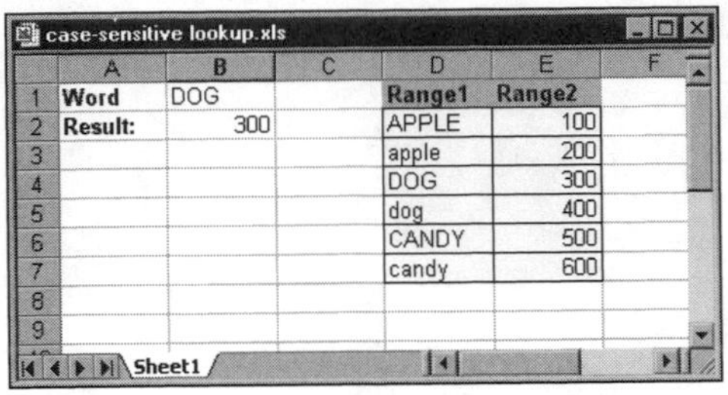

	A	B	C	D	E
1	Word	DOG		Range1	Range2
2	Result:	300		APPLE	100
3				apple	200
4				DOG	300
5				dog	400
6				CANDY	500
7				candy	600

Figure 8-8: Using an array formula to perform a case-sensitive lookup

The array formula that follows is in cell B2. This formula does a case-sensitive lookup in *Range1* and returns the corresponding value in *Range2*.

```
{=INDEX(Range2,MATCH(TRUE,EXACT(Value,Range1),0))}
```

The formula looks up the word *DOG* (uppercase) and returns 300. The following standard LOOKUP formula returns 400.

```
=LOOKUP(Value,Range1,Range2)
```

Choosing among multiple lookup tables

You can, of course, have any number of lookup tables in a worksheet. In some cases, your formula may need to decide which lookup table to use. Figure 8-9 shows an example.

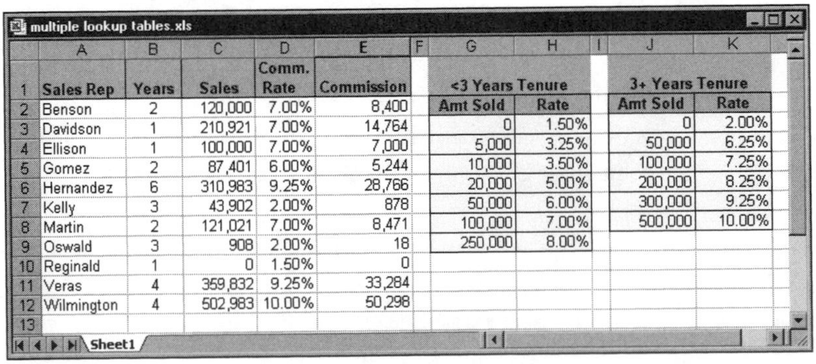

	A	B	C	D	E	G	H	J	K
1	Sales Rep	Years	Sales	Comm. Rate	Commission	<3 Years Tenure		3+ Years Tenure	
2	Benson	2	120,000	7.00%	8,400	Amt Sold	Rate	Amt Sold	Rate
3	Davidson	1	210,921	7.00%	14,764	0	1.50%	0	2.00%
4	Ellison	1	100,000	7.00%	7,000	5,000	3.25%	50,000	6.25%
5	Gomez	2	87,401	6.00%	5,244	10,000	3.50%	100,000	7.25%
6	Hernandez	6	310,983	9.25%	28,766	20,000	5.00%	200,000	8.25%
7	Kelly	3	43,902	2.00%	878	50,000	6.00%	300,000	9.25%
8	Martin	2	121,021	7.00%	8,471	100,000	7.00%	500,000	10.00%
9	Oswald	3	908	2.00%	18	250,000	8.00%		
10	Reginald	1	0	1.50%	0				
11	Veras	4	359,832	9.25%	33,284				
12	Wilmington	4	502,983	10.00%	50,298				

Figure 8-9: This worksheet demonstrates the use of multiple lookup tables.

This workbook calculates sales commission and contains two lookup tables: G3:H9 (named *Table1*) and J3:K8 (named *Table2*). The commission rate for a particular sales representative depends on two factors: the sales rep's years of service (column B) and the amount sold (column C). Column D contains formulas that look up the commission rate from the appropriate table. For example, the formula in cell D2 is:

```
=VLOOKUP(C2,IF(B2<3,Table1,Table2),2)
```

The second argument for the VLOOKUP function consists of an IF formula that uses the value in column B to determine which lookup table to use.

The formula in column E simply multiplies the sales amount in column C by the commission rate in column D. The formula in cell E2, for example, is:

```
=C2*D2
```

 You can access the workbook shown in Figure 8-9 on the companion CD-ROM.

Determining letter grades for test scores

A common use of a lookup table is to assign letter grades for test scores. Figure 8-10 shows a worksheet with student test scores. The range E2:F6 (named *GradeList*) displays a lookup table used to assign a letter grade to a test score.

	A	B	C	D	E	F	G
1	Student	Score	Grade		Score	Grade	
2	Adams	36	F		0	F	
3	Baker	68	D		40	D	
4	Camden	50	D		70	C	
5	Dailey	77	C		80	B	
6	Gomez	92	A		90	A	
7	Hernandez	100	A				
8	Jackson	74	C				
9	Maplethorpe	45	D				
10	Paulson	60	D				
11	Ramirez	89	B				
12	Sosa	99	A				
13	Thompson	91	A				
14	Wilson	59	D				
15							
16							
17							
18							

Figure 8-10: Looking up letter grades for test scores

The companion CD-ROM contains a workbook that demonstrates both formulas in this section.

Column C contains formulas that use the VLOOKUP function and the lookup table to assign a grade based on the score in column B. The formula in C2, for example, is:

```
=VLOOKUP(B2,GradeList,2)
```

When the lookup table is small (as in the example shown in with Figure 8-10), you can use a literal array in place of the lookup table. The formula that follows, for example, returns a letter grade without using a lookup table. Rather, the information in the lookup table is hard-coded into a literal array. See Chapter 12 for more information about literal arrays.

```
=VLOOKUP(B2,{0,"F";40,"D";70,"C";80,"B";90,"A"},2)
```

Calculating a grade point average

A student's grade point average (GPA) is a numerical measure of the average grade received for classes taken. This discussion assumes a letter grade system, in which each letter grade is assigned a numeric value (A=4, B=3, C=2, D=1, and F=0). The GPA comprises an average of the numeric grade values, weighted by the credit hours of the course. A one-hour course, for example, receives less weight than a three-hour course. The GPA ranges from 0 (all Fs) to 4.00 (all As).

Figure 8-11 shows a worksheet with information for a student. This student took five courses, for a total of 13 credit hours. Range B2:B6 is named *CreditHours*. The grades for each course appear in column C (Range C2:C6 is named *Grades*). Column D uses a lookup formula to calculate the grade value for each course. The lookup formula in cell D2, for example, follows. This formula uses the lookup table in G2:H6 (named *GradeTable*).

```
=VLOOKUP(C2,GradeTable,2,FALSE)
```

Formulas in column E calculate the weighted values. The formula in E2 is:

```
=D2*B2
```

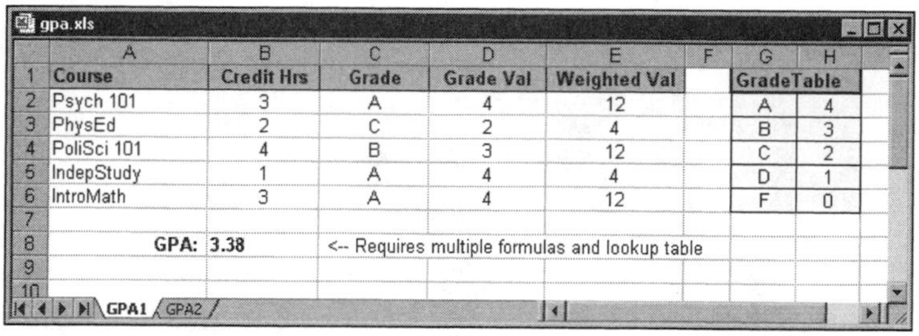

Figure 8-11: Using multiple formulas to calculate a GPA

Cell B8 computes the GPA using the following formula:

```
=SUM(E2:E6)/SUM(B2:B6)
```

The preceding formulas work fine, but you can streamline the GPA calculation quite a bit. In fact, you can use a single array formula to make this calculation and avoid using the lookup table and the formulas in columns D and E. This array formula does the job:

```
{=SUM((MATCH(Grades,{"F","D","C","B","A"},0)-1)*CreditHours)
/SUM(CreditHours)}
```

You can access a workbook that demonstrates both the multiformula and the array formula techniques on the companion CD-ROM.

Performing a two-way lookup

Figure 8-12 shows a worksheet with a table that displays product sales by month. The user enters a month in cell B1 and a product name in cell B2.

The companion CD-ROM contains the workbook shown in Figure 8-12.

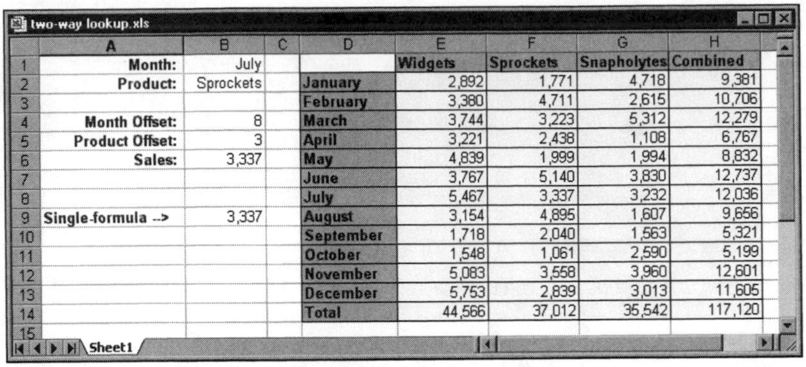

two-way lookup.xls

	A	B	C	D	E	F	G	H
1	Month:	July			Widgets	Sprockets	Snapholytes	Combined
2	Product:	Sprockets		January	2,892	1,771	4,718	9,381
3				February	3,380	4,711	2,615	10,706
4	Month Offset:	8		March	3,744	3,223	5,312	12,279
5	Product Offset:	3		April	3,221	2,438	1,108	6,767
6	Sales:	3,337		May	4,839	1,999	1,994	8,832
7				June	3,767	5,140	3,830	12,737
8				July	5,467	3,337	3,232	12,036
9	Single-formula -->	3,337		August	3,154	4,895	1,607	9,656
10				September	1,718	2,040	1,563	5,321
11				October	1,548	1,061	2,590	5,199
12				November	5,083	3,558	3,960	12,601
13				December	5,753	2,839	3,013	11,605
14				Total	44,566	37,012	35,542	117,120
15								

Sheet1

Figure 8-12: This table demonstrates a two-way lookup.

To simplify things, the worksheet uses the following named ranges:

Name	Refers To
Month	B1
Product	B2
Table	D1:H14
MonthList	D1:D14
ProductList	D1:H1

The following formula (in cell B4) uses the MATCH function to return the position of the *Month* within the *MonthList* range. For example, if the month is January, the formula returns 2 because January is the second item in the *MonthList* range (the first item is a blank cell, D1).

```
=MATCH(Month,MonthList,0)
```

The formula in cell B5 works similarly, but uses the *ProductList* range.

```
=MATCH(Product,ProductList,0)
```

The final formula, in cell B6, returns the corresponding sales amount. It uses the INDEX function with the results from cells B4 and B5.

```
=INDEX(Table,B4,B5)
```

You can, of course, combine these formulas into a single formula as shown here:

```
=INDEX(Table,MATCH(Month,MonthList,0),MATCH(Product,ProductList,0))
```

 TIP If use Excel 97 or later, you can use the Lookup Wizard add-in to create this type of formula (see Figure 8-13).

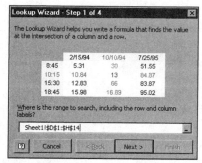

Figure 8-13: The Lookup Wizard add-in can create a formula that performs a two-way lookup.

 TIP Another way to accomplish a two-way lookup is to provide a name for each row and column of the table. A quick way to do this is to select the table and use Insert → Name → Create. After creating the names, you can use a simple formula, such as:= Sprockets July

This formula, which uses the range intersection operator (a space), returns July sales for Sprockets. See Chapter 3 for details.

Performing a two-column lookup

Some situations may require a lookup based on the values in two columns. Figure 8-14 shows an example.

ON THE CD

The workbook shown in Figure 8-14 also appears on the companion CD-ROM.

	A	B	C	D	E	F
				Make	**Model**	**Code**
1	**Make:**	Jeep		Chevy	Blazer	C-094
2	**Model:**	Grand Cherokee		Chevy	Tahoe	C-823
3	**Code:**	J-701		Ford	Explorer	F-772
4				Ford	Expedition	F-229
5				Isuzu	Rodeo	I-897
6				Isuzu	Trooper	I-900
7				Jeep	Cherokee	J-983
8				Jeep	Grand Cherokee	J-701
9				Nissan	Pathfinder	N-231
10				Toyota	4Runner	T-871
11				Toyota	Land Cruiser	T-981
12						
13						

two-column lookup.xls — Sheet1

Figure 8-14: This workbook performs a lookup using information in two columns (D and E).

The lookup table contains automobile makes and models, and a corresponding code for each. The worksheet uses named ranges, as shown here:

F2:F12	*Code*
B1	*Make*
B2	*Model*
D2:D12	*Range1*
E2:E12	*Range2*

The following array formula displays the corresponding code for an automobile make and model.

```
{=INDEX(Price,MATCH(Make&Model,Range1&Range2,0))}
```

This formula works by concatenating the contents of *Make* and *Model*, and then searching for this text in an array consisting of the concatenated corresponding text in *Range1* and *Range2*.

Determining the address of a value within a range

Most of the time, you want your lookup formula to return a value. You may, however, need to determine the cell address of a particular value within a range. For example, Figure 8-15 shows a worksheet with a range of numbers that occupy a single column (named *Data*). Cell B1, which contains the value to look up, is named *Target*.

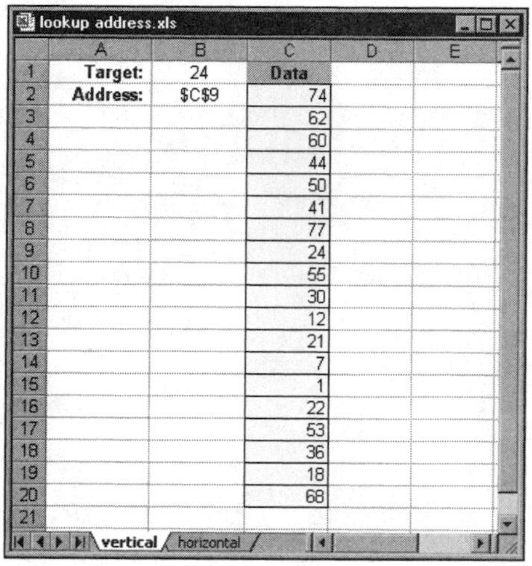

Figure 8-15: The formula in cell B2 returns the address in the Data range for the value in cell B1.

The formula in cell B2, which follows, returns the address of the cell in the *Data* range that contains the *Target* value.

```
=ADDRESS(ROW(Data)+MATCH(Target,Data,0)-1,COLUMN(Data))
```

If the *Data* range occupies a single row, use this formula to return the address of the *Target* value:

```
=ADDRESS(ROW(Data),COLUMN(Data)+MATCH(Target,Data,0)-1)
```

The companion CD-ROM contains the workbook shown in Figure 8-15.

If the *Data* range contains more than one instance of the *Target* value, the address of the first occurrence is returned. If the *Target* value is not found in the *Data* range, the formula returns #N/A.

Looking up a value using the closest match

The VLOOKUP and HLOOKUP functions are useful in the following situations:

◆ You need to identify an exact match for a target value. Use FALSE as the function's fourth argument.

◆ You need to locate an approximate match. If the function's fourth argument is TRUE or omitted and an exact match is not found, the next largest value less than the lookup value is returned.

But what if you need to look up a value based on the *closest* match? Neither VLOOKUP nor HLOOKUP can do the job.

Figure 8-16 shows a worksheet with student names in column A and values in column B. Range B2:B20 is named *Data*. Cell E2, named *Target*, contains a value to search for in the *Data* range. Cell E3, named *ColOffset*, contains a value that represents the column offset from the *Data* range.

	A	B	C	D	E	F
1	**Student**	**Data**				
2	Ann	9,101		**Target Value -->**	8025	
3	Betsy	8,873		**Column Offset -->**	-1	
4	Chuck	6,000				
5	David	9,820		**Student:**	Leslie	
6	George	10,500				
7	Hilda	3,500				
8	James	12,873				
9	John	5,867				
10	Keith	8,989				
11	Leslie	8,000				
12	Michelle	1,124				
13	Nora	9,099				
14	Paul	6,800				
15	Peter	5,509				
16	Rasmusen	5,460				
17	Sally	8,400				
18	Theresa	7,777				
19	Violet	3,600				
20	Wendy	5,400				
21						

Figure 8-16: This workbook demonstrates how to perform a lookup using the closest match.

You can access the workbook shown in Figure 8-16 on the companion CD-ROM.

The array formula that follows identifies the closest match to the *Target* value in the *Data* range, and returns the names of the corresponding student in column A (i.e., the column with an offset of -1). The formula returns Leslie (with a matching value of 8,000 – the one closest to the *Target* value of 8,025).

```
{=INDIRECT(ADDRESS(ROW(Data)+MATCH(MIN(ABS(Target-Data)),
ABS(Target-Data),0)-1,COLUMN(Data)+ColOffset))}
```

If two values in the *Data* range are equidistant from the *Target* value, the formula uses the first one in the list.

The value in *ColOffset* can be negative (for a column to the left of *Data*), positive (for a column to the right of *Data*), or 0 (for the actual closest match value in the *Data* range).

Looking up a value using linear interpolation

Interpolation refers to the process of estimating a missing value by using existing values. To illustrate, refer to Figure 8-17. Column D contains a list of values (named *x*), and column E contains corresponding values (named *y*).

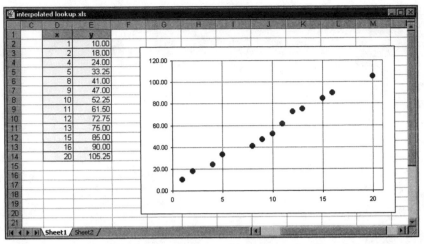

Figure 8-17: This workbook demonstrates a table lookup using linear interpolation.

The worksheet also contains a chart that depicts the relationship between the x range and the y range graphically. As you can see, there is a linear relationship between the corresponding values in the x and y ranges – as x increases, so does y. Notice that the values in the x range are not strictly consecutive. For example, the x range doesn't contain the following values: 3, 6, 7, 14, 17, 18, and 19.

You can create a lookup formula that looks up a value in the x range and returns the corresponding value from the y range. But what if you want to estimate the y value for a missing x value? A normal lookup formula does not return a very good result because it simply returns an existing y value (not an estimated y value). For example, the following formula looks up the value 3, and returns 18.00 (the value that corresponds to 2 in the x range).

```
=LOOKUP(3,x,y)
```

In such a case, you probably want to interpolate. In other words, because the lookup value (3) is halfway between existing x values (2 and 4), you want the formula to return a y value of 21.000 – a value halfway between the corresponding y values 18.00 and 24.00.

FORMULAS TO PERFORM A LINEAR INTERPOLATION

Figure 8-18 shows a worksheet with formulas in column B. The value to be looked up is entered into cell B1. The final formula, in cell B16, returns the result. If the value in B3 is found in the x range, the corresponding y value is returned. If the value in B3 is not found, the formula in B16 returns an estimated y value, obtained using linear interpolation.

	A	B	C	D	E	
	interpolated lookup.xls					
1	X-value to look up:	3		x	y	
2				1	10.00	
3	Matching row:	2		2	18.00	
4	Exact match?	FALSE		4	24.00	
5				5	33.25	
6	1st row:	2		8	41.00	
7	2nd row:	3		9	47.00	
8				10	52.25	
9	1st x value:	2		11	61.50	
10	2nd x value:	4		12	72.75	
11				13	75.00	
12	1st looked up y value:	18		15	85.00	
13	2nd looked up y value:	24		16	90.00	
14				20	105.25	
15	Adjustment factor:	0.5				
16	Interpolated lookup:	21.00				
17						
18						

Figure 8-18: Column B contains formulas that perform a lookup using linear interpolation.

 The companion CD-ROM contains the workbook shown in Figure 8-18.

It's critical that the values in the *x* range appear in ascending order. If B1 contains a value less than the lowest value in x or greater than the largest value in x, the formula returns an error value. Table 8-2 lists and describes these formulas.

TABLE 8-2 FORMULAS FOR A LOOKUP USING LINEAR INTERPOLATION

Cell	Formula	Description
B3	=LOOKUP(B1,x,x)	Performs a standard lookup, and returns looked-up value in the *x* range.
B4	=B1=B3	Returns TRUE if the looked-up value equals the value to be looked up.
B6	=MATCH(B3,x,0)	Returns the row number of the *x* range that contains the matching value.
B7	=IF(B4,B6,B6+1)	Returns the same row as the formula in B6 if an exact match is found. Otherwise, it adds 1 to the result in B6.
B9	=INDEX(x,B6)	Returns the *x* value that corresponds to the row in B6.

B10	`=INDEX(x,B7)`	Returns the *x* value that corresponds to the row in B7.
B12	`=LOOKUP(B9,x,y)`	Returns the *y* value that corresponds to the *x* value in B9.
B13	`=LOOKUP(B10,x,y)`	Returns the *y* value that corresponds to the *x* value in B10
B15	`=IF(B4,0,(B1-B3)/(B10-B9))`	Calculates an adjustment factor based on the difference between the *x* values.
B16	`=B12+((B13-B12)*B15)`	Calculates the estimated *y* value using the adjustment factor in B15.

COMBINING THE LOOKUP AND TREND FUNCTIONS

Another slightly different approach, which you may find preferable to performing lookup using linear interpolation, uses the LOOKUP and TREND functions. One advantage is that it requires only one formula (see Figure 8-19).

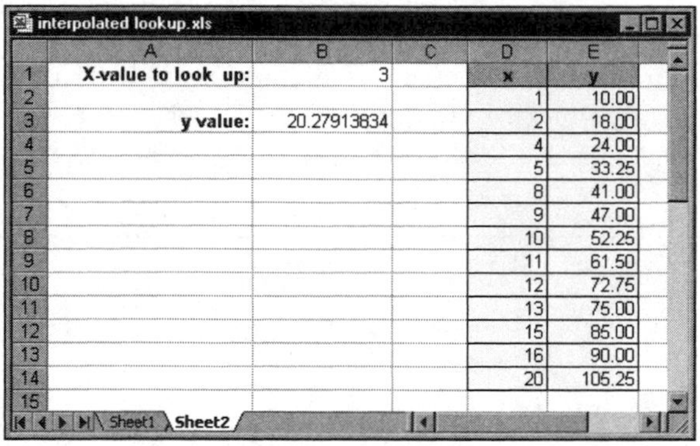

Figure 8-19: This worksheet uses a formula that utilizes the LOOKUP function and the TREND function.

The formula in cell B3 follows. This formula uses an IF function to make a decision. If an exact match is found in the *x* range, the formula returns the corresponding *y* value (using the LOOKUP function). If an exact match is not found, the formula uses the TREND function to return the calculated "best-fit" *y* value (it does not perform a linear interpolation).

```
=IF(B1=LOOKUP(B1,x,x),LOOKUP(INDEX(x,MATCH(LOOKUP(B1,x,x),x,0)),x,y)
,TREND(y,x,B1))
```

Summary

This chapter presented an overview of the functions available to perform table lookups. It included many formula examples demonstrating basic lookups, as well as not-so-basic lookups.

The next chapter discusses useful formulas for summarizing information contained in a database.

Chapter 9

Databases and Lists

IN THIS CHAPTER

◆ Basic information about using lists or worksheet databases

◆ Using AutoFiltering to filter a list using simple criteria

◆ Using advanced filtering to filter a list using more complex criteria

◆ Understanding how to create a criteria range for use with advanced filtering or database functions

◆ Using the SUBTOTAL function to summarize data in a list

A WORKSHEET DATABASE (also known as a list) is an organized collection of information. More specifically, it consists of a row of headers (descriptive text), followed by additional rows of data comprising values or text. This chapter provides an over-view of Excel's worksheet database features and presents some powerful formulas to help you get a handle on even the most unwieldy database.

Worksheet Lists or Databases

Figure 9-1 shows an example of a worksheet list (or database). This particular list has its headers in row 1 and has 10 rows of data. Notice that the data consists of several different types: text, numerical values, dates, and logical values. Column C contains a formula that calculates the monthly salary from the value in column B.

People often refer to the columns in a list as *fields* and to the rows as *records*. Using this terminology, the list shown in the figure has six fields (Name, Annual Salary, Monthly Salary, Location, Date Hired, and Exempt) and 10 records.

	A	B	C	D	E	F
1	Name	Annual Salary	Monthly Salary	Location	Date Hired	Exempt
2	James Brackman	$42,400	$3,533	New York	03/01/1998	FALSE
3	Michael Orenthal	$20,900	$1,742	New Jersey	04/16/1997	FALSE
4	Francis Jenikins	$67,700	$5,642	Arizona	11/12/1998	TRUE
5	Peter Yates	$19,950	$1,663	Arizona	04/05/1999	FALSE
6	Walter Franklin	$43,000	$3,583	Arizona	03/28/1999	FALSE
7	Louise Victor	$48,500	$4,042	Connecticut	07/05/1997	FALSE
8	Sally Rice	$24,500	$2,042	New York	06/16/1997	FALSE
9	Charles K. Barkley	$52,000	$4,333	Connecticut	09/09/1998	FALSE
10	Melinda Hindquest	$102,000	$8,500	New York	06/04/1997	TRUE
11	Linda Harper	$24,000	$2,000	Arizona	02/16/1999	FALSE
12						
13						

Figure 9-1: A simple worksheet list

The size of a list that you develop in Excel is limited by the size of a single work-sheet. In other words, a list can have no more than 256 fields and can consist of no more than 65,535 records (one row contains the field names). A list of this size re-quires a great deal of memory and, even then, may prove impossible. At the other extreme, a list can consist of a single cell – not very useful, but still considered a list.

A list having 65,535 records is a new feature in Excel 97 or later versions. In versions of Excel prior to Excel 97, a list is limited to 16,383 records because worksheets contain only 16,384 rows.

Why are lists used?

People use worksheet lists for a wide variety of purposes. For some users, a list sim-ply keeps track of information (for example, customer information); others use lists to store data that ultimately appears in a report. Common list operations include:

◆ Entering data into the list

◆ Filtering the list to display only the rows that meet certain criteria

◆ Sorting the list

◆ Inserting formulas to calculate subtotals

◆ Creating formulas to calculate results on the list, filtered by certain criteria

◆ Creating a summary table of the data in the list (often done by using a pivot table)

When creating lists, it helps to plan the organization of your list information. This sidebar on designing lists has guidelines to help you create lists.

Designing a List

Although Excel is quite accommodating with regard to the information that is stored in a list, planning the organization of your list information is important and makes the list easier to work with. Remember the following guidelines when you create lists:

◆ **Insert descriptive labels (one for each column) in the first row (the** *header row*) **of the list.** If you use lengthy labels, consider using the Wrap Text format so that you don't have to widen the columns.

◆ **Make sure each column contains the same type of information.** For example, don't mix dates and text in a single column.

◆ **Consider using formulas that perform calculations on other fields in the same record.** If you use formulas that refer to cells outside the list, make these absolute references; otherwise, you get unexpected results when you sort the list.

◆ **Don't leave any empty rows within the list.** For list operations, Excel determines the list boundaries automatically, and an empty row signals the end of the list.

◆ **Keep the list on a worksheet by itself, to obtain the best results.** If you must place other information on the same worksheet as the list, place the information above or below the list. In other words, don't use the cells to the left or right of a list.

◆ **Freeze the first row.** Select the cell in the first column and first row of your table, then choose Window → Freeze Panes to make sure that you can see the headings when you scroll the list.

◆ **Preformat the entire column to ensure that the data has the same format.** For example, if a column contains dates, format the entire column with the same date format.

Using AutoFilter

Filtering a list involves the process of hiding all rows in the list except those rows that meet some criteria that you specify. For example, if you have a list of customers, you can filter the list to show only those who live in New Jersey. Filtering is a common (and very useful) technique.

Excel provides two ways to filter a list. AutoFilter is useful for simple filtering criteria. Advanced filtering (discussed later in this chapter) is for more complex filtering.

AutoFiltering basics

To use Excel's AutoFilter feature to filter a list, place the cell pointer anywhere within the list and then choose Data → Filter → AutoFilter. Excel determines the range occupied by the list and adds drop-down arrows to the field names in the header row (as shown in Figure 9-2). The status bar displays *Filter Mode* to remind you that AutoFiltering is in effect.

Name	Annual Salary	Monthly Salary	Location	Date Hired	Exempt
James Brackman	$42,400	$3,533	New York	03/01/1998	FALSE
Michael Orenthal	$20,900	$1,742	New Jersey	04/16/1997	FALSE
Francis Jenikins	$67,700	$5,642	Arizona	11/12/1998	TRUE
Peter Yates	$19,950	$1,663	Arizona	04/05/1999	FALSE
Walter Franklin	$43,000	$3,583	Arizona	03/28/1999	FALSE
Louise Victor	$48,500	$4,042	Connecticut	07/05/1997	FALSE
Sally Rice	$24,500	$2,042	New York	06/16/1997	FALSE
Charles K. Barkley	$52,000	$4,333	Connecticut	09/09/1998	FALSE
Melinda Hindquest	$102,000	$8,500	New York	06/04/1997	TRUE
Linda Harper	$24,000	$2,000	Arizona	02/16/1999	FALSE

Figure 9-2: When you choose the Data → Filter → AutoFilter command, Excel adds drop-down arrows to the field names in the header row.

When you click the arrow in one of these drop-down lists, the list expands to show the unique items in that column. Select an item, and Excel hides all rows except those that include the selected item. You can filter the list using a single field or multiple fields. The drop-down arrow changes color to remind you that you filtered the list by a value in that column.

AutoFiltering has a limit. Only the first 999 unique items in the column appear in the drop-down list. If your list exceeds this limit, you can use advanced filtering, which I describe later.

Besides showing every item in the column, the drop-down list offers five other choices:

◆ **All:** Displays all items in the column. Use this to remove filtering for a column.

◆ **Top 10:** Filters to display the "top 10" items in the list. Actually, this represents a misnomer; you can display the "top n" items (you choose the number).

◆ **Custom:** Enables you to filter the list by multiple items (see Figure 9-3).

◆ **Blanks:** Filters the list by showing rows that contain blanks in this column. This option is available only if the column contains one or more blank cells.

◆ **NonBlanks:** Filters the list by showing rows that contain nonblanks in this column. This option is available only if the column contains one or more blank cells.

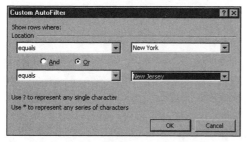

Figure 9-3: The Custom AutoFilter dialog box gives you more filtering options.

Excel automatically creates a hidden name (_FilterDatabase) for the range occupied by the filtered list. You can use this name in a VBA macro or in a formula. To select the filtered data range, press Ctrl+G to bring up the Go To dialog box. The hidden name does not appear in the list of names, so you need to enter it manually. Type **_FilterDatabase** in the Reference field and click OK.

Custom AutoFiltering is useful, but it definitely has limitations. For example, if you want to filter a list to show only three values in a field (such as New York or New Jersey or Connecticut), you can't do it through AutoFiltering. Such filtering tasks require the advanced filtering feature, which I discuss later in this chapter.

To display the entire unfiltered list again, click the arrow and choose All — the first item on the drop-down list. Or, you can select Data → Filter → Show All. To exit AutoFilter mode and remove the drop-down arrows from the field names, choose Data → Filter → AutoFilter again.

Counting and summing filtered data

After you filter the list, the status bar displays a message that tells you how many rows qualify. For example, it may display *9 of 36 records found*. This message disappears when the sheet is calculated.

You can, however, create a formula to display the number of filtered records. The formula that follows, for example, displays the number of filtered records by using the SUBTOTAL function, with 3 as the first argument.

```
=SUBTOTAL(3,A5:A400)
```

You should put this formula in a row above or below the list. Otherwise, filtering the list may hide the row that contains the formula. Also, make sure that the range argument begins with the first row of the list and extends (at least) to the last row of the list.

To display the sum of filtered records, use 9 as the first argument for the SUBTOTAL function. The following formula, for example, returns the sum of the filtered values in column C.

```
=SUBTOTAL(9,C5:C400)
```

Figure 9-4 shows the result of these formulas when applied to a filtered list.

	A	B	C	D	E
1	Count of qualifying records:		9		
2	Total Sales for qualifying records:		36,761		
3					
4	**Month**	**Region**	**Sales**		
8	Feb	North	5,584		
11	Mar	North	3,531		
14	Apr	North	5,955		
17	May	North	3,286		
20	Jun	North	4,705		
23	Jul	North	3,436		
26	Aug	North	3,292		
29	Sep	North	3,779		
32	Oct	North	3,193		
41					
42					

Figure 9-4: The formulas in cells C1 and C2 use the SUBTOTAL function.

The SUBTOTAL function is the only function that handles data hidden by AutoFiltering. If you have other formulas that refer to data in a filtered list, these formulas don't adjust to use only the visible cells. For example, if a cell contains a formula that sums values in column C, the formula continues to show the sum for *all* the values in column C — not just those in the visible rows.

Filling in the Gaps

When you import data, you can end up with a worksheet that looks something like the one in the accompanying figure. In this example, an entry in column A applies to several rows of data. If you sort such a list, you can end up with a mess and you won't be able to tell who sold what.

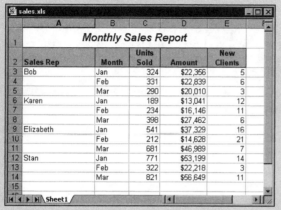

When you have a small list, you can enter the missing cell values manually. But if you have a huge database, you need a better way of filling in those cell values. Here's how:

1. Select the range (A3:A14 in this example).

2. Press Ctrl+G to display the Go To dialog box.

3. In the Go To dialog box, click Special.

4. Select the Blanks option.

5. In the formula bar, type = followed by the address of the first cell with an entry in the column (=A3 in this example), and press Ctrl+Enter.

6. Reselect the range and choose Edit → Copy.

7. Select Edit → Paste Special, choose the Values option, and click OK.

Using Advanced Filtering

In many cases, AutoFiltering does the job just fine. But if you run up against its limitations, you need to use advanced filtering. Advanced filtering is much more flexible than AutoFiltering, but it takes a bit of up-front work to use it. Advanced filtering provides you with the following capabilities:

- You can specify more complex filtering criteria.
- You can specify computed filtering criteria.
- You can extract a copy of the rows that meet the criteria to another location.

Setting up a criteria range

Before you can use the advanced filtering feature, you must set up a *criteria range,* a designated range on a worksheet that conforms to certain requirements. The criteria range holds the information that Excel uses to filter the list. It must conform to the following specifications:

- Consist of at least two rows, and the first row must contain some or all field names from the list
- The other rows of the criteria range must consist of your filtering criteria

Although you can put the criteria range anywhere in the worksheet, you should avoid putting it in rows where you placed the list. Because Excel hides some of these rows when filtering the list, you may find that your criteria range is no longer visible after filtering. Therefore, you should generally place the criteria range above or below the list.

Figure 9-5 shows a criteria range, located in A1:D2, above the list that it uses. Only some field names appear in the criteria range. You don't need to include in the criteria range field names for fields that you don't use in the selection criteria.

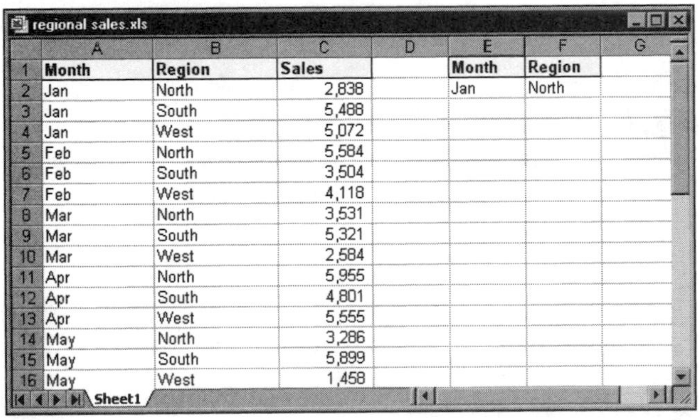

	A	B	C	D	E	F	G
1	Month	Region	Sales		Month	Region	
2	Jan	North	2,838		Jan	North	
3	Jan	South	5,488				
4	Jan	West	5,072				
5	Feb	North	5,584				
6	Feb	South	3,504				
7	Feb	West	4,118				
8	Mar	North	3,531				
9	Mar	South	5,321				
10	Mar	West	2,584				
11	Apr	North	5,955				
12	Apr	South	4,801				
13	Apr	West	5,555				
14	May	North	3,286				
15	May	South	5,899				
16	May	West	1,458				

Figure 9-5: A criteria range for a list

In this example, the criteria range has only one row of criteria. The fields in each row of the criteria range (except for the header row) are joined with an AND operator. Therefore, after applying the advanced filter, the list shows only the rows in which the Month column equals *Jan* AND the Region column equals *North*. You may find specifying criteria in the criteria range a bit tricky. I discuss this topic in detail later in this chapter. See "Specifying Advanced Filter Criteria."

Filtering a list

To perform the filtering, select any cell within your list. Then choose Data→Filter→Advanced filter. Excel displays the Advanced Filter dialog box, shown in Figure 9-6. Excel guesses your List range (you can change it if necessary), but you need to specify the criteria range. To filter the list in place (i.e., hide rows that don't qualify), select the option labeled Filter the list, in-place. If you select the Copy to another location option, you need to specify a range in the Copy to box. Click OK, and Excel filters the list by the criteria that you specify.

Figure 9-6: The Advanced Filter dialog box

To make things easier on you when you use the Advanced Filter dialog box, you can create some named ranges. If you name a range *Criteria*, the reference for the range appears automatically in the Criteria range box. You can also define the name *Database* for the range of data to be filtered, and define the name *Extract* for the area where you want to paste the rows. These ranges appear automatically in the List range and Copy to boxes of the Advanced Filter dialog box.

When you copy filtered records to another location (in other words, when you select the Copy to another location option), you can specify which columns to include in the copy. Before displaying the Advanced Filter dialog box, copy the desired field labels to the first row of the area where you plan to paste the filtered rows. In the Advanced Filter dialog box, specify a reference to the copied column labels in the Copy to box. The copied rows then include only the columns for which you copied the labels.

Working with Data in a List

Excel's Data → Form command displays a dialog box to help you work with a list. This dialog enables you to enter new data, delete rows, and search for rows that match certain criteria.

Excel's Data Form is handy, but by no means ideal. If you like the idea of using a dialog box to work with data in a list, check out my Enhanced Data Form add-in. It offers many advantages over Excel's Data Form.

Once you install the add-in, activate any cell in a list and then choose Data → JWalk Enhanced Data Form. Data that makes up the current record appears in the dialog box. Use the horizontal scrollbar (or the Previous/Next buttons) to scroll through the database. Changes you make to the data are written to the database, and undo is available. The form handles an unlimited number of fields; and a wildcard-capable search window permits quick retrieval of the desired record based on any field.

You can access the JWalk Enhanced Data Form add-in on the companion CD-ROM.

Specifying Advanced Filter Criteria

Recent enhancements to list-related features in Excel have focused exclusively on AutoFiltering. As far as I can tell, the advanced filter technique has not changed at all since the initial release of Excel. In fact, specifying advanced filtering criteria remains one of the most confusing aspects of Excel. This section presents plenty of examples to help you understand how to create a criteria range that extracts the information you need.

The examples in this section use the list shown in Figure 9-7. This list, which has 125 records and eight fields, was designed to use a good assortment of data types: values, text strings, logicals, and dates. The list occupies the range A8:H133.

	A	B	C	D	E	F	G	H
7								
8	ListPrice	Date Listed	Area	Bedrooms	Baths	SquareFt	Type	Pool
9	$350,000	01/08/2000	N. County	3	2.5	1,991	Condo	FALSE
10	$215,000	01/10/2000	Central	3	1.75	2,157	Single Family	TRUE
11	$315,000	01/12/2000	S. County	2	2	1,552	Condo	FALSE
12	$379,000	01/16/2000	N. County	4	3	3,000	Single Family	FALSE
13	$248,500	01/26/2000	?	4	2.5	2,101	Single Family	TRUE
14	$297,500	01/28/2000	S. County	4	3.5	2,170	Single Family	FALSE
15	$259,900	02/01/2000	N. County	4	3	1,734	Condo	FALSE
16	$325,000	02/05/2000	S. County	4	3	2,800	Condo	TRUE
17	$208,750	02/07/2000	S. County	4	3	2,207	Single Family	TRUE
18	$227,500	02/07/2000	S. County	4	3	1,905	Condo	FALSE
19	$259,900	02/07/2000	N. County	3	2.5	2,122	Condo	FALSE
20	$405,000	02/10/2000	N. County	2	3	2,444	Single Family	TRUE
21	$236,900	02/11/2000	S. County	2	2	1,483	Condo	FALSE
22	$240,000	02/11/2000	S. County	3	2.5	1,595	Condo	FALSE
23	$304,900	02/13/2000	S. County	4	3	2,350	Single Family	FALSE
24	$349,900	02/17/2000	N. County	4	3	2,290	Single Family	TRUE
25	$249,000	02/25/2000	Central	4	3	1,940	Single Family	TRUE
26	$229,500	02/28/2000	Central	4	3	2,041	Single Family	FALSE
27	$359,900	03/01/2000	N. County	3	3	1,839	Condo	FALSE
28	$335,000	03/06/2000	Central	3	2.5	2,000	Single Family	TRUE
29	$360,000	03/06/2000	S. County	5	3	2,112	Single Family	TRUE
30	$349,000	03/11/2000	N. County	4	2.5	2,730	Condo	TRUE
31	$249,000	03/13/2000	S. County	3	2.5	1,730	Condo	FALSE
32	$309,950	03/15/2000	Central	4	3	2,800	Single Family	FALSE
33	$325,000	03/22/2000	Central	3	2.5	1,752	Single Family	FALSE
34	$285,000	03/31/2000	Central	2	1	2,036	Single Family	FALSE
35	$375,000	04/01/2000	Central	4	3	2,368	Single Family	TRUE

Figure 9-7: This list stores information about real estate listings.

The workbook shown in Figure 9-7 is available on the companion CD-ROM.

Specifying a single criterion

The examples in this section use a single-selection criterion. In other words, the contents of a single field determine the record selection.

You also can use AutoFiltering to perform this type of filtering.

To select only the records that contain a specific value in a specific field, enter the field name in the first row of the criteria range, and the value to match in the second row. Figure 9-8, for example, shows the criteria range (A1:A2) that selects records containing the value 4 in the Bedrooms field.

	A	B	C	D	E	F	G	H
1	**Bedrooms**							
2	4							
3								
4								
5								
6								
7								
8	**ListPrice**	**Date Listed**	**Area**	**Bedrooms**	**Baths**	**SquareFt**	**Type**	**Pool**
9	$350,000	01/08/2000	N. County	3	2.5	1,991	Condo	FALSE
10	$215,000	01/10/2000	Central	3	1.75	2,157	Single Family	TRUE
11	$315,000	01/12/2000	S. County	2	2	1,552	Condo	FALSE
12	$379,000	01/16/2000	N. County	4	3	3,000	Single Family	FALSE
13	$248,500	01/26/2000	?	4	2.5	2,101	Single Family	TRUE
14	$297,500	01/28/2000	S. County	4	3.5	2,170	Single Family	FALSE
15	$259,900	02/01/2000	N. County	4	3	1,734	Condo	FALSE

Figure 9-8: The criteria range (A1:A2) selects records that describe properties with four bedrooms.

Note that the criteria range does not need to include all of the fields from the list. If you work with different sets of criteria, you may find it more convenient to list all of the field names in the first row of your criteria range.

USING COMPARISON OPERATORS

You can use comparison operators to refine your record selection. For example, you can select records based on any of the following:

◆ Homes that have at least four bedrooms

◆ Homes with a square footage less than 2,000

◆ Homes with a list price of no more than $200,000

To select the records that describe homes that have at least four bedrooms, make the following entries in the criterion range:

```
A1:     Bedrooms
A2:     >=4
```

Table 9-1 lists the comparison operators that you can use with text or value criteria. If you don't use a comparison operator, Excel assumes the equal sign operator (=).

TABLE **9-1** COMPARISON OPERATORS

Operator	Comparison Type
=	Equal to
>	Greater than
>=	Greater than or equal to
<	Less than
<=	Less than or equal to
< >	Not equal to

Table 9-2 shows examples of some criteria that use comparison operators.

TABLE **9-2** EXAMPLES OF COMPARISON OPERATORS

Criteria	Selects
>100	Records that contain a value greater than 100
<>0	Records that contain a value not equal to 0
=500	Records that contain a value of 500 (omitting the equal sign gives the same result)
<5000	Records that contain a value less than 5000
>=5000	Records that contain a value less than or equal to 5000

USING WILDCARD CHARACTERS

Criteria that use text also can make use of two "wildcard" characters: an asterisk (*) matches any number of characters; a question mark (?) matches any single character. Table 9-3 shows examples of criteria that use text. Some of these are a bit counter-intuitive. For example, to select records that match a single character, you must enter the criterion as a formula (refer to the last entry in the table).

TABLE 9-3 EXAMPLES OF TEXT CRITERIA

Criteria	Selects
="January"	Records that contain the text *January* (and nothing else).
January	Records that contain the text *January* (and nothing else).
C	Records that contain text that begins with the letter C.
<>C*	Records that contain any text, except text that begins with the letter C.
>K	Records that contain text that begins with the letters L through Z.
County	Records that contain text that includes the word *COUNTY*.
Sm*	Records that contain text that begins with the letters *SM*.
s*s	Records that contain text that begins with S and ends with S.
s?s	Records that contain three-letter text that begins with S and ends with S.
<>*c	Records that contain text that does not end with the letter C.
<>???????	All records that don't contain exactly five letters.
<>*c*	Records that do not contain the letter C.
~?	Records that contain a single question mark character.
=	Records that contain a blank.
="<>"	Records that contain any nonblank entry.
="=c"	Records that contain the single character C. You must enter this exactly as shown: as a formula, with an initial equal sign.

 The text comparisons are not case sensitive. For example, si* matches *Simpson* as well as *sick*.

Specifying multiple criteria

Often, you may want to select records based on criteria that use more than one field or multiple values within a single field. These selection criteria involve logical OR or AND comparisons. Following are a few examples of the types of multiple criteria that you can apply to the real estate database.

- ◆ A list price less than $250,000, and square footage of at least 2,000

- ◆ Single-family home with a pool

- ◆ At least four bedrooms, at least three bathrooms, and square footage less than 3,000

- ◆ A home listed for no more than one month, with a list price greater than $300,000

- ◆ A condominium with square footage between 1,000 and 1,500

- ◆ A single-family home listed in the month of March

To join criteria with an AND operator, use multiple columns in the criteria range. Figure 9-9 shows a criteria range that selects records with a list price of less than $250,000, and a square footage of at least 2,000.

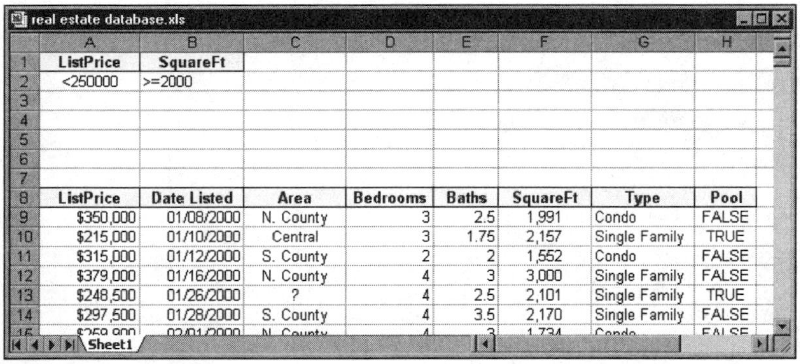

Figure 9–9: This criteria range uses multiple columns that select records using a logical AND operation.

Figure 9-10 shows another example. This criteria range selects records that were listed in the month of March. Notice that the field name (Date Listed) appears twice in the criteria range. The criteria selects the records in which the Date Listed date is greater than or equal to March 1 AND the Date Listed date is less than April 1.

	real estate database.xls								
	A	B	C	D	E	F	G	H	
1	Date Listed	Date Listed							
2	>=3/1/2000	<4/1/2000							
3									
4									
5									
6									
7									
8	ListPrice	Date Listed	Area	Bedrooms	Baths	SquareFt	Type	Pool	
9	$350,000	01/08/2000	N. County	3	2.5	1,991	Condo	FALSE	
10	$215,000	01/10/2000	Central	3	1.75	2,157	Single Family	TRUE	
11	$315,000	01/12/2000	S. County	2	2	1,552	Condo	FALSE	
12	$379,000	01/16/2000	N. County	4	3	3,000	Single Family	FALSE	
13	$248,500	01/26/2000	?	4	2.5	2,101	Single Family	TRUE	

Figure 9-10: This criteria range selects records that describe properties that were listed in the month of March.

To join criteria with a logical OR operator, use more than one row in the criteria range. A criteria range can have any number of rows, each of which joins with the others via an OR operator. Figure 9-11 shows a criteria range (A1:C3) with two rows of criteria.

	real estate database.xls								
	A	B	C	D	E	F	G	H	
1	Type	SquareFt	ListPrice						
2	Condo	>=1800							
3	Single Family		<210000						
4									
5									
6									
7									
8	ListPrice	Date Listed	Area	Bedrooms	Baths	SquareFt	Type	Pool	
9	$350,000	01/08/2000	N. County	3	2.5	1,991	Condo	FALSE	
16	$325,000	02/05/2000	S. County	4	3	2,800	Condo	TRUE	
17	$208,750	02/07/2000	S. County	4	3	2,207	Single Family	TRUE	
18	$227,500	02/07/2000	S. County	4	3	1,905	Condo	FALSE	
19	$259,900	02/07/2000	N. County	3	2.5	2,122	Condo	FALSE	
27	$359,900	03/01/2000	N. County	3	3	1,839	Condo	FALSE	
30	$349,000	03/11/2000	N. County	4	2.5	2,730	Condo	TRUE	
36	$369,900	04/04/2000	N. County	4	3	1,988	Condo	FALSE	

Figure 9-11: This criteria range has two sets of criteria, each of which is in a separate row.

In this example, the filtered list shows the rows that meet either of the following conditions:

◆ A condo with a square footage of at least 1,800, OR

◆ A single-family home with a list price under $210,000

You cannot perform this type of filtering using AutoFiltering.

Specifying computed criteria

Using computed criteria can make filtering even more powerful. Computed criteria filter the list based on one or more calculations. Figure 9-12 shows a criteria range that selects records in which the list price is less than the average list price of all records. The formula in cell B2 is:

```
=ListPrice>AVERAGE(A:A)
```

	Above Avg						
	TRUE						
ListPrice	**Date Listed**	**Area**	**Bedrooms**	**Baths**	**SquareFt**	**Type**	**Pool**
$350,000	01/08/2000	N. County	3	2.5	1,991	Condo	FALSE
$315,000	01/12/2000	S. County	2	2	1,552	Condo	FALSE
$379,000	01/16/2000	N. County	4	3	3,000	Single Family	FALSE
$297,500	01/28/2000	S. County	4	3.5	2,170	Single Family	FALSE
$325,000	02/05/2000	S. County	4	3	2,800	Condo	TRUE

Figure 9-12: This criteria range uses computed criteria.

Keep these following points in mind when using computed criteria.

◆ Computed criteria formulas are always logical formulas: They must return either TRUE or FALSE.

◆ You can use the field label in your formula. In the preceding example, ListPrice is not a named range. It is a field label in the database. Alternatively, you can use a reference to the cell in the first data row in the field of interest (not a reference to the cell that contains the field name). In this example, the cell in the first data row for the ListPrice field is cell A9. The following formula returns the same result as the previous example:

```
=A9>AVERAGE(A:A)
```

◆ Ignore the values returned by formulas in the criteria range. These refer to the first row of the list. Sometimes, using a field label in the formula results in an error value such as #NAME? or #VALUE!. You can just ignore this error. It does not affect how the list is filtered.

♦ When you use computed criteria, do not use an existing field label in your criteria range. In Figure 9-12, notice that cell B1 contains *Above Avg,* which is not a field name from the list. A computed criteria essentially computes a new field for the list. Therefore, you must supply a new field name in the first row of the criteria range. Or, if you prefer, you can simply leave the field name cell blank.

♦ You can use a reference to an entire column in a computed criteria formula. In the preceding example, the AVERAGE function used A:A as its argument. If you do so, the criteria formula must be in a different column than the column referenced. Failure to do so results in a circular reference. If you prefer, you can simply use the actual address of the column within your list.

♦ You can use any number of computed criteria and mix and match them with noncomputed criteria.

♦ If your computed formula refers to a value outside the list, use an absolute reference rather than a relative reference. For example, use $C$1 rather than C1.

COMPUTED CRITERIA EXAMPLES

Figure 9-13 shows another example of computed criteria. This criteria selects records in which the sum of the bedrooms and bathrooms is greater than 8. Notice that the computed criteria formula returns an error value because the formula refers to field names. The filtering works correctly, despite the error.

```
=Bedrooms+Baths>8
```

Alternatively, you can write this formula to refer to the first data row in the list:

```
=D9+E9>8
```

Using this formula does not return an error, but the formula isn't as easy to understand.

	ListPrice	Date Listed	Area	Bedrooms	Baths	SquareFt	Type	Pool
8								
58	$545,000	06/09/2000	N. County	8	4	5,800	Single Family	FALSE
74	$574,900	08/09/2000	S. County	5	4	4,700	Single Family	FALSE
84	$229,500	09/05/2000	N. County	6	3	2,700	Single Family	TRUE

Figure 9–13: This criteria range uses computed criteria.

Following is another example of a computed criteria formula. This formula selects the records listed within the past 60 days.

```
=Date Listed>TODAY()-60
```

USING ARRAYS WITH COMPUTED CRITERIA

Excel also supports arrays in computed criteria formulas. To see how this may be useful, consider a situation in which you want to identify properties that don't have a "half bath." Filter out records that have 3.5, 4.5, or some other noninteger value in the Baths field. Figure 9-14 displays one example. The criteria range, A1:A7, uses six OR criteria to make the selection.

	ListPrice	Date Listed	Area	Bedrooms	Baths	SquareFt	Type	Pool
					Baths			
					2			
					3			
					4			
					5			
					6			
					7			
11	$315,000	01/12/2000	S. County	2	2	1,552	Condo	FALSE
12	$379,000	01/16/2000	N. County	4	3	3,000	Single Family	FALSE
15	$259,900	02/01/2000	N. County	4	3	1,734	Condo	FALSE
16	$325,000	02/05/2000	S. County	4	3	2,800	Condo	TRUE

Figure 9-14: Using six OR criteria to select records with noninteger bathrooms

Another option uses this single-computed criteria formula:

```
=IF(OR(Baths={2,3,4,5,6,7}),TRUE)
```

This formula returns TRUE if the value in the Bath field equals any of the values in the array.

Using Database Functions with Lists

To create formulas that return results based on filtering criteria, use Excel's database worksheet functions. These functions all begin with the letter D and are listed in the Database category of the Paste Function dialog box. Table 9-4 lists Excel's database functions.

TABLE 9-4 EXCEL'S DATABASE WORKSHEET FUNCTIONS

Function	Description
DAVERAGE	Returns the average of database entries that match a criteria
DCOUNT	Counts the cells containing numbers from a specified database and criteria
DCOUNTA	Counts nonblank cells from a specified database and criteria
DGET	Extracts from a database a single record that matches the specified criteria
DMAX	Returns the maximum value from selected database entries
DMIN	Returns the minimum value from selected database entries
DPRODUCT	Multiplies the values in a particular field of records that match the criteria in a database
DSTDEV	Estimates the standard deviation, based on a sample of selected database entries
DSTDEVP	Calculates the standard deviation, based on the entire population of selected database entries
DSUM	Adds the numbers in the field column of records in the database that match the criteria
DVAR	Estimates variance, based on a sample from selected database entries
DVARP	Calculates variance, based on the entire population of selected database entries

The database functions all require a separate criteria range, which is specified as the last argument for the function. The database functions use exactly the same type of criteria range as discussed earlier in "Specifying Advanced Filter Criteria."

Refer to Figure 9-15. The formula in cell E5, which follows, uses the DSUM function to calculate the sum of values in a list that meet certain criteria. Specifically, the formula returns the sum of the Sales column for records in which the Month is "Feb" and the Region is "North."

```
=DSUM(Database,3,Criteria)
```

In this case, the list is named *Database*, 3 is the field number of the column you are summing, and *Criteria* is the name of the criteria range (E1:F2).

	A	B	C	D	E	F	G
1	Month	Region	Sales		Month	Region	
2	Jan	North	2,838		Feb	North	
3	Jan	South	5,488				
4	Jan	West	5,072				
5	Feb	North	5,584		5,584	<-- DSUM	
6	Feb	South	3,504				
7	Feb	West	4,118				
8	Mar	North	3,531				
9	Mar	South	5,321				
10	Mar	West	2,584				
11	Apr	North	5,955				
12	Apr	South	4,801				

Figure 9-15: Using the DSUM function to sum a list using a criteria range

You may find it cumbersome to set up a criteria range every time you need to use a database function. Fortunately, Excel provides some alternative ways to perform conditional sums and counts. Refer to Chapter 7 for examples that use SUMIF, COUNTIF, and various other techniques.

If you're an array formula aficionado, you might be tempted to use a literal array in place of the criteria range. In theory, the following array formula *should* work (and would eliminate the need for a separate criteria range). Unfortunately, the database functions do not support arrays, and this formula simply returns a #VALUE! error.

```
{=DSUM(Database,3,{"Month","Region";"Feb","North"})}
```

In the original release of Excel 97, the database functions do not work correctly if the first argument refers to a range that contains more than 32,768 rows. Excel 97 SR-1 corrected this problem.

Working with a Lotus 1-2-3 File?

If you open a 1-2-3 file in Excel, be aware that Excel evaluates the database criteria ranges differently. This may affect the results obtained when using advanced filtering and database functions.

Continued

> ## Working with a Lotus 1-2-3 File? *(Continued)*
>
> For example, in 1-2-3 a criteria such as "John" finds only rows with cells that contain the text "John." When you open a 1-2-3 file in Excel, the "transition formula evaluation" is in effect. If you don't change this setting, the criteria ranges will be evaluated as they are in 1-2-3.
>
> But if you select Tools → Options, and clear the Transition formula evaluation checkbox (in the Transition tab of the Options dialog box), Excel evaluates the criteria range using its rules (which are different). For example, the "John" criteria finds any rows that contain cells with text beginning with "John"; this includes cells that contain "John," "John Smith," and "Johnson."

Appendix A contains more information about working with 1-2-3 files.

Summarizing a list with a data table

This section describes a technique that you can use to summarize the information in a database. It uses the Data → Table command to create a dynamic summary table. A pivot table is often your best choice for this type of thing, but this technique offers one advantage: the data table is updated automatically (you do not need to refresh it, as in a pivot table).

Figure 9-16 shows part of a simple sales list that occupies five columns. The list contains a monthly sales total (column E) for each sales representative, along with the number of sales contacts made (column D) and the sales rep's region (either North or South, in column C). For example, in January, Bob (a sales rep for the North region) made 58 contacts for total sales of $283,800.

The list contains 76 records, and the entire list (A1:E77) is named *Database*. Range G1:H2 stores a criteria range for the list. This range is named *Criteria*. The goal is to create a summary table that shows key information by month. Figure 9-17 shows the summary table in G8:K23 — created using the Data → Table command.

The workbook shown in Figure 9-17 is available on the companion CD-ROM. For comparison, the workbook also contains a pivot table summary, plus a table that uses array formulas (as described in Chapter 7).

data table summary.xls

	A	B	C	D	E
1	Month	Sales Rep	Region	Contacts	Sales
2	Jan	Bob	North	58	283,800
3	Jan	Frank	North	35	507,200
4	Jan	Paul	South	25	107,600
5	Jan	Randy	South	47	391,600
6	Jan	Mary	South	39	226,700
7	Feb	Bob	North	44	558,400
8	Feb	Jill	North	46	350,400
9	Feb	Frank	North	74	411,800
10	Feb	Paul	South	29	154,200
11	Feb	Randy	South	45	258,000
12	Feb	Mary	South	52	233,800
13	Mar	Bob	North	30	353,100
14	Mar	Jill	North	44	532,100
15	Mar	Frank	North	57	258,400
16	Mar	Paul	South	13	286,000
17	Mar	Randy	South	14	162,200
18	Mar	Mary	South	36	134,300
19	Apr	Bob	North	54	595,500
20	Apr	Jill	North	44	480,100
21	Apr	Frank	North	79	555,500

data table

Figure 9-16: A data table is a good way to summarize this list.

data table summary.xls

	B	C	D	E	F	G	H	I	J	K
1	Sales Rep	Region	Contacts	Sales		Month	Region			
2	Bob	North	58	283,800		Jan	North			
3	Frank	North	35	507,200						
4	Paul	South	25	107,600						
5	Randy	South	47	391,600						
6	Mary	South	39	226,700						
7	Bob	North	44	558,400						
8	Jill	North	46	350,400			Sales Reps	Contacts	Sales	Sales/Contact
9	Frank	North	74	411,800			2	93	791,000	8,505
10	Paul	South	29	154,200		Jan	2	93	791,000	8,505
11	Randy	South	45	258,000		Feb	3	164	1,320,600	8,052
12	Mary	South	52	233,800		Mar	3	131	1,143,600	8,730
13	Bob	North	30	353,100		Apr	3	177	1,631,100	9,215
14	Jill	North	44	532,100		May	3	173	1,064,300	6,152
15	Frank	North	57	258,400		Jun	3	132	1,001,200	7,585
16	Paul	South	13	286,000		Jul	3	166	872,300	5,255
17	Randy	South	14	162,200		Aug	3	127	1,082,100	8,520
18	Mary	South	36	134,300		Sep	3	148	1,239,300	8,374
19	Bob	North	54	595,500		Oct	3	147	962,100	6,545
20	Jill	North	44	480,100		Nov	4	162	1,004,522	6,201
21	Frank	North	79	555,500		Dec	4	205	1,219,183	5,947
22	Paul	South	36	328,200						
23	Randy	South	31	154,200		TOTALS		1,825	13,331,305	7,423

data table / pivot table / array form

Figure 9-17: Use the Data → Table command to create this summary table.

To create this data table:

1. Enter the month names in G10:G21.

2. Enter the descriptive labels shown in H8:K8.

3. Enter the formulas from Table 9-5 into cells in row 9.

4. Select the range G9:K21.

5. Choose Data → Table. Excel displays the Table dialog box shown in Figure 9-18.

6. In the Table dialog box, enter **G2** into the field labeled Column input cell (leave the Row input cell field empty).

7. Click OK.

TABLE 9-5 FORMULAS TO ENTER

Cells	Formula
H9	=DCOUNTA(Database,2,Criteria)
I9	=DSUM(Database,4,Criteria)
J9	=DSUM(Database,5,Criteria)
KO	=J9/I9

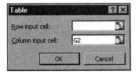

Figure 9-18: The Table dialog box

Excel inserts a single array formula into H10:K21. The formula is:

```
=TABLE(,G2)
```

This formula uses the information in the cells to the left (G10:G21) and above (H9:K9) to perform calculations. It evaluates the formulas in row 9, substituting the corresponding month in column G. In other words, the single criteria range is being treated as if it were a series of criteria ranges.

You can enter a region name (either North or South) in cell H2 and the data table will show the information for that region. If H2 is blank, the data table shows information for all regions.

Creating Subtotals

Excel's Data → Subtotals command is a handy tool that inserts formulas into a list automatically. These formulas use the SUBTOTAL function, which actually does more than simply sum data. To use this feature, your list must be sorted, because the formulas are inserted whenever the value in a specified field changes.

Figure 9-19 shows an example of a list that is appropriate for subtotals. This list is sorted by the Month field, and then by the Region field.

Month	State	Region	Contacts	Sales
Jan	California	West	58	283,800
Jan	Washington	West	35	507,200
Jan	Oregon	West	39	226,700
Jan	New York	East	25	107,600
Jan	New Jersey	East	47	391,600
Feb	California	West	44	558,400
Feb	Washington	West	74	411,800
Feb	Oregon	West	46	350,400
Feb	New York	East	52	233,800
Feb	New Jersey	East	29	154,200
Mar	California	West	30	353,100
Mar	Washington	West	57	258,400
Mar	Oregon	West	44	532,100
Mar	New York	East	36	134,300
Mar	New Jersey	East	14	162,200

Figure 9-19: This list is a good candidate for subtotals, which are inserted at each change of the month and at each change of the region.

To insert subtotal formulas into a list automatically, move the cell pointer anywhere in the list and choose Data → Subtotals. You will see the Subtotal dialog box, shown in Figure 9-20.

Figure 9-20: The Subtotal dialog box automatically inserts subtotal formulas into a sorted list.

The Subtotal dialog box

The Subtotal dialog box offers the following choices:

- At each change in: This drop-down list displays all fields in your list. You must have sorted the list by the field that you choose.
- Use function: Choose from 11 functions (Sum is the default).
- Add subtotal to: This list box shows all the fields in your list. Place a checkmark next to the field or fields that you want to subtotal.
- Replace current subtotals: If checked, Excel removes any existing subtotal formulas and replaces them with the new subtotals.
- Page break between groups: If checked, Excel inserts a manual page break after each subtotal.
- Summary below data: If checked, Excel places the subtotals below the data (the default). Otherwise, the subtotal formulas appear above the totals.
- Remove All: This button removes all subtotal formulas in the list.

When you click OK, Excel analyzes the list and inserts formulas as specified – and even creates an outline for you. Figure 9-21 shows a worksheet after adding two sets of subtotals: one that summarizes by month, and another that summarizes by region.

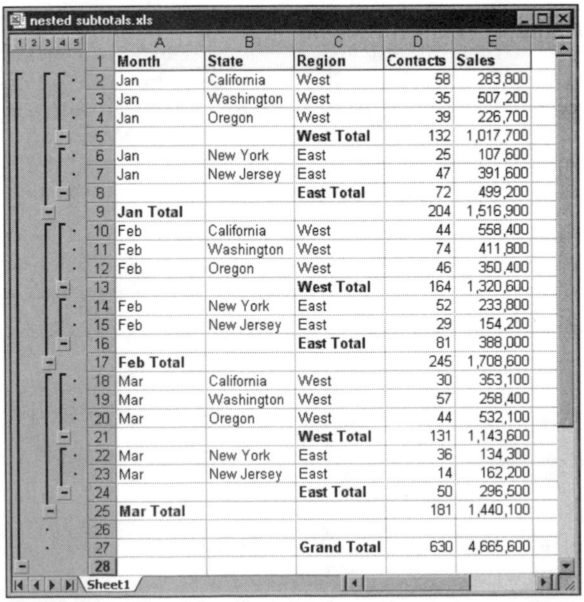

	A	B	C	D	E
1	**Month**	**State**	**Region**	**Contacts**	**Sales**
2	Jan	California	West	58	283,800
3	Jan	Washington	West	35	507,200
4	Jan	Oregon	West	39	226,700
5			**West Total**	132	1,017,700
6	Jan	New York	East	25	107,600
7	Jan	New Jersey	East	47	391,600
8			**East Total**	72	499,200
9	**Jan Total**			204	1,516,900
10	Feb	California	West	44	558,400
11	Feb	Washington	West	74	411,800
12	Feb	Oregon	West	46	350,400
13			**West Total**	164	1,320,600
14	Feb	New York	East	52	233,800
15	Feb	New Jersey	East	29	154,200
16			**East Total**	81	388,000
17	**Feb Total**			245	1,708,600
18	Mar	California	West	30	353,100
19	Mar	Washington	West	57	258,400
20	Mar	Oregon	West	44	532,100
21			**West Total**	131	1,143,600
22	Mar	New York	East	36	134,300
23	Mar	New Jersey	East	14	162,200
24			**East Total**	50	296,500
25	**Mar Total**			181	1,440,100
26					
27			**Grand Total**	630	4,665,600
28					

Figure 9-21: Excel adds the subtotal formulas automatically – and even creates an outline.

If you add subtotals to a filtered list, the subtotals may no longer be accurate when you remove the filter.

The formulas all use the SUBTOTAL worksheet function. For example, the formula in cell E9 (total sales for January) is:

```
=SUBTOTAL(9,E2:E7)
```

Although this formula refers to two other cells that contains a SUBTOTAL formula (E5 and E8), those cells are not included in the sum to avoid double-counting.

You can use the outline controls to adjust the level of detail shown. Figure 9-22, for example, shows only the summary rows from the subtotaled list. These rows contain the SUBTOTAL formulas.

	Month	State	Region	Contacts	Sales
5			West Total	132	1,017,700
8			East Total	72	499,200
9	Jan Total			204	1,516,900
13			West Total	164	1,320,600
16			East Total	81	388,000
17	Feb Total			245	1,708,600
21			West Total	131	1,143,600
24			East Total	50	296,500
25	Mar Total			181	1,440,100
26					
27			Grand Total	630	4,665,600
28					

Figure 9-22: Using the outline controls to hide the detail and display only the summary rows

About the SUBTOTAL function

You can, of course, use the SUBTOTAL function in formulas that you create manually. Using the Data → Subtotals command is usually easier. The first argument for the SUBTOTAL function determines the actual function used (see Table 9-6). For example, when the first argument is 1, the SUBTOTAL function works like the AVERAGE function.

TABLE 9-6 FIRST ARGUMENT OPTIONS FOR THE SUBTOTAL FUNCTION

Value	Function
1	AVERAGE
2	COUNT
3	COUNTA
4	MAX
5	MIN
6	PRODUCT
7	STDEV
8	STDEVP
9	SUM
10	VAR
11	VARP

Summary

This chapter presented various formula techniques relevant to working with a list. A list (also known as a worksheet database) is an organized collection of information. The first row contains field names, and subsequent rows contain data (records). AutoFiltering presents a useful method of filtering a list using simple criteria; for more complex criteria you need to use advanced filtering, which requires a criteria range. This chapter also discussed Excel's database functions (which also require a criteria range) and the SUBTOTAL function.

Chapter 10 switches gears and covers common financial formulas.

Chapter 10

Financial Calculations

IN THIS CHAPTER

◆ A brief overview of the Excel functions that deal with the time value of money

◆ Formulas that perform various types of loan calculations

◆ Formulas that perform various types of investment calculations

◆ An overview of Excel's depreciation functions

IT'S A SAFE BET that the most common use of Excel is to perform calculations involving money. Every day, people make hundreds of thousands of financial decisions based on the numbers that are calculated in a spreadsheet. These decisions range from simple (*Can I afford to buy a new car?*) to complex (*Will purchasing XYZ Corporation result in a positive cash flow in the next 18 months?*). This chapter discusses basic financial calculations that you can perform with the assistance of Excel.

The Time Value of Money

Depending on how you look at it, the face value of money may not be what it seems. A key consideration is the *time value* of money. This concept involves calculating the value of money in the past, present, or future. It is based on the premise that money increases in value over time because of *interest* earned by the money. In other words, a dollar invested today will be worth more tomorrow.

For example, imagine that your rich uncle decided to give away some money and asked you to choose one of the following options:

◆ Receive $8,000 today

◆ Receive $9,500 in one year

◆ Receive $12,000 in five years

◆ Receive $150 per month for five years

If your goal is to maximize the amount received, you need to take into account not only the face value of the money, but also the *time value* of the money when it arrives in your hands.

The time value of money depends on your perspective. In other words, you're either a lender or a borrower. When you take out a loan to purchase an automobile you're a borrower, and the institution that provides the funds to you is the lender. When you invest money in a bank savings account, you're a lender; you're lending your money to the bank, and the bank is borrowing it from you.

Several concepts contribute to the time value of money:

♦ Present Value (PV). This is the *principal* amount. If you deposit $5,000 in a bank CD, this amount represents the principal, or present value, of the money you invested. If you borrow $15,000 to purchase a car, this amount represents the principal or present value of the loan. Present Value may be positive or negative.

♦ Future Value (FV). This is the principal plus interest. If you invest $5,000 for five years and earn 6 percent annual interest, you receive $6,312.38 at the end of the five-year term. The amount is the future value of your $5,000 investment. If you take out a three-year auto loan for $15,000 and pay 7 percent annual interest, you pay a total of $16,673.16. This amount represents the principal plus the interest you paid. Future Value may be positive or negative.

♦ Payment (PMT). This is either principal, or principal plus interest. If you deposit $100 per month into a savings account, $100 is the payment. If you have a monthly mortgage payment of $825, the $825 is made up of principal and interest.

♦ Interest Rate. Interest is a percentage of the principal, usually expressed on an annual basis. For example, you might earn 5.5 percent annual interest on a bank CD. Or, your mortgage loan may have a 7.75 percent interest rate.

♦ Period. This represents the point in time when interest is paid or earned. For example, a bank CD that pays interest quarterly or an auto loan that requires monthly payments.

♦ Term. This is the amount of time of interest. A 12-month bank CD has a term of one year. A 30-year mortgage loan has a term of 30 years.

Loan Calculations

Now, let's look at how to calculate various components of a loan. Think of a loan as consisting of the following components:

- ◆ The loan amount
- ◆ The interest rate
- ◆ The number of payment periods
- ◆ The periodic payment amount

If you know any three of these components, you can create a formula to calculate the unknown component.

 The loan calculations in this section all assume a fixed-rate loan with a fixed term.

Worksheet functions for calculating loan information

This section describes five functions: PMT, PPMT, IPMT, RATE, and PV. For information about the arguments used in these functions, see the sidebar, "Financial Function Arguments."

THE PMT FUNCTION
The PMT function returns the loan payment (principal plus interest) per period, assuming constant payment amounts and a fixed interest rate. The syntax for the PMT function is:

```
PMT(rate,nper,pv,fv,type)
```

The following formula returns the monthly payment amount for a $5,000 loan with a 6 percent annual percentage rate. The loan has a term of four years (48 months).

```
=PMT(.06/12,48,-5000)
```

This formula returns $117.43, the monthly payment for the loan. Notice that the third argument (*pv*, for present value) is negative.

THE PPMT FUNCTION
The PPMT function returns the *principal* part of a loan payment for a given period, assuming constant payment amounts and a fixed interest rate. The syntax for the PPMT function is:

```
PPMT(rate,per,nper,pv,fv,type)
```

The following formula returns the amount paid to principal for the first month of a \$5,000 loan with a 6 percent annual percentage rate. The loan has a term of four years (48 months).

```
=PPMT(.06/12,1,48,-5000)
```

The formula returns \$92.43 for the principal, which is about 78.7 percent of the total loan payment. If we change the second argument to 48 (to calculate the principal amount for the last payment), the formula returns \$116.84, or about 99.5 percent of the total loan payment.

 To calculate the cumulative principal paid between any two payment periods, use the CUMPRINC function, which is available only when you install the Analysis ToolPak add-in. This function uses two additional arguments: *start_period* and *end_period*.

THE IPMT FUNCTION

The IPMT function returns the *interest* part of a loan payment for a given period, assuming constant payment amounts and a fixed interest rate. The syntax for the IPMT function is:

```
IPMT(rate,per,nper,pv,fv,type)
```

The following formula returns the amount paid to interest for the first month of a \$5,000 loan with a 6 percent annual percentage rate. The loan has a term of four years (48 months).

```
=IPMT(.06/12,1,48,-5000)
```

This formula returns an interest amount of \$25.00. By the last payment period for the loan, the interest payment is only \$0.58.

 To calculate the cumulative interest paid between any two-payment periods, use the CUMIPMT function, which is available only when you install the Analysis ToolPak add-in. This function uses two additional arguments: *start_period* and *end_period*.

THE RATE FUNCTION

The RATE function returns the periodic interest rate of a loan, given the number of payment periods, the periodic payment amount, and the loan amount. The syntax for the RATE function is:

```
RATE(nper,pmt,pv,fv,type,guess)
```

The following formula calculates the annual interest rate for a 48-month loan for $5,000 that has a monthly payment amount of $117.43.

```
=RATE(48,117.43,-5000)*12
```

This formula returns 6.00 percent. Notice that the result of the function multiplies by 12 to get the annual percentage rate.

THE NPER FUNCTION

The NPER function returns the number of payment periods for a loan, given the loan's amount, interest rate, and periodic payment amount. The syntax for the NPER function is:

```
NPER(rate, pmt, pv, fv, type)
```

The following formula calculates the number of payment periods for a $5,000 loan that has a monthly payment amount of $117.43. The loan has a 6 percent annual interest rate.

```
=NPER(0.06/12,117.43,-5000)
```

This formula returns 47.997 (i.e., 48 months). The monthly payment was rounded to the nearest penny, causing the minor discrepancy.

THE PV FUNCTION

The PV function returns the present value (that is, the original loan amount) for a loan, given the interest rate, the number of periods, and the period payment amount. The syntax for the PV function is:

```
PV(rate,nper,pmt,fv,type)
```

The following formula calculates the original loan amount for a 48-month loan that has a monthly payment amount of $117.43. The annual interest rate is 6 percent.

```
=PV(0.06/12,48,-117.43)
```

This formula returns $5,000.21. The monthly payment was rounded to the near-est penny, causing the $0.21 discrepancy.

Financial Function Arguments

Here are some of the arguments you'll see when working with financial functions:

◆ rate: The interest rate per period. If the rate is expressed as an annual interest rate, you must divide it by the number of periods.

◆ nper: The total number of payment periods.

◆ per: A particular period. The period must be less than or equal to nper.

◆ pmt: The payment made each period (a constant value that does not change over the life of the annuity).

◆ fv: The future value after the last payment is made. If you omit fv, it is assumed to be 0 (the future value of a loan, for example, is 0).

◆ type: Indicates when payments are due — either 0 (due at the end of the period) or 1 (due at the beginning of the period). If you omit type, it is assumed to be 0.

A loan calculation example

Figure 10-1 shows a worksheet set up to calculate the periodic payment amount for a loan. The loan amount is in cell B1, and the annual interest rate is in cell B2. Cell B3 contains the payment period expressed in months. For example, if B3 is 1, the payment is due monthly. If B3 is 3, the payment is due quarterly. Cell B4 contains the number of periods of the loan. The example shown in this figure calculates the payment for a $10,000 loan at 9.5 percent annual interest, with monthly payments for 36 months. The formula in cell B6 is:

```
=PMT(B2*(B3/12),B4,-B1)
```

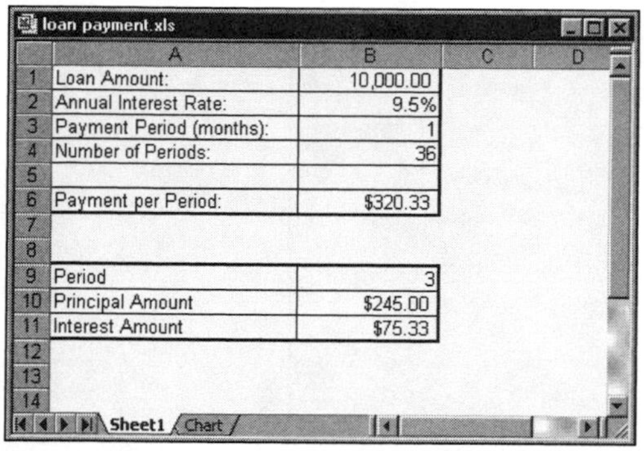

Figure 10-1: Using the PMT function to calculate a loan payment amount

Notice that the first argument is an expression that calculates the *periodic inter-est rate* using the annual interest rate and the payment period. Therefore, if payments are made quarterly on a three-year loan, the payment period is 3, the number of periods is 12, and the periodic interest rate would be calculated as the annual interest rate multiplied by 3/12.

In the worksheet in Figure 10-1, range A9:B11 is set up to calculate the principal and interest amount for a particular payment period. Cell B9 contains the payment period used by the formulas in B10:B11 (it must be less than or equal to the value in B4).

The formula in cell B10, shown here, calculates the amount of the payment that goes toward principal for the payment period in cell B9.

```
=PPMT(B2*(B3/12),B9,B4,-B1)
```

The following formula, in cell B11, calculates the amount of the payment that goes toward interest for the payment period in cell B9:

```
=IPMT(B2*(B3/12),B9,B4,-B1)
```

You should note that the sum of B10 and B11 always remains equal to the total loan payment calculated in cell B6. However, the relative proportion of principal and interest amounts varies with the payment period (an increasingly larger proportion of the payment is applied toward principal as the loan progresses). Figure 10-2 shows this graphically.

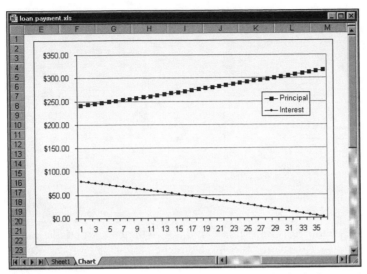

Figure 10-2: This chart shows the relative interest and principal amounts for the payment periods of a loan.

The workbook shown in Figure 10-1 and Figure 10-2 is available on the companion CD-ROM.

Credit card payments

Did you ever wonder how long it would take to pay off a credit card balance if you make the minimum payment amount each month? Figure 10-3 shows a worksheet set up to make this type of calculation.

	A	B	C
1	Credit Card Balance	$1,000.00	
2	Annual Interest Rate:	18.25%	
3	Minimum Payment Pct:	2.00%	
4	Minimum Monthly Payment Amount:	$20.00	
5	Your **Actual** Monthly Payment:	$20.00	
6			
7	No. of Payments Required:	94.7	
8	Total Amount Paid:	$1,893.29	
9	Total Interest Paid:	$893.29	
10			

Figure 10-3: This worksheet calculates the number of payments required to pay off a credit card balance.

The workbook shown in Figure 10-3 is available on the companion CD-ROM.

Range B1:B5 stores input values. In this example, the credit card has a balance of $1,000 and the lender charges 18.25 percent annual percentage rate (APR). The minimum payment is 2.00 percent (typical of many credit card lenders). Therefore, the minimum payment amount for this example is $20. You can enter another value in cell B5. For example, you may choose to pay $50 per month.

Range B7:B9 holds formulas that perform various calculations. The formula in B7, which follows, calculates the number of months required to pay off the balance.

```
=NPER(B2/12,B5,-B1,0)
```

The formula in B8 calculates the total amount you will pay. This formula is:

```
=B7*B5
```

The formula in cell B9 calculates the total interest paid:

```
=B8-B1
```

In this example, it would take more than seven years to pay off the credit card balance if you only make the minimum payment amount. This assumes, of course, that you make no additional charges on the account. This example may help explain why you receive so many credit card solicitations in the mail.

Figure 10-4 shows some additional calculations for the credit card example. For example, if you want to pay off the credit card in 12 months, you need to make monthly payments of $91.80. (This results in total payments of $1,101.59 and total interest of $101.59.) The formula in B13 is:

```
=PMT($B$2/12,A13,-$B$1)
```

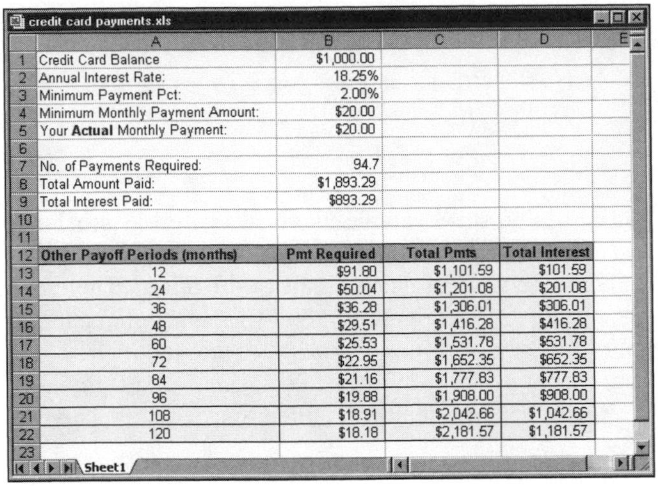

credit card payments.xls

	A	B	C	D
1	Credit Card Balance	$1,000.00		
2	Annual Interest Rate:	18.25%		
3	Minimum Payment Pct:	2.00%		
4	Minimum Monthly Payment Amount:	$20.00		
5	Your **Actual** Monthly Payment:	$20.00		
6				
7	No. of Payments Required:	94.7		
8	Total Amount Paid:	$1,893.29		
9	Total Interest Paid:	$893.29		
10				
11				
12	**Other Payoff Periods (months)**	**Pmt Required**	**Total Pmts**	**Total Interest**
13	12	$91.80	$1,101.59	$101.59
14	24	$50.04	$1,201.08	$201.08
15	36	$36.28	$1,306.01	$306.01
16	48	$29.51	$1,416.28	$416.28
17	60	$25.53	$1,531.78	$531.78
18	72	$22.95	$1,652.35	$652.35
19	84	$21.16	$1,777.83	$777.83
20	96	$19.88	$1,908.00	$908.00
21	108	$18.91	$2,042.66	$1,042.66
22	120	$18.18	$2,181.57	$1,181.57
23				

Sheet1

Figure 10-4: Column B shows the payment required to pay off the credit card balance for various payoff periods.

Creating a loan amortization schedule

A loan amortization schedule is a table of values that depicts various information for each payment period of a loan. Figure 10-5 shows a worksheet that uses formulas to calculate an amortization schedule.

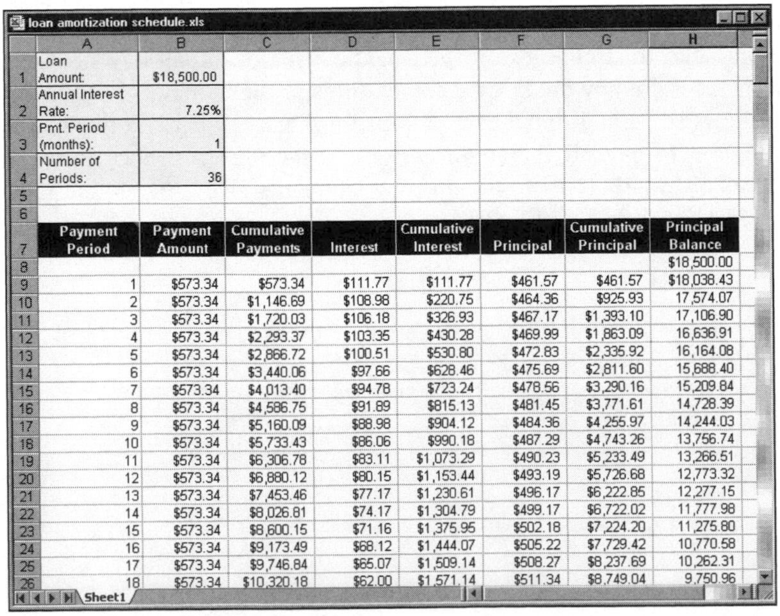

loan amortization schedule.xls

	A	B	C	D	E	F	G	H
1	Loan Amount:	$18,500.00						
2	Annual Interest Rate:	7.25%						
3	Pmt. Period (months):	1						
4	Number of Periods:	36						
5								
6								
7	**Payment Period**	**Payment Amount**	**Cumulative Payments**	**Interest**	**Cumulative Interest**	**Principal**	**Cumulative Principal**	**Principal Balance**
8								$18,500.00
9	1	$573.34	$573.34	$111.77	$111.77	$461.57	$461.57	$18,038.43
10	2	$573.34	$1,146.69	$108.98	$220.75	$464.36	$925.93	17,574.07
11	3	$573.34	$1,720.03	$106.18	$326.93	$467.17	$1,393.10	17,106.90
12	4	$573.34	$2,293.37	$103.35	$430.28	$469.99	$1,863.09	16,636.91
13	5	$573.34	$2,866.72	$100.51	$530.80	$472.83	$2,335.92	16,164.08
14	6	$573.34	$3,440.06	$97.66	$628.46	$475.69	$2,811.60	15,688.40
15	7	$573.34	$4,013.40	$94.78	$723.24	$478.56	$3,290.16	15,209.84
16	8	$573.34	$4,586.75	$91.89	$815.13	$481.45	$3,771.61	14,728.39
17	9	$573.34	$5,160.09	$88.98	$904.12	$484.36	$4,255.97	14,244.03
18	10	$573.34	$5,733.43	$86.06	$990.18	$487.29	$4,743.26	13,756.74
19	11	$573.34	$6,306.78	$83.11	$1,073.29	$490.23	$5,233.49	13,266.51
20	12	$573.34	$6,880.12	$80.15	$1,153.44	$493.19	$5,726.68	12,773.32
21	13	$573.34	$7,453.46	$77.17	$1,230.61	$496.17	$6,222.85	12,277.15
22	14	$573.34	$8,026.81	$74.17	$1,304.79	$499.17	$6,722.02	11,777.98
23	15	$573.34	$8,600.15	$71.16	$1,375.95	$502.18	$7,224.20	11,275.80
24	16	$573.34	$9,173.49	$68.12	$1,444.07	$505.22	$7,729.42	10,770.58
25	17	$573.34	$9,746.84	$65.07	$1,509.14	$508.27	$8,237.69	10,262.31
26	18	$573.34	$10,320.18	$62.00	$1,571.14	$511.34	$8,749.04	9,750.96

Sheet1

Figure 10-5: A loan amortization schedule

The loan parameters are entered into B1:B4, and the formulas beginning in row 9 use these values for the calculations. Table 10-1 shows the formulas in row 9 of the schedule. These formulas were copied down to row 488. Therefore, the worksheet can calculate amortization schedules for a loan with as many as 480 payment periods. The worksheet uses conditional formatting to hide the data in rows that extend beyond the loan term.

TABLE 10-1 FORMULAS USED TO CALCULATE AN AMORTIZATION SCHEDULE

Cell	Formula	Description
A9	=A8+1	Returns the payment number
B9	=PMT($B$2*($B$3/12),$B$4,-$B$1)	Calculates the periodic payment amount
C9	=C8+B9	Calculates the cumulative payment amounts
D9	=IPMT($B$2*($B$3/12),A9,$B$4,-$B$1)	Calculates the interest portion of the periodic payment
E9	=E8+D9	Calculates the cumulative interest paid
F9	=PPMT($B$2*($B$3/12),A9,$B$4,-$B$1)	Calculates the principal portion of the periodic payment
G9	=G8+F9	Calculates the cumulative amount applied toward principal
H9	=H8-F9	Returns the principal balance at the end of the period

Loan Amortization Wizard

If you create lots of amortization schedules, an add-in that I developed may interest you. The Loan Amortization Wizard uses a five-step dialog box sequence to specify the loan parameters, plus other options (such as formatting and the presence or absence of an outline). It then creates a new workbook with formulas, per your specifications.

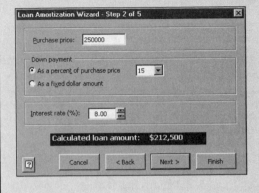

 The accompanying CD-ROM contains the Loan Amortization Wizard add-in. It requires Microsoft Excel 97 or later.

Summarizing loan options using a data table

Excel's Data → Table command is a handy tool to summarize various loan options. This section describes how to create one-way and two-way data tables.

 A workbook that demonstrates one- and two-way data tables is available on the companion CD-ROM.

CREATING A ONE-WAY DATA TABLE

A one-way data table shows the results of any number of calculations for different values of a single input cell.

Figure 10-6 shows a one-way data table (in B10:I13) that displays three calculations (payment amount, total payments, and total interest) for a loan, using seven interest rates ranging from 7.00 percent to 8.50 percent. In this example, the input cell is cell B2.

	A	B	C	D	E	F	G	H	I
	loan data tables.xls								
1	Loan Amount:	$10,000.00							
2	Annual Interest Rate:	7.25%							
3	Pmt. Period (months):	1							
4	Number of Periods:	36							
5									
6	Payment Amount:	$309.92							
7	Total Payments:	$11,156.95							
8	Total Interest:	$1,156.95							
9									
10			7.00%	7.25%	7.50%	7.75%	8.00%	8.25%	8.50%
11	Payment Amount:	$309.92	$308.77	$309.92	$311.06	$312.21	$313.36	$314.52	$315.68
12	Total Payments:	$11,156.95	$11,115.75	$11,156.95	$11,198.24	$11,239.62	$11,281.09	$11,322.66	$11,364.31
13	Total Interest:	$1,156.95	$1,115.75	$1,156.95	$1,198.24	$1,239.62	$1,281.09	$1,322.66	$1,364.31
14									
15									
16									

‖ ◀ ▶ ▶‖ \ 1-way / 2-way /

Figure 10-6: Using a one-way data table to display three loan calculations for various interest rates

To create this one-way data table do the following:

1. Enter the formulas that return the results for use in the data table. In this example, the formulas are in B6:B8.

2. Enter various values for a single input cell in successive columns. In this example, the input value is interest rate, and the values for various interest rates appear in C10:I10.

3. Create a reference to the formula cells in the column to the left of the input values. In this example, the range B11:B13 contains simple formulas that reference other cells. For example, B11 contains the following formula:

   ```
   =B6
   ```

4. Select the rectangular range that contains the entries from the previous steps. In this example, select B10:I13.

5. Select the Data → Table command. Excel displays the Table dialog box shown in Figure 10-7.

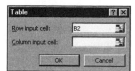

Figure 10-7: Excel's Table dialog box

6. For the Row input cell field, specify the cell reference that corresponds to the variable in your Data Table column header row. In this example, the Row input cell is B2.

7. Leave the Column input cell field empty.

8. Click OK. Excel inserts an array formula that uses the TABLE function with a single argument.

9. If you like, you can format the data table. For example, you might want to apply shading to the row and column headers.

Note that the array formula is not entered into the entire range that you selected in Step 4. The first column and first row of your selection are not changed.

TIP When you create a data table, the leftmost column of the data table (the column that contains the references entered in Step 3) contains the calculated values for the input cell. In this example, those values are repeated in column D. You might want to "hide" the values in column B by making the font color the same color as the background.

CREATING A TWO-WAY DATA TABLE

A two-way data table shows the results of a single calculation for different values of two input cells. Figure 10-8 shows a two-way data table (in B10:I16) that displays a calculation (payment amount) for a loan, using seven interest rates and six loan amounts.

	A	B	C	D	E	F	G	H	I
1	Loan Amount:	$10,000.00							
2	Annual Interest Rate:	7.25%							
3	Pmt. Period (months):	1							
4	Number of Periods:	36							
5									
6	Payment Amount:	$309.92							
7	Total Payments:	$11,156.95							
8	Total Interest:	$1,156.95							
9					*Interest Rate*				
10		$309.92	7.00%	7.25%	7.50%	7.75%	8.00%	8.25%	8.50%
11		$9,000.00	$277.89	$278.92	$279.96	$280.99	$282.03	$283.07	$284.11
12		$9,500.00	$293.33	$294.42	$295.51	$296.60	$297.70	$298.79	$299.89
13	*Loan Amount*	$10,000.00	$308.77	$309.92	$311.06	$312.21	$313.36	$314.52	$315.68
14		$10,500.00	$324.21	$325.41	$326.62	$327.82	$329.03	$330.24	$331.46
15		$11,000.00	$339.65	$340.91	$342.17	$343.43	$344.70	$345.97	$347.24
16		$11,500.00	$355.09	$356.40	$357.72	$359.04	$360.37	$361.70	$363.03
17									
18									

Figure 10-8: Using a two-way data table to display payment amounts for various loan amounts and interest rates

To create this two-way data table do the following:

1. Enter a formula that returns the results that will be used in the data table. In this example, the formula is in cell B6. The formulas in B7:B8 are not used.

2. Enter various values for the first input in successive columns. In this example, the first input value is interest rate, and the values for various interest rates appear in C10:I10.

3. Enter various values for the second input cell in successive rows, to the left and below the input values for the first input. In this example, the second input value is loan amount, and the values for various loan amounts are in B11:B16.

4. Create a reference to the formula that will be calculated in the table. This reference goes in the upper left corner of the data table range. In this example, cell B10 contains the following formula:

   `=B6`

5. Select the rectangular range that contains the entries from the previous steps. In this example, select B10:I16.

6. Select the Data → Table command. Excel displays the Table dialog box.

7. For the Row input cell field, specify the cell reference that corresponds to the first input cell. In this example, the Row input cell is B2.

8. For the Column input cell field, specify the cell reference that corresponds to the second input cell. In this example, the Row input cell is B1.

9. Click OK. Excel inserts an array formula that uses the TABLE function with two arguments.

After you create the two-way data table, you can change the calculated cell by changing the cell reference in the upper left cell of the data table. In this example, you can change the formula in cell B10 to =B8 so the data table displays total interest rather than payment amounts.

TIP
If you find that using data tables slows down the calculation of your workbook, select Tools → Options. In the Options dialog box, click the Calculation tab and change the calculation mode to Automatic except tables.

Calculating a loan with irregular payments

So far, the loan calculation examples in this chapter have involved loans with regular periodic payments. In some cases, loan payback is irregular. For example, you may loan some money to friends or family members without formal agreements as to how they will pay the money back.

Figure 10-9 shows a worksheet set up to keep track of such a loan. The annual interest rate for the loan is stored in cell B1 (named *APR*). The original loan amount and loan date are stored in row 5. Formulas, beginning in row 6, track the loan payments and perform calculations.

	Payment Number	Payment Amount	Payment Date	Amount to Interest	Amount to Principal	Cumulative Payments	Cumulative Interest	Loan Balance
1	Interest Rate (APR):	5.50%						
2								
3								
5	Original Loan	($10,000.00)	06/01/98					$10,000.00
6	1	$200.00	07/18/98	$70.82	$129.18	$200.00	$70.82	$9,870.82
7	2	$200.00	08/02/98	$22.31	$177.69	$400.00	$93.13	$9,693.13
8	3	$200.00	09/17/98	$67.19	$132.81	$600.00	$160.32	$9,560.32
9	4	$100.00	12/02/98	$109.49	($9.49)	$700.00	$269.81	$9,569.81
10	5	$250.00	01/12/99	$59.12	$190.88	$950.00	$328.93	$9,378.93
11	Addition to Principal	($500.00)	01/25/99	$0.00	($500.00)	$950.00	$328.93	$9,878.93
12	6	$200.00	02/04/99	$32.51	$167.49	$1,150.00	$361.43	$9,711.43
13	7	$100.00	02/20/99	$23.41	$76.59	$1,250.00	$384.85	$9,634.85
14	8	$200.00	03/01/99	$13.07	$186.93	$1,450.00	$397.91	$9,447.91
15	9	$250.00	03/16/99	$21.35	$228.65	$1,700.00	$419.27	$9,219.27
16	10	$200.00	04/02/99	$23.62	$176.38	$1,900.00	$442.89	$9,042.89
17	11	$200.00	04/19/99	$23.16	$176.84	$2,100.00	$466.05	$8,866.05
18	12	$300.00	05/04/99	$20.04	$279.96	$2,400.00	$486.09	$8,586.09
19	13	$100.00	05/16/99	$15.53	$84.47	$2,500.00	$501.62	$8,501.62
20	14	$200.00	06/02/99	$21.78	$178.22	$2,700.00	$523.39	$8,323.39
21	15	$200.00	06/19/99	$21.32	$178.68	$2,900.00	$544.72	$8,144.72
22	16	$100.00	07/05/99	$19.64	$80.36	$3,000.00	$564.35	$8,064.35
23	17	$100.00	07/15/99	$12.15	$87.85	$3,100.00	$576.50	$7,976.50
24	Addition to Principal	($500.00)	09/01/99	$0.00	($500.00)	$3,100.00	$576.50	$8,476.50
25	18	$100.00	11/02/99	$79.19	$20.81	$3,200.00	$655.70	$8,455.70
26	19	$100.00	11/15/99	$16.56	$83.44	$3,300.00	$672.26	$8,372.26
27	20	$200.00	12/15/99	$37.85	$162.15	$3,500.00	$710.11	$8,210.11

Figure 10-9: This worksheet tracks loan payments that are made on an irregular basis.

Column B stores the payment amount made on the date in column C. Notice that the payments are not made on a regular basis. Also, notice that in two cases (row 11 and row 24) the payment amount is negative. These entries represent additional borrowed money added to the loan balance. Formulas in columns D and E calculate the amount of the payment credited toward interest and principal. Columns F and G keep a running tally of the cumulative payments and interest amounts. Formulas in column H compute the new loan balance after each payment. Table 10-2 lists and describes the formulas in row 6.

TABLE 10-2 FORMULAS TO CALCULATE A LOAN WITH IRREGULAR PAYMENTS

Cell	Formula	Description
D6	=IF(B6>0,(((C6-C5)/365)*H5)*APR,0)	If the payment is positive, the formula calculates the interest. If the payment is negative (an addition to the loan), the formula displays 0.
E6	=B6-D6	The formula subtracts the interest amount from the payment to calculate the amount credited to principal.
F6	=IF(B6>0,F5+B6,F5)	If the payment is positive, the formula adds the payment to the running total. If the payment is negative, the formula displays the running total following the previous payment.
G6	=IF(B6>0,G5+D6,G5)	If the payment is positive, the formula adds the interest to the running total. If the payment is negative, the formula displays the running total following the previous payment.
H6	=H5-E6	The formula calculates the new loan balance.

The workbook shown in Figure 10-9 is available on the companion CD-ROM.

Investment Calculations

Investment calculations involve calculating interest on fixed-rate investments, such as bank savings accounts, CDs, and annuities. You can make these interest calculations for investments that consist of a single deposit or multiple deposits.

The companion CD-ROM contains a workbook with all of the interest calculation examples in this section.

Future value of a single deposit

Many investments consist of a single deposit that earns interest over the term of the investment. This section describes calculations for simple interest and compound interest.

CALCULATING SIMPLE INTEREST

Simple interest refers to the fact that interest payments are not compounded. The basic formula for computing interest is

```
Interest = Principal * Rate * Term
```

For example, suppose you deposit $1,000 into a bank CD that pays a 5 percent simple annual interest rate. After one year, the CD matures and you withdraw your money. The bank adds $50, and you walk away with $1,050. In this case, the interest earned is calculated by multiplying the principal ($1,000) by the interest rate (.05) by the term (one year).

If the investment term is less than one year, the simple interest rate is adjusted accordingly, based on the term. For example, $1,000 invested in a six-month CD that pays 5 percent simple annual interest earns $25 when the CD matures. In this case, the annual interest rate multiplies by 6/12.

Figure 10-10 shows a worksheet set up to make simple interest calculations. The formula in cell B7, shown here, calculates the interest due at the end of the term:

```
=B3*B4*B5
```

Figure 10-10: This worksheet calculates simple interest payments.

The formula in B8 simply adds the interest to the original investment amount.

CALCULATING COMPOUND INTEREST

Most fixed-term investments pay interest using some type of compound interest calculation. Compound interest refers to the fact that interest is credited to the investment balance, and the investment then earns interest on the interest.

For example, suppose you deposit $1,000 into a bank CD that pays 5 percent annual interest rate, compounded monthly. Each month, the interest is calculated on the balance and that amount is credited to your account. The next month's interest calculation will be based on a higher amount since it also includes the previous month's interest payment. One way to calculate the final investment amount involves a series of formulas (see Figure 10-11).

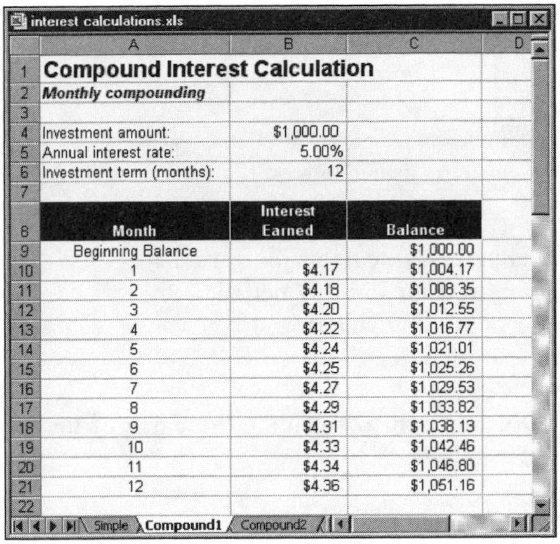

Investment amount:	$1,000.00	
Annual interest rate:	5.00%	
Investment term (months):	12	
Month	Interest Earned	Balance
Beginning Balance		$1,000.00
1	$4.17	$1,004.17
2	$4.18	$1,008.35
3	$4.20	$1,012.55
4	$4.22	$1,016.77
5	$4.24	$1,021.01
6	$4.25	$1,025.26
7	$4.27	$1,029.53
8	$4.29	$1,033.82
9	$4.31	$1,038.13
10	$4.33	$1,042.46
11	$4.34	$1,046.80
12	$4.36	$1,051.16

Figure 10-11: Using a series of formulas to calculate compound interest

Column B contains formulas to calculate the interest for one month. For example, the formula in B10 is:

```
=C9*($B$5*(1/12))
```

The formulas in column C simply add the monthly interest amount to the balance. For example, the formula in C10 is:

```
=C9+B10
```

At the end of the 12-month term, the CD balance is $1,051.16. In other words, monthly compounding results in an additional $1.16 (compared to simple interest).

You can use Excel's FV function to calculate the final investment amount without using a series of formulas. Figure 10-12 shows a worksheet set up to calculate compound interest. Cell B6 is an input cell that holds the number of compounding periods per year. For monthly compounding, the value in B6 would be 12. For quarterly compounding, the value would be 4. For daily compounding, the value would be 365. Cell B7 holds the term of the investment expressed in years.

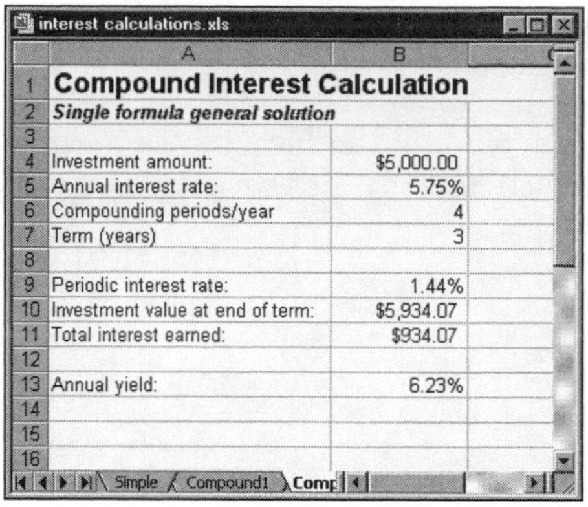

Figure 10-12: Using a single formula to calculate compound interest

Cell B9 contains the following formula that calculates the periodic interest rate. This value is the interest rate used for each compounding period.

```
=B5*(1/B6)
```

The formula in cell B10 uses the FV function to calculate the value of the investment at the end of the term. The formula is:

```
=FV(B9,B6*B7,,-B4)
```

The first argument for the FV function is the periodic interest rate, which is calculated in cell B9. The second argument represents the total number of compounding periods. The third argument (pmt) is omitted, and the fourth argument is the original investment amount (expressed as a negative value).

The total interest is calculated with a simple formula in cell B11:

```
=B10-B4
```

Another formula, in cell B13, calculates the annual yield on the investment:

```
=(B11/B4)/B7
```

For example, suppose you deposit $5,000 into a three-year CD, with a 5.75 percent annual interest rate compounded quarterly. In this case, the investment has four compounding periods per year, so you enter 4 into cell B6. The term is three years, so you enter 3 into cell B7. The formula in B10 returns $5,934.07.

Perhaps you want to see how this stacks up against a competitor's account that offers daily compounding. Figure 10-13 shows a calculation with daily compounding, using a $5,000 investment (compare this to Figure 10-11). As you can see, the difference is very small ($934.07 vs. $941.28). Over a period of three years, the account with daily compounding earns a total of $7.21 more interest.

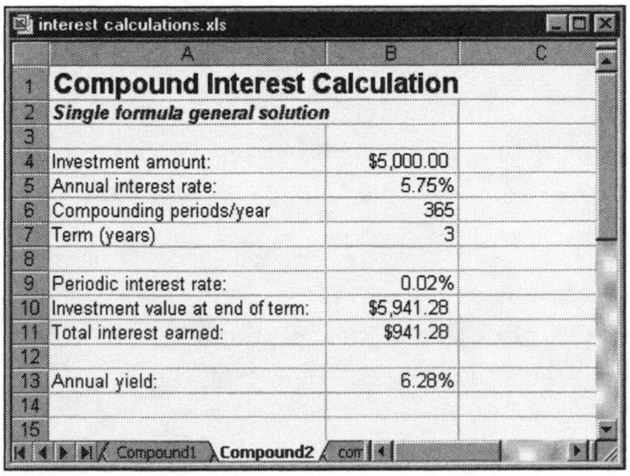

Figure 10-13: Calculating interest using daily compounding

CALCULATING INTEREST WITH CONTINUOUS COMPOUNDING

The term *continuous compounding* refers to interest that is accumulated continuously. In other words, the investment has an infinite number of compounding periods per year. The following formula calculates the future value of a $5,000 investment at 5.75 percent compounded continuously for three years:

```
=5000*EXP(0.0575*3)
```

The formula returns $5,941.36, which is an additional $0.08 compared to daily compounding.

NOTE

It's possible to calculate compound interest without using the FV function. The general formula to calculate compound interest is:

```
Principal * (1 + periodic rate) ^ number of periods
```

For example, consider a five-year, $5,000 investment that earns an annual interest rate of 5 percent compounded monthly. The formula to calculate the future value of this investment is:

```
=5000*(1+.05/12)^(12*5)
```

The Rule of 72

Need to make an investment decision, but don't have a computer handy? You can use the "Rule of 72" to determine the number of years required to double your money at a particular interest rate, using annual compounding. Just divide 72 by the interest rate. For example, consider a $10,000 investment at 6 percent interest. How many years will it take to turn that 10 grand into 20 grand? Take 72, divide it by 6, and you get 12 years. What if you can get a 7 percent interest rate? If so, you can double your money in a little over 10 years.

How accurate is the Rule of 72? The table that follows shows Rule of 72 estimated values vs. the actual values for various interest rates. As you can see, this simple rule is remarkably accurate. However, for interest rates that exceed 30 percent, the accuracy drops off considerably.

Interest Rate	Rule of 72	Actual
1%	72.00	69.66
2%	36.00	35.00
3%	24.00	23.45
4%	18.00	17.67
5%	14.40	14.21
6%	12.00	11.90
7%	10.29	10.24
8%	9.00	9.01
9%	8.00	8.04
10%	7.20	7.27
15%	4.80	4.96
20%	3.60	3.80
25%	2.88	3.11
30%	2.40	2.64

The Rule of 72 also works in reverse. For example, if you want to double your money in six years, divide 6 into 72; you'll discover that you need to find an investment that pays an annual interest rate of about 12 percent.

Future value of a series of deposits

Now, consider another type of investment, one in which you make a regular series of deposits. This type of investment is known as an *annuity*.

The worksheet functions discussed in the "Loan Calculations" section also apply to annuities, but you need to use the perspective of a lender, not a borrower. A simple example of this type of investment is a holiday club savings program offered by some companies. A fixed amount is deducted from each of your paychecks and deposited into an interest-earning account. At the end of the year, you withdraw the money (with accumulated interest) to use for holiday expenses.

Suppose you deposit $200 at the beginning of each month (for 12 months) into an account that pays 4.25 percent annual interest compounded monthly. The following formula calculates the future value of your series of deposits.

```
=FV(0.0425/12,12,-200,,1)
```

This formula returns $2,455.97, which represents the total of your deposits ($2,400) plus the interest ($55.97). The last argument for the FV function is 1, which means that you make payments at the beginning of the month. Figure 10-14 shows a worksheet set up to calculate annuities. Table 10-3 describes the contents of this sheet.

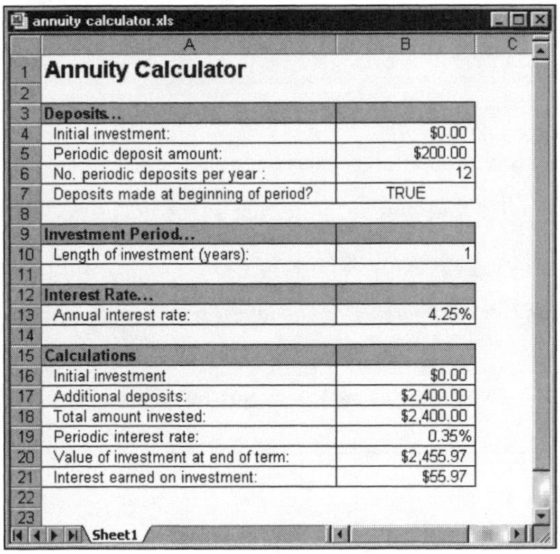

Figure 10-14: This worksheet contains formulas to calculate annuities.

The workbook shown in Figure 10-14 is available on the companion CD-ROM.

TABLE 10-3 THE ANNUITY CALCULATOR WORKSHEET

Cell	Formula	Description
B4	None (input cell)	Iinitial investment (can be 0)
B5	None (input cell)	The amount deposited on a regular basis
B6	None (input cell)	The number of deposits made in 12 months
B7	None (input cell)	TRUE if you make deposits at the beginning of period, FALSE otherwise
B10	None (input cell)	The length of the investment, in years (can be fractional)
B13	None (input cell)	The annual interest rate
B16	=B4	Displays the initial investment amount
B17	=B5*B6*B10	Calculates the total of all regular deposits
B18	=B16+B17	Adds the initial investment to the sum of the deposits
B19	=B13*(1/B6)	Calculates the periodic interest rate
B20	=FV(B19,B6*B10,-B5,-B4,IF(B7,1,0))	Calculates the future value of the investment
B21	=B20-B18	Calculates the interest earned from the investment

Depreciation Calculations

Excel offers five functions to calculate depreciation of an asset over time. Depreciating an asset places a value on the asset at a point in time, based on the original value and its useful life. The function that you choose depends on the type of depreciation method that you use.

Table 10-4 summarizes Excel's depreciation functions and the arguments used by each. For complete details, consult Excel's online Help system.

TABLE 10-4 EXCEL'S DEPRECIATION FUNCTIONS

Function	Depreciation Method	Arguments*
SLN	Straight-line. The asset depreciates by the same amount each year of its life.	Cost, Salvage, Life
DB	Declining balance. Computes depreciation at a fixed rate.	Cost, Salvage, Life, Period, [Month]
DDB	Double-declining balance. Computes depreciation at an accelerated rate. Depreciation is highest in the first period, and decreases in successive periods.	Cost, Salvage, Life, Period, Month, [Factor]
SYD	Sum of the year's digits. Allocates a large depreciation in the earlier years of an asset's life.	Cost, Salvage, Life, Period
VDB	Variable-declining balance. Computes the depreciation of an asset for any period (including partial periods) using the double-declining balance method or some other method you specify.	Cost, Salvage, Life, Start Period, End Period, [Factor], [NoSwitch]

*Arguments in brackets are optional

The arguments for the depreciation functions are described as follows:

◆ *Cost*: Original cost of the asset.

◆ *Salvage*: Salvage cost of the asset after it has fully depreciated.

◆ *Life*: Number of periods over which the asset will depreciate.

◆ *Period*: Period in the Life for which the calculation is being made.

◆ *Month*: Number of months in the first year; if omitted, Excel uses 12.

◆ *Factor*: Rate at which the balance declines; if omitted, it is assumed to be 2 (that is, double-declining).

♦ *Rate*: Interest rate per period. If you make payments monthly, for example, you must divide the annual interest rate by 12.

♦ *No-switch*: True or False. Specifies whether to switch to straight-line depreciation when depreciation is greater than the declining balance calculation.

Figure 10-15 shows depreciation calculations using the SLN, DB, DDB, and SYD functions. The asset's original cost, $10,000, is assumed to have a useful life of 10 years, with a salvage value of $1,000. The range labeled Depreciation Amount shows the annual depreciation of the asset. The range labeled Value of Asset shows the asset's depreciated value over its life.

	A	B	C	D	E	F
	depreciation.xls					
1	Asset:	Office Furniture				
2	Original Cost:	$10,000				
3	Life (years):	10				
4	Salvage Value:	$1,000				
5						
6	**Depreciation Amount**					
7	Year	SLN	DB	DDB	SYD	
8	1	$900.00	$2,060.00	$2,000.00	$1,636.36	
9	2	$900.00	$1,635.64	$1,600.00	$1,472.73	
10	3	$900.00	$1,298.70	$1,280.00	$1,309.09	
11	4	$900.00	$1,031.17	$1,024.00	$1,145.45	
12	5	$900.00	$818.75	$819.20	$981.82	
13	6	$900.00	$650.08	$655.36	$818.18	
14	7	$900.00	$516.17	$524.29	$654.55	
15	8	$900.00	$409.84	$419.43	$490.91	
16	9	$900.00	$325.41	$335.54	$327.27	
17	10	$900.00	$258.38	$268.44	$163.64	
18						
19						
20	**Value of Asset**					
21	Year	SLN	DB	DDB	SYD	
22	0	$10,000.00	$10,000.00	$10,000.00	$10,000.00	
23	1	$9,100.00	$7,940.00	$8,000.00	$8,363.64	
24	2	$8,200.00	$6,304.36	$6,400.00	$6,890.91	
25	3	$7,300.00	$5,005.66	$5,120.00	$5,581.82	
26	4	$6,400.00	$3,974.50	$4,096.00	$4,436.36	
27	5	$5,500.00	$3,155.75	$3,276.80	$3,454.55	
28	6	$4,600.00	$2,505.67	$2,621.44	$2,636.36	
29	7	$3,700.00	$1,989.50	$2,097.15	$1,981.82	
30	8	$2,800.00	$1,579.66	$1,677.72	$1,490.91	
31	9	$1,900.00	$1,254.25	$1,342.18	$1,163.64	
32	10	$1,000.00	$995.88	$1,073.74	$1,000.00	
33						

Depreciation / VBD /

Figure 10-15: A comparison of four depreciation functions

 The companion CD-ROM contains the workbook shown in Figure 10-15.

Figure 10-16 shows a chart that graphs the asset's value. As you can see, the SLN function produces a straight line; the other functions produce a curved line because the depreciation is greater in the earlier years of the asset's life.

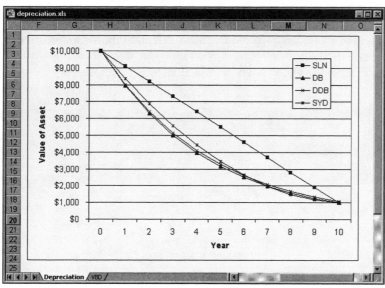

Figure 10-16: This chart shows an asset's value over time, using four depreciation functions.

The VBD function is useful if you need to calculate depreciation for multiple periods (for example, years 2 and 3). Figure 10-17 shows a worksheet set up to calculate depreciation using the VBD function. The formula in cell B12 is:

```
=VDB(B2,B4,B3,B6,B7,B8,B9)
```

	A	B	C
1	Asset:	Office Furniture	
2	Original Cost:	$10,000	
3	Life (years):	10	
4	Salvage Value:	$1,000	
5			
6	Starting Period:	0	
7	Ending Period:	3	
8	Factor:	2	
9	No-Switch:	TRUE	
10			
11			
12	Depreciation -->	$4,880.00	
13			
14			

Figure 10-17: Using the VBD function to calculate depreciation for multiple periods

The formula displays the depreciation for the first three years of an asset (starting period of 0 and ending period of 3).

Summary

This chapter presented examples of basic financial calculations for loans, investments, and depreciation.

The next chapter covers a wide variety of miscellaneous calculations.

Chapter 11

Miscellaneous Calculations

IN THIS CHAPTER

- ◆ Conversion factors for a wide variety of measurement units
- ◆ Formulas for calculating the various parts of a right triangle
- ◆ Calculations for area, surface, circumference, and volume
- ◆ Matrix functions to solve simultaneous equations
- ◆ Formulas that demonstrate various ways to round numbers

THIS CHAPTER CONTAINS reference information that may be useful to you at some point. Consider it a cheat sheet to help you remember the stuff you may have learned, but have long since forgotten.

Unit Conversions

You know the distance from New York to London in miles, but your European office needs the numbers in kilometers. What's the conversion factor? The information in this section contains many useful conversion factors that you can use in your formulas.

Excel's CONVERT function (available only when you install the Analysis ToolPak add-in) can calculate many unit conversions (refer to the online help for complete details). In some cases, however, you may find it more efficient to create your own conversion formulas. If so, you need to know the specific conversion factor for the measurement units.

Using the unit conversion tables

To convert from one measurement unit to another, locate the appropriate conversion table in this section and determine the conversion factor. For example, to convert meters to inches, use the Distance Conversion Factors table. Refer to the third row of the table (labeled Meter) and then locate the column labeled Inch. The meter-to-inch conversion factor is 39.37007874.

You can then use the conversion factor in a formula. For example, if cell A1 contains the value in meters, enter the following formula to convert it to inches:

```
=A1*39.37007874
```

Converting metric units

To convert to or from other metric units, you need to use an additional metric conversion factor from Table 11-1. To use this table, multiply the basic metric unit by the metric conversion factor. For example, consider the meter unit of distance measurement. A kilometer is 1 meter times 1E+03, or 1,000 meters. A millimeter, conversely, is 1 meter times 1E-03, or 1/1,000 meters.

 The companion CD-ROM includes a workbook that contains all of the conversion tables in this chapter.

TABLE 11-1 METRIC CONVERSION FACTORS

Metric Prefix	Metric Conversion Factor
Exa	1E+18
Peta	1E+15
Tera	1E+12
Giga	1E+09
Mega	1E+06
Kilo	1E+03
Hecto	1E+02
Deci	1E-01

Metric Prefix	Metric Conversion Factor
Centi	1E-02
Milli	1E-03
Micro	1E-06
Nano	1E-09
Pico	1E-12
Femto	1E-15
Atto	1E-18

If you want to convert from a metric unit to a nonmetric unit, *multiply* the distance conversion factor by the metric conversion factor. If you convert from a nonmetric unit to a metric unit, *divide* the distance conversion factor by the metric conversion factor.

For example, suppose cell A1 contains a value in millimeters and you need to convert it to inches. Multiply the value in A1 by the meter-to-inch conversion factor (39.37007874) and multiply the result by the metric conversion factor (1E-03). The resulting formula is:

```
=A1*39.37007874*1E-03
```

Now, assume cell A1 contains a value in inches, and you need to convert it to millimeters. In this case, the inch-to-meter distance unit conversion factor is 0.0254 and the metric conversion factor is 1E-03. The formula to convert from inches to millimeters is:

```
=A1*0.0254/1E-03
```

Distance conversions

Table 11-2 shows conversion factors for six common units of measurement. For details on using this table, see the subsection, "Using the Unit Conversion Tables" earlier in the chapter.

TABLE 11-2 DISTANCE CONVERSION FACTORS

	Foot	Inch	Meter	Nautical Mile	Statute Mile	Yard
Foot	1	12	0.3048	0.000164579	0.000189394	0.333333333
Inch	0.083333333	1	0.0254	1.37149E-05	1.57828E-05	0.0277777778
Meter	3.280839895	39.37007874	1	0.000539957	0.000621371	1.093613298
Nautical mile	6076.115486	72913.38583	1852	1	1.150779448	2025.371828
Statute mile	5280	63360	1609.344	0.868976242	1	1759.999999
Yard	3	36	0.9144	0.000493737	0.000568182	1

TABLE 11-3 WEIGHT CONVERSION FACTORS

	Gram	Ounce	Pound
Gram	1	0.035274	0.002205
Ounce	28.34952	1	0.0625
Pound	453.5923	16	1

TABLE 11-4 LIQUID MEASUREMENT CONVERSION FACTORS

	Cup	Fluid Ounce	Gallon	Liter	Pint	Quart	Table-spoon	Teaspoon
Cup	1	8	0.0625	0.23664	0.5	0.25	16	48
Fluid ounce	0.125	1	0.007813	0.02958	0.0625	0.03125	2	6
Gallon	16	128	1	3.786235	8	4	256	768
Liter	4.225833	33.80667	0.264115	1	2.112917	1.056458	67.61333	202.84
Pint	2	16	0.125	0.473279	1	0.5	32	96
Quart	4	32	0.25	0.946559	2	1	64	192
Tablespoon	0.0625	0.5	0.003906	0.01479	0.03125	0.015625	1	3
Teaspoon	0.020833	0.166667	0.001302	0.00493	0.010417	0.005208	0.333333	1

TABLE 11-5 SURFACE MEASUREMENT CONVERSION FACTORS

	Acre	Hectare	Square Foot	Square Inch	Square Meter	Square Mile	Square Yard
Acre	1	0.404685642	43560	6272640	4046.856422	0.0015625	4839.999997
Hectare	2.471053815	1	107639.1042	15500031	10000	0.003861022	11959.90046

Continued

TABLE 11-5 SURFACE MEASUREMENT CONVERSION FACTORS (*Continued*)

	Acre	Hectare	Square Foot	Square Inch	Square Meter	Square Mile	Square Yard
Square Foot	2.29568E-05	9.2903E-06	1	144	0.09290304	3.58701E-08	0.11111111
Square Inch	1.59423E-07	6.4516E-08	0.006944444	1	0.00064516	2.49098E-10	0.000771605
Square Meter	0.000247105	1E-04	10.76391042	1550.0031	1	3.86102E-07	1.195990046
Square Mile	640	258.998811	27878400	4014489600	2589988.11	1	3097599.998
Square Yard	0.000206612	8.36127E-05	9	1296	0.836127361	3.22831E-07	1

TABLE 11-6 SURFACE MEASUREMENT CONVERSION FACTORS

	Cubic Foot	Cubic Inch	Cubic Meter	Cubic Yard
Cubic Foot	1	1728	0.028316847	0.037037037
Cubic Inch	0.000578704	1	1.63871E-05	2.14335E-05
Cubic Meter	35.31466672	61023.74409	1	1.307950618
Cubic Yard	27	46656	0.764554859	1

TABLE 11–7 FORCE CONVERSION FACTORS

	Dyne	Newton	Pound Force
Dyne	1	0.00001	2.25E-06
Newton	100000	1	0.224809
Pound force	444822.2	4.448222	1

TABLE 11–8 ENERGY CONVERSION FACTORS

	BTU	Calorie (IT)	Calorie (Th'mic)	Electron Volt	Erg	Foot-pound	Horse power-hour	Joule	Watt-hour
BTU	1	251.9966	252.1655	6.59E+21	1.06E+10	25036.98	0.000393	1055.058	0.293072
Calorie (IT)	0.003968	1	1.00067	2.61E+19	41867928	99.35441	1.56E-06	4.186795	0.001163
Calorie (Th'mic)	0.003966	0.99933	1	2.61E+19	41839890	99.28787	1.56E-06	4.183991	0.001162
Electron volt	1.52E-22	3.83E-20	3.83E-20	1	1.6E-12	3.8E-18	5.97E-26	1.6E-19	4.45E-23
Erg	9.48E-11	2.39E-08	2.39E-08	6.24E+11	1	2.37E-06	3.73E-14	1E-07	2.78E-11
Foot-pound	3.99E-05	0.010065	0.010072	2.63E+17	421399.8	1	1.57E-08	0.04214	1.17E-05

Continued

TABLE 11-8 ENERGY CONVERSION FACTORS (Continued)

	BTU	Calorie (IT)	Calorie (Th'mic)	Electron Volt	Erg	Foot-pound	Horse power-hour	Joule	Watt-hour
Horsepower-hour	2544.426	641186.8	641616.4	1.68E+25	2.68E+13	63704732	1	2684517	745.6997
Joule	0.000948	0.238846	0.239006	6.24E+18	9999995	23.73042	3.73E-07	1	0.000278
Watt-hour	3.412133	859.8459	860.4221	2.25E+22	3.6E+10	85429.48	0.001341	3599.998	1

TABLE 11-9 TIME CONVERSION FACTORS

	Day	Hour	Minute	Second	Year
Day	1	24	1440	86400	0.002738
Hour	0.041667	1	60	3600	0.000114
Minute	0.000694	0.016667	1	60	1.9E-06
Second	1.16E-05	0.000278	0.016667	1	3.17E-08
Year	365.25	8766	525960	31557600	1

Weight conversions

Table 11-3 shows conversion factors for three common units of weight. For details on using this table, see the subsection "Using the Unit Conversion Tables" earlier in the chapter.

Liquid measurement conversions

Table 11-4 shows conversion factors for eight common liquid measurement units. For details on using this table, see the subsection "Using the Unit Conversion Tables" earlier in the chapter.

Surface conversions

Table 11-5 shows conversion factors for seven common units of surface (or area). For details on using this table, see the subsection "Using the Unit Conversion Tables" earlier in the chapter.

Surface measurement conversions

Table 11-6 shows conversion factors for four common surface measurement units. For details on using this table, see the subsection "Using the Unit Conversion Tables" earlier in this chapter.

Force conversions

Table 11-7 shows conversion factors for three common units of force. For details on using this table, see the subsection "Using the Unit Conversion Tables" earlier in this chapter.

Energy conversions

Table 11-8 shows conversion factors for nine common units of energy. For details on using this table, see the subsection "Using the Unit Conversion Tables" earlier in this chapter.

Time conversions

Table 11-9 shows conversion factors for five common units of time. For details on using this table, see the subsection "Using the Unit Conversion Tables" earlier in this chapter.

Temperature conversions

This section presents formulas for conversion among three units of temperature: Fahrenheit, Celsius, and Kelvin. Temperature conversions, unlike the unit conversions discussed previously in this chapter, do not use a simple conversion factor. Rather, you need to use a formula to calculate the conversion. The formulas in Table 11-10 assume that the temperature for conversion is in a cell named *temp*.

TABLE 11-10 TEMPERATURE CONVERSION FORMULAS

Type of Conversion	Formula
Fahrenheit to Celsius	=(temp-32)*(5/9)
Fahrenheit to Kelvin	=(temp-32)*(5/9)+273
Celsius to Fahrenheit	=(temp*1.8)+32
Celsius to Kelvin	=temp+273
Kelvin to Celsius	=temp-273
Kelvin to Fahrenheit	=((temp-273)*1.8)+32

Solving Right Triangles

A right triangle has six components: three sides and three angles. Figure 11-1 shows a right triangle with its various parts labeled. Angles are labeled A, B, and C; sides are labeled Hypotenuse, Base, and Height. Angle C is always 90 degrees (or PI/2 radians). If you know any two of these components (not including Angle C, which is always known), you can use formulas to solve for the others.

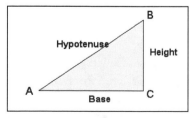

Figure 11-1: A right triangle's components

Need to Convert Other Units?

This chapter, of course, doesn't list every possible unit conversion factor. To calculate other unit conversions, you need to find the appropriate conversion factor. The Internet is a good source for such information. Use any Web search engine and enter search terms that correspond to the units you use. Likely, you'll find the information you need.

Also, you can download a copy of Josh Madison's popular (and free) Convert software. This excellent program can handle just about any conceivable unit conversion you throw at it. The URL is:

```
http://www.joshmadison.com/software/
```

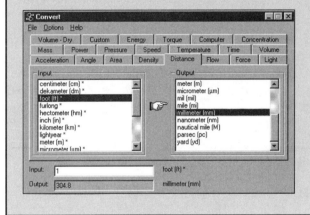

The Pythagorean theorem states that

```
Height^2 + Base^2 = Hypotenuse^2
```

Therefore, if you know two sides of a right triangle, you can calculate the remaining side. The formula to calculate a right triangle's height (given the length of the hypotenuse and base) is:

```
=SQRT(ABS((hypotenuse^2)-(base^2)))
```

The formula to calculate a right triangle's base (given the length of the hypotenuse and height) is:

```
=SQRT(ABS((hypotenuse^2)-(height^2)))
```

The formula to calculate a right triangle's hypotenuse (given the length of the base and height) is:

```
=SQRT(ABS((height^2)+(Base_Length^2)))
```

Other useful trigonometric identities are:

```
SIN(A)=Height/Hypotenuse
SIN(B)=Base/Hypotenuse
COS(A)=Base/Hypotenuse
COS(B)=Height/Hypotenuse
TAN(A)=Height/Base
SIN(A)=Base/Height
```

Excel's trigonometric functions all assume that the angle arguments are in radians. To convert degrees to radians, use the RADIANS function. To convert radians to degrees, use the DEGREES function.

If you know the height and base, you can use the following formula to calculate the angle formed by the hypotenuse and base (Angle A).

```
=ATAN(height/base)
```

The preceding formula returns radians. To convert to degrees, use this formula:

```
=DEGREES(ATAN(height/base))
```

If you know the height and base, you can use the following formula to calculate the angle formed by the hypotenuse and height (Angle B):

```
=PI()/2-ATAN(height/base)
```

The preceding formula returns radians. To convert to degrees, use this formula:

```
=90-DEGREES(ATAN(height/base))
```

The companion CD-ROM contains a workbook with formulas that calculate various parts of a right triangle — given two known parts. These formulas give you some insight on working with right triangles.

Figure 11-2 shows a workbook that contains formulas to calculate the various parts of a right triangle.

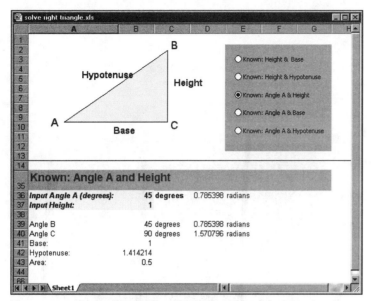

Figure 11-2: This workbook is useful for working with right triangles.

Area, Surface, Circumference, and Volume Calculations

This section contains formulas for calculating the area, surface, circumference, and volume for common two- and three-dimensional shapes.

Calculating the area and perimeter of a square

To calculate the area of a square, square the length of one side. The following formula calculates the area of a square for a cell named *side*.

```
=side^2
```

To calculate the perimeter of a square, multiply one side by 4. The following formula uses a cell named *side* to calculate the perimeter of a square.

```
=side*4
```

Calculating the area and perimeter of a rectangle

To calculate the area of a rectangle, multiply its height by its base. The following formula returns the area of a rectangle, using cells named *height* and *base*.

```
=height*base
```

To calculate the perimeter of a rectangle, multiply the height by 2, and add it to the width multiplied by 2. The following formula returns the perimeter of a rectangle, using cells named *height* and *width*.

```
=(height*2)+(width*2)
```

Calculating the area and perimeter of a circle

To calculate the area of a circle, multiply the square of the radius by π. The following formula returns the area of a circle. It assumes that a cell named *radius* contains the circle's radius.

```
=PI()*(radius^2)
```

The radius of a circle is equal to one-half of the diameter.

To calculate the circumference of a circle, multiply the diameter of the circle by π. The following formula calculates the circumference of a circle using a cell named *diameter*.

```
=diameter*PI()
```

The diameter of a circle is the radius times 2.

Calculating the area of a trapezoid

To calculate the area of a trapezoid, add the two parallel sides, multiply by the height, and then divide by 2. The following formula calculates the area of a trapezoid, using cells named *side* and *height*.

```
=((side*2)*height)/2
```

Calculating the area of a triangle

To calculate the area of a triangle, multiply the base by the height, and then divide by 2. The following formula calculates the area of a triangle, using cells named *base* and *height*.

```
=(base*height)/2
```

Calculating the surface and volume of a sphere

To calculate the surface of a sphere, multiply the square of the radius by π, and then multiply by 4. The following formula returns the surface of a sphere, the radius of which is in a cell named *radius*:

```
=PI()*(radius^2)*4
```

To calculate the volume of a sphere, multiply the cube of the radius by 4 times π, and then divide by 3. The following formula calculates the volume of a sphere. The cell named *radius* contains the sphere's radius.

```
=((radius^4)*(4*PI()))/3
```

Calculating the surface and volume of a cube

To calculate the surface area of a cube, square one side and multiply by 6. The following formula calculates the surface of a cube using a cell named *side*, which contains the length of a side of the cube:

```
=(side^2)*6
```

To calculate the volume of a cube, raise the length of one side to the third power. The following formula returns the volume of a cube, using a cell named *side*:

```
=side^3
```

Calculating the surface and volume of a cone

The following formula calculates the surface of a cone (including the surface of the base). This formula uses cells named *radius* and *height*:

```
=PI()*radius*(SQRT(height^2+radius^2)+radius))
```

To calculate the volume of a cone, multiply the square of the radius of the base by π, multiply by the height, and then divide by 3. The following formula returns the volume of a cone, using cells named *radius* and *height*:

```
=(PI()*(radius^2)*height)/3
```

Calculating the volume of a cylinder

To calculate the volume of a cylinder, multiply the square of the radius of the base by π, and then multiply by the height. The following formula calculates the volume of a cylinder, using cells named *radius* and *height*:

```
=(PI()*(radius^2)*height)
```

Calculating the volume of a pyramid

Calculate the area of the base, then multiply by the height and divide by 3. This next formula calculates the volume of a pyramid. It assumes cells named *width* (the width of the base), *length* (the length of the base), and *height* (the height of the pyramid).

```
=(width*length*height)/3
```

Solving Simultaneous Equations

This section describes how to use formulas to solve simultaneous linear equations. The following is an example of a set of simultaneous linear equations:

```
3x + 4y = 8
4x + 8y = 1
```

Solving a set of simultaneous equations involves finding the values for x and y that satisfy both equations. For this set of equations, the solution is as follows:

```
x = 7.5
y = -3.625
```

The number of variables in the set of equations must be equal to the number of equations. The preceding example uses two equations with two variables. Three equations are required to solve for three variables (x, y, and z).

The general steps for solving a set of simultaneous equations follow. See Figure 11-3, which uses the equations presented at the beginning of this section.

1. Express the equations in standard form. If necessary, use simple algebra to rewrite the equations such that the variables all appear on the left side of the equal sign. The two equations that follow are identical, but the second one is in standard form.

   ```
   3x -8 = -4y
   3x + 4y = 8
   ```

2. Place the coefficients in an n-by-n range of cells, where n represents the number of equations. In Figure 11-3, the coefficients are in the range G6:H7.

3. Place the constants (the numbers on the right side of the equal sign) in a vertical range of cells. In Figure 11-3, the constants are in the range J6:J7.

4. Use an array formula to calculate the inverse of the coefficient matrix. In Figure 11-3, the following array formula is entered into the range G10:H11.

```
{=MINVERSE(G6:H7)}
```

5. Use an array formula to multiply the inverse of the coefficient matrix by the constant matrix. In Figure 11-3, the following array formula is entered into the range H14:H15. This range holds the solution.

```
{=MMULT(G10:H11,J6:J7)}
```

Chapter 14 demonstrates how to use iteration to solve some simultaneous equations.

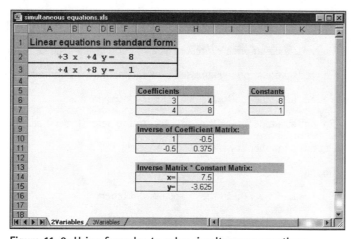

Figure 11-3: Using formulas to solve simultaneous equations

You can access the workbook shown in Figure 11-3 on the companion CD-ROM. This workbook solves simultaneous equations with two or three variables.

Rounding Numbers

Excel provides quite a few functions that round values in various ways. Table 11-11 summarizes these functions.

It's important to understand the difference between rounding a value and formatting a value. When you format a number to display a specific number of decimal places, formulas that refer to that number use the actual value — which may differ from the displayed value. When you round a number, formulas that refer to that value use the rounded number.

TABLE 11-11 EXCEL'S ROUNDING FUNCTIONS

Function	Description
CEILING	Rounds a number up (away from zero) to the nearest specified multiple
DOLLARDE*	Converts a dollar price expressed as a fraction into a decimal number
DOLLARFE*	Converts a dollar price expressed as a decimal into a fractional number
EVEN	Rounds a number up to the nearest even integer
FLOOR	Rounds a number down (toward zero) to the nearest specified multiple
INT	Rounds a number down to make it an integer
MROUND*	Rounds a number to a specified multiple
ODD	Rounds a number up to the nearest odd integer
ROUND	Rounds a number to a specified number of digits
ROUNDDOWN	Rounds a number down (toward zero) to a specified number of digits
ROUNDUP	Rounds a number up (away from zero) to a specified number of digits
TRUNC	Truncates a number to a specified number of significant digits

In the above table, there is an asterisk next to some of the functions. This means that the function is only available when the Analysis ToolPak add-in is installed.

Chapter 6 contains examples of rounding time values.

The following sections provide examples of formulas that use various types of rounding.

Basic rounding formulas

The ROUND function is useful for basic rounding to a specified number of digits. You specify the number of digits in the second argument for the ROUND function. For example, the formula that follows returns 123.40 (the value is rounded to one decimal place).

=ROUND(123.37,1)

If the second argument for the ROUND function is zero, the value is rounded to the nearest integer. The formula that follows, for example, returns 123.00.

=ROUND(123.37,0)

The second argument for the ROUND function can also be negative. In such a case, the number is rounded to the left of the decimal point. The following formula, for example, returns 123.00.

=ROUND(123.37,-1)

The ROUND function rounds either up or down. But how does it handle a number such as 12.5, rounded to no decimal places? You'll find that the ROUND function rounds such numbers away from zero. The formula that follows, for instance, returns 13.0.

=ROUND(12.5,0)

The next formula returns -13.00 (the rounding occurs away from zero).

=ROUND(-12.5,0)

To force rounding to occur in a particular direction, use the ROUNDUP or ROUNDDOWN functions. The following formula, for example, returns 12.0. The value rounds down.

```
=ROUNDDOWN(12.5,0)
```

The formula that follows returns 13.0. The value rounds up to the nearest whole value.

```
=ROUNDUP(12.43,0)
```

Rounding to the nearest multiple

The MROUND function (part of the Analysis ToolPak add-in) is useful for rounding values to the nearest multiple. For example, you can use this function to round a number to the nearest 5 (133 rounded to the nearest 5 is 135).

Rounding dollar values

Often, you need to round dollar values to the nearest penny. For example, a calculated price may be something like $45.78923. In such a case, you should round the calculated price to an even penny. This may sound simple, but there are actually three ways to round such a value:

◆ Round it up to the nearest penny.

◆ Round it down to the nearest penny.

◆ Round it to the nearest penny (the rounding may be up or down).

The following formula assumes a dollars and cents value is in cell A1. The formula rounds the value to the nearest penny. For example, if cell A1 contains $12.421, the formula returns $12.42.

```
=ROUND(A1,2)
```

If you need to round the value up to the nearest penny, use the CEILING function. The following formula rounds the value in cell A1 up to the nearest penny. If, for example, cell A1 contains $12.421, the formula returns $12.43.

```
=CEILING(A1,0.01)
```

To round a dollar value down, use the FLOOR function. The following formula, for example, rounds the dollar value in cell A1 down to the nearest penny. If cell A1 contains $12.421, the formula returns $12.42.

```
=FLOOR(A1,0.01)
```

To round a dollar value up to the nearest nickel, use this formula:

```
=CEILING(A1,0.05)
```

Working with fractional dollars

The DOLLARFR and DOLLARDE functions are useful when working with fractional dollar value, as in stock market quotes. To access these functions, you must install the Analysis ToolPak add-in.

Consider the value $9.25. You can express the decimal part as a fractional value ($9 1/4, $9 2/8, $9 4/16, and so on). The DOLLARFR function takes two arguments: the dollar amount and the denominator for the fractional part. The following formula, for example, returns 9.1 (the .1 decimal represents 1/4).

```
=DOLLARFR(9.25,4)
```

It's important to understand that you cannot use the value returned by the DOLLARFR function in other calculations. To perform calculations on such a value, you need to convert it back to a decimal value by using the DOL-LARDE function.

The DOLLARDE function converts a dollar value expressed as a fraction to a decimal amount. It also uses a second argument to specify the denominator of the fractional part. The following formula, for example, returns 9.25.

```
=DOLLARDE(9.1,4)
```

The DOLLARDE and DOLLARFR functions aren't limited to dollar values. For example, you can use these functions to work with feet and inches. You might have a value that represents 8.5 feet. Use the following formula to express this value in terms of feet and inches. The formula returns 8.06 (which represents 8 feet, six inches).
```
=DOLLARFR(8.5,12)
```

Using the INT and TRUNC functions

On the surface, the INT and TRUNC functions seem similar. Both convert a value to an integer. The TRUNC function simply removes the fractional part of a number. The INT function rounds a number down to the nearest integer, based on the value of the fractional part of the number.

In practice, INT and TRUNC return different results only when using negative numbers. For example, the following formula returns -14.0:

```
=TRUNC(-14.2)
```

The next formula returns -15.0 because -14.3 is rounded down to the next lower integer.

```
=INT(-14.2)
```

The TRUNC function takes an additional (optional) argument that's useful for truncating decimal values. For example, the formula that follows returns 54.33 (the value truncated to two decimal places):

```
=TRUNC(54.3333333,2)
```

Rounding to an even or odd integer

The ODD and EVEN functions are provided for situations in which you need to round a number up to the nearest odd or even integer. These functions take a single argument and return an integer value. The EVEN function rounds its argument up to the nearest even integer. The ODD function rounds its argument up to the nearest odd integer. Table 11-12 shows some examples of these functions.

TABLE 11-12 RESULTS USING THE EVEN AND ODD FUNCTIONS

Number	EVEN Function	ODD Function
-3.6	-4	-5
-3.0	-4	-3
-2.4	-4	-3
-1.8	-2	-3
-1.2	-2	-3
-0.6	-2	-1
0.0	0	1

Number	EVEN Function	ODD Function
0.6	2	1
1.2	2	3
1.8	2	3
2.4	4	3
3.0	4	3
3.6	4	5

Rounding to n significant digits

In some cases, you may need to round a value to a particular number of significant digits. For example, you might want to express the value 1,432,187 in terms of two significant digits (that is, as 1,400,000). The value 9,187,877 expressed in terms of three significant digits is 9,180,000.

If the value is an integer, the following formula does the job. This formula rounds the integer in cell A1 to two significant digits. To round to a different number of significant digits, replace the 2 in this formula with a different number.

```
=ROUNDDOWN(A1,2-LEN(A1))
```

For nonintegers, the solution gets a bit trickier. The formula that follows provides a more general solution that rounds the value in cell A1 to the number of significant digits specified in cell A2. This formula works for both integers and nonintegers.

```
=ROUND(A1,A2-1-INT(LOG10(ABS(A1))))
```

For example, if cell A1 contains 1.27845 and cell A2 contains 3, the formula returns 1.28000 (the value, rounded to three significant digits).

Summary

This chapter covered several topics: unit conversions, trigonometric formulas, calculations for various two- and three-dimensional shapes, simultaneous equations, and rounding.

In the next chapter, we turn to array formulas.

Part III

Array Formulas

Chapter 12

Introducing Arrays

IN THIS CHAPTER

◆ The definition of an array and an array formula

◆ One-dimensional versus two-dimensional arrays

◆ How to work with array constants

◆ Techniques for working with array formulas

◆ Examples of multicell array formulas

◆ Examples of array formulas that occupy a single cell

One of Excel's most interesting (and most powerful) features is its ability to work with arrays in a formula. Although Excel is no longer unique in this area (recent versions of Quattro Pro also support arrays), its implementation is still the most elegant. This chapter introduces the concept of arrays and is required reading for anyone who wants to become a master of Excel formulas. Chapter 13 continues with lots of useful examples.

Array Formulas

If you do any computer programming, you've probably been exposed to the concept of an array. An *array* is simply a collection of items operated on collectively or individually. In Excel, an array can be one-dimensional or two-dimensional. These dimensions correspond to rows and columns. For example, a *one-dimensional array* can be stored in a range that consists of one row (a horizontal array) or one column (a vertical array). A *two-dimensional array* can be stored in a rectangular range of cells. Excel doesn't support three-dimensional arrays.

But, as you'll see, arrays need not be stored in cells. You can also work with arrays that exist only in Excel's memory. You can then use an *array formula* to manipulate this information and return a result. An array formula can occupy multiple cells, or reside in a single cell.

This section presents two examples of array formulas. One is of an array formula that occupies multiple cells, and the other is of another array formula that occupies only one cell.

A multicell array formula

Figure 12-1 shows a simple worksheet set up to calculate product sales. Normally, you would calculate the value in column D (total sales per product) with a formula such as the one that follows, and then copy this formula down the column.

```
=B2*C2
```

After copying the formula, the worksheet contains six formulas in column D.

Figure 12-1: The range D2:D7 contains a single array formula.

	A	B	C	D	E
1	Product	Units Sold	Unit Price	Total	
2	AR-988	3	$50	$150	
3	BZ-011	10	$100	$1,000	
4	MR-919	5	$20	$100	
5	TR-811	9	$10	$90	
6	TS-333	3	$60	$180	
7	ZL-001	1	$200	$200	
8					
9					
10					

Another alternative uses a *single* formula (an array formula) to calculate all six values in D2:D7. This single formula occupies six cells and returns an array of six values.

To create a single array formula to perform the calculations do the following:

1. Select a range to hold the results. In this case, the range is D2:D7.

2. Enter the following formula:

   ```
   =B2:B7*C2:C7
   ```

3. Normally, you press Enter to enter a formula. Because this is an array formula, press Ctrl+Shift+Enter.

The formula is entered into all six of the selected cells. If you examine the formula bar, you'll see the following:

```
{=B2:B7*C2:C7}
```

Excel places brackets around the formula to indicate that it's an array formula.

This formula performs its calculations and returns a six-item array. The array formula actually works with two other arrays, both of which happen to be stored in ranges. The values for the first array are stored in B2:B7, and the values for the second array are stored in C2:C7.

Because it's not possible to display more than one value in a single cell, six cells are required to display the resulting array. That explains why you selected six cells before you entered the array formula.

This array formula, of course, returns exactly the same values as these six normal formulas entered into individual cells in D2:D7:

```
=B2*C2
=B3*C3
=B4*C4
=B5*C5
=B6*C6
=B7*C7
```

Using a single array formula rather than individual formulas does offer a few advantages:

◆ It's a good way of ensuring that all formulas in a range are identical.

◆ Using a multicell array formula makes it less likely you will overwrite a formula accidentally. You cannot change one cell in a multicell array formula.

◆ Using a multicell array formula will almost certainly prevent novices from tampering with your formulas.

A single-cell array formula

Now, it's time to take a look at a single-cell array formula. Refer again to Figure 12-1. The following array formula occupies a single cell:

```
{=SUM(B2:B7*C2:C7)}
```

You can enter this formula into any cell. But when you enter this formula, make sure you use Ctrl+Shift+Enter (and don't type the brackets).

This array formula returns the sum of the total product sales. It's important to understand that this formula does not rely on the information in column D. In fact, you can delete column D and the formula will still work.

This formula works with two arrays, both of which are stored in cells. The first array is stored in B2:B7, and the second array is stored in C2:C7. The formula multiplies the corresponding values in these two arrays and creates a new array (which exists only in memory). The SUM function then operates on this new array and returns the sum of its values.

Creation of an array constant

The examples in the previous section used arrays stored in worksheet ranges. The examples in this section demonstrate an important concept: An array does not have to be stored in a range of cells. This type of array, which is stored in memory, is referred to as an *array constant*.

You create an array constant by listing its items and surrounding them with brackets. Here's an example of a five-item vertical array constant:

{1,0,1,0,1}

The following formula uses the SUM function, with the preceding array constant as its argument. The formula returns the sum of the values in the array (which is 3).

=SUM({1,0,1,0,1})

 When you specify an array directly (as shown previously), you must provide the brackets around the array elements. When you enter an array formula, on the other hand, you do not supply the brackets.

At this point, you probably don't see any advantage to using an array constant. The formula that follows, for example, returns the same result as the previous formula.

=SUM(1,0,1,0,1)

Following is a formula that uses two array constants:

=SUM({1,2,3,4}*{5,6,7,8})

This formula creates a new array (in memory) that consists of the product of the corresponding elements in the two arrays. The new array is:

{5,12,21,32}

This new array is then used as an argument for the SUM function, which returns the result (70). The formula is equivalent to the following formula, which doesn't use arrays:

=SUM(1*5,2*6,3*7,4*8)

A formula can work with both an array constant and an array stored in a range. The following formula, for example, returns the sum of the values in A1:D1, each multiplied by the corresponding element in the array constant.

```
=SUM((A1:D1*{1,2,3,4}))
```

This formula is equivalent to:

```
=SUM(A1*1,B1*2,C1*3,D1*4)
```

Array constant elements

An array constant can contain numbers, text, logical values (TRUE or FALSE), and even error values such as #N/A. Numbers can be in integer, decimal, or scientific format. You must enclose text in double quotation marks (for example, "Tuesday"). You can use different types of values in the same array constant, as in this example:

```
{1,2,3,TRUE,FALSE,TRUE,"Moe","Larry","Shemp"}
```

An array constant cannot contain formulas, functions, or other arrays. Numeric values cannot contain dollar signs, commas, parentheses, or percent signs. For example, the following is an invalid array constant:

```
{SQRT(32),$56.32,12.5%}
```

Dimensions of an Array

As stated previously, an array can be either one-dimensional or two-dimensional. A one-dimensional array's orientation can be either vertical or horizontal.

One-dimensional horizontal arrays

The elements in a one-dimensional horizontal array are separated by commas. The following example is a one-dimensional horizontal array constant:

```
{1,2,3,4,5}
```

To display this array in a range requires five cells in a row. To enter this array into a range, select a range of cells that consists of one row and five columns. Then, enter ={1,2,3,4,5} and press Ctrl+Shift+Enter.

If you enter this array into a horizontal range that consists of more than five cells, the extra cells will contain #NA (which denotes unavailable values). If you enter this array into a *vertical* range of cells, only the first item (1) will appear in each cell.

The following example is another horizontal array; it has seven elements and is made up of text strings:

```
{"Sun","Mon","Tue","Wed","Thu","Fri","Sat"}
```

One-dimensional vertical arrays

The elements in a one-dimensional vertical array are separated by semicolons. The following is a six-element vertical array constant:

```
{10;20;30;40;50;60}
```

Displaying this array in a range requires six cells in a column. To enter this array into a range, select a range of cells that consists of six rows and one column. Then, enter ={10;20;30;40;50;60} and press Ctrl+Shift+Enter.

The following is another example of a vertical array; this one has four elements:

```
{"Widgets";"Sprockets";"Do-Dads";"Thing-A-Majigs"}
```

Two-dimensional arrays

A two-dimensional array uses commas to separate its horizontal elements, and semicolons to separate its vertical elements. The following example shows a 3 × 4 array constant.

```
{1,2,3,4;5,6,7,8;9,10,11,12}
```

To display this array in a range requires 12 cells. To enter this array into a range, select a range of cells that consists of three rows and four columns. Then, type ={1,2,3,4;5,6,7,8;9,10,11,12} and press Ctrl+Shift+Enter. Figure 12-2 shows how this array appears when entered into a range.

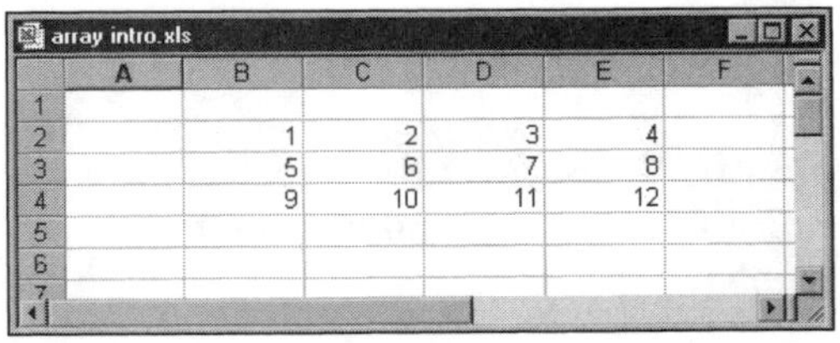

Figure 12-2: A 3 × 4 array, entered into a range of cells

If you enter an array into a range that has more cells than array elements, Excel displays #NA into the extra cells. Figure 12-3 shows a 3 × 4 array entered into a 10 × 5 cell range.

	A	B	C	D	E	F	G
1							
2		1	2	3	4	#N/A	
3		5	6	7	8	#N/A	
4		9	10	11	12	#N/A	
5		#N/A	#N/A	#N/A	#N/A	#N/A	
6		#N/A	#N/A	#N/A	#N/A	#N/A	
7		#N/A	#N/A	#N/A	#N/A	#N/A	
8		#N/A	#N/A	#N/A	#N/A	#N/A	
9		#N/A	#N/A	#N/A	#N/A	#N/A	
10		#N/A	#N/A	#N/A	#N/A	#N/A	
11		#N/A	#N/A	#N/A	#N/A	#N/A	
12							
13							

Figure 12–3: A 3 × 4 array, entered into a 10 × 5 cell range

Each row of a two-dimensional array must contain the same number of items. The array that follows, for example, is not valid because the third row contains only two items:

```
{1,2,3,4;5,6,7,8;9,10,11}
```

Naming Array Constants

You can create an array constant, give it a name, and then use this named array in a formula. Technically, a named array is a named formula.

Chapter 3 covers the topic of names and named formulas in detail.

Figure 12-4 shows a named array being created using the Define Name dialog box. The name of the array is *DayNames*, and it refers to the following array:

```
{"Sun","Mon","Tue","Wed","Thu","Fri","Sat"}
```

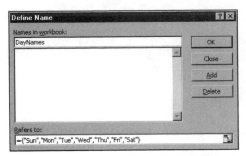

Figure 12-4: Creating a named array constant

Notice that, in the Define Name dialog box, the array is defined using a leading equal sign (=). Without this equal sign, the array is interpreted as a text string rather than an array. Also, you must type the brackets when defining a named array constant; Excel does not enter them for you.

After creating this named array, you can use it in a formula. Figure 12-5 shows a worksheet that contains a single array formula entered into the range A1:G1. The formula is:

```
{=DayNames}
```

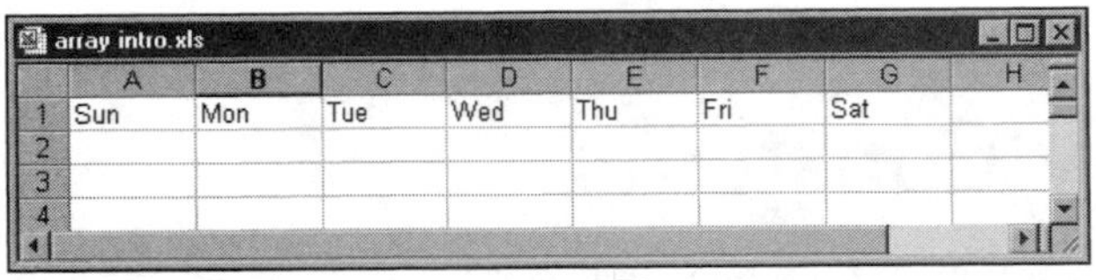

Figure 12-5: Using a named array in an array formula

Because commas separate the array elements, the array has a horizontal orientation. Use semicolons to create a vertical array. Or you can use Excel's TRANSPOSE function to insert a horizontal array into a vertical range of cells (see "Transposing an Array," later in this chapter).

You also can access individual elements from the array by using Excel's INDEX function. The following formula, for example, returns *Wed*, the fourth item in the *DayNames* array:

```
=INDEX(DayNames,4)
```

Working with Array Formulas

This section deals with the mechanics of selecting cells that contain arrays, and entering and editing array formulas. These procedures differ a bit from working with ordinary ranges and formulas.

Entering an array formula

When you enter an array formula into a cell or range, you must follow a special procedure so Excel knows that you want an array formula rather than a normal formula. You enter a normal formula into a cell by pressing Enter. You enter an array formula into one or more cells by pressing Ctrl+Shift+Enter.

You can easily identify an array formula, because the formula is enclosed in brackets in the formula bar. The following formula, for example, is an array formula:

```
{=SUM(LEN(A1:A5))}
```

Don't enter the brackets when you create an array formula; Excel inserts them for you. If the result of an array formula consists of more than one value, you must select all of the cells in the results range *before* you enter the formula. If you fail to do this, only the first element of the result is returned.

Selecting an array formula range

You can select the cells that contain a multicell array formula manually, by using the normal cell selection procedures. Or, you can use either of the following methods:

♦ Activate any cell in the array formula range. Select Edit→Go To (or press F5), click the Special button, and then choose the Current Array option. Click OK to close the dialog box.

♦ Activate any cell in the array formula range and press Ctrl+/ to select the entire array.

Editing an array formula

If an array formula occupies multiple cells, you must edit the entire range as though it is a single cell. The key point to remember is that you can't change just one element of an array formula. If you attempt to do so, Excel displays the messages shown in Figure 12-6.

Figure 12-6: Excel's warning message reminds you that you can't edit
just one cell of a multicell array formula.

The following rules apply to multicell array formulas. (If you try to do any of
these things, Excel lets you know about it.)

◆ You can't change the contents of any individual cell that makes up an
array formula.

◆ You can't move cells that make up part of an array formula (but you can
move an entire array formula).

◆ You can't delete cells that form part of an array formula (but you can
delete an entire array).

◆ You can't insert new cells into an array range. This rule includes inserting
rows or columns that would add new cells to an array range.

To edit an array formula, select all the cells in the array range and activate the
formula bar as usual (click it or press F2). Excel removes the brackets from the formula while you edit it. Edit the formula and then press Ctrl+Shift+Enter to enter the
changes. All of the cells in the array now reflect your editing changes.

 If you fail to press Ctrl+Shift+Enter after editing an array formula, the formula will no longer be an array formula...

You can't change any individual cell that makes up a multicell array formula.
However, you can apply formatting to the entire array or to only parts of it.

Expanding or contracting a multicell array formula

Often, you may need to expand a multicell array formula (to include more cells) or contract it (to include fewer cells). Doing so requires a few steps:

1. Select the entire range that contains the array formula.

2. Press F2 to enter Edit mode.

3. Press Ctrl+Enter. This step enters an identical (non-array) formula into each selected cell.

4. Change your range selection to include additional or fewer cells.

5. Press F2.

6. Press Ctrl+Shift+Enter.

Array Formulas: The Downside

If you've followed along in this chapter, you probably understand some of the advantages of using array formulas. The main advantage, of course, is that an array formula enables you to perform otherwise impossible calculations. As you gain more experience with arrays, you undoubtedly will discover some disadvantages.

Array formulas are one of the least understood features of Excel. Consequently, if you plan to share a workbook with someone who may need to make modifications, you should probably avoid using array formulas. Encountering an array formula when you don't know what it is can be very confusing.

You may also discover that you can easily forget to enter an array formula by pressing Ctrl+Shift+Enter. If you edit an existing array, you still must use these keys to complete the edits. Except for logical errors, this is probably the most common problem that users have with array formulas. If you press Enter by mistake after editing an array formula, just double-click the cell to get back into Edit mode, and then press Ctrl+Shift+Enter.

Another potential problem with array formulas is that they can slow your worksheet's recalculations, especially if you use very large arrays. On a faster system, this may not be a problem. But, conversely, using an array formula is almost always faster than using a custom VBA function.

Multicell Array Formulas

This section contains examples that demonstrate additional features of array formulas that are entered into a range of cells. These features include creating arrays from values, performing operations, using functions, transposing arrays, and generating consecutive integers.

Creating an array from values in a range

The following array formula creates an array from a range of cells. Figure 12-7 shows a workbook with some data entered into A1:C4. The range D8:F11 contains a single array formula:

```
{=A1:C4}
```

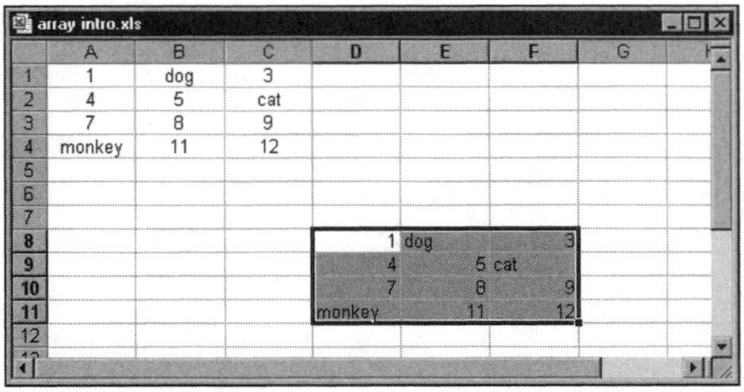

Figure 12-7: Creating an array from a range

The array in D8:F11 is linked to the range A1:C4. Change any value in A1:C4 and the corresponding cell in D8:F11 reflects that change.

Creating an array constant from values in a range

In the previous example, the array formula in D8:F11 essentially created a link to the cells in A1:C4. It's possible to "sever" this link and create an array constant made up of the values in A1:C4.

To do so, select the cells that contain the array formula (the range D8:F11, in this example). Then press F2 to edit the array formula. Press F9 to convert the cell references to values. Press Ctrl+Shift+Enter to reenter the array formula (which now uses an array constant). The array constant is:

{1,"dog",3;4,5,"cat";7,8,9;"monkey",11,12}

Figure 12-8 shows how this looks in the formula bar.

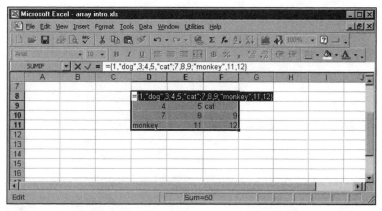

Figure 12-8: After pressing F9, the formula bar displays the array constant.

Performing operations on an array

So far, most of the examples in this chapter simply entered arrays into ranges. The following array formula creates a rectangular array and multiplies each array element by 2:

{={1,2,3,4;5,6,7,8;9,10,11,12}*2}

Figure 12-9 shows the result when you enter this formula into a range.

	A	B	C	D	E	F	G
15							
16							
17		2	4	6	8		
18		10	12	14	16		
19		18	20	22	24		
20							
21							

Figure 12-9: Performing a mathematical operation on an array

The following array formula multiplies each array element by itself. Figure 12-10 shows the result when you enter this formula into a range.

{={1,2,3,4;5,6,7,8;9,10,11,12}*{1,2,3,4;5,6,7,8;9,10,11,12}}

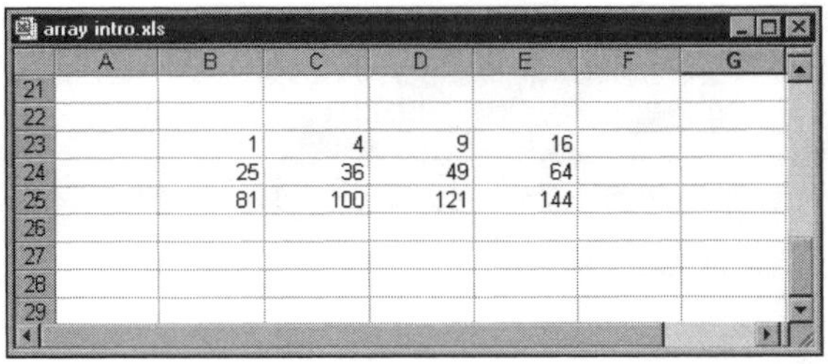

Figure 12-10: Multiplying each array element by itself

The following array formula is a simpler way of obtaining the same result:

```
{={1,2,3,4;5,6,7,8;9,10,11,12}^2}
```

If the array is stored in a range (such as A1:C4), the array formula returns the square of each value in the range, as follows:

```
{=A1:C4^2}
```

Using functions with an array

As you might expect, you also can use functions with an array. The following array formula, which you can enter into a 10-cell vertical range, calculates the square root of each array element:

```
{=SQRT({1;2;3;4;5;6;7;8;9;10})}
```

If the array is stored in a range, an array formula such as the one that follows returns the square root of each value in the range:

```
{=SQRT(A1:C4)}{=SQRT(A1:A10)}
```

Transposing an array

When you transpose an array, you essentially convert rows to columns and columns to rows. In other words, you can convert a horizontal array to a vertical array (and vice versa). Use Excel's TRANSPOSE function to transpose an array.

Consider the following one-dimensional horizontal array constant:

```
{1,2,3,4,5}
```

You can enter this array into a vertical range of cells by using the TRANSPOSE function. To do so, select a range of five cells that occupy five rows and one column. Then, enter the following formula and press Ctrl+Shift+Enter:

```
=TRANSPOSE({1,2,3,4,5})
```

The horizontal array is transposed, and the array elements appear in the vertical range.

Transposing a two-dimensional array works in a similar manner. Figure 12-11 shows a two-dimensional array entered into a range normally, and entered into a range using the TRANSPOSE function. The formula in A1:D3 is:

```
{={1,2,3,4;5,6,7,8;9,10,11,12}}
```

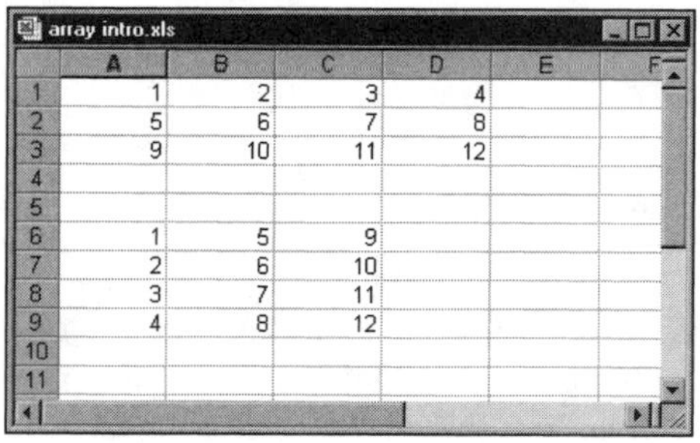

Figure 12-11: Using the TRANSPOSE function to transpose a rectangular array

The formula in A6:C9 is:

```
{=TRANSPOSE({1,2,3,4;5,6,7,8;9,10,11,12})}
```

You can, of course, use the TRANSPOSE function to transpose an array stored in a range. The following formula, for example, uses an array stored in A1:C4 (four rows, three columns). You can enter this array formula into a range that consists of three rows and four columns.

```
{=TRANSPOSE(A1:C4)}
```

Generating an array of consecutive integers

As you will see in Chapter 13, it's often useful to generate an array of consecutive integers for use in an array formula. Excel's ROW function, which returns a row number, is ideal for this. Consider the array formula shown here, entered into a vertical range of 12 cells:

```
{=ROW(1:12)}
```

This formula generates a 12-element array that contains integers from 1 to 12. To demonstrate, select a range that consists of 12 rows and one column, and enter the array formula into the range. You'll find that the range is filled with 12 consecutive integers (see Figure 12-12).

	A	B	C	D
1				
2		1		
3		2		
4		3		
5		4		
6		5		
7		6		
8		7		
9		8		
10		9		
11		10		
12		11		
13		12		
14				

Figure 12–12: Using an array formula to generate consecutive integers

If you want to generate an array of consecutive integers, a formula like the one shown previously is good — but not perfect. To see the problem, insert a new row above the range that contains the array formula. You'll find that Excel adjusts the row references so the array formula now reads:

```
{=ROW(2:13)}
```

The formula that originally generated integers from 1 to 12 now generates integers from 2 to 13.

For a better solution, use this formula:

```
{=ROW(INDIRECT("1:12"))}
```

This formula uses the INDIRECT function, which takes a text string as its argument. Excel does not adjust the references contained in the argument for the INDIRECT function. Therefore, this array formula *always* returns integers from 1-12.

 Chapter 13 contains several examples that use the technique for generating consecutive integers.

> ## Worksheet Functions That Return an Array
>
> Several of Excel's worksheet functions use arrays; you must enter a formula that uses one of these functions into multiple cells as an array formula. These functions are FORECAST, FREQUENCY, GROWTH, LINEST, LOGEST, MINVERSE, MMULT, and TREND. Consult the online help for more information.

Single-Cell Array Formulas

The examples in the previous section all used a multicell array formula — a single array formula entered into a range of cells. The real power of using arrays becomes apparent when you use single-cell array formulas. This section contains examples of array formulas that occupy a single cell.

Counting characters in a range

Suppose you have a range of cells that contains text entries (see Figure 12-13). If you need to get a count of the total number of characters in that range, the "traditional" method involves creating a formula like the one that follows and copying it down the column:

`=LEN(A1)`

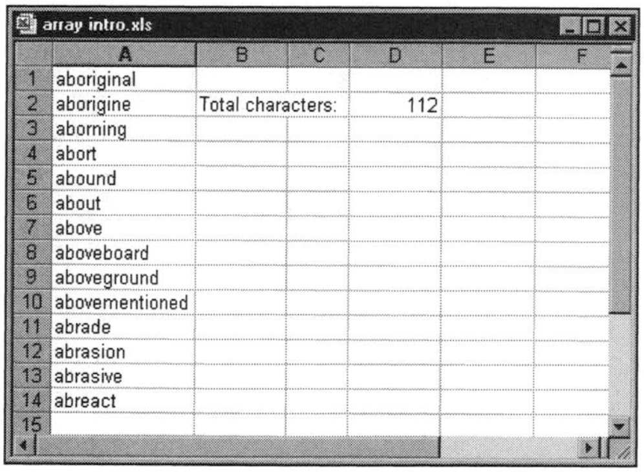

Figure 12-13: A single array formula can count the number of characters in a range of text.

Then, you use a SUM formula to calculate the sum of the values returned by the intermediate formulas.

The following array formula does the job without using any intermediate formulas:

```
{=SUM(LEN(A1:A14))}
```

The array formula uses the LEN function to create a new array (in memory) that consists of the number of characters in each cell of the range. In this case, the new array is:

```
{1,10,9,8,5,6,5,5,10,11,14,6,8,8,7}
```

The array formula is then reduced to:

```
=SUM({1,10,9,8,5,6,5,5,10,11,14,6,8,8,7})
```

Summing the three smallest values in a range

The following formula returns the sum of the three smallest values in a range named *Data:*

```
{=SUM(SMALL(Data,{1,2,3}))}
```

The function uses an array constant as the second argument for the SMALL function. This generates a new array, which consists of the three smallest values in the range. This array is then passed to the SUM function, which returns the sum of the values in the new array.

Figure 12-14 shows an example in which the range A1:A10 is named *Data*. The SMALL function is evaluated three times – each time with a different second argument. The first time, the SMALL function has a second argument of 1, and it returns -5. The second time, the second argument for the SMALL function is 2, and it returns 0 (the second smallest value in the range). The third time, the SMALL function has a second argument of 3, and it returns the third smallest value of 2.

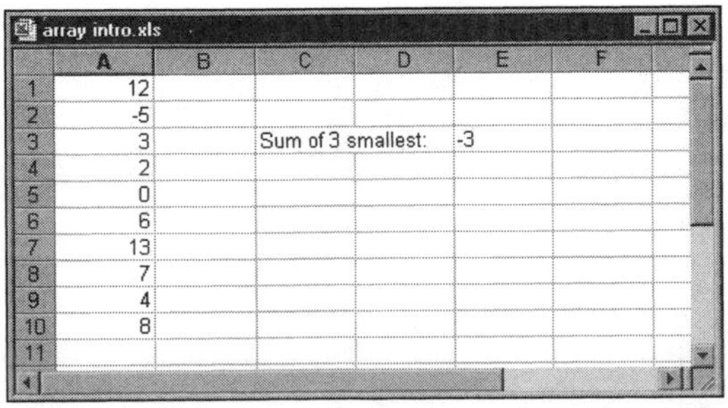

Figure 12-14: An array formula returns the sum of the three smallest values in A1:A10.

Therefore, the array that's passed to the SUM function is:

```
{-5,0,2}
```

The formula returns the sum of the array (-3).

Counting text cells in a range

The following array formula uses the IF function to examine each cell in a range. It then creates a new array (of the same size and dimensions as the original range) that consists of 1s and 0s, depending on whether the cell contains text. This new array is then passed to the SUM function, which returns the sum of the items in the array. The result is a count of the number of text cells in the range.

```
{=SUM(IF(ISTEXT(A1:D5),1,0))}
```

This general array formula type (i.e., an IF function nested in a SUM function) is very useful for counting. Refer to Chapter 7 for additional examples.

Figure 12-15 shows an example of the preceding formula in cell C8. The array created by the IF Function is:

```
{0,1,1,1;1,0,0,0;1,0,0,0;1,0,0,0;1,0,0,0}
```

array intro.xls					
	A	B	C	D	E	F
1		Jan	Feb	Mar		
2	Region 1	7	4	9		
3	Region 2	8	2	8		
4	Region 3	12	1	9		
5	Region 4	14	6	10		
6						
7						
8	No. of text cells:		7			
9						

Figure 12-15: An array formula returns the number of text cells in the range.

Notice that this array contains four rows of three elements (the same dimensions as the range).

A variation on this formula follows:

```
{=SUM(ISTEXT(A1:D5)*1)}
```

This formula eliminates the need for the IF function and takes advantage of the fact that:

```
TRUE * 1 = 1
```

and

```
FALSE * 1 = 0
```

Eliminating intermediate formulas

One of the main benefits of using an array formula is that you can eliminate intermediate formulas in your worksheet. This makes your worksheet more compact, and eliminates the need to display irrelevant calculations. Figure 12-16 shows a worksheet that contains pre-test and post-test scores for students. Column D contains formulas that calculate the changes between the pre-test and the post-test scores. Cell D17 contains a formula, shown here, that calculates the average of the values in column D:

```
=AVERAGE(D2:D15)
```

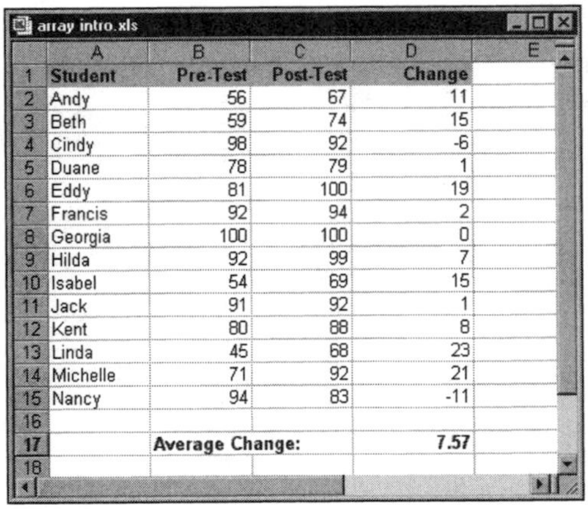

	A	B	C	D	E
1	Student	Pre-Test	Post-Test	Change	
2	Andy	56	67	11	
3	Beth	59	74	15	
4	Cindy	98	92	-6	
5	Duane	78	79	1	
6	Eddy	81	100	19	
7	Francis	92	94	2	
8	Georgia	100	100	0	
9	Hilda	92	99	7	
10	Isabel	54	69	15	
11	Jack	91	92	1	
12	Kent	80	88	8	
13	Linda	45	68	23	
14	Michelle	71	92	21	
15	Nancy	94	83	-11	
16					
17			Average Change:	7.57	
18					

Figure 12-16: Without an array formula, calculating the average change requires intermediate formulas in column D.

With an array formula, you can eliminate column D. The following array formula calculates the average of the changes, but does not require the formulas in column D:

```
{=AVERAGE(C2:C15-B2:B15)}
```

How does it work? The formula uses two arrays, the values of which are stored in two ranges (B2:B15 and C2:C15). The formula creates a *new* array that consists of the differences between each corresponding element in the other arrays. This new array is stored in Excel's memory, not in a range. The AVERAGE function then uses this new array as its argument and returns the result.

The new array consists of the following elements:

```
{11,15,-6,1,19,2,0,7,15,1,8,23,21,-11}
```

The formula, therefore, is reduced to:

```
=AVERAGE({11,15,-6,1,19,2,0,7,15,1,8,23,21,-11})
```

You can use additional array formulas to calculate other measures for the data in this example. For instance, the following array formula returns the largest change (i.e., the greatest improvement). This formula returns 23, which represents Linda's test scores.

```
{=MAX(C2:C15-B2:B15)}
```

The following array formula returns the smallest change (that is, the least improvement). This formula returns -11, which represents Nancy's test scores.

```
{=MIN(C2:C15-B2:B15)}
```

Using an array in lieu of a range reference

If your formula uses a function that requires a range reference, you may be able to replace that range reference with an array constant. This is useful in situations in which the values in the referenced range do not change.

A notable exception to using an array constant in place of a range reference in a function is with the database functions that use a reference to a criteria range (for example, DSUM). Unfortunately, using an array constant instead of a reference to a criteria range does not work.

Figure 12-17 shows a worksheet that uses a lookup table to display a word that corresponds to an integer. For example, looking up a value of 9 returns *Nine* from the lookup table in D1:E10. The formula in cell C1 is:

```
=VLOOKUP(B1,D1:E10,2,FALSE)
```

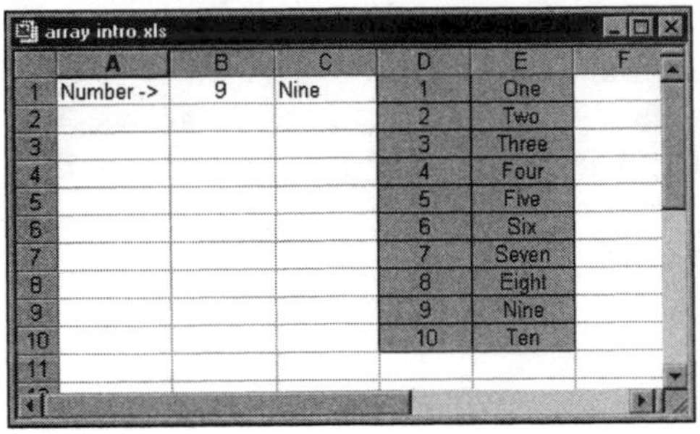

Figure 12-17: You can replace the lookup table in D1:E10 with an array constant.

You can use a two-dimensional array in place of the lookup range. The following formula returns the same result as the previous formula, but it does not require the lookup range in D1:E1:

```
=VLOOKUP(B1,{1,"One";2,"Two";3,"Three";4,"Four";5,"Five";
6,"Six";7,"Seven";8,"Eight";9,"Nine";10,"Ten"},2,FALSE)
```

Summary

This chapter introduced the concept of *arrays*, a collection of items that reside in a range or in Excel's memory. An array formula operates on a range and returns a single value or an array of values.

The next chapter continues this discussion and presents several useful examples that help clarify the concept.

Chapter 13

Performing Magic with Array Formulas

IN THIS CHAPTER

- ◆ More examples of single-cell array formulas
- ◆ More examples of multicell array formulas
- ◆ Returning an array from a custom VBA function

THE PREVIOUS CHAPTER provided an introduction to arrays and array formulas, and presented some basic examples to whet your appetite. This chapter continues the saga, and provides many useful examples that further demonstrate the power of this feature.

I selected the examples in this chapter to provide a good assortment of the various uses for array formulas. Most can be used as-is. You will, of course, need to adjust the range names or references used. Also, you can modify many of the examples easily to work in a slightly different manner.

 Each of the examples in this chapter is demonstrated in a file on the companion CD-ROM.

More Single-Cell Array Formulas

You enter single-cell array formulas into a single cell. These array formulas work with arrays contained in a range, or that exist in memory.

Summing a range that contains errors

You've probably discovered that Excel's SUM function doesn't work if you attempt to sum a range that contains one or more error values (such as #DIV/0! or #NA). Figure 13-1 shows an example. The SUM formula in cell C9 returns an error value because the range that it sums (C2:C8) contains errors.

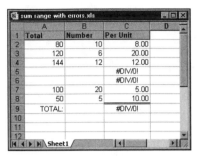

Figure 13-1: An array formula can sum a range of values, even if the range contains errors.

The following array formula returns a sum of the values in a range named *Data*, even if the range contains error values:

```
{=SUM(IF(ISERROR(Data),"",Data))}
```

This formula works by creating a new array that contains the original values, but without the errors. The IF function effectively filters out error values by replacing them with an empty string. The SUM function then works on this "filtered" array. This technique also works with other functions, such as MIN and MAX.

 You may want to use a function other than ISERROR. The ISERROR function returns TRUE for any error value: #N/A, #VALUE!, #REF!, #DIV/0!, #NUM!, #NAME?, or #NULL!. The ISERR function returns TRUE for any error except #N/A. The ISNA function returns TRUE only if the cell contains a #N/A.

Counting the number of error values in a range

The following array formula is similar to the previous example, but it returns a count of the number of error values in a range named *Data*.

```
{=SUM(IF(ISERROR(Data),1,0))}
```

This formula creates an array that consists of 1s (if the corresponding cell contains an error) and 0s (if the corresponding cell does not contain an error value).

You can simplify the formula a bit by removing the third argument for the IF function. If this argument is not specified, the IF function returns FALSE if the condition is not satisfied (that is, the cell does not contain an error value). The array formula shown here performs exactly like the previous formula, but doesn't use the third argument for the IF function:

```
{=SUM(IF(ISERROR(Data),1))}
```

Actually, you can simplify the formula even more:

```
{=SUM(ISERROR(Data)*1)}
```

This version of the formula relies on the fact that:

```
TRUE * 1 = 1
```

and

```
FALSE * 1 = 0
```

Summing based on a condition

Often, you need to sum values based on one or more conditions. The array formula that follows, for example, returns the sum of the positive values (it excludes negative values) in a range named *Data*:

```
{=SUM(IF(Data>0,Data))}
```

The IF function creates a new array that consists only of positive values. This array is passed to the SUM function. The *Data* range can consist of any number of rows and columns.

You also can use Excel's SUMIF function for this example. The following function, which is not an array formula, returns the same result:

```
=SUMIF(Data,">0")
```

SUMIF, however, can't be used for multiple conditions. For example, if you want to sum only values that are greater than 0 and less than 5, you need an array formula. This array formula does the job:

```
{=SUM((Data>0)*(Data<=5)*Data)}
```

 Contrary to what you might expect, you cannot use the AND function in an array formula. The following array formula, while quite logical, doesn't return the correct result:

```
{=SUM(IF(AND(Data>0,Data<=5),Data))}
```

You also can combine criteria using an OR condition. For example, to sum the values that are less than 0 or greater than 5, use the following array formula:

```
{=SUM(IF(NOT(NOT((Data<0)+(Data>5))),Data))}
```

As with the AND function, you cannot use the OR function in an array formula. The following formula, for example, does not return the correct result:

`{=SUM(IF(OR(Data<0,Data>5),Data))}`

For an explanation of the workarounds required for using logical functions in an array formula, refer to the following sidebar, "Illogical Behavior from Logical Functions."

Illogical Behavior from Logical Functions

Excel's AND and OR functions are logical functions that return TRUE or FALSE. Unfortunately, these functions do not perform as expected when used in an array formula.

As shown here, columns A and B contain logical values. The AND function returns TRUE if all of its arguments are TRUE. Column C contains nonarray formulas that work as expected. For example, cell C3 contains the following function:

`=AND(A3,B3)`

	A	B	C	D	E
logical functions in array formulas.xls					
1					
2	Condition 1	Condition 2	Non-Array Formulas	Array with AND {=AND(A3:A6,B3:B6)}	Array formula: {=A3:A6*B3:B6}
3	TRUE	TRUE	TRUE	FALSE	1
4	TRUE	FALSE	FALSE	FALSE	0
5	FALSE	TRUE	FALSE	FALSE	0
6	FALSE	FALSE	FALSE	FALSE	0
7					
8					

The range D3:D6 contains this array formula:

`{=AND(A3:A6,B3:B6)}`

You might expect this array formula to return the following array:

`{TRUE,FALSE,FALSE,FALSE}`

Rather, it returns only a single item: FALSE. In fact, both the AND function and the OR function always return a single result (never an array). Even when using array constants, the AND function still returns only a single value. For example, this array formula does not return an array:

`{=AND({TRUE,TRUE,FALSE,FALSE},{TRUE,FALSE,TRUE,FALSE})}`

I don't know whether or not the formula not returning an array is by design or if it's a bug. In any case, it certainly is inconsistent with how the other functions operate.

Column E contains another array formula, which follows, that returns an array of 0s and 1s. These 0s and 1s correspond to FALSE and TRUE, respectively.

```
{=A3:A6*B3:B6}
```

In array formulas, you must use this syntax in place of the AND function.

The following array formula, which uses the OR function, does not return an array (as you might expect):

```
=OR(A3:A6,B3:B6)
```

Rather, you can use a formula such as the following, which *does* return an array comprising logical OR using the corresponding elements in the ranges:

```
=NOT(NOT(A3:A6+B3:B6))
```

The NOT function works as expected: When used in an array formula, it *does* return an array.

Summing the n largest values in a range

The following array formula returns the sum of the 10 largest values in a range named *Data:*

```
{=SUM(LARGE(Data,ROW(INDIRECT("1:10"))))}
```

The LARGE function is executed 10 times, each time with a different second argument (1, 2, 3, and so on up to 10). The results of these calculations are stored in a new array, and that array is used as the argument for the SUM function.

To sum a different number of values, replace the 10 in the argument for the INDIRECT function with another value. To sum the n *smallest* values in a range, use the SMALL function instead of the LARGE function.

Computing an average that excludes zeros

Figure 13-2 shows a simple worksheet that calculates average sales. The formula in cell B11 is:

```
=AVERAGE(B2:B9)
```

	A	B	C	D	E	F
1	Sales Person	Sales				
2	Abner	23,991				
3	Baker	15,092				
4	Charleston	0				
5	Davis	11,893				
6	Ellerman	32,116				
7	Flugelhart	29,089				
8	Gallaway	0				
9	Harrison	33,211				
10						
11		18,174	<-- Average with zeros			
12		24,232	<-- Average without zeros (array formula)			
13						

Figure 13-2: The calculated average includes cells that contain a 0.

This formula, of course, calculates the average of the values in B2:B9. Two of the sales staff had the week off, however, so this average doesn't accurately describe the average sales per representative.

 The AVERAGE function ignores blank cells, but does not ignore cells that contain 0.

The following array formula returns the average of the range, but excludes the cells that contain 0.

```
{=AVERAGE(IF(B2:B9<>0,B2:B9))}
```

This formula creates a new array that consists only of the non-zero values in the range. The AVERGAGE function then uses this new array as its argument. You also can get the same result with a regular (nonarray) formula:

```
=SUM(B2:B9)/COUNTIF(B2:B9,"<>0")
```

This formula uses the COUNTIF function to count the number of non-zero values in the range. This value is divided into the sum of the values.

Determining if a particular value appears in a range

To determine whether a particular value appears in a range of cells, you can choose the Edit → Find command and do a search of the worksheet. But, you also can make this determination by using an array formula.

Figure 13-3 shows a worksheet with a list of names in A3:E22 (named *NameList*). An array formula in cell D1 checks the name entered into cell C1 (named *TheName*). If the name exists in the list of names, the formula displays the text *Found*. Otherwise, it displays *Not Found*.

	A	B	C	D	E
1	Enter a Name -->		Michelle	Found	
2					
3	Al	Daniel	Harold	Lyle	Richard
4	Allen	Dave	Ian	Maggie	Rick
5	Andrew	David	Jack	Margaret	Robert
6	Anthony	Dennis	James	Marilyn	Rod
7	Arthur	Don	Jan	Mark	Roger
8	Barbara	Donald	Jeff	Marvin	Ronald
9	Bernard	Doug	Jeffrey	Mary	Russ
10	Beth	Douglas	Jerry	Matt	Sandra
11	Bill	Ed	Jim	Mel	Scott
12	Bob	Edward	Joe	Merle	Simon
13	Brian	Eric	John	Michael	Stacy
14	Bruce	Fran	Joseph	Michelle	Stephen
15	Cark	Frank	Karl	Mike	Steven
16	Carl	Fred	Kathy	Norman	Stuart
17	Charles	Gary	Keith	Patrick	Susan
18	Chris	George	Kenneth	Paul	Terry
19	Chuck	Glenn	Kevin	Peter	Thomas
20	Clark	Gordon	Larry	Phillip	Timothy
21	Curt	Greg	Leonard	Ray	Vincent
22	Dan	Gregory	Louise	Rebecca	William
23					

Figure 13-3: Using an array formula to determine if a range contains a particular value

The array formula in cell D1 is:

```
{=IF(OR(TheName=NameList),"Found","Not Found")}
```

This formula compares *TheName* to each cell in the *NameList* range. It builds a new array that consists of logical TRUE or FALSE values. The OR function returns TRUE if any one of the values in the new array is TRUE. The IF function uses this result to determine which message to display.

A simpler form of this formula follows. This formula displays TRUE if the name is found; otherwise it displays FALSE.

```
{=OR(TheName=NameList)}
```

Counting the number of differences in two ranges

The following array formula compares the corresponding values in two ranges (named *MyData* and *YourData*) and returns the number of differences in the two ranges. If the contents of the two ranges are identical, the formula returns 0.

```
{=SUM(IF(MyData=YourData,0,1))}
```

The two ranges must be the same size and of the same dimensions.

This formula works by creating a new array of the same size as the ranges being compared. The IF function fills this new array with 0s and 1s (0 if a difference is found, 1 if the corresponding cells are the same). The SUM function then returns the sum of the array.

Returning the location of the maximum value in a range

The following array formula returns the row number of the maximum value in a single-column range named *Data*:

```
{=MIN(IF(Data=MAX(Data),ROW(Data), ""))}
```

The IF function creates a new array that corresponds to the *Data* range. If the corresponding cell contains the maximum value in *Data*, then the array contains the row number; otherwise, it contains an empty string. The MIN function uses this new array as its second argument, and returns the smallest value – the row number of the maximum value in *Data*.

If the *Data* range contains more than one cell that has the maximum value, the row of the first maximum cell is returned.

The following array formula is similar to the previous one, but it returns the actual cell address of the maximum value in the *Data* range. It uses the ADDRESS function, which takes two arguments: a row number and a column number.

```
{=ADDRESS(MIN(IF(Data=MAX(Data),ROW(Data), "")),COLUMN(Data))}
```

Finding the row of a value's nth occurrence in a range

The following array formula returns the row number within a single-column range named *Data* that contains the *n*th occurrence of a cell named *Value*:

```
{=SMALL(IF(Data=Value,ROW(Data), ""),n)}
```

The IF function creates a new array that consists of the row number of values from the *Data* range that are equal to *Value*. Values from the Data range that are not equal to *Value* are replaced with an empty string. The SMALL function works on this new array, and returns the *n*th smallest row number.

The formula returns #NUM! if the *Value* is not found or if *n* exceeds the number of the values in the range.

Returning the longest text in a range

The following array formula displays the text string in a range (named *Data*) that has the most characters. If multiple cells contain the longest text string, the first cell is returned.

```
{=INDEX(Data,MATCH(MAX(LEN(Data)),LEN(Data),FALSE),1)}
```

This formula creates four new arrays:

- ◆ Array #1: An array that consists of the length of each cell in the *Data* range (created by the LEN function)

- ◆ Array #2: Another array identical to Array #1

- ◆ Array #3: An array that contains the maximum value in Array #1 (created by the MAX function)

- ◆ Array #4: An array that contains the offset of the cell that contains the maximum length (created by the MATCH function)

The INDEX function works with these arrays and returns the contents of the cell that contains the most characters. This function works only if the *Data* range consists of a single column.

Determining if a range contains valid values

You might have a list of items that you need to check against another list. For example, you might import a list of part numbers into a range named *MyList*, and you want to ensure that all of the part numbers are valid. You can do this by comparing the items in the imported list to the items in a master list of part numbers (named *Master*).

The following array formula returns TRUE if every item in the range named *MyList* is found in the range named *Master*. Both of these ranges must consist of a single column, but they don't need to contain the same number of rows.

```
{=ISNA(MATCH(TRUE,ISNA(MATCH(MyList,Master,0)),0))}
```

The array formula that follows returns the number of invalid items. In other words, it returns the number of items in *MyList* that do not appear in *Master*.

```
{=SUM(1*ISNA(MATCH(MyList,Master,0)))}
```

To return the first invalid item in *MyList*, use the following array formula:

```
{=INDEX(MyList,MATCH(TRUE,ISNA(MATCH(MyList,Master,0)),0))}
```

Summing the digits of an integer

The following array formula calculates the sum of the digits in an integer, which is stored in cell A2. For example, if A2 contains the value 132, the formula returns 6 (the sum of 1, 3, and 2).

```
{=SUM(MID(A2,ROW(INDIRECT("1:"&LEN(A2))),1)*1)}
```

To understand how this formula works, let's start with the ROW function, shown here:

```
=ROW(INDIRECT("1:"&LEN(A2)))
```

This function returns an array of consecutive integers beginning with 1 and ending with the number of digits in the value in cell A2. For example, if cell A2 contains the value 132, then the LEN function returns 3 and the array generated by the ROW functions is:

```
{1,2,3}
```

 For more information about using the INDIRECT function to return this array, see Chapter 12.

This array is then used as the second argument for the MID function. The MID part of the formula, simplified a bit and expressed as values, is the following:

```
=MID(132,{1,2,3},1)*1
```

This function generates an array with three elements:

```
{4,0,9}{1,3,2}
```

By simplifying again and adding the SUM function, the formula looks like this:

```
=SUM({4,0,9})=SUM({1,3,2})
```

This produces the result of 6.

The values in the array created by the MID function are multiplyied by 1 because the MID function returns a string. Multiplying by 1 forces a numeric value result. Alternatively, you can use the VALUE function to force a numeric string to become a numeric value.

Notice that the formula does not work with a negative value because the negative sign is not a numeric value. The following formula solves this problem by using the ABS function to return the absolute value of the number. Figure 13-4 shows a worksheet that uses this formula in column B.

```
{=SUM(VALUE(MID(ABS(A2),ROW(INDIRECT("1:"&LEN(ABS(A2)))),1)))}
```

	A	B	C
1	Number	Sum of Digits	
2	132	6	
3	9	9	
4	111111	6	
5	980991	36	
6	-980991	36	
7	409	13	
8		0	
9	12	3	
10	123	6	
11			
12			

Figure 13-4: An array formula calculates the sum of the digits in an integer.

Summing rounded values

Figure 13-5 shows a simple worksheet that demonstrates a common spreadsheet problem: rounding errors. As you can see, the grand total in cell E5 appears to display an incorrect amount (that is, it's off by a penny). The values in column E use a number format that displays two decimal places. The actual values, however, consist of additional decimal places that do not display due to rounding (as a result of the number format). The net effect of these rounding errors is a seemingly incorrect total. The total — actually $168.320997 — displays as $168.32.

The following array formula creates a new array that consists of values in column E, rounded to two decimal places.

```
{=SUM(ROUND(E2:E4,2))}
```

This formula returns $168.31.

summing rounded values.xls				
A	**B**	**C**	**D**	**E**
Description	**Quantity**	**Unit Price**	**Discount**	**Total**
Widgets	6	$11.69	5.23%	$66.47
Sprockets	8	$9.74	5.23%	$73.84
Snapholytes	3	$9.85	5.23%	$28.00
GRAND TOTAL				**$168.32**

Figure 13-5: Using an array formula to correct rounding errors

You also can eliminate these types of rounding errors by using the ROUND function in the formula that calculates each row total in column E. This technique does not require an array formula.

Refer to Chapter 11 for more information about Excel's functions that are relevant to rounding.

Summing every nth value in a range

Suppose you have a range of values and you want to compute the sum of every third value in the list — the first, the fourth, the seventh, and so on. You can't accomplish this task with a standard formula, but an array formula does the job.

Refer to the data in Figure 13-6. The values are stored in a range named *Data*, and the value of n is in cell E6 (named *n*).

sum every nth.xls								
	A	**B**	**C**	**D**	**E**	**F**	**G**	**H**	**I**
1		Data							
2		1							
3		2							
4		3							
5		4							
6		5		N:	3	= nth value			
7		6			70	= Result returned by a single array formula			
8		7							
9		8							
10		9							
11		10							
12		11							
13		12							
14		13							
15		14							
16		15							
17		16							
18		17							
19		18							
20		19							
21									

Figure 13-6: An array formula returns the sum of every nth value in the range.

The following array formula returns the sum of every nth value in the range.

```
{SUM(IF(MOD(ROW(INDIRECT("1:"&COUNT(Data)))-1,n)=0,Data,""))}
```

This formula generates an array of consecutive integers, and the MOD function uses this array as its first argument. The second argument for the MOD function is the value of *n*. The MOD function creates another array, which consists of the remainders (after each row number is divided by *n*). If the array item is 0 (i.e., the row is evenly divisible by *n*), the corresponding item in the *Data* range will be included in the sum.

You'll find that this formula fails when *n* is 0 (i.e., sums no items). The modified array formula that follows uses an IF function to handle this case:

```
{=IF(n=0,0,SUM(IF(MOD(ROW(INDIRECT("1:"&COUNT(data)))-
1,n)=0,data,"")))}
```

This formula works only when the *Data* range consists of a single column of values. It does not work for a rectangular range, or for a single row of values.

To make the formula work with a horizontal range, you need to transpose the array of integers generated by the ROW function. The modified array formula that follows works only with a horizontal *Data* range:

```
{=IF(n=0,0,SUM(IF(MOD(TRANSPOSE(ROW(INDIRECT("1:"&COUNT(Data))))-
1,n)=0,Data,"")))}
```

Removing non-numeric characters from a string

The following array formula extracts a number from a string that contains text. For example, consider the string *ABC145Z*. The formula returns the numeric part, 145.

```
{=MID(A1,MATCH(0,(ISERROR(MID(A1,ROW(INDIRECT("1:"&LEN(A1))),1)
*1)*1),0),LEN(A1)-SUM((ISERROR(MID(A1,ROW
(INDIRECT("1:"&LEN(A1))),1)*1)*1)))}
```

This formula works only with a single embedded number. For example, it fails with a string such as *X45Z99*.

Determining the closest value in a range

The array formula that follows returns the value in a range named *Data* that is closest to a another value (named *Target*):

```
{=INDEX(Data,MATCH(SMALL(ABS(Target-Data),1),ABS(Target-Data),0))}
```

If two values in the *Data* range are equidistant from the *Target* value, the formula returns the first one in the list. Figure 13-7 shows an example of this formula. In this case, the *Target* value is 45. The array formula in cell D3 returns 48 – the value closest to 45.

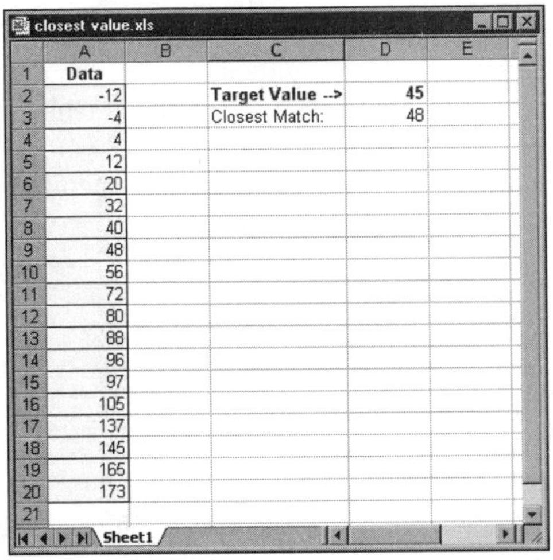

Figure 13-7: An array formula returns the closest match.

Returning the last value in a column

Suppose you have a worksheet that you update frequently by adding new data to columns. You might need a way to reference the last value in column A (the value most recently entered). If column A contains no empty cells, the solution is relatively simple and doesn't require an array formula:

```
=OFFSET(A1,COUNTA(A:A)-1,0)
```

This formula uses the COUNTA function to count the number of nonempty cells in column A. This value (minus 1) is used as the second argument for the OFFSET function. For example, if the last value is in row 100, COUNTA returns 100. The OFFSET function returns the value in the cell 99 rows down from cell A1, in the same column.

If column A has one or more empty cells interspersed – frequently the case – the preceding formula won't work because the COUNTA function doesn't count the empty cells.

The following array formula returns the contents of the last nonempty cell in the first 500 rows of column A:

```
{=INDIRECT(ADDRESS(MAX((ROW(1:500)*(A1:A500<>""))),COLUMN(A:A)))}
```

You can, of course, modify the formula to work with a column other than column A. To use a different column, change the four column references from A to whatever column you need. If the last nonempty cell occurs in a row beyond row 500, you need to change the two instances of "500" to a larger number. The fewer rows referenced in the formula, the faster the calculation speed.

 You cannot use this formula, as written, in the same column with which it's working. Attempting to do so generates a circular reference. You can, however, modify it. For example, to use the function in cell A1, change the references so they begin with row 2.

Returning the last value in a row

The following array formula is similar to the previous formula, but it returns the last nonempty cell in a row (in this case, row 1):

```
=INDIRECT(ADDRESS(1,(MAX((TRANSPOSE(ROW(1:256))*(1:1<>"")))))))
```

To use this formula for a different row, change the first argument for the ADDRESS function, and change the 1:1 reference to correspond to the row.

Ranking data with an array formula

Often, computing the rank orders for the values in a range of data is helpful. If you have a worksheet that contains the annual sales figures for 20 salespeople, for example, you may want to know how each person ranks, from highest to lowest.

If you've used Excel's RANK function, you may have noticed that the ranks produced by this function don't handle ties the way that you may like. For example, if two values are tied for third place, the RANK function gives both of them a rank of 3. You may prefer to assign each an average (or midpoint) of the ranks—in other words, a rank of 3.5 for both values tied for third place.

Figure 13-8 shows a worksheet that uses two methods to rank a column of values (named *Sales*). The first method (column C) uses Excel's RANK function. Column D uses array formulas to compute the ranks.

The following is the array formula in cell D2:

```
{=SUM(1*(B2<=Sales))-(SUM(1*(B2=Sales))-1)/2}
```

This formula copied to the cells below it.

	A	B	C	D	E	F	G
1	Salesperson	Sales	Excel's Rank Function	Ranks With Array Formula			
2	Adams	123,000	6	6			
3	Bigelow	98,000	9	10			
4	Fredericks	98,000	9	10	Assigned middle rank		
5	Georgio	98,000	9	10			
6	Jensen	25,000	12	12			
7	Juarez	101,000	8	8			
8	Klein	305,000	1	1			
9	Lynch	145,000	3	3.5			
10	Mayne	145,000	3	3.5	Assigned average rank		
11	Roberton	121,000	7	7			
12	Slokum	124,000	5	5			
13	Wu	150,000	2	2			
14							

Figure 13-8: Ranking data with Excel's RANK function and with array formulas

NOTE Each ranking is computed with a separate array formula, not with an array formula entered into multiple cells.

Each array function works by computing the number of higher values and subtracting one half of the number of equal values minus 1.

Creating a dynamic crosstab table

A crosstab table tabulates or summarizes data across two dimensions. Take a look at the data in Figure 13-9. This worksheet shows a simple expense account listing. Each item consists of the date, the expense category, and the amount spent. Each column of data is a named range, indicated in the first row.

Array formulas summarize this information into a handy table that shows the total expenses – by category – for each day. Cell F3 contains the following array formula, which copied to the remaining 14 cells in the table:

```
{=SUM(IF($E3&F$2=Date&Category,Amount))}
```

These array formulas display the totals for each day, by category.

The formula sums the values in the *Amount* range, but does so only if the row and column names in the summary table match the corresponding entries in the *Date* and *Category* ranges. It does the comparison by concatenating (using the & operator) the row and column names and comparing the resulting string to the concatenation of the corresponding *Date* and *Category* values. If the two match, the SUM function kicks in and adds the corresponding value in the *Amount* range.

You can customize this technique to hold any number of different categories and any number of dates. You can eliminate the dates, in fact, and substitute people's names, departments, regions, and so on.

dynamic crosstab.xls

	A	B	C	D	E	F	G	H	I
1	Date	Category	Amount						
2	04-Jan	Food	23.50			Transp	Food	Lodging	
3	04-Jan	Transp	15.00		04-Jan	160.50	49.57	65.95	
4	04-Jan	Food	9.12		05-Jan	20.00	27.80	89.00	
5	04-Jan	Food	16.95		06-Jan	0.00	101.96	75.30	
6	04-Jan	Transp	145.50		07-Jan	11.50	25.00	112.00	
7	04-Jan	Lodging	65.95						
8	05-Jan	Transp	20.00						
9	05-Jan	Food	7.80						
10	05-Jan	Food	20.00						
11	05-Jan	Lodging	89.00						
12	06-Jan	Food	9.00						
13	06-Jan	Food	3.50						
14	06-Jan	Food	11.02						
15	06-Jan	Food	78.44						
16	06-Jan	Lodging	75.30						
17	07-Jan	Transp	11.50						
18	07-Jan	Food	15.50						
19	07-Jan	Food	9.50						
20	07-Jan	Lodging	112.00						
21									

Sheet1

Figure 13-9: You can use array formulas to summarize data such as this in a dynamic crosstab table.

You also can use Excel's pivot table feature to summarize data in this way. However, pivot tables do not update automatically when the data changes, so the array formula method I just described has at least one advantage.

More Multicell Array Formulas

The previous chapter introduced array formulas entered into multicell ranges. In this section, I present a few more array multicell formulas. Most of these formulas return some or all of the values in a range, but rearranged in some way.

Returning only positive values from a range

The following array formula works with a single-column vertical range (named *Data*). The array formula is entered into a range that's the same size as *Data*, and returns only the positive values in the *Data* range (0s and negative numbers are ignored).

```
{=INDEX(Data,SMALL(IF(Data>0,ROW(INDIRECT("1:"&ROWS(Data)))),
ROW(INDIRECT("1:"&ROWS(Data))))))}
```

As you can see in Figure 13-10, this formula works but not perfectly. The *Data* range is A2:A21, and the array formula is entered into C2:C21. However, the array formula displays #NUM! error values for cells that don't contain a value.

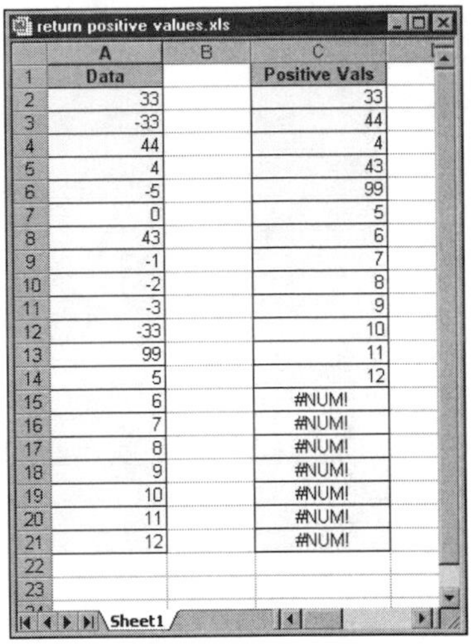

Figure 13-10: Using an array formula to return only the positive values in a range

This more complex array formula avoids the error value display:

```
{=IF(ISERR(SMALL(IF(Data>0,ROW(INDIRECT("1:"&ROWS(Data)))),
ROW(INDIRECT("1:"&ROWS(Data))))),"",INDEX(Data,SMALL(IF
(Data>0,ROW(INDIRECT("1:"&ROWS(Data)))),ROW(INDIRECT
("1:"&ROWS(Data))))))}
```

Returning nonblank cells from a range

The following formula is a variation on the formula in the previous section. This array formula works with a single-column vertical range named *Data*. The array formula is entered into a range of the same size as *Data*, and returns only the non-blank cell in the *Data* range.

```
{=IF(ISERR(SMALL(IF(Data<>"",ROW(INDIRECT("1:"&ROWS(Data)))),
ROW(INDIRECT("1:"&ROWS(Data))))),"",INDEX(Data,SMALL(IF(Data
<>"",ROW(INDIRECT("1:"&ROWS(Data)))),ROW(INDIRECT("1:"&ROWS
(Data))))))}
```

Reversing the order of the cells in a range

The following array formula works with a single-column vertical range (named *Data*). The array formula, which is entered into a range of the same size as *Data*, returns the values in *Data* — but in reverse order.

```
{=IF(INDEX(Data,ROWS(data)-ROW(INDIRECT("1:"&ROWS(Data)))+1)
="","",INDEX(Data,ROWS(Data)-ROW(INDIRECT("1:"&ROWS(Data)))
+1))}
```

Figure 13-11 shows this formula in action. The range A2:A20 is named *Data*, and the array formula is entered into the range C2:C20.

	A	B	C	D	E
1	**Data Entry Range**		**Reversed**		
2	first		10		
3	second		9		
4	third		8		
5	fourth		7th		
6	5th		6th		
7	6th		5th		
8	7th		fourth		
9	8		third		
10	9		second		
11	10		first		

Figure 13-11: A multicell array formula reverses the order of the values in the range.

Sorting a range of values dynamically

Suppose your worksheet contains a single-column vertical range named *Data*. The following array formula – entered into a range with the same number of rows as *Data* – returns the values in *Data*, sorted from highest to lowest. This formula works only with numeric values, not with text.

```
{=LARGE(Data,ROW(INDIRECT("1:"&ROWS(Data))))}
```

To sort the values in *Data* from lowest to highest, use this array formula:

```
{=SMALL(Data,ROW(INDIRECT("1:"&ROWS(Data))))}
```

This formula can be useful if you need to have your data entry sorted immediately. Start by defining the range name *Data* as your data entry range. Then, enter the array formula into another range with the same number of rows as *Data*.

You'll find that the array formula returns #NUM! for cells that don't have a value. This can be annoying if you're entering data. The modified version, which follows, is more complex, but it eliminates the display of the error value.

```
{=IF(ISERR(LARGE(Data,ROW(INDIRECT("1:"&ROWS(Data))))),"",
LARGE(Data,ROW(INDIRECT("1:"&ROWS(Data)))))}
```

Returning a list of unique items in a range

If you have a single-column range named *Data*, the following array formula returns a list of the unique items in the range:

```
{=INDEX(Data,SMALL(IF(MATCH(Data,Data,0)=
ROW(INDIRECT("1:"&ROWS(Data))),MATCH(Data,Data,0),""),
ROW(INDIRECT("1:"&ROWS(Data)))))}
```

This formula does not work if the *Data* range contains any blank cells. The unfilled cells of the array formula display #NUM!. Figure 13-12 shows an example. Range A2:A20 is named *Data*, and the array formula is entered into range C2:C20.

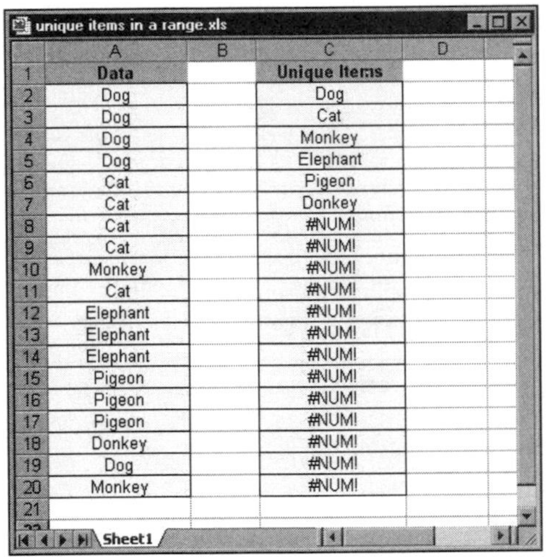

	A	B	C	D
1	Data		Unique Items	
2	Dog		Dog	
3	Dog		Cat	
4	Dog		Monkey	
5	Dog		Elephant	
6	Cat		Pigeon	
7	Cat		Donkey	
8	Cat		#NUM!	
9	Cat		#NUM!	
10	Monkey		#NUM!	
11	Cat		#NUM!	
12	Elephant		#NUM!	
13	Elephant		#NUM!	
14	Elephant		#NUM!	
15	Pigeon		#NUM!	
16	Pigeon		#NUM!	
17	Pigeon		#NUM!	
18	Donkey		#NUM!	
19	Dog		#NUM!	
20	Monkey		#NUM!	
21				

Figure 13-12: Using an array formula to return unique items from a list

Displaying a calendar in a range

Figure 13-13 shows a calendar displayed in a range of cells. The worksheet has two defined named: *m* (for the month) and *y* (for the year). A single array formula, entered into 42 cells, displays the corresponding calendar. The following array formula is entered into the range B6:H11:

```
{=IF(MONTH(DATE(y,m,1))<>MONTH(DATE(y,m,1)-(WEEKDAY(DATE(y,m,1))-
1)+{0;7;14;21;28;35}+
{0,1,2,3,4,5,6}),"",DATE(y,m,1)-(WEEKDAY(DATE(y,m,1))-
1)+{0;7;14;21;28;35}+{0,1,2,3,4,5,6}))}
```

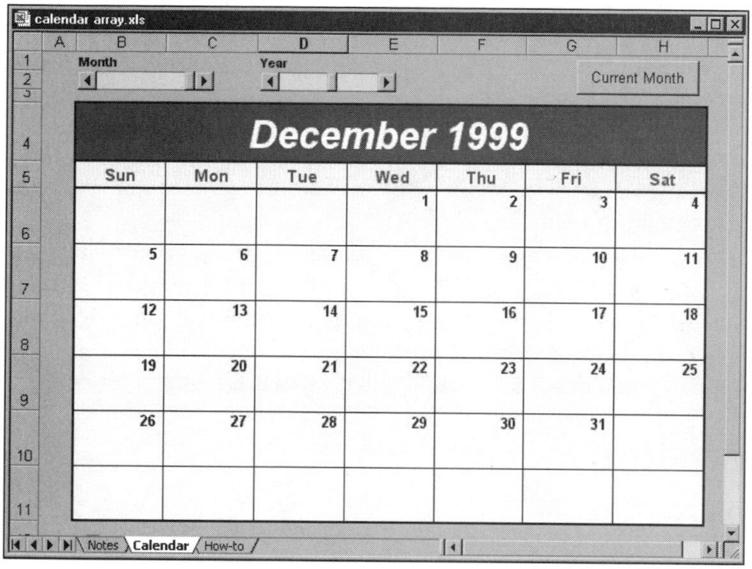

Figure 13-13: Displaying a calendar using a single array formula

The array formula actually returns date values, but the cells are formatted to display only the day portion of the date. Also, notice that the array formula uses array constants. You can simplify the array formula quite a bit by removing the IF function:

```
{=DATE(y,m,1)-(WEEKDAY(DATE(y,m,1))-1)+{0;7;14;21;28;35}+
{0,1,2,3,4,5,6}}
```

See Chapter 12 for more information about array constants.

This version of the formula displays the days from the preceding month and the next month. The IF function checks each date to make sure it's in the current month. If not, the IF function returns an empty string.

Returning an Array from a Custom VBA Function

The chapter's final example demonstrates one course of action you can take if you can't figure out a particular array formula. If Excel doesn't provide the tools you need, you need to create your own.

For example, I struggled for several hours in an attempt to create an array formula that returns a sorted list of text entries. Although you can create an array formula that returns a sorted list of *values* (see "Sorting a Range of Values Dynamically," earlier in this chapter), doing the same for text entries alluded me.

Therefore, I created a custom VBA function called SORTED, which I list here:

```
Function SORTED(rng, Optional ascending) As Variant
    Dim SortedData() As Variant
    Dim CellCount As Long
    Dim Temp As Variant, i As Long, j As Long
    CellCount = rng.Count
    ReDim SortedData(1 To CellCount)

'   Check optional argument
    If IsMissing(ascending) Then ascending = True

'   Exit with an error if not a single column
    If rng.Columns.Count > 1 Then
        SORTED = CVErr(xlErrValue)
        Exit Function
    End If

'   Transfer data to SortedData
    For i = 1 To CellCount
        SortedData(i) = rng(i)
        If TypeName(SortedData(i)) = "Empty" _
          Then SortedData(i) = ""
    Next i
    On Error Resume Next

'   Sort the SortedData array
    For i = 1 To CellCount
        For j = i + 1 To CellCount
            If SortedData(j) <> "" Then
                If ascending Then
                    If SortedData(i) > SortedData(j) Then
                        Temp = SortedData(j)
```

```
                        SortedData(j) = SortedData(i)
                        SortedData(i) = Temp
                End If
            Else
                If SortedData(i) < SortedData(j) Then
                    Temp = SortedData(j)
                    SortedData(j) = SortedData(i)
                    SortedData(i) = Temp
                End If
            End If
        End If
        Next j
    Next i

'   Transpose it
    SORTED = Application.Transpose(SortedData)
End Function
```

Refer to Part V for information about creating custom VBA functions.

The SORTED function takes two arguments: a range reference and an optional second argument that specifies the sort order. The default sort order is ascending order. If you specify FALSE as the second argument, the range is returned sorted in descending order.

Once the SORTED Function procedure is entered into a VBA module, you can use the SORTED function in your formulas. The following array formula, for example, returns the contents of a single-column range named *Data*, but sorted in ascending order. You enter this formula into a range the same size as the *Data* range.

```
{=SORTED(Data)}
```

This array formula returns the contents of the *Data* range, but sorted in descending order:

```
{=SORTED(Data,False)}
```

As you can see, using a custom function results in a much more compact formula. Custom functions, however, are usually much slower than formulas that use Excel's built-in functions.

Figure 13-14 shows an example of this function used in an array formula. Range A2:A17 is named *Data*, and the array formula is entered into range C2:C17.

Figure 13-14: Using a custom worksheet function in an array formula

Summary

This chapter provided many examples of useful array formulas. You can use these formulas as is, or adapt them to your needs. It also presented a custom worksheet function that returns an array.

The next chapter presents intentional circular references.

Part IV

Miscellaneous Formula Techniques

Chapter 14

Intentional Circular References

IN THIS CHAPTER

◆ General information regarding how Excel handles circular references

◆ Why you might want to use an intentional circular reference

◆ How Excel determines calculation and iteration settings

◆ Examples of formulas that use intentional circular references

◆ Potential problems when using intentional circular references

WHEN MOST SPREADSHEET USERS hear the term *circular reference*, they immediately think of an error condition. Generally, a circular reference is an accident – something that you need to correct. Sometimes, however, a circular reference can be a good thing. This chapter presents some examples that demonstrate intentional circular references.

Understanding Circular References

When you are entering formulas in a worksheet, you occasionally may see a message from Excel, like the one shown in Figure 14-1. This is Excel's way of telling you that the formula you just entered will result in a *circular reference*. A circular reference occurs when a formula refers to its own cell, either directly or indirectly. For example, you create a circular reference if you enter the following formula into cell A10 because the formula refers to the cell that contains the formula.

```
=SUM(A1:A10)
```

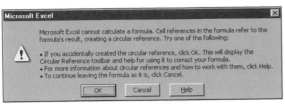

Figure 14-1: Excel's way of telling you that your formula contains a circular reference

Every time the formula in A10 is calculated, it must be recalculated because A10 has changed. In theory, the calculation would continue forever while the value in cell A10 tried to reach infinity.

Correcting an accidental circular reference

When you see the circular reference message after entering a formula, Excel gives you three options:

◆ Click OK to attempt to locate the circular reference (Excel's Circular Reference toolbar is displayed). This also has the annoying side effect of displaying a help screen whether you need it or not.

◆ Click Cancel to enter the formula as is.

◆ Click Help to read about circular references in the online help.

Most circular reference errors are caused by simple typographical or range selection errors. For example, when creating a SUM formula in cell A10, you might accidentally select A1:A10 instead of A1:A9.

If you know the source of the problem, click Cancel. Excel displays a message in the status bar to remind you that a circular reference exists. In this case, the message reads Circular: A10. If you activate a different workbook, the message simply displays Circular (without the cell reference). You can then edit the formula and fix the problem.

If you get the circular message area, but you don't know what formula caused the problem, you can click OK. When you do so, Excel displays the Help topic on circular references and the Circular Reference toolbar (see Figure 14-2). On the Circular Reference toolbar, click the first cell in the Navigate Circular Reference drop-down list box, and then examine the cell's formula. If you cannot determine whether that cell caused the circular reference, click the next cell in the Navigate Circular Reference box. Continue to review the formulas until the status bar no longer displays Circular.

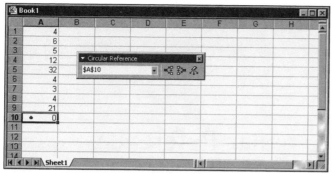

Figure 14-2: The Circular Reference toolbar

 Excel won't display its Circular Reference dialog box if you have the Iteration setting turned on. You can check this in the Options dialog box (in the Calculation tab). I discuss more about this setting later.

Understanding indirect circular references

Usually, a circular reference is quite obvious and, therefore, easy to identify and correct. Sometimes, however, circular references are indirect. In other words, a formula may refer to a formula that refers to a formula that refers back to the original formula. In some cases, you need to conduct a bit of detective work to figure out the problem.

About Circular References

For a practical, real-life demonstration of a circular reference, refer to the sidebar, "More About Circular References," later in this chapter.

For more information about tracking down a circular reference, refer to Chapter 19.

Intentional Circular References

As mentioned previously, you can use a circular reference to your advantage in some situations. A circular reference, if set up properly, can be the functional equivalent of a Do-Loop construct used in a programming language such as VBA. An intentional circular reference introduces recursion or iteration into a problem. Each intermediate "answer" from a circular reference calculation is used in the subsequent calculation. Eventually, the solution converges to the final value.

By default, Excel does not permit circular references. You must explicitly tell Excel that you want it to perform iterative calculations in your workbook. You do this on the Calculation tab of the Options dialog box (see Figure 14-3).

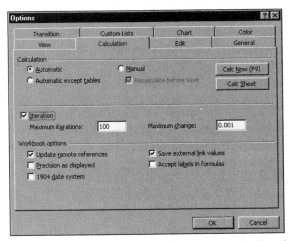

Figure 14-3: To calculate a circular reference, the Iteration checkbox must be checked.

Figure 14-4 shows a simple example of a worksheet that uses an intentional circular reference. A company has a policy of contributing five percent of its net profit to charity. The contribution itself, however, is considered an expense and therefore subtracted from the net profit figure. This produces a circular reference.

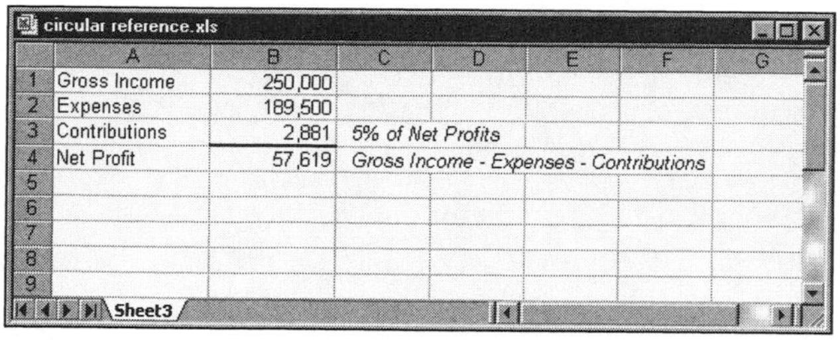

Figure 14-4: The company also deducts the five-percent contribution of net profits as an expense, creating an intentional circular reference.

> **NOTE** The circular reference cannot be resolved unless the Iteration setting is turned on.

The cells in column B are named, using the text in column A. The *Contributions* cell (B3) contains the following formula:

```
=5%*Net_Profit
```

The *Net_Profit* cell (B4) contains the following formula:

```
=Gross_Income-Expenses-Contributions
```

These formulas produce a resolvable circular reference. Excel keeps calculating until the formula results converge on a solution.

> **ON THE CD** You can access the workbook shown in Figure 14-4 on the companion CD-ROM. For your convenience, the worksheet includes a button that, when clicked, displays the Calculation tab of the Options dialog box. This makes it easy to experiment with various iteration settings.

Understanding iterations

The Calculation tab of the Options dialog box contains three controls relevant to circular references:

◆ Iteration checkbox: If unchecked, Excel does not perform iterative calculations, and Excel displays a warning dialog box if you create a formula that has a circular reference. When creating an intentional circular reference, this checkbox must be checked.

◆ Maximum iterations: Determines the maximum number of iterations that Excel will perform. This value cannot exceed 32,767.

◆ Maximum change: Determines when iteration stops. For example, if this setting is .01, iterations will stop when a calculation produces a result that differs by less than 10 percent of the previous value.

Calculation continues until Excel reaches the number of iterations specified in the Maximum iterations box, or until a recalculation changes all cells by less than the amount you set in the Maximum Change box (whichever is reached first). Depending on your application, you may need to adjust the settings in the Maximum iterations field or the Maximum change field. For a more accurate solution, make the Maximum change field smaller. If the result doesn't converge after 100 iterations, you can increase the Maximum iterations field.

To get a feel for how this works, open the example workbook presented in the previous section. Then:

1. Access the Calculation tab in the Options dialog box and make sure the Iteration checkbox is checked.

2. Set the Maximum iterations setting to 1.

3. Set the Maximum change setting to .001.

4. Enter a different value into the *Gross_Income* cell (cell B1).

5. Press F9 to calculate the sheet.

Because the Maximum iteration setting is 1, pressing F9 performs just one iteration. You'll find that the *Contributions* cell has not converged. Press F9 a few more times, and you'll see the result converge on the solution. When the solution is found, pressing F9 has no noticeable effect. If the Maximum iterations setting is a large value, the solution appears almost immediately (unless it involves some slow calculations).

How Excel Determines Calculation and Iteration Settings

It's important to understand that all open workbooks use the same calculation and iteration settings. For example, if you have two workbooks open, you cannot have one of them set to automatic calculation and the other set to manual calculation. Although you can save a workbook with particular settings (for example, manual calculation with no iterations), those settings can change if you open another workbook.

Excel follows these general rules to determine which calculation and iteration settings to use:

◆ The first workbook opened uses the calculation mode saved with that workbook. If you open other workbooks, they use the same calculation mode.

For example, suppose you have two workbooks: Book1 and Book2. Book1 has its Iteration setting turned off (the default setting), and Book2 (which uses intentional circular references) has its Iteration setting turn on. If you open Book1 and then Book2, both workbooks will have the iteration setting turned off. If you open Book2 and then Book1, both workbooks will have their iteration setting turned on.

◆ Changing the calculation mode for one workbook changes the mode for all workbooks.

If you have both Book1 and Books2 open, changing the calculation mode or Iteration setting of either workbook affects both workbooks.

◆ All worksheets in a workbook use the same mode of calculation.

◆ If you have all workbooks closed and you create a new workbook, the new workbook uses the same calculation mode as the last closed workbook. One exception: if you create the workbook from a template. If so, the workbook uses the calculation mode specified in the template.

◆ If the mode of calculation in a workbook changes, and you save the file, the current mode of calculation is saved with the workbook.

Circular Reference Examples

Following are a few more examples of using intentional circular references. They demonstrate creating circular references for time stamping a cell, calculating an all-time high value, solving a recursive equation, and solving simultaneous equations.

For these examples to work properly, the Iteration setting must be in effect. Select Tools → Options, and click the Calculation tab. Make sure the Iteration checkbox is checked.

Time stamping a cell entry

Figure 14-5 shows a worksheet designed such that entries in column A are "time stamped" in column B. The formulas in column B monitor the corresponding cell in column A. When you insert an entry in column A, the formula enters the current date and time.

	A	B	C	D	E
1	Data Entry	Time Stamp			
2	54.5	6/10/99 1:32 PM			
3	509.32	6/10/99 1:33 PM			
4	54.98	6/11/99 10:20 AM			
5	52.87	6/11/99 10:20 AM			
6					
7					
8					
9					
10					
11					
12					

Figure 14-5: Using circular reference formulas to time stamp entries in column A

The workbook shown in Figure 14-5 is available on the companion CD-ROM.

The formula in cell B2, which is copied down to other cells in column B, is:

```
=IF(ISBLANK(A2),"",IF(B2="",NOW(),B2))
```

This formula uses an IF function to check cell A2. If the cell is empty, the formula returns an empty string. If A2 is not empty, the formula checks the value in cell B2 (that is a self-reference). If B2 is empty, the formula returns the date and time. Using the second IF statement ensures that the NOW function does not recalculate.

Calculating an all-time high value

Figure 14-6 shows a worksheet that displays the sales made by sales representatives. This sheet is updated every month – new sales figures replace the values in column B.

	A	B	C	D	E	F	G
1	**April Sales**		98,223	<-- All-Time High!			
2							
3	**Sales Rep**	**Amount Sold**					
4	Jackson	59,874					
5	Smith	56,892					
6	Lopez	32,445					
7	Peterson	55,678					
8	Rayez	33,455					
9							
10							

Figure 14-6: Using a circular reference formula to keep track of the highest value ever entered in column B

The formula in cell C1 keeps track of the all-time high sales – the largest value *ever* entered into column B. This formula, which uses a circular reference, is as follows:

```
=MAX(B:B,C1)
```

The formula uses the MAX function to return the maximum value in column B, or in cell C1. In this example, the formula displays 98,223. This is a value from a previous month (in other words, a value not currently in column B).

ON THE CD The companion CD-ROM contains the workbook shown in Figure 14-6.

Generating unique random integers

You can take advantage of a circular reference to generate unique random integers in a range. The worksheet in Figure 14-7 generates 15 random integers between 1 and 30 in column A. The integers are generated such that they produce unique numbers (that is, not duplicated). You might want to use this technique to generate random lottery number picks.

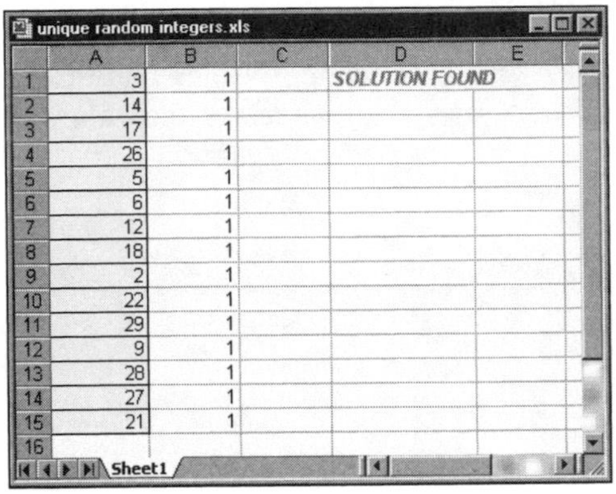

Figure 14-7: Using circular reference formulas to generate unique random integers in column A

Column B contains formulas that count the number of times a particular number appears in the range A1:A15. For example, the formula in cell B1 follows. This formula displays the number of times the value in cell A1 appears in the range A1:A15:

```
=COUNTIF($A$1:$A$15,A1)
```

Each formula in column A contains a circular reference. The formula examines the sum of the cells in column B. If this sum does not equal 15, a new random integer is generated. When the sum of the cells in column B equals 15, the values in column A are all unique. The formula in cell A1 is:

```
=IF(SUM($B$1:$B$15)<>15,INT(RAND()*30+1),A1)
```

Cell D1, which follows, contains a formula that displays the status. If the sum of the cells in column B does not equal 15, the formula displays the text CALC AGAIN (press F9 to perform more iterations). When column B contains all 1s, the formula displays *SOLUTION FOUND.*

```
=IF(SUM(B1:B15)<>15,"CALC AGAIN","SOLUTION FOUND")
```

To generate a new set of random integers, select any cell in column B. Then press F2 to edit the cell, and press Enter to reenter it. The number of calculations required depends on:

◆ The Iteration setting on the Calculation tab of the Options dialog box. If you specify a higher number of iterations, you have a better chance of finding 15 unique values.

◆ The number of values requested, compared to the number of possible values. This example seeks 15 unique integers from a pool of 30. Fewer calculations are required if, for example, you request 15 unique values from a pool of 100.

Solving a recursive equation

A recursive equation is an equation in which a variable appears on both sides of the equal sign. The following equations represent examples of recursive equations.

```
x = 1/(x+1)
x = COS(x)
x = SQRT(X+5)
x = 2^(1/x)
x = 5 + (1/x)
```

To solve a recursive equation, make sure that the Iteration setting is turned on. Then, convert the equation into a self-referencing formula. To solve the first equation, enter the following formula into cell A1:

```
=1/(A1+1)
```

The formula converges at 0.618033988749895, the value of x that satisfies the equation.

Sometimes, this technique doesn't work. For example, consider the following recursive equation.

```
x = 5 + (1/x)
```

If you enter the formula that follows into cell A1, you'll find that it returns a #DIV/0! error because the iterations begin with 0 (and dividing by 0 results in an error).

```
=5+(1/A1)
```

To solve this type of equation, you need to use two cells. The following step-by-step instructions demonstrate.

1. Enter any non-zero value in cell A1.

2. Enter the following formula in cell A2:

   =5+(1/A1)

3. Enter the following formula in cell A1:

   =A2

Both cells A1 and A2 display 5.19258235429625, the value of x that satisfies the equation. Note that, in Step 1, entering a non-zero value essentially provides a non-zero *seed* for the recursion. After you replace this value with the formula (in Step 3), the initial value in cell A1 was still used as the starting value for the formula in cell A2.

 Because of the way Excel performs calculations, it's critical that the seed cell is to the left of or above the formula.

Figure 14-8 shows a worksheet that calculates several recursive equations. Note that the equations in rows 5 and 6 require a seed value. The formulas in column E use the values in column C to provide a check of the results. For example, the formula in cell E2 is:

=1/(C2+1)

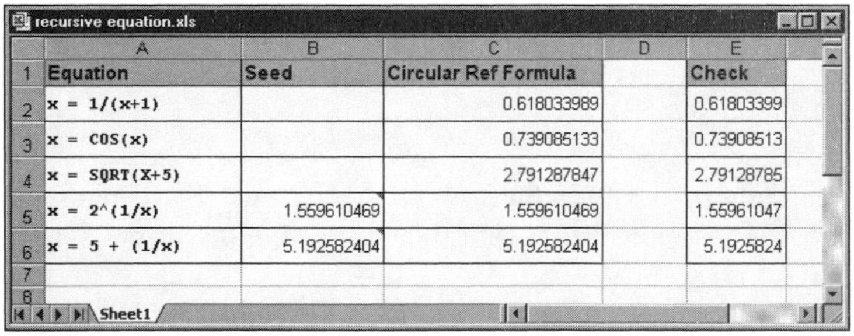

	A	B	C	D	E
1	Equation	Seed	Circular Ref Formula		Check
2	x = 1/(x+1)		0.618033989		0.61803399
3	x = COS(x)		0.739085133		0.73908513
4	x = SQRT(X+5)		2.791287847		2.79128785
5	x = 2^(1/x)	1.559610469	1.559610469		1.55961047
6	x = 5 + (1/x)	5.192582404	5.192582404		5.1925824
7					
8					

Figure 14–8: This workbook uses circular references to calculate several recursive equations.

 You can access the workbook shown in Figure 14-8 on the companion CD-ROM.

Solving simultaneous equations using a circular reference

In some cases, you can use circular references to solve simultaneous equations. Consider the two simultaneous equations listed here:

```
3x + 4y = 8
3x + 8y = 20
```

The goal is to find the value of *x* and the value of *y* that satisfies both equations. First, rewrite the equations to express them in terms of *x* and *y*. The following equation is the first equation, expressed in terms of *x*.

```
x = (8 - 4y)/3
```

The following equation is the second equation, expressed in terms of y.

```
y = (20 - 3x)/8
```

As shown in Figure 14-9, cell B5 is named *X* and cell B6 is named *Y*. The formulas in these cells mirror the previous equations. The formula in B5 (*X*) is:

```
=(8-(4*Y))/3
```
The formula is cell B6 (*Y*) is:

```
=(20-(3*X))/8
```

The figure also shows a chart that plots the two equations. The intersection of the two lines represents the values of *X* and *Y* that solve the equations.

Note the circular reference. The *X* cell refers to the *Y* cell, and the *Y* cell refers to the *X* cell. These cells converge to display the solution:

```
X = -1.333
Y = 3.000
```

Using intentional circular references to solve simultaneous equations is more of an interesting demonstration than a practical approach. You'll find that some iterative calculations never converge. In other words, successive recalculations will never *hone in* on a solution. For example, consider the simultaneous equations that follow. A solution *does* exist, but you cannot use circular references to find it.

```
x = 4 - y/2
y = 3 + 2x
```

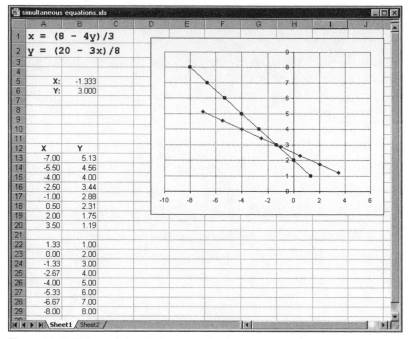

Figure 14–9: This worksheet solves two simultaneous equations.

The best approach for solving simultaneous equations with Excel involves the use of matrices. See Chapter 11 for examples.

XREF

ON THE CD

The companion CD-ROM contains a workbook with two sets of simultaneous equations. You can solve one set by using intentional circular references; you cannot solve the other set using this technique.

More About Circular References

For a practical, real-life demonstration of a circular reference, refer to the sidebar, "About Circular References," earlier in this chapter.

Potential Problems with Intentional Circular References

Although intentional circular references can be useful, using this feature has some potential problems. To take advantage of an intentional circular reference, the Iteration setting must be in effect. When the Iteration setting is in effect, Excel does not warn you of circular references. Therefore, you run the risk of creating an *accidental* circular reference without even knowing about it.

If a circular reference formula generates an error value, the error value can be propagated to all other formulas involved in the circular reference. Therefore, you may need to use the ISERROR function inside of an IF function to test for error values.

The number of iterations specified in the Maximum iteration field applies to all formulas in the workbook — not just those that use circular references. If your workbook contains many complex formulas, these additional iterations can slow things down considerably. Therefore, when you use intentional circular references, keep your worksheets very simple.

You may need to distribute a workbook that uses intentional circular references to other users. If Excel's Iteration setting is not active when you open the workbook, Excel displays the circular reference error message, which probably confuses all but the most sophisticated users.

Summary

This chapter provided an overview of how Excel handles circular references. Although most circular references indicate an error, there are some benefits to writing formulas that use intentional circular references. To take advantage of a circular reference, the Iteration setting must be in effect.

The next chapter demonstrates how formulas can expand your chart-making capabilities.

Chapter 15

Charting Techniques

IN THIS CHAPTER

- ◆ Creating charts from any number of worksheets or different workbooks

- ◆ Plotting functions with one and two variables

- ◆ Creating awesome designs with formulas

- ◆ Working with linear and nonlinear trendlines

- ◆ Useful charting tricks for working with charts

EXCEL'S CHARTING CAPABILITIES are downright awesome. As you know, a chart is a visual display of virtually any type of numeric data that's stored in a worksheet. Excel supports more than 100 different chart types; you have almost complete control over nearly every aspect of each chart. This chapter, which assumes that you're familiar with Excel's charting feature, demonstrates some useful charting techniques – most of which involve formulas.

Representing Data in Charts

Basically, a *chart* presents a table of numbers visually. Displaying data in a well conceived chart can make the data more understandable; and you often can make your point more quickly as a result. Because a chart presents a picture, charts are particularly useful for understanding a lengthy series of numbers and their interrelationships. Making a chart helps you to spot trends and patterns that you otherwise could not identify when examining a range of numbers.

You create charts from numbers that appear in a worksheet. You can enter these numbers directly, or you can derive them as the result of formulas. Normally, the data used by a chart resides in a single worksheet, within one file, but that's not a strict requirement. A single chart can use data from any number of worksheets, or even from different workbooks.

Understanding the SERIES formula

A chart consists of one or more data series, and each data series appears as a line, column, bar, and so on. The SERIES formula determines the data used in each series in a chart. When you select a data series in a chart, its SERIES formula appears in the formula bar. This is not a "real" formula. In other words, you can't use it in a cell and you can't use worksheet functions within the SERIES formula. You can, however, edit the arguments in the SERIES formula. A SERIES formula has the following syntax:

```
=SERIES(name, category_labels, values, order)
```

The arguments you can use in the SERIES function include:

- *name* – (Optional) The name used in the legend. If the chart has only one series, the name argument is used as the title.

- *category_labels* – (Optional) The range that contains the labels for the category axis. If omitted, Excel uses consecutive integers beginning with 1.

- *values* – (Required) The range that contains the values.

- *order* – (Required) An integer that specifies the plotting order of the series (relevant only if the chart has more than one series).

Range references in a SERIES formula are always absolute, and they always include the sheet name. For example:

```
=SERIES(Sheet1!$B$1,,Sheet1!$B$2:$B$7,1)
```

A range reference can consist of a noncontiguous range. If so, each range is separated by a comma and the argument is enclosed in parentheses. In the following SERIES formula, the values range consists of B2:B3 and B5:B7:

```
=SERIES(,,(Sheet1!$B$2:$B$3,Sheet1!$B$5:$B$7),1)
```

Although a SERIES formula can refer to data in other worksheets, the data for a series must reside on a single sheet. The following SERIES formula, for example, is not valid because the data series references two different worksheets.

```
=SERIES(,,(Sheet1!$B$2,Sheet2!$B$2),1)
```

USING NAMES IN A SERIES FORMULA

You can substitute range names for the range references in a SERIES formula. When you do so, Excel changes the reference in the SERIES formula to include the workbook name. For example, the SERIES formula shown here uses a range named *MyData* (located in a workbook named budget.xls). Excel added the workbook name and exclamation point.

```
=SERIES(Sheet1!$B$1,,budget.xls!MyData,1)
```

Using names in a series formula provides a significant advantage: If you change the range reference for the name, the chart automatically reflects the new data. In the preceding SERIES formula, for example, assume the range named *MyData* refers to A1:A20. The chart displays the 20 values in that range. You can then use the Insert→Name→Define command to redefine *MyData* as a different range, say A1:A30. The chart then displays the 30 data points defined by *MyData* (no chart editing is necessary).

As I noted previously, a SERIES formula cannot use worksheet functions. You *can*, however, create named formulas (which use functions) and use these named formulas in your SERIES formula. As you see later in this chapter, this technique enables you to perform charting tricks that seem impossible.

UNLINKING A CHART SERIES FROM ITS DATA RANGE

Normally, an Excel chart uses data stored in a range. Change the data in the range, and the chart updates automatically. In some cases, you may want to "unlink" the chart from its data ranges and produce a *static chart* – a chart that never changes. For example, if you plot data generated by various what-if scenarios, you may want to save a chart that represents some baseline so you can compare it with other scenarios. There are two ways to create such a chart:

♦ *Paste it as a picture:* Activate the chart and choose Edit→Copy. Then, press the Shift key and select Edit→Paste Picture (the Paste Picture command is available only if you press Shift when you select the Edit menu). The result is a picture of the copied chart.

♦ *Convert the range references to arrays:* Click a chart series and then click the formula bar to activate the SERIES formula. Press F9 to convert the ranges to arrays. Repeat this for each series in the chart. This technique (as opposed to creating a picture) enables you to continue to edit the chart.

Chart-Making Tips

Here I present a number of chart-making tips that you might find helpful.

◆ To create a chart with a single keystroke, select the data you want to chart and press F11. The result is a new chart sheet that contains a chart of the default chart type.

◆ You can size the chart in a chart sheet according to the window size by using the View → Sized with Window command. When you enable this setting, the chart adjusts itself when you resize the workbook window (it always fits perfectly in the window). In this mode, the chart that you're working on may or may not correspond to how it looks when printed.

◆ If you have many charts of the same type to create, changing the default chart format to the chart type with which you're working is much more efficient than separately formatting each chart. Then, you can create all of your charts without having to select the chart type. To change the default chart type, select Chart → Chart Type and choose the new default chart type. Then, click the Set as default chart type button.

◆ To print an embedded chart on a separate page, select the chart and choose File → Print (or click the Print button). Excel prints the chart on a page by itself and does *not* print the worksheet.

◆ If you don't want a particular embedded chart to appear on your printout, right-click the chart and choose Format Chart Area from the shortcut menu. Click the Properties tab in the Format Chart Area dialog box and remove the checkmark from the Print object checkbox.

◆ Sometimes, using a mouse to select a particular chart element is tricky. You may find it easier to use the keyboard to select a chart element. When a chart is activated, press the up arrow or down arrow to cycle through all parts in the chart. When a data series is selected, press the right arrow or left arrow to select individual points in the series.

◆ When you select a chart element, you'll find that many of the toolbar buttons that you normally use for worksheet formatting also work with the selected chart element. For example, if you select the chart's Plot Area, you can change its color by using the Fill Color tool on the Formatting toolbar. If you select an element that contains text, you can use the Font Color tool to change the color of the text.

◆ Prior to Excel 97, clicking an embedded chart selected the chart object. You could then adjust its properties. To activate the chart, you actually had to double-click it. Beginning with Excel 97, clicking an embedded chart activates the chart contained inside the chart object. You can adjust the chart object's properties by using the Properties tab of the Format Chart dialog box. To select the chart object itself, press Ctrl while you click the chart. You may want to select the chart object to change its name by using the Name box.

◆ You can delete all data series from a chart. If you do so, the chart appears empty. It retains its settings, however. Therefore, you can add a data series to an empty chart and it again will look like a chart.

◆ For more control over positioning your chart, press Ctrl while you click the chart. Then, use the arrow keys to move the chart one pixel at a time.

◆ To create a line that continues through a point that has no information, type the formula =NA() in the blank cells in your range.

Creating links to cells

You can add cell links to various elements of a chart. Adding cell links can make your charts more dynamic. You can set dynamic links for chart titles, data labels, additional descriptive text, and pictures.

ADDING TITLE LINKS

The labels in a chart (Chart Title, Category Axis Title, and Value Axis Title) are normally not linked to any cell. In other words, they contain static text that changes only when you edit them manually. You can, however, create a link so a title refers to a worksheet cell.

To create a linked title, first make sure the chart contains the chart element title that you want. You can use the Chart Wizard to add titles to a chart that doesn't already have them. Next, select the title and click in the formula bar. Type an equal sign and then click the cell that contains the title text. The result is a formula that contains the sheet reference and the cell reference as an absolute reference (for example, =Sheet1!$A$1). Press Enter to attach the formula to the chart title. Figure 15-1 shows a chart in which the Chart Title is linked to cell A1.

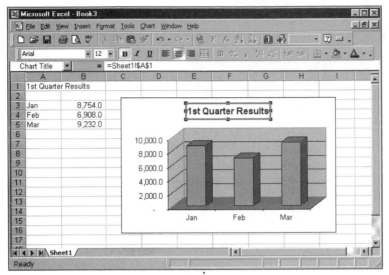

Figure 15-1: The Chart Title linked to cell A1

ADDING LINKS TO DATA LABELS

You probably know that Excel enables you to label each data point in a chart. You do this on the Data Labels tab in the Format Data Series dialog box. Unfortunately, this feature isn't very flexible. For example, you can't specify a range that contains the labels. You can, however, edit individual data labels. To do so, click once on the data label to select all data labels, then click again to select the single data label. Once a single data label is selected, you can add any text you like. Or, you can specify a link to a cell by clicking the formula bar and entering a reference formula (such as =Sheet1!$A$1).

The Power Utility Pak includes a handy utility that makes it easy to add data labels to your charts by specifying a worksheet range. You can access a trial version of Power Utility Pak on the companion CD-ROM, and you can use the coupon in the back of the book to order a copy at a discount.

ADDING TEXT LINKS

You might want your chart to display some other text (such as a descriptive note) that's stored in a cell. Doing so is easy. First, activate the chart. Then, click in the formula bar, type an equal sign, and click the cell that contains the text. Press Enter. Excel creates a Text Box in the center of your chart (see Figure 15-2). You can drag this Text Box to its desired location and apply any type of formatting you like.

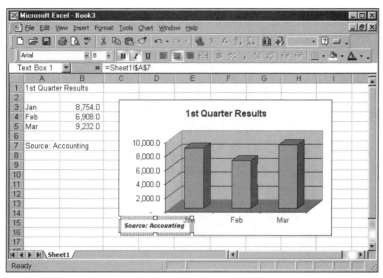

Figure 15-2: A Text Box linked to a cell

To add an unlinked Text Box, just select the chart, type the text in the formula bar, and press Enter.

ADDING PICTURE LINKS

Excel has a feature that enables you to display a data table inside of a chart. You can select this option in Step 3 of the Chart Wizard. The data table option displays a table that shows the values used in a chart. This can be a handy feature, but it's not very flexible. For example, you have limited formatting options, and you have no control over the position of the data table (it always appears below the chart). A linked picture of a range presents an alternative to the data table (see Figure 15-3 for an example).

To create a linked picture in a chart, first create the chart as you normally would. Then, perform the following steps:

1. Select the range that you would like to include in the chart.

2. Select Edit → Copy.

3. Activate the chart.

4. Press Shift, and then select Edit → Paste Picture. This pastes an *unlinked* picture of the range.

5. To create the link, select the picture and then type a reference to the range in the formula bar. You can do this easily by typing an equal sign and then reselecting the range.

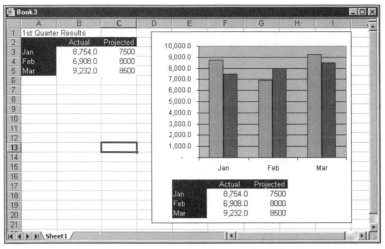

Figure 15-3: This chart contains a linked picture of the A2:C5 range.

The picture now contains a live link to the range. If you change the values or cell formatting, the changes will reflect in the linked picture.

Charting progress toward a goal

You're probably familiar with a "thermometer" type display that shows the percentage of a task that's completed. It's relatively easy to create such a display in Excel, which can track progress toward a goal, for example. The trick involves creating a chart that uses a single cell (which holds a percentage value) as a data series.

Figure 15-4 shows a worksheet set up to track daily progress toward a goal: 1,000 new customers in a 15-day period. Cell B18 contains the goal value, and cell B19 contains a simple sum formula:

```
=SUM(B2:B16)
```

Cell B21 contains a formula that calculates the percent of goal:

```
=B19/B18
```

As you enter new data in column B, the formulas display the current results.

To create the chart, select cell B21 and click the Chart Wizard button. Notice the blank row before cell B21. Without this blank row, Excel uses the entire data block for the chart, not just the single cell. Since B21 is isolated from the other data, the Chart Wizard uses only the single cell. In Step 1 of the Chart Wizard dialog, specify a Column chart with the first subtype (Clustered Column). Click Next twice, and make some additional adjustments on the Step 3 page: add a Chart Title (Title tab), remove Category (x) axis (Axes tab), remove the legend (Legend tab), and specify Show value (Data Labels tab). Click Finish to create the chart.

	A	B	C	D	E	F	
		New					
1	Day	Customers			New Customer		
2	Day 1	90			Promotion		
3	Day 2	83		100%			
4	Day 3	132					
5	Day 4	87		90%			
6	Day 5	102					
7	Day 6	132		80%			
8	Day 7			70%			
9	Day 8						
10	Day 9			60%			
11	Day 10						
12	Day 11			50%			
13	Day 12						
14	Day 13			40%			
15	Day 14						
16	Day 15			30%	63%		
17	New Customers						
18	Goal:	1,000		20%			
19	Total:	626					
20				10%			
21		63%		0%			
22							

Figure 15-4: This chart displays progress toward a goal.

Then, make some additional customizations. Double-click the column to display the Format Data Series dialog. Click the Options tab, and set the Gap width to 0 (which makes the column occupy the entire width of plot area). You also may want to change the pattern used in the column. Do this in the Patterns tab. The example uses a gradient fill effect. Next, double-click the vertical axis to bring up the Format Axis dialog. In the Scale tab, set the Minimum to 0 and the Maximum to 1.

You can make other cosmetic changes as you like. For example, you may want to change the chart's width to make it look more like a thermometer, as well as adjust fonts, colors, and so on.

ON THE CD   The workbook that contains the progress chart also appears on the companion CD-ROM.

Creating a Gantt chart

Gantt charts represent the time required to perform each task in a project. Figure 15-5 shows data used to create the simple Gantt chart shown in Figure 15-6. Creating a Gantt chart isn't difficult when using Excel, but it does require some setup work.

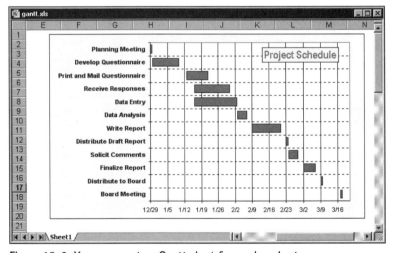

Figure 15-5: Data used in the Gantt chart

Figure 15-6: You can create a Gantt chart from a bar chart.

You can access a workbook that demonstrates setting up a Gantt chart on the companion CD-ROM.

Follow these steps to create this chart:

1. Enter the data as shown in Figure 15-5. The formula in cell D2, which was copied to the rows below it, is

```
=B2+C2-1
```

2. Use the Chart Wizard to create a stacked bar chart from the range A2:C13. Use the second subtype, labeled *Stacked Bar.*

3. In Step 2 of the Chart Wizard, select the Columns option. Also, notice that Excel incorrectly uses the first two columns as the Category axis labels.

4. In Step 2 of the Chart Wizard, click the Series tab and add a new data series. Then, set the chart's series to the following:

   Series 1: B2:B13

   Series 2: C2:C13

   Category (x) axis labels: A2:A13

5. In Step 3 of the Chart Wizard, remove the legend and then click Finish to create an embedded chart.

6. Adjust the height of the chart so that all the axis labels are visible. You can also accomplish this by using a smaller font size.

7. Access the Format Axis dialog box for the horizontal axis. Adjust the horizontal axis Minimum and Maximum scale values to correspond to the earliest and latest dates in the data (note that you can enter a date into the Minimum or Maximum edit box). You also may want to change the date format for the axis labels.

8. Access the Format Axis dialog box for the vertical axis. In the Scale tab, select the option labeled Categories in reverse order, and also set the option labeled Value (Y) axis crosses at maximum category.

9. Select the first data series and access the Format Data Series dialog box. On the Patterns tab, set Border to None and Area to None. This makes the first data series invisible.

10. Apply other formatting as desired.

Creating a comparative histogram

With a bit of creativity, you can create charts that you thought impossible with Excel. For example, Figure 15-7 shows a comparative histogram chart. Such a chart, sometimes known as a *population pyramid*, often displays population data.

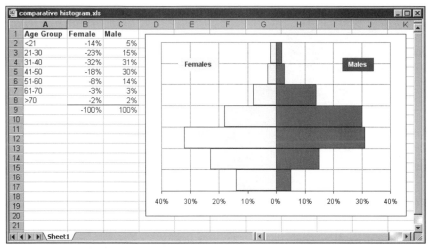

Figure 15-7: Producing this comparative histogram chart requires a few tricks.

   The companion CD-ROM contains a workbook that demonstrates a comparative histogram chart.

Follow these steps to create the chart:

1. Enter the data as shown in Figure 15-7. Notice that the values for females are entered as negative numbers.

2. Select A1:C8 and create a 2D bar chart. Use the subtype labeled *Clustered Bar*.

3. Apply the following custom number format to the horizontal axis:

   0%;0%;0%

   This custom format eliminates the negative signs in the percentages.

4. Select the vertical axis and access the Format Axis dialog box. Click the Patterns tab and remove all tick marks. Set the Tick mark labels option to Low. This keeps the axis in the center of the chart but displays the axis labels at the left side.

5. Select either of the data series and then access the Format Data Series dialog box. Click the Options tab and set the Overlap to 100 and the Gap width to 0.

6. Delete the legend.

7. Add two Text Boxes to the chart (Females and Males), to substitute for the legend.

8. Apply other formatting as desired.

Handling Missing Data

Sometimes, data that you chart may lack one or more data points. Excel offers several ways to handle the missing data. You don't specify these options in the Format Data Series dialog box (as you might expect). Rather, you must select the chart, choose Tools → Options, and then click the Chart tab, shown here.

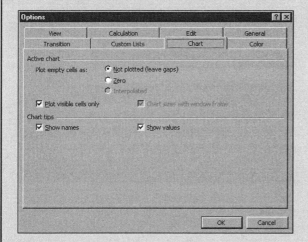

This setting applies only to the active chart. You must have an active chart when you open the Options dialog box. Otherwise, the option is grayed. This is an excellent example of a setting that shows up in an unexpected dialog box.

The options that you set apply to the entire active chart, and you can't set a different option for different series in the same chart. The following are the options in the Chart panel for the active chart:

◆ Not plotted (leave gaps): Missing data gets ignored, causing the data series to have a gap.

◆ Zero: Missing data is treated as zero.

◆ Interpolated: Missing data is calculated by using data on either side of the missing point(s). This option is available only for line charts.

Creating a box plot

A box plot (sometimes known as a quartile plot) is often used to summarize data. Figure 15-8 shows a box plot created for four groups of data. The raw data appears in columns A through D. The range G2:J7, used in the chart, contains formulas that summarize the data. Table 15-1 shows the formulas in column G (which were copied to the three columns to the right).

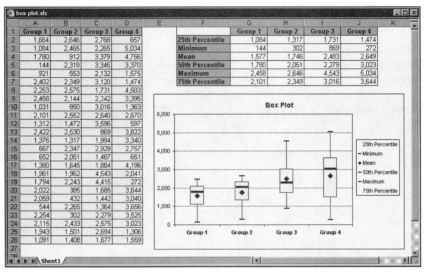

Figure 15-8: This box plot summarizes the data in columns A through D.

TABLE 15-1 FORMULAS USED TO CREATE A BOX PLOT

Cell	Calculation	Formula
G2	25th Percentile	=QUARTILE(A2:A26,1)
G3	Minimum	=MIN(A2:A26)
G4	Mean	=AVERAGE(A2:A26)
G5	50th Percentile	=QUARTILE(A2:A26,2)
G6	Maximum	=MAX(A2:A26)
G7	75th Percentile	=QUARTILE(A2:A26,3)

Follow these steps to create the box plot:

1. Select the range F1:J7.

2. Click the Chart Wizard button.

3. In Step 1 of the Chart Wizard, select a Line chart type and the fourth chart subtype (Line with markers). Click Next.

4. In Step 2 of the Chart Wizard, select the Rows option. Click Finish to create the chart.

5. Activate the first data series (25th Percentile), open the Format Data Series dialog box, and click the Patterns tab. Set the Line option to None. Set the Marker Style to None. Click the Options tab and place a checkmark next to High-low lines and Up-down bars. Adjust the colors if desired.

6. Activate the second data series (Minimum), open the Format Data Series dialog box, and click the Patterns tab. Set the Line option to None. Set the Marker Style to a horizontal bar. Adjust the colors if desired.

7. Activate the third data series (Mean), open the Format Data Series dialog box, and click the Patterns tab. Set the Line option to None. Set the Marker Style to a diamond shape. Adjust the colors if desired.

8. Activate the fourth data series (50th Percentile), open the Format Data Series dialog box, and click the Patterns tab. Set the Line option to None. Set the Marker Style to a horizontal bar. Adjust the colors if desired.

9. Activate the fifth data series (Maximum), open the Format Data Series dialog box, and click the Patterns tab. Set the Line option to None. Set the Marker Style to a horizontal bar. Adjust the colors if desired.

10. Activate the sixth data series (75th Percentile), open the Format Data Series dialog box, and click the Patterns tab. Set the Line option to None. Set the Marker Style to None. Adjust the colors if desired.

TIP

After performing all of these steps, you may want to create a custom chart type to simplify the creation of additional box plots. Activate the chart, and select Chart → Chart Type. Click the Custom Types tab and choose the User-defined option. Click the Add button and specify a name and description for your chart.

Plotting every nth data point

Normally, Excel doesn't plot data that resides in a hidden row or column. You can sometimes use this to your advantage, because it's an easy way to control what data appears in the chart.

Suppose you have a lot of data in a column, and you want to plot only every tenth data point. One way to accomplish this is to use AutoFilter in conjunction with a formula. Figure 15-9 shows a worksheet with AutoFilter in effect. The chart plots only the data in the visible (filtered) rows and ignores the values in the hidden rows.

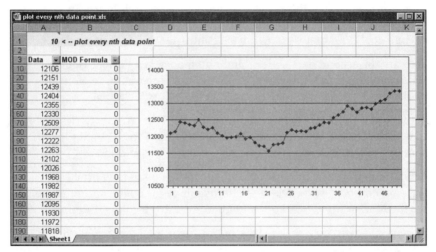

Figure 15-9: This chart plots every nth data point (specified in A1) by ignoring data in the rows hidden by AutoFiltering.

The workbook shown in Figure 15-9 also appears on the companion CD-ROM.

Cell A1 contains the value 10. The value in this cell determines which rows to hide. Column C contains identical formulas that use the value in cell A1. For example, the formula in cell C3 appears like:

```
=MOD(ROW(),$A$1)
```

This formula uses the MOD function to calculate the remainder when the row number (returned by the ROW function) is divided by the value in A1. As a result, every *n*th cell (the value in cell A1 determines *n*) contains 0. Then, use the Data → Filter → AutoFilter command to turn on AutoFiltering. Set up the AutoFilter to display only the rows that contain a 0 in column B. Note that if you change the value in cell A1, you need to respecify the AutoFilter criteria for column B (the rows will not hide automatically).

TIP In some cases, you may not like the idea that hidden data is not displayed in your chart. To override this, activate the chart and select the Tools → Options command. In the Options dialog box, click the Chart tab and remove the checkmark from the checkbox labeled Plot visible cells only.

Updating a data series automatically

It's not difficult to change the data range used by a chart, but in some cases you may prefer a chart that updates automatically when you enter new data. If you have a chart that displays daily sales, for example, you probably need to change the chart's data range each day you add new data. This section describes a way to force Excel to update the chart's data range whenever you add new data to your worksheet.

ON THE CD A workbook that demonstrates automatically updating a data series appears on the companion CD-ROM.

To force Excel to update your chart automatically when you add new data, follow these steps:

1. Create the worksheet shown in Figure 15-10.

2. Select Insert → Name → Define to bring up the Define Name dialog box. In the Names in workbook field, enter **Date**. In the Refers to field, enter this formula:

   ```
   =OFFSET(Sheet1!$A$2,0,0,COUNTA(Sheet1!$A:$A)-1)
   ```

3. Click Add. Notice that the OFFSET function refers to the first data point (cell A2) and uses the COUNTA function to get the number of data points in the column. Because column A has a heading in row 1, the formula subtracts 1 from the number.

4. Type **Sales** in the Names in workbook field. Enter this in the Refers to field:

```
=OFFSET(Sheet1!$B$2,0,0,COUNTA(Sheet1!$B:$B)-1)
```

5. Click Add and then OK to close the dialog box.

6. Activate the chart and select the data series.

7. Replace the range references with the names that you defined in Steps 2 and 4. The formula should read:

```
=SERIES(,Sheet1!Date,Sheet1!Sales,1)
```

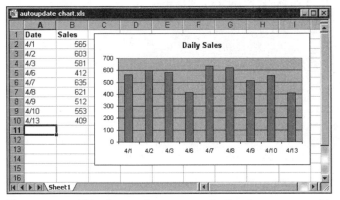

Figure 15-10: This chart updates automatically whenever you add new data to columns A and B.

After you perform these steps, the chart updates automatically when you add data to columns A and B.

To use this technique for your own data, make sure that the first argument for the OFFSET function refers to the first data point and that the argument for COUNTA refers to the entire column of data. Also, if the columns used for the data contain any other entries, COUNTA returns an incorrect value.

Plotting the last n data points

You can use a technique that makes your chart show only the most recent data points in a column. For example, you can create a chart that always displays the most recent 12 months of data (see Figure 15-11).

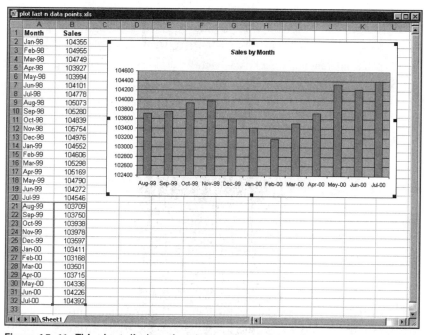

Figure 15-11: This chart displays the 12 most recent data points.

The instructions that follow describe how to create the chart in this figure:

1. Create a worksheet like the one shown in Figure 15-11.

2. Select Insert → Name → Define to bring up the Define Name dialog box. In the Names in workbook field, enter **Dates**. In the Refers to field, enter this formula:

   ```
   =OFFSET(Sheet1!$A$1,COUNTA(Sheet1!$A:$A)-12,0,12,0)
   ```

3. Click Add. Notice that the OFFSET function refers to cell A1 (not the cell with the first month).

4. Type **Sales** in the Names in workbook field. Enter this in the Refers to field:

   ```
   =OFFSET(Sheet1!$B$1,COUNTA(Sheet1!$B:$B)-12,0,12,1)
   ```

5. Click Add and then click OK to close the dialog box.

6. Activate the chart and select the data series.

7. Replace the range references with the names that you defined in Steps 2 and 4. The formula should read:

```
=SERIES(,Sheet1!Dates,Sheet1!Sales,1)
```

 To plot a different number of data points, adjust the formulas entered in Steps 2 and 4. Replace both occurrences of 12 with your new value.

Plotting Data Interactively

This section describes two techniques that you can use to get maximum value out of a single chart. As you'll see, the user determines data plotted by the chart — either by activating a row or selecting from a drop-down list.

Plotting based on the active row

Figure 15-12 shows a chart that displays the data in the row that contains the cell pointer. When you move the cell pointer, press F9 and the chart displays the data from that row.

The chart uses two named formulas, each with a mixed reference (the column part is absolute, but the row part is relative). The following names assume that cell A3 was active when the names were created. *ChartTitle* is defined as:

```
=OFFSET($A3,0,0)
```

ChartData is defined as:

```
=OFFSET($A3,0,1,1,5)
```

The SERIES formula for the chart's data series uses these named formulas. The SERIES formula looks like this:

```
=SERIES(Sheet1!ChartTitle,Sheet1!$B$2:$F$2,Sheet1!ChartData,1)
```

When the worksheet is recalculated, the named formulas get updated based on the active cell.

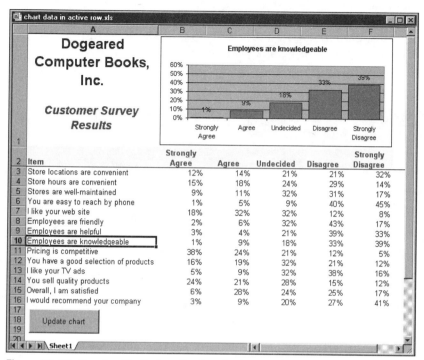

Figure 15-12: Pressing F9 displays the data in the row that contains the cell pointer.

 You can access the workbook shown in Figure 15-12 on the companion CD-ROM.

The worksheet contains a button that executes a simple VBA macro that determines if the cell pointer appears in a row that contains data (in other words, rows 3 through 16). If so, the sheet is calculated. If not, nothing happens. The macro listing follows:

```
Sub UpdateChart()
    If ActiveCell.Row > 2 And ActiveCell.Row < 17 Then _
      ActiveSheet.Calculate
End Sub
```

Selecting data from a combo box

Figure 15-13 shows a chart that displays data as specified by a drop-down control (known as a Combo Box). The chart uses the data in B1:E2, but the month selected in the Combo Box determines the contents of these cells. Range A6:D17 contains the monthly data, and formulas in B2:E2 display the data using the value in cell A2. For example, when cell A4 contains the value 4, the chart displays data for April (the fourth month).

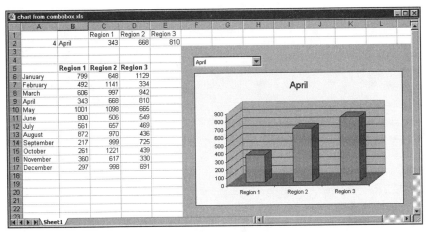

Figure 15-13: Selecting data to plot using a Combo Box

The formula in cell B2 looks like this:

```
=INDEX(A6:A17,$A$2)
```

This formula was copied to C2:E2.

The key here is to get the Combo Box to display the month names and place the selected month index into cell A2. To create the Combo Box:

1. Select View → Toolbars → Forms to display the Forms toolbar.

2. On the Forms toolbar, click the control labeled Combo Box, and drag it into the worksheet to create the control.

3. Double-click the Combo Box to display the Format Control dialog box.

4. In the Format Control dialog box, click the Control tab.

5. Specify A6:A17 as the Input range, and A2 as the Cell link.

You'll find that the Combo Box displays the month names and puts the index number of the selected month into cell A2. The formulas in row 2 display the appropriate data, which displays in the chart.

The workbook that contains the Combo Box example appears on the companion CD-ROM.

Plotting functions with one variable

Excel's charting tools can plot various mathematical and trigonometric functions. For example, Figure 15-14 shows a plot of the SIN function, for values of x (expressed in radians) from -5 to +5 in increments of 0.5. The function is expressed as:

```
y = SIN(x)
```

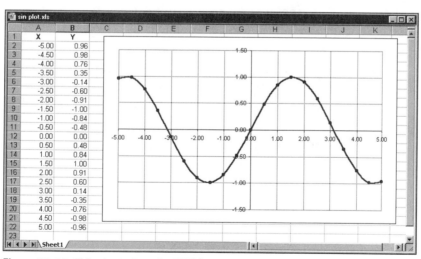

Figure 15-14: This chart plots the SIN(x).

The chart is an XY Scatter chart, with the x values stored in column A and the y values in column B. Each pair of x and y values appears as a data point in the chart, and the points connect with a line.

CREATING PLOTS

The key to creating plots of functions, of course, lies in coming up with two data ranges: one for the x values and one for the y values. The y values will be generated by formulas.

When plotting functions, make sure you select the XY chart type. If you use any other chart type, Excel always uses equal increments on the x-axis.

A BETTER WAY TO PLOT FUNCTIONS

You can use a technique developed by Stephen Bullen, an Excel expert extraordinaire, who resides in the United Kingdom. This method plots functions or formulas automatically without actually generating any values in the worksheet! This is one of the most impressive Excel applications I've seen.

The companion CD-ROM features a workbook that demonstrates Stephen's technique.

Figure 15-15 shows an example that plots the following function for 50 x values ranging from -5 to +5:

```
y = (x^3)*(x^2)
```

Stephen's technique uses two defined names: *Cht_X* and *Cht_Y*. The SERIES function in the chart, which uses these defined names, looks like this:

```
=SERIES(,Sheet1!Cht_X,Sheet1!Cht_Y,1)
```

To plot a function using this worksheet:

1. Enter the formula *as text* into cell B6.

2. Enter the beginning value for x into cell C9.

3. Enter the ending value for x into cell C10.

4. Specify the number of points to plot in cell C11.

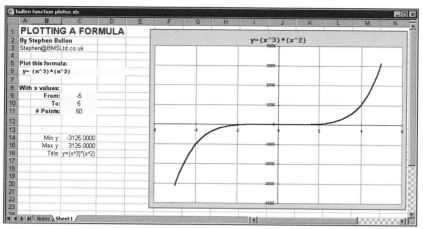

Figure 15-15: Plotting functions using a technique developed by Stephen Bullen

So how does it work? Let's start by analyzing the *Cht_X* formula, which generates the x values for the chart series:

```
=$C$9+(ROW(OFFSET($B$1,0,0,$C$11,1))-1)*($C$10-$C$9)/($C$11-1)
```

This formula uses the OFFSET function to generate an array of *n* values, where the value in cell C11 determines *n*. The array begins with the value in C9 and ends with the value in C11. The following expression calculates the increment between successive x values (calculated by subtracting the ending value from the beginning value, and dividing by the number of points minus 1).

```
=($C$10-$C$9)/($C$11-1)
```

As an example, when x begins with -3, ends with 3, and contains 5 data points, the following array is created:

```
{-3, -1.5, 0, 1.5, 3}
```

The *Cht_Y* formula uses the EVALUATE function to create an array of y values for the chart:

```
=EVALUATE(SUBSTITUTE(Sheet1!$B$6&"+x*0","x","Cht_X"))
```

EVALUATE is an XLM macro function, and it cannot be used in a worksheet formula. This function essentially evaluates a string expression and returns a result. Although you cannot use the EVALUATE function in a worksheet formula, you *can* use it in a name.

Suppose B6 contains the string *SIN(x)*, and the first x value is -3. The *Cht_Y* formula for the first data point is:

```
=EVALUATE(SUBSTITUTE("SIN(x)+x*0","x","Cht_X"))
```

The SUBSTITUTE function replaces each occurrence of *x* with *Cht_X*, and returns the string:

```
SIN(Cht_X)+Cht_X*0
```

The EVALUATE function grabs the first value (-3) from the array generated by the *Cht_X* formula, evaluates the following expression, and returns the result as the first y value:

```
SIN(-3)-3*0
```

 Because the formula replaces each occurrence of x with *Cht_X*, this technique does not work when you use functions that contain the letter X (for example, EXP or MAX).

The workbook contains additional formulas in the range C14:C16. The formula in C14 displays the minimum value in the array created by the *Cht_Y* formula.

```
=MIN(Cht_Y)
```

Cell C15 contains a formula to display the maximum of the y values:

```
= MAX(Cht_Y)
```

The formula in cell C16 serves as the chart's title:

```
=A6&B6&TEXT(NOW(),"")
```

This formula concatenates cells A6 and B6 and uses the NOW function to force an update of the chart.

Plotting functions with two variables

The preceding section described how to plot functions that use a single variable. For example, you can plot the following function for various values of x:

```
y = x^2
```

You also can plot functions that use two variables. For example, the following function calculates a value of z for various values of two variables (x and y):

```
z = SIN(x) * COS(y)
```

Figure 15-16 shows a surface chart that plots the value of z for x values ranging from -3.0 to 0, and for y values ranging from 2.0 to 5.0. Both x and y use an increment of 0.15.

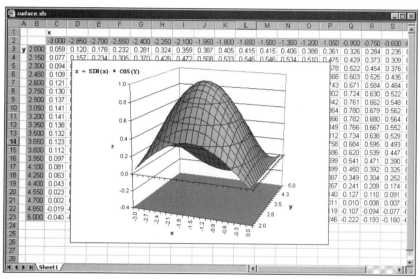

Figure 15-16: Using a surface chart to plot a function with two variables

If you work with surface charts, you may notice that this chart type has some serious limitations. Ideally, you want to create an "XYZ surface chart," in which you supply various values for X, Y, and Z. Unfortunately, Excel does not support this type of chart. Actually, a surface chart essentially shows a 3-D view of what looks like a rubber sheet stretched over a 3-D column chart. The example in Figure 15-16 contains 21 data series (corresponding to values of y), each of which contains 21 data points (corresponding to values of x).

To create a meaningful 3-D surface chart, you need to start with a 2-D range with the upper left cell empty. The top row should contain increasing or decreasing values of x with a constant difference between each x value. The left column should contain increasing or decreasing values of y with a constant difference between y values. The z values fill in the remaining cells corresponding to the respective x-y pair. Select the entire range as the source data for the chart.

"Secret" Formatting Tips for Surface Charts

You may discover that Excel does not permit you to select an individual data series in a surface chart. Because of this, you cannot perform the types of formatting normally available in the Format Data Series dialog box.

You can apply some types of formatting to a Surface chart, but Excel makes you jump through a few hoops to get to the proper dialog box — Format Legend Key (see the accompanying figure). To get to this dialog box, make sure the Surface chart displays a legend. Then, click the legend to select it and then click any legend key (a colored square to the left of the legend entry). Double-click the selected legend key and you'll get the Format Legend Key dialog box.

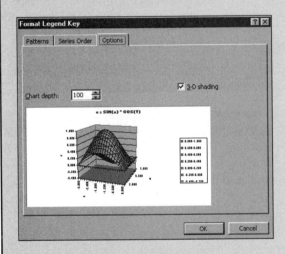

◆ Use the Patterns tab to change the color of the selected legend key; this also changes the color of the corresponding data series. If you would like your Surface chart to display using a single color, you need to change each legend key.

◆ Use the Options tab to change the depth of the chart. You can change the chart's depth by changing this setting while *any* legend key is selected.

◆ You can also apply 3-D shading in the Options tab. Again, this setting applies to the entire chart, not just the data series that corresponds to the selected legend entry.

Creating Awesome Designs

Figure 15-17 shows an example of an XY chart that displays "hypocycloid" curves using random values. This type of curve is the same as that generated by Hasbro's popular SpiroGraph toy, which you may remember from childhood.

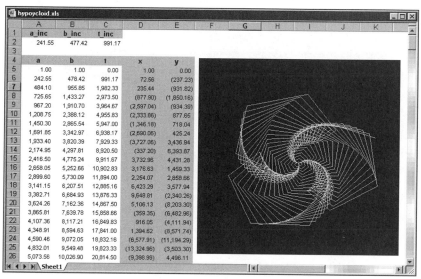

Figure 15-17: A hypocycloid curve

 The companion CD-ROM contains a workbook with a more sophisticated example of the technique shown in Figure 15-17.

The chart uses data in columns D and E (the *x* and *y* ranges). These columns contain formulas that rely on data in columns A through C. The first column (column D) consists of the following formula:

```
=(A5-B5)*COS(C5)+B5*COS((A5/B5-1)*C5)
```

The formula in the second column (column E) is as follows:

```
=(A5-B5)*SIN(C5)-B5*SIN((A5/B5-1)*C5)
```

Pressing F9 recalculates the worksheet, which generates new increment values (random) for columns A through C and creates a new display in the chart. The variety (and beauty) of charts generated using these formulas may amaze you. Figure 15-18 shows a few more examples.

Figure 15–18: Additional examples of hypocycloid curves, randomly generated

Working with Trendlines

With some charts, you may want to plot a trendline that describes the data. A *trendline* points out general trends in your data. In some cases, you can forecast future data with trendlines. A single series can have more than one trendline.

In general, only XY Scatter charts should use a trendline. If you use a different chart type (such as Column or Line), the x-values are assumed to be a series of integers that begin with 1.

Excel makes adding a trendline to a chart quite simple. Although you might expect this option to appear in the Format Data Series dialog box, it doesn't. You must go to the Add Trendline dialog box, shown in Figure 15-19, which you access by selecting Chart → Add Trendline. This command is available only when a data series is selected.

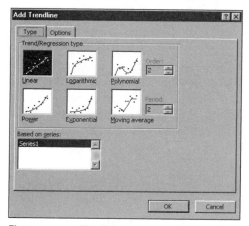

Figure 15-19: The Add Trendline dialog box offers several types of automatic trendlines.

The type of trendline that you choose depends on your data. Linear trends are the most common type, but you can describe some data more effectively with another type. When you click the Options tab in the Add Trendline dialog box, Excel displays the options shown in Figure 15-20.

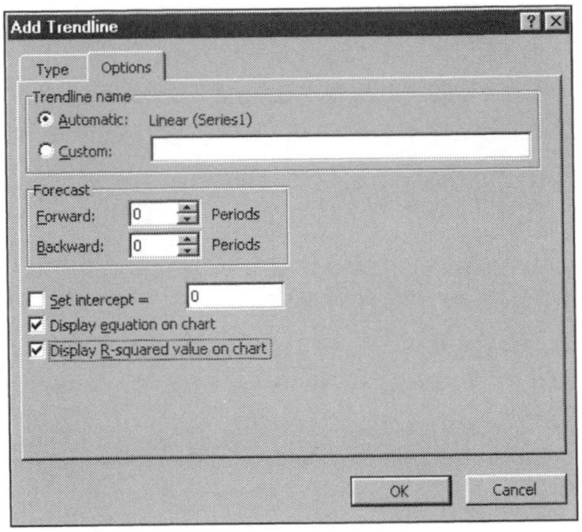

Figure 15-20: The Options tab in the Add Trendline dialog box

The Options tab enables you to specify a name to appear in the legend and the number of periods that you want to forecast. Additional options enable you to set the intercept value, specify that the equation used for the trendline should appear on the chart, and choose whether the R-squared value appears on the chart.

When Excel inserts a trendline, it may look like a new data series, but it's not. It's a new chart element with a name, such as Series 1 Trendline 1. You can double-click a trendline to change its formatting or its options.

Linear trendlines

Figure 15-21 shows two charts. The chart on the left depicts a data series without a trendline. As you can see, the data seems to be "linear" over time. The chart on the right is the same chart, but with a linear trendline that shows the trend in the data.

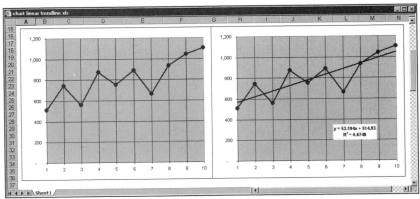

Figure 15-21: Before (left chart) and after (right chart) adding a linear trendline to a chart

The workbook shown in Figure 15-21 also appears on the companion CD-ROM.

The second chart also uses the options to display the equation and the R-squared value. In this example, the equation is:

```
y = 53.194x + 514.93
```

The R-squared value is 0.6748.

To display more or fewer decimal places in the equation and R-squared value, select the box and click the Increase Decimal or Decrease Decimal button on the Formatting toolbar.

What do these numbers mean? You can describe a straight line with an equation of the form:

```
y = mx +b
```

For each value of x (in this case, column B), you can calculate the predicted value of y (the value on the trendline) by using this equation. The variable *m* represents the slope of the line and b represents the y-intercept. For example, the month of February has an x value of 2 and a y value of 743. The predicted value for February, obtained using the following formula, is 621.318:

```
=(53.194*2)+514.93
```

The R-squared value, sometime referred to as the *coefficient of determination*, ranges in value from 0 to 1. This value indicates how closely the estimated values for the trendline correspond to your actual data. A trendline is most reliable when its R-squared value is at or near 1.

CALCULATING THE SLOPE AND Y-INTERCEPT

As you know, Excel can display the equation for the trendline in a chart. This equation shows the slope (m) and y-intercept (b) of the best-fit trendline. You can calculate the value of the slope and y-intercept yourself, using the LINEST function in a formula.

Figure 15-22 shows 10 data points (x values in column B, y values in column C). The formula that follows is an array formula that displays its result (the slope and y-intercept) in two cells.

```
{=LINEST(C2:C11,B2:B11) }
```

chart linear trendline.xls

	A	B	C	D	E	F	G	H
1	Month	X	Actual Y				m	b
2	Jan	1	512				53.19394	514.9333
3	Feb	2	743					
4	Mar	3	559					
5	Apr	4	875					
6	May	5	755					
7	Jun	6	890					
8	Jul	7	663					
9	Aug	8	934					
10	Sep	9	1,042					
11	Oct	10	1,102					
12	Nov	11						
13	Dec	12						
14								

Sheet1

Figure 15-22: Using the LINEST function to calculate slope and y-intercept

Figure 15-22 shows the formula entered into cells G2:H2. Select these two cells, type the formula (without the brackets), and press Ctrl+Shift+Enter. Cell F2 displays the slope; cell G2 displays the y-intercept.

CALCULATING PREDICTED VALUES

Once you know the values for the slope and y-intercept, you can calculate the predicted y value for each x. Figure 15-23 shows the result. Cell D2 contains the following formula, which is copied down the column.

```
=(B2*$G$2)+$H$2
```

chart linear trendline.xls

	A	B	C	D	E	F	G	H
1	Month	X	Actual Y	Predicted Y			m	b
2	Jan	1	512	568.12727			53.19394	514.9333
3	Feb	2	743	621.32121				
4	Mar	3	559	674.51515				
5	Apr	4	875	727.70909				
6	May	5	755	780.90303				
7	Jun	6	890	834.09697				
8	Jul	7	663	887.29091				
9	Aug	8	934	940.48485				
10	Sep	9	1,042	993.67879				
11	Oct	10	1,102	1046.87273				
12	Nov	11		1100.06667				
13	Dec	12		1153.26061				
14								

Sheet1

Figure 15-23: Column D contains formulas that calculate the predicted values for y.

The calculated values in column D represent the values used to plot the linear trendline. You can calculate predicted values of y without first computing the slope and y-intercept. You do so with an array formula that uses the TREND function. Select D2:D11, type the following formula (without the brackets), and press Ctrl+Shift+Enter.

```
{=TREND(C2:C11,B2:B11)}
```

LINEAR FORECASTING

When your chart contains a trendline, you can instruct Excel to forecast and plot additional values. You do this on the Options tab in the Format Trendline dialog box (or the Options tab in the Add Trendline dialog box). Just specify the number of periods to forecast. Figure 15-24 shows a chart that forecasts results for two subsequent periods.

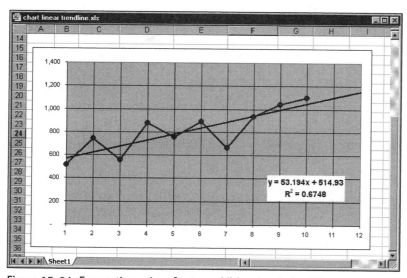

Figure 15-24: Forecasting values for two additional periods of time.

If you know the values of the slope and y-intercept (see "Calculating the Slope and Y-Intercept," earlier in the chapter), you can calculate forecasts for other values of x. For example, to calculate the value of y when x = 11 (November), use the following formula:

```
=(53.194*11)+514.93
```

You can also forecast values by using the FORECAST function. The following formula, for example, forecasts the value for November (that is, x = 11) using known x and known y values.

```
=FORECAST(11,C2:C11,B2:B11)
```

CALCULATING R-SQUARED

The accuracy of forecasted values depends on how well the linear trendline fits your actual data. The value of R-squared represents the degree of fit. R-squared values closer to 1 indicate a better fit and more accurate predictions. In other words, you can interpret R-squared as the proportion of the variance in y attributable to the variance in x.

As described previously, you can instruct Excel to display the R-squared value in the chart. Or, you can calculate it directly in your worksheet using the RSQ function. The following formula calculates R-squared for x values in B1:B11 and y values for C1:C11:

```
=RSQ(B2:B11,C2:C11)
```

 The value of R-squared calculated by the RSQ function is valid only for a linear trendline.

Nonlinear trendlines

Curve fitting refers to the process of making projections beyond a data range (extrapolation) or making estimates between acquired data points (interpolation). Besides linear trendlines, an Excel chart can display trendlines of the following types:

◆ Logarithmic: Used when the rate of change in the data increases or decreases quickly, and then flattens out

◆ Power: Used when the data consists of measurements that increase at a specific rate. The data cannot contain zero or negative values.

◆ Exponential: Used when data values rise or fall at increasingly higher rates. The data cannot contain zero or negative values.

◆ Polynomial: Used when data fluctuates. You can specify the order of the polynomial (from 2 to 6) depending on the number of fluctuations in the data.

The Type tab in the Trendline dialog box offers the option of Moving average, which really isn't a trendline. This option, however, can be useful for smoothing out "noisy" data. The Moving average option enables you to specify the number of data points to include in each average. For example, if you select 5, Excel averages every five data points.

Earlier in this chapter, I described how to calculate the slope and y-intercept for the linear equation that describes a linear trendline. Nonlinear trendlines also have equations, as described in the sections that follow.

The companion CD-ROM contains a workbook with the nonlinear trendline examples described in this section.

LOGARITHMIC TRENDLINE
The equation for a logarithmic trendline appears like this:

```
y = (c * LN(x)) - b
```

Figure 15-25 shows a chart with a logarithmic trendline added. A single array formula in E2:F2 calculates the values for c and b. The formula is:

```
{=LINEST(C2:C11,LN(B2:B11))}
```
Column C shows the predicted y values for each value of *x*, using the calculated values for b and c. For example, the formula in cell C2 is:

```
=($E$2*LN(A2))+$F$2
```

As you can see, a logarithmic trendline does not provide a good fit for this data. The R-square value is low, and the trendline does not match the data.

POWER TRENDLINE
The equation for a power trendline looks like:

```
y = c * x^b
```

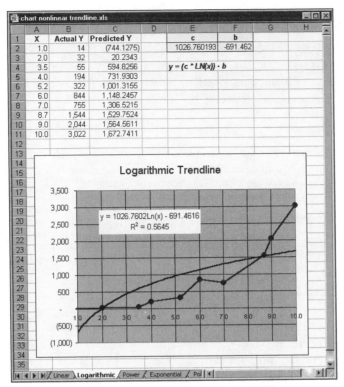

Figure 15-25: A chart displaying a logarithmic trendline

Figure 15-26 shows a chart with a power trendline added. The first element in a two-cell array formula in E2:F2 calculates the values for b. The formula is:

```
=LINEST(LN(B2:B11),LN(A2:A11),,TRUE)
```

The following formula, in cell F3, calculates the value for c:

```
=EXP(F2)
```

Column C shows the predicted y values for each value of x, using the calculated values for b and c. For example, the formula in cell C2 is:

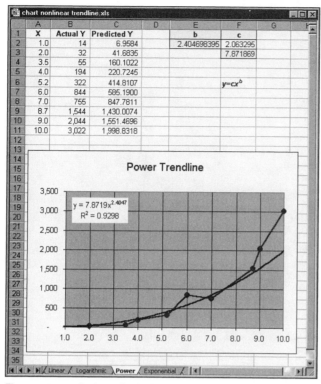

Figure 15-26: A chart displaying a power trendline

```
=$F$3*(A2^$E$2)
```

EXPONENTIAL TRENDLINE

The equation for an exponential trendline looks like this:

y = c * EXP(b * x)Figure 15-27 shows a chart with an exponential trendline
added. The first element in a two-cell array formula in F2:G2 calculates the values
for b. The formula is:

```
{=LINEST(LN(B2:B11),A2:A11)}
```

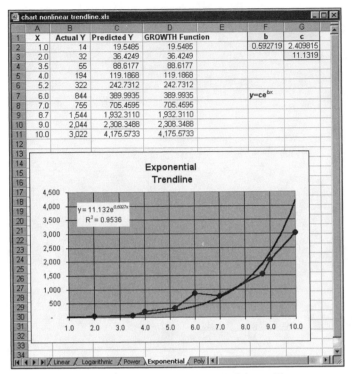

Figure 15–27: A chart displaying an exponential trendline

The following formula, in cell G3, calculates the value for c:

```
=EXP(G2)
```

Column C shows the predicted y values for each value of x, using the calculated values for b and c. For example, the formula in cell C2 is:

```
=$G$3*EXP($F$2*A2)
```

Column D uses the GROWTH function in an array formula to generate predicted y values. The array formula, entered in D2:D10, appears like this:

```
{=GROWTH(B2:B11,A2:A11)}
```

POLYNOMIAL TRENDLINE

When you request a polynomial trendline, you also need to specify the order of the polynomial (ranging from 2 through 6). The equation for an exponential trendline depends on the order. The following equation, for example, is for a third-order polynomial trendline:

$$y = (c3 * x^3) + (c2 * x^2) + (c1 * x^1) + b$$

Notice that there are three c coefficients (one for each order).

Figure 15-28 shows a chart with a third-order polynomial trendline added. A four-element array formula entered in F2:I2 caluculates the values for each of three c coefficients and the b coefficient. The formula is:

```
{=LINEST(B2:B11,A2:A11^{1,2,3})}
```

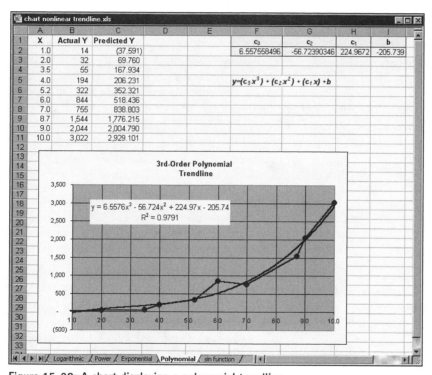

Figure 15-28: A chart displaying a polynomial trendline

Column C shows the predicted y values for each value of x, using the calculated values for b and the three c coefficients. For example, the formula in cell C2 is:

```
=($F$2*A2^3)+($G$2*A2^2)+($H$2*A2)+$I$2
```

Useful Chart Tricks

This section contains a number of useful charting tricks that I've accumulated over the years. These tricks include storing multiple charts on a chart sheet, viewing an embedded chart in a window, changing worksheet values by dragging data points in a chart, and animating charts.

Storing multiple charts on a chart sheet

Most Excel users would agree that a chart sheet holds a single chart. Most of the time, that's a true statement. However, it's certainly possible to store multiple charts on a single chart sheet. In fact, Excel enables you to do this directly. If you activate an embedded chart and then select Chart→Location, Excel displays its Chart Location dialog box. If you select the As new sheet option and specify an existing chart sheet as the location, you see the dialog box shown in Figure 15-29. Click OK and the chart appears on top of the chart in the chart sheet.

Figure 15-29: Excel enables you to relocate an embedded chart to an existing chart sheet.

Generally, you'll want to add embedded charts to an *empty* chart sheet. To create an empty chart sheet, select a single blank cell and press F11.

By storing multiple charts on a chart sheet, you can take advantage of the View→Sized with Window command to automatically scale the charts to the window size and dimensions. Figure 15-30 shows an example of a chart sheet that contains eight embedded charts.

Viewing an embedded chart in a window

When you activate an embedded chart, the chart actually is contained in a window that is normally *invisible*. To see an embedded chart in its own window, right-click the embedded chart and select Chart Window from the shortcut menu. The embedded chart remains on the worksheet, but the chart also appears in its own floating window. You can move and resize this window (but you can't maximize it). If you move the window, you'll notice that the embedded chart still displays in its original location. Activating any other window makes the embedded chart window invisible again.

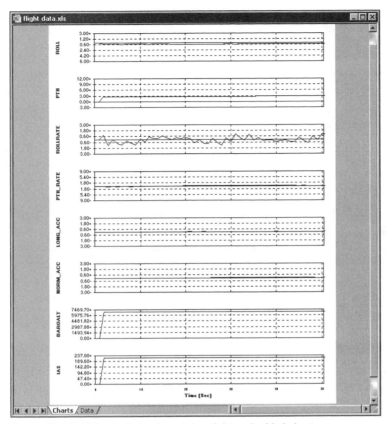

Figure 15-30: This chart sheet contains eight embedded charts.

Changing a worksheet value by dragging a data point

Excel provides an interesting chart-making feature that also can prove somewhat dangerous. This feature enables you to change the value in a worksheet by dragging the data markers on two-dimensional line charts, bar charts, column charts, XY charts, and bubble charts.

Here's how it works. Select an individual data point in a chart series (not the entire series) and then drag the point in the direction in which you want to adjust the value. As you drag the data marker, the corresponding value in the worksheet changes to correspond to the data point's new position on the chart. Figure 15-31 shows the result of dragging the data points around on an XY chart with five data series.

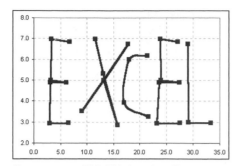

Figure 15-31: This XY chart has five data series.

If the value of a data point that you move is the result of a formula, Excel displays its Goal Seek dialog box. Use this dialog box to specify the cell that Excel should adjust to make the formula produce the result that you pointed out on the chart. This technique is useful if you know what a chart should look like and you want to determine the values that will produce the chart. Obviously, this feature also can be dangerous, because you inadvertently can change values that you shouldn't – so exercise caution.

Using animated charts

Most people don't realize it, but Excel is capable of performing simple animations using shapes and charts (animations require macros). Consider the XY chart shown in Figure 15-32.

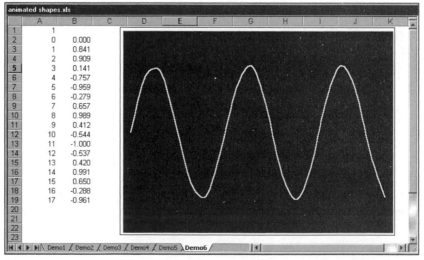

Figure 15-32: A simple VBA procedure turns this chart into an interesting animation.

The x values (column A) depend on the value in cell A1. The value in each row represents the previous row's value, plus the value in A1. Column B contains formulas that calculate the SIN of the corresponding value in column A. The following simple procedure produces an interesting animation. It simply changes the value in cell A1, which causes the values in the x and y ranges to change.

```
Sub AnimateChart()
    Range("A1") = 0
    For i = 1 To 150
        Range("A1") = Range("A1") + 0.035
    Next i
    Range("A1") = 0
End Sub
```

The companion CD-ROM contains a workbook that features this animated chart, plus several other animation examples.

Creating a "clock" chart

Figure 15-33 shows an XY chart formatted to look like a clock. It not only *looks* like a clock, but it also functions like a clock. There is really no reason why anyone would need to display a clock such as this on a worksheet, but creating the workbook was challengeing, and you may find it instructive.

	Hour Hand		Minute Hand		Second Hand		Numbers	
	x	y	x	y	x	y	x	y
	0.000	0.000	0.000	0.000	0.000	0.000	0.000	1.000
	-0.477	-0.150	0.383	-0.702	0.845	0.089	0.500	0.866
							0.866	0.500
							1.000	0.000
							0.866	-0.500
							0.500	-0.866
							0.000	-1.000
							-0.500	-0.866
							-0.866	-0.500
							-1.000	0.000
							-0.866	0.500
							-0.500	0.866

Figure 15-33: This fully functional clock is actually an XY chart in disguise.

The chart uses four data series: one for the hour hand, one for the minute hand, one for the second hand, and one for the numbers. The last data series draws a circle with 12 points. The numbers consist of manually entered data labels. (See the sidebar, "Plotting a Circle.")

The formulas listed in Table 15-2 calculate the data series for the clock hands (the range G4:L4 contains zero values, not formulas).

TABLE **15-2 FORMULAS USED TO GENERATE A CLOCK CHART**

Cell	Description	Formula
G5	Origin of hour hand	=0.5*SIN((HOUR(NOW())+(MINUTE(NOW())/60))*(2*PI()/12))
H5	End of hour hand	=0.5*COS((HOUR(NOW())+(MINUTE(NOW())/60))*(2*PI()/12))
I5	Origin of minute hand	=0.8*SIN((MINUTE(NOW())+(SECOND(NOW())/60))*(2*PI()/60))
J5	End of minute hand	=0.8*COS((MINUTE(NOW())+(SECOND(NOW())/60))*(2*PI()/60))
K5	Origin of second hand	=0.85*SIN(SECOND(NOW())*(2*PI()/60))
L5	End of second had	=0.85*COS(SECOND(NOW())*(2*PI()/60))

This workbook uses a simple VBA procedure, which recalculates the worksheet every second.

In addition to the clock chart, the workbook contains a text box that displays the time using the NOW() function, as shown in Figure 15-34. Normally hidden, you can display this text box by deselecting the *Analog clock* checkbox. A simple VBA procedure attached to the checkbox hides and unhides the chart, depending on the status of the checkbox.

The workbook with the animated clock example appears on the companion CD-ROM. The CD also includes a different version of this file that uses VBA procedures instead of formulas.

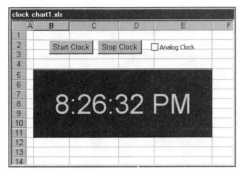

Figure 15-34: Displaying a digital clock in a worksheet is much easier, but not as fun to create.

When you examine the workbook, keep the following points in mind.

◆ The ChartObject, named *ClockChart*, covers up a range named *DigitalClock* – used to display the time digitally.

◆ The two buttons on the worksheet are from the Forms toolbar, and each has a VBA procedure assigned to it (StartClock and StopClock).

◆ The CheckBox control (named *cbClockType*) on the worksheet is from the Forms toolbar, not from the Control Toolbox toolbar. Clicking the object executes a procedure named cbClockType_Click, which simply toggles the Visible property of the ChartObject. When invisible, the digital clock is revealed.

◆ The chart is an XY chart with four Series objects. These series represent the hour hand, the minute hand, the second hand, and the 12 numbers.

◆ The UpdateClock procedure executes when you click the Start Clock button. This procedure determines which clock is visible and performs the appropriate updating.

◆ The UpdateClock procedure uses the OnTime method of the Application object. This method enables you to execute a procedure at a specific time. Before the UpdateClock procedure ends, it sets up a new OnTime event that occurs in one second. In other words, the UpdateClock procedure is called every second.

◆ The UpdateClock procedure uses some basic trigonometry to determine the angles at which to display the hands on the ciock.

Plotting a Circle

You can create an XY chart that draws a perfect circle. To do so, you need two ranges, one for the x values and another for the y values. The number of data points in the series determines the *smoothness* of the circle. Or, you simply select the Smoothed line option in the Format Series dialog box (Patterns tab) for the data series.

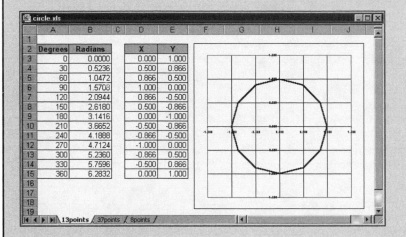

The example shown (available on the companion CD-ROM) uses 13 points to create the circle. If you work in degrees, generate a series of values such as the ones shown in column A. The series starts with 0 and has 30-degree increments. If you work in radians (column B), the first series starts with 0 and increments by PI/6.

The ranges used in the chart appear in columns D and E. If you work in degrees, the formula in D3 is:

```
=SIN(RADIANS(A3))
```

The formula in E3 is:

```
=COS(RADIANS(A3))
```

If you work in radians, use this formula in D3:

```
=SIN(A3)
```

And use this formula in E3:

```
=COS(A3)
```

The formulas in D3 and E3 simply copy down to subsequent rows.

To plot a circle with more data points, you need to adjust the increment value in columns A and B (or C and D if working in radians). The final value should be the same as those shown in row 15. In degrees, the increment is 360 divided by the number of data points -1. In radians, the increment is π divided by the number of data points - 1,divided by 2.

Drawing with an XY chart

The final example has absolutely no practical value, but you may find it interesting (and maybe even a bit entertaining). The worksheet consists of an embedded XY chart, along with a number of controls. (These controls, from the Forms toolbar, are not ActiveX controls.)

The workbook that demonstrates drawing with an XY chart appears on the companion CD-ROM.

Clicking one of the arrow buttons draws a line in the chart, the size of which is determined by the step value, set with one of the Spin controls. With a little practice (and patience) you can create simple sketches. Figure 15-35 shows an example.

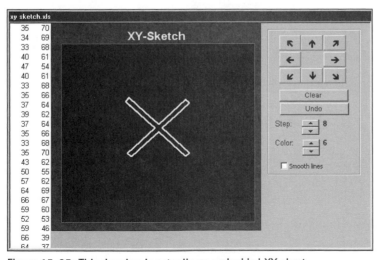

Figure 15-35: This drawing is actually an embedded XY chart.

Clicking an arrow button executes a macro that adds two values to a range: an X value and a Y value. It then redefines two range names (XRange and YRange) used in the chart's SERIES formula. Particularly handy is the multilevel Undo button. Clicking this button simply erases the last two values in the range, and then redefines the range names. Additional accoutrements include the capability to change the color of the lines and the capability to display smoothed lines.

Summary

This chapter presented details on the SERIES formula used in charts, and presented several examples of non-standard charts that you can produce with Excel. The chapter also discussed various types of trendlines and provided techniques for plotting functions. It presented a variety of useful chart tips and techniques that you can adapt for use with your charts.

The next chapter covers formula techniques with pivot tables.

Chapter 16

Pivot Tables

EXCEL'S PIVOT TABLE feature probably represents the most technologically sophisticated component in Excel. This chapter may seem a bit out of place in this book. After all, a pivot table does its job without using formulas. That's exactly the point. If you haven't yet discovered the power of pivot tables, this chapter will demonstrate how using a pivot table can serve as an excellent alternative to creating many complex formulas.

About Pivot Tables

A pivot table is essentially a dynamic summary report generated from a database. The database can reside in a worksheet or in an external file. A pivot table can help transform endless rows and columns of numbers into a meaningful presentation of the data.

For example, a pivot table can create frequency distributions and cross-tabulations of several different data dimensions. In addition, you can display subtotals and any level of detail that you want. Perhaps the most innovative aspect of a pivot table lies in its interactivity. After you create a pivot table, you can rearrange the information in almost any way imaginable, and even insert special *formulas* that perform new calculations. You even can create post hoc groupings of summary items (for example, combine Northern Region totals with Western Region totals).

As far as I can tell, the term *pivot table* is unique to Excel. The name stems from the fact that you can rotate the table's row and column headings around the core data area to give you different views of your summarized data.

One minor drawback to using a pivot table is that, unlike a formula-based summary report, a pivot table does not update automatically when you change the source data. This does not pose a serious problem, however, since a single click of the Refresh toolbar button forces a pivot table to use the latest data.

A pivot table example

The best way to understand the concept of a pivot table is to see one. Start with Figure 16-1, which shows the data used in creating the pivot table in this chapter.

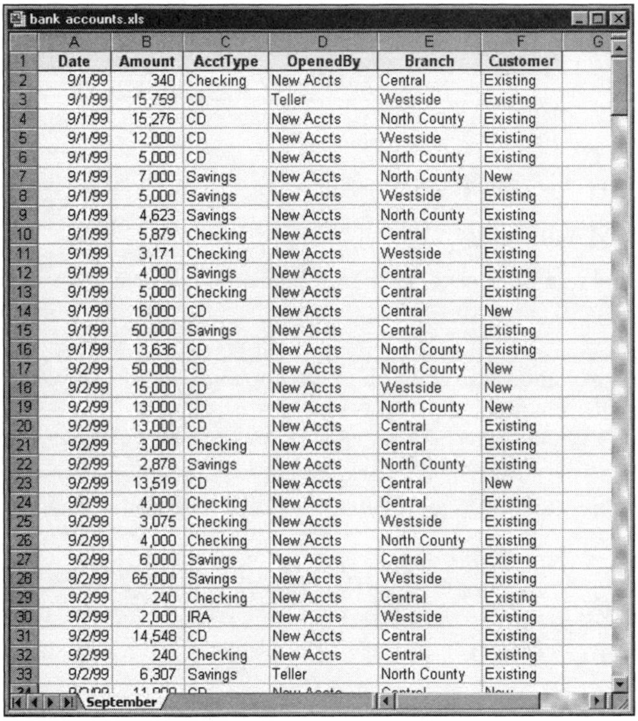
bank accounts.xls

	Date	Amount	AcctType	OpenedBy	Branch	Customer
2	9/1/99	340	Checking	New Accts	Central	Existing
3	9/1/99	15,759	CD	Teller	Westside	Existing
4	9/1/99	15,276	CD	New Accts	North County	Existing
5	9/1/99	12,000	CD	New Accts	Westside	Existing
6	9/1/99	5,000	CD	New Accts	North County	Existing
7	9/1/99	7,000	Savings	New Accts	North County	New
8	9/1/99	5,000	Savings	New Accts	Westside	Existing
9	9/1/99	4,623	Savings	New Accts	North County	Existing
10	9/1/99	5,879	Checking	New Accts	Central	Existing
11	9/1/99	3,171	Checking	New Accts	Westside	Existing
12	9/1/99	4,000	Savings	New Accts	Central	Existing
13	9/1/99	5,000	Checking	New Accts	Central	Existing
14	9/1/99	16,000	CD	New Accts	Central	New
15	9/1/99	50,000	Savings	New Accts	Central	Existing
16	9/1/99	13,636	CD	New Accts	North County	Existing
17	9/2/99	50,000	CD	New Accts	North County	New
18	9/2/99	15,000	CD	New Accts	Westside	New
19	9/2/99	13,000	CD	New Accts	North County	New
20	9/2/99	13,000	CD	New Accts	Central	Existing
21	9/2/99	3,000	Checking	New Accts	Central	Existing
22	9/2/99	2,878	Savings	New Accts	North County	Existing
23	9/2/99	13,519	CD	New Accts	Central	New
24	9/2/99	4,000	Checking	New Accts	Central	Existing
25	9/2/99	3,075	Checking	New Accts	Westside	Existing
26	9/2/99	4,000	Checking	New Accts	North County	Existing
27	9/2/99	6,000	Savings	New Accts	Central	Existing
28	9/2/99	65,000	Savings	New Accts	Westside	Existing
29	9/2/99	240	Checking	New Accts	Central	Existing
30	9/2/99	2,000	IRA	New Accts	Westside	Existing
31	9/2/99	14,548	CD	New Accts	Central	Existing
32	9/2/99	240	Checking	New Accts	Central	Existing
33	9/2/99	6,307	Savings	Teller	North County	Existing

September

Figure 16-1: This database is used to create a pivot table.

This database consists of daily new-account information for a three-branch bank. The database contains 350 records, and tracks:

- The date that each account was opened
- The opening amount
- The account type (CD, checking, savings, or IRA)
- Who opened the account (a teller or a new-account representative)
- The branch at which it was opened (Central, Westside, or North County)
- Whether a new customer or an existing customer opened the account

The workbook shown in Figure 16-1 also appears on the companion CD-ROM.

The bank accounts database contains a lot of information. But in its current form, the data does not reveal much. To make the data more useful, you need to summarize it. Summarizing a database is essentially the process of answering questions about the data. Following are a few questions that may be of interest to the bank's management:

◆ What is the total deposit amount for each branch, broken down by account type?

◆ How many accounts were opened at each branch, broken down by account type?

◆ What's the dollar distribution of the different account types?

◆ What types of accounts do tellers open most often?

◆ How does the Central branch compare to the other two branches?

◆ Which branch opens the most accounts for new customers?

You could, of course, write formulas to answer these questions. Often, however, a pivot table presents a better choice. Creating a pivot table takes only a few seconds and doesn't require a single formula.

Figure 16-2 shows a pivot table created from the database displayed in Figure 16-1. This pivot table shows the amount of new deposits, broken down by branch and account type. This particular summary represents one of dozens of summaries that you can produce from this data.

bank accounts.xls				
	A	B	C	D	E
1					
2					
3	Sum of Amount	Branch			
4	AcctType	Central	North County	Westside	Grand Total
5	CD	859,438	830,139	344,962	2,034,539
6	Checking	208,208	92,225	90,597	391,030
7	IRA	63,380	134,374	10,000	207,754
8	Savings	332,349	152,607	154,000	638,956
9	Grand Total	1,463,375	1,209,345	599,559	3,272,279
10					
11					

Sheet1 / September /

Figure 16-2: A simple pivot table

Figure 16-3 shows another pivot table generated from the bank data. This pivot table uses a page field for the Customer item. In this case, the pivot table displays the data only for existing customers. Notice the changes in the orientation of the table; branches appear in rows and account types appear in columns.

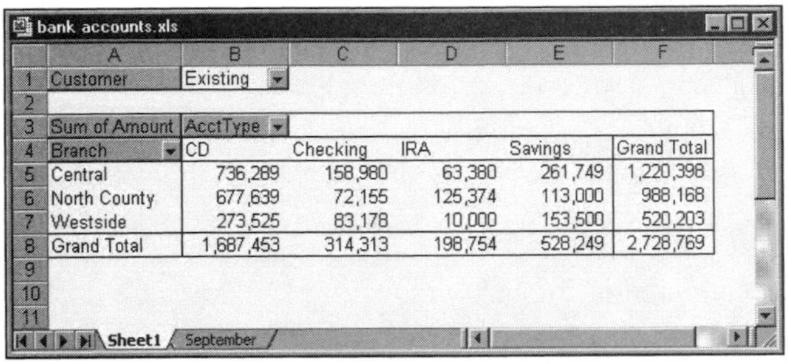
bank accounts.xls

Customer	Existing				
Sum of Amount	AcctType				
Branch	CD	Checking	IRA	Savings	Grand Total
Central	736,289	158,980	63,380	261,749	1,220,398
North County	677,639	72,155	125,374	113,000	988,168
Westside	273,525	83,178	10,000	153,500	520,203
Grand Total	1,687,453	314,313	198,754	528,249	2,728,769

Figure 16-3: A pivot table that uses a page field

Data appropriate for a pivot table

Not all data can be used to create a pivot table. The data that you summarize must be in the form of a database. You can store the database in either a worksheet (sometimes known as a list) or an external database file. Although Excel can convert any database to a pivot table, not all databases benefit.

Generally speaking, fields in a database table can consist of two types:

- Data: Contains a value or data to be summarized. In Figure 16-1, the Amount field is a data field.
- Category: Describes the data. In Figure 16-1, the Date, AcctType, OpenedBy, Branch, and Customer fields are category fields because they describe the data in the Amount field.

A single database table can have any number of data fields and category fields. When you create a pivot table, you usually want to summarize one or more of the data fields. Conversely, the values in the category fields appear in the pivot table as rows, columns, or pages.

Exceptions exist, however, and you may find Excel's pivot table feature useful even for databases that don't contain actual numerical data fields. The database in Figure 16-4, for example, doesn't contain any numerical data, but you can create a useful pivot table that counts the items in fields rather than sums them.

Employee	Month Born	Sex
Amos	January	Male
Baker	December	Female
Carlos	November	Female
Davidson	April	Female
Elinore	January	Male
Frankindorf	February	Male
Galiaga	May	Male
Hessidia	February	Female
Iniz	September	Male
Jacobs	October	Female
Kent	June	Female
Lopez	March	Female
Martin	February	Male
Nu	September	Female
Oswald	July	Male
Parkinson	March	Female
Quincy	January	Female

Figure 16-4: This database doesn't have any numerical fields, but you can use it to generate a pivot table.

You can summarize information in pivot tables by using methods other than summing. For example, the pivot table that you see in Figure 16-5 cross-tabulates the Month Born field by the Sex field; the intersecting cells show the count for each combination of month and gender.

Count of Employee	Sex		
Month Born	Female	Male	Grand Total
January	2	2	4
February	1	2	3
March	2		2
April	1	1	2
May	1	1	2
June	1		1
July	1	1	2
August	1	1	2
September	1	1	2
October	1	1	2
November	2	1	3
December	1		1
Grand Total	15	11	26

Figure 16-5: This pivot table summarizes non-numeric fields by displaying a count rather than a sum.

Pivot Table Terminology

Understanding the terminology associated with pivot tables is the first step in mastering this feature. Refer to the accompanying figure to get your bearings.

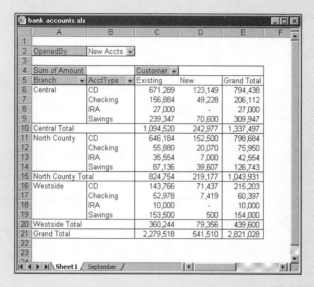

◆ **Column field:** A field that has a column orientation in the pivot table. Each item in the field occupies a column. In the figure, Customer represents a column field that contains two items (Existing and New). You can have nested column fields.

◆ **Data area:** The cells in a pivot table that contain the summary data. Excel offers several ways to summarize the data (sum, average, count, and so on). In the figure, the Data area includes C6:E21.

◆ **Grand totals:** A row or column that displays totals for all cells in a row or column in a pivot table. You can specify that grand totals be calculated for rows, columns, or both (or neither). The pivot table in the figure shows grand totals for both rows and columns.

◆ **Group:** A collection of items treated as a single item. You can group items manually or automatically (group dates into months, for example). The pivot table in the figure does not have any defined groups.

◆ **Item:** An element in a field that appears as a row or column header in a pivot table. In the figure, Existing and New are items for the Customer field. The Branch field has three items: Central, North County, and Westside. AcctType has four items: CD, Checking, IRA, and Savings.

- ◆ Page field: A field that has a page orientation in the pivot table — similar to a slice of a three-dimensional cube. You can display only one item (or all items) in a page field at one time. In the figure, OpenedBy represents a page field that displays the New Accts item; the pivot table shows data only for New Accts.

- ◆ Refresh: To recalculate the pivot table after making changes to the source data.

- ◆ Row field: A field that has a row orientation in the pivot table. Each item in the field occupies a row. You can have nested row fields. In the figure, Branch and AcctType both represent row fields.

- ◆ Source data: The data used to create a pivot table. It can reside in a worksheet or an external database.

- ◆ Subtotals: A row or column that displays subtotals for detail cells in a row or column in a pivot table. The pivot table in the figure displays subtotals for each branch.

Creating a Pivot Table

You create a pivot table using a series of steps presented in the PivotTable and PivotChart Wizard. You access this wizard by choosing Data → PivotTable and PivotChart Report. Then, carry out the steps outlined here.

This discussion assumes you use Excel 2000. The procedure differs slightly in earlier versions of Excel.

Step1: Specifying the data location

When you choose Data → PivotTable and PivotChart Report, you'll see the dialog box shown in Figure 16-6.

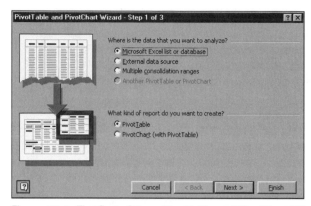

Figure 16-6: The first of three PivotTable and PivotChart Wizard dialog boxes

In this step, you identify the data source. Excel is quite flexible in the data that you can use for a pivot table. (See the sidebar, "Pivot Table Data Sources.") This example uses a worksheet database.

You see different dialog boxes while you work through the Wizard, depending on the location of the data that you want to analyze. The following sections present the Wizard's dialog boxes for data located in an Excel list or database, in the context of describing the various possible data sources.

Pivot Table Data Sources

The data used in a pivot table can come from a variety of sources, including Excel databases or lists, data sources external to Excel, multiple tabled ranges, and other pivot tables. I describe these sources here.

Excel list or database

Usually, the data that you analyze is stored in a worksheet database (also known as a list). Databases stored in a worksheet have a limit of 65,535 records and 256 fields. Working with a database of this size isn't efficient, however (and memory may not even permit it). The first row in the database should contain field names. No other rules exist. The data can consist of values, text, or formulas.

External data source

If you use the data in an external database for a pivot table, use Query (a separate application) to retrieve the data. You can use dBASE files, SQL server data, or other data that your system is set up to access. Step 2 of the PivotTable and PivotChart Wizard prompts you for the data source. Note that in Excel 2000, you also can create a pivot table from an OLAP (OnLine Analytical Processing) database.

Multiple consolidation ranges

You also can create a pivot table from multiple tables. This procedure is equivalent to consolidating the information in tables. When you create a pivot table to consolidate information in tables, you have the added advantage of using all of the pivot table tools while working with the consolidated data.

Another pivot table

Excel enables you to create a pivot table from an existing pivot table. Actually, this is a bit of a misnomer. The pivot table that you create is based on the *data* that the first pivot table uses (not the pivot table itself). If the active workbook has no pivot tables, this option is grayed — meaning you can't choose it. If you need to create more than one pivot table from the same set of data, the procedure is more efficient (in terms of memory usage) if you create the first pivot table and then use that pivot table as the source for subsequent pivot tables.

Step 2: Specifying the data

To move on to the next step of the Wizard, click the Next button. Step 2 of the PivotTable and PivotChart Wizard prompts you for the data. Remember, the dialog box varies depending on your choice in the first dialog box; Figure 16-7 shows the dialog box that appears when you select an Excel list or database in Step 1.

Figure 16-7: In Step 2, you specify the data range.

If you place the cell pointer anywhere within the worksheet database when you select Data → PivotTable Report, Excel identifies the database range automatically in Step 2 of the PivotTable and PivotChart Wizard.

You can use the Browse button to open a different worksheet and select a range. To move on to Step 3, click the Next button.

TIP   If the source range for a pivot table is named *Database*, you can use Excel's built-in Data Form to add new data to the range. The named range will extend automatically to include the new records.

Step 3: Completing the pivot table

Figure 16-8 shows the dialog box for the final step of the PivotTable and PivotChart Wizard. In this step, you specify the location for the pivot table.

Figure 16-8: In Step 3, you specify the pivot table's location.

If you select the New worksheet option, Excel inserts a new worksheet for the pivot table. If you select the Existing worksheet option, the pivot table appears on the current worksheet (you can specify the starting cell location).

At this point, you can click the Options button to select some options that determine how the table appears. (Refer to the sidebar "Pivot Table Options.") You can set these options at any time after you create the pivot table, so you do not need to do so before creating the pivot table.

You can set up the actual layout of the pivot table by using either of two techniques:

◆ By clicking the Layout button in Step 3 of the PivotTable and PivotChart Wizard. You then can use a dialog box to lay out the pivot table.

◆ By clicking the Finish button to create a blank pivot table. You then can use the PivotTable toolbar to lay out the pivot table.

I describe both of these options in the following subsections.

USING A DIALOG BOX TO LAY OUT A PIVOT TABLE

When you click the Layout button of the Wizard's last dialog box, you get the dialog box shown in Figure 16-9. The fields in the database appear as buttons along the right side of the dialog box. Simply drag the buttons to the appropriate area of the pivot table diagram (which appears in the center of the dialog box).

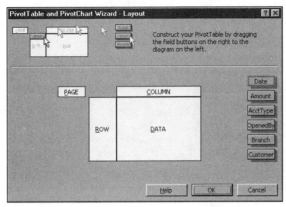

Figure 16-9: Specify the table layout

 For versions prior to Excel 2000, this dialog box appears as Step 4 of the Wizard. For these versions, this is the only way to lay out a pivot table.

The pivot table diagram has four areas:

◆ Page: Values in the field appear as page items in the pivot table.

◆ Row: Values in the field appear as row items in the pivot table.

◆ Data: The field is summarized in the pivot table.

◆ Column: Values in the field appear as column items in the pivot table.

You can drag as many field buttons as you want to any of these locations, and you don't have to use all the fields. Any fields that you don't use simply don't appear in the pivot table.

When you drag a field button to the Data area, the PivotTable and PivotChart Wizard apply the Sum function if the field contains numeric values; they apply the Count function if the field contains non-numeric values.

While you set up the pivot table, you can double-click a field button to customize it. You can specify, for example, to summarize a particular field as a Count or other function. You also can specify which items in a field to hide or omit. If you drag a field button to an incorrect location, just drag it off the table diagram to get rid of it. Note that you can customize fields at any time after you create the pivot table; I demonstrate this later in the chapter.

Figure 16-10 shows how the dialog box looks after dragging some field buttons to the pivot table diagram. This pivot table displays the sum of the Amount field, broken down by AcctType (as rows) and Customer (as columns). In addition, the Branch field appears as a page field. Click OK to redisplay the PivotTable and PivotChart Wizard – Step 3 of the dialog box.

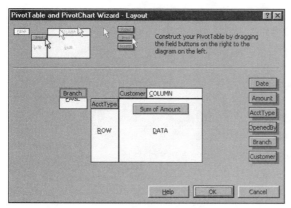

Figure 16-10: The table layout after dragging field buttons to the pivot table diagram

USING THE PIVOTTABLE TOOLBAR TO LAY OUT A PIVOT TABLE

You may prefer to lay out your pivot table directly in the worksheet, using the PivotTable toolbar. The technique closely resembles the one just described, because you still drag and drop fields. But in this case, you drag fields from the toolbar into the worksheet.

 You cannot use this technique with versions prior to Excel 2000.

Complete the first two steps of the PivotTable and PivotChart Wizard. If you want, set options for the pivot table by using the Options button that appears in the third dialog box of the Wizard. Don't bother with the Layout button, however.

Select a location for the pivot table and choose Finish. Excel displays a pivot table template similar to the one you see in Figure 16-11. The template provides you with hints about where to drop various types of fields.

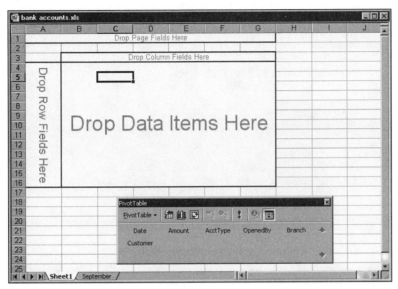

Figure 16-11: Use the PivotTable toolbar to drag and drop fields onto the pivot table template that Excel displays.

Drag and drop fields from the PivotTable toolbar onto the template. As you point at buttons on the toolbar, you'll see tool tips that instruct you to drag the field to the template. Excel continues to update the pivot table as you drag and drop fields; for this reason, you'll find this method easiest to use if you drag and drop data items last.

If you make a mistake, simply drag the field off the template and drop it any-place on the worksheet — Excel removes it from the pivot table template. All fields remain on the PivotTable toolbar, even if you use them.

THE FINISHED PRODUCT

Figure 16-12 shows the result of this example. Notice that the page field displays as a drop-down box. You can choose which item in the page field to display by choosing it from the list. You also can choose an item called All, which displays all the data.

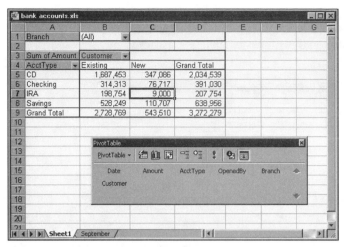

Figure 16-12: The pivot table created by the PivotTable and PivotChart Wizard

Pivot Table Options

Excel provides plenty of options that determine how your pivot table looks and works. To access these options, click the Options button in the final step of the PivotTable and PivotChart Wizard to display the PivotTable Options dialog box. You also can access this dialog box after you create the pivot table. Right-click any cell in the pivot table and then select Options from the shortcut menu. The accompanying figure shows the PivotTable Options dialog box. Following, I list its choices:

◆ Name: You can provide a name for the pivot table. Excel provides default names in the form of PivotTable1, PivotTable2, and so on.

◆ Grand totals for columns: Check this box if you want Excel to calculate grand totals for items displayed in columns.

◆ Grand totals for rows: Check this box if you want Excel to calculate grand totals for items displayed in rows.

◆ AutoFormat table: Check this box if you want Excel to apply one of its AutoFormats to the pivot table. Excel uses the AutoFormat even if you rearrange the table layout.

◆ Subtotal hidden page items: Check this box if you want Excel to include hidden items in the page fields in the subtotals.

◆ Merge labels: Check this box if you want Excel to merge the cells for outer row and column labels. Doing so may make the table more readable.

◆ Preserve formatting: Check this box if you want Excel, when it updates the pivot table, to keep any of the formatting that you applied.

◆ Repeat item labels on each printed page: Check this box to set row titles that appear on each page when you print a PivotTable report.

◆ Mark Totals with *: Available only if you generated the pivot table from an OLAP data source. If checked, displays an asterisk after every subtotal and grand total to indicate that these values include any hidden items as well as displayed items.

◆ Page layout: You can specify the order in which you want the page fields to appear.

◆ Fields per column: You can specify the number of page fields to show before starting another row of page fields.

◆ For error values, show: You can specify a value to show for pivot table cells that display an error.

◆ For empty cells, show: You can specify a value to show for empty pivot table cells.

◆ Set print titles: Check this box to set column titles that appear at the top of each page when you print a PivotTable report.

Continued

Pivot Table Options *(Continued)*

◆ Save data with table layout: If you check this option, Excel stores an additional copy of the data (called a *pivot table cache*), enabling Excel to recalculate the table more quickly when you change the layout. If memory is an issue, you should keep this option unchecked (which slows updating a bit).

◆ Enable drilldown: If checked, you can double-click a cell in the pivot table to view details.

◆ Refresh on open: If checked, the pivot table refreshes whenever you open the workbook.

◆ Refresh every *x* minutes: If you are connected to an external database, you can specify how often you want the pivot table refreshed while the workbook is open.

◆ Save password: If you use an external database that requires a password, you can store the password as part of the query so that you don't have to reenter it.

◆ Background query: If checked, Excel runs the external database query in the background while you continue your work.

◆ Optimize memory: This option reduces the amount of memory used when you refresh an external database query.

Grouping Pivot Table Items

One of the more useful features of a pivot table is the ability to combine items into groups. To group objects, select them, right-click, and choose Group and Outline→ Group from the shortcut menu.

When a field contains dates, Excel can create groups automatically. Figure 16-13 shows a simple database table with two fields: Date and Sales. This table has 371 records, and covers dates between June 1, 1999 and October 27, 2000. The goal is to summarize the sales information by month.

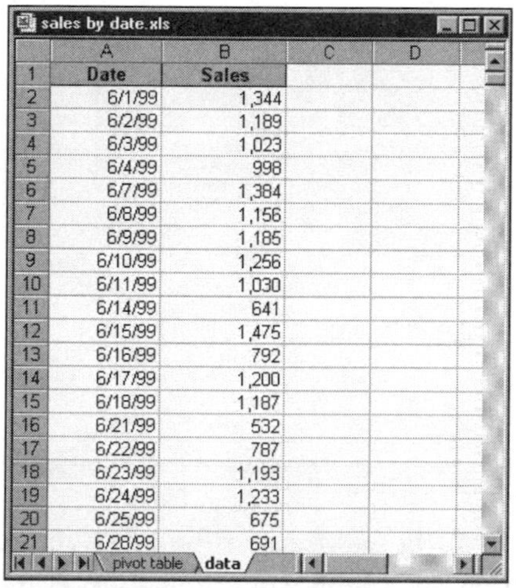

	A	B	C	D
1	Date	Sales		
2	6/1/99	1,344		
3	6/2/99	1,189		
4	6/3/99	1,023		
5	6/4/99	998		
6	6/7/99	1,384		
7	6/8/99	1,156		
8	6/9/99	1,185		
9	6/10/99	1,256		
10	6/11/99	1,030		
11	6/14/99	641		
12	6/15/99	1,475		
13	6/16/99	792		
14	6/17/99	1,200		
15	6/18/99	1,187		
16	6/21/99	532		
17	6/22/99	787		
18	6/23/99	1,193		
19	6/24/99	1,233		
20	6/25/99	675		
21	6/28/99	691		

Figure 16-13: You can use a pivot table to summarize the sales data by month.

Figure 16-14 shows a pivot table created from the data. Not surprisingly, it looks exactly like the input data because the dates have not been grouped. To group the items by month, right-click the Data heading and select Group and Outline→Group. You'll see the Grouping dialog box shown in Figure 16-15.

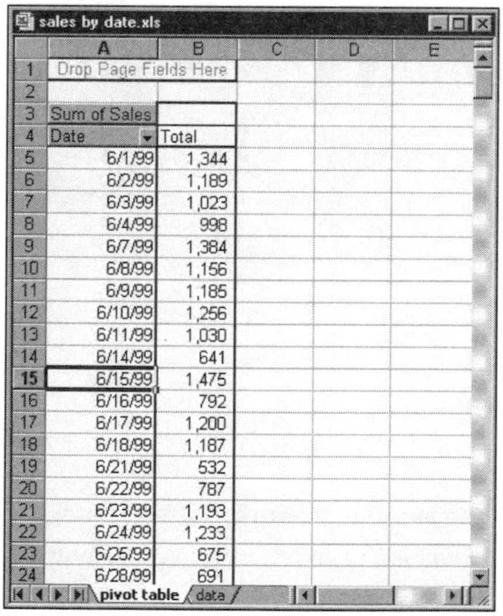

	A	B	C	D	E
1	Drop Page Fields Here				
2					
3	Sum of Sales				
4	Date	Total			
5	6/1/99	1,344			
6	6/2/99	1,189			
7	6/3/99	1,023			
8	6/4/99	998			
9	6/7/99	1,384			
10	6/8/99	1,156			
11	6/9/99	1,185			
12	6/10/99	1,256			
13	6/11/99	1,030			
14	6/14/99	641			
15	6/15/99	1,475			
16	6/16/99	792			
17	6/17/99	1,200			
18	6/18/99	1,187			
19	6/21/99	532			
20	6/22/99	787			
21	6/23/99	1,193			
22	6/24/99	1,233			
23	6/25/99	675			
24	6/28/99	691			

Figure 16-14: The pivot table, before grouping by month

Figure 16-15: Use the Grouping dialog box to group items in
a pivot table.

In the list box, select Months and Years, and verify that the starting and ending
dates are correct. Click OK. The Date items in the pivot table are grouped by years
and by months (see Figure 16-16).

Years	Date	Total
Sum of Sales		
1999	Jun	23,378
	Jul	22,186
	Aug	21,081
	Sep	23,021
	Oct	21,254
	Nov	21,198
	Dec	23,042
2000	Jan	20,863
	Feb	22,883
	Mar	24,590
	Apr	21,095
	May	23,625
	Jun	20,226
	Jul	20,127
	Aug	22,341
	Sep	22,291
	Oct	20,607
Grand Total		373,808

Figure 16-16: The pivot table, after grouping by month

If you select only Months in the Grouping list box, months in different years
combine together. For example, the June item would display sales for both
1999 and 2000.

Copying a Pivot Table

A pivot table is a special type of *object*, and you cannot manipulate it as you may expect. For example, you can't insert a new row or enter formulas within the pivot table. If you want to manipulate a pivot table in ways not normally permitted, make a copy of it.

To copy a pivot table, select the table and choose Edit → Copy. Then, activate a new worksheet and choose Edit → Paste Special. Select the Values option and click OK. The contents of the pivot table are copied to the new location so you can do whatever you like. You also may want to repeat the Edit → Paste Special command and select Formats (to copy the formatting from the pivot table).

Note that the copied information is no longer linked to the source data. If the source data changes, your copied pivot table does not reflect these changes.

Creating a Calculated Field or Calculated Item

Once you create a pivot table, you can create two types of *formulas* for further analysis:

- ♦ A calculated field: A new field created from other fields in the pivot table. A calculated field must reside in the Data area of the pivot table (you can't use a calculated field in the Page, Row, or Column areas).

- ♦ A calculated item: A calculated item uses the contents of other items within a field of the pivot table. A calculated item must reside in the Page, Row, or Column area of a pivot table (you can't use a calculated item in the Data area).

The formulas used to create calculated fields and calculated items are not standard Excel formulas. In other words, you do not enter the formulas into cells. Rather, you enter these formulas in a dialog box, and they are stored along with the pivot table data.

Excel 2000 enables you to use an OLAP database as the source for a pivot table. You can't, however, create calculated fields or items in a pivot table based on an OLAP database.

The examples in this section use the database table shown in Figure 16-17. The table consists of five fields and 48 records. Each record describes monthly sales information for a particular sales representative. For example, Amy is a sales rep for the North region, and she sold 152 units in January for total sales of $23,040.

calculated field and item.xls

	A	B	C	D	E
1	SalesRep	Region	Month	Sales	Units Sold
2	Amy	North	Jan	$23,040	239
3	Amy	North	Feb	$24,131	79
4	Amy	North	Mar	$24,646	71
5	Amy	North	Apr	$22,047	71
6	Amy	North	May	$24,971	157
7	Amy	North	Jun	$24,218	92
8	Amy	North	Jul	$25,735	175
9	Amy	North	Aug	$23,638	87
10	Amy	North	Sep	$25,749	557
11	Amy	North	Oct	$24,437	95
12	Amy	North	Nov	$25,355	706
13	Amy	North	Dec	$25,899	180
14	Bob	North	Jan	$20,024	103
15	Bob	North	Feb	$23,822	267
16	Bob	North	Mar	$24,854	96
17	Bob	North	Apr	$22,838	74
18	Bob	North	May	$25,320	231
19	Bob	North	Jun	$24,733	164
20	Bob	North	Jul	$21,184	68
21	Bob	North	Aug	$23,174	114
22	Bob	North	Sep	$25,999	84
23	Bob	North	Oct	$22,639	260

Pivot Table | Data

Figure 16-17: This data demonstrates calculated fields and calculated items.

Figure 16-18 shows the basic pivot table created from the data. The examples that follow will create:

- A calculated field, to compute average sales per unit
- A calculated item, to summarize the data by quarters

calculated field and item.xls

	A	B	C	D	E	F
1	Region	(All)				
2						
3	Total Sales	SalesRep				
4	Month	Amy	Bob	Chuck	Doug	Grand Total
5	Jan	$23,040	$20,024	$19,886	$26,264	$89,214
6	Feb	$24,131	$23,822	$23,494	$29,953	$101,400
7	Mar	$24,646	$24,854	$21,824	$25,041	$96,365
8	Apr	$22,047	$22,838	$22,058	$29,338	$96,281
9	May	$24,971	$25,320	$20,280	$25,150	$95,721
10	Jun	$24,218	$24,733	$23,965	$27,371	$100,287
11	Jul	$25,735	$21,184	$23,032	$25,044	$94,995
12	Aug	$23,638	$23,174	$21,273	$29,506	$97,591
13	Sep	$25,749	$25,999	$21,584	$29,061	$102,393
14	Oct	$24,437	$22,639	$19,625	$27,113	$93,814
15	Nov	$25,355	$23,949	$19,832	$25,953	$95,089
16	Dec	$25,899	$23,179	$20,583	$28,670	$98,331
17	Grand Total	$293,866	$281,715	$257,436	$328,464	$1,161,481
18						
19						

Pivot Table | Data

Figure 16-18: This pivot table was created from the data in Figure 16-7.

Creating a calculated field in a pivot table

Because a pivot table is a special type of data range, you can't insert new rows or columns within the pivot table. This means that you can't insert formulas to perform calculations with the data in a pivot table. However, you can create calculated fields for a pivot table. A *calculated field* consists of a calculation that can involve other fields.

A calculated field is basically a way to display new information in a pivot table. It essentially presents an alternative to creating a new *data* field in your source database. A calculated field cannot be used as a Row, Column, or Page field.

In the sales example, for instance, suppose you want to calculate the average sales amount per unit. You can compute this value by dividing the Sales field by the Units Sold field. The result shows a new field (a calculated field) for the pivot table.

Use the following procedure to create a calculated field that consists of the Sales field divided by the Units Sold field:

1. Move the cell pointer anywhere within the pivot table.

2. Right-click and choose Formulas → Calculated Field from the shortcut menu. Excel displays the Insert Calculated Field dialog box, shown in Figure 16-19.

3. Enter a descriptive name for the field and specify the formula. The formula can use other fields and worksheet functions. For this example, the calculated field name is Avg Unit Price, and the formula appears as the following:

   ```
   =Sales/'Units Sold'
   ```

4. Click Add to add this new field.

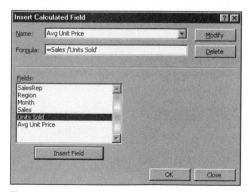

Figure 16-19: The Insert Calculated Field dialog box

You can create the formula manually by typing it, or by double-clicking items in the Fields list box. Double-clicking an item transfers it to the Formula field. Because the Units Sold field contains a space, Excel adds single quotes around the field name.

After you create the calculated field, Excel adds it to the Data area of the pivot table. You can treat it just like any other field, with one exception: you can't move it to the Page, Row, or Column area (it must remain in the Data area).

Figure 16-20 shows the pivot table after adding the calculated field. The new field displays as Sum of Avg Unit Price (you can change this, if desired). The calculated field also appears on the PivotTable toolbar, along with the other fields available for use in the pivot table.

calculated field and item.xls

Month	Data	Amy	Bob	Chuck	Doug	Grand Total
	Region	(All)				
			SalesRep			
Jan	Total Sales	$23,040	$20,024	$19,886	$26,264	$89,214
	Sum of Avg Unit Price	$96	$194	$209	$285	$169
Feb	Total Sales	$24,131	$23,822	$23,494	$29,953	$101,400
	Sum of Avg Unit Price	$305	$89	$159	$35	$75
Mar	Total Sales	$24,646	$24,854	$21,824	$25,041	$96,365
	Sum of Avg Unit Price	$347	$259	$263	$291	$287
Apr	Total Sales	$22,047	$22,838	$22,058	$29,338	$96,281
	Sum of Avg Unit Price	$311	$309	$230	$132	$208
May	Total Sales	$24,971	$25,320	$20,280	$25,150	$95,721
	Sum of Avg Unit Price	$159	$110	$45	$104	$88
Jun	Total Sales	$24,218	$24,733	$23,965	$27,371	$100,287
	Sum of Avg Unit Price	$263	$151	$32	$288	$90
Jul	Total Sales	$25,735	$21,184	$23,032	$25,044	$94,995
	Sum of Avg Unit Price	$147	$312	$149	$305	$198
Aug	Total Sales	$23,638	$23,174	$21,273	$29,506	$97,591
	Sum of Avg Unit Price	$272	$203	$28	$286	$91
Sep	Total Sales	$25,749	$25,999	$21,584	$29,061	$102,393
	Sum of Avg Unit Price	$46	$310	$189	$199	$114
Oct	Total Sales	$24,437	$22,639	$19,625	$27,113	$93,814
	Sum of Avg Unit Price	$257	$87	$236	$226	$168
Nov	Total Sales	$25,355	$23,949	$19,832	$25,953	$95,089
	Sum of Avg Unit Price	$36	$220	$283	$320	$98
Dec	Total Sales	$25,899	$23,179	$20,583	$28,670	$98,331
	Sum of Avg Unit Price	$144	$50	$116	$145	$96
Total Total Sales		$293,866	$281,715	$257,436	$328,464	$1,161,481
Total Sum of Avg Unit Price		$117	$138	$86	$142	$118

Figure 16-20: This pivot table uses a calculated field.

> The formulas that you develop also can use worksheet functions, but the functions cannot refer to cells or named ranges.

Inserting a calculated item into a pivot table

The previous section describes how to create a calculated field. Excel also enables you to create a *calculated item* for a pivot table field. The sales example uses a field named Month, which consists of text strings. You can create a calculated item (called Qtr-1, for example) that displays the sum of Jan, Feb, and Mar.

You also can do this by grouping the items – but using grouping hides the individual months and shows only the total of the group. Creating a calculated item for quarterly totals shows the total and the individual months.

To create a calculated item to sum the data for Jan, Feb, and Mar, use these steps:

1. Move the cell pointer to a Row, Column, or Page area of the pivot table. The cell pointer cannot be in the Data area.

2. Right-click and choose Formulas → Calculated Item from the shortcut menu. Excel displays the Insert Calculated Item dialog box, as shown in Figure 16-21.

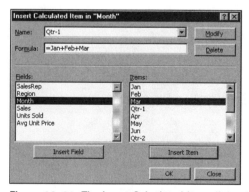

Figure 16-21: The Insert Calculated Item dialog box

3. Enter a name for the new item and specify the formula. The formula can use items in other fields, but can't use worksheet functions. For this example, the new item is named Qtr-1, and the formula appears as follows:

```
=Jan+Feb+Mar
```

4. Click Add.

5. Repeat Steps 3 and 4 to create additional calculated items for Qtr-2 (=Apr+May+Jun), Qtr-3 (=Jul+Aug+Sep), and Qtr-4 (=Oct+Nov+Dec).

6. Click OK to close the dialog box.

 If you use a calculated item in your pivot table, you may need to turn off the Grand Total display to avoid double counting.

After you create the items, they appear in the pivot table. Figure 16-22 shows the pivot table after adding four calculated items. Notice that the calculated items are added to the end of the Month items. You can rearrange the items by selecting and dragging. Figure 16-23 shows the pivot table after rearranging the items logically. (I also made the calculated items bold.)

Month	Amy	Bob	Chuck	Doug	Grand Total
Jan	$23,040	$20,024	$19,886	$26,264	$89,214
Feb	$24,131	$23,822	$23,494	$29,953	$101,400
Mar	$24,646	$24,854	$21,824	$25,041	$96,365
Apr	$22,047	$22,838	$22,058	$29,338	$96,281
May	$24,971	$25,320	$20,280	$25,150	$95,721
Jun	$24,218	$24,733	$23,965	$27,371	$100,287
Jul	$25,735	$21,184	$23,032	$25,044	$94,995
Aug	$23,638	$23,174	$21,273	$29,506	$97,591
Sep	$25,749	$25,999	$21,584	$29,061	$102,393
Oct	$24,437	$22,639	$19,625	$27,113	$93,814
Nov	$25,355	$23,949	$19,832	$25,953	$95,089
Dec	$25,899	$23,179	$20,583	$28,670	$98,331
Qtr-1	$71,817	$68,700	$65,204	$81,258	$286,979
Qtr-2	$71,236	$72,891	$66,303	$81,859	$292,289
Qtr-3	$75,122	$70,357	$65,889	$83,611	$294,979
Qtr-4	$75,691	$69,767	$60,040	$81,736	$287,234

Figure 16-22: This pivot table uses a calculated item.

	A	B	C	D	E	F	G
	calculated field and item.xls						
1	Region	(All)					
2							
3	Total Sales	SalesRep					
4	Month	Amy	Bob	Chuck	Doug	Grand Total	
5	Jan	$23,040	$20,024	$19,886	$26,264	$89,214	
6	Feb	$24,131	$23,822	$23,494	$29,953	$101,400	
7	Mar	$24,646	$24,854	$21,824	$25,041	$96,365	
8	**Qtr-1**	**$71,817**	**$68,700**	**$65,204**	**$81,258**	**$286,979**	
9	Apr	$22,047	$22,838	$22,058	$29,338	$96,281	
10	May	$24,971	$25,320	$20,280	$25,150	$95,721	
11	Jun	$24,218	$24,733	$23,965	$27,371	$100,287	
12	**Qtr-2**	**$71,236**	**$72,891**	**$66,303**	**$81,859**	**$292,289**	
13	Jul	$25,735	$21,184	$23,032	$25,044	$94,995	
14	Aug	$23,638	$23,174	$21,273	$29,506	$97,591	
15	Sep	$25,749	$25,999	$21,584	$29,061	$102,393	
16	**Qtr-3**	**$75,122**	**$70,357**	**$65,889**	**$83,611**	**$294,979**	
17	Oct	$24,437	$22,639	$19,625	$27,113	$93,814	
18	Nov	$25,355	$23,949	$19,832	$25,953	$95,089	
19	Dec	$25,899	$23,179	$20,583	$28,670	$98,331	
20	**Qtr-4**	**$75,691**	**$69,767**	**$60,040**	**$81,736**	**$287,234**	
21							
22							

Pivot Table / Data

Figure 16-23: The pivot table, after rearranging the calculated items

A calculated item appears in a pivot table only if the field on which it is based also appears. If you remove or pivot a field from either the Row or Column category into the Data category, the calculated item does not appear.

Summary

This chapter presented an introduction to pivot tables and demonstrated how to create a pivot table, group items, and calculated fields and calculated items. A pivot table often provides an excellent alternative to creating formulas for summarizing a database.

The next chapter discusses the use of conditional formatting and data validation.

Chapter 17

Conditional Formatting and Data Validation

IN THIS CHAPTER

◆ An overview of Excel's conditional formatting feature

◆ Practical examples of using conditional formatting formulas

◆ An overview of Excel's data validation feature

◆ Practical examples of using data validation formulas

THIS CHAPTER EXPLORES TWO very useful Excel features: conditional formatting and data.

validation. You may not think these features have much to do with formulas. But as you'll see, when you toss formulas into the mix, these features can perform some amazing feats.

 Excel 97 introduced conditional formatting and data validation. Therefore, this chapter does not apply if you use an earlier version of Excel.

Conditional Formatting

Conditional formatting enables you to apply cell formatting selectively and automatically. For example, you can set things up such that all negative values in a range have a light yellow background color. When you enter or change a value in the range, Excel examines the value and evaluates the conditional formatting rules for the cell. If the value is negative, the background is shaded. If not, no formatting is applied.

Conditional formatting is very useful for quickly identifying erroneous cell entries, or cells of a particular type. You can use a format (such as bright red cell shading) to make a particular cell easy to identify.

455

Is this a handy feature? No doubt. But dig a little deeper and you'll see that a lot more lurks in the shadows, and this feature can do things you may not have thought possible. The key, as you'll see, is specifying your conditions by using formulas. In this section, I describe Excel's conditional formatting feature and point out some of its limitations as well as a potentially serious design flaw.

Specifying conditional formatting

To apply conditional formatting to a cell or range:

1. Select the cell or range.

2. Choose Format → Conditional Formatting. Excel displays its Conditional Formatting dialog box, shown in Figure 17-1.

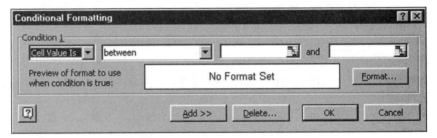

Figure 17-1: The Conditional Formatting dialog box

3. In the drop-down box, select either Cell Value Is (for simple conditional formatting) or Formula Is (for formatting based on a formula).

4. Specify the condition (or enter a formula).

5. Click the Format button and specify the formatting to apply if the condition is TRUE.

6. To add additional conditions (up to two more), click Add and then repeat Steps 3–5.

7. Click OK.

After performing these steps, the cell or range will be formatted based on the conditions you specify. This formatting, of course, is dynamic: If you change the contents of a cell, Excel reevaluates the new contents and applies or removes the formatting accordingly.

Formatting types you can apply

When you click the Format button in the Conditional Formatting dialog box, you get the Format Cells dialog box shown in Figure 17-2. This is a modified version of the standard Format Cells dialog box. It does not have the Number, Alignment, and Protection tabs, but it includes a Clear button. You can specify any of the following formats:

♦ Font style (regular, bold, or italic)

♦ Font underline

♦ Font color

♦ Font strikethrough

♦ Border outline

♦ Border line style

♦ Border line color

♦ Cell shading color

♦ Cell background pattern

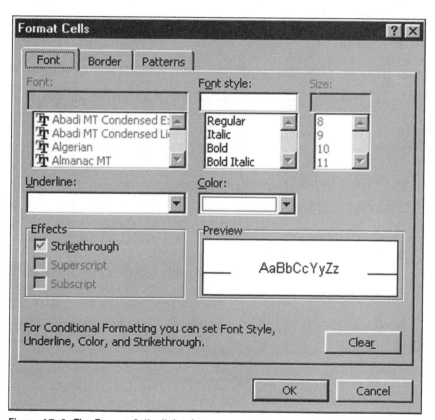

Figure 17–2: The Format Cells dialog box

Notice that you can't specify the font size; presumably because the font size can affect row heights. The designers probably decided that changing row heights automatically could be distracting, or introduce other problems such as pagination when printing.

TIP The colors available in the Format Cells dialog box are the 56 colors in the workbook's color palette. If none of these colors is satisfactory, you can modify the workbook's color palette. To do so, select Tools → Options, and click the Color tab in the Options dialog box. Select a color and click the Modify button to change the color. But exercise caution because changing a color may affect other color formatting in your workbook.

Specifying conditions

The leftmost drop-down list in the Conditional Formatting dialog box enables you to choose one of two options:

- ◆ Cell Value Is: for simple conditions
- ◆ Formula Is: for more complex, formula-based conditions

I discuss these two classes of conditions in the sections that follow.

SIMPLE CONDITIONS

When you select Cell Value Is, you can specify conditions of the following types:

- ◆ between (you specify two values)
- ◆ not between (you specify two values)
- ◆ equal to (you specify one value)
- ◆ not equal to (you specify one value)
- ◆ greater than (you specify one value)
- ◆ less than (you specify one value)
- ◆ greater than or equal to (you specify one value)
- ◆ less than or equal to (you specify one value)

You can either enter the value(s) directly, or specify a cell reference.

FORMULA-BASED CONDITIONS

When you select Formula Is, you can specify a formula. Do so by specifying a cell that contains a formula, or by entering a formula directly into the dialog box (see Figure 17-3).

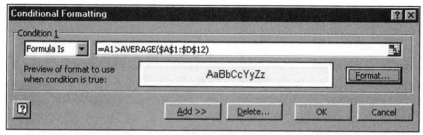

Figure 17-3: Entering a formula directly into the Conditional Formatting dialog box

 You must specify a logical formula that returns either TRUE or FALSE. If the formula evaluates to TRUE, the condition is satisfied and the conditional formatting is applied. If the formula evaluates to FALSE, the conditional formatting is not applied.

As you'll see by studying the examples later in this chapter, the real power of conditional formatting is apparent when you enter a formula directly into the Conditional Formatting dialog box.

If the formula that you enter into the Conditional Formatting dialog box contains a cell reference, that reference is considered a relative reference, based on the upper left cell in the selected range. For example, suppose you want to set up a conditional formatting condition that applies shading to blank cells in the range B2:B10. Follow these steps:

1. Select the range B2:B10.

2. Choose Format → Conditional Formatting.

3. Select the Formula Is item from the drop-down list.

4. Enter the following formula in the formula box:

   ```
   =B2=""
   ```

5. Click the Format button and specify a pattern for the cell shading.

6. Click OK twice.

Notice that the formula entered contains a reference to the upper left cell in the selected range. To demonstrate that the reference is relative, select cell B5 and examine its conditional formatting formula. You'll see that the conditional formatting formula for this cell is:

```
=B5=""
```

Generally, when entering a conditional formatting formula for a range of cells, you'll use a reference to the upper left cell in the selected range. One exception: when you need to refer to a specific cell. For example, suppose you select range A1:B20, and you want to apply formatting to all cells in the range that exceed the value in cell C1. Enter this conditional formatting formula:

```
=A1>$C$1
```

In this case, the reference to cell C1 is an absolute reference; it will not be adjusted for the cells in the selected range. In other words, the conditional formatting formula for cell A2 looks like:

```
=A2>$C$1
```

The relative cell reference is adjusted, but the absolute cell reference is not.

Working with conditional formats

This section describes some additional information about conditional formatting that you might find useful.

Changing Font Color Using Custom Number Formats

In some cases, you can avoid conditional formatting and take advantage of a custom number format that changes font color conditionally. For example, the custom number format that follows displays positive values in black, negative values in red, and zero values in blue.

```
[Black]General;[Red]-General;[Blue]General
```

For more information about creating custom number formats, refer to Appendix C.

MULTIPLE CONDITIONS

As noted above, you can specify as many as three conditions by clicking the Add button in the Conditional Formatting dialog box. For example, you might enter the following three conditions (and specify different formatting for each):

```
Cell Value Is less than 0
Cell Value Is equal to 0
Cell Value is greater than 0
```

In this case, the sign of the value (negative, 0, or positive) determines the applied formatting.

If none of the specified conditions is TRUE, the cells keep their existing formats. If you specify multiple conditions and more than one condition is TRUE, Excel applies only the formatting for the first TRUE condition. For example, you may specify the following two conditions:

```
Cell Value Is between 1 and 12
Cell Value Is less than 6
```

Entering a value of 4 satisfies both conditions. Therefore, the cell will be formatted using the format specified for the first condition.

BE CAREFUL WHEN PASTING

It's important to keep in mind that it's very easy (too easy) to wipe out the conditional formatting in a cell or range by pasting copied data to the cell.

Copying a cell and pasting it to a cell or range that contains conditional formatting wipes out the conditional formatting in the destination range. You get no warning. This, of course, is a serious design flaw on the part of Microsoft—one that you should keep in mind if you use conditional formatting in your workbook.

COPYING CELLS THAT CONTAIN CONDITIONAL FORMATTING

Conditional formatting information is stored with a cell much like standard formatting information is stored with a cell. This means that when you copy a cell that contains conditional formatting, the conditional formatting is also copied.

TIP To copy only the conditional formats, select cells you want to format and include at least one cell in the selection that has the conditional formats you want to copy. Select Format → Conditional Formatting and then click OK.

Inserting rows or columns within a range that contains conditional formatting causes the new cells to have the same conditional formatting.

DELETING CONDITIONAL FORMATTING

When you press Del to delete the contents of a cell, you do not delete the conditional formatting for the cell (if any). To remove all conditional formats (as well as all other cell formatting), select the cells and choose Edit → Clear → Formats.

To remove only conditional formatting (and leave the other formatting intact) you need to use the Conditional Formatting dialog box. Select the cells, then choose Format → Conditional Formatting. Click the Delete button in the Conditional Formatting dialog box and you get another dialog box (see Figure 17-4) that enables you to specify the conditions that you want to delete. This dialog box always displays checkboxes for three conditions, even if you haven't defined that many conditions.

Figure 17-4: Use the Delete Conditional Formatting dialog box to remove one or more conditions.

TIP You also can remove conditional formatting from a cell by simply copying a cell that *doesn't* have conditional formatting and then pasting it to the cell or range. This, of course, also copies other formatting as well.

LOCATING CELLS THAT CONTAIN CONDITIONAL FORMATTING

You cannot tell, just by looking at a cell, whether it contains conditional formatting. You can, however, use Excel's Go To dialog box to select such cells.

Select Edit → Go To (or press F5) to display the Go To dialog box. Click the Special button, and then select the Conditional formats option (see Figure 17-5). To select all cells on the worksheet containing conditional formatting, select the All option. To select only the cells that contain the same conditional formatting as the active cell, select the Same option. Click OK and the cells will be selected for you.

Figure 17-5: Use the Go To Special dialog box to locate cells that contain conditional formatting.

USING REFERENCES TO OTHER SHEETS

If you enter a conditional formatting formula that uses one or more references to other sheets, Excel responds with an error message. If you need to refer to a cell on a different sheet, you must create a reference to that cell. For example, if you need to refer to cell A1 on Sheet3, you can use a simple formula such as:

```
=Sheet3!A1
```

Conditional formatting formulas

This section contains a number of examples that demonstrate various uses for conditional formatting. Each of these examples uses a formula entered directly into the Conditional Formatting dialog box. You decide the type of formatting that you apply conditionally.

 You can access all of the examples in this section on the companion CD-ROM.

IDENTIFYING NON-NUMERIC DATA

The following conditional formatting formula applies formatting to cell A1 only if the cell contains text:

```
=ISTEXT(A1)
```

To apply this conditional formatting formula to a range, select the range first. The argument for the ISTEXT function should be the upper left cell in the range.

IDENTIFYING ABOVE-AVERAGE CELLS

I applied the following conditional formatting formula to range A1:D12. It applies formatting to all cells in the range A1:D12 that are above the average (see Figure 17-6).

```
=A1>AVERAGE($A$1:$D$12)
```

	A	B	C	D	E
1	1	12	23	34	
2	36	13	24	35	
3	3	14	25	2	
4	4	15	26	37	
5	5	16	27	38	
6	41	17	28	6	
7	7	18	12	40	
8	8	19	30	41	
9	9	20	31	42	
10	10	43	32	21	
11	11	22	33	44	
12	29	23	34	45	
13					
14					

Figure 17-6: Using conditional formatting to highlight all above-average cells

Notice that the first cell reference (A1) is a relative reference, but the range argument for the AVERAGE formula is absolute.

IDENTIFYING DATES IN A PARTICULAR MONTH

Conditional formatting, of course, also works with dates. The conditional formatting formula that follows applies formatting only if the cell contains a date in the month of June:

```
=MONTH(A1)=6
```

This formula assumes that cell A1 is the upper left cell in the selected range. It works by using the MONTH function, which returns the month for a date.

The MONTH function does not distinguish between dates and non-dates. In other words, the MONTH function is applied to all cells, even if they don't contain a date.

IDENTIFYING TODAY'S DATE

Excel's TODAY function returns the current date. If you have a series of dates in a worksheet, you can use conditional formatting to make it easy to identify data for the current date. The conditional formatting formula that follows applies formatting only if the cell contains the current date. This assumes that you selected a range beginning with cell A1 when you entered the conditional formatting formula.

```
=A1=TODAY()
```

IDENTIFYING WEEKEND DATES

Excel's WEEKDAY function returns an integer that represents the day of the week (1 is Sunday, 2 is Monday, and so on). You can use this function in a custom formatting formula to identify weekends. The following custom formatting formula applies formatting to cells that contain a date that falls on a Saturday or Sunday (see Figure 17-7).

```
=OR(WEEKDAY(A1)=7,WEEKDAY(A1)=1)
```

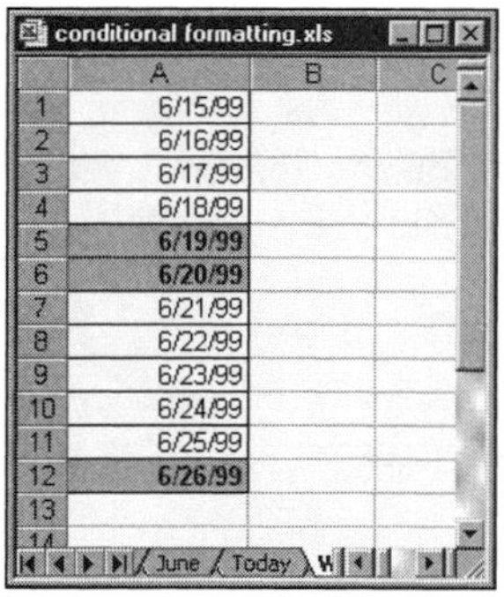

Figure 17-7: Using conditional formatting to highlight cells that contain a weekend date

This formula uses the OR function, so it returns TRUE if the WEEKDAY function returns either 7 or 1. You'll find that the WEEKDAY function returns 7 if its argument is an empty cell. Therefore, you should use this formula:

```
=IF(ISBLANK(A1),"",OR(WEEKDAY(A1)=7,WEEKDAY(A1)=1))
```

HIDING ERROR VALUES

You can use conditional formatting to *hide* error values in your cells. In this case, hiding the contents of a cell consists of setting its font color equal to its background color. The following conditional formatting formula applies formatting to the cell if it returns an error value (for example, #DIV/0!):

```
=ISERROR(A1)
```

The applied formatting sets the font color to the background color.

 Although setting the background color equal to the font color technique works, it's usually not the best way to handle the display of error values. Cells that reference the erroneous cell display an error, and the user easily can change the background color. A better approach is to use an IF function, which displays an empty string if the formula returns an error. The following formula displays an empty string if B1/C1 generates an error:

```
=IF(ISERR(B1/C1),"",(B1/C1))
```

IDENTIFYING THE MAXIMUM VALUE IN A RANGE

Excel's MAX function returns the maximum value in a range. If you want to make this value stand out, you can use a conditional formatting formula such as this one:

```
=A1=MAX($A$1:$A$30)
```

In this case, the conditional formatting is applied to all cells in A1:A30, and the maximum value in that range will be formatted. You can, of course, modify this formula to use the MIN function (which returns the smallest value in a range).

IDENTIFYING THE THREE LARGEST VALUES IN A RANGE

Excel's LARGE function returns the *n*th largest value in a range (*n* is specified as the second argument). The following conditional formatting formula applies formatting to the three largest values in the range A1:A30.

```
=OR(A1=LARGE($A$1:$A$30,1),A1=LARGE($A$1:$A$30,2),
A1=LARGE($A$1:$A$30,3))
```

Notice that the formula uses the OR function, with three arguments. If any of the three arguments evaluates to TRUE, then the OR function returns TRUE.

DISPLAYING ALTERNATE ROW SHADING

The conditional formatting formula that follows was applied to the range A1:D18, shown in Figure 17-8, to apply shading to alternate rows. This formula is quite useful for making your spreadsheets easier to read.

```
=MOD(ROW(),2)=0
```

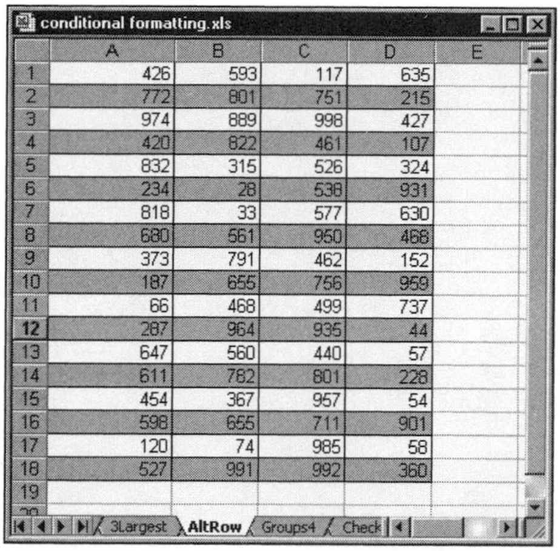

	A	B	C	D	E
1	426	593	117	635	
2	772	801	751	215	
3	974	889	998	427	
4	420	822	461	107	
5	832	315	526	324	
6	234	28	538	931	
7	818	33	577	630	
8	680	561	950	468	
9	373	791	462	152	
10	187	655	756	959	
11	66	468	499	737	
12	287	964	935	44	
13	647	560	440	57	
14	611	782	801	228	
15	454	367	957	54	
16	598	655	711	901	
17	120	74	985	58	
18	527	991	992	360	
19					

Figure 17-8: Using conditional formatting to apply formatting to alternate rows

This formula uses the ROW function (which returns the row number) and the MOD function (which returns the remainder of its first argument divided by its second argument). For cells in even numbered rows, the MOD function returns 0, and cells in that row are formatted. For alternate shading of columns, use the COLUMN function instead of the ROW function.

You can use variations on this conditional formatting formula to get other types of row shading. For example, the conditional formatting formula that follows shades every third row:

```
=MOD(ROW(),3)=0
```

The following conditional formatting formula applies alternate shading in groups of four rows (four rows shaded, followed by four rows not shaded):

```
=MOD(INT((ROW()-1)/4)+1,2)
```

Need checkerboard shading, as shown in Figure 17-9? This conditional formatting formula does just that:

```
=MOD(ROW(),2)=MOD(COLUMN(),2)
```

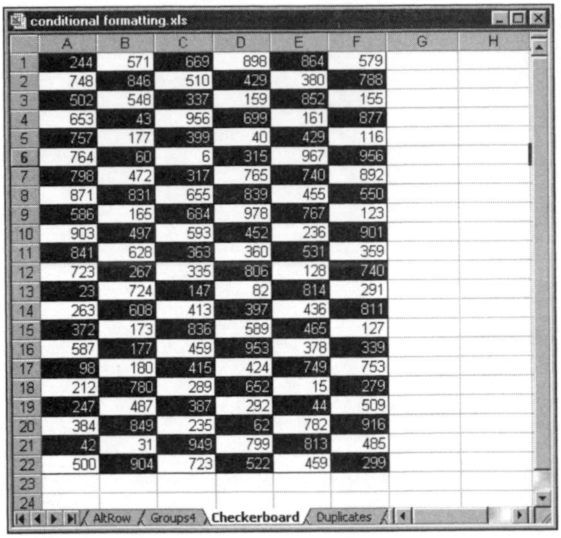

	A	B	C	D	E	F
1	244	571	669	898	864	579
2	748	846	510	429	380	788
3	502	548	337	159	852	155
4	653	43	956	699	161	877
5	757	177	399	40	429	116
6	764	60	6	315	967	956
7	798	472	317	765	740	892
8	871	831	655	839	455	550
9	586	165	684	978	767	123
10	903	497	593	452	236	901
11	841	628	363	360	531	359
12	723	267	335	806	128	740
13	23	724	147	82	814	291
14	263	608	413	397	436	811
15	372	173	836	589	465	127
16	587	177	459	953	378	339
17	98	180	415	424	749	753
18	212	780	289	652	15	279
19	247	487	387	292	44	509
20	384	849	235	62	782	916
21	42	31	949	799	813	485
22	500	904	723	522	459	299

Figure 17-9: Using conditional formatting to create a checkerboard effect

IDENTIFYING DUPLICATE VALUES IN A RANGE

You might find it helpful to identify duplicate values within a range (see Figure 17-10). You can use a conditional formatting formula such as the one that follows. In this case, formatting is applied to all cells that are not unique within the range A1:A12.

```
=IF(COUNTIF($A$1:$D$12,A1)>1,TRUE,FALSE)
```

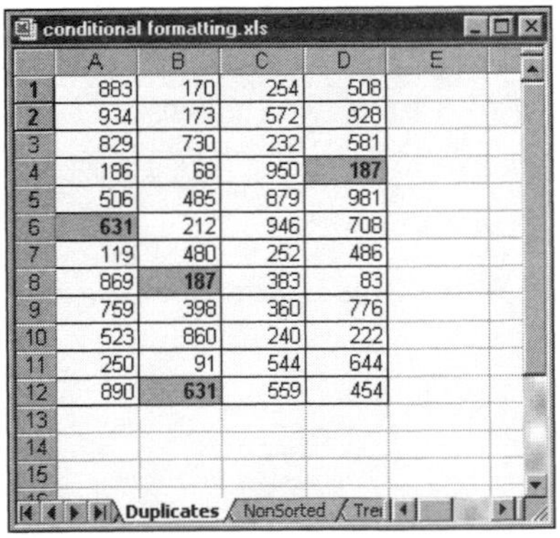

	A	B	C	D
1	883	170	254	508
2	934	173	572	928
3	829	730	232	581
4	186	68	950	187
5	506	485	879	981
6	631	212	946	708
7	119	480	252	486
8	869	187	383	83
9	759	398	360	776
10	523	860	240	222
11	250	91	544	644
12	890	631	559	454

Figure 17-10: Using conditional formatting to identify duplicate values in a range

To apply formatting only to non-duplicated values in a range, use a formula such as this:

```
=IF(COUNTIF($A$1:$D$12,A1)=1,TRUE,FALSE)
```

IDENTIFYING NON-SORTED VALUES IN A RANGE

If you have a single-column range of values that should be in ascending order, you can use a conditional formatting formula to quickly spot values out of order. This example assumes that your sorted values begin in cell A1. Select the range of values beginning with A2, and then specify the following conditional formatting formula:

```
=A2<A1
```

Conditional formatting will be applied to any cell that is less than the cell above it.

IDENTIFYING UPWARD OR DOWNWARD TRENDS

In some cases, you might find it helpful to visually identify upward or downward trends in a column of data. This example assumes that the data begins in cell A1. You need to select the range beginning in A2 and then specify two conditions, as follows:

```
=A2>A1
=A2<A1
```

Specify a different format for each condition, so you can spot the trends without creating a chart. Figure 17-11 shows an example.

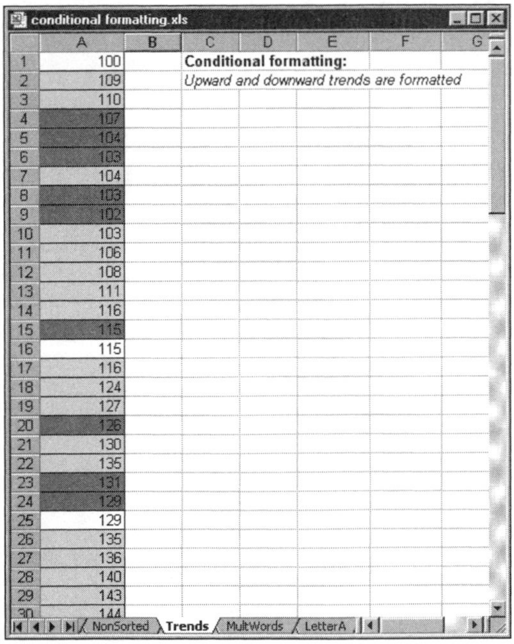

Figure 17-11: Use conditional formatting to identify upward and downward trends

IDENTIFYING CELLS CONTAINING MORE THAN ONE WORD

You also can use conditional formatting with text. For example, you can use the following conditional formatting formula to apply formatting to cells that contain more than one word.

```
=LEN(SUBSTITUTE(TRIM(A1),CHAR(32),CHAR(32)&CHAR(32)) )
-LEN(TRIM(A1))+1>1
```

This formula assumes that the selected range begins in cell A1. The formula works by counting the space characters in the cell (using the TRIM function to strip out multiple spaces). If the count is greater than 1, the formula returns TRUE and the conditional formatting is applied.

IDENTIFYING CELLS CONTAINING A SPECIFIC CHARACTER

The conditional formatting formula that follows applies formatting to cells (beginning in cell A1) that contain the letter A (either upper- or lowercase).

```
=LEN(A1)-LEN(SUBSTITUTE(SUBSTITUTE(A1,"A",""),"a","")))>0
```

DISPLAYING A RESULT ONLY WHEN ALL DATA IS ENTERED

This example uses conditional formatting to display a result only when you have entered all the necessary data. In Figure 17-12, a formula in cell B5 calculates the sum of the four values above. The objective is to hide the total until you enter all four values.

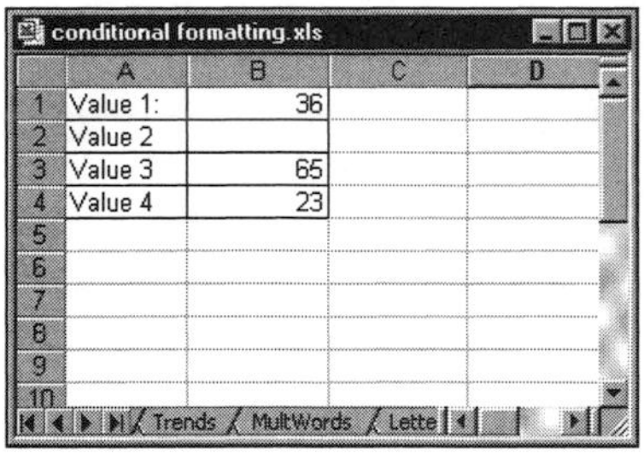

Figure 17-12: Conditional formatting hides the contents of A5:B5 unless you enter a value for each cell in B1:B4.

Select A5:B5 and format these cells so the font color matches the background color. For example, make the font color white. This effectively makes these two cells invisible. With A5:B5 still selected, enter the following conditional formatting formula:

```
=AND($B$1:$B$4<>"")
```

This formula returns TRUE only when all of the cells in B1:B4 are not empty. Specify the conditioning of your choice. For example, you can make the background color black. Figure 17-13 shows the result when you have entered all of the required data.

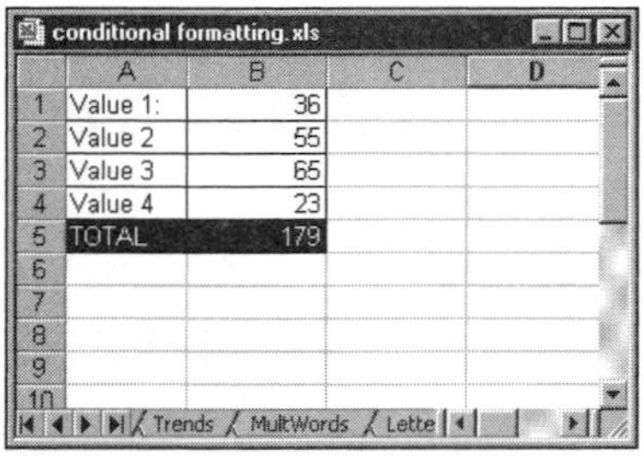

Figure 17–13: Because B1:B4 contains data, you can view the contents of A5:B5.

IDENTIFYING POSITIVE CHANGES

Figure 17-14 shows data for a group of students who took two tests. Conditional formatting is used to highlight the rows in which the students' post-test scores were higher than their pre-test scores.

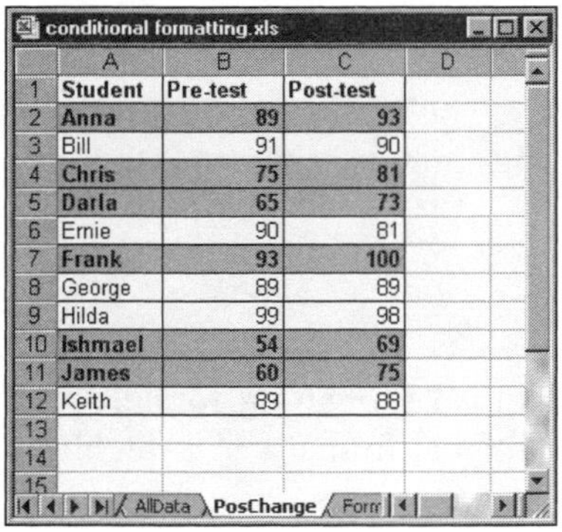

Figure 17–14: Using conditional formatting to identify students who scored higher on the post-test

The conditional formatting formula for the range A2:C12 is:

```
=$C2>$B2
```

Notice that this formula uses mixed references. The column part is absolute, but the row part is relative.

Using custom functions in conditional formatting formulas

Conditional formatting formulas also work with custom worksheet functions created using VBA. This section provides four examples.

Part V provides an overview of VBA, with specific information about creating custom worksheet functions.

IDENTIFYING FORMULA CELLS

Oddly, Excel does not have a function that determines whether a cell contains a formula. When Excel lacks a feature, you often can overcome the limitation by using VBA. The VBA function listed below uses VBA's HasFormula property. The function returns TRUE if the cell (specified as its argument) contains a formula; otherwise, it returns FALSE.

```
Function ISFORMULACELL(cell) As Boolean
    ISFORMULACELL = cell.HasFormula
End Function
```

After you enter this function into a VBA module, you can use the function in your worksheet formulas. For example, the following formula returns TRUE if cell A1 contains a formula:

```
=ISFORMULACELL(A1)
```

And, you also can use this function in a conditional formatting formula. The worksheet in Figure 17-15, for example, uses conditional formatting to highlight all cells that contain a formula.

IDENTIFYING DATE CELLS

Excel also lacks a function to determine whether a cell contains a date. The following VBA function, which uses VBA's IsDate function, fills this gap. The custom HASDATE function returns TRUE if the cell contains a date.

```
Function HASDATE(cell) As Boolean
    HASDATE = IsDate(cell)
End Function
```

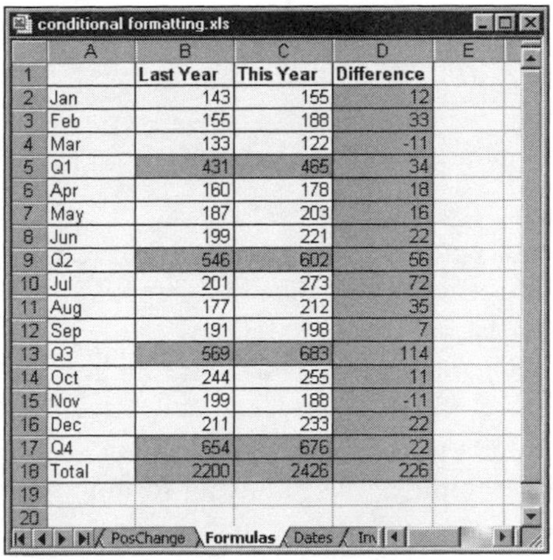
conditional formatting.xls

	A	B	C	D	E
1		Last Year	This Year	Difference	
2	Jan	143	155	12	
3	Feb	155	188	33	
4	Mar	133	122	-11	
5	Q1	431	465	34	
6	Apr	160	178	18	
7	May	187	203	16	
8	Jun	199	221	22	
9	Q2	546	602	56	
10	Jul	201	273	72	
11	Aug	177	212	35	
12	Sep	191	198	7	
13	Q3	569	683	114	
14	Oct	244	255	11	
15	Nov	199	188	-11	
16	Dec	211	233	22	
17	Q4	654	676	22	
18	Total	2200	2426	226	
19					
20					

PosChange Formulas Dates Im

Figure 17-15: Using a custom VBA function to apply conditional formatting to cells that contain a formula

You can use this function to improve the conditional formatting formulas presented earlier in this chapter (see "Identifying Dates in a Particular Month" and "Identifying Weekends"). Neither of the conditional formatting formulas presented could distinguish between cells that contain a date and cells that contain a normal value. You can use the AND function to ensure that the formatting applies only to date cells.

The following conditional formatting formula applies formatting to cell A1 if it contains a date and the month is June:

```
=AND(HASDATE(A1),MONTH(A1)=6)
```

The following conditional formatting formula applies formatting to cell A1 if it contains a date and the date falls on a weekend:

```
=AND(HASDATE(A1),OR(WEEKDAY(A1)=7,WEEKDAY(A1)=1))
```

IDENTIFYING LINK FORMULAS

You may want to identify cells that contain a link formula (a formula that uses a reference in a different workbook). The following VBA function returns TRUE if the cell contains a formula that contains an external link. The HASLINK function uses VBA's versatile Like operator.

```
Function HASLINK(cell)
    HASLINK = cell.Formula Like "*[[]*"
End Function
```

To apply conditional formatting to cells that contain a link, you can create a conditional formatting formula such as the following:

```
=HASLINK(A1)
```

IDENTIFYING INVALID DATA

You might have a situation in which the data entered must adhere to some very specific rules, and you'd like to apply special formatting if the data entered is not valid. You might have part numbers that consist of seven characters: four upper-case alphabetic characters, followed by a hyphen, and then a two-digit number. For example: ADSS-09 or DYUU-43.

You can write a conditional formatting formula to determine if part numbers adhere to this structure, but the formula is very complex. The following formula, for example, returns TRUE only if the value in A1 meets the part number rules specified above.

```
=AND(LEN(A1)=7,AND(LEFT(A1)>="A",LEFT(A1)<="Z"),
AND(MID(A1,2,1)>="A",MID(A1,2,1)<="Z"),AND(MID(A1,3,1)>="A",
MID(A1,3,1)<="Z"),AND(MID(A1,4,1)>="A",MID(A1,4,1)<="Z"),
MID(A1,5,1)="-",AND(VALUE(MID(A1,6,2))>=0,
VALUE(MID(A1,6,2))<=99))
```

For a simpler approach, write a custom VBA worksheet function. VBA's Like operator makes this sort of comparison relatively easy. The following VBA Function procedure listed returns TRUE if its argument does not correspond to the part number rules outlined previously.

```
Function INVALIDPART(n) As Boolean
    If n Like "[A-Z][A-Z][A-Z][A-Z]-##" Then
        INVALIDPART = False
    Else
        INVALIDPART = True
    End If
End Function
```

After defining this function in a VBA module, you can enter the following conditional formatting formula to apply special formatting if cell A1 contains an invalid part number.

```
=INVALIDPART(A1)
```

Figure 17-16 shows a range that uses the INVALIDPART function in a conditional formatting formula. Cells that contain invalid part numbers have a colored background.

Figure 17-16: Using conditional formatting to highlight cells with invalid entries

Data Validation

The data validation feature, available in Excel 97 and later versions, is similar in many respects to the conditional formatting feature. This feature enables you to set up certain rules that dictate what you can enter into a cell. For example, you may want to limit data entry to whole numbers between 1 and 12. If the user makes an invalid entry, you can display a custom message such as the one shown in Figure 17-17.

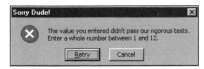

Figure 17-17: Displaying a message when the user makes an invalid entry

As with the conditional formatting feature, you can use a formula to specify your data validation criteria.

 The data validation feature suffers the same problem as conditional formatting: If the user copies a cell and pastes it to a cell that contains data validation, the data validation rules are deleted and the cell then accepts any type of data.

Specifying validation criteria

To specify the type of data allowable in a cell or range:

1. Select the cell or range.

2. Choose Data → Validation. Excel displays its Data Validation dialog box.

3. Click the Settings tab (see Figure 17-18).

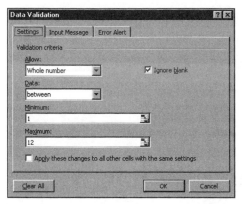

Figure 17-18: The Settings tab of the Data Validation dialog box

4. Choose an option from the drop-down box labeled Allow. To specify a formula, select Custom.

5. Specify the conditions by selecting from the drop-down box labeled Data. Your selection determines what other controls you can access.

6. Click the Input Message tab (see Figure 17-19) and specify which message to display when a user selects the cell. You can use this optional step to tell the user what type of data is expected.

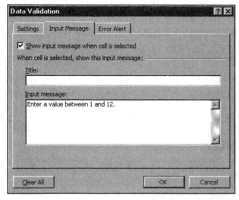

Figure 17-19: The Input Message tab of the Data Validation dialog box

7. Click the Error Alert tab (see Figure 17-20) and specify which error message to display when a user makes an invalid entry. The selection for Style determines what choices users have when they make invalid entries. To prevent an invalid entry, choose Stop. This step is optional.

8. Click OK.

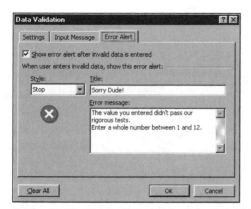

Figure 17-20: The Error Alert tab of the Data Validation dialog box

After performing these steps, the cell or range contains the validation criteria you specified.

Types of validation criteria you can apply

The Settings tab of the Data Validation dialog box enables you to specify any of the following data validation criteria:

◆ Any value. Selecting this option removes any existing data validation. Note, however, that the input message, if any, still displays if the checkbox is checked in the Input Message tab.

◆ Whole number. The user must enter a whole number. You specify a valid range of whole numbers by using the Data drop-down list. For example, you can specify that the entry must be a whole number greater than or equal to 100.

◆ Decimal. The user must enter a number. You specify a valid range of numbers by using the Data drop-down list. For example, you can specify that the entry must be greater than or equal to 0, and less than or equal to 1.

◆ List. The user must choose from a list of entries you provide. Specify the range (which must be a single row or column) that contains the list using the Source control. If you have a short list, you can enter it directly into the Source control. Each item must be separated by a comma.

TIP If you specify a range for a list, it must be on the same sheet. If your list is in a range on a different worksheet, you can provide a name for the range and then use the name as your list source.

◆ Date. The user must enter a date. You specify a valid date range by using the Data drop-down list. For example, you can specify that the entered data must be greater than or equal to January 1, 2000, and less than or equal to December 31, 2000.

◆ Time. The user must enter a time. You specify a valid date range by using the Data drop-down list. For example, you can specify that the entered data must be greater than 12:00 PM.

◆ Text length. The length of the data (number of characters) is limited. You specify a valid length by using the Data drop-down list. For example, you can specify that the length of the entered data be 1 (a single alphanumeric character).

◆ Custom. A logical formula determines the validity of the user's entry. You can enter the formula directly into the Formula control, or specify a cell reference that contains a formula. This chapter contains examples of useful formulas.

The Settings tab of the Data Validation dialog box contains two other options:

◆ Ignore blank. If checked, blank entries are allowed.

◆ Apply these changes to all other cells with the same setting. If checked, the changes you make apply to all other cells that contain the original data validation criteria.

It's important to understand that, even with data validation in effect, the user could enter invalid data. If the Style setting in the Error Alert tab of the Data Validation dialog box is set to anything except Stop, invalid data *can* be entered.

TIP After your data is entered, you can look for entries that are outside the limits you set. When you click Circle Invalid Data on the Auditing toolbar, circles appear around cells that contain incorrect entries (see Figure 17-21). If you correct an invalid entry, the circle disappears.

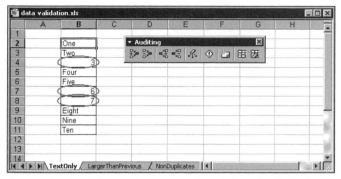

Figure 17-21: Circles are drawn around invalid entries (cells that contain a value).

Using formulas for data validation rules

For simple data validation, the data validation feature is quite straightforward and easy to use. But the real power of this feature becomes apparent when you use data validation formulas.

The formula that you specify must be a logical formula that returns either TRUE or FALSE. If the formula evaluates to TRUE, the data is considered valid and remains in the cell. If the formula evaluates to FALSE, a message box appears that displays the message specified in the Error Alert tab of the Data Validation dialog box.

As noted earlier, you specify a formula in the Data Validation dialog box by selecting the Custom option in the Allow drop-down list of the Settings tab. You can enter the formula directly into the Formula control, or enter a reference to a cell that contains a formula.

If the formula that you enter contains a cell reference, that reference will be considered to be a relative reference, based on the upper left cell in the selected range. This works exactly the same as using a formula for conditional formatting (see "Formula-Based Conditions," earlier in this chapter).

Using data validation formulas to accept only specific entries

Each of the following data validation examples uses a formula entered directly into the Data Validation dialog box. You can set up these formulas to accept only text, a certain value, non-duplicate entries, or text that begins with a specific letter.

All of the examples in this section are available on the companion CD-ROM.

ACCEPTING TEXT ONLY

To force a range to accept only text (no values), use the following data validation formula:

```
=ISTEXT(A1)
```

This formula assumes that the upper left cell in the selected range is cell A1.

ACCEPTING A LARGER VALUE THAN THE PREVIOUS CELL

The following data validation formula allows the user to enter a value only if it's greater than the value in the cell directly above it.

```
=A2>A1
```

This formula assumes that A2 is the upper left cell in the selected range. Note that you can't use this formula for a cell in row 1.

ACCEPTING NON–DUPLICATE ENTRIES ONLY

The following data validation formula does not permit the user to make a duplicate entry in the range A1:C20:

```
=COUNTIF($A$1:$C$20,A1)=1
```

This formula assumes that A1 is the upper left cell in the selected range. Note that the first argument for COUNTIF is an absolute reference. The second argument is a relative reference, and it adjusts for each cell in the validation range. Figure 17-22 shows this validation criteria in effect, using a custom error alert message.

ACCEPTING TEXT THAT BEGINS WITH "A"

The following data validation formula demonstrates how to check for a specific character. In this case, the formula ensures that the user's entry is a text string that beings with the letter A (either upper- or lowercase).

```
=LEFT(A1)="a"
```

This formula assumes that the upper left cell in the selected range is cell A1.

The following formula is variation of this validation formula. In this case, the formula ensures that the entry begins with the letter A and contains exactly five characters.

```
=COUNTIF(A1,"A????")=1
```

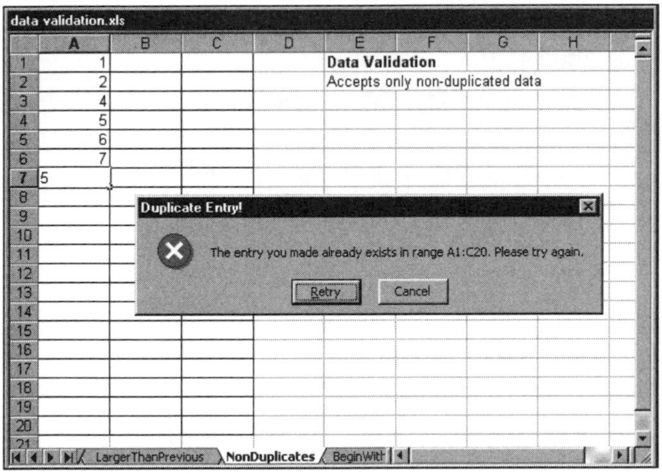

Figure 17-22: Using data validation to prevent duplicate entries in a range

Using Custom Worksheet Functions in Data Validation Formulas

Earlier in this chapter, I described how to use custom VBA functions for custom formatting (see "Using Custom Functions in Conditional Formatting Formulas"). For some reason, Excel does not permit you to use a custom VBA function in a data validation formula. If you attempt to do so, you get the following (erroneous) error message: *A named range you specified cannot be found.*

The workaround uses the custom function in a cell formula, and then specifies a data validation formula that refers to that cell.

Part V of this book covers custom VBA functions.

Summary

This chapter provided an overview of two useful features available in Excel 97 or later: conditional formatting and data validation. It also provided many examples of using formulas in conjunction with these features.

The next chapter covers creating megaformulas.

Chapter 18

Creating Megaformulas

IN THIS CHAPTER

◆ What is a megaformula, and why would you want to use such a thing

◆ How to create a megaformula

◆ Examples of megaformulas

◆ Pros and cons of using megaformulas

THIS CHAPTER DESCRIBES a useful technique that lets you combine several formulas into a single formula — what I call a *megaformula*. This technique can eliminate intermediate formulas and may even speed up recalculation. The downside, as you'll see, is that the formula is virtually incomprehensible and is impossible to edit.

What Is a Megaformula?

Often, spreadsheets require intermediate formulas to produce a desired result. In other words, a formula may depend on other formulas, which in turn depend on other formulas. After you get all these formulas working correctly, you often can eliminate the intermediate formulas and create a single (and more complex) formula. For lack of a better term, I call such a formula a *megaformula*.

What are the advantages of employing megaformulas? They use fewer cells (less clutter), and recalculation may be faster. And, you can impress people you know with your formula-building abilities. The disadvantages? The formula probably will be impossible to decipher or modify — even by the person who created it.

 The techniques described in this chapter helped to create many of the complex formulas presented elsewhere in this book.

A limitation to the megaformula technique is that Excel formulas can contain no more than 1,024 characters.

Creating a Megaformula: A Simple Example

Creating a megaformula basically involves copying formula text and pasting it into another formula. Let's start with a relatively simple example. Examine the spreadsheet shown in Figure 18-1. This sheet uses formulas to calculate mortgage loan information.

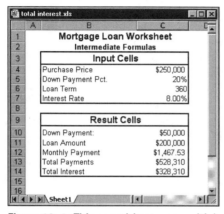

Figure 18-1: This spreadsheet uses multiple formulas to calculate mortgage loan information.

The Result Cells section of the worksheet uses information entered into the Input Cells section, and contains the formulas shown in Table 18-1.

TABLE **18-1** FORMULAS USED TO CALCULATE TOTAL INTEREST

Cell	Formula	What It Does
C10	=C4*C5	Calculates the down payment amount
C11	=C4-C10	Calculates the loan amount
C12	=PMT(C7/12,C6,-C11)	Calculates the monthly payment
C13	=C12*C6	Calculates the total payments
C14	=C13-C11	Calculates the total interest

Suppose you're *really* interested in the total interest paid (cell C14). You could, of course, simply hide the rows that contain the extraneous information. But, it's also possible to create a single formula that does the work of several intermediary formulas.

The formula that calculates total interest depends on other formulas (in C10 and C13). In addition, the formula in C13 depends on the formula in C12. And cell C12, in turn, depends on C10. Therefore, calculating the total interest uses five formulas. The steps that follow describe how to create a single formula to calculate total interest so you can eliminate the intermediate formulas. C14 contains the following formula:

```
=C13-C11
```

The steps that follow describe how to convert this formula into a megaformula.

1. Substitute the formula contained in cell C13 for the reference to cell C13. Before doing this, add parentheses around the formula in C13. Now, the formula in C14 is:

   ```
   =(C12*C6)-C11
   ```

2. Substitute the formula contained in cell C12 for the reference to cell C12. Now, the formula in C14 is:

   ```
   =(PMT(C7/12,C6,-C11)*C6)-C11
   ```

3. Substitute the formula contained in cell C11 for the two references to cell C11. Before copying the formula, you need to insert parentheses around it. Now, the formula in C14 is:

   ```
   =(PMT(C7/12,C6,-(C4-C10))*C6)-(C4-C10)
   ```

4. Substitute the formula contained in C10 for the two references to cell C10. Before copying the formula, insert parentheses around it. After doing so, the formula in C14 is:

   ```
   =(PMT(C7/12,C6,-(C4-(C4*C5)))*C6)-(C4-(C4*C5))
   ```

At this point, the formula contains references only to input cells. You can safely delete the formulas in C10:C13. The single megaformula now does the work previously performed by the intermediary formulas.

Unless you're a world-class Excel formula wizard, it's quite unlikely that you could arrive at that formula without first creating intermediate formulas.

I designed this previous exercise to demonstrate how to create a megaformula. This technique is *not* the most efficient way to calculate total interest on a loan. Excel provides a more direct way to make that calculation: Use the CUMIPMT function contained in the Analysis ToolPak.

Creating a megaformula essentially involves substituting formula text for cell references in a formula. You perform substitutions until the megaformula contains no references to formula cells. At each step along the way, you can check your work by ensuring that the formula continues to display the same result. In the previous example, a few of the steps required you to use parentheses around the copied formula.

Megaformula Examples

To demonstrate the process of creating a megaformula, let's look at three specific examples. These examples provide a thorough introduction to applying the megaformula technique for streamlining a variety of tasks, including cleaning up a list of names by removing middle names and initials, returning the position of the last space character in a string, and determining if a credit card number is valid.

Copying Text from a Formula

Creating megaformulas involves copying formula text and then replacing a cell reference with the copied text. To copy the contents of a formula, activate the cell and press F2. Then, select the formula text (without the equal sign) by pressing Shift+Home, followed by Shift+right arrow. Then, press Ctrl+C to copy the selected text to the clipboard. Activate the cell that contains the megaformula and press F2. Use the arrow keys, and hold down Shift to select the cell reference you want to replace. Finally, press Ctrl+V to replace the selected text with the clipboard contents.

In some cases, you need to insert parentheses around the copied formula text to make the formula calculate correctly. If the formula returns a different result after you paste the formula text, press Ctrl+Z to undo the paste. Insert parentheses around the formula you want to copy and try again.

Using a megaformula to remove middle names

Consider a worksheet with a column of people's names, like the one shown in Figure 18-2. Suppose you have a worksheet with thousands of such names, and you need to remove all the middle names and middle initials from the names. Editing the cells manually takes hours, so you opt for a formula-based solution. Notice that not all the names have a middle name or initial, which makes the task a bit trickier. Although this is not a difficult task, it normally involves several intermediate formulas.

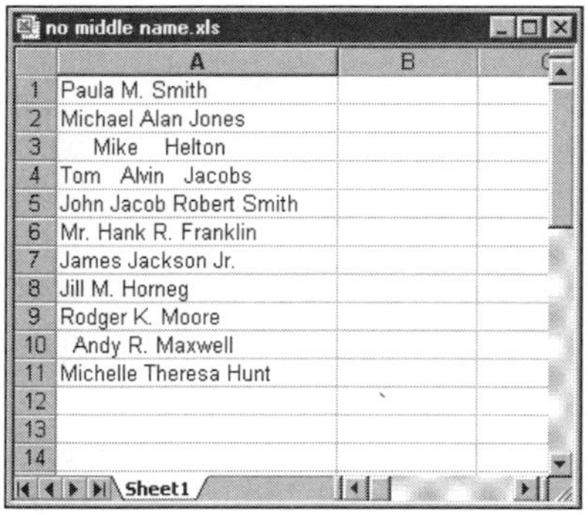

no middle name.xls

	A	B
1	Paula M. Smith	
2	Michael Alan Jones	
3	Mike Helton	
4	Tom Alvin Jacobs	
5	John Jacob Robert Smith	
6	Mr. Hank R. Franklin	
7	James Jackson Jr.	
8	Jill M. Horneg	
9	Rodger K. Moore	
10	Andy R. Maxwell	
11	Michelle Theresa Hunt	
12		
13		
14		

Sheet1

Figure 18-2: The goal is to remove the middle name or middle initial from each name.

Figure 18-3 shows the results of the more conventional solution, which requires six intermediate formulas as shown in Table 18-2. The names are in column A; column H displays the end result. Columns B through G hold the intermediate formulas.

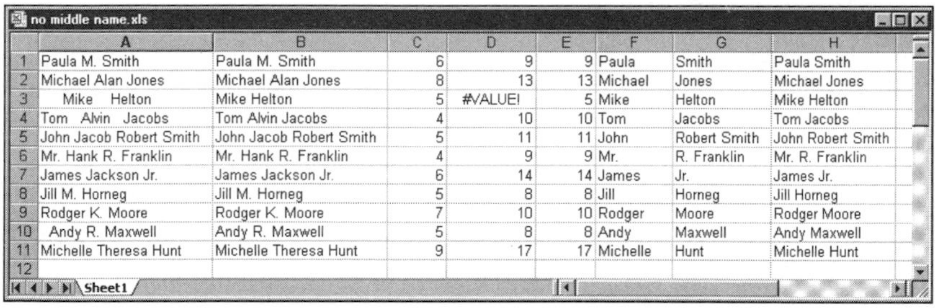

no middle name.xls

	A	B	C	D	E	F	G	H
1	Paula M. Smith	Paula M. Smith	6	9	9	Paula	Smith	Paula Smith
2	Michael Alan Jones	Michael Alan Jones	8	13	13	Michael	Jones	Michael Jones
3	Mike Helton	Mike Helton	5	#VALUE!	5	Mike	Helton	Mike Helton
4	Tom Alvin Jacobs	Tom Alvin Jacobs	4	10	10	Tom	Jacobs	Tom Jacobs
5	John Jacob Robert Smith	John Jacob Robert Smith	5	11	11	John	Robert Smith	John Robert Smith
6	Mr. Hank R. Franklin	Mr. Hank R. Franklin	4	9	9	Mr.	R. Franklin	Mr. R. Franklin
7	James Jackson Jr.	James Jackson Jr.	6	14	14	James	Jr.	James Jr.
8	Jill M. Horneg	Jill M. Horneg	5	8	8	Jill	Horneg	Jill Horneg
9	Rodger K. Moore	Rodger K. Moore	7	10	10	Rodger	Moore	Rodger Moore
10	Andy R. Maxwell	Andy R. Maxwell	5	8	8	Andy	Maxwell	Andy Maxwell
11	Michelle Theresa Hunt	Michelle Theresa Hunt	9	17	17	Michelle	Hunt	Michelle Hunt
12								

Sheet1

Figure 18-3: Removing the middle names and initials requires six intermediate formulas.

TABLE 18-2 INTERMEDIATE FORMULAS IN THE FIRST ROW OF SHEET1 IN FIGURE 18-3

Cell	Intermediate Formula	What It Does
B1	=TRIM(A1)	Removes excess spaces
C1	=FIND(" ",B1,1)	Locates the first space
D1	=FIND(" ",B1,C1+1)	Locates the second space
E1	=IF(ISERROR(D1),C1,D1)	Uses the first space if no second space exists
F1	=LEFT(B1,C1)	Extracts the first name
G1	=RIGHT(B1,LEN(B1)-E1)	Extracts the last name
H1	=F1&" "&G1	Concatenates the two names

 Notice that the result isn't perfect. For example, this method fails if a name has two middle names (such as John Jacob Robert Smith). That occurs because the formula simply searches for the second space character in the name. In this example, the megaformula returns *John Robert Smith*. Later in this chapter, I present an array formula method to identify the last space character in a string.

With a bit of work, you can eliminate all the intermediate formulas and replace them with a single megaformula. You do so by creating all the intermediate formulas and then going back into the final result formula (in this case, the formula in column H) and replacing each cell reference with a copy of the formula in the cell referred to (without the equal sign). Fortunately, you can use the clipboard to copy and paste (see the sidebar, "Copying Text from a Formula"). Keep repeating this process until cell H1 contains nothing but references to cell A1. You end up with the following megaformula in one cell:

```
=LEFT(TRIM(A1),FIND(" ",TRIM(A1),1)-1)&" "&RIGHT
(TRIM(A1),LEN(TRIM(A1))-IF(ISERROR(FIND(" ",
TRIM(A1),FIND(" ",TRIM(A1),1)+1)),FIND(" ",TRIM(A1),1),
FIND(" ",TRIM(A1),FIND(" ",TRIM(A1),1)+1)))
```

When you're satisfied that the megaformula works, you can delete the columns that hold the intermediate formulas because they are no longer used.

THE STEP-BY-STEP PROCEDURE

If you're still not clear about this process, take a look at these step-by-step procedures.

1. Examine the formula in H1. This formula contains two cell references (F1 and G1).

   ```
   =F1&" "&G1
   ```

2. Activate cell G1 and copy the contents of the formula (without the equal sign) to the clipboard.

3. Activate cell H1 and replace the reference to cell G1 with the clipboard contents. Now, cell H1 contains the following formula:

   ```
   =F1&" "&RIGHT(B1,LEN(B1)-E1)
   ```

4. Activate cell F1 and copy the contents of the formula (without the equal sign) to the clipboard.

5. Activate cell H1 and replace the reference to cell F1 with the clipboard contents. Now, the formula in cell H1 is:

   ```
   =LEFT(B1,C1-1)&" "&RIGHT(B1,LEN(B1)-E1)
   ```

6. Now, cell H1 contains references to three cells (B1, C1, and E1). The formulas in those cells will replace each of the three references.

7. Replace the reference to cell E1 with the formula in E1. The result is:

   ```
   =LEFT(B1,C1-1)&" "&RIGHT(B1,LEN(B1)-IF(ISERROR(D1),C1,D1))
   ```

8. Notice that the formula in cell H1 now contains two references to cell D1. Copy the formula from D1 and replace both of the references to cell D1. The formula now looks like this:

   ```
   =LEFT(B1,C1-1)&" "&RIGHT(B1,LEN(B1)-IF(ISERROR(FIND
   (" ",B1,C1+1)),C1,FIND(" ",B1,C1+1)))
   ```

9. Replace the four references to cell C1 with the formula contained in cell C1. The formula in cell H1 is:

   ```
   =LEFT(B1,FIND(" ",B1,1)-1)&" "&RIGHT(B1,LEN(B1)-IF
   (ISERROR(FIND(" ",B1,FIND(" ",B1,1)+1)),FIND(" ",B1,1),
   FIND(" ",B1,FIND(" ",B1,1)+1)))
   ```

10. Finally, replace the nine references to cell B1 with the formula in cell B1. The result is:

    ```
    =LEFT(TRIM(A1),FIND(" ",TRIM(A1),1)-1)&" "&RIGHT(TRIM(A1),
    LEN(TRIM(A1))-IF(ISERROR(FIND(" ",TRIM(A1),FIND(" ",
    TRIM(A1),1)+1)),FIND(" ",TRIM(A1),1),FIND(" ",TRIM(A1),
    FIND(" ",TRIM(A1),1)+1)))
    ```

Notice that the formula in cell H1 now contains references only to cell A1. The megaformula is complete, and it performs exactly the same tasks as all the intermediate formulas (which you can delete).

 You can access the workbook for removing middle names and initials on the companion CD-ROM.

COMPARING SPEED AND EFFICIENCY

Because a megaformula is so complex, you may think that using one slows down recalculation. Actually, that's not the case. As a test, I created a workbook that used the megaformula 65,536 times. Then, I created another workbook that used six intermediate formulas to compute the 65,536 results. I compared the results with a custom VBA function that performs the same operation. Table 18-3 shows the statistics regarding the three methodologies.

TABLE 18-3 COMPARING INTERMEDIATE FORMULAS, A MEGAFORMULA, AND A VBA FUNCTION

Method	Recalculation Time (Seconds)	File Size
Intermediate formulas	10.8	24.4MB
Megaformula	6.2	8.9MB
VBA function	106.7	8.6MB

The actual results will of course vary depending on system speed and the amount of memory installed.

As you can see, using a megaformula in this case resulted in faster recalculations as well as a *much* smaller workbook. The VBA function was much slower — in fact, it wasn't even in the same ballpark. This is fairly typical of VBA functions; they are always slower than built-in Excel functions.

Using a megaformula to return a string's last space character position

As previously noted, the "remove middle name" example presented earlier contains a flaw: To identify the last name, the formula searches for the second space character. A better solution is to search for the *last* space character. Unfortunately, Excel doesn't provide any simple way to locate the first position of a character from the *end* of a string. The example in this section solves that problem and describes a way to determine the position of the first occurrence of a specific character beginning from the end of a text string.

 This technique involves arrays, so you might want to review the material in Part IV to familiarize yourself with this topic.

This example describes how to create a megaformula that returns the character position of the last *space character* in a string. You can, of course, modify the formula to work with any other character.

CREATING THE INTERMEDIATE FORMULAS
The general plan is to create an array of characters in the string, but in reverse order. Once that array is created, we can use the MATCH function to locate the first space character in the array.

Refer to Figure 18-4, which shows the results of the intermediate formulas. Cell A1 contains an arbitrary name, which happens to be composed of 12 characters. The range B1:B12 contains the following array formula:

```
{=ROW(INDIRECT("1:"&LEN(A1)))}
```

	A	B	C	D	E	F	G
1	Jim E. Brown	1	12	n	6	7	
2		2	11	w			
3		3	10	o			
4		4	9	r			
5		5	8	B			
6		6	7				
7		7	6	.			
8		8	5	E			
9		9	4				
10		10	3	m			
11		11	2	i			
12		12	1	J			

first character from end of string.xls

Figure 18-4: These intermediate formulas will eventually be converted to a single megaformula.

You enter this formula into the entire B1:B12 range by selecting the range, typing the formula, and pressing Ctrl+Shift+Enter. Remember not to type the brackets.

Excel adds the brackets to indicate an array formula. This formula returns an array of 12 consecutive integers.

The range C1:C12 contains the following array formula:

```
{=LEN(A1)+1-B1:B12}
```

This formula essentially reverses the integers generated in column B. The range D1:D12 contains the following array formula:

```
{=MID(A1,C1:C12,1)}
```

This formula uses the MID function to extract the characters in cell A1. The MID function uses the array in C1:C12 as its second argument. The result is an array of characters in reverse order. The formula in cell E1 is:

```
=MATCH(" ",D1:D12,0)
```

This formula, which is *not* an array formula, uses the MATCH function to return the position of the first space character in the range D1:D12. In the example shown in Figure 18-4, the formula returns 6, which means that the first space character is six characters from the end of the text in A1. The formula in cell F1 is:

```
=LEN(A1)+1-E1
```

This formula returns the character position of the last space in the string.

You may wonder how all of these formulas can possibly be combined into a single formula. Keep reading for the answer.

CREATING THE MEGAFORMULA

At this point, cell F1 contains the result we are looking for. The challenge is consolidating all of those intermediate formulas into a single formula. The goal is to produce a formula that contains only references to cell A1. These steps will get you to that goal.

1. The formula in F1 contains a reference to E1. Replace that reference with the text of the formula in E1. As a result, the formula in F1 becomes:

   ```
   =LEN(A1)+1-MATCH(" ",D1:D12,0)
   ```

2. Now, the formula contains a reference to D1:D12. This range contains a single array formula. Replacing the reference to D1:D12 with the array formula results in the following formula in F1:

   ```
   {=LEN(A1)+1-MATCH(" ",MID(A1,C1:C12,1),0)}
   ```

Because an array formula replaced the reference in cell F1, you now must enter the formula in F1 as an array formula (enter it with Ctrl+Shift+Enter).

3. Now, the formula in F1 contains a reference to C1:C12, which also contains an array formula. Replace the reference to C1:C12 with the array formula in C1:C12 to get this formula in F1:

   ```
   {=LEN(A1)+1-MATCH(" ",MID(A1,LEN(A1)+1-B1:B12,1),0)}
   ```

4. Next, replace the reference to B1:B12 with the array formula in B1:B12. The result is:

   ```
   {=LEN(A1)+1-MATCH(" ",MID(A1,LEN(A1)+1-ROW(INDIRECT
   ("1:"&LEN(A1))),1),0)}
   ```

Now, the array formula in F1 refers only to cell A1 — exactly what we want. The megaformula does all of the work, and you can delete all of the intermediate formulas.

Although you use a 12-digit value and arrays stored in 12-row ranges to create the formula, the final formula does not use any of these range references. Consequently, the megaformula works with a value of any length.

PUTTING THE MEGAFORMULA TO WORK

Figure 18-5 displays a worksheet with names in column A. Column B contains the megaformula developed in the previous section. Column C contains a formula that extracts the characters beginning after the last space — the last name.

	A	B	C	D	E
1	Paula M. Smith	9	Smith		
2	Michael Alan Jones	13	Jones		
3	Mike Helton	5	Helton		
4	Tom Alvin Jacobs	10	Jacobs		
5	John Jacob Robert Smith	18	Smith		
6	Mr. Hank R. Franklin	12	Franklin		
7	James Jackson Jr.	14	Jr.		
8	Jill M. Horneg	8	Horneg		
9	Rodger K. Moore	10	Moore		
10	Andy R. Maxwell	8	Maxwell		
11	Michelle Theresa Hunt	17	Hunt		
12					
13					
14					
15					

first character from end of string.xls

Sheet1 \ Sheet2

Figure 18-5: Column B contains a megaformula that returns the character position of the last space of the names in column A.

Cell C1, for example, contains this formula:

```
=RIGHT(A1,LEN(A1)-B1)
```

If you like, you can eliminate the formulas in column B and create a specialized formula that returns the last name. To do so, substitute the formula in B1 for the reference to B1 in the formula. The result is the following array formula:

```
{=RIGHT(A1,LEN(A1)-(LEN(A1)+1-MATCH(" ",MID(A1,LEN(A1)+1-
ROW(INDIRECT("1:"&LEN(A1))),1),0)))}
```

You must insert parentheses around the formula text copied from cell B1. Without the parentheses, the formula does not evaluate correctly.

The workbook for locating a string's last space character is available on the companion CD-ROM.

Using a megaformula to determine the validity of a credit card number

You may not know it, but you can determine the validity of a credit card number by using a relatively complex algorithm to analyze the digits of the number. In addition, you can determine the type of credit card by examining the initial digits and the length of the number. Table 18-4 shows information about four major credit cards.

TABLE 18-4 INFORMATION ABOUT FOUR CREDIT CARDS

Credit Card	Prefix Digits	Total Digits
Mastercard	51–55	16
Visa	4	13 or 16
American Express	34 or 37	15
Discover	6011	16

"Validity," in this case, means whether the credit card number *itself* is a valid number. This technique, of course, cannot determine if the number represents an active credit card account.

You can test the validity of a credit card account number by processing its checksum digits. All account numbers used in major credit cards use a "mod 10" check digit algorithm. The general process follows these steps:

1. Add leading zeros to the account number to make the total digits equal 16.

2. Beginning with the first digit, double the value of alternate digits of the account number. If the result is a two-digit number, add the two digits together.

3. Add the eight values generated in Step 2 to each of the skipped digits of the original number.

4. If the sum obtained in Step 3 is evenly divisible by 10, the number is a valid credit card number.

The example described in this section describes a megaformula that determines if a credit card number is a valid number.

THE BASIC FORMULAS

Figure 18-6 shows a worksheet set up to analyze a credit card number and determine its validity. This workbook uses quite a few formulas to make the determination.

In this workbook, the credit card number is entered in cell F1, with no spaces or hyphens. The formula in cell F2 follows. This formula appends leading zeros, if necessary, to make the card number exactly 16 digits. The other formulas use the string in cell F2.

```
=REPT("0",16-LEN(F1))&F1
```

When entering a credit card number that contains more than 15 digits, you must be careful that Excel does not round the number to 15 digits. You can precede the number with an apostrophe or preformat the cell as Text (using the Number Format tab of the Format Cells dialog box).

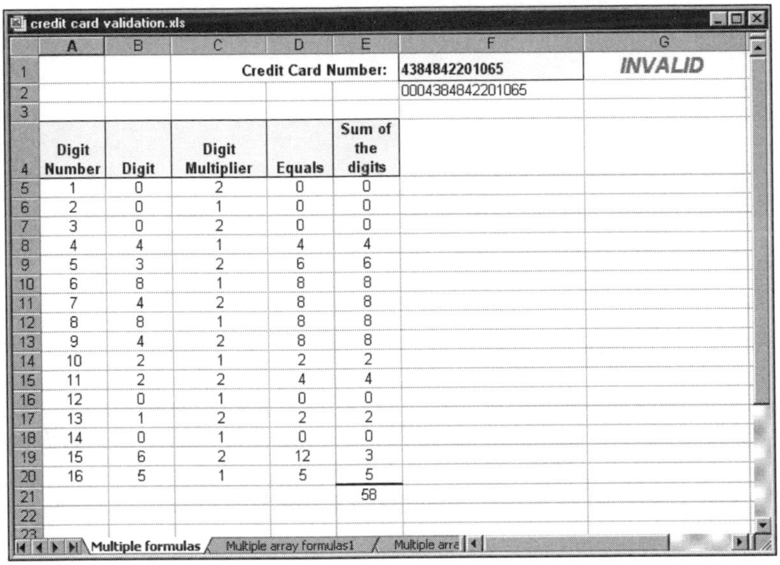
credit card validation.xls

	A	B	C	D	E	F	G
1			Credit Card Number:			4384842201065	INVALID
2						0004384842201065	
3							
4	Digit Number	Digit	Digit Multiplier	Equals	Sum of the digits		
5	1	0	2	0	0		
6	2	0	1	0	0		
7	3	0	2	0	0		
8	4	4	1	4	4		
9	5	3	2	6	6		
10	6	8	1	8	8		
11	7	4	2	8	8		
12	8	8	1	8	8		
13	9	4	2	8	8		
14	10	2	1	2	2		
15	11	2	2	4	4		
16	12	0	1	0	0		
17	13	1	2	2	2		
18	14	0	1	0	0		
19	15	6	2	12	3		
20	16	5	1	5	5		
21					58		
22							

Multiple formulas / Multiple array formulas1 / Multiple arra

Figure 18-6: The formulas in this workbook determine the validity of a credit card number.

Column A contains a series of integers from 1 to 16, representing the digit positions of the credit card. Column B contains formulas that extract each digit from cell F2. For example, the formula in cell B5 is:

```
=MID($F$2,A5,1)
```

Column C contains the multipliers for each digit: alternating 2s and 1s. Column D contains formulas that multiply the digit by the multiplier. For example, the formula in cell D5 is:

```
=B5*C5
```

Column E contains formulas that sum the digits displayed in column D. A single digit value in column D is returned directly. For two-digit values, the sum of the digits is displayed in Column E. For example, if column D displays 14, the formula in column E returns 5 (i.e., 1 + 4). The formula that accomplishes this is:

```
=INT((D5/10)+MOD((D5),10))
```

Cell E21 contains a simple SUM formula to add the values in column E:

```
=SUM(E5:E20)
```

The formula in cell G1, which follows, calculates the remainder when cell E21 is divided by 10. If the remainder is 0, the card number is valid and the formula displays *VALID*. Otherwise, the formula displays *INVALID*.

```
=IF(MOD(E21,10)=0,"VALID","INVALID")
```

CONVERT TO ARRAY FORMULAS

It's important to understand that the megaformula that we'll create will be an array formula because the intermediary formulas occupy multiple rows – not just a single row as in the previous examples.

First, you have to convert all of the formulas to array formulas. Note that columns A and C consist of values, not formulas. To use the values in a megaformula, they must be generated by formulas – more specifically, array formulas.

Enter the following array formula into the range A5:A20. This array formula returns a series of 16 consecutive integers.

```
{=ROW(INDIRECT("1:16"))}
```

For column B, select B5:B20 and enter the following array formula:

```
{=MID($F$2,A5:A20,1)}
```

Next, column C requires an array formula that generates alternating values of 2 and 1. Such a formula, entered into the range C5:C20, is shown here:

```
{=(MOD(ROW(INDIRECT("1:16")),2)+1)}
```

For column D, select D5:D20 and enter the following array formula:

```
{=B5:B20*C5:C20}
```

Finally, select E5:E20 and enter this array formula:

```
{=INT((D5:D20/10)+MOD((D5:D20),10))}
```

Now, there are five columns of 20 rows, but only five actual formulas.

BUILD THE MEGAFORMULA

To build the megaformula for this task, start with the cell that has the final result – cell G1. The original formula in G1 is:

```
=IF(MOD(E21,10)=0,"VALID","INVALID")
```

First, replace the reference to cell E21 with the formula in E21. Doing so results in the following formula in cell G1:

```
=IF(MOD(SUM(E5:E20),10)=0,"VALID","INVALID")
```

Next, replace the reference to E5:E20 with the array formula contained in that range. Now, the formula becomes an array formula so you must enter it with Ctrl+Shift+Enter. After the replacement, the formula in G1 is:

```
{=IF(MOD(SUM(INT((D5:D20/10)+MOD((D5:D20),10))),10)=0,
"VALID","INVALID")}
```

You can replace the two references to range D5:D20 with the array formula contained in D5:20. Doing so results in the following formula in cell G1:

```
{=IF(MOD(SUM(INT((B5:B20*C5:C20/10)+MOD((B5:B20*C5:C20),10))),
10)=0,"VALID","INVALID")}
```

Next, replace the references to cell C5:C20 with the array formula in C5:C20. Note that you must have a set of parentheses around the copied formula text. The result is as follows:

```
{=IF(MOD(SUM(INT((B5:B20*(MOD(ROW(INDIRECT("1:16")),2)+1)/10)+
MOD((B5:B20*(MOD(ROW(INDIRECT("1:16")),2)+1)),10))),10)=0,
"VALID","INVALID")}
```

Replacing the references to B5:B20 with the array formula contained in B5:B20 yields the following:

```
{=IF(MOD(SUM(INT((MID($F$2,A5:A20,1)*(MOD(ROW(INDIRECT("1:16")),2)
+1)/10)+MOD((MID($F$2,A5:A20,1)*(MOD(ROW(INDIRECT("1:16")),
2)+1)),10))),10)=0,"VALID","INVALID")}
```

Next, substitute the array formula in range A5:A20 for the references to that range. The resulting formula is:

```
{=IF(MOD(SUM(INT((MID($F$2,ROW(INDIRECT("1:16")),1)*(MOD(ROW
(INDIRECT("1:16")),2)+1)/10)+MOD((MID($F$2,ROW(INDIRECT("1:16")),1)*
(MOD(ROW(INDIRECT("1:16")),2)+1)),10))),10)=0,"VALID","INVALID")}
```

Next, substitute the formula in cell F2 for the references to cell F2. After making the substitutions, the formula is as follows:

```
{=IF(MOD(SUM(INT((MID(REPT("0",16-LEN(F1))&F1,
```

```
ROW(INDIRECT("1:16")),1)*(MOD(ROW(INDIRECT("1:16")),2)+1)/
10)+MOD((MID(REPT("0",16-LEN(F1))&F1,ROW(INDIRECT("1:16")),1)*
(MOD(ROW(INDIRECT("1:16")),2)+1)),10))),10)=0,"VALID",
"INVALID")}
```

Now, you can delete the now superfluous intermediate formulas. The final megaformula, a mere 229 characters in length, does the work of 51 intermediary formulas!

 You can access the credit card number validation workbook on the companion CD-ROM.

The Pros and Cons of Megaformulas

If you followed the examples in this chapter, you probably realize that the main advantage of creating a megaformula is to eliminate intermediate formulas. Doing so can streamline your worksheet, reduce the size of your workbook files, and even result in faster recalculations.

The downside? Creating a megaformula does, of course, require some additional time and effort. And, as you've undoubtedly noticed, a megaformula is virtually impossible for anyone (even me) to figure out. If you decide to use megaformulas, make sure that the intermediate formulas are performing correctly before you start building a megaformula. Even better, keep a copy of the intermediate formulas somewhere in case you discover an error or need to make a change.

Summary

This chapter described a useful technique that involves combining multiple formulas into a single, complex formula (a megaformula). I presented several examples of creating such formulas.

The next chapter takes a look at formulas you can create for debugging purposes.

Chapter 19

Tools and Methods for Debugging Formulas

IN THIS CHAPTER

◆ What is formula debugging

◆ How to identify and correct common formula errors

◆ A description of Excel's auditing tools

◆ Auditing tools available from third-party providers

ERRORS HAPPEN. AND WHEN you create Excel formulas, errors happen very frequently. This chapter describes common formula errors and discusses tools and methods you can use to help create formulas that work as they are intended to work.

Formula Debugging?

The term *debugging* refers to the process of identifying and correcting errors in a computer program. Strictly speaking, an Excel formula is not a computer program. Formulas, however, are subject to the same types of problems that occur in a computer program. If you create a formula that doesn't work as it should, you need to identify and correct the problem.

The ultimate goal in developing a spreadsheet solution, is to generate accurate results. For simple worksheets, this isn't difficult, and you usually can tell whether the results are correct. But as your worksheets grow in size or complexity, ensuring accuracy becomes more difficult.

Making a change in a worksheet — even a relatively minor change — may produce a ripple effect that introduces errors in other cells. For example, accidentally entering a value into a cell that formerly held a formula is all too easy to do. This simple error can have a major impact on other formulas, and you may not discover the problem until long after you make the change. Or, you may *never* discover the problem.

Research on Spreadsheet Errors

Using a spreadsheet can be hazardous to your company's bottom line. It's far too easy to simply assume that your spreadsheet produces accurate results. If you use the results of a spreadsheet to make a major decision, it's especially important to make sure that the formulas return accurate and meaningful results.

Researchers have conducted quite a few studies that deal with spreadsheet errors. Generally, these studies have found that between 20 and 40 percent of all spreadsheets contain some type of error. If this type of research interests you, I urge you to check out the Spreadsheet Research (SSR) Web site maintained by Raymond R. Panko of the University of Hawaii. The URL is:

`http://www.cba.hawaii.edu/panko/`

Formula Problems and Solutions

Formula errors tend to fall into one of the following four general categories:

◆ Syntax errors: There is a problem with the syntax of a formula. For example, a formula may have mismatched parentheses, or you may have spelled a function name incorrectly.

◆ Logical errors: A formula doesn't return an error, but it contains a logical flaw that causes it to return an incorrect result.

◆ Incorrect reference errors: The logic of the formula is correct, but the formula uses an incorrect cell reference. For example, the range reference in a SUM formula may not include all of the data you want to sum. Or, a formula may erroneously refer to its own cell, producing a circular reference.

◆ Incomplete calculation errors: The formulas simply aren't calculated fully. Microsoft has acknowledged some problems with Excel's calculation engine. To ensure that your formulas are fully calculated, use Ctrl+Alt+F9.

Syntax errors are usually the easiest to identify and correct. In most cases, you will know about syntax errors. For example, Excel won't permit you to enter a formula with mismatched parentheses. Other syntax errors also usually result in an error display. The other three error categories are more difficult to identify.

The remainder of this section describes some common formula problems and offers advice on identifying and correcting them.

Mismatched parentheses

In a formula, every left parenthesis must have a corresponding right parenthesis. If your formula has mismatched parentheses, Excel usually won't permit you to enter it. An exception involves a simple formula that uses a function. For example, if you enter the formula that follows (missing a closing parenthesis), Excel accepts the formula and provides the missing parenthesis.

```
=SUM(A1:A500
```

A formula may have an equal number of left and right parentheses, but the parentheses may not match properly. For example, consider the following formula, which converts a text string so that the first character is uppercase and the remaining characters are lowercase. This formula has five pairs of parentheses, and they match properly.

```
=UPPER(LEFT(A1))&RIGHT(LOWER(A1),LEN(A1)-1)
```

The following formula also has five pairs of parentheses, but mismatched ones. The result displays a syntactically correct formula that simply returns the wrong result.

```
=UPPER(LEFT(A1)&RIGHT(LOWER(A1),LEN(A1)-1))
```

Often, having parentheses in the wrong location results in a syntax error. It's usually a message that tells you that you entered too many or too few arguments for a function.

 TIP   Excel can help you out with mismatched parentheses. When you edit a formula, move the cursor to a parenthesis and pause. Excel displays it (and its matching parenthesis) in bold for about one second.

Cells are filled with

When a cell is filled with a series of pound signs (#), it could mean either of two things:

◆ The column is not wide enough to accommodate the formatted numeric value. To correct it, you can make the column wider or use a different number format.

◆ The cell contains a formula that returns an invalid date or time. For example, Excel does not support dates prior to 1900 or the use of negative time values. Attempting to display either of these results in a cell filled with pound signs. Widening the column does not fix it.

Using Formula AutoCorrect

When you enter a formula that has a syntax error, Excel attempts to determine the problem and offers a suggested correction. For example, if you enter the following formula (which has a syntax error), Excel displays the dialog box shown in the accompanying figure.

```
=SUM(A1:A12)/3B
```

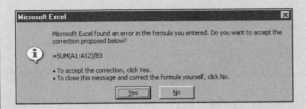

Exercise caution when accepting corrections for your formulas from Excel, because it doesn't always guess correctly. For example, I entered the following formula (which has mismatched parentheses):

```
=AVERAGE(SUM(A1:A12,SUM(B1:B12))
```

Excel proposed the following correction to the formula:

```
=AVERAGE(SUM(A1:A12,SUM(B1:B12)))
```

You may be tempted to accept the suggestion without even thinking. In this case, the proposed formula is syntactically correct — but not what I intended. The correct formula is:

```
=AVERAGE(SUM(A1:A12),SUM(B1:B12))
```

Blank cells are not blank

Some Excel users have discovered that pressing the Spacebar seems to erase the contents of a cell. Actually, pressing the Spacebar inserts a space character, which isn't the same as erasing the cell.

For example, the following formula returns the number of non-empty cells in range A1:A10. If you "erase" any of these cells by using the Spacebar, these cells will be included in the count, and the formula will return an incorrect result.

```
=COUNTA(A1:A10)
```

If your formula doesn't ignore blank cells the way it should, check to make sure that the blank cells are really blank cells.

Tracing Error Values

The Trace Error button on the Auditing toolbar helps you to identify the cell that is causing an error value to appear. Often, an error in one cell is the result of an error in a precedent cell. Activate a cell that contains an error, and click the Trace Error button. Excel draws arrows to indicate the error source.

Formulas returning an error

A formula may return any of the following error values:

◆ #DIV/0!

◆ #NA

◆ #NAME?

◆ #NULL!

◆ #NUM!

◆ #REF!

◆ #VALUE!

The sections that follow summarize possible problems that may cause these errors.

#DIV/0! ERRORS

Division by zero is not permitted. If you attempt to do so, Excel displays its familiar #DIV/0! error value.

Because Excel considers a blank cell to be zero, you also get this error if your formula divides by a missing value. This is a common problem when you create formulas for data that you haven't entered yet. Figure 19-1 shows an example. The formula in cell D2, which was copied to the cells below it, is:

```
=(C2-B2)/C2
```

This formula calculates the percent change between the values in columns B and C. Data isn't available for months beyond May, so the formula returns a #DIV/0! error.

To avoid the error display, you can use an IF function to check for a blank cell in column C:

```
=IF(ISBLANK(C2),"",(C2-B2)/C2)
```

Book1

	A	B	C	D	E
1	Month	Last Year	This Year	Change	
2	January	132	173	23.7%	
3	February	134	135	0.7%	
4	March	150	145	-3.4%	
5	April	165	189	12.7%	
6	May	173	198	12.6%	
7	June	145		#DIV/0!	
8	July	168		#DIV/0!	
9	August	201		#DIV/0!	
10	September	187		#DIV/0!	
11	October	175		#DIV/0!	
12	November	198		#DIV/0!	
13	December	221		#DIV/0!	
14					

Sheet1

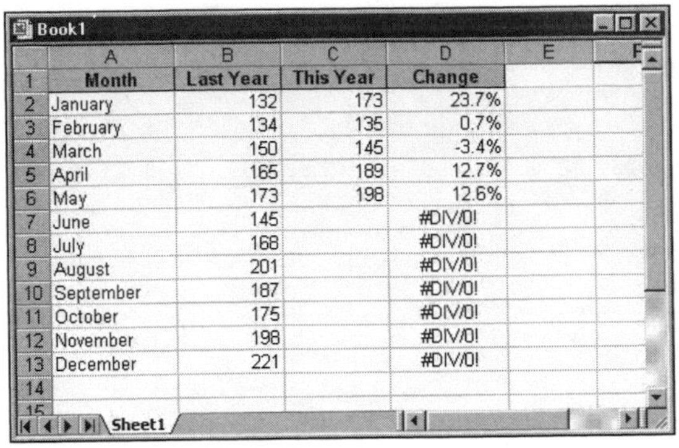

Figure 19-1: #DIV/0! errors occur when the data in column C is missing.

This formula displays an empty string if cell C2 is blank; otherwise, it displays the calculated value.

Another approach is to use an IF function to check for *any* error condition. The following formula, for example, displays an empty string if the formula results in any type of error. Unlike the previous formula, this one does not display an error if cell C3 contains a 0.

```
=IF(ISERROR((C2-B2)/C2),"",(C2-B2)/C2)
```

#N/A ERRORS

The #N/A error occurs if any cell referenced by a formula displays #N/A.

> NOTE
>
> Some users like to enter =NA() or #N/A explicitly for missing data. This method makes it perfectly clear that the data is not available and hasn't been deleted accidentally.

The #N/A error also occurs when a lookup function (HLOOKUP, LOOKUP, MATCH, or VLOOKUP) cannot find a match.

#NAME? ERRORS

The #NAME? error occurs under these conditions:

- The formula contains an undefined range or cell name.
- The formula contains text that Excel *interprets* as an undefined name. A misspelled function name, for example, generates a #NAME? error.
- The formula uses a worksheet function that's defined in an add-in, and the add-in is not installed.

Excel has a bit of a problem with range names. If you delete a name for a cell or range and the name is used in a formula, the formula continues to use the name, although it is no longer defined. As a result, the formula displays #NAME?. You might expect Excel automatically to convert the names to their corresponding cell references, but that's not what happens.

#NULL! ERRORS

The #NULL! error occurs when a formula attempts to use an intersection of two ranges that don't actually intersect. Excel's intersection operator is a space. The following formula, for example, returns #NULL! because the two ranges do not intersect.

```
=SUM(B5:B14 A16:F16)
```

The following formula does not return #NULL!. It displays the contents of cell B9, which represents the intersection of the two ranges.

```
=SUM(B5:B14 A9:F9)
```

#NUM! ERRORS

A formula returns a #NUM! error if:

- You pass a non-numerical argument to a function when a numerical argument is expected.

- A function that uses iteration cannot calculate a result. Examples of functions that use iteration are IRR and RATE.

- A formula returns a value that is too large or too small. Excel supports values between 1E-307 and 1E+307.

#REF! ERRORS

The #REF! error occurs when a formula uses an invalid cell reference. This error can occur when you copy a cell that contains a formula. For example, assume the following formula is in cell A2.

```
=A1-1
```

If you copy the cell to any cell in row 1, the formula returns #REF! because it attempts to refer to a nonexistent cell.

#VALUE! ERRORS

The #VALUE! error is very common, and can occur under the following conditions:

◆ An argument for a function is of an incorrect data type or the formula attempts to perform an operation using incorrect data. For example, a formula that adds a value to a text string returns the #VALUE! error.

◆ A function's argument is a range, when it should be a single value.

◆ A custom worksheet function is not calculated. With some versions of Excel, inserting or moving a sheet may cause this error. You can use Ctrl+Alt+F9 to force a recalculation.

◆ You forget to press Ctrl+Shift+Enter when entering an array formula.

Absolute/relative reference problems

As described in Chapter 2, a cell reference can be relative (for example, A1), absolute, (for example, $A$1), or mixed (for example, $A1 or A$1). The type of cell reference you use in a formula is relevant only if the formula will be copied to other cells.

A common problem is to use a relative reference when you should use an absolute reference. As shown in Figure 19-2, cell C1 contains a tax rate, which is used in the formulas in column C. The formula in cell C4 is:

```
=B4+(B4*$C$1)
```

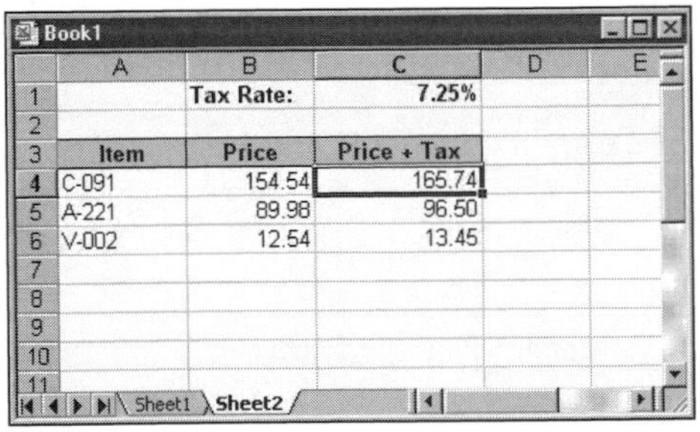

Figure 19-2: Formulas in the range C4:C6 use an absolute reference to cell C1.

Notice that the reference to cell C1 is an absolute reference. When the formula is copied to other cells in column C, the formula continues to refer to cell C1. If the reference to cell C1 were a relative reference, the copied formulas would return an incorrect result.

> ## Pay Attention to the Colors
>
> When you edit a cell that contains a formula, Excel color-codes the cell and range references in the formula. Excel also outlines the cells and ranges used in the formula by using corresponding colors. Therefore, you can see at a glance the cells used in the formula.
>
> You also can manipulate the colored outline to change the cell or range reference. To change the references that are used, drag the outline's border or drag the outline's fill handle (at the lower-right corner of the outline).

Operator precedence problems

Excel has some straightforward rules about the order in which mathematical operations are performed. In Table 19-1, operations with a lower precedence are performed before operations with a higher precedence. This table, for example, shows that multiplication has a higher precedence than addition. Therefore, multiplication is performed first.

TABLE 19-1 OPERATOR PRECEDENCE IN EXCEL FORMULAS

Symbol	Operator	Precedence
-	Negation	1
%	Percent	2
^	Exponentiation	3
* and /	Multiplication and division	4
+ and -	Addition and subtraction	5
&	Text concatenation	6
=, <, >, and <>	Comparison	7

When in doubt (or simply to clarify your intentions), you should use parentheses to ensure that operations are performed in the correct order. For example, the following formula multiplies A1 by A2, and then adds 1 to the result. The multiplication is performed first, because it has a higher order of precedence.

```
= 1+A1*A2
```

A clearer version of this formula follows. The parentheses are not necessary, but, in this case, the order of operations is perfectly obvious.

```
=1+(A1*A2)
```

Notice that the negation operator symbol is exactly the same as the subtraction operator symbol. This, as you might expect, can cause some confusion. Consider these two formulas:

```
=-3^2
=0-3^2
```

The first formula, as expected, returns 9. The second formula, however, returns -9. Squaring a number always produces a positive result, so how is it that Excel can return the −9 result?

In the first formula, the minus sign is a negation operator and has the highest precedence. In the second example, the minus sign is a subtraction operator, which has a lower precedence than the exponentiation operator. Therefore, the value 3 is squared and the result is subtracted from zero, which produces a negative result.

 Excel is a bit unusual in interpreting the negation operator. Other spreadsheet products (for example, 1-2-3 and Quattro Pro) return -9 for both formulas. In addition, Excel's VBA language also returns -9 for these expressions!

Using parentheses, as in the following formula, causes Excel to interpret the operator as a minus sign rather than a negation operator. This formula returns 9.

```
=0+(-3^2)
```

Formulas are not calculated

If you use custom worksheet functions written in VBA, you may find that formulas that use these functions fail to get recalculated and may display incorrect results. To force a recalculation of all formulas, press Ctrl+Alt+F9.

 Prior to Excel 2000, this key combination was not documented.

Actual vs. displayed values

You may encounter a situation in which values in a range don't appear to add up properly. For example, Figure 19-3 shows a worksheet with the following formula entered into each cell in the range B2:B4:

```
=1/3
```

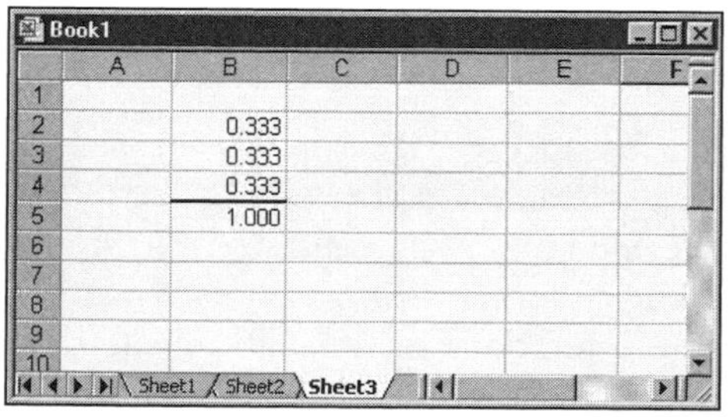

Figure 19-3: A simple demonstration of numbers that appear to add up incorrectly

Cell B5 contains the following formula:

```
=SUM(B2:B4)
```

All of the cells are formatted to display with three decimal places. As you can see, the formula in cell B5 appears to display an incorrect result (you might expect it to display 0.999). The formula, of course, *does* return the correct result. The formula uses the *actual* values in the range B2:B4, not the displayed values.

You can instruct Excel to use the displayed values by checking the Precision as displayed checkbox on the Calculation tab of the Options dialog box (choose Tools → Options to display this dialog box).

Selecting the Precision as displayed option also affects normal values (non-formulas) entered into cells. For example, if a cell contains the value 4.68 and is displayed with no decimal places (that is, 5) selecting the Precision as displayed option converts 4.68 to 5.00. This change is permanent and you cannot restore the original value if you later uncheck the Precision as displayed option.

Floating point number errors

Computers, by their very nature, do not have infinite precision. Excel stores numbers in binary format using eight bytes, which can handle numbers with 15-digit accuracy. Some numbers cannot be expressed precisely using eight bytes, so the number stores as an approximation.

To demonstrate how this may cause problems, enter the following formula into cell A1:

```
=(5.1-5.2)+1
```

The result should be 0.9. However, if you format the cell to display 15 decimal places, you'll discover that Excel calculates the formula with a result of 0.899999999999999. This occurs because the operation in parentheses is performed first, and this intermediate result stores in binary format using an approximation. The formula then adds 1 to this value, and the approximation error is propagated to the final result.

In many cases, this type of error does not present a problem. However, if you need to test the result of that formula using a logical operator, it *may* present a problem. For example, the following formula (which assumes the previous formula is in cell A1) returns FALSE:

```
=A1=.9
```

One solution to this type of error is to use Excel's ROUND function. The following formula, for example, returns TRUE because the comparison is made using the value in A1 rounded to one decimal place:

```
=ROUND(A1,1)=0.9
```

Here's another example of a "precision" problem. Try entering the following formula:

```
=1.333+1.225-1.333-1.225
```

If you use Excel 97 or later, the formula returns 0. Previous versions return 2.22044604925031E-16 (a number very close to zero).

 Beginning with Excel 97, if an addition or subtraction operation results in a value at or very close to zero, the calculation engine compensates for any error introduced as a result of converting an operand to and from binary. When you perform the previous example in Excel 97 and later, it correctly displays 0.

"Phantom link" errors

You may open a workbook and see a message such as the one shown in Figure 19-4. This message sometimes appears even when a workbook contains no linked formulas.

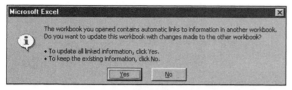

Figure 19-4: Excel's way of asking you if you want to update links in a workbook

In the vast majority of cases, this phantom link problem occurs because of an erroneous name. Select Insert → Name → Define and scroll through the list of names. If you see a name that refers to #REF!, delete the name.

 These phantom links may be created when you copy a worksheet that contains names. See Chapter 3 for more information about names.

Circular reference errors

A circular reference is a formula that contains a reference to the cell that contains the formula. The reference may be direct or indirect. For help tracking down a circular reference, see "Excel Auditing Tools," later in this chapter.

 As described in Chapter 14, there are some situations in which you create an intentional circular reference.

Excel's Auditing Tools

Excel includes a number of tools that can help you track down formula errors. This section describes the auditing tools built into Excel.

Identifying cells of a particular type

The Go To Special dialog box enables you to specify the type of cells that you want Excel to select. To display this dialog box, choose Edit→Go To (or press F5 or Ctrl+G). The Go To dialog box appears. Click the Special button, which displays the Go To Special dialog box, as shown in Figure 19-5.

Figure 19-5: The Go To Special dialog box

 If you select a multicell range before choosing Edit→Go To, the command operates only within the selected cells. If a single cell is selected, the command operates on the entire worksheet.

You can use the Go To Special dialog box to select cells of a certain type, which often can help in identifying errors. For example, if you choose the Formulas option, Excel selects all the cells that contain a formula. If you zoom the worksheet out to a small size, you can get a good idea of the worksheet's organization (see Figure 19-6). It also may help you spot a common error: a formula that has been replaced accidentally with a value. If you find a cell that's not selected amid a group of selected formula cells, chances are good that the cell formerly contained a formula that has been replaced by a value.

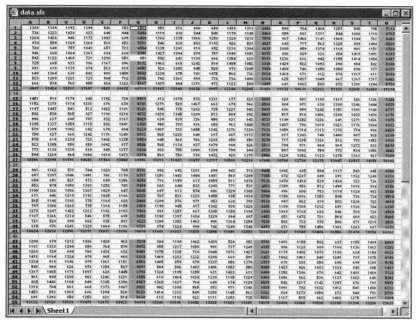

Figure 19-6: Zooming out and selecting all formula cells can give you a good overview of how the worksheet is designed.

Viewing formulas

You can become familiar with an unfamiliar workbook by displaying the formulas rather than the results of the formulas. Select Tools → Options, and check the checkbox labeled Formulas on the View tab. You may want to create a new window for the workbook before issuing this command. That way, you can see the formulas in one window and the results in the other. Use the Window → New Window command to open a new window.

You can use Ctrl+' to toggle between formula view and normal view.

Figure 19-7 shows an example of a worksheet displayed in two windows. The window on the top shows the normal view (formula results), and the window on the bottom displays the formulas.

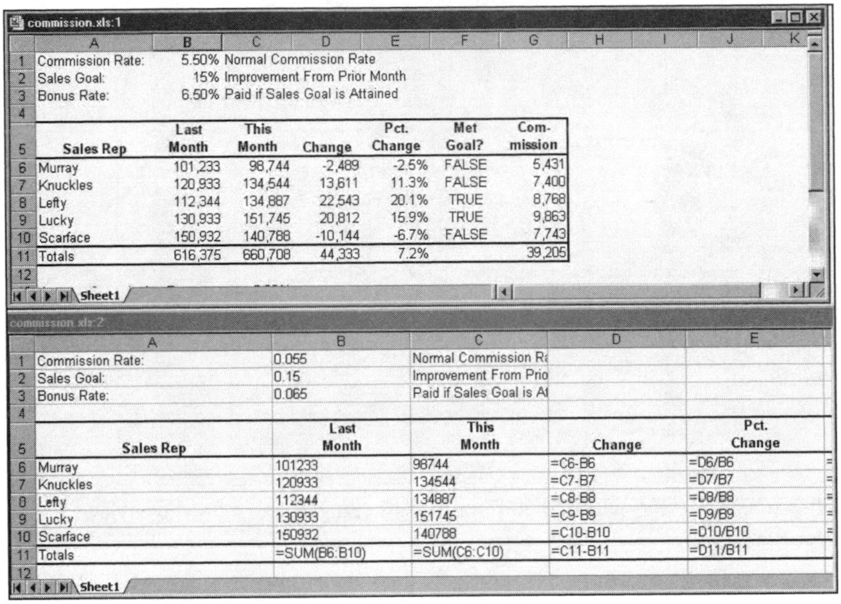

Figure 19-7: Displaying formulas (bottom window) and their results (top window)

Tracing cell relationships

To understand how to trace cell relationships, you need to familiarize yourself with the following two concepts:

♦ Cell precedents: Applicable only to cells that contain a formula, a formula cell's precedents are all the cells that contribute to the formula's result. A *direct precedent* is a cell that you use directly in the formula. An *indirect precedent* is a cell that isn't used directly in the formula but is used by a cell to which you refer in the formula.

♦ Cell dependents: These are formula cells that depend on a particular cell. A cell's dependents consist of all formula cells that use the cell. Again, the formula cell can be a direct dependent or an indirect dependent.

Often, identifying cell precedents for a formula cell sheds light on why the formula isn't working correctly. Conversely, knowing which formula cells depend on a particular cell is helpful. For example, if you're about to delete a formula, you may want to check whether it has any dependents.

IDENTIFYING PRECEDENTS

You can identify cells used by a formula in the active cell in a number of ways:

◆ Press F2. Cells used directly by the formula are outlined in color; the color corresponds to the cell reference in the formula. This technique is limited to identifying cells on the same sheet as the formula.

◆ Select Edit → Go To (or press F5) to display the Go To dialog box. Then click the Special button to display the Go To Special dialog box. Select the Precedents option, and then select either Direct only (for direct precedents only) or All levels (for direct and indirect precedents). Click OK, and Excel highlights the precedent cells for the formula. This technique is limited to identifying cells on the same sheet as the formula.

◆ Press Ctrl+[to select all direct precedent cells on the active sheet.

◆ Press Ctrl+Shift+[to select all precedent cells (direct and indirect) on the active sheet.

◆ Display the Auditing toolbar (select Tools → Auditing → Show Auditing Toolbar). Click the Trace Precedents button to draw arrows to indicate a cell's precedents. Click this button multiple times to see additional levels of precedents. Figure 19-8 shows a worksheet with precedent arrows drawn to indicate the precedents for the formula in cell C13.

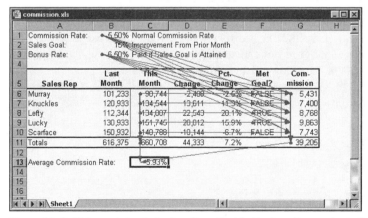

Figure 19-8: This worksheet displays lines that indicate cell precedents for the formula in cell C13.

IDENTIFYING DEPENDENTS

You can identify formula cells that use a particular cell in a number of ways.

- Select Edit → Go To (or press F5) to display the Go To dialog box. Then click the Special button to display the Go To Special dialog box. Select the Dependents option, and then select either Direct only (for direct dependents only) or All levels (for direct and indirect dependents). Click OK; Excel highlights the cells that depend on the active cell. This technique is limited to identifying cells on the active sheet only.

- Press Ctrl+] to select all direct dependent cells on the active sheet.

- Press Ctrl+Shift+] to select all dependent cells (direct and indirect) on the active sheet.

- Display the Auditing toolbar (select Tools → Auditing → Show Auditing Toolbar). Click the Trace Dependents button to draw arrows to indicate a cell's dependents. Click this button multiple times to see additional levels of dependents.

Tracing error values

The Trace Error button on the Auditing toolbar helps you to identify the cell that is causing an error value to appear. Often, an error in one cell is the result of an error in a precedent cell. Activate a cell that contains an error, and click the Trace Error button. Excel draws arrows to indicate the error source.

Fixing circular reference errors

If you accidentally create a circular reference formula, Excel displays a warning message. If you click OK, Excel displays the Circular Reference toolbar (see Figure 19-9). If you can't figure out the source of the problem, use the Navigate Circular Reference tools (a drop-down list control) on the toolbar to select a cell involved in the circular reference. Start by selecting the first cell listed. Then, work your way down the list until you figure out the problem.

Figure 19-9: The Circular Reference toolbar

Third-Party Auditing Tools

A few third-party auditing tools for Excel are available — namely the Power Utility Pak, the Spreadsheet Detective, and the Excel Auditor. I describe them in the following subsections.

Power Utility Pak

My Power Utility Pak includes a number of useful utilities relevant to auditing a worksheet. These utilities are:

♦ Workbook Summary Report: Produces a handy summary report of the entire workbook

♦ Workbook Link Report: Produces a report that describes all links in the workbook

♦ Worksheet Map: Creates a handy *map* that makes it easy to identify cells of various types (see Figure 19-10)

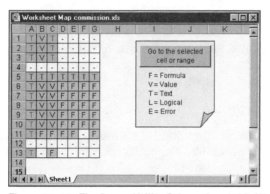

Figure 19-10: The Power Utility Pak produced this Worksheet Map.

♦ Compare Sheets or Ranges: Performs a cell-by-cell comparison of two worksheets or ranges.

♦ Date Report: Creates a useful report that may help you identify potential year-2000 problems.

♦ Name Lister: Lists all names in a workbook. Unlike Excel's Define Name dialog box, this utility also lists hidden names.

♦ Formula Report: Generates a useful listing of all formulas in a worksheet (see Figure 19-11). This is much more useful than Excel's formula view.

♦ VBA Project Summary Report: Generates a report that describes the VBA procedures contained in a workbook.

ON THE CD   A trial version of Power Utility Pak is available on the companion CD-ROM. You can use the coupon in the back of the book to order a copy at a significant discount.

Formula Report for commission.xls

Workbook: C:\Excel Files\commission.xls
Worksheet name: Sheet1
Number of formulas: 21
Report generated: 9/15/99 8:53:46 AM

Address	Row	Col	Display	No. Format	Formula	RC Formula	Precedents	Direct Precedents
D6	6	4	-2,489	#,##0	=C6-B6	=RC[-1]-RC[-2]	2	2
E6	6	5	-2.5%	0.0%	=D6/B6	=RC[-1]/RC[-3]	3	2
D7	7	4	13,611	#,##0	=C7-B7	=RC[-1]-RC[-2]	2	2
E7	7	5	11.3%	0.0%	=D7/B7	=RC[-1]/RC[-3]	3	2
D8	8	4	22,543	#,##0	=C8-B8	=RC[-1]-RC[-2]	2	2
E8	8	5	20.1%	0.0%	=D8/B8	=RC[-1]/RC[-3]	3	2
D9	9	4	20,812	#,##0	=C9-B9	=RC[-1]-RC[-2]	2	2
E9	9	5	15.9%	0.0%	=D9/B9	=RC[-1]/RC[-3]	3	2
D10	10	4	-10,144	#,##0	=C10-B10	=RC[-1]-RC[-2]	2	2
E10	10	5	-6.7%	0.0%	=D10/B10	=RC[-1]/RC[-3]	3	2
B11	11	2	616,375	#,##0	=SUM(B6:B10)	=SUM(R[-5]C:R[-1]C)	5	5
C11	11	3	660,708	#,##0	=SUM(C6:C10)	=SUM(R[-5]C:R[-1]C)	5	5
D11	11	4	44,333	#,##0	=C11-B11	=RC[-1]-RC[-2]	12	2
E11	11	5	7.2%	0.0%	=D11/B11	=RC[-1]/RC[-3]	13	2
G6	6	7	5,431	#,##0	=IF(F6,C6*$B$3,C6*$B$1)	=IF(RC[-1],RC[-4]*R3C2,RC[-4]*R1C2)	7	4
G7	7	7	7,400	#,##0	=IF(F7,C7*$B$3,C7*$B$1)	=IF(RC[-1],RC[-4]*R3C2,RC[-4]*R1C2)	7	4
G8	8	7	8,768	#,##0	=IF(F8,C8*$B$3,C8*$B$1)	=IF(RC[-1],RC[-4]*R3C2,RC[-4]*R1C2)	7	4
G9	9	7	9,863	#,##0	=IF(F9,C9*$B$3,C9*$B$1)	=IF(RC[-1],RC[-4]*R3C2,RC[-4]*R1C2)	7	4
G10	10	7	7,743	#,##0	=IF(F10,C10*$B$3,C10*$B$1)	=IF(RC[-1],RC[-4]*R3C2,RC[-4]*R1C2)	7	4
G11	11	7	39,205	#,##0	=SUM(G6:G10)	=SUM(R[-5]C:R[-1]C)	32	5
C13	13	3	5.93%	0.00%	=G11/C11	=R[-2]C[4]/R[-2]C	34	2

Sheet1

Figure 19-11: The Power Utility Pak can generate a useful report that lists all formulas in a worksheet.

Spreadsheet Detective

The Spreadsheet Detective, available from Southern Cross Software, is a comprehensive auditing tool for Excel workbooks. For complete information (including a free evaluation version), visit the URL listed here:

```
http://www.uq.net.au/detective/home.html
```

Excel Auditor

The Excel Auditor is available from Byg Software, based in the U.K. This product includes many tools to help you identify and correct spreadsheet errors. For complete information, visit the URL listed here:

```
http://www.bygsoftware.com
```

Summary

This chapter discussed the types of formula errors you are likely to encounter. I described how to identify such errors and some general guidelines on correcting them. I also described the auditing tools built into Excel plus three third-party auditing tools that you may find helpful.

The next chapter is the first of four chapters to provide information about creating custom worksheet functions using VBA.

Part V

Developing Custom Worksheet Functions

Chapter 20

Introducing VBA

IN THIS CHAPTER

◆ An introduction to VBA, the programming language built into Excel

◆ How to use the Visual Basic Editor

◆ How to work in the code windows of the VB Editor

THIS CHAPTER INTRODUCES YOU to Visual Basic for Applications (VBA). VBA is Excel's programming language – the language used to create custom worksheet functions. Before you can create custom functions using VBA, you need to have some basic background knowledge of VBA as well as some familiarity with the Visual Basic Editor.

About VBA

Excel 5 was the first application on the market to feature Visual Basic for Applications. VBA is best thought of as Microsoft's common application scripting language. It's included now with all Office 2000 applications, and it's also available in applications from other vendors. In Excel, VBA has two primary uses:

◆ It enables you to automate spreadsheet tasks

◆ It enables you to create custom functions that you can use in your worksheet formulas

 Excel also includes another way of creating custom functions using the XLM macro language. XLM is pretty much obsolete, but it is still supported for compatibility purposes. This book completely ignores the XLM language and focuses on VBA.

VBA is a complex topic – far too complex to be covered completely in this book. Since this book deals with formulas, I hone in on one aspect of VBA: creating

custom worksheet functions. You can use a custom worksheet function (sometimes known as a user-defined function) in formulas.

If your goal is to become a VBA expert, this book nudges you in that direction, but it doesn't get you to your final destination. Rather, you might want to check out one of my other books: *Excel 2000 Programming For Dummies*, or *Microsoft Excel 2000 Power Programming with VBA*. Both books cover all aspects of VBA programming for Excel.

Introducing the Visual Basic Editor

Before you can begin creating custom functions, you need to become familiar with the Visual Basic Editor, or VB Editor, for short. The VB Editor enables you to work with VBA modules, which are containers for your VBA code.

In Excel 5 and Excel 95, a VBA module appeared as a separate sheet in a workbook. Beginning with Excel 97, VBA modules no longer show up as sheets in a workbook. Rather, you use the VB Editor to view and work with VBA modules. In Excel 97 and later, VBA modules are still stored with workbook files; they just aren't visible unless you activate the VB Editor.

This chapter assumes that you use Excel 97 or later. Previous versions do not have a separate VB Editor.

Activating the VB Editor

When you work in Excel, you can switch to the VB Editor using any of the following techniques:

- ◆ Press Alt+F11.
- ◆ Select Tools → Macro → Visual Basic Editor.
- ◆ Click the Visual Basic Editor button, located on the Visual Basic toolbar (not visible, by default).

Figure 20-1 shows the VB Editor. Chances are that your VB Editor window won't look exactly like the window shown in the figure. This window is highly customizable. You can hide windows, change their sizes, "dock" them, rearrange them, and so on.

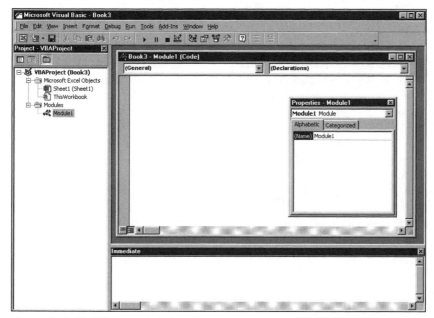

Figure 20-1: The Visual Basic Editor window

The VB Editor components

The VB Editor consists of a number of components. I briefly describe some of the key components in the sections that follow.

MENU BAR

The VB Editor menu bar, of course, works like every other menu bar you've encountered. It contains commands that you use to work with the various components in the VB Editor. The VB Editor also features shortcut menus. Right-click virtually anything in a VB Editor window, and you get a shortcut menu of common commands.

TOOLBARS

The standard toolbar, directly under the menu bar by default, is one of six VB Editor toolbars available. VB Editor toolbars work just like those in Excel: You can customize toolbars, move them around, display other toolbars, and so forth.

PROJECT WINDOW

The Project window displays a tree diagram that consists of every workbook currently open in Excel (including add-ins and hidden workbooks). In the VB Editor, each workbook is known as a *project*. I discuss the Project window in more detail in the next section ("Using the Project Window"). If the Project window is not visible, press Ctrl+R.

CODE WINDOW

A code window contains VBA code. Every item in a project has an associated code window. To view a code window for an object, double-click the object in the Project window. For example, to view the code window for the Sheet1 object for a particular workbook, double-click Sheet1 in the Project window. Unless you've added some VBA code, the code window will be empty. I discuss code windows later on in this chapter (see "Working with Code Windows").

PROPERTIES WINDOW

The Properties window contains a list of all properties for the selected object. Use this window to examine and change properties. You can use the F4 shortcut key to display the Properties window.

IMMEDIATE WINDOW

The Immediate window is most useful for executing VBA statements directly, testing statements, and debugging your code. This window may or may not be visible. If the Immediate window isn't visible, press Ctrl+G. To close the Immediate window, click the Close button on its title bar.

Using the project window

When you work in the VB Editor, each Excel workbook and add-in that's currently open is considered a project. You can think of a project as a collection of objects arranged as an outline. You can expand a project by clicking the plus sign (+) at the left of the project's name in the Project window. You contract a project by clicking the minus sign (-) to the left of a project's name. Figure 20-2 shows the Project window with three projects listed (one add-in and two workbooks).

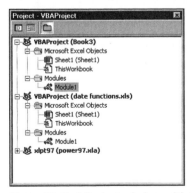

Figure 20-2: A Project window with three projects listed

If you try to expand a project protected with a password, you'll be prompted to enter the password.

Every project expands to show at least one "node" called Microsoft Excel Objects. This node expands to show an item for each worksheet and chart sheet in the workbook (each sheet is considered an object), and another object called ThisWorkbook (which represents the Workbook object). If the project has any VBA modules, the project listing also shows a Modules node with the modules listed there. A project also may contain a node called Forms that contains UserForm objects (also known as custom dialog boxes).

ADDING A NEW VBA MODULE

A new Excel workbook does not have any VBA modules. To add a VBA module to a project, select the project's name in the Project window and choose Insert → Module.

When you create custom functions, they *must* reside in a standard VBA module, not in a code window for a Sheet object or the ThisWorkbook object. If the code for your custom function does not reside in a VBA module, it will not work!

RENAMING A MODULE

VBA modules have names such as Module1, Module2, and so on. To rename a VBA module, select it in the Project window and then change the Name property using the Properties window. (A VBA module has only one property – Name.) If the Properties window is not visible, press F4 to display it. Figure 20-3 shows a VBA module that has had its name changed to MyModule.

REMOVING A VBA MODULE

If you would like to remove a VBA module from a project, select the module's name in the Project window and choose File → Remove *xxx* (where *xxx* is the name of the module). You'll be asked if you want to export the module before removing it. Exporting a module makes a backup of the module's contents. You can import an exported module into any other project.

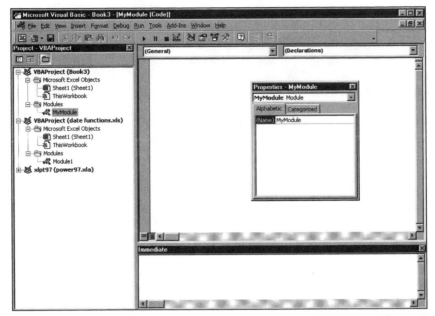

Figure 20-3: Use the Properties window to change the name of a VBA module.

Using code windows

Each object in a project has an associated code window. To summarize, these objects can be:

◆ The workbook itself (the item named ThisWorkbook in the Project window)

◆ A worksheet or chart sheet in a workbook (for example, Sheet1 or Chart1 in the Project window)

◆ A VBA module

◆ A class module (a special type of module that enables you to create new object classes)

◆ A UserForm

This book focuses exclusively on VBA modules, the location where custom worksheet functions are stored.

MINIMIZING AND MAXIMIZING WINDOWS

At any given time, the VB Editor may have lots of code windows. Figure 20-4 shows an example.

Figure 20-4: Code window overload

Code windows are much like worksheet windows in Excel. You can minimize them, maximize them, hide them, rearrange them, and so on. Most people find it much easier to maximize the code window on which they're working. Sometimes, however, you may want to have two or more code windows visible. For example, you might want to compare the code in two modules, or copy code from one module to another.

Minimizing a code window gets it out of the way. You also can click the Close button in a code window's title bar to close the window completely. To open it again, just double-click the appropriate object in the Project window.

You can't close a workbook from the VB Editor. You must reactivate Excel and close it from there.

STORING VBA CODE

In general, a code window can hold three types of code:

♦ *Sub procedures.* A *procedure* is a set of instructions that performs some action. For example, you might have a Sub procedure that combines various parts of a workbook into a concise report.

◆ *Function procedures.* A *function* is a set of instructions that returns a single value or an array (similar in concept to a worksheet function such as SUM). You can use Function procedures in worksheet formulas.

◆ *Declarations.* A *declaration* is information about a variable that you provide to VBA. For example, you can declare the data type for variables you plan to use.

A single VBA module can store any number of procedures and declarations.

This book focuses exclusively on Function procedures. A Function procedure is the only type of procedure that you can use in worksheet formulas.

Entering VBA code

Before you can do anything meaningful, you must have some VBA code in a code window. For Function procedures, the code window will always be a VBA module. You can add code to a VBA module in three ways:

◆ Use your keyboard to type it

◆ Use Excel's macro-recorder feature to record your actions and convert them into VBA code

◆ Copy the code from another module and paste it into the module in which you are working

ENTERING CODE MANUALLY

Sometimes, the most direct route is the best one. Type the code using your keyboard. Entering and editing text in a VBA module works just as you expect. You can select text and copy it, or cut and paste it to another location.

Use the Tab key to indent the lines that logically belong together (e.g., the conditional statements between an If and an End If statement). Indentation isn't necessary, but it makes the code easier to read.

A single instruction in VBA can be as long as you like. For readability sake, however, you might want to break a lengthy instruction into two or more lines. To do so, end the line with a space followed by an underscore character, and then press Enter and continue the instruction on the following line. The following code, for example, is a single statement split over three lines.

```
If IsNumeric(MyCell) Then _
    Result = "Number" Else _
    Result = "Non-Number"
```

Notice that I indented the last two lines of this statement. Doing so is optional, but it helps clarify the fact that these four lines comprise a single statement.

After you enter an instruction, the VB Editor performs the following actions to improve readability:

◆ It inserts spaces between operators. If you enter Ans=1+2 (without any spaces), for example, VBA converts it to

```
Ans = 1 + 2
```

◆ The VB Editor adjusts the case of the letters for keywords, properties, and methods. If you enter the following text:

```
user=application.username
```

VBA converts it to

```
user = Application.UserName
```

◆ Because variable names are not case sensitive, the VB Editor adjusts the names of all variables with the same letters so that their case matches the case of letters that you most recently typed. For example, if you first specify a variable as myvalue (all lowercase) and then enter the variable as MyValue (mixed case), VBA changes all other occurrences of the variable to MyValue. An exception occurs if you declare the variable with Dim or a similar statement; in this case, the variable name always appears as it was declared.

◆ The VB Editor scans the instruction for syntax errors. If it finds an error, it changes the color of the line and may display a message describing the problem. Use the VB Editor's Tools → Options command to display the Options dialog box, where you control the error color (with the Editor Format tab) and whether the error message is displayed (with the Auto Syntax Check option on the Editor tab).

Like Excel, the VB Editor has multiple levels of Undo and Redo. Therefore, if you find that you mistakenly deleted an instruction, you can click the Undo button (or press Ctrl+Z) repeatedly until the instruction returns. After undoing the action, you can press F4 to redo previously undone changes.

USING THE MACRO RECORDER

Another way to get code into a VBA module is to record your actions using Excel's macro recorder. No matter how hard you try, there is absolutely no way to record a Function procedure (the type of procedure that it used for a custom worksheet function). All recorded macros are Sub procedures. But using the macro recorder *can* help you identify various properties that you can use in your custom functions. For example, turn on the macro recorder to record your actions while you change the user name. Follow these steps in Excel:

1. Select Tools → Macro → Record New Macro.

2. In the Record Macro dialog box, accept the default settings and click OK to begin recording. Excel displays a small toolbar named Stop Recording.

3. Select Tools → Options.

4. In the Options dialog box, click the General tab.

5. Make a change (any change) to the User Name box.

6. Click OK to close the Options dialog box.

7. Click the Stop Recording button on the Stop Recording toolbar.

8. Press Alt+F11 to activate the VB Editor.

9. In the Project window, select the project that corresponds to your workbook. You'll find a VBA procedure that looks something like this:

```
Sub Macro1()
'
' Macro1 Macro
' Macro recorded 12/1/99 by Bob Smith
'
    With Application
        .UserName = "Robert Smith"
        .StandardFont = "Arial"
        .StandardFontSize = "10"
        .DefaultFilePath = "d:\xlfiles"
        .EnableSound = False
        .RollZoom = False
    End With
End Sub
```

Note that this is a Sub procedure, not a Function procedure. In other words, you can't use this procedure in a worksheet formula. If you examine the code, however, you'll see a reference to the UserName property. You can use this information when creating a Function procedure. For example, the following Function procedure uses the UserName property. This function, when used in a worksheet formula, returns the name of the user.

```
Function USER()
    USER = Application.UserName
End Function
```

You can consult the online help system to identify various properties, but using the macro recorder is often more efficient if you don't know exactly what you're looking for. Once you identify what you need, you can check the online help for details.

COPYING VBA CODE

So far, this section has covered entering code directly and recording your actions to generate VBA code. The final method of getting code into a VBA module is to copy it from another module. For example, you may have written a custom function for one project that also would be useful in your current project. Rather than reenter the code, you can open the workbook, activate the module, and use the normal Clipboard copy-and-paste procedures to copy it into your current VBA module.

You also can copy VBA code from other sources. For example, you might find a listing on a Web page or in a newsgroup. In such a case, you can select the text in your browser (or newsreader), copy it to the Clipboard, and then paste it into a module.

Saving your project

As when working with any application, you should save your work frequently while working in the VB Editor. To do so, use the File → Save command, press Ctrl+S, or click the Save button on the standard toolbar.

 When you save your project, you actually save your Excel workbook. By the same token, if you save your workbook in Excel, you also save the changes made in the workbook's VB project.

The VB Editor does not have a File → Save As command. To save your project with a different name, activate Excel and use Excel's File → Save As command.

Summary

This chapter provided an introduction to VBA, the language used to create custom worksheet functions. I introduced the various components of the VB Editor and described several ways to enter code into a VBA module.

The next chapter covers the basics of VBA Function procedures.

Chapter 21

Function Procedure Basics

IN THIS CHAPTER

- ◆ Why you might want to create custom functions

- ◆ An introductory VBA Function example

- ◆ About VBA Function procedures

- ◆ How to use the Paste Function dialog box to add a function description and assign a function category

- ◆ Tips for testing and debugging functions

- ◆ How to create an add-in to hold your custom functions

PREVIOUS CHAPTERS DISCUSSED Excel's common worksheet functions and how you can use them to build more complex formulas. These functions, as well as those available in the Analysis ToolPak add-in, provide a great deal of flexibility when creating formulas. However, situations that call for custom functions can arise. This chapter discusses the reasons you might want to use custom functions, how you create a VBA Function procedure, and methods for testing and debugging them.

Why Create Custom Functions?

You are, of course, familiar with Excel's worksheet functions—even novices know how to use the most common worksheet functions, such as SUM, AVERAGE, and IF. Excel includes more than 300 predefined worksheet functions, plus additional functions available through the Analysis ToolPak add-in.

As you know, you can use Visual Basic for Applications (VBA) to create additional worksheet functions—sometimes referred to as custom functions or *user-defined functions* (UDFs). With all the functions available in Excel and VBA, you may wonder why you would ever need to create new functions. The answer: to simplify your work and give your formulas more power.

Often, for example, you can create a custom function that can significantly shorten your formulas. Shorter formulas are more readable and easier to work with. However, it's important to understand that custom functions in your formulas are usually much slower than built-in functions. But on a fast system, the speed difference often goes unnoticed.

The process of creating a custom function is not difficult. In fact, many people (authors included) *enjoy* creating custom functions. This book provides you with the information you need to create your own functions. In this and subsequent chapters, you'll find many custom function examples that you can adapt for your own use.

An Introductory VBA Function Example

Without further ado, let's take a look at a simple VBA Function procedure. This function, named USER, doesn't accept any arguments. When used in a worksheet formula, this function simply displays the user's name, in uppercase characters. To create this function:

1. Start with a new workbook (not necessary, but let's keep it simple for starters).

2. Press Alt+F11 to activate the VB Editor.

3. Click your workbook's name in the Project window.

4. Choose Insert → Module to add a VBA module.

5. Type the following code in the code window.

```
Function USER()
'    Returns the user's name
     USER = Application.UserName
     USER = UCase(USER)
End Function
```

 I gave this warning in the previous chapter, but it's worth repeating: When you create a custom function, make sure it resides in a normal VBA module — not in a code module for a Sheet or ThisWorkbook.

To try out the User function, activate Excel (press Alt+F11) and enter the following formula into any cell in the workbook.

```
=USER()
```

If you entered the VBA code correctly, the Function procedure executes and your name displays (in uppercase characters) in the cell.

 If your formula returns an error, make sure that the VBA code for the USER function is in a VBA module (not a module for a Sheet or ThisWorkbook object). Also, make sure that the module is in the project associated with the workbook into which you enter the formula.

When Excel calculates your worksheet, it encounters the custom function named USER. Each instruction in the function is evaluated, and the result is returned to your worksheet. You can use this function any number of times in any number of cells.

You'll find that this custom function works just like any other worksheet function. You can insert it in a formula by using the Insert → Function command or the Paste Function button on the Standard toolbar (in the Paste Function dialog box, custom functions appear in the User Defined category). As with any other function, you can use it in a more complex formula. For example, try this:

```
="Hello "&USER()
```

Or, use this formula to display the number of characters in your name:

```
=LEN(USER())
```

If you don't like the fact that your name is in uppercase, edit the procedure as follows:

```
Function USER()
'   Returns the user's name
    USER = Application.UserName
End Function
```

After editing the function, reactivate Excel and press F9 to recalculate. Any cell that uses the USER function displays a different result.

What Custom Worksheet Functions Can't Do

As you develop custom worksheet functions, you should understand a key point. A function procedure used in a worksheet formula must be "passive." In other words, it cannot change things in the worksheet.

You may be tempted to try to write a custom worksheet function that changes the formatting of a cell. For example, it might be useful to have a function that changes the color of text in a cell based on the cell's value. Try as you might, such a function is impossible to write — everybody tries this, and no one succeeds. No matter what you do, the function always returns an error because the code attempts to change something on the worksheet. Remember that a function can return only a value. It cannot perform actions with objects.

About Function Procedures

Function procedures have a structure. Here, we'll look at some of the technical details that apply to Function procedures. These are general guidelines for declaring functions, naming functions, using custom functions in formulas, and using arguments in custom functions.

Declaring a function

The official syntax for declaring a function is as follows:

```
[Public | Private][Static] Function name [(arglist)][As type]
    [statements]
    [name = expression]
    [Exit Function]
    [statements]
    [name = expression]
End Function
```

- ◆ *Public* indicates that the function is accessible to all other procedures in all other modules in the workbook (optional).

- ◆ *Private* indicates that the function is accessible only to other procedures in the same module (optional). If you use the Private keyword, your functions will not appear in the Insert Function dialog box.

◆ *Static* indicates that the values of variables declared in the function are preserved between calls (optional).

◆ *Function* is a keyword that indicates the beginning of a Function procedure (required).

◆ *Name* can be any valid variable name. When the function finishes, the single-value result is assigned to the function's name (required).

◆ *Arglist* is a list (one or more) of variables that represent arguments passed to the function. The arguments are enclosed in parentheses. Use a comma to separate arguments (arguments are optional).

◆ *Type* is the data type returned by the function (optional).

◆ *Statements* are valid VBA statements (optional).

◆ *Exit Function* is a statement that causes an immediate exit from the function (optional).

◆ *End Function* is a keyword that indicates the end of the function (required).

Choosing a name for your function

Each function must have a unique name, and function names must adhere to a few rules:

◆ You can use alphabetic characters, numbers, and some punctuation characters, but the first character must be alphabetic.

◆ You can use any combination of upper- and lowercase.

◆ You can't use a name that looks like a worksheet cell's address (such as J21). Actually, you *can* use such a name for a function, but Excel won't interpret it as a function.

◆ VBA does not distinguish between case. To make a function name more readable, you can use mixed case (InterestRate rather than interestrate).

◆ You can't use spaces or periods. To make function names more readable, you can use the underscore character (Interest_Rate).

◆ The following characters cannot be embedded in a function's name: #, $, %, &, or !. These are type declaration characters that have a special meaning in VBA.

◆ A function name can consist of as many as 255 characters — but no one creates function names that long!

Using functions in formulas

Using a custom VBA function in a worksheet formula is like using a built-in work-sheet function, except that you must ensure that Excel can locate the Function procedure. If the Function procedure is in the same workbook as the formula, you don't have to do anything special. If it's in a different workbook, you may have to tell Excel where to find it.

You can do so in three ways:

◆ *Precede the function's name with a file reference.* For example, if you want to use a function called CountNames that's defined in a workbook named Myfuncs.xls, you can use a formula such as the following:

```
=Myfuncs.xls!CountNames(A1:A1000)
```

If you insert the function with the Paste Function dialog box, the workbook reference is inserted automatically.

◆ *Set up a reference to the workbook.* You do so with the VB Editor's Tools → References command (see Figure 21-1). If the function is defined in a referenced workbook, you don't need to use the worksheet name. Even when the dependent workbook is assigned as a reference, the Paste Function dialog box continues to insert the workbook reference (even though it's not necessary).

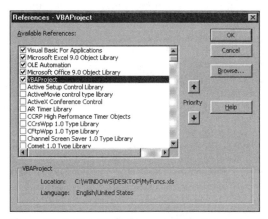

Figure 21-1: Use the References dialog box to create a reference to a project that contains a custom VBA function.

By default, all projects are named VBAProject — and that's the name that appears in the Available References list in the References dialog box. To make sure you select the correct project in the References dialog box, keep your eye on the bottom of the dialog box, which shows the workbook name for the selected item.

♦ *Create an add-in.* When you create an add-in from a workbook that has Function procedures, you don't need to use the file reference when you use one of the functions in a formula; the add-in must be installed, however. I discuss add-ins later in this chapter (see "Creating Add-Ins").

Using function arguments

Custom functions, like Excel's built-in functions, vary in their use of arguments. Keep the following points in mind regarding VBA Function procedure arguments.

♦ Arguments can be variables (including arrays), constants, literals, or expressions.

♦ A function can have no argument.

♦ A function can have a fixed number of required arguments (from 1 to 60).

♦ A function can have a combination of required and optional arguments.

See Chapter 23 for examples of functions that use various types of arguments.

Using the Paste Function Dialog Box

Excel's Paste Function dialog box is a handy tool that enables you to choose a particular worksheet function from a list of available functions. The Paste Function dialog box also displays a list of your custom worksheet functions and prompts you for the function's arguments.

Custom Function procedures defined with the Private keyword do not appear in the Paste Function dialog box.

By default, custom functions are listed under the User Defined category, but you can have them appear under a different category. You also can add some text that describes the function.

Adding a function description

When you select a function in the Paste Function dialog box, a brief description of the function appears (see Figure 21-2).

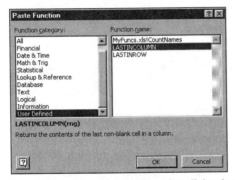

Figure 21-2: Excel's Paste Function dialog box displays a brief description of the selected function.

If you don't provide a description for your custom function, the Paste Function dialog box displays the following text: *Choose the help button for help on this function and its arguments.* In most cases, of course, that description is not accurate.

The following steps describe how to provide a description for a custom function.

1. Create your function in the VB Editor.

2. Activate Excel, and select Tools → Macro → Macros (or press Alt+F8).

   The Macro dialog box lists available Sub procedures, but not functions.

3. Type the name of your function in the Macro Name box.

4. Click the Options button to display the Macro Options dialog box. If the Options button is not disabled, you probably spelled the function's name incorrectly.

5. Enter the function description in the Description box (see Figure 21-3). The Shortcut key field is irrelevant for functions.

6. Click OK, and then Cancel.

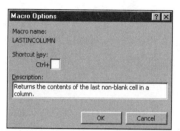

Figure 21–3: Providing a function description in the Macro Options dialog box

When you use the Paste Function dialog box to enter a function, the formula palette kicks in after you click OK. For built-in functions, the formula palette displays a description for each of the function's arguments. Unfortunately, it is not possible to provide such descriptions for your custom function arguments.

Specifying a function category

Oddly, Excel does not provide a direct way to assign a custom function to a particular function category. If you would like your custom function to appear in a function category other than User Defined, you need to execute some VBA code when you open the workbook (or add-in) that contains the function definition.

The following Sub procedure, which must be placed in the code module for the ThisWorkbook object, executes whenever you open the workbook. This procedure assigns the function named COMMISSION to the Financial category (category number 1).

```
Private Sub Workbook_Open()
    Application.MacroOptions Macro:="COMMISSION", Category:=1
End Sub
```

You will, of course, substitute the actual name of your function and you can specify a different function category. The Workbook_Open procedure can contain any number of statements — one for each of your functions.

Table 21-1 lists the function category numbers that you can use. Notice that a few of these categories (10–13) normally do not display in the Paste Function dialog box. If you assign your function to one of these categories, the category then appears.

TABLE **21-1** FUNCTION CATEGORIES

Category Number	Category Name
0	All (no specific category)
1	Financial
2	Date & Time
3	Math & Trig
4	Statistical
5	Lookup & Reference
6	Database
7	Text
8	Logical
9	Information
10	Commands
11	Customizing
12	Macro Control
13	DDE/External
14	User Defined
15	Engineering

Testing and Debugging Functions

Naturally, testing and debugging your custom function are the next important steps you must take to ensure that it carries out the calculation you intend. VBA code that you write can contain three general types of errors:

- Syntax errors: An error in writing the statement — for example, a misspelled keyword, a missing operator, or mismatched parentheses. The VB Editor lets you know about syntax errors by displaying a pop-up error box. You can't use the function until you correct all syntax errors.

- Run-time errors: Errors that occur as the function executes. For example, attempting to perform a mathematical operation on a string variable generates a run-time error. Unless you spot it beforehand, you won't be aware of a run-time error until it occurs.

- Logical errors: Code that runs, but simply returns the wrong result

To force the code in a VBA module to be checked for syntax errors, select Debug → Compile. This highlights the first syntax error, if any. Correct the error and issue the command again until you find all of the errors.

An error in code is sometimes called a bug. The process of locating and correcting such an error is known as debugging.

When you test a Function procedure by using a formula in a worksheet, run-time errors can be difficult to locate because (unlike syntax errors) they do not appear in a pop-up error box. If a run-time error occurs, the formula that uses the function simply returns an error value (#VALUE!). This section describes several approaches to debugging custom functions.

When you test a custom function, it's a good idea to use the function in only one formula in the worksheet.

Using VBA's MsgBox statement

The MsgBox statement, when used in your VBA code, displays a pop-up box. You can use MsgBox statements at strategic locations within your code to monitor the value of specific variables. The example that follows is a Function procedure that should reverse a text string passed as its argument. For example, passing *Hello* as the argument should return *olleH*. If you try to use this function in a formula, however, you see that it doesn't work — it contains a logical error.

```
Function REVERSETEXT(text) As String
'   Returns its argument, reversed
    TextLen = Len(text)
    For i = TextLen To 1 Step -1
        REVERSETEXT = Mid(text, i, 1) & REVERSETEXT
    Next i
End Function
```

You can insert a temporary MsgBox statement to help you figure out the source of the problem. Here's the function again, with the MsgBox statement inserted within the loop:

```
Function REVERSETEXT(text) As String
'   Returns its argument, reversed
    TextLen = Len(text)
    For i = TextLen To 1 Step -1
        REVERSETEXT = Mid(text, i, 1) & REVERSETEXT
        MsgBox REVERSETEXT
    Next i
End Function
```

When this function is evaluated, a pop-up message box appears — once for each time through the loop. The message box shows the current value of REVERSETEXT. In other words, this technique enables you to monitor the results as the function is executed. Figure 21-4 shows an example.

The information displayed in the series of message boxes shows that the text string is being built within the loop, but the new text is being added to the beginning of the string, not the end. The corrected assignment statement is:

```
REVERSETEXT = REVERSETEXT = Mid(text, i, 1)
```

When the function is working properly, make sure you remove all of the MsgBox statements. They get very annoying.

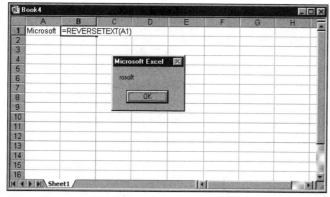

Figure 21-4: Use a MsgBox statement to monitor the value of a variable as a Function procedure executes.

To display more than one variable in a message box, you need to concatenate the variables and insert a space character in between each. The statement below, for example, displays the value of three variables (x, y, and z) in a message box.

```
MsgBox x & " " & y & " " & z
```

If you omit the blank space, you cannot distinguish the separate values.

Using Debug.Print statements in your code

If you find that using MsgBox statements is too intrusive, a better option is to insert some temporary code that writes values directly to VB Editor's Immediate window (see the sidebar, "Using the Immediate Window"). You use the Debug.Print statement to write the values of selected variables.

For example, if you want to monitor a value inside of a loop, use a routine such as the one that follows.

```
Function VOWELCOUNT(r)
    Count = 0
    For i = 1 To Len(r)
        Ch = UCase(Mid(r, i, 1))
        If Ch Like "[AEIOU]" Then
            Count = Count + 1
            Debug.Print Ch, i
        End If
    Next i
    VOWELCOUNT = Count
End Function
```

In this case, the value of two variables (Ch and i) print to the Immediate window whenever the Debug.Print statement is encountered. Figure 21-5 shows the result when the function has an argument of *California*.

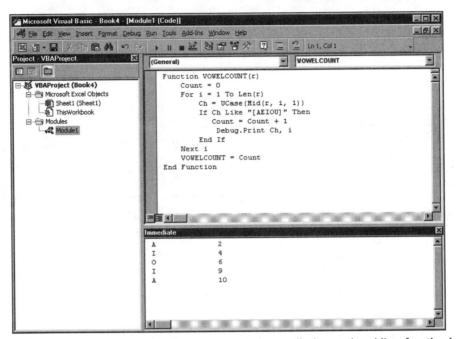

Figure 21-5: Using the VB Editor's Immediate window to display results while a function is running

When your function is debugged, make sure you remove the Debug.Print statements.

Calling the function from a Sub procedure

Another way to test a Function procedure is to call the function from a Sub procedure. To do so, just add a temporary Sub procedure to the module, and insert a statement that calls your function. This is particularly useful because run-time errors display as they occur.

The following Function procedure contains an error (a run-time error). As I noted previously, the run-time errors do not display when testing a function by using a worksheet formula. Rather, the function simply returns an error (#VALUE!).

```
Function REVERSETEXT(text) As String
'   Returns its argument, reversed
```

```
    TextLen = Len(text)
    For i = TextLen To 1 Step -1
        REVERSETEXT = REVERSETEXT And Mid(text, i, 1)
    Next i
End Function
```

To help identify the source of the run-time error, insert the Sub procedure listed below.

```
Sub Test()
    x = REVERSETEXT("Hello")
    MsgBox x
End Sub
```

This Sub procedure simply calls the REVERSETEXT function and assigns the result to a variable named *x*. The MsgBox statement displays the result.

You can execute the Sub procedure directly from the VB Editor. Just move the cursor anywhere within the procedure and select Run → Run Sub/UserForm (or, just press F5). When you execute the Test procedure, you see the error message shown in Figure 21-6.

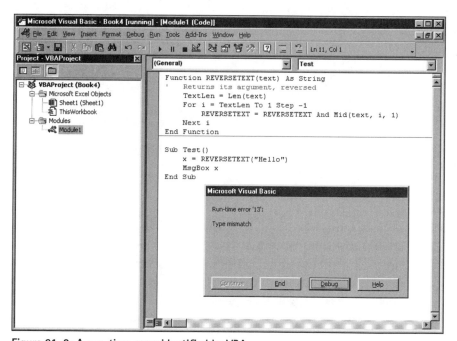

Figure 21-6: A run-time error identified by VBA

Click the Debug button, and the VB Editor highlights the statement causing the problem (see Figure 21-7). The error message doesn't tell you how to correct the error, but it does narrow your choices. Once you know the statement that's causing the error, you can examine it more closely or use the Immediate window (see the sidebar, "Using the Immediate Window") to help locate the exact problem.

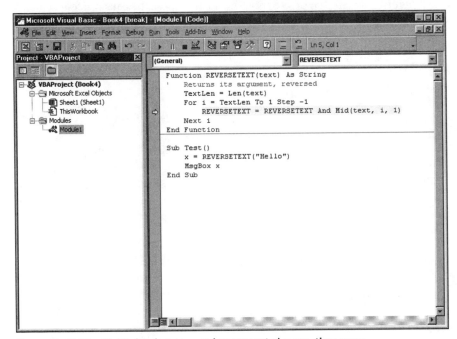

Figure 21-7: The highlighted statement has generated a run-time error.

In this case, the problem is the user of the And operator instead of the concatenation operator (&). The correct statement is:

```
REVERSETEXT = REVERSETEXT & Mid(text, i, 1)
```

When you click the Debug button, the procedure is still running — it's just halted and is in "break mode." After you make the correction, press F5 to continue execution, press F8 to continue execution on a line-by-line basis, or click the Rest button to halt execution.

Using the Immediate Window

The VB Editor's Immediate window can be helpful when debugging code. To activate the Immediate window, press Ctrl+G.

You can type VBA statements in the Immediate window and see the result immediately. For example, type the following code in the Immediate window and press Enter:

```
Print Sqr(1156)
```

The VB Editor prints the result of this square root operation (34). To save a few keystrokes, you can use a single question mark (?) in place of the Print keyword.

The Immediate window is particularly useful for debugging run-time errors when VBA is in break mode. For example, you can use the Immediate window to check the current value for variables, or to check the data type of a variable.

Often, errors occur because data is of the wrong type. The following statement, for example, displays the data type of a variable named Counter (which you think is an Integer variable).

```
? TypeName(Counter)
```

If you discover that Counter is a data type other than Integer, you may have solved your problem.

Setting a breakpoint in the function

Another debugging option is to set a breakpoint in your code. Execution pauses when VBA encounters a breakpoint. You can then use the Immediate window to check the values of variable, or you can use F8 to step through your code line by line.

To set a breakpoint, move the cursor to the statement at which you want to pause execution, and select Debug → Toggle Breakpoint (or press F9). This highlights the statement to remind you that a breakpoint is in effect (you also see a dot in the code window margin). You can set any number of breakpoints in your code. To remove a breakpoint, move the cursor to the statement and press F9. Figure 21-8 shows a Function procedure that contains a breakpoint.

```
Book4 - Module1 (Code)
(General)                              REVERSETEXT

Function REVERSETEXT(text) As String
'   Returns its argument, reversed
    TextLen = Len(text)
    For i = TextLen To 1 Step -1
        REVERSETEXT = REVERSETEXT And Mid(text, i, 1)
    Next i
End Function
```

Figure 21-8: The highlighted statement contains a breakpoint.

Creating Add-Ins

If you create some custom functions that you use frequently, you might want to store these functions in an add-in file. A primary advantage is that you can use the functions in formulas in any workbook without a filename qualifier.

Assume that you have a custom function named ZapSpaces, and it's stored in Myfuncs.xls. To use this function in a formula in a workbook other than Myfuncs.xls, you need to enter the following formula:

```
=Myfuncs.xls!ZapSpaces(A1:C12)
```

If you create an add-in from Myfuncs.xls and the add-in is loaded, you can omit the file reference and enter a formula such as the following:

```
= ZapSpaces(A1:C12)
```

Creating an add-in from a workbook is simple. The following steps describe how to create an add-in from a normal workbook file:

1. Develop your functions, and make sure they work properly.

2. Activate the VB Editor, and select the workbook in the Project window. Choose Tools → *xxx* Properties, and click the Protection tab. Select the *Lock project for viewing* checkbox, and enter a password (twice). Click OK.

   You only need to do this step if you want to prevent others from viewing or modifying your macros or custom dialog boxes.

3. Choose File → Properties, click the Summary tab, and enter a brief, descriptive title in the *Title* field and a longer description in the *Comments* field.

   This step is not required, but it makes the add-in easier to use by displaying descriptive text in the Add-Ins dialog box.

4. Select File → Save As.

5. In the Save As dialog box, select *Microsoft Excel add-in (*.xla)* from the *Save as type* drop-down list.

6. Click Save. A copy of the workbook is saved (with an .xla extension), and the original XLS workbook remains open.

A workbook you convert to an add-in must have at least one worksheet. For example, if your workbook contains only chart sheets or Excel 5/95 dialog sheets, the *Microsoft Excel add-in (*.xla)* option does not appear in the Save As dialog box.

With previous versions of Excel (before Excel 97), to modify an add-in, you had to open the original XLS file, make your changes, and then recreate the add-in. For Excel 97 and later versions, this is no longer necessary. As long as the add-in is not protected, you can make changes to the add-in in the VB Editor. If the add-in is protected, you must enter the password to unprotect it. Therefore, with Excel 97 or later, keeping an XLS version of your add-in is not necessary.

Once you create your add-in, you can install it using the standard procedure: Select Tools → Add-Ins, and click the Browse button in the Add-Ins dialog box. Then, locate your *.xla file.

A Few Words About Security

Microsoft has never promoted Excel as a product that creates applications with secure source code. The password feature provided in Excel is sufficient to prevent casual users from accessing parts of your application that you want to keep hidden. But, the truth is, several password-cracking utilities are available. If you must absolutely be sure that no one ever sees your code or formulas, Excel is not your best choice as a development platform.

Summary

This chapter covered some essential details to help you develop effective custom functions. It discussed the type of arguments that you can use, and described how to make your function appear in a specific category in the Paste Function dialog box. The chapter also presented some techniques to help debug functions and ended with instructions for creating an add-in to hold your functions.

The next chapter discusses VBA programming concepts.

Chapter 22

VBA Programming Concepts

IN THIS CHAPTER

◆ Introducing an example function procedure

◆ Using comments in your code

◆ Understanding VBA's language elements, including variables, data types, and constants

◆ Using assignment expressions in your code

◆ Declaring arrays and multidimensional arrays

◆ Using VBA's built-in functions

◆ Controlling the execution of your Function procedures

◆ Using ranges in your code

THIS CHAPTER DISCUSSES some of the key language elements and programming concepts in VBA. If you've used other programming languages, much of this information may sound familiar. VBA has a few unique wrinkles, however, so even experienced programmers may find some new information.

An Introductory Example Function Procedure

To get the ball rolling, let's start with an example Function procedure. This function, named REMOVESPACES, accepts a single argument and returns that argument without any spaces. For example, the following formula returns *ThisIsATest*.

```
=REMOVESPACES("This Is A Test")
```

To create this function, insert a VBA module into a project, and then enter the following Function procedure into the code window of the module:

```
Function REMOVESPACES(cell) As String
'   Removes all spaces from cell
    Dim CellLength As Integer
    Dim Temp As String
    Dim i As Integer
    CellLength = Len(cell)
    Temp = ""
    For i = 1 To CellLength
        Character = Mid(cell, i, 1)
        If Character <> Chr(32) Then Temp = Temp & Character
    Next i
    REMOVESPACES = Temp
End Function
```

Let's look closely at this function's code line by line.

♦ The first line of the function is called the function's declaration line. Notice that the procedure starts with the keyword *Function*, followed by the name of the function (REMOVESPACES). This function uses only one argument (cell); the argument's name is enclosed in parentheses. *As String* defines the data type of the function's return value. The "As" part of the function declaration is optional.

♦ The second line is simply a comment (optional) that describes what the function does.

♦ The next three lines use the Dim keyword to declare the three variables used in the procedure: CellLength, Temp, and i. Declaring a variable isn't necessary, but (as you'll see later) it's an excellent practice.

♦ The procedure's next line assigns a value to a variable named CellLength. This statement uses VBA's Len function to determine the length of the contents of the argument (cell).

♦ The next statement creates a variable named Temp and assigns it an empty string.

♦ The next four statements comprise a For-Next loop. The statements between the For statement and the Next statement are executed a number of times; the value of CellLength determines the number of times. For example, assume the cell passed as the argument contains the text "Bob Smith." The statements within the loop would execute nine times — one time for each character in the string.

◆ Within the loop, the Character variable holds a single character that is extracted using VBA's Mid function (which works just like Excel's MID function). The If statement determines if the character is not a space (VBA's Chr function is equivalent to Excel's CHAR function). If it's not a space, then the character is appended to the end of the string stored in the Temp variable. If the character is a space, the Temp variable is unchanged and the next character is processed.

◆ When the loop finishes, the Temp variable holds all characters originally passed to the function in the cell argument, except for the spaces.

◆ The string contained in the Temp variable is assigned to the function's name. This string is the value that the function returns.

◆ The Function procedure ends with an End Function statement.

The REMOVESPACES procedure uses some common VBA language elements, including:

◆ A comment (the line preceded by the apostrophe)

◆ Variable declarations

◆ Three assignment statements

◆ Two built-in VBA functions (Len and Mid)

◆ A looping structure (For-Next)

◆ An If-Then structure

◆ String concatenation (using the & operator)

Not bad for a first effort, eh? The remainder of this chapter provides more information on these (and many other) programming concepts.

Using Comments

A *comment* is descriptive text embedded within your code. VBA completely ignores the text of a comment. It's a good idea to use comments liberally to describe what you do (the purpose of a particular VBA instruction is not always obvious).

You can use a complete line for your comment, or you can insert a comment *after* an instruction on the same line. A comment is indicated by an apostrophe. VBA ignores any text that follows an apostrophe — except when the apostrophe is contained within quotation marks — up until the end of the line. For example, the following statement does not contain a comment, even though it has an apostrophe:

```
Result = "Can't calculate"
```

The following example shows a VBA Function procedure with three comments:

```
Function MyFunc()
'   This function does nothing of value
    x = 0    'x represents nothingness
'   Return the result
    MyFunc = x
End Function
```

When developing a function, you may want to test it without including a particular instruction or group of instructions. Instead of deleting the instruction, simply convert it to a comment by inserting an apostrophe at the beginning. VBA then ignores the instruction(s) when the routine is executed. To convert the comment back to an instruction, delete the apostrophe.

The VB Editor's Edit toolbar contains two very useful buttons. Select a group of instructions and then use the Comment Block button to convert the instructions to comments. The Uncomment Block button converts a group of comments back to instructions.

Using Variables, Data Types, and Constants

A *variable* is a named storage location in your computer's memory. Variables can accommodate a wide variety of *data types* – from simple Boolean values (True or False) to large, double-precision values (see the following section). You assign a value to a variable by using the assignment operator, which is an equal sign.

Following are some examples of assignment expressions that use various types of variables. The variable names are to the left of the equal sign. Each statement assigns the value to the right of the equal sign to the variable on the left.

```
x = 1
InterestRate = 0.075
LoanPayoffAmount = 243089
DataEntered = False
x = x + 1
MyNum = YourNum * 1.25
TheKing = "Jim Leyritz"
DateStarted = #3/14/99#
```

VBA has many *reserved words*, which are words that you cannot use for variable or procedure names. If you attempt to use one of these words, you get an error message. For example, although the reserved word *Next* might make a very descriptive variable name, the following instruction generates a syntax error:

```
Next = 132
```

Unfortunately, syntax error messages sometimes aren't descriptive. The preceding instruction generates this error message: *Compile Error: Expected: variable*. It would be nice if the error message read something like *Reserved word used as a variable*. So if an instruction produces a strange error message, check the online help to make sure your variable name doesn't have a special use in VBA.

Defining data types

VBA makes life easy for programmers because it can automatically handles all the details involved in dealing with data. *Data type* refers to how data is stored in memory – as integers, real numbers, strings, and so on.

Although VBA can take care of data typing automatically, it does so at a cost: slower execution and less efficient use of memory. If you want optimal speed for your functions, you need to be familiar with data types. Generally, it's best to use the data type that uses the smallest number of bytes – yet still can handle all the data that will be assigned to it. When VBA works with data, execution speed is a function of the number of bytes VBA has at its disposal. In other words, the fewer bytes used by data, the faster VBA can access and manipulate the data. Table 22-1 lists VBA's assortment of built-in data types.

TABLE 22-1 VBA'S DATA TYPES

Data Type	Bytes Used	Range of Values
Byte	1 byte	0 to 255
Boolean	2 bytes	TRUE or FALSE
Integer	2 bytes	−32,768 to 32,767
Long	4 bytes	−2,147,483,648 to 2,147,483,647

Continued

TABLE 22-1 VBA'S DATA TYPES (*Continued*)

Data Type	Bytes Used	Range of Values
Single	4 bytes	–3.402823E38 to –1.401298E–45 (for negative values); 1.401298E–45 to 3.402823E38 (for positive values)
Double	8 bytes	–1.79769313486231E308 to –4.94065645841247E–324 (negative values); 4.94065645841247E–324 to 1.79769313486232E308 (positive values)
Currency	8 bytes	–922,337,203,685,477.5808 to 922,337,203,685,477.5807
Decimal	14 bytes	+/–79,228,162,514,264,337,593,543,950,335 with no decimal point; +/– 7.9228162514264337593543950335 with 28 places to the right of the decimal
Date	8 bytes	January 1, 0100 to December 31, 9999
Object	4 bytes	Any object reference
String (variable-length)	10 bytes + string length	0 to approximately 2 billion
String (fixed-length)	Length of string	1 to approximately 65,400
Variant (with numbers)	16 bytes	Any numeric value up to the range of a double data type
Variant (with characters)	22 bytes + string length	0 to approximately 2 billion

---

Declaring variables

Before you use a variable in a procedure, you may want to *declare* it — that is, tell VBA its name and data type. Declaring variables provides two main benefits:

◆ *Your procedures run faster and use memory more efficiently.* The default data type, variant, causes VBA to repeatedly perform time-consuming checks and reserve more memory than necessary. If VBA knows the data type for a variable, it doesn't have to investigate; and it can reserve just enough memory to store the data.

◆ *You avoid problems involving misspelled variable names.* Say that you use an undeclared variable named CurrentRate. At some point in your procedure, however, you insert the statement CurentRate = .075. This misspelled variable name, which is very difficult to spot, likely will cause your function to return an incorrect result.

You declare a variable by using the Dim keyword. For example, the following statement declares a variable named Count to be an integer.

```
Dim Count As Integer
```

You also can declare several variables with a single Dim statement. For example,

```
Dim x As Integer, y As Integer, z As Integer
Dim First As Long, Last As Double
```

Unlike some languages, VBA does not permit you to declare a group of variables to be a particular data type by separating the variables with commas. For example, the following statement — although valid — does *not* declare all the variables as integers:

```
Dim i, j, k As Integer
```

In the preceding statement, only k is declared to be an integer. To declare all variables as integers, use this statement:

```
Dim i As Integer, j As Integer, k As Integer
```

If you don't declare the data type for a variable that you use, VBA uses the default data type, variant. Data stored as a variant acts like a chameleon: It changes type, depending on what you do with it. The following procedure demonstrates how a variable can assume different data types.

```
Function VariantDemo()
    MyVar = "123"
    MyVar = MyVar / 2
    MyVar = "Answer: " & MyVar
    VariantDemo = MyVar
End Function
```

Forcing Yourself to Declare All Variables

To force yourself to declare all the variables that you use, include the following as the first instruction in your VBA module:

```
Option Explicit
```

This statement causes your procedure to stop whenever VBA encounters an undeclared variable name. VBA issues an error message (*Compile error: Variable not defined*), and you must declare the variable before you can proceed.

To ensure that the Option Explicit statement appears in every new VBA module, enable the Require Variable Declaration option on the Editor tab of the VB Editor's Options dialog box.

In the VariantDemo Function procedure, MyVar starts out as a three-character text string that looks like a number. Then this "string" is divided by two and MyVar becomes a numeric data type. Next, MyVar is appended to a string, converting MyVar back to a string. The function returns the final string: *Answer: 61.5.*

Using constants

A variable's value may, and often does, change while a procedure is executing (that's why it's called a variable). Sometimes, you need to refer to a named value or string that never changes: a *constant*.

 If you attempt to change the value of a constant in a VBA procedure, you get an error — as you would expect. A constant is a constant, not a variable.

You declare a constant by using the Const statement at the top of your procedure. Here are some examples:

```
Const NumQuarters as Integer = 4
Const Rate = .0725, Period = 12
Const CompanyName as String = "Acme Snapholytes"
```

The second statement declares two constants with a single statement, but it doesn't declare a data type. Consequently, the two constants are variants. Because a constant never changes its value, you normally want to declare your constants as a specific data type. The *scope* of a constant depends on where it is declared within your module:

- To make a constant available within a single procedure only, declare it after the Sub or Function statement to make it a local constant.

- To make a constant available to all procedures in a module, declare it before the first procedure in the module.

- To make a constant available to all modules in the workbook, use the Public keyword and declare the constant before the first procedure in a module.

Using constants throughout your code in place of hard-coded values or strings is an excellent programming practice. For example, if your procedure needs to refer to a specific value — such as an interest rate — several times, it's better to declare the value as a constant and use the constant's name rather than its value in your expressions. This technique makes your code more readable, and makes it easier to change should the need arise — you have to change only one instruction rather than several.

Using strings

Like Excel, VBA can manipulate both numbers and text (strings). There are two types of strings in VBA:

- *Fixed-length strings* are declared with a specified number of characters. The maximum length is 65,535 characters.

- *Variable-length strings* theoretically can hold up to 2 billion characters.

Each character in a string takes 1 byte of storage. When you declare a string variable with a Dim statement, you can specify the maximum length if you know it (that is, a fixed-length string), or you can let VBA handle it dynamically (a variable-length string). Working with fixed-length strings is slightly more efficient in terms of memory usage.

In the following example, the MyString variable is declared to be a string with a maximum length of 50 characters. YourString is also declared as a string, but with an unspecified length.

```
Dim MyString As String * 50
Dim YourString As String
```

Using dates

You can use a string variable to store a date, of course, but then you can't perform date calculations using the variable. Using the Date data type is a better way to work with dates.

A variable defined as a Date uses 8 bytes of storage and can hold dates ranging from January 1, 0100, to December 31, 9999. That's a span of nearly 10,000 years — more than enough for even the most aggressive financial forecast! The Date data type also is useful for storing time-related data. In VBA, you specify dates and times by enclosing them between two pound signs (#).

The range of dates that VBA can handle is much larger than Excel's own date range — which begins with January 1, 1900. Therefore, be careful that you don't attempt to use a date in a worksheet that lies outside of Excel's acceptable date range.

Here are some examples of declaring variables and constants as Date data types:

```
Dim Today As Date
Dim StartTime As Date
Const FirstDay As Date = #1/1/2001#
Const Noon = #12:00:00#
```

Date variables display dates according to your system's short date format, and times appear according to your system's time format (either 12 or 24 hours). You can modify these system settings by using the Regional Settings option in the Windows Control Panel.

Using Assignment Expressions

An *assignment expression* is a VBA instruction that evaluates an expression and assigns the result to a variable or an object. An *expression* is a combination of keywords, operators, variables, and constants that yield a string, number, or object. An expression can perform a calculation, manipulate characters, or test data.

If you know how to create formulas in Excel, you'll have no trouble creating expressions in VBA. With a worksheet formula, Excel displays the result in a cell. Conversely, you can assign a VBA expression to a variable or use it as a property value.

VBA uses the equal sign (=) as its assignment operator. Note the following examples of assignment statements (the expressions are to the right of the equal sign):

```
x = 1
x = x + 1
x = (y * 2) / (z  * 2)
MultiSheets = True
```

Often, expressions use functions — VBA's built-in functions, Excel's worksheet functions, or custom functions that you develop in VBA. I discuss VBA's built-in functions later in this chapter.

Operators play a major role in VBA. Familiar operators describe mathematical operations, including addition (+), multiplication (*), division (/), subtraction (-), exponentiation (^), and string concatenation (&). Less familiar operators are the backslash (\) used in integer division, and the Mod operator used in modulo arithmetic. The Mod operator returns the remainder of one number divided by another. For example, the following expression returns 2:

```
17 Mod 3
```

VBA also supports the same comparative operators used in Excel formulas: equal to (=), greater than (>), less than (<), greater than or equal to (>=), less than or equal to (<=), and not equal to (<>). In addition, VBA provides a full set of logical operators, as shown in Table 22-2.

TABLE 22-2 VBA'S LOGICAL OPERATORS

Operator	What It Does
Not	Performs a logical negation on an expression
And	Performs a logical conjunction on two expressions
Or	Performs a logical disjunction on two expressions
XoR	Performs a logical exclusion on two expressions
Eqv	Performs a logical equivalence on two expressions
Imp	Performs a logical implication on two expressions

The order of precedence for operators in VBA exactly matches that in Excel. Of course, you can add parentheses to change the natural order of precedence.

Using Arrays

An *array* is a group of elements of the same type that have a common name; you refer to a specific element in the array using the array name and an index number. For example, you may define an array of 12 string variables so that each variable corresponds to the name of a different month. If you name the array MonthNames, you can refer to the first element of the array as MonthNames(0), the second element as MonthNames(1), and so on, up to MonthNames(11).

Declaring an array

You declare an array with a Dim or Public statement just as you declare a regular variable. You also can specify the number of elements in the array. You do so by specifying the first index number, the keyword To, and the last index number – all inside parentheses. For example, here's how to declare an array comprising exactly 100 integers:

```
Dim MyArray(1 To 100) As Integer
```

TIP

When you declare an array, you need to specify only the upper index, in which case VBA assumes that 0 is the lower index. Therefore, the following two statements have the same effect:

```
Dim MyArray(0 to 100) As Integer
Dim MyArray(100) As Integer
```

In both cases, the array consists of 101 elements.

If you would like VBA to assume that 1 is the lower index for all arrays that declare only the upper index, include the following statement before any procedures in your module:

```
Option Base 1
```

Declaring multidimensional arrays

The array examples in the preceding section were one-dimensional arrays. VBA arrays can have up to 60 dimensions, although it's rare to need more than three dimensions (a 3-D array). The following statement declares a 100-integer array with two dimensions (2-D):

```
Dim MyArray(1 To 10, 1 To 10) As Integer
```

You can think of the preceding array as occupying a 10 × 10 matrix. To refer to a specific element in a 2-D array, you need to specify two index numbers. For example, here's how you can assign a value to an element in the preceding array:

```
MyArray(3, 4) = 125
```

A *dynamic array* doesn't have a preset number of elements. You declare a dynamic array with a blank set of parentheses:

```
Dim MyArray() As Integer
```

Before you can use a dynamic array in your code, however, you must use the ReDim statement to tell VBA how many elements are in the array (or ReDim Preserve if you want to keep the existing values in the array). You can use the ReDim statement any number of times, changing the array's size as often as you like.

Arrays crop up later in this chapter in the sections that discuss looping.

Using VBA's Built-in Functions

VBA has a variety of built-in functions that simplify calculations and operations. Many of VBA's functions are similar (or identical) to Excel's worksheet functions. For example, the VBA function UCase, which converts a string argument to uppercase, is equivalent to the Excel worksheet function UPPER.

TIP

To display a list of VBA functions while writing your code, type **VBA** followed by a period (.). The VB Editor displays a list of all functions (see Figure 22-1). If this doesn't work for you, make sure that you select the Auto List Members option. Choose Tools → Options, and click the Editor tab. In addition to functions, the list that displays also includes built-in constants. The VBA functions are all described in the online help. To view help, just move the cursor over a function name and press F1.

Here's a statement that calculates the square root of a variable using VBA's Sqr function, and then assigns the result to a variable named x.

```
x = Sqr(MyValue)
```

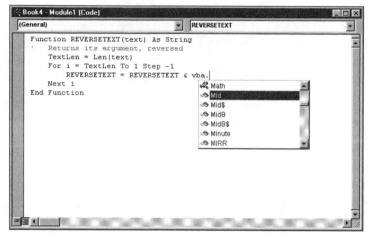

Figure 22-1: Displaying a list of VBA functions in the VB Editor

Knowledge of VBA's functions can save you lots of work. For example, consider the REMOVESPACES Function procedure presented at the beginning of this chapter. That function uses a For-Next loop to examine each character in a string and builds a new string. A much simpler (and more efficient) version of that Function procedure uses VBA's Replace function. Following is a rewritten version of the Function procedure.

```
Function REMOVESPACES(cell) As String
'    Removes all spaces from cell
    REMOVESPACES = Replace(cell, " ", "")
End Function
```

TIP   The Replace function is new to the version of VBA included with Excel 2000. This function is not available if you use an earlier versions of Excel.

You can use many (but not all) of Excel's worksheet functions in your VBA code. To use a worksheet function in a VBA statement, just precede the function name with Application and a dot.

The following code demonstrates how to use an Excel worksheet function in a VBA statement. Excel's infrequently used ROMAN function converts a decimal number into a Roman numeral.

```
DecValue = 1999
RomanValue = Application.Roman(DecValue)
```

The variable RomanValue contains the string MCMXCIX. Fans of old movies are often dismayed when they learn that Excel doesn't have a function to convert a Roman numeral to its decimal equivalent. You can, of course, create such a function yourself. Are you up for a challenge?

It's important to understand that you cannot use worksheet functions that have an equivalent VBA function. For example, VBA cannot access Excel's SQRT worksheet function because VBA has its own version of that function: Sqr. Therefore, the following statement generates an error:

```
x = Application.SQRT(123)    'error
```

Controlling Execution

Some VBA procedures start at the top and progress line by line to the bottom. Often, however, you need to control the flow of your routines by skipping over some statements, executing some statements multiple times, and testing conditions to determine what the routine does next.

This section discusses several ways of controlling the execution of your VBA procedures:

◆ If-Then constructs

◆ Select Case constructs

◆ For-Next loops

◆ Do While loops

◆ Do Until loops

◆ On Error statements

The If-Then construct

Perhaps the most commonly used instruction grouping in VBA is the If-Then construct. This instruction is one way to endow your applications with decision-making capability. The basic syntax of the If-Then construct is:

```
If condition Then true_instructions [Else false_instructions]
```

The If-Then construct executes one or more statements conditionally. The Else clause is optional. If included, it enables you to execute one or more instructions when the condition you test is not true.

The following Function procedure demonstrates an If-Then structure without an Else clause. The example deals with time. VBA uses the same date-and-time serial number system as Excel. The time of day is expressed as a fractional value — for example, noon is represented as .5. VBA's Time function returns a value that represents the time of day, as reported by the system clock. In the example that follows, the function starts out by assigning an empty string to GreetMe. The If-Then statement checks the time of day. If the time is before noon, the Then, part of the statement executes and the function returns *Good Morning*.

```
Function GreetMe()
    GreetMe = ""
    If Time < 0.5 Then GreetMe= "Good Morning"
End Function
```

The following function uses two If-Then statements. It displays either Good Morning or Good Afternoon:

```
Function GreetMe()
    If Time < 0.5 Then GreetMe = "Good Morning"
    If Time >= 0.5 Then GreetMe = "Good Afternoon"
End Function
```

Notice that the second If-Then statement uses >= (greater than or equal to). This covers the extremely remote chance that the time is precisely 12:00 noon when the function is executed.

Another approach is to use the Else clause of the If-Then construct. For example,

```
Function GreetMe()
    If Time < 0.5 Then GreetMe = "Good Morning" Else _
       GreetMe = "Good Afternoon"
End Function
```

Notice that the preceding example uses the line continuation sequence (a space followed by an underscore); If-Then-Else is actually a single statement.

The following is another example that uses the If-Then construct. This Function procedure calculates a discount, based on a quantity. It accepts one argument (quantity) and returns the appropriate discount based on that value.

```
Function Discount(quantity)
    If quantity <= 5 Then Discount = 0
    If quantity >= 6 Then Discount = 0.1
    If quantity >= 25 Then Discount = 0.15
    If quantity >= 50 Then Discount = 0.2
    If quantity >= 75 Then Discount = 0.25
End Function
```

Notice that each If-Then statement in this procedure is always executed, and the value for Discount can change as the function is executed. The final value, however, is the desired value.

The preceding examples all used a single statement for the Then clause of the If-Then construct. Often, however, you need to execute multiple statements if a condition is True. You still can use the If-Then construct, but you need to use an End If statement to signal the end of the statements that comprise the Then clause. Here's an example that executes two statements if the If clause is True.

```
If x > 0 Then
    y = 2
    z = 3
End If
```

You also can use multiple statements for an If-Then-Else construct. Here's an example that executes two statements if the If clause is True, and two other statements if the If clause is not True.

```
If x > 0 Then
    y = 2
    z = 3
Else
    y = -2
    z = -3
End If
```

The Select Case construct

The Select Case construct is useful for choosing among three or more options. This construct also works with two options and is a good alternative to If-Then-Else. The syntax for Select Case is as follows:

```
Select Case testexpression
    [Case expressionlist-n
        [instructions-n]]
    [Case Else
        [default_instructions]]
End Select
```

The following example of a Select Case construct shows another way to code the GreetMe examples presented in the preceding section:

```
Function GreetMe()
    Select Case Time
        Case Is < 0.5
            GreetMe = "Good Morning"
        Case 0.5 To 0.75
            GreetMe = "Good Afternoon"
        Case Else
            GreetMe = "Good Evening"
    End Select
End Function
```

And here's a rewritten version of the Discount function from the previous section, this time using a Select Case construct:

```
Function Discount(quantity)
    Select Case quantity
        Case Is <= 5
            Discount = 0
        Case 6 To 24
            Discount = 0.1
        Case 25 To 49
            Discount = 0.15
        Case 50 To 74
            Discount = 0.2
        Case Is >= 75
            Discount = 0.25
    End Select
End Function
```

Any number of instructions can be written below each Case statement; they all execute if that case evaluates to True.

Looping blocks of instructions

Looping is the process of repeating a block of VBA instructions within a procedure. You may know the number of times to loop, or it may be determined by the values of variables in your program. VBA offers a number of looping constructs:

◆ For-Next Loops

◆ Do While Loops

◆ Do Until Loops

FOR-NEXT LOOPS

Following is the syntax for a For-Next loop:

```
For counter = start To end [Step stepval]
    [instructions]
    [Exit For]
    [instructions]
Next [counter]
```

The following listing is an example of a For-Next loop that doesn't use the optional Step value or the optional Exit For statement. This function accepts two arguments and returns the sum of all integers between (and including) the arguments.

```
Function SumIntegers(first, last)
    total = 0
    For num = first To last
        total = total + num
    Next num
    SumIntegers = total
End Function
```

The following formula, for example, returns 55 — the sum of all integers from 1 to 10.

```
=SumIntegers(1,10)
```

In this example, *num* (the loop counter variable) starts out with the same value as the *first* variable and increases by 1 each time the loop repeats. The loop ends when *num* is equal to the last variable. The total variable simply accumulates the various values of *num* as it changes during the looping.

 When you use For-Next loops, you should understand that the loop counter is a normal variable — nothing special. As a result, you can change the value of the loop counter within the block of code executed between the For and Next statements. This is, however, a *ba-a-ad* practice and can cause unpredictable results. In fact, you should take special precautions to ensure that your code does not change the loop counter.

You also can use a Step value to skip some values in the loop. Here's the same function rewritten to sum *every other* integer between the first and last arguments.

```
Function SumIntegers2(first, last)
    total = 0
    For num = first To last Step 2
        total = total + num
    Next num
    SumIntegers2 = Total
End Function
```

The following formula returns 25, the sum of 1, 3, 5, 7, and 9.

```
=SumIntegers2(1,10)
```

For-Next loops also can include one or more Exit For statements within the loop. When this statement is encountered, the loop terminates immediately — as the following example demonstrates.

```
Function RowOfLargest(c)
    NumRows = Rows.Count
    MaxVal = Application.Max(Columns(c))
    For r = 1 To NumRows
        If Cells(r, c) = MaxVal Then
            RowOfLargest = r
            Exit For
        End If
    Next r
End Function
```

The RowOfLargest function accepts a column number (1 through 256) for its argument, and then returns the row number of the largest value in that column. It starts by getting a count of the number of rows in the worksheet (this varies, depending on the Excel version). This number is assigned to the NumRows variable. The maximum value in the column is calculated by using Excel's MAX function, and this value is assigned to the MaxVal variable.

The For-Next loop checks each cell in the column. If any cell it checks is equal to MaxVal, the row number (variable *r*, the loop counter) is assigned to the function's name and the Exit For statement ends the procedure. Without the Exit For statement, the loop continues to check all cells in the column — which could take quite a long time!

The previous examples use relatively simple loops. But you can have any number of statements in the loop, and you can even nest For-Next loops inside other For-Next loops. Following is VBA code that uses nested For-Next loops to initialize a 10 × 10 × 10 array with the value –1. When the three loops finish executing, each of the 1,000 elements in MyArray contains –1.

```
Dim MyArray(1 to 10, 1 to 10, 1 to 10)
For i = 1 To 10
    For j = 1 To 10
        For k = 1 To 10
            MyArray(i, j, k) = -1
        Next k
    Next j
Next i
```

DO WHILE LOOPS

A Do While loop is another type of looping structure available in VBA. Unlike a For-Next loop, a Do While loop executes while a specified condition is met. A Do While loop can have either of two syntaxes:

```
Do [While condition]
    [instructions]
    [Exit Do]
    [instructions]
Loop
```

   or

```
Do
    [instructions]
    [Exit Do]
    [instructions]
Loop [While condition]
```

As you can see, VBA enables you to put the While condition at the beginning or the end of the loop. The difference between these two syntaxes involves the point in time when the condition is evaluated. In the first syntax, the contents of the loop may never be executed. In the second syntax, the contents of the loop are always executed at least one time.

The following example is the RowOfLargest function presented in the previous section, rewritten to use a Do While loop (using the first syntax).

```
Function RowOfLargest(c)
    NumRows = Rows.Count
    MaxVal = Application.Max(Columns(c))
    r = 1
    Do While Cells(r, c) <> MaxVal
        r = r + 1
    Loop
    RowOfLargest = r
End Function
```

The variable *r* starts out with a value of 1 and increments within the Do While loop. The looping continues as long as the cell being evaluated is not equal to *MaxVal*. When the cell is equal to *MaxVal*, the loop ends and the function is assigned the value of *r*. Notice that if the maximum value is in row 1, the looping does not occur.

The following procedure uses the second Do While loop syntax. The loop always executes at least once.

```
Function RowOfLargest(c)
    NumRows = Rows.Count
    MaxVal = Application.Max(Columns(c))
    r = 0
    Do
        r = r + 1
    Loop While Cells(r, c) <> MaxVal
    RowOfLargest = r
End Function
```

Do While loops also can contain one or more Exit Do statements. When an Exit Do statement is encountered, the loop ends immediately.

DO UNTIL LOOPS

The Do Until loop structure closely resembles the Do While structure. The difference is evident only when the condition is tested. In a Do While loop, the loop executes *while* the condition is true. In a Do Until loop, the loop executes *until* the condition is true. Do Until also has two syntaxes:

```
Do [Until condition]
    [instructions]
    [Exit Do]
    [instructions]
```

```
Loop
```

   or

```
Do
    [instructions]
    [Exit Do]
    [instructions]
Loop [Until condition]
```

The following example demonstrates the first syntax of the Do Until loop. This example makes the code a bit clearer because it avoids the negative comparison required in the Do While example.

```
Function RowOfLargest(c)
    NumRows = Rows.Count
    MaxVal = Application.Max(Columns(c))
    r = 1
    Do Until Cells(r, c) = MaxVal
        r = r + 1
    Loop
    RowOfLargest = r
End Function
```

Finally, the following function is the same procedure, but it is rewritten to use the second syntax of the Do Until loop.

```
Function RowOfLargest(c)
    NumRows = Rows.Count
    MaxVal = Application.Max(Columns(c))
    r = 0
    Do
        r = r + 1
        Loop Until Cells(r, c) = MaxVal
    RowOfLargest = r
End Function
```

The On Error statement

Undoubtedly, you've used one of Excel's worksheet functions in a formula and discovered that the formula returns an error value (for example, #VALUE!). A formula can return an error value in a number of situations, including:

   ◆ You omitted one or more required argument.

- ◆ An argument was not the correct data type (for example, text instead of a value).

- ◆ An argument is outside of a valid numeric range (division by zero, for example).

In many cases, you can ignore error handling within your functions. If the user doesn't provide the proper number of arguments, the function simply returns an error value. It's up to the user to figure out the problem. This is how Excel's worksheet functions handle errors.

In other cases, you want your code to know if errors occurred and then do something about them. Excel's On Error statement enables you to identify and handle errors.

To simply ignore an error, use the following statement:

```
On Error Resume Next
```

If you use this statement, you can determine if an error occurs by checking the value of the Err object, which returns an error number. If Err is equal to zero, an error did not occur. If Err is equal to anything else, an error *did* occur.

The following example is a function that returns the name of a cell or range. If the cell or range does not have a name, an error occurs and the formula that uses the function returns a #VALUE! error.

```
Function RANGENAME(rng)
    RANGENAME = rng.Name.Name
End Function
```

The following list shows an improved version of the function. The On Error Resume Next statement causes VBA to ignore the error. The If Err statement checks to see if an error occurs. If so, the function returns an empty string.

```
Function RANGENAME(rng)
    On Error Resume Next
    RANGENAME = rng.Name.Name
    If Err <> 0 Then RANGENAME = ""
End Function
```

The following statement instructs VBA to watch for errors, and if an error occurs, continues executing at a different named location — in this case, a statement labeled ErrHandler.

```
On Error GoTo ErrHandler
```

The following Function procedure demonstrates this statement. The DIVIDETWO function accepts two arguments (*num1* and *num2*) and returns the result of *num1* divided by *num2*.

```
Function DIVIDETWO(num1, num2)
    On Error GoTo ErrHandler
    DIVIDETWO = num1 / num2
    Exit Function
ErrHandler:
    DIVIDETWO = "ERROR"
End Function
```

The On Error GoTo statement instructs VBA to jump to the statement labeled ErrHandler if an error occurs. As a result, the function returns a string (*ERROR*) if any type of error occurs while the function is executing. Note the use of the Exit Function statement. Without this statement, the code continues executing and the error handling code *always* executes. In other words, the function would always returns *ERROR*.

It's important to understand that the DIVIDETWO function is *non-standard* in its approach. Returning a string when an error occurs (*ERROR*) is not how Excel's functions work. Rather, they return an actual error value.

Chapter 23 contains several examples of the On Error statement, including an example that demonstrates how to return an actual error value from a function.

Using Ranges

Many of the custom functions that you develop will work with the data contained in a cell or in a range of cells. Recognize that a range can be a single cell or a group of cells. This section describes some key concepts to make this task easier. The information in this section is intended to be practical, rather than comprehensive. If you want more details, consult the online help.

Chapter 23 contains many practical examples of functions that use ranges. Studying those examples helps to clarify the information in this section.

The For Each-Next construct

Often, your Function procedures need to loop through a range of cells. For example, you might write a function that accepts a range as an argument. Your code needs to examine each cell in the range and do something. The For Each-Next construct is very useful for this sort of thing. The syntax of the For Each-Next construct is:

```
For Each element In group
    [instructions]
    [Exit For]
    [instructions]
Next [element]
```

The following Function procedure accepts a range argument and returns the sum of the squared values in the range.

```
Function SUMOFSQUARES(rng)
    total = 0
    For Each cell In rng
        total = total + cell ^ 2
    Next cell
    SUMOFSQUARES = total
End Function
```

Following is a worksheet formula that uses the SumOfSquares function.

```
=SumOfSquares(A1:C100)
```

In this case, the function's argument is a range that consists of 300 cells. The SumOfSquares function works equally well with a range of any size.

 In the preceding example, *cell* and *rng* are both variable names. There's nothing special about either name; you can replace them with any valid variable name.

Referencing a range

VBA code can reference a range in a number of different ways:

◆ The Range property

- ◆ The Cells property
- ◆ The Offset property

THE RANGE PROPERTY

You can use the Range property to refer to a range directly, using a cell address or name. The following example assigns the value in cell A1 to a variable named Init. In this case, the statement accesses the range's Value property.

```
Init = Range("A1").Value
```

Besides the Value property, VBA enables you to access a number of other properties of a range. For example, the statement that follows counts the number of cells in a range and assigns the value to the Cnt variable.

```
Cnt = Range("A1:C300").Count
```

The Range property also is useful for referencing a single cell in a multicell range. For example, you may create a function that is supposed to accept a single-cell argument. If the user specifies a multicell range as the argument, you can use the Range property to extract the upper left cell in the range. The following example uses the Range property (with an argument of "A1") to return the value in the upper left cell of the range represented by the cell argument.

```
Function Square(cell)
    Value = cell.Range("A1").Value
    Square = Value ^ 2
End Function
```

Assume the user enters the following formula:

```
=Square(C5:C12)
```

The Square function works with the upper left cell in C5:C12 (which is C5), and returns the value squared.

Many of Excel's worksheet functions work in this way. For example, if you specify a multicell range as the first argument for the LEFT function, Excel uses the upper left cell in the range. However, if you specify a multicell range as the argument for the SQRT function, Excel returns an error.

THE CELLS PROPERTY

Another way to reference a range is to use the Cells property. The Cells property accepts two arguments (a row number and a column number) and returns a single cell. The following statement assigns the value in cell A1 to a variable named FirstCell:

```
FirstCell = Cells(1, 1).Value
```

The statement that follows returns the upper left cell in the range C5:C12.

```
UpperLeft = Range("C5:C12").Cells(1,1)
```

 TIP If you use the Cells property without an argument, it returns a range that consists of all cells on the worksheet. In the following example, the TotalCells variable contains the total number of cells in the worksheet.

```
TotalCells = Cells.Count
```

The following statement uses Excel's COUNTA function to determine the number of non-empty cells in the worksheet:

```
NonEmpty = Application.COUNTA(Cells))
```

THE OFFSET PROPERTY

The Offset property (like the Range and Cells properties) also returns a Range object. The Offset property is used in conjunction with a range. It takes two arguments that correspond to the relative position from the upper left cell of the specified Range object. The arguments can be positive (down or right), negative (up or left), or zero. The following example returns the value one cell below cell A1 (i.e., cell A2), and assigns it to a variable named NextCell:

```
NextCell = Range("A1").Offset(1,0).Value
```

The following Function procedure accepts a single-cell argument and uses a For-Next loop to return the sum of the 10 cells below it:

```
Function SumBelow(cell)
    Total = 0
    For i = 1 To 10
        Total = Total + cell.Offset(i, 0)
    Next i
    SumBelow = Total
End Function
```

Some useful properties of ranges

In previous sections, you saw examples that used the Value property for a range. VBA gives you access to many additional range properties. Some of the more useful properties for function writers are briefly described in the sections that follow. For complete information on a particular property, refer to Excel's online help.

THE FORMULA PROPERTY

The Formula property returns the formula (as a string) contained in a cell. If you try to access the Formula property for a range that consists of more than one cell, you get an error. If the cell doesn't have a formula, this property returns the cell's value. The following function simply displays the formula for the upper left cell in a range:

```
Function CELLFORMULA(cell)
    CELLFORMULA = cell.Range("A1").Formula
End Function
```

You can use the HasFormula property to determine if a cell has a formula.

THE ADDRESS PROPERTY

The Address property returns the address of a range as a string. By default, it returns the address as an absolute reference (for example, $A$1:$C$12). The following function, which isn't all that useful, returns the address of a range.

```
Function RANGEADDRESS(rng)
    RANGEADDRESS = rng.Address
End Function
```

For example, the following formula returns the string *$A$1:$C$3*:

```
=RANGEADDRESS(A1:C3)
```

THE COUNT PROPERTY

The Count property returns the number of cells in a range. The following function uses the Count property:

```
Function CELLCOUNT(rng)
    CELLCOUNT = rng.Count
End Function
```

The following formula returns 9:

```
=CELLCOUNT(A1:C3)
```

THE PARENT PROPERTY

The Parent property returns an object that corresponds to an object's *container* object. For a Range object, the Parent property returns a Worksheet object (the worksheet that contains the range).

The following function uses the Parent property and returns the name of the worksheet of the range passed as an argument:

```
Function SHEETNAME(rng)
    SHEETNAME = rng.Parent.Name
End Function
```

The following formula, for example, returns the string *Sheet1:*

```
=SHEETNAME(Sheet1!A16)
```

THE NAME PROPERTY

The Name property returns a Name object for a cell or range. To get the actual cell or range name, you need to access the Name property of the Name object. If the cell or range doesn't have a name, the Name property returns an error.

The following Function procedure displays the name of a range or cell passed as its argument. If the range or cell doesn't have a name, the function returns an empty string. Note the use of On Error Resume Next. This handles situations in which the range doesn't have a name.

```
Function RANGENAME(rng)
    On Error Resume Next
    RANGENAME = rng.Name.Name
    If Err <> 0 Then RANGENAME = ""
End Function
```

THE NUMBERFORMAT PROPERTY

The NumberFormat property returns the number format (as a string) assigned to a cell or range. The following function simply displays the number format for the upper left cell in a range:

```
Function NUMBERFORMAT(cell)
    NUMBERFORMAT = cell.Range("A1").NumberFormat
End Function
```

THE FONT PROPERTY

The Font property returns a Font object for a range or cell. To actually do anything with this Font object, you need to access its properties. For example, a Font object has properties such as Bold, Italic, Name, Color, and so on. The following function returns TRUE if the upper left cell of its argument is formatted as bold:

```
Function ISBOLD(cell)
    ISBOLD = cell.Range("A1").Font.Bold
End Function
```

THE COLUMNS AND ROWS PROPERTIES

The Columns and Rows properties work with columns or rows in a range. For example, the following function returns the number of columns in a range by accessing the Count property:

```
Function COLUMNCOUNT(rng)
    COLUMNCOUNT = rng.Columns.Count
End Function
```

THE ENTIREROW AND ENTIRECOLUMN PROPERTIES

The EntireRow and EntireColumn properties enable you to work with an entire row or column for a particular cell. The following function accepts a single cell argument and then uses the EntireColumn property to get a range consisting of the cell's entire column. It then uses Excel's COUNTA function to return the number of non-empty cells in the column.

```
Function NONEMPTY(cell)
    NONEMPTY = Application.CountA(cell.EntireColumn)
End Function
```

THE HIDDEN PROPERTY

The Hidden property is used with rows or columns. It returns TRUE if the row or column is hidden. If you try to access this property for a range that doesn't consist of an entire row or column, you get an error. The following function accepts a single cell argument and returns TRUE if either the cell's row or the cell's column is hidden:

```
Function CELLISHIDDEN(cell)
    If cell.EntireRow.Hidden Or cell.EntireColumn.Hidden Then
        CELLISHIDDEN = True
    Else
        CELLISHIDDEN = False
    End If
End Function
```

The Set keyword

An important concept in VBA is the ability to create a new Range object and assign it to a variable — more specifically, an object *variable*. You do so by using the Set keyword. The following statement creates an object variable named MyRange:

```
Set MyRange = Range("A1:A10")
```

After the statement executes, you can use the MyRange variable in your code in place of the actual range reference. Examples in subsequent sections help clarify this concept.

The Intersect function

The Intersect function returns a range that consists of the intersection of two other ranges. For example, consider the two ranges selected in Figure 22-2. These ranges, D3:D10 and B5:F5, contain one cell in common (D5). In other words, D5 is the intersection of D3:D10 and B5:F5.

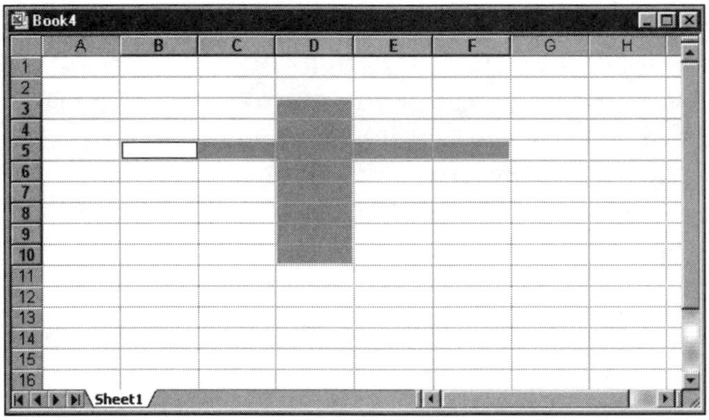

Figure 22-2: Use the Intersect function to work with the intersection of two ranges.

The following Function procedure accepts two range arguments and returns the count of the number of cells the ranges have in common:

```
Function CELLSINCOMMON(rng1, rng2)
    On Error Resume Next
    CELLSINCOMMON = 0
    Set CommonCells = Intersect(rng1, rng2)
    If Err = 0 Then CELLSINCOMMON = CommonCells.Count
End Function
```

The CELLSINCOMMON function uses the Intersect function to create a range object named CommonCells. Note the use of On Error Resume Next. This statement is necessary because the Intersect function returns an error if the ranges have no cells in common. If the error occurs, it is ignored. The final statement checks the value of Err. If 0, then no error occurs and the function returns the value of the Count property for the CommonCells object. If an error does occur, then Err has a value other than 0 and the function returns 0.

The Union function

The Union function combines two or more ranges into a single range. The following statement uses the Union function to create a range object that consists of the first and third columns of a worksheet:

```
Set TwoCols = Union(Range("A:A"), Range("C:C"))
```

The Union function can take any number of arguments.

The UsedRange property

The UsedRange property returns a Range object that represents the used range of the worksheet. Press Ctrl+End to activate the lower right cell of the used range. The UsedRange property can be *very useful* in making your functions more efficient.

Consider the Function procedure that follows. This function accepts a range argument and returns the number of formula cells in the range.

```
Function FORMULACOUNT(rng)
    cnt = 0
    For Each cell In rng
        If cell.HasFormula Then cnt = cnt + 1
    Next cell
    FORMULACOUNT = cnt
End Function
```

In many cases, the preceding function works just fine. But what if the user enters a formula such as this?

```
=FORMULACOUNT("A:A")
```

With an argument that consists of one or more entire columns, the function does not work well because it loops through every cell in the range – even those that are well beyond the area of the sheet that's actually used. The following function is rewritten to make it more efficient:

```
Function FORMULACOUNT(rng)
    cnt = 0
    Set WorkRange = Intersect(rng, rng.Parent.UsedRange)
    For Each cell In WorkRange
        If cell.HasFormula Then cnt = cnt + 1
    Next cell
    FORMULACOUNT = cnt
End Function
```

This function creates a Range object named WorkRange that consists of the intersection of the range passed as an argument and the used range of the worksheet. In other words, WorkRange consists of a subset of the range argument that only includes cells in the used range of the worksheet.

Summary

This chapter provided an introduction to VBA's language elements, including variables, data types, constants, and arrays. It also discussed the various methods you can use to control the flow of execution of your Function procedures. The chapter also presented several examples of functions that demonstrate how to work with ranges and use VBA's built-in functions.

The next, and final, chapter contains examples of custom functions.

Chapter 23

VBA Function Examples

IN THIS CHAPTER

- ◆ Simple custom function examples

- ◆ Custom function for determining a cell's data type

- ◆ Custom function for making a single worksheet function act like multiple functions

- ◆ Custom function for generating random numbers and selecting cells at random

- ◆ Custom functions for calculating sales commissions

- ◆ Custom functions for manipulating text

- ◆ Custom functions for counting and summing cells

- ◆ Custom functions that deal with dates

- ◆ Custom function example for returning the last nonempty cell in a column or row

- ◆ Custom functions that work with multiple worksheets

- ◆ Advanced custom function techniques

- ◆ Custom functions that use Windows API functions

THIS CHAPTER IS JAM-PACKED with a wide variety of useful (or potentially useful) VBA custom functions. You can use many of the functions as written. You may need to modify other functions to meet your particular needs. It is important to note that, for maximum speed and efficiency, these function procedures declare all variables that are used.

Simple Functions

The functions in this section are relatively simple, but they can be very useful. Most of these are based on the fact that VBA can obtain lots of useful information that's not normally available for use in a formula. For example, your VBA code can access a cell's HasFormula property to determine if a cell contains a formula. Oddly, Excel does not have a built-in worksheet function that tells you this.

The companion CD-ROM contains a workbook that includes all of the functions in this section.

Does a cell contain a formula?

The CELLHASFORMULA function that follows accepts a single-cell argument and returns TRUE if the cell has a formula.

```
Function CELLHASFORMULA(cell) As Boolean
'    Returns TRUE if cell has a formula
     CELLHASFORMULA = cell.Range("A1").HasFormula
End Function
```

If a range argument is passed to the function, the function works with the upper left cell in the range.

Returning a cell's formula

The CELLFORMULA function that follows returns the formula for a cell, as a string. If the cell does not have a formula, it returns an empty string.

```
Function CELLFORMULA(cell) As String
'    Returns the formula in cell, or an
'    empty string if cell has no formula
     Dim UpperLeft As Range
     Set UpperLeft = cell.Range("A1")
     If UpperLeft.HasFormula Then
         CELLFORMULA = UpperLeft.Formula
     Else
         CELLFORMULA = ""
     End If
End Function
```

This function creates a Range object variable named UpperLeft. This variable represents the upper left cell in the argument passed to the function.

> ## Is the cell Using the Functions in This Chapter
>
> If you see a function listed in this chapter that you find useful, you can use it in your own workbook. All of the Function procedures in this chapter are available on the companion CD-ROM. Just open the appropriate workbook (see Appendix E), activate the VB Editor, and copy and paste the function listing to a VBA module in your workbook. If you prefer, you can collect a number of functions and create an add-in (see Chapter 21 for details).
>
> It's impossible to anticipate every function you'll ever need. However, the examples in this chapter cover a wide variety of topics, so it's likely that you can locate an appropriate function and adapt the code for your own use.

hidden?

The CELLISHIDDEN function that follows accepts a single cell argument and returns TRUE if the cell is hidden. It is considered a hidden cell if either its row or its column is hidden.

```
Function CELLISHIDDEN(cell) As Boolean
'    Returns TRUE if cell is hidden
    Dim UpperLeft As Range
    Set UpperLeft = cell.Range("A1")
    If UpperLeft.EntireRow.Hidden Or _
       UpperLeft.EntireColumn.Hidden Then
        CELLISHIDDEN = True
    Else
        CELLISHIDDEN = False
    End If
End Function
```

Returning a worksheet name

The SHEETNAME function that follows accepts a single argument (a range) and returns the name of the worksheet that contains the range. It uses the Parent property of the Range object. The Parent property returns an object — the object that contains the Range object.

```
Function SHEETNAME(rng) As String
'    Returns the sheet name for rng
    SHEETNAME = rng.Parent.Name
End Function
```

The following function is a variation on this theme. It doesn't use an argument. Rather it relies on the fact that a function can determine the cell from which it was called by using Application.Caller.

```
Function SHEETNAME() As String
'    Returns the sheet name of the cell that
'    contains the function
     SHEETNAME = Application.Caller.Parent.Name
End Function
```

In this function, Application.Caller returns a Range object that corresponds to the cell that contains the function. For example, suppose you have the following formula in cell A1:

```
=SHEETNAME()
```

When the SHEETNAME function is executed, Application.Caller returns a Range object corresponding to the cell that contains the function. The Parent property returns the worksheet; the Name property returns the name of the worksheet.

Returning a workbook name

The next function, WORKBOOKNAME, returns the name of the workbook for a range reference. Notice that it uses the Parent property twice. The first Parent property returns a Worksheet object; the second Parent property returns a Workbook object.

```
Function WORKBOOKNAME() As String
'    Returns the workbook name of the cell
'    that contains the function
     WORKBOOKNAME = Application.Caller.Parent.Parent.Name
End Function
```

Returning the application's name

The following function, while not very useful, carries this discussion of object parents to the next logical level: accessing the Parent property three times. This function returns the name of the Application object, which always is the string *Microsoft Excel.*

```
Function APPNAME() As String
'    Returns the application name of the cell
'    that contains the function
     APPNAME = Application.Caller.Parent.Parent.Parent.Name
End Function
```

Understanding Object Parents

Objects in Excel are arranged in a hierarchy. At the top of the hierarchy is the Application object (Excel itself). Excel contains other objects, these objects contain other objects, and so on. The following depicts how a Range object fits into this scheme.

Application Object (Excel)

Workbook Object

Worksheet Object

Range Object

In the lingo of object-oriented programming, a Range object's parent is the Worksheet object that contains it. A Worksheet object's parent is the workbook that contains the worksheet. And, a Workbook object's parent is the Application object. Armed with this knowledge, you can make use of the Parent property to create a few useful functions.

Returning Excel's version number

The following function returns Excel's version number. For example, if you use Excel 2000, it returns 9.0.

```
Function EXCELVERSION() as Variant
'    Returns Excel's version number
     EXCELVERSION = Application.Version
End Function
```

Returning cell formatting information

This section contains a number of custom functions that return information about a cell's formatting. These functions are useful if you need to sort data based on formatting (for example, sorting all bold cells together).

The functions in this section use an Application.Volatile True statement. This causes the function to be reevaluated when the workbook is calculated. You'll find, however, that these functions don't always return the correct value. This is because changing cell formatting, for example, does not trigger Excel's recalculation engine. To force a global recalculation (and update all of the custom functions), press Ctrl+Alt+F9.

The following function returns TRUE if its single-cell argument has bold formatting.

```
Function ISBOLD(cell) As Boolean
'   Returns TRUE if cell is bold
    Application.Volatile True
    ISBOLD = cell.Range("A1").Font.Bold
End Function
```

The following function returns TRUE if its single-cell argument has italic formatting.

```
Function ISITALIC(cell) As Boolean
'   Returns TRUE if cell is italic
    Application.Volatile True
    ISITALIC = cell.Range("A1").Font.Italic
End Function
```

Both of the preceding functions return an error if the cell has mixed formatting — for example, only some characters are bold. The following function returns TRUE only if all characters in the cell are bold. It works by looping through each character in the cell.

```
Function ALLBOLD(cell) As Boolean
'   Returns TRUE if all characters in cell
'   are bold
    Application.Volatile True
    Dim UpperLeft As Range
    Dim i As Integer
    Set UpperLeft = cell.Range("A1")
    ALLBOLD = True
    For i = 1 To UpperLeft.Characters.Count
        If Not UpperLeft.Characters(i).Font.Bold Then
            ALLBOLD = False
            Exit Function
        End If
    Next i
End Function
```

The FILLCOLOR function that follows returns an integer that corresponds to the color index of the cell's interior (the cell's fill color). If the cell's interior is not filled, the function returns –4142.

```
Function FILLCOLOR(cell) As Integer
'   Returns an integer corresponding to
```

```
'    cell's interior color
     Application.Volatile True
     FILLCOLOR = cell.Range("A1").Interior.ColorIndex
End Function
```

The following function returns the number format string for a cell.

```
Function NUMBERFORMAT(cell) As String
'    Returns a string that represents
'    the cell's number format
     Application.Volatile True
     NUMBERFORMAT = cell.Range("A1").NumberFormat
End Function
```

Determining a Cell's Data Type

Excel provides a number of built-in functions that can help determine the type of data contained in a cell. These include ISTEXT, ISLOGICAL, and ISERROR. In addition, VBA includes functions such as ISEMPTY, ISDATE, and ISNUMERIC.

The following function accepts a range argument and returns a string (*Blank, Text, Logical, Error, Date, Time*, or *Value*) that describes the data type of the upper left cell in the range.

```
Function CELLTYPE(cell)
'    Returns the cell type of the upper left
'    cell in a range
     Dim UpperLeft As Range
     Application.Volatile
     Set UpperLeft = cell.Range("A1")
     Select Case True
         Case UpperLeft.NumberFormat = "@"
             CELLTYPE = "Text"
         Case IsEmpty(UpperLeft)
             CELLTYPE = "Blank"
         Case WorksheetFunction.IsText(UpperLeft)
             CELLTYPE = "Text"
         Case WorksheetFunction.IsLogical(UpperLeft)
             CELLTYPE = "Logical"
         Case WorksheetFunction.IsErr(UpperLeft)
             CELLTYPE = "Error"
         Case IsDate(UpperLeft)
             CELLTYPE = "Date"
         Case InStr(1, UpperLeft.Text, ":") <> 0
             CELLTYPE = "Time"
```

```
        Case IsNumeric(UpperLeft)
            CELLTYPE = "Value"
    End Select
End Function
```

Figure 23-1 shows the CELLTYPE function in use. Column B contains formulas that use the CELLTYPE function with an argument from column A. For example, cell B1 contains the following formula:

```
=CELLTYPE(A1)
```

	A	B	C	D	E
1	1	Value	A simple value		
2	8.6	Value	Formula that returns a value		
3	Budget Sheet	Text	Simple text		
4	FALSE	Logical	Logical formula		
5	TRUE	Logical	Logical value		
6	#DIV/0!	Error	Formula error		
7	04/12/1999	Date	Formula that returns a date		
8	4:00 PM	Time	A time		
9	143	Text	Value preceded by apostrophe		
10	434	Text	Cell formatted as Text		
11	A1:C4	Text	Text with a colon		
12		Blank	Empty cell		
13		Text	Cell with a single space		
14		Blank	Blank cell		
15					
16					
17					

celltype function.xls — Sheet1

Figure 23-1: The CELLTYPE function returns a string that describes the contents of a cell.

A workbook that demonstrates the CELLTYPE function is available on the companion CD-ROM.

A Multifunctional Function

This section demonstrates a technique that may be helpful in some situations: making a single worksheet function act like multiple functions. The following VBA function, named STATFUNCTION, takes two arguments: the range (rng) and the operation (op). Depending on the value of op, the function returns a value computed using any of the following worksheet functions: AVERAGE, COUNT, MAX, MEDIAN, MIN, MODE, STDEV, SUM, or VAR. For example, you can use this function in your worksheet:

```
=STATFUNCTION(B1:B24,A24)
```

The result of the formula depends on the contents of cell A24, which should be a string such as *Average, Count, Max,* and so on. You can adapt this technique for other types of functions.

```
Function STATFUNCTION(rng, op)
    Select Case UCase(op)
        Case "SUM"
            STATFUNCTION = Application.Sum(rng)
        Case "AVERAGE"
            STATFUNCTION = Application.Average(rng)
        Case "MEDIAN"
            STATFUNCTION = Application.Median(rng)
        Case "MODE"
            STATFUNCTION = Application.Mode(rng)
        Case "COUNT"
            STATFUNCTION = Application.Count(rng)
        Case "MAX"
            STATFUNCTION = Application.Max(rng)
        Case "MIN"
            STATFUNCTION = Application.Min(rng)
        Case "VAR"
            STATFUNCTION = Application.Var(rng)
        Case "STDEV"
            STATFUNCTION = Application.StDev(rng)
        Case Else
            STATFUNCTION = CVErr(xlErrNA)
    End Select
End Function
```

Figure 23-2 shows the STATFUNCTION function used in conjunction with a drop-down list generated by Excel's Data → Validation command. The formula in cell C14 is:

```
=STATFUNCTION(C1:C12,B14)
```

 The workbook shown in Figure 23-2 is available on the companion CD-ROM.

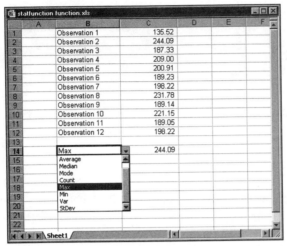

Figure 23-2: Selecting an operation from the list displays the result in cell B14.

Generating Random Numbers

This section presents two functions that deal with random numbers. One generates random numbers that don't change. The other selects a cell at random from a range.

Generating random numbers that don't change

You can use Excel's RAND function to quickly fill a range of cells with random values. But, as you may have discovered, the RAND function generates a new random number whenever the worksheet is recalculated. If you prefer to generate random numbers that don't change with each recalculation, use the STATICRAND Function procedure that follows:

```
Function STATICRAND()
'   Returns a random number that doesn't
'   change when recalculated
    STATICRAND = Rnd
End Function
```

The STATICRAND function uses VBA's built-in Rand function, which, like Excel's RAND function, returns a random number between 0 and 1. When you use STATIC-RAND, however, the random numbers do not change when the sheet is calculated.

Pressing F9 does not generate new values from the STATICRAND function, but pressing Ctrl+Alt+F9 (Excel's "global recalc" key combination) does.

If you want to generate a series of random integers between 0 and 1000, you can use a formula such as

```
=INT(STATICRAND()*1000)
```

Controlling Function Recalculation

When you use a custom function in a worksheet formula, when is it recalculated?

Custom functions behave like Excel's built-in worksheet functions. Normally, a custom function is recalculated only when it needs to be recalculated — that is, when you modify any of a function's arguments — but you can force functions to recalculate more frequently. Adding the following statement to a Function procedure makes the function recalculate whenever any cell changes:

```
Application.Volatile True
```

The Volatile method of the Application object has one argument (either True or False). Marking a function procedure as volatile forces the function to be calculated whenever calculation occurs in *any* cell in the worksheet.

For example, the custom STATICRAND function presented in this chapter can be changed to emulate Excel's RAND() function by using the Volatile method, as follows:

```
Function NONSTATICRAND()
'   Returns a random number that
'   changes when the sheet is recalculated
    Application.Volatile True
    NONSTATICRAND = Rnd
End Function
```

Using the False argument of the Volatile method causes the function to be recalculated only when one or more of its arguments change (if a function has no arguments, this method has no effect). By default, all functions work as if they include an Application.Volatile False statement.

Selecting a cell at random

The following function, named DRAWONE, randomly chooses one cell from an input range and returns the cell's contents.

```
Function DRAWONE(rng)
'    Chooses one cell at random from a range
     DRAWONE = rng(Int((rng.Count) * Rnd + 1))
End Function
```

If you use this function, you find that it is not recalculated when the worksheet is calculated. In other words, the function is not a volatile function (see the sidebar, "Controlling Function Recalculation," earlier in this chapter). You can make the function volatile by adding the following statement:

```
Application.Volatile True
```

After doing so, the DRAWONE function displays a new random cell value whenever the sheet is calculated.

I present two additional functions that deal with randomization later in this chapter (see "Advanced Function Techniques").

Calculating Sales Commissions

Sales managers often need to calculate the commissions earned by their sales forces. The calculations in the function example presented here are based on a sliding scale — employees who sell more earn a higher commission rate (see Table 23-1). For example, a salesperson with sales between $10,000 and $19,999 qualifies for a commission rate of 10.5 percent.

TABLE 23-1 COMMISSION RATES FOR MONTHLY SALES

Monthly Sales	Commission Rate
0 - $9,999	8.0%
$10,000 - $19,999	10.5%

Monthly Sales	Commission Rate
$20,000 - $39,999	12.0%
$40,000+	14.0%

There are several ways to calculate commissions for various sales amounts entered into a worksheet. You can use a complex formula with nested IF functions, such as the following:

```
=IF(AND(A1>=0,A1<=9999.99),A1*0.08,
IF(AND(A1>=10000,A1<=19999.99),A1*0.105,
IF(AND(A1>=20000,A1<=39999.99),A1*0.12,
IF(A1>=40000,A1*0.14,0))))
```

This may not be the best approach for a couple of reasons. First, the formula is overly complex, making it difficult to understand. Second, the values are hard-coded into the formula, making the formula difficult to modify. And if you have more than seven commission rates, you run up against Excel's limit on nested functions.

A better approach is to use a lookup table function to compute the commissions. For example:

```
=VLOOKUP(A1,Table,2)*A1
```

Using VLOOKUP is a good alternative, but it may not work if the commission structure is more complex. (See the following subsection, "A Function for a More Complex Commission Structure."). Yet another approach is to create a custom function.

A function for a simple commission structure

The COMMISSION function that follows accepts a single argument (Sales) and computes the commission amount.

```
Function COMMISSION(Sales)
'   Calculates sales commissions
    Const Tier1 As Double = 0.08
    Const Tier2 As Double = 0.105
    Const Tier3 As Double = 0.12
    Const Tier4 As Double = 0.14
    Select Case Sales
        Case 0 To 9999.99
            COMMISSION = Sales * Tier1
```

```
        Case 1000 To 19999.99
            COMMISSION = Sales * Tier2
        Case 20000 To 39999.99
            COMMISSION = Sales * Tier3
        Case Is >= 40000
            COMMISSION = Sales * Tier4
    End Select
End Function
```

The following worksheet formula, for example, returns 3,000 (the sales amount, 25,000, qualifies for a commission rate of 12 percent):

```
=COMMISSION(25000)
```

This function is very easy to understand and maintain. It uses constants to store the commission rates and a Select Case structure to determine which commission rate to use.

A function for a more complex commission structure

If the commission structure is more complex, you may need to use additional arguments for your COMMISSION function. Imagine that the aforementioned sales manager implements a new policy to help reduce turnover: The total commission paid increases by 1 percent for every year a salesperson stays with the company.

A modified COMMISSION function follows. This function now takes two arguments: the monthly sales (Sales) and the number of years employed (Years).

```
Function COMMISSION2(Sales, Years) As Single
'   Calculates sales commissions based on
'   years in service
    Const Tier1 As Double = 0.08
    Const Tier2 As Double = 0.105
    Const Tier3 As Double = 0.12
    Const Tier4 As Double = 0.14
    Select Case Sales
        Case 0 To 9999.99
            COMMISSION2 = Sales * Tier1
        Case 1000 To 19999.99
            COMMISSION2 = Sales * Tier2
        Case 20000 To 39999.99
            COMMISSION2 = Sales * Tier3
        Case Is >= 40000
            COMMISSION2 = Sales * Tier4
    End Select
    COMMISSION2 = COMMISSION2 + (COMMISSION2 * Years / 100)
End Function
```

Figure 23-3 shows the COMMISSION2 function in use. The formula in cell D2 is

```
=COMMISSION2(B2,C2)
```

	A	B	C	D	E
1	Sales Rep	Amount Sold	Years Employed	Commission	
2	Adams, Robert	5,010.54	1	404.85	
3	Baker, Sheila	9,833.91	0	786.71	
4	Clarke, Edward	12,500.32	2	1,338.78	
5	Davis, Don	35,988.22	3	4,448.14	
6	Elfin, Bill	41,822.99	3	6,030.88	
7	Franklin, Ben	8,090.32	1	653.70	
8	Gomez, Chris	11,098.32	2	1,188.63	
9	Harley, Mary	48,745.23	5	7,165.55	
10					
11					
12					

commission function.xls — Sheet1

Figure 23-3: Calculating sales commissions based on sales amount and years employed

The workbook shown in Figure 23-3 is available on the companion CD-ROM.

Text Manipulation Functions

Text strings can be manipulated with functions in a variety of ways, including reversing the display of a text string, scrambling the characters in a text string, or extracting specific characters from a text string. This section offers a number of function examples that manipulate text strings.

The companion CD-ROM contains a workbook that demonstrates all of the functions in this section.

Reversing a string

The REVERSETEXT function that follows returns the text in a cell backwards.

```
Function REVERSETEXT(text) As String
'    Returns its argument, reversed
     Dim TextLen As Integer
```

```
    Dim i As Integer
    TextLen = Len(text)
    For i = TextLen To 1 Step -1
        REVERSETEXT = REVERSETEXT & Mid(text, i, 1)
    Next i
End Function
```

The following formula, for example, returns *naivE*.

```
=REVERSETEXT("Evian")
```

The function uses a For-Next loop with a negative Step value. This causes the characters in the argument to process in reverse order. It uses the concatenation operator (&) to build the result string.

Scrambling text

The following function returns the contents of its argument randomized. For example, using *Microsoft* as the argument may return *oficMorts,* or some other random permutation.

```
Function SCRAMBLE(text)
'   Scrambles its single-cell argument
    Dim TextLen As Integer
    Dim i As Integer
    Dim RandPos As Integer
    Dim Char As String * 1
    Set text = text.Range("A1")
    TextLen = Len(text)
    For i = 1 To TextLen
        Char = Mid(text, i, 1)
        RandPos = Int((TextLen - 1 + 1) * Rnd + 1)
        Mid(text, i, 1) = Mid(text, RandPos, 1)
        Mid(text, RandPos, 1) = Char
    Next i
    SCRAMBLE = text
End Function
```

Returning an acronym

The ACRONYM function returns the first letter (in uppercase) of each word in its argument. For example, the following formula returns *IDG*.

```
=ACRONYM("International Data Group")
```

The listing for the ACRONYM Function procedure follows:

```
Function ACRONYM(text) As String
'    Returns an acronym for text
    Dim TextLen As Integer
    Dim i As Integer
    text = Application.Trim(text)
    TextLen = Len(text)
    ACRONYM = Left(text, 1)
    For i = 2 To TextLen
        If Mid(text, i, 1) = Chr(32) Then
            ACRONYM = ACRONYM & Mid(text, i + 1, 1)
        End If
    Next i
    ACRONYM = UCase(ACRONYM)
End Function
```

This function uses Excel's TRIM function to remove any extra spaces from the argument. The first character in the argument always is the first character in the result. The For-Next loop examines each character. If it's a space, then the character *after* the space is appended to the result. Finally, the result converts to uppercase using VBA's UCase function.

Does the text match a pattern?

The function that follows returns TRUE if a string matches a pattern composed of text and wildcard characters. The ISLIKE function is remarkably simple and is essentially a *wrapper* for VBA's useful Like operator.

```
Function ISLIKE(text As String, pattern As String) As Boolean
'    Returns true if the first argument is like the second

    ISLIKE = text Like pattern
End Function
```

Wildcard characters are * (matches any number of characters), ? (matches any single character), and # (matches any single digit). In addition, the pattern argument can consist of a list of characters enclosed in brackets.

The following formula returns TRUE because ? matches any single character. If the first argument were "Unit12", the function would return FALSE.

```
=ISLIKE("Unit1","Unit?")
```

The ISLIKE function also works with values. The following formula, for example, returns TRUE if cell A1 contains a value that begins with 1 and has exactly three numeric digits.

```
=ISLIKE(A1,"1##")
```

The following formula returns TRUE because the first argument is a single character contained in the list of characters specified in the second argument.

```
=ISLIKE("a","[aeiou]")
```

If the character list begins with an exclamation point (!), the comparison is made with characters *not* in the list. For example, the following formula returns TRUE because the first argument is a single character that does not appear in the second argument's list.

```
=ISLIKE("g","[!aeiou]")
```

Does a cell contain text?

Chapter 5 described how a number of Excel's worksheet functions are not reliable at times when dealing with text in a cell. The CELLHASTEXT function that follows returns TRUE if the cell argument contains text or contains a value formatted as Text.

```
Function CELLHASTEXT(cell) As Boolean
'    Returns TRUE if cell contains a string
'    or cell is formatted as Text
    Dim UpperLeft as Range
    CELLHASTEXT = False
    Set UpperLeft = cell.Range("A1")
    If UpperLeft.NumberFormat = "@" Then
        CELLHASTEXT = True
        Exit Function
    End If
    If Not IsNumeric(UpperLeft) Then
        CELLHASTEXT = True
        Exit Function
    End If
End Function
```

The following formula returns TRUE if cell A1 contains a text string or if the cell is formatted as Text.

```
=CELLHASTEXT(A1)
```

Extracting the nth element from a string

The EXTRACTELEMENT function is a custom worksheet function that extracts an element from a text string based on a specified separator character. Assume cell A1 contains the following text:

```
123-456-789-9133-8844
```

The following formula, for example, returns the string *9133* – the fourth element in the string. The string uses a hyphen (-) as the separator.

```
=EXTRACTELEMENT(A1,4,"-")
```

The EXTRACTELEMENT function uses three arguments:

- Txt: The text string from which you're extracting. This can be a literal string or a cell reference.

- *n*: An integer that represents the element to extract

- Separator: A single character used as the separator

If you specify a space as the Separator character, multiple spaces are treated as a single space (almost always what you want). If *n* exceeds the number of elements in the string, the function returns an empty string.

The VBA code for the EXTRACTELEMENT function follows:

```
Function EXTRACTELEMENT(Txt, n, Separator) As String
'   Returns the nth element of a text string, where the
'   elements are separated by a specified separator character

    Dim Txt1 As String, TempElement As String
    Dim ElementCount As Integer, i As Integer

    Txt1 = Txt
'   If space separator, remove excess spaces
    If Separator = Chr(32) Then Txt1 = Application.Trim(Txt1)

'   Add a separator to the end of the string
    If Right(Txt1, Len(Txt1)) <> Separator Then _
        Txt1 = Txt1 & Separator

'   Initialize
```

```
        ElementCount = 0
        TempElement = ""

'   Extract each element
    For i = 1 To Len(Txt1)
        If Mid(Txt1, i, 1) = Separator Then
            ElementCount = ElementCount + 1
            If ElementCount = n Then
'               Found it, so exit
                EXTRACTELEMENT = TempElement
                Exit Function
            Else
                TempElement = ""
            End If
        Else
            TempElement = TempElement & Mid(Txt1, i, 1)
        End If
    Next i
    EXTRACTELEMENT = ""
End Function
```

Spelling out a number

The SPELLDOLLARS function returns a number spelled out in text — as on a check. For example, the following formula returns the string *One hundred twenty-three and 45/100 dollars*.

```
=SPELLDOLLARS(123.45)
```

Figure 23-4 shows some additional examples of the SPELLDOLLARS function. Column C contains formulas that use the function. For example, the formula in C1 is:

```
=SPELLDOLLARS(A1)
```

Note that negative numbers are spelled out and enclosed in parentheses.

 The SPELLDOLLARS function is too lengthy to list here, but you can view the complete listing in the workbook on the companion CD-ROM.

	A	B	C	D	
1	32		Thirty-Two and 00/100 Dollars		
2	37.56		Thirty-Seven and 56/100 Dollars		
3	-32		(Thirty-Two and 00/100 Dollars)		
4	-26.44		(Twenty-Six and 44/100 Dollars)		
5	-4		(Four and 00/100 Dollars)		
6	1.56		One and 56/100 Dollars		
7	1		One and 00/100 Dollars		
8	6.56		Six and 56/100 Dollars		
9	12.12		Twelve and 12/100 Dollars		
10	1000000		One Million and 00/100 Dollars		
11	10000000000		Ten Billion and 00/100 Dollars		
12					

Figure 23-4: Examples of the SPELLDOLLARS function

Counting and Summing Functions

Chapter 7 contains many formula examples to count and sum cells based on various criteria. If you can't arrive at a formula-based solution for a counting or summing problem, it's likely that you can create a custom function. This section contains three functions that perform counting or summing.

The companion CD-ROM contains a workbook that demonstrates the functions in this section.

Counting cells between two values

The COUNTBETWEEN function accepts three arguments:

◆ *rng*: A range reference

◆ *num1*: The lower limit

◆ *num2*: The upper limit

The function returns the number of cells in rng that are greater than or equal to num1 and less than or equal to num2.

```
Function COUNTBETWEEN(rng, num1, num2)
'    Counts number of values between num1 and num2
    Dim CellCount As Integer
    Dim cell As Range
    Set rng = Intersect(rng.Parent.UsedRange, rng)
```

```
    CellCount = 0
    For Each cell In rng
        If cell.Value >= num1 And cell.Value <= num2 Then _
          CellCount = CellCount + 1
    Next cell
    COUNTBETWEEN = CellCount
End Function
```

The COUNTBETWEEN function uses the Intersect function to create a range limited to the sheet's used range. This is so the function won't have to process cells in the sheet's unused area (particularly important if the range argument consists of an entire column, for example).

Counting visible cells in a range

The COUNTVISIBLE function that follows accepts a range argument and returns the number of visible cells in the range. A cell is not visible if it resides in a hidden row or a hidden column.

```
Function COUNTVISIBLE(rng)
'    Counts visible cells
    Dim CellCount As Long
    Dim cell As Range
    Application.Volatile
    CellCount = 0
    Set rng = Intersect(rng.Parent.UsedRange, rng)
    For Each cell In rng
        If Not IsEmpty(cell) Then
            If Not cell.EntireRow.Hidden And _
                Not cell.EntireColumn.Hidden Then _
                CellCount = CellCount + 1
        End If
    Next cell
    COUNTVISIBLE = CellCount
End Function
```

This function loops though each cell in the range and first checks to see if the cell is empty. If it's not empty, then it checks the Hidden properties of the cell's row and column. If either the row or column is hidden, then the CellCount variable increments.

The COUNTVISIBLE function is useful when you work with AutoFilters or outlines. Both of these features make use of hidden rows. Hiding and unhiding rows and columns do not trigger a worksheet recalculation. Therefore, you may need to press Ctrl+Alt+F9 to force a complete recalculation.

> Excel's SUBTOTAL function (with a first argument of 2 or 3) is also useful for counting visible cells in an AutoFiltered list. The SUBTOTAL function, however, doesn't work properly if cells are hidden in a non-filtered list.

Summing visible cells in a range

The SUMVISIBLE function is based on the COUNTVISIBLE function in the previous section. This function accepts a range argument and returns the sum of the visible cells in the range. A cell is not visible if it resides in a hidden row or a hidden column.

```
Function SUMVISIBLE(rng)
'   Sums only visible cells
    Dim CellSum As Long
    Dim cell As Range
    Application.Volatile
    CellSum = 0
    Set rng = Intersect(rng.Parent.UsedRange, rng)
    For Each cell In rng
        If IsNumeric(cell) Then
            If Not cell.EntireRow.Hidden And _
              Not cell.EntireColumn.Hidden Then _
              CellSum = CellSum + cell
        End If
    Next cell
    SUMVISIBLE = CellSum
End Function
```

Hiding or unhiding rows and columns does not trigger a worksheet recalculation. Therefore, you may need to press Ctrl+Alt+F9 to force a complete recalculation.

> Excel's SUBTOTAL function (with a first argument of 9) is also useful for summing visible cells in an AutoFiltered list. The SUBTOTAL function, however, doesn't work properly if cells are hidden in a non-filtered list.

Date Functions

Chapter 6 presented a number of useful Excel functions and formulas for calculating dates, times, and time periods by manipulating date and time serial values. This section presents additional functions that deal with dates.

The companion CD-ROM contains a workbook that demonstrates the Date functions presented in this section.

Calculating the next Monday

The NEXTMONDAY function that follows accepts a date argument and returns the date of the following Monday.

```
Function NEXTMONDAY(d As Date) As Date
    Dim TestDay As Date
    TestDay = d + 1
    Do Until WeekDay(TestDay) = 2
        TestDay = TestDay + 1
    Loop
    NEXTMONDAY = TestDay
End Function
```

This function uses VBA's WeekDay function, which returns an integer that represents the day of the week for a date (1 = Sunday, 2 = Monday, and so on).

The following formula returns 12/27/99 — the first Monday after Christmas day, 1999 (which is a Saturday):

```
=NEXTMONDAY(DATE(1999,12,25))
```

Calculating the next day of the week

The NEXTDAY function, which follows, is a variation on the NEXTMONDAY function. This function accepts two arguments: a date and an integer between 1 and 7 that represents a day of the week (1 = Sunday, 2 = Monday, and so on). The NEXTDAY function returns the date for the next specified day of the week.

```
Function NEXTDAY(d As Date, day As Integer) As Variant
'   Returns the next specified day
    Dim TestDay As Date
```

```
'   Make sure day is between 1 and 7
    If day < 1 Or day > 7 Then
        NEXTDAY = CVErr(xlErrNA)
        Exit Function
    End If

    TestDay = d + 1
    Do Until WeekDay(TestDay) = day
        TestDay = TestDay + 1
    Loop
    NEXTDAY = TestDay
End Function
```

Which week of the month?

The MONTHWEEK function that follows returns an integer that corresponds to the week of the month for a date.

```
Function MONTHWEEK(d As Date) As Variant
'   Returns the week of the month for a date
    Dim FirstDay As Integer

'   Check for valid date argument
    If Not IsDate(d) Then
        MONTHWEEK = CVErr(xlErrNA)
        Exit Function
    End If

'   Get first day of the month
    FirstDay = WeekDay(DateSerial(Year(d), Month(d), 1))

'   Calculate the week number
    MONTHWEEK = Application.RoundUp((FirstDay + day(d) - 1) / 7, 0)
End Function
```

Working with dates before 1900

Many users are surprised to discover that Excel cannot work with dates prior to the year 1900. To correct this deficiency, I created an add-in called Extended Date Functions. This add-in enables you to work with dates in the years 0100 through 9999.

The companion CD-ROM contains a copy of the Extended Date Functions add-in.

When installed, the Extended Date Function add-in gives you access to eight new worksheet functions:

- ◆ XDATE(y,m,d,fmt): Returns a date for a given year, month, and day. As an option, you can provide a date formatting string.

- ◆ XDATEADD(xdate1,days,fmt): Adds a specified number of days to a date. As an option, you can provide a date formatting string.

- ◆ XDATEDIF(xdate1,xdate2): Returns the number of days between two dates.

- ◆ XDATEYEARDIF(xdate1,xdate2): Returns the number of full years between two dates (useful for calculating ages).

- ◆ XDATEYEAR(xdate1): Returns the year of a date.

- ◆ XDATEMONTH(xdate1): Returns the month of a date.

- ◆ XDATEDAY(xdate1): Returns the day of a date.

- ◆ XDATEDOW(xdate1): Returns the day of the week of a date (as an integer between 1 and 7).

These functions do not make any adjustments for changes made to the calendar in 1582. Consequently, working with dates prior to October 15, 1582 may not yield correct results.

Returning the Last Nonempty Cell in a Column or Row

This section presents two useful functions: LASTINCOLUMN, which returns the contents of the last nonempty cell in a column, and LASTINROW, which returns the contents of the last nonempty cell in a row. Chapter 13 presented array formulas for this task, but you may prefer to use a custom function.

The companion CD-ROM contains a workbook that demonstrates the functions presented in this section.

Each of these functions accepts a range as its single argument. The range argument can be a column reference (for LASTINCOLUMN) or a row reference (for LASTINROW). If the supplied argument is not a complete column or row reference (such as 3:3 or D:D), the function uses the column or row of the upper-left cell in the range. For example, the following formula returns the contents of the last nonempty cell in column B:

=LASTINCOLUMN(B5)

The following formula returns the contents of the last nonempty cell in row 7:

=LASTINROW(C7:D9)

These functions are quite fast because they examine only the cells in the intersection of the specified column or row and the worksheet's used range.

The LASTINCOLUMN function

The LASTINCOLUMN function follows:

```
Function LASTINCOLUMN(rng As Range)
    Dim WorkRange As Range
    Dim i As Integer, CellCount As Integer
    Application.Volatile
    Set WorkRange = rng.Columns(1).EntireColumn
    Set WorkRange = Intersect(WorkRange.Parent.UsedRange, _
        WorkRange)
    CellCount = WorkRange.Count
    For i = CellCount To 1 Step -1
        If Not IsEmpty(WorkRange(i)) Then
            LASTINCOLUMN = WorkRange(i).Value
            Exit Function
        End If
    Next i
End Function
```

The LASTINROW Function

The LASTINROW function follows:

```
Function LASTINROW(rng As Range) As Variant
    Dim WorkRange As Range
    Dim i As Integer, CellCount As Integer
    Application.Volatile
    Set WorkRange = rng.Rows(1).EntireRow
    Set WorkRange = Intersect(WorkRange.Parent.UsedRange, _
      WorkRange)
    CellCount = WorkRange.Count
    For i = CellCount To 1 Step -1
        If Not IsEmpty(WorkRange(i)) Then
            LASTINROW = WorkRange(i).Value
            Exit Function
        End If
    Next i
End Function
```

Multisheet Functions

You may need to create a function that works with data contained in more than one worksheet within a workbook. This section contains two VBA functions that enable you to work with data across multiple sheets, including a function that overcomes an Excel limitation when copying formulas to other sheets.

 The companion CD-ROM contains a workbook that demonstrates the multisheet functions presented in this section.

Returning the maximum value across all worksheets

If you need to determine the maximum value in a cell (for example, B1) across a number of worksheets, use a formula such as this:

```
=MAX(Sheet1:Sheet4!B1)
```

This formula returns the maximum value in cell B1 for Sheet1, Sheet4, and all of the sheets in between. But what if you add a new sheet (Sheet5) after Sheet4? Your formula doesn't adjust automatically, so you need to edit it to include the new sheet reference:

```
=MAX(Sheet1:Sheet5!B1)
```

The function that follows accepts a single-cell argument, and returns the maximum value in that cell across all worksheets in the workbook. The following formula, for example, returns the maximum value in cell B1 for all sheets in the workbook.

```
=MAXALLSHEETS(B1)
```

If you add a new sheet, you do not need to edit the formula.

```
Function MAXALLSHEETS(cell)
    Dim MaxVal As Double
    Dim Addr As String
    Dim Wksht As Object
    Application.Volatile
    Addr = cell.Range("A1").Address
    MaxVal = -9.9E+307
    For Each Wksht In cell.Parent.Parent.Worksheets
        If Wksht.Name = cell.Parent.Name And _
          Addr = Application.Caller.Address Then
        ' avoid circular reference
        Else
            If IsNumeric(Wksht.Range(Addr)) Then
                If Wksht.Range(Addr) > MaxVal Then _
                  MaxVal = Wksht.Range(Addr).Value
            End If
        End If
    Next Wksht
    If MaxVal = -9.9E+307 Then MaxVal = 0
    MAXALLSHEETS = MaxVal
End Function
```

The For Each statement uses the following expression to access the workbook:

```
cell.Parent.Parent.Worksheets
```

The parent of the cell is a worksheet, and the parent of the worksheet is the workbook. Therefore, the For Each-Next loop cycles among all worksheets in the workbook. The first If statement inside of the loop performs a check to see if the cell being checked is the cell that contains the function. If so, that cell is ignored to avoid a circular reference error.

 You can modify the MAXALLSHEETS function easily to perform other cross-worksheet calculations: Minimum, Average, Sum, and so on.

The SHEETOFFSET function

A recurring complaint about Excel is its poor support for relative sheet references. For example, suppose you have a multisheet workbook, and you enter a formula such as this on Sheet2:

=Sheet1!A1+1

This formula works fine. However, if you copy the formula to the next sheet (Sheet3), the formula continues to refer to Sheet1. Or, if you insert a sheet between Sheet1 and Sheet2, the formula continues to refer to Sheet1 (most likely, you want it to refer to the newly inserted sheet). In fact, you cannot create formulas that re-fer to worksheets in a relative manner. However, you can use the SHEETOFFSET function to overcome this limitation.

THE SHEETOFFSET FUNCTION: TAKE ONE

Following is a VBA Function procedure named SHEETOFFSET.

```
Function SHEETOFFSET(offset, ref)
'    Returns cell contents at ref, in sheet offset
    Application.Volatile
    SHEETOFFSET = Sheets(Application.Caller.Parent.Index _
      + offset).Range(ref.Address)
End Function
```

The SHEETOFFSET function accepts two arguments:

◆ *offset*: The sheet offset, which can be positive, negative, or 0.

◆ *ref*: A single-cell reference. If the *offset* argument is 0, the cell reference must not be the same as the cell that contains the formula. If so, you get a circular reference error.

The following formula returns the value in cell A1 of the sheet before the sheet that contains the formula:

```
=SHEETOFFSET(-1,A1)
```

The following formula returns the value in cell A1 of the sheet after the sheet that contains the formula:

```
=SHEETOFFSET(1,A1)
```

This function works fine in most cases. For example, you can copy the formula to other sheets and the relative referencing will be in effect in all of the copied formulas. And, if you insert a worksheet, the sheet reference adjusts automatically.

But this function has a problem: If your workbook contains non-worksheet sheets (that is, chart sheets or Excel 5 dialog sheets), the function fails because it looks for a cell that doesn't exist.

THE SHEETOFFSET FUNCTION: TAKE TWO

You can, nevertheless, use an improved version of the SHEETOFFSET function. This version of the function uses a second function named WorksheetIndex. The WorksheetIndex function returns the worksheet index for a Worksheet object passed as an argument. It then uses the value to identify another worksheet. This version of SHEETOFFSET, which follows, essentially ignores any non-worksheet sheets in the workbook.

```
Function SHEETOFFSET(offset, Ref)
'   Returns cell contents at Ref, in sheet offset
    Dim WksIndex As Integer
    Application.Volatile
    WksIndex = WorksheetIndex(Application.Caller.Parent)
    SHEETOFFSET = Worksheets(WksIndex + offset).Range(Ref.Address)
End Function


Private Function WorksheetIndex(x As Worksheet) As Integer
'   Returns the Worksheets (not Sheets) Index
    Dim Wks As Worksheet, WksNum As Integer
    WksNum = 1
    For Each Wks In x.Parent.Worksheets
        If x.Name = Wks.Name Then
            WorksheetIndex = WksNum
            Exit Function
        End If
        WksNum = WksNum + 1
    Next Wks
```

```
End Function
```

Notice that because the WorksheetIndex function is not designed for use in a formula, it is declared with the Private keyword. Doing so prevents it from appearing in the Paste Function dialog box.

Advanced Function Techniques

Now, let's turn to some even more advanced functions. The examples in this section demonstrate some special techniques you can use with your custom functions.

◆ Returning an error value from a function

◆ Returning an array from a function

◆ Using optional function arguments

◆ Using an indefinite number of function arguments

◆ Using Windows API functions

Returning an error value

In some cases, you might want your custom function to return a particular error value. Consider the REVERSETEXT function, which I presented earlier in this chapter.

```
Function REVERSETEXT(text) As String
'    Returns its argument, reversed
    Dim TextLen As Integer
    Dim i As Integer
    TextLen = Len(text)
    For i = TextLen To 1 Step -1
        REVERSETEXT = REVERSETEXT & Mid(text, i, 1)
    Next i
End Function
```

This function reverses the contents of its single-cell argument (which can be text or a value). If the argument is a multicell range, the function returns #VALUE! Assume that you want this function to work only with strings. If the argument doesn't contain a string, you want the function to return an error value (#N/A).

You might be tempted to simply assign a string that looks like an Excel formula error value. For example:

```
REVERSETEXT = "#N/A"
```

Although the string *looks* like an error value, it is not treated as such by other formulas that may reference it. To return a *real* error value from a function, use VBA's CVErr function, which converts an error number to a real error.

Fortunately, VBA has built-in constants for the errors that you want to return from a custom function. These constants are listed here:

- ◆ xlErrDiv0
- ◆ xlErrNA
- ◆ xlErrName
- ◆ xlErrNull
- ◆ xlErrNum
- ◆ xlErrRef
- ◆ xlErrValue

The revised REVERSETEXT function follows:

```
Function REVERSETEXT(text) As Variant
'    Returns its argument, reversed
    Dim TextLen As Integer
    Dim i As Integer
    If Not IsNumeric(text) Then
        TextLen = Len(text)
        For i = TextLen To 1 Step -1
            REVERSETEXT = REVERSETEXT & Mid(text, i, 1)
        Next i
    Else
        REVERSETEXT = CVErr(xlErrNA)
    End If
End Function
```

This function uses VBA's IsNumeric function to determine if the argument is not numeric (i.e., contains text). If so, the function proceeds normally. If the cell doesn't contain text, the function returns the #N/A error.

The data type for the function's return value was changed to variant because the function now can return something other than a string.

Returning an array from a function

Most functions that you develop with VBA return a single value. It's possible, however, to write a function that returns multiple values in an array.

Part III deals with arrays and array formulas. Specifically, these chapters provide examples of a single formula that returns multiple values in separate cells. As you'll see, you can also create custom functions that return arrays.

VBA includes a useful function called Array. The Array function returns a variant that contains an array. It's important to understand that the array returned is not the same as a normal array composed of elements of the variant type. In other words, a variant array is not the same as an array of variants.

If you're familiar with using array formulas in Excel, you have a head start understanding VBA's Array function. You enter an array formula into a cell by pressing Ctrl+Shift+Enter. Excel inserts brackets around the formula to indicate that it's an array formula. See Chapter 12 for more details on array formulas.

The lower bound of an array created by using the Array function is always 0. Unlike other types of arrays, it is not affected by the lower bound specified with the Option Base statement.

The MONTHNAMES function that follows demonstrates how to return an array from a Function procedure.

```
Function MONTHNAMES() As Variant
    MONTHNAMES = Array( _
        "Jan", "Feb", "Mar", "Apr", _
        "May", "Jun", "Jul", "Aug", _
        "Sep", "Oct", "Nov", "Dec")
End Function
```

Figure 23-5 shows a worksheet that uses the MONTHNAMES function. You enter the function by selecting A1:L1, and then entering the following formula:

```
{=MONTHNAMES()}
```

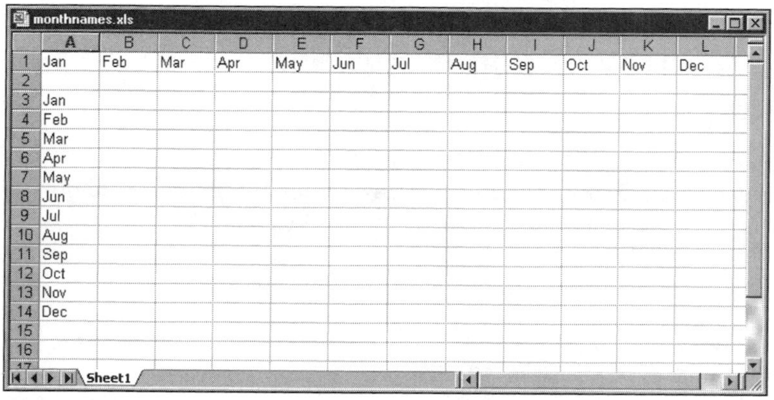

Figure 23-5: The MONTHNAMES function entered as an array formula

> **NOTE** As with any array formula, you must press Ctrl+Shift+Enter to enter the formula. Do not enter the brackets. Excel inserts the brackets for you.

The MONTHNAMES function, as written, returns a horizontal array in a single row. To display the array in a vertical range in a single column (as in A3:A14 in Figure 23-5), select the range and enter the following formula:

```
{=TRANSPOSE(MONTHNAMES())}
```

Alternatively, you can modify the function so it does the transposition. The following function uses Excel's TRANSPOSE function to return a vertical array.

```
Function VMONTHNAMES() As Variant
    VMONTHNAMES = Application.Transpose(Array( _
        "Jan", "Feb", "Mar", "Apr", _
        "May", "Jun", "Jul", "Aug", _
        "Sep", "Oct", "Nov", "Dec"))
End Function
```

A workbook that demonstrates MONTHNAMES and VMONTHNAMES is available on the companion CD-ROM.

Returning an array of nonduplicated random integers

The RANDOMINTEGERS function returns an array of nonduplicated integers. The function is intended to be used in a multicell array formula. Figure 23-6 shows a worksheet that uses the following formula in the range A1:D10.

```
{=RANDOMINTEGERS()}
```

	A	B	C	D	E	F	G
1	39	37	10	30			
2	36	19	9	8			
3	13	21	18	7			
4	12	34	40	20			
5	35	16	33	31			
6	17	22	11	2			
7	32	24	14	23			
8	4	25	28	6			
9	1	27	38	26			
10	15	5	29	3			
11							
12							

Figure 23-6: An array formula generates nonduplicated consecutive integers, arranged randomly.

This formula was entered into the entire range using Ctrl+Shift+Enter. The formula returns an array of nonduplicated integers, arranged randomly. Because 40 cells contain the formula, the integers range from 1 to 40. The code for RANDOM-INTEGERS follows:

```
Function RANDOMINTEGERS()
    Dim FuncRange As Range
    Dim V() As Variant, ValArray() As Variant
    Dim CellCount As Double
    Dim i As Integer, j As Integer
    Dim r As Integer, c As Integer
    Dim Temp1 As Variant, Temp2 As Variant
    Dim RCount As Integer, CCount As Integer
```

```vba
    Randomize

'   Create Range object
    Set FuncRange = Application.Caller

'   Return an error if FuncRange is too large
    CellCount = FuncRange.Count
    If CellCount > 1000 Then
        RANDOMINTEGERS = CVErr(xlErrNA)
        Exit Function
    End If

'   Assign variables
    RCount = FuncRange.Rows.Count
    CCount = FuncRange.Columns.Count
    ReDim V(1 To RCount, 1 To CCount)
    ReDim ValArray(1 To 2, 1 To CellCount)

'   Fill array with random numbers
'   and consecutive integers
    For i = 1 To CellCount
        ValArray(1, i) = Rnd
        ValArray(2, i) = i
    Next i

'   Sort ValArray by the random number dimension
    For i = 1 To CellCount
        For j = i + 1 To CellCount
            If ValArray(1, i) > ValArray(1, j) Then
                Temp1 = ValArray(1, j)
                Temp2 = ValArray(2, j)
                ValArray(1, j) = ValArray(1, i)
                ValArray(2, j) = ValArray(2, i)
                ValArray(1, i) = Temp1
                ValArray(2, i) = Temp2
            End If
        Next j
    Next i

'   Put the randomized values into the V array
    i = 0
    For r = 1 To RCount
        For c = 1 To CCount
            i = i + 1
            V(r, c) = ValArray(2, i)
```

```
        Next c
    Next r
    RANDOMINTEGERS = V
End Function
```

 This workbook containing the RANDOMINTEGERS function is available on the companion CD-ROM.

Randomizing a range

The RANGERANDOMIZE function that follows accepts a range argument and returns an array that consists of the input range – in random order.

```
Function RANGERANDOMIZE(rng)
    Dim V() As Variant, ValArray() As Variant
    Dim CellCount As Double
    Dim i As Integer, j As Integer
    Dim r As Integer, c As Integer
    Dim Temp1 As Variant, Temp2 As Variant
    Dim RCount As Integer, CCount As Integer
    Randomize

'   Return an error if rng is too large
    CellCount = rng.Count
    If CellCount > 1000 Then
        RANGERANDOMIZE = CVErr(xlErrNA)
        Exit Function
    End If

'   Assign variables
    RCount = rng.Rows.Count
    CCount = rng.Columns.Count
    ReDim V(1 To RCount, 1 To CCount)
    ReDim ValArray(1 To 2, 1 To CellCount)

'   Fill ValArray with random numbers
'   and values from rng
    For i = 1 To CellCount
        ValArray(1, i) = Rnd
        ValArray(2, i) = rng(i)
    Next i
```

```
'    Sort ValArray by the random number dimension
     For i = 1 To CellCount
         For j = i + 1 To CellCount
             If ValArray(1, i) > ValArray(1, j) Then
                 Temp1 = ValArray(1, j)
                 Temp2 = ValArray(2, j)
                 ValArray(1, j) = ValArray(1, i)
                 ValArray(2, j) = ValArray(2, i)
                 ValArray(1, i) = Temp1
                 ValArray(2, i) = Temp2
             End If
         Next j
     Next i

'    Put the randomized values into the V array
     i = 0
     For r = 1 To RCount
         For c = 1 To CCount
             i = i + 1
             V(r, c) = ValArray(2, i)
         Next c
     Next r
     RANGERANDOMIZE = V
End Function
```

The code closely resembles that for the RANDOMINTEGERS function. Figure 23-7 shows the function in use. The array formula in C2:C11 is:

```
{=RANGERANDOMIZE(A2:A11)}
```

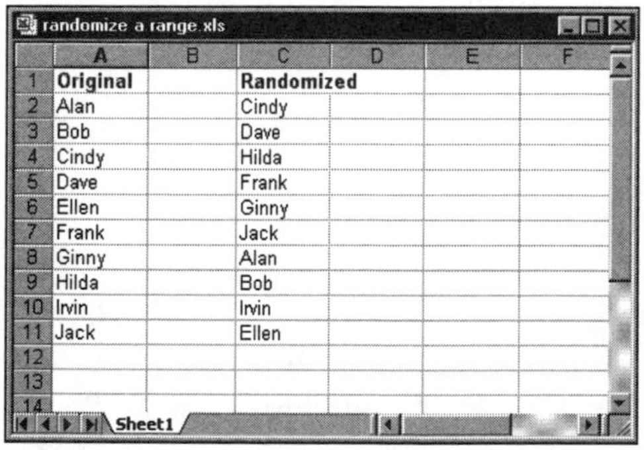

Figure 23-7: The RANGERANDOMIZE function returns the contents of a range, in random order.

This formula returns the contents of A2:A11, but in random order.

 The workbook containing the RANGERANDOMIZE function is available on the companion CD-ROM.

Using optional arguments

Many of Excel's built-in worksheet functions use optional arguments. For example, the LEFT function returns characters from the left side of a string. Its official syntax is:

```
LEFT(text,num_chars)
```

The first argument is required, but the second is optional. If you omit the optional argument, Excel assumes a value of 1.

Custom functions that you develop in VBA also can have optional arguments. You specify an optional argument by preceding the argument's name with the keyword *Optional*. Following is a simple function that returns the user's name.

```
Function USER()
    USER = Application.UserName
End Function
```

Suppose that, in some cases, you want the user's name to be returned in uppercase letters. The following function uses an optional argument.

```
Function USER(Optional UpperCase As Boolean)
    If IsMissing(UpperCase) Then UpperCase = False
    If UpperCase Then
        USER = Ucase(Application.UserName)
    Else
        USER = Application.UserName
    End If
End Function
```

If the argument is False or omitted, the user's name is returned without any changes. If the argument is True, then the user's name converts to uppercase (using VBA's Ucase function) before it is returned. Notice that the first statement in the procedure uses the IsMissing function to determine if the argument was supplied or not. If the argument is missing, the statement sets the UpperCase variable to False (the default value).

All of the following formulas are valid (and the first two have the same effect):

```
=USER()
=USER(False)
=USER(True)
```

Using an indefinite number of arguments

Some of Excel's worksheet functions take an indefinite number of arguments. A familiar example is the SUM function, which has the following syntax:

```
SUM(number1,number2...)
```

The first argument is required, but you can have as many as 29 additional arguments. Here's an example of a formula that uses the SUM function with four range arguments:

```
=SUM(A1:A5,C1:C5,E1:E5,G1:G5)
```

You can mix and match the argument types. For example, the following example uses three arguments: a range, followed by a value, and finally an expression.

```
=SUM(A1:A5,12,24*3)
```

You can create function procedures that have an indefinite number of arguments. The trick is to use an array as the last (or only) argument, preceded by the keyword *ParamArray*.

 ParamArray can apply only to the *last* argument in the procedure. It is always a variant data type, and it is always an optional argument (although you don't use the Optional keyword).

A SIMPLE EXAMPLE OF INDEFINITE ARGUMENTS

A Function procedure that can have any number of single-value arguments follows. It simply returns the sum of the arguments.

```
Function SIMPLESUM(ParamArray arglist() As Variant) As Double
    For Each arg In arglist
        SIMPLESUM = SIMPLESUM + arg
    Next arg
End Function
```

The following formula returns the sum of the single-cell arguments:

```
=SIMPLESUM(A1,A5,12)
```

The most serious limitation of the SIMPLESUM function is that it doesn't handle multicell ranges. This improved version does:

```
Function SIMPLESUM(ParamArray arglist() As Variant) As Double
    For Each arg In arglist
        If TypeName(arg) = "Range" Then
            For Each cell In arg
                SIMPLESUM = SIMPLESUM + cell
            Next cell
        Else
            SIMPLESUM = SIMPLESUM + arg
        End If
    Next arg
End Function
```

This function checks each entry in the Arglist array. If the entry is a range, then the code uses a For Each-Next loop to sum the cells in the range.

Even this improved version certainly is not a substitute for Excel's SUM function. Try it out using various types of arguments and you'll see that it fails unless each argument is a value or a range reference. Also, if an argument consists of an entire column, you'll find that the function is *very* slow since it evaluates every cell – even the empty ones.

EMULATING EXCEL'S SUM FUNCTION

This section presents a Function procedure called MYSUM. Unlike the SIMPLESUM function listed in the previous section, MYSUM emulates Excel's SUM function perfectly.

Before you look at the code for the MYSUM function, take a minute to think about Excel's SUM function. This very versatile function can have any number of arguments (even "missing" arguments), and the arguments can be numerical values, cells, ranges, text representations of numbers, logical values, and even embedded functions. For example, consider the following formula:

```
=SUM(A1,5,"6",,TRUE,SQRT(4),B1:B5)
```

This formula – which is a valid formula – contains all of the following types of arguments, listed here in the order of their presentation:

◆ A single cell reference (A1)

◆ A literal value (5)

- ◆ A string that looks like a value ("6")

- ◆ A missing argument

- ◆ A logical value (TRUE)

- ◆ An expression that uses another function (SQRT)

- ◆ A range reference (B1:B5)

Following is the listing for the MYSUM function that handles all these argument types.

```
Function MYSUM(ParamArray n() As Variant) As Variant
' Emulates Excel's SUM function
  Dim i As Integer
  Dim TmpRng As Range
  Dim cell As Range
  Dim ErrCode As String
  MYSUM = 0
' Process each iument
  For i = 0 To UBound(n)
'    Skip missing iuments
    If Not IsMissing(n(i)) Then
'        What type of argument is it?
        Select Case TypeName(n(i))

            Case "Range"
'               Create temp range to handle full row/column args
                Set TmpRng = Intersect(n(i).Parent.UsedRange, n(i))
                For Each cell In TmpRng
                    If Application.IsError(cell) Then
                        ErrCode = CStr(cell)
                        MYSUM = CVErr(Right(ErrCode, Len(ErrCode) _
                            - InStr(ErrCode, " ")))
                        Exit Function
                    End If
                    If cell = True Or cell = False Then
                        MYSUM = MYSUM + 0
                    Else
                        If IsNumeric(cell) Then MYSUM = MYSUM + cell
                    End If
                Next cell

            Case "Error" 'return the error
                MYSUM = n(i)
```

```
            Exit Function

        Case Else
'            Check for literal TRUE and compensate
            If n(i) = "True" Then MYSUM = MYSUM + 2
            MYSUM = MYSUM + n(i)
        End Select
    End If
  Next i
End Function
```

 A workbook containing the MYSUM function is available on the companion CD-ROM.

As you study the code for MYSUM, keep the following points in mind:

◆ Missing arguments (determined by the IsMissing function) are simply ignored.

◆ The procedure uses VBA's TypeName function to determine the type of argument. Each argument type is handled differently.

◆ For a range argument, the function loops through each cell in the range and adds its value to a running total.

◆ The data type for the function is a variant because the function needs to return an error if any of its arguments is an error value.

◆ If an argument contains an error (for example, #DIV0!), the MYSUM function simply returns the error—just like Excel's SUM function.

◆ Excel's SUM function considers a text string to have a value of 0 unless it appears as a literal argument (an actual value, not a variable). Therefore, MYSUM adds the cell's value only if it can be evaluated as a number. (VBA's IsNumeric function is used for this.)

◆ Dealing with Boolean arguments is tricky. For MYSUM to emulate SUM exactly, it needs to test for a literal TRUE in the argument list and compensate for the difference (that is, add 2 to –1 to get 1).

◆ For range arguments, the function uses the Intersect function to create a temporary range that consists of the intersection of the range and the sheet's used range. This handles cases in which a range argument consists of a complete row or column, which takes forever to evaluate.

You may wonder about the relative speeds of SUM and MYSUM. MYSUM, of course, is much slower, but just how much slower depends on the speed of your system and the formulas themselves. On one system, a worksheet with 1,000 SUM formulas recalculates instantly. After replacing the SUM functions with MYSUM functions, it takes about 12 seconds. MYSUM may be improved a bit, but it can never come close to SUM's speed.

The point of this example is not to create a new SUM function. Rather, it demonstrates how to create custom worksheet functions that look and work like those built into Excel.

Using Windows API Functions

VBA can borrow procedures from other files that have nothing to do with Excel or VBA — for example, the Dynamic Link Library (DLL) files that Windows and other software use. As a result, you can do things with VBA that otherwise would be outside the language's scope.

The examples in this section require 32-bit Excel — Excel 95 or later. They do not work with earlier versions of Excel.

The Windows API (Application Programming Interface) is a set of functions available to Windows programmers. When you call a Windows function from VBA, you access the Windows API. Many of the Windows resources used by Windows programmers are available in DLLs, which store programs and functions and are linked at run-time rather than at compile time.

Before you can use a Windows API function, you must declare the function at the top of a standard VBA module, above the first procedure. Declaring an API function is a bit tricky; you must declare it precisely. The declaration statement tells VBA:

◆ Which API function you use

◆ In which library the API function is located

◆ The API function's arguments

After you declare an API function, you can use it in your VBA code.

The subsections that follow present several VBA functions that make use of Windows API functions.

When debugging functions that use API calls, system crashes are not uncommon. Therefore, make sure you save your work frequently.

Determining the current video mode

The following function example uses Windows API calls to determine a system's current video mode (resolution). The VIDEO function takes one argument: a string, either *width* or *height*.

```
'API declaration
Declare Function GetSystemMetrics Lib "user32" _
  (ByVal nIndex As Long) As Long

Public Const SM_CXSCREEN = 0
Public Const SM_CYSCREEN = 1

Function VIDEO(dimension)
    Select Case UCase(dimension)
        Case "HEIGHT"
            VIDEO = GetSystemMetrics(SM_CYSCREEN)
        Case "WIDTH"
            VIDEO = GetSystemMetrics(SM_CXSCREEN)
        Case Else
            VIDEO = CVErr(xlErrNA)
    End Select
End Function
```

The following formulas demonstrate the VIDEO function:

```
=VIDEO("height")
=VIDEO("width")
```

The companion CD-ROM contains a workbook that demonstrates the VIDEO function.

Getting disk information

In some cases, you might need to know about the disk drives attached to the system. The Function procedure examples in this section make use of Windows API functions to determine a variety of useful information about storage devices. The VBA functions in this section use two API calls. The declarations are listed here:

```
Private Declare Function GetDRIVETYPE32 Lib "kernel32" _
  Alias "GetDRIVETYPEA" (ByVal nDrive As String) As Long

Private Declare Function GetLogicalDriveStrings _
  Lib "kernel32" Alias "GetLogicalDriveStringsA" (ByVal _
  nBufferLength As Long, ByVal lpBuffer As String) As Long
```

THE DRIVEEXISTS FUNCTION

The following function takes one argument (a drive letter) and returns TRUE if the specified drive exists.

```
Function DRIVEEXISTS(DriveLetter As String) As Boolean
'    Returns True if a specified drive letter exists
    Dim Buffer As String * 255
    Dim BuffLen As Long
    Dim DLetter As String * 1
    Dim i As Integer

    DLetter = Left(DriveLetter, 1)
    BuffLen = GetLogicalDriveStrings(Len(Buffer), Buffer)

    DRIVEEXISTS = False
'    Search for the string
    For i = 1 To BuffLen
        If Ucase(Mid(Buffer, i, 1)) = Ucase(DLetter) Then
'            Found it
            DRIVEEXISTS = True
            Exit Function
        End If
    Next i
End Function
```

The following formula returns TRUE if drive E exists, and FALSE if it does not exist:

```
=DRIVEEXISTS("E")
```

THE DRIVETYPE FUNCTION

The DRIVETYPE function that follows takes one argument (a drive letter) and returns one of the following strings that describes the type of drive: *Local, Removable, Fixed, Remote, CD-ROM, RAM Disk,* or *Unknown Drive Type.*

```
Function DRIVETYPE(DriveLetter As String) As String
'    Returns a string that describes the drive type
     Dim DLetter As String * 2
     Dim DriveCode As Integer

     DLetter = Left(DriveLetter, 1) & ":"
     DriveCode = GetDriveType32(DLetter)

     Select Case DriveCode
         Case 1: DRIVETYPE = "Local"
         Case 2: DRIVETYPE = "Removable"
         Case 3: DRIVETYPE = "Fixed"
         Case 4: DRIVETYPE = "Remote"
         Case 5: DRIVETYPE = "CD-ROM"
         Case 6: DRIVETYPE = "RAM Disk"
         Case Else: DRIVETYPE = "Unknown Drive Type"
     End Select
End Function
```

The following formula returns a string that describes drive D. For example, if drive D is a CD-ROM, the formula returns *CD-ROM*.

```
=DRIVETYPE("D")
```

The preceding formula returns *Local* for a drive letter that doesn't exist. Therefore, you can use the following formula to test for the existence of the drive letter. This formula returns NA if drive D does not exist; otherwise it returns the drive type.

```
=IF(DRIVEEXISTS("D"),DRIVETYPE("D"),NA())
```

 The companion CD-ROM contains a workbook that demonstrates the DRI-VEEXISTS and DRIVETYPE functions.

Summary

This chapter presented many examples of custom VBA Function procedures that you can use in your worksheet formulas. You can use many of these functions as-is. You may need to adapt others to suit your specific needs.

Appendix A

Working with Imported 1-2-3 Files

Lotus 1-2-3 used to be the leading spreadsheet. That distinction, of course, now belongs to Excel. Many users, however, continue to use 1-2-3. You may be in a position in which you need to import a file generated by 1-2-3. If so, the information in this appendix may be helpful to you.

About 1-2-3 Files

Many versions of 1-2-3 have surfaced over the years, and 1-2-3 files exist in several formats. Table A-1 describes the 1-2-3 files you may encounter.

TABLE A-1 LOTUS 1-2-3 FILE TYPES

File Extension	Description
WKS	Generated by 1-2-3 for DOS Release 1.0 and 1.0a. These files consist of a single sheet. Excel can read and write these files.
WK1	Generated by 1-2-3 for DOS Release 2.x. These files consist of a single sheet, and may have a companion *.FMT or *.ALL file that contains formatting information. Excel can read these files, but saves only the active sheet.
WK3	Generated by 1-2-3 for DOS Release 3.x and 1-2-3 for Windows Release 1.0. These files may contain multiple sheets, and may have a companion *.FM3 file that contains formatting information. Excel can read and write these files.
WK4	Generated by 1-2-3 for Windows Release 4.0. These files may contain multiple sheets. Excel can read and write these files.
123	Generated by 1-2-3 for Windows Release 5 and Millenium Edition. Excel can neither read nor write these files.

When importing or exporting 1-2-3 files, do not expect a perfect translation. Excel's online help describes the limitations.

Got a Case of File Bloat?

When you import a 1-2-3 file and save it as an Excel file, you may find that the file becomes very large, making it very slow to open and save. The most likely cause is that the imported 1-2-3 file contains entire columns that are preformatted. When Excel imports such a file, it converts all formatted cells — even if they're empty. The solution is to select all blank rows below the last used cell in your worksheet, then delete those rows. Resave the workbook, and it should be a more manageable size.

Lotus 1-2-3 Formulas

In some cases, you may find that the formulas in an imported 1-2-3 file work perfectly in Excel. In other cases, some formulas may not convert correctly and you may need to do some tweaking or rewriting.

Excel evaluates some formulas differently than 1-2-3. These formulas fall into three categories:

♦ Those that use text in calculation

♦ Those that use logical operators (TRUE and FALSE)

♦ Those that use database criteria

To force Excel to use 1-2-3's method of evaluating formulas, select Tools → Options. In the Options dialog box, click the Transition tab and place a checkmark next to the Transition formula evaluation option.

 When you open a 1-2-3 file, the Transition formula evaluation checkbox is selected automatically for that sheet to ensure that Excel calculates the formulas according to Lotus 1-2-3 rules.

If you plan to make extensive use of an imported 1-2-3 file, you might want to consider translating any formulas that aren't evaluated correctly, and turning off the Transition formula evaluation option. Doing so helps to avoid confusion among users unfamiliar with 1-2-3.

The following sections provide some tips on how to convert your 1-2-3 formulas so they work properly in Excel (without the Transition formula evaluation setting).

Let Excel Teach You

If you're moving up from an older DOS version of 1-2-3, you may be surprised to know that Excel can help you with the transition. The secret lies in the Help → Lotus 1-2-3 Help command. Selecting this command displays a dialog box with the 1-2-3 commands listed along the left side (see the accompanying figure).

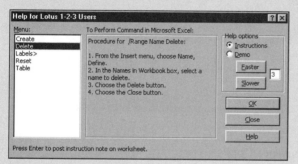

Select the 1-2-3 command sequence, and Excel displays instructions, or even demonstrates the corresponding menu command. For example, if you're a veteran 1-2-3 for DOS user, you know that you use / rnd (for Range Name Delete) to delete a name. If you enter this command sequence in Excel's Help for Lotus 1-2-3 Users dialog box, you see instructions that describe how to perform that operation in Excel.

Text in calculations

In 1-2-3, cells that contain text are considered to have a value of 0 when the cell is used in a formula that uses mathematical operators. Excel, on the other hand, returns an error.

If the Transition formula evaluation option is set, Excel considers text to have a value of 0.

The following formula is perfectly valid in 1-2-3 (and it returns 12). In Excel, the formula returns a #VALUE! error.

```
="Dog"+12
```

Similarly, if cell A1 contains the text *Dog*, and cell A2 contains the value 12, the following formula is valid in 1-2-3, but returns an error in Excel:

```
=A1+A2
```

Excel, however, does permit references to text cells in function arguments, and it treats such values as 0. For example, the following formula works fine in both 1-2-3 and Excel, even if the range A1:A10 contains text:

```
=SUM(A1:A10)
```

You can take advantage of this fact to convert a 1-2-3 formula such as =A1+A2 to the following:

```
=SUM(A1,A2)
```

Logical operators

Boolean expressions in 1-2-3 are evaluated to 1 or 0. Excel displays these values as TRUE or FALSE. TRUE is equivalent to 1-2-3's 1, and FALSE is equivalent to 1-2-3's 0.

 If the Transition formula evaluation option is set, Excel displays 0 for FALSE and 1 for TRUE.

In 1-2-3, for example, the following formula displays either 1 or 0, depending on the contents of cells A1 and A2. In Excel, the formula returns either TRUE or FALSE.

```
=A1<A2
```

This distinction may be important if your worksheet uses IF functions that check for 0 or 1. For example, the following formula has different results in 1-2-3 and Excel:

```
=IF(A1<A2=1,B1,B2)
```

To fix this formula so it works properly in Excel, change it to:

```
=IF(A1<A2,B1,B2)
```

Lotus 1-2-3 uses the following logical operators: #AND#, #NOT#, and #OR#. Excel uses logical functions (AND, NOT, and OR) in place of these. For example, the following 1-2-3 formula returns the string *yes* if cell A1=12 and cell A2=12, and the string *no* if both cells are not equal to 12:

```
@IF(A1=12#AND#A2=12,"yes","no")
```

The equivalent 1-2-3 formula is:

```
=IF(AND(A1=12,A2=12),"yes","no")
```

Database criteria

If your imported worksheet uses database criteria ranges (i.e., advanced filtering), be especially careful. Database criteria ranges are evaluated differently when you extract data, find data, and use database functions. For example, the criteria "Ben" finds only rows where the value *Ben* is contained in the cell. In Excel, the criteria "Ben" finds rows in which the contents of the cell begins with *Ben* — including *Benjamin, Benny,* and *Benito.*

If the Transition formula evaluation option is set, Excel works exactly like 1-2-3 in using database criteria.

What About 1-2-3 Macros?

Excel can execute some 1-2-3 macros — the keystroke macros developed using early versions of 1-2-3. These macros are stored directly in a worksheet and represent keystrokes sent to the interface. Don't expect perfect compatibility, however.

Typically, these keystroke macros are given a range name such as \t. This macro is executed by typing Ctrl+T. These special names are valid if they are contained in an imported file. But, you'll find that you cannot create such a name in Excel.

If you convert 1-2-3 files to Excel, the best approach is to recreate the macros using VBA. You'll get much better performance and the macros will be easier to maintain.

Lotus 1-2-3 Function Compatibility

Most of the worksheet functions in 1-2-3 have equivalents in Excel. In some cases, however, the correspondence is not perfect. Fortunately, Excel's online help provides a thorough description of the differences between the worksheet functions available in 1-2-3 and in Excel.

Function equivalents

Table A-2 lists 1-2-3 functions that have equivalent Excel functions. It's important to understand that in some cases the correspondence is not exact. Also, for some Excel functions, you must enter the arguments in a different order.

TABLE A-2 EXCEL EQUIVALENTS FOR 1-2-3 FUNCTIONS

Lotus 1-2-3 Function	Equivalent Excel Function
@	INDIRECT
@@	INDIRECT
@ABS	ABS
@ACCRUED	ACCRINT
@ACOS	ACOS
@ACOSH	ACOSH
@ASIN	ASIN
@ASINH	ASINH
@ATAN	ATAN
@ATAN2	ATAN2
@ATANH	ATANH
@AVEDEV	AVEDEV
@AVG	AVERAGEA
@BESSELI	BESSELI
@BESSELJ	BESSELJ
@BESSELK	BESSELK
@BESSELY	BESSELY

Lotus 1-2-3 Function	Equivalent Excel Function
@BIN2DEC	BIN2DEC
@BIN2HEX	BIN2HEX
@BIN2OCT	BIN2OCT
@BINOMIAL	BINOMDIST
@CELL	CELL
@CELLPOINTER	CELL
@CHAR	CHAR
@CHAR	CHAR
@CHIDIST	CHIINV
@CHIDIST	CHIDIST
@CHOOSE	CHOOSE
@CLEAN	CLEAN
@CODE	CODE
@COLS	COLUMNS
@COLUMN	COLUMN
@COMBIN	COMBIN
@CONFIDENCE	CONFIDENCE
@CONVERT	CONVERT
@CORREL	CORREL, PEARSON
@COS	COS
@COSH	COSH
@COUNT	COUNTA
@COUNTBLANK	COUNTBLANK
@COUNTIF	COUNTIF
@COUPDAYBS	COUPDAYBS
@COUPDAYS	COUPDAYS

Continued

TABLE A-2 EXCEL EQUIVALENTS FOR 1-2-3 FUNCTIONS *(Continued)*

Lotus 1-2-3 Function	Equivalent Excel Function
@COUPDAYSNC	COUPDAYSNC
@COUPNCD	COUPNCD
@COUPNUM	COUPNUM
@COUPPCD	COUPPCD
@COV	COVAR
@CRITBINOMIAL	CRITBINOM
@CTERM	NPER
@D360	DAYS360
@DATE	DATE
@DATEVALUE	DATEVALUE
@DAVG	DAVERAGE
@DAVG	DAVERAGE
@DAY	DAY
@DAYS	DAYS360
@DAYS360	DAYS360
@DB	DB
@DCOUNT	DCOUNTA
@DDB	DDB
@DEC2BIN	DEC2BIN
@DEC2FRAC	DOLLARFR
@DEC2HEX	DEC2HEX
@DEC2OCT	DEC2OCT
@DEGTORAD	RADIANS
@DEVSQ	DEVSQ
@DGET	DGET
@DISC	DISC

Lotus 1-2-3 Function	Equivalent Excel Function
@DMAX	DMAX
@DMIN	DMIN
@DPURECOUNT	DCOUNT, DCOUNTA
@DSTD	DSTDEVP
@DSTDS	DSTDEV
@DSUM	DSUM
@DURATION	DURATION
@DVAR	DVARP
@DVARS	DVAR
@ERF	ERF
@ERFC	ERFC
@EVEN	EVEN
@EXACT	EXACT
@EXP	EXP
@EXPONDIST	EXPONDIST
@FACT	FACT
@FALSE	FALSE
@FDIST	FINV, FDIST
@FIND	FIND
@FISHER	FISHER
@FISHERINV	FISHERINV
@FORECAST	FORECAST
@FRAC2DEC	DOLLARDE
@FTEST	FTEST
@FV	FV
@FVAL	FV

Continued

TABLE A-2 EXCEL EQUIVALENTS FOR 1-2-3 FUNCTIONS *(Continued)*

Lotus 1-2-3 Function	Equivalent Excel Function
@GAMMALN	GAMMALN
@GEOMEAN	GEOMEAN
@HARMEAN	HARMEAN
@HEX2BIN	HEX2BIN
@HEX2DEC	HEX2DEC
@HEX2OCT	HEX2OCT
@HLOOKUP	HLOOKUP
@HOUR	HOUR
@HYPGEOMDIST	HYPGEOMDIST
@IF	IF
@INDEX	INDEX
@INFO	INFO
@INT	TRUNC
@INTRATE	INTRATE
@IPAYMT	CUMIPMT, IMPT
@IRATE	RATE
@IRR	IRR
@ISEMPTY	ISBLANK
@ISERR	ISERR, ISERROR
@ISNUMBER	ISNONTEXT, ISNUMBER
@ISRANGE	ISREF
@ISSTRING	ISTEXT
@KURTOSIS	KURT
@LARGE	LARGE
@LEFT	LEFT
@LENGTH	LEN

Lotus 1-2-3 Function	Equivalent Excel Function
@LN	LN
@LOG	LOG, LOG10
@LOGINV	LOGINV
@LOGNORMDIST	LOGNORMDIST
@LOWER	LOWER
@MATCH	MATCH
@MAX	MAXA
@MDURATION	MDURATION
@MEDIAN	MEDIAN
@MID	MID
@MIN	MINA
@MINUTE	MINUTE
@MIRR	MIRR
@MOD	MOD
@MODE	MODE
@MONTH	MONTH
@N	N
@NA	NA
@NEGBINOMDIST	NEGBINOMDIST
@NETWORKDAYS	NETWORKDAYS
@NEXTMONTH	EOMONTH, EDATE
@NORMAL	NORMINV, NORMDIST, NORMSDIST
@NORMSINV	NORMSINV
@NOW	NOW
@NPER	NPER
@NPV	NPV

Continued

TABLE A-2 EXCEL EQUIVALENTS FOR 1-2-3 FUNCTIONS *(Continued)*

Lotus 1-2-3 Function	Equivalent Excel Function
@OCT2BIN	OCT2BIN
@OCT2DEC	OCT2DEC
@OCT2HEX	OCT2HEX
@ODD	ODD
@PAYMT	PMT
@PERCENTILE	PERCENTILE
@PERMUT	PERMUT
@PI	PI
@PMT	PMT
@POISSON	POISSON
@PPAYMT	CUMPRINC, PPMT
@PRANK	PERCENTRANK
@PRICE	PRICE
@PRICEDISC	PRICEDISC
@PRICEMAT	PRICEMAT
@PROB	PROB
@PRODUCT	PRODUCT
@PROPER	PROPER
@PUREAVG	AVERAGE, AVERAGEA
@PURECOUNT	COUNT, COUNTA
@PUREMAX	MAX, MAXA
@PUREMIN	MIN, MINA
@PURESTD	STDEVP, STDEVPA
@PURESTDS	STDEV, STDEVA
@PUREVAR	VARP, VARPA
@PUREVARS	VAR, VARA

Lotus 1-2-3 Function	Equivalent Excel Function
@PV	PV
@PVAL	PV
@QUARTILE	QUARTILE
@QUOTIENT	QUOTIENT
@RADTODEG	DEGREES
@RAND	RAND
@RANDBETWEEN	RANDBETWEEN
@RANK	RANK
@RATE	RATE
@RECEIVED	RECEIVED
@REGRESSION	INTERCEPT
@REPEAT	REPT
@REPLACE	REPLACE
@RIGHT	RIGHT
@RIGHT	RIGHT
@ROUND	ROUND
@ROUNDDOWN	INT, ROUNDDOWN
@ROUNDM	CEILING, FLOOR
@ROUNDUP	ROUNDUP
@ROW	ROW
@ROWS	ROWS
@RSQ	RSQ
@S	T
@SECOND	SECOND
@SERIESSUM	SERIESSUM
@SIGN	SIGN

Continued

TABLE A-2 EXCEL EQUIVALENTS FOR 1-2-3 FUNCTIONS *(Continued)*

Lotus 1-2-3 Function	Equivalent Excel Function
@SIN	SIN
@SINH	SINH
@SKEWNESS	SKEW
@SLN	SLN
@SMALL	SMALL
@SQRT	SQRT
@SQRTPI	SQRTPI
@STANDARDIZE	STANDARDIZE
@STD	STDEVPA
@STDS	STDEVA
@STEYX	STEYX
@STRING	FIXED, TEXT
@SUM	SUM
@SUMIF	SUMIF
@SUMPRODUCT	SUMPRODUCT
@SUMSQ	SUMSQ
@SUMX2MY2	SUMX2MY2
@SUMX2PY2	SUMX2PY2
@SUMXMY2	SUMXMY2
@SYD	SYD
@TAN	TAN
@TANH	TANH
@TBILLEQ	TBILLEQ
@TBILLPRICE	TBILLPRICE
@TBILLYIELD	TBILLYIELD
@TDIST	TDIST, TINV

Lotus 1-2-3 Function	Equivalent Excel Function
@TERM	NPER
@TIME	TIME
@TIMEVALUE	TIMEVALUE
@TODAY	TODAY
@TRIM	TRIM
@TRIMMEAN	TRIMMEAN
@TRUE	TRUE
@TRUNC	TRUNC
@TTEST	TTEST
@UPPER	UPPER
@VALUE	VALUE
@VAR	VARPA
@VARS	VARA
@VDB	VDB
@VLOOKUP	VLOOKUP
@WEEKDAY	WEEKDAY
@WEIBULL	WEIBULL
@WORKDAY	WORKDAY
@YEAR	YEAR
@YEARFRAC	YEARFRAC
@YIELD	YIELD
@YIELDDISC	YIELDDISC
@YIELDMAT	YIELDMAT
@ZTEST	ZTEST

Converting database functions

There's a common problem with 1-2-3's database functions (for example, @DSUM and @DCOUNT). Lotus 1-2-3 enables you to specify your criteria as an argument. Refer to Figure A-1, which shows a 1-2-3 file imported into Excel. The following formula (in cell E4) was not translated correctly and displays a #NAME? error.

```
=DCOUNTA(A1:C18,"Product",AND(PRODUCT="Widget",MONTH="January"))
```

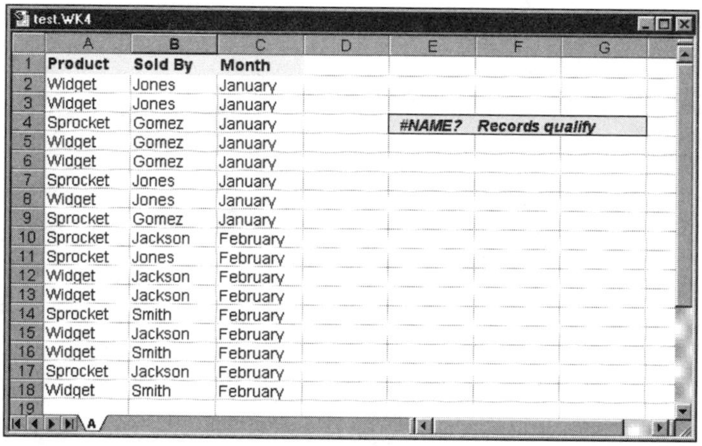

Figure A-1: This imported 1-2-3 file uses a @DCOUNT function with a criterion argument not supported by Excel.

The original 1-2-3 formula was written to return the count of records in which the Product is *Widget* and the Month is *January*. The original 1-2-3 formula (before conversion by Excel) was:

```
@DCOUNT(A1:C18,"Product",PRODUCT="Widget" #AND#MONTH="January")
```

Unfortunately, Excel's database functions do not allow you to specify the criteria as an argument. Rather, you need to:

◆ Set up a special criteria range for the DCOUNTA function

◆ Use a different function – in this case, the COUNTIF function.

Figure A-2 shows a criteria range in E1:F2. The following formula returns the count of records in which the Product is *Widget* and the Month is *January*.

```
=DCOUNT(A1:C18,"Product",E1:F2)
```

	A	B	C	D	E	F	G	
1	**Product**	**Sold By**	**Month**		**Product**	**Month**		
2	Widget	Jones	January		Widget	January		
3	Widget	Jones	January					
4	Sprocket	Gomez	January		*5 Records qualify*			
5	Widget	Gomez	January					
6	Widget	Gomez	January					
7	Sprocket	Jones	January					
8	Widget	Jones	January					
9	Sprocket	Gomez	January					
10	Sprocket	Jackson	February					
11	Sprocket	Jones	February					
12	Widget	Jackson	February					
13	Widget	Jackson	February					
14	Sprocket	Smith	February					
15	Widget	Jackson	February					
16	Widget	Smith	February					
17	Sprocket	Jackson	February					
18	Widget	Smith	February					
19								
20								

Figure A-2: Using a criteria range for the DCOUNT formula

Alternatively, you can use an array formula, which doesn't require a criteria range. The following formula is the Excel equivalent of the incorrectly translated @DCOUNT formula:

```
{=SUM((A2:A18="Widget")*(C2:C18="January"))}
```

Enter an array formula using Ctrl+Shift+Enter. Do not type the brackets; Excel inserts them for you. For more information about array formulas, see Part III. For additional counting techniques, see Chapter 7.

Appendix B

Excel's Function Reference

THIS APPENDIX contains a complete listing of Excel's worksheet functions. The functions are arranged alphabetically in tables by categories used by the Paste Function dialog box. Some of these functions are available only when you install a particular add-in.

Excel Functions by Category

Tables B-1 through B-10 present the following 10 categories of Excel functions: database, date and time, engineering, financial, information, logical, lookup and reference, math and trig, statistical, and text. As you'll see, some of these functions are only available if you install an add-in program – Analysis ToolPak, ODBC, or Microsoft Query. For more information about a particular function, including its arguments, select the function in the Paste Function dialog box and click the Help button (or press F1). Table B-1 lists Excel's database functions.

TABLE B-1 DATABASE CATEGORY FUNCTIONS

Function	What It Does
DAVERAGE	Returns the average of selected database entries
DCOUNT	Counts the cells containing numbers from a specified database and criteria
DCOUNTA	Counts nonblank cells from a specified database and criteria
DGET	Extracts from a database a single record that matches the specified criteria
DMAX	Returns the maximum value from selected database entries
DMIN	Returns the minimum value from selected database entries
DPRODUCT	Multiplies the values in a particular field of records that match the criteria in a database

Continued

TABLE **B-1** DATABASE CATEGORY FUNCTIONS *(Continued)*

Function	What It Does
DSTDEV	Estimates the standard deviation based on a sample of selected database entries
DSTDEVP	Calculates the standard deviation based on the entire population of selected database entries
DSUM	Adds the numbers in the field column of records in the database that match the criteria
DVAR	Estimates variance based on a sample from selected database entries
DVARP	Calculates variance based on the entire population of selected database entries
SQL.CLOSE**	Terminates a SQL.OPEN connection
SQL.BIND**	Specifies where to place SQL.EXEC.QUERY results
SQL.ERROR**	Returns error information on SQL* functions
SQL.EXEC.QUERY**	Executes a SQL statement on a SQL.OPEN connection
QUERYGETDATA***	Gets external data using Microsoft Query
QUERYGETDATA DIALOG***	Displays a dialog box to get data using Microsoft Query
SQL.GET.SCHEMA**	Returns information on a SQL.OPEN connection
SQL.OPEN**	Makes a connection to a data source via ODBC
QUERYREFRESH***	Updates a data range using Microsoft Query
SQL.REQUEST**	Requests a connection and executes a SQL query
SQL.RETRIEVE**	Retrieves SQL.EXEC.QUERY results
SQL.RETRIEVE.TO. FILE**	Retrieves SQL.EXEC.QUERY results to a file

** Available only when the ODBC add-in is installed.
*** Available only when the MS Query add-in is installed.

Table B-2 lists Excel's date and time functions.

TABLE B-2 DATE AND TIME CATEGORY FUNCTIONS

Function	What It Does
DATE	Returns the serial number of a particular date
DATEVALUE	Converts a date in the form of text to a serial number
DAY	Converts a serial number to a day of the month
DAYS360	Calculates the number of days between two dates, based on a 360-day year
EDATE*	Returns the serial number of the date that is the indicated number of months before or after the start date
EOMONTH*	Returns the serial number of the last day of the month before or after a specified number of months
HOUR	Converts a serial number to an hour
MINUTE	Converts a serial number to a minute
MONTH	Converts a serial number to a month
NETWORKDAYS*	Returns the number of whole workdays between two dates
NOW	Returns the serial number of the current date and time
SECOND	Converts a serial number to a second
TIME	Returns the serial number of a particular time
TIMEVALUE	Converts a time in the form of text to a serial number
TODAY	Returns the serial number of today's date
WEEKDAY	Converts a serial number to a day of the week
WEEKNUM*	Returns the week number in the year
WORKDAY*	Returns the serial number of the date before or after a specified number of workdays
YEAR	Converts a serial number to a year
YEARFRAC*	Returns the year fraction representing the number of whole days between start_date and end_date

*Available only when the Analysis ToolPak add-in is installed.

Table B-3 lists Excel's engineering functions.

**TABLE B-3 ENGINEERING CATEGORY FUNCTIONS AVAILABLE IN THE ANALYSIS
TOOLPAK ADD-IN**

Function	What It Does
BESSELI	Returns the modified Bessel function In(x)
BESSELJ	Returns the Bessel function Jn(x)
BESSELK	Returns the modified Bessel function Kn(x)
BESSELY	Returns the Bessel function Yn(x)
BIN2DEC	Converts a binary number to decimal
BIN2HEX	Converts a binary number to hexadecimal
BIN2OCT	Converts a binary number to octal
COMPLEX	Converts real and imaginary coefficients into complex numbers
CONVERT	Converts a number from one measurement system to another
DEC2BIN	Converts a decimal number to binary
DEC2HEX	Converts a decimal number to hexadecimal
DEC2OCT	Converts a decimal number to octal
DELTA	Tests whether two values are equal
ERF	Returns the error function
ERFC	Returns the complementary error function
FACTDOUBLE	Returns the double factorial of a number
GESTEP	Tests whether a number is greater than a threshold value
HEX2BIN	Converts a hexadecimal number to binary
HEX2DEC	Converts a hexadecimal number to decimal
HEX2OCT	Converts a hexadecimal number to octal
IMABS	Returns the absolute value (modulus) of a complex number
IMAGINARY	Returns the imaginary coefficient of a complex number
IMARGUMENT	Returns the argument theta — an angle expressed in radians
IMCONJUGATE	Returns the complex conjugate of a complex number

Function	What It Does
IMCOS	Returns the cosine of a complex number
IMDIV	Returns the quotient of two complex numbers
IMEXP	Returns the exponential of a complex number
IMLN	Returns the natural logarithm of a complex number
IMLOG2	Returns the base-2 logarithm of a complex number
IMLOG10	Returns the base-10 logarithm of a complex number
IMPOWER	Returns a complex number raised to an integer power
IMPRODUCT	Returns the product of two complex numbers
IMREAL	Returns the real coefficient of a complex number
IMSIN	Returns the sine of a complex number
IMSQRT	Returns the square root of a complex number
IMSUB	Returns the difference of two complex numbers
IMSUM	Returns the sum of complex numbers
OCT2BIN	Converts an octal number to binary
OCT2DEC	Converts an octal number to decimal
OCT2HEX	Converts an octal number to hexadecimal

Table B-4 lists Excel's financial functions.

TABLE B-4 FINANCIAL CATEGORY FUNCTIONS

Function	What It Does
ACCRINT*	Returns the accrued interest for a security that pays periodic interest
ACCRINTM*	Returns the accrued interest for a security that pays interest at maturity
AMORDEGRC*	Returns the depreciation for each accounting period
AMORLINC*	Returns the depreciation for each accounting period

Continued

TABLE B-4 FINANCIAL CATEGORY FUNCTIONS *(Continued)*

Function	What It Does
COUPDAYBS*	Returns the number of days from the beginning of the coupon period to the settlement date
COUPDAYS*	Returns the number of days in the coupon period that contains the settlement date
COUPDAYSNC*	Returns the number of days from the settlement date to the next coupon date
COUPNCD*	Returns the next coupon date after the settlement date
COUPNUM*	Returns the number of coupons payable between the settlement date and maturity date
COUPPCD*	Returns the previous coupon date before the settlement date
CUMIPMT*	Returns the cumulative interest paid between two periods
CUMPRINC*	Returns the cumulative principal paid on a loan between two periods
DB	Returns the depreciation of an asset for a specified period, using the fixed-declining balance method
DDB	Returns the depreciation of an asset for a specified period, using the double-declining balance method or some other method that you specify
DISC*	Returns the discount rate for a security
DOLLARDE*	Converts a dollar price (expressed as a fraction) into a dollar price (expressed as a decimal number)
DOLLARFR*	Converts a dollar price (expressed as a decimal number) into a dollar price (expressed as a fraction)
DURATION*	Returns the annual duration of a security with periodic interest payments
EFFECT*	Returns the effective annual interest rate
FV	Returns the future value of an investment
FVSCHEDULE*	Returns the future value of an initial principal after applying a series of compound interest rates
INTRATE*	Returns the interest rate for a fully invested security
IPMT	Returns the interest payment for an investment for a given period
IRR	Returns the internal rate of return for a series of cash flows
ISPMT	Returns the interest associated with a specific loan payment

Function	What It Does
ISPMT	Returns the interest associated with a specific loan payment
MDURATION*	Returns the Macauley modified duration for a security with an assumed par value of $100
MIRR	Returns the internal rate of return where positive and negative cash flows are financed at different rates
NOMINAL*	Returns the annual nominal interest rate
NPER	Returns the number of periods for an investment
NPV	Returns the net present value of an investment based on a series of periodic cash flows and a discount rate
ODDFPRICE*	Returns the price per $100 face value of a security with an odd first period
ODDFYIELD*	Returns the yield of a security with an odd first period
ODDLPRICE*	Returns the price per $100 face value of a security with an odd last period
ODDLYIELD*	Returns the yield of a security with an odd last period
PMT	Returns the periodic payment for an annuity
PPMT	Returns the payment on the principal for an investment for a given period
PRICE*	Returns the price per $100 face value of a security that pays periodic interest
PRICEDISC*	Returns the price per $100 face value of a discounted security
PRICEMAT*	Returns the price per $100 face value of a security that pays interest at maturity
PV	Returns the present value of an investment
RATE	Returns the interest rate per period of an annuity
RECEIVED*	Returns the amount received at maturity for a fully invested security
SLN	Returns the straight-line depreciation of an asset for one period
SYD	Returns the sum-of-years' digits depreciation of an asset for a specified period
TBILLEQ*	Returns the bond-equivalent yield for a Treasury bill
TBILLPRICE*	Returns the price per $100 face value for a Treasury bill
TBILLYIELD*	Returns the yield for a Treasury bill

Continued

TABLE B-4 FINANCIAL CATEGORY FUNCTIONS *(Continued)*

Function	What It Does
VDB	Returns the depreciation of an asset for a specified or partial period using a declining balance method
XIRR*	Returns the internal rate of return for a schedule of cash flows that is not necessarily periodic
XNPV*	Returns the net present value for a schedule of cash flows that is not necessarily periodic
YIELD*	Returns the yield on a security that pays periodic interest
YIELDDISC*	Returns the annual yield for a discounted security; for example, a Treasury bill
YIELDMAT*	Returns the annual yield of a security that pays interest at maturity

Available only when the Analysis ToolPak add-in is installed.

Table B-5 lists Excel's information functions.

TABLE B-5 INFORMATION CATEGORY FUNCTIONS

Function	What It Does
CELL	Returns information about the formatting, location, or contents of a cell
ERROR.TYPE	Returns a number corresponding to an error type
INFO	Returns information about the current operating environment
ISBLANK	Returns TRUE if the value is blank
ISERR	Returns TRUE if the value is any error value except #N/A
ISERROR	Returns TRUE if the value is any error value
ISEVEN*	Returns TRUE if the number is even
ISLOGICAL	Returns TRUE if the value is a logical value
ISNA	Returns TRUE if the value is the #N/A error value
ISNONTEXT	Returns TRUE if the value is not text
ISNUMBER	Returns TRUE if the value is a number

Function	What It Does
ISODD*	Returns TRUE if the number is odd
ISREF	Returns TRUE if the value is a reference
ISTEXT	Returns TRUE if the value is text
N	Returns a value converted to a number
NA	Returns the error value #N/A
TYPE	Returns a number indicating the data type of a value

Available only when the Analysis ToolPak add-in is installed.

Table B-6 lists Excel's logical functions.

TABLE B-6 LOGICAL CATEGORY FUNCTIONS

Function	What It Does
AND	Returns TRUE if all of its arguments are TRUE
FALSE	Returns the logical value FALSE
IF	Specifies a logical test to perform
NOT	Reverses the logic of its argument
OR	Returns TRUE if any argument is TRUE
TRUE	Returns the logical value TRUE

Table B-7 lists Excel's lookup and reference functions.

TABLE B-7 LOOKUP AND REFERENCE CATEGORY FUNCTIONS

Function	What It Does
ADDRESS	Returns a reference as text to a single cell in a worksheet
AREAS	Returns the number of areas in a reference

Continued

TABLE **B-7** LOOKUP AND REFERENCE CATEGORY FUNCTIONS *(Continued)*

Function	What It Does
CHOOSE	Chooses a value from a list of values
COLUMN	Returns the column number of a reference
COLUMNS	Returns the number of columns in a reference
GETPIVOTDATA	Returns data stored in a PivotTable
HLOOKUP	Looks in the top row of an array and returns the value of the indicated cell
HYPERLINK	Creates a shortcut that opens a document on your hard drive, a server, or the Internet
INDEX	Uses an index to choose a value from a reference or array
INDIRECT	Returns a reference indicated by a text value
LOOKUP	Looks up values in a vector or array
MATCH	Looks up values in a reference or array
OFFSET	Returns a reference offset from a given reference
ROW	Returns the row number of a reference
ROWS	Returns the number of rows in a reference
TRANSPOSE	Returns the transpose of an array
VLOOKUP	Looks in the first column of an array and moves across the row to return the value of a cell

Table B-8 lists Excel's mathematical and trigonometric functions.

TABLE **B-8** MATH AND TRIG CATEGORY FUNCTIONS

Function	What It Does
ABS	Returns the absolute value of a number
ACOS	Returns the arccosine of a number
ACOSH	Returns the inverse hyperbolic cosine of a number
ASIN	Returns the arcsine of a number

Function	What It Does
ASINH	Returns the inverse hyperbolic sine of a number
ATAN	Returns the arctangent of a number
ATAN2	Returns the arctangent from x and y coordinates
ATANH	Returns the inverse hyperbolic tangent of a number
CEILING	Rounds a number to the nearest integer or to the nearest multiple of significance
COMBIN	Returns the number of combinations for a given number of objects
COS	Returns the cosine of a number
COSH	Returns the hyperbolic cosine of a number
DEGREES	Converts radians to degrees
EVEN	Rounds a number up to the nearest even integer
EXP	Returns e raised to the power of a given number
FACT	Returns the factorial of a number
FLOOR	Rounds a number down, toward 0
GCD*	Returns the greatest common divisor
INT	Rounds a number down to the nearest integer
LCM*	Returns the least common multiple
LN	Returns the natural logarithm of a number
LOG	Returns the logarithm of a number to a specified base
LOG10	Returns the base-10 logarithm of a number
MDETERM	Returns the matrix determinant of an array
MINVERSE	Returns the matrix inverse of an array
MMULT	Returns the matrix product of two arrays
MOD	Returns the remainder from division
MROUND*	Returns a number rounded to the desired multiple
MULTINOMIAL*	Returns the multinomial of a set of numbers
ODD	Rounds a number up to the nearest odd integer

Continued

TABLE **B-8 MATH AND TRIG CATEGORY FUNCTIONS** *(Continued)*

Function	What It Does
PI	Returns the value of pi
POWER	Returns the result of a number raised to a power
PRODUCT	Multiplies its arguments
QUOTIENT*	Returns the integer portion of a division
RADIANS	Converts degrees to radians
RAND	Returns a random number between 0 and 1
RANDBETWEEN*	Returns a random number between the numbers that you specify
ROMAN	Converts an Arabic numeral to Roman, as text
ROUND	Rounds a number to a specified number of digits
ROUNDDOWN	Rounds a number down, toward 0
ROUNDUP	Rounds a number up, away from 0
SERIESSUM*	Returns the sum of a power series based on the formula
SIGN	Returns the sign of a number
SIN	Returns the sine of the given angle
SINH	Returns the hyperbolic sine of a number
SQRT	Returns a positive square root
SQRTPI*	Returns the square root of (*number* * pi)
SUBTOTAL	Returns a subtotal in a list or database
SUM	Adds its arguments
SUMIF	Adds the cells specified by a given criteria
SUMPRODUCT	Returns the sum of the products of corresponding array components
SUMSQ	Returns the sum of the squares of the arguments
SUMX2MY2	Returns the sum of the difference of squares of corresponding values in two arrays
SUMX2PY2	Returns the sum of the sum of squares of corresponding values in two arrays

Function	What It Does
SUMXMY2	Returns the sum of squares of differences of corresponding values in two arrays
TAN	Returns the tangent of a number
TANH	Returns the hyperbolic tangent of a number
TRUNC	Truncates a number to an integer

Available only when the Analysis ToolPak add-in is attached.

Table B-9 lists Excel's statistical functions.

TABLE B-9 STATISTICAL CATEGORY FUNCTIONS

Function	What It Does
AVEDEV	Returns the average of the absolute deviations of data points from their mean
AVERAGE	Returns the average of its arguments
AVERAGEA	Returns the average of its arguments and includes evaluation of text and logical values
BETADIST	Returns the cumulative beta probability density function
BETAINV	Returns the inverse of the cumulative beta probability density function
BINOMDIST	Returns the individual term binomial distribution probability
CHIDIST	Returns the one-tailed probability of the chi-squared distribution
CHIINV	Returns the inverse of the one-tailed probability of the chi-squared distribution
CHITEST	Returns the test for independence
CONFIDENCE	Returns the confidence interval for a population mean
CORREL	Returns the correlation coefficient between two data sets
COUNT	Counts how many numbers are in the list of arguments
COUNTA	Counts how many values are in the list of arguments

Continued

TABLE **B-9** STATISTICAL CATEGORY FUNCTIONS *(Continued)*

Function	What It Does
COUNTBLANK	Counts the number of blank cells in the argument range
COUNTIF	Counts the number of cells that meet the criteria you specify in the argument
COVAR	Returns covariance — the average of the products of paired deviations
CRITBINOM	Returns the smallest value for which the cumulative binomial distribution is less than or equal to a criterion value
DEVSQ	Returns the sum of squares of deviations
EXPONDIST	Returns the exponential distribution
FDIST	Returns the F probability distribution
FINV	Returns the inverse of the F probability distribution
FISHER	Returns the Fisher transformation
FISHERINV	Returns the inverse of the Fisher transformation
FORECAST	Returns a value along a linear trend
FREQUENCY	Returns a frequency distribution as a vertical array
FTEST	Returns the result of an F-test
GAMMADIST	Returns the gamma distribution
GAMMAINV	Returns the inverse of the gamma cumulative distribution
GAMMALN	Returns the natural logarithm of the gamma function, $G(x)$
GEOMEAN	Returns the geometric mean
GROWTH	Returns values along an exponential trend
HARMEAN	Returns the harmonic mean
HYPGEOMDIST	Returns the hypergeometric distribution
INTERCEPT	Returns the intercept of the linear regression line
KURT	Returns the kurtosis of a data set
LARGE	Returns the *k*th largest value in a data set
LINEST	Returns the parameters of a linear trend
LOGEST	Returns the parameters of an exponential trend

Function	What It Does
LOGINV	Returns the inverse of the lognormal distribution
LOGNORMDIST	Returns the cumulative lognormal distribution
MAX	Returns the maximum value in a list of arguments, ignoring logical values and text
MAXA	Returns the maximum value in a list of arguments, including logical values and text
MEDIAN	Returns the median of the given numbers
MIN	Returns the minimum value in a list of arguments, ignoring logical values and text
MINA	Returns the minimum value in a list of arguments, including logical values and text
MODE	Returns the most common value in a data set
NEGBINOMDIST	Returns the negative binomial distribution
NORMDIST	Returns the normal cumulative distribution
NORMINV	Returns the inverse of the normal cumulative distribution
NORMSDIST	Returns the standard normal cumulative distribution
NORMSINV	Returns the inverse of the standard normal cumulative distribution
PEARSON	Returns the Pearson product moment correlation coefficient
PERCENTILE	Returns the kth percentile of values in a range
PERCENTRANK	Returns the percentage rank of a value in a data set
PERMUT	Returns the number of permutations for a given number of objects
POISSON	Returns the Poisson distribution
PROB	Returns the probability that values in a range are between two limits
QUARTILE	Returns the quartile of a data set
RANK	Returns the rank of a number in a list of numbers
RSQ	Returns the square of the Pearson product moment correlation coefficient
SKEW	Returns the skewness of a distribution
SLOPE	Returns the slope of the linear regression line

Continued

TABLE **B-9** STATISTICAL CATEGORY FUNCTIONS *(Continued)*

Function	What It Does
SMALL	Returns the *k*th smallest value in a data set
STANDARDIZE	Returns a normalized value
STDEV	Estimates standard deviation based on a sample, ignoring text and logical values
STDEVA	Estimates standard deviation based on a sample, including text and logical values
STDEVP	Calculates standard deviation based on the entire population, ignoring text and logical values
STDEVPA	Calculates standard deviation based on the entire population, including text and logical values
STEYX	Returns the standard error of the predicted *y*-value for each *x* in the regression
TDIST	Returns the student's t-distribution
TINV	Returns the inverse of the student's t-distribution
TREND	Returns values along a linear trend
TRIMMEAN	Returns the mean of the interior of a data set
TTEST	Returns the probability associated with a student's t-Test
VAR	Estimates variance based on a sample, ignoring logical values and text
VARA	Estimates variance based on a sample, including logical values and text
VARP	Calculates variance based on the entire population, ignoring logical values and text
VARPA	Calculates variance based on the entire population, including logical values and text
WEIBULL	Returns the Weibull distribution
ZTEST	Returns the two-tailed P-value of a z-test

Table B-10 lists Excel's text functions.

TABLE **B-10** TEXT CATEGORY FUNCTIONS

Function	What It Does
CHAR	Returns the character specified by the code number
CLEAN	Removes all nonprintable characters from text
CODE	Returns a numeric code for the first character in a text string
CONCATENATE	Joins several text items into one text item
DOLLAR	Converts a number to text, using currency format
EXACT	Checks to see whether two text values are identical
FIND	Finds one text value within another (case-sensitive)
FIXED	Formats a number as text with a fixed number of decimals
LEFT	Returns the leftmost characters from a text value
LEN	Returns the number of characters in a text string
LOWER	Converts text to lowercase
MID	Returns a specific number of characters from a text string, starting at the position that you specify
PROPER	Capitalizes the first letter in each word of a text value
REPLACE	Replaces characters within text
REPT	Repeats text a given number of times
RIGHT	Returns the rightmost characters from a text value
SEARCH	Finds one text value within another (not case-sensitive)
SUBSTITUTE	Substitutes new text for old text in a text string
T	Converts its arguments to text
TEXT	Formats a number and converts it to text
TRIM	Removes spaces from text
UPPER	Converts text to uppercase
VALUE	Converts a text argument to a number

Appendix C

Custom Number Formats

THE ABILITY TO CREATE CUSTOM number formats is one of Excel's most powerful features. Although Excel provides lots of built-in number formats, you may find that none of these suit your needs. This appendix describes how to create custom number formats and provides many examples.

About Number Formatting

By default, all cells use the General number format. This is basically a "what you type is what you get" format. But if the cell is not wide enough to show the entire number, the General format rounds numbers with decimals and uses scientific notation for large numbers. In many cases, you may want to format a cell using something other than the General number format.

The key thing to remember about number formatting is that it affects only how a value is *displayed*. The actual number remains intact, and any formulas that use a formatted number use the actual number.

Automatic number formatting

Excel is smart enough to perform some formatting for you automatically. For example, if you enter 12.3% into a cell, Excel knows that you want to use a percentage format and applies it for you automatically. If you use commas to separate thousands (such as 123,456), Excel applies comma formatting for you. And if you precede your value with a dollar sign, Excel formats the cell for currency.

 A new feature in Excel 2000 makes it easier to enter values into cells formatted as a percentage. Select Tools → Options, and click the Edit tab in the Options dialog box. If the checkbox labeled Enable automatic percent entry is checked, you can simply enter a normal value into a cell formatted to display as a percent (for example, enter **12.5** for 12.5%). If this checkbox is not checked, you must enter the value as a decimal (for example, **.125** for 12.5%).

Excel automatically applies a built-in number format to a cell based on the following criteria:

◆ If a number contains a slash (/), it may be converted to a date format or a fraction format.

◆ If a number contains a hyphen (-), it may be converted to a date format.

◆ If a number contains a colon (:), or is followed by a space and the letter A or P, it may be converted to a time format.

◆ If a number contains the letter E (in uppercase or lowercase letters), it may be converted to scientific notation or exponential format.

To avoid automatic number formatting when you enter a value, preformat the cell with the desired number format, or precede your entry with an apostrophe (this makes the entry text).

Formatting numbers using toolbar buttons

The Formatting toolbar contains several buttons that enable you to quickly apply common number formats. When you click one of these buttons, the selected cells takes on the specified number format. Table C-1 summarizes the formats that these Formatting toolbar buttons perform.

These five toolbar buttons actually apply predefined styles to the selected cells. Access Excel's styles by using the Format → Style command.

TABLE C-1 NUMBER-FORMATTING BUTTONS ON THE FORMATTING TOOLBAR

Button Name	Formatting Applied
Currency Style	Adds a dollar sign to the left, separates thousands with a comma, and displays the value with two digits to the right of the decimal point
Percent Style	Displays the value as a percentage, with no decimal places

Button Name	Formatting Applied
Comma Style	Separates thousands with a comma and displays the value with two digits to the right of the decimal place
Increase Decimal	Increases the number of digits to the right of the decimal point by one
Decrease Decimal	Decreases the number of digits to the right of the decimal point by one

Using shortcut keys to format numbers

Another way to apply number formatting is to use shortcut keys. Table C-2 summarizes the shortcut key combinations that you can use to apply common number formatting to the selected cells or range.

TABLE C-2 NUMBER-FORMATTING KEYBOARD SHORTCUTS

Key Combination	Formatting Applied
Ctrl+Shift+~	General number format (i.e., unformatted values)
Ctrl+Shift+$	Currency format with two decimal places (negative numbers appear in parentheses)
Ctrl+Shift+%	Percentage format, with no decimal places
Ctrl+Shift+^	Scientific notation number format, with two decimal places
Ctrl+Shift+#	Date format with the day, month, and year
Ctrl+Shift+@	Time format with the hour, minute, and a.m. or p.m.
Ctrl+Shift+!	Two decimal places, thousands separator, and a hyphen for negative values

Using the Format Cells dialog box to format numbers

For optimal control of number formatting, use the Number tab of the Format Cells dialog box. Select the cells to format, and then choose Format → Cells. The Number tab of the Format Cells dialog box displays 12 categories of number formats from which to choose. When you select a category from the list box, the right side of the dialog box changes to display appropriate options. For example, Figure C-1 shows how the dialog box looks when you click the Currency category.

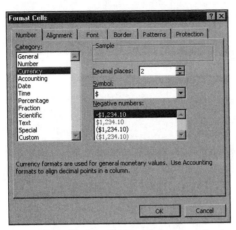

Figure C-1: Options for the Currency category

Following I list the number-format categories, along with some general comments:

- **General:** The default format; it displays numbers as integers, decimals, or in scientific notation if the value is too wide to fit in the cell.

- **Number:** Enables you to specify the number of decimal places, whether to use a comma to separate thousands, and how to display negative numbers (with a minus sign, in red, in parentheses, or in red and in parentheses).

- **Currency:** Enables you to specify the number of decimal places, whether to use a dollar sign, and how to display negative numbers (with a minus sign, in red, in parentheses, or in red and in parentheses). This format always uses a comma to separate thousands.

- **Accounting:** Differs from the Currency format in that the dollar signs always line up vertically.

- **Date:** Enables you to choose from 15 date formats.

- **Time:** Enables you to choose from eight time formats.

- **Percentage:** Enables you to choose the number of decimal places; always displays a percent sign.

◆ Fraction: Enables you to choose from among nine fraction formats.

◆ Scientific: Displays numbers in exponential notation (with an E): 2.00E+05 = 200,000. 2.05E+05 = 205,000. You can choose the number of decimal places to display to the left of E.

◆ Text: When applied to a value, causes Excel to treat the value as text (even if it looks like a value). This feature is useful for items such as numerical part numbers.

◆ Special: Contains four additional number formats (Zip Code, Zip Code +4, Phone Number, and Social Security Number).

◆ Custom: Enables you to define custom number formats not included in any of the other categories.

If the cell displays a series of pound signs (such as ########), it means that the column is not wide enough to display the value by using the number format that you selected. Either make the column wider or change the number format. You don't see this condition too often because Excel usually adjusts column widths automatically to accommodate entries as you make them. A series of pound signs also can mean that the cell contains an invalid date or time.

Formatting Numbers in Charts

When you create a chart, the number formatting on the chart is linked to the worksheet cells that contain the numbers. For example, the values displayed on the chart's value axis or data labels use the same number format as the values used to create the chart. If you like, you can apply number formats (including custom number formats) to values that appear in charts.

Generally, you can double-click any part of a chart that displays a number. This brings up the appropriate Format dialog box. Click the Number tab and specify the desired number format. You can choose from a built-in format, or use a custom number format.

To reestablish links between a chart's number formats and the worksheet number formatting, select the Linked to source checkbox on the Number tab of the Format dialog box.

Creating a Custom Number Format

Figure C-2 shows how the Format Cells dialog box looks when you select the Custom category. This category enables you to create number formats not included in any of the other categories. As you can see, Excel gives you a great deal of flexibility in creating custom number formats.

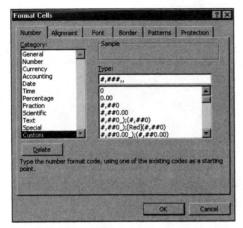

Figure C-2: The Custom category enables you to create custom number formats.

 Custom number formats are stored with the worksheet. To make the custom format available in a different workbook, you can just copy a cell that uses the custom format to the other workbook.

About custom number formats

You construct a number format by specifying a series of codes as a *number format string*. You enter this code sequence in the Type field after you select the Custom category on the Number tab of the Format Cells dialog box. Here's an example of a simple number format code:

```
0.000
```

This code consists of placeholders and a decimal point; it tells Excel to display the value with three digits to the right of the decimal place. Here's another example:

```
00000
```

This custom number format has five placeholders and displays the value with five digits (no decimal point). This is a good format to use when the cell holds a zip code (in fact, this is the code actually used by the ZIP Code format in the Special category). When you format the cell with this number format and then enter a zip code such as 06604 (Bridgeport, CT), the value is displayed with the leading zero. If you enter this number into a cell with the General number format, it displays 6604 (no leading zero).

Scroll through the list of number formats in the Custom category in the Format Cells dialog box to see many more examples. In many cases, you can use one of these codes as a starting point, and only slight customization will be needed.

Parts of a number format string

A custom format string enables you to specify different format codes for positive numbers, negative numbers, zero values, and text. You do so by separating the codes with a semicolon. The codes are arranged in the following structure:

```
Positive format; Negative format; Zero format; Text format
```

If you use only one section, the format string applies to all values. If you use two sections, the first section applies to positive values and zeros, the second to negative values. If you use three sections, the first section applies to positive values, the second to negative values, and the third to zeros.

The following is an example of a custom number format that specifies a different format for each of these types:

```
[Green]General;[Red]General;[Black]General;[Blue]General
```

This example takes advantage of the fact that colors have special codes. A cell formatted with this custom number format displays its contents in a different color, depending on the value. When a cell is formatted with this custom number format, a positive number is green, a negative number is red, a zero is black, and text is blue.

If you want to apply cell formatting automatically (such as text or background color) based on the cell's contents, a better solution is to use Excel's Conditional Formatting feature (available in Excel 97 or later). Chapter 17 discusses this feature.

> ## Preformatting Cells
>
> Usually, you'll apply number formats to cells that already contain values. You also can format cells with a specific number format *before* you make an entry. Then, when you enter information, it takes on the format that you specified. You can preformat specific cells, entire rows or columns, or even the entire worksheet.
>
> Rather than preformat an entire worksheet, however, you can change the number format for the Normal style (unless you specify otherwise, all cells use the Normal style). Change the Normal style by selecting Format → Style. In the Style dialog box, click the Modify button and then choose the new number format for the Normal style.

Custom number format codes

Table C-3 lists the formatting codes available for custom formats, along with brief descriptions. I use most of these codes in examples later in this appendix.

TABLE C-3 CODES USED TO CREATE CUSTOM NUMBER FORMATS

Code	Comments
General	Displays the number in General format
#	Digit placeholder
0 (zero)	Digit placeholder
?	Digit placeholder
.	Decimal point
%	Percentage
,	Thousands separator
E- E+ e- e+	Scientific notation
$ - + / ( ) : space	Displays this character
\	Displays the next character in the format
*	Repeats the next character, to fill the column width
_ (underscore)	Leaves a space equal to the width of the next character
"text"	Displays the text inside the double quotation marks

Code	Comments
@	Text placeholder
[*color*]	Displays the characters in the color specified
[COLOR *n*]	Displays the corresponding color in the color palette, where *n* is a number from 0 to 56
[condition value]	Enables you to set your own criteria for each section of a number format

Table C-4 lists the codes used to create custom formats for dates and times.

TABLE C-4 CODES USED IN CREATING CUSTOM FORMATS FOR DATES AND TIMES

Code	Comments
M	Displays the month as a number without leading zeros (1–12)
Mm	Displays the month as a number with leading zeros (01–12)
Mmm	Displays the month as an abbreviation (Jan–Dec)
Mmmm	Displays the month as a full name (January–December)
Mmmmm	Displays the first letter of the month (J–D)
D	Displays the day as a number without leading zeros (1–31)
Dd	Displays the day as a number with leading zeros (01–31)
Ddd	Displays the day as an abbreviation (Sun–Sat)
Dddd	Displays the day as a full name (Sunday–Saturday)
Yy or yyyy	Displays the year as a two-digit number (00–99), or as a four-digit number (1900–2078)
H or hh	Displays the hour as a number without leading zeros (0–23), or as a number with leading zeros (00–23)
M or mm	Displays the minute as a number without leading zeros (0–59), or as a number with leading zeros (00–59)

Continued

TABLE C-4 *(Continued)*

Code	Comments
S or ss	Displays the second as a number without leading zeros (0–59), or as a number with leading zeros (00–59)
[ ]	Displays hours greater than 24, or minutes or seconds greater than 60
AM/PM	Displays the hour using a 12-hour clock; if no AM/PM indicator is used, the hour uses a 24-hour clock

Custom Number Format Examples

The remainder of this appendix consists of useful examples of custom number formats. You can use most of these format codes as-is. Others may require slight modification to meet your needs.

Scaling values

You can use a custom number format to scale a number. For example, if you work with very large numbers, you may want to display the numbers in thousands (i.e., displaying 1,000,000 as 1,000). The actual number, of course, will be used in calculations that involve that cell.

DISPLAYING VALUES IN THOUSANDS OR HUNDREDS

The following format string displays values without the last three digits to the left of the decimal place, and no decimal places. In other words, the value appears as if it's divided by 1,000 and rounded to no decimal places.

#,###,

A variation of this format string follows. A value with this number format appears as if it's divided by 1,000 and rounded to two decimal places.

#,###.00,

Where Did Those Number Formats Come From?

Excel may create custom number formats without you realizing it. When you use the Increase Decimal or Decrease Decimal button on the Formatting toolbar, new number formats are created that appear on the Number tab of the Format Cells dialog box. (To access this dialog box, click Cells on the Format menu.) For example, if you click the Increase Decimal button five times, the following custom number formats are created:

```
0.0
0.000
0.0000
0.000000
```

A format string for two decimal places is not created because that format string is built-in.

The following table shows examples of these number formats:

Value	Number Format	Display
123456	#,###,	123
1234565	#,###,	1,235
-323434	#,###,	-323
123123.123	#,###,	123
499	#,###,	(blank)
500	#,###,	1
123456	#,###.00,	123.46
1234565	#,###.00,	1,234.57
-323434	#,###.00,	-323.43
123123.123	#,###.00,	123.12
499	#,###.00,	.50
500	#,###.00,	.50

DISPLAYING VALUES IN HUNDREDS

The following format string displays values in hundreds, with two decimal places. A value with this number format appears as if it's divided by 100, and rounded to two decimal places.

`0"."00`

The following table shows examples of these number formats:

Value	Number Format	Display
546	0"."00	5.46
100	0"."00	1.00
9890	0"."00	98.90
500	0"."00	5.00
-500	0"."00	-5.00
0	0"."00	0.00

DISPLAYING VALUES IN MILLIONS

The following format string displays values in millions, with no decimal places. A value with this number appears as if it's divided by 1,000,000, and rounded to no decimal places.

`#,###,,`

A variation of this format string follows. A value with this number appears as if it's divided by 1,000,000, and rounded to two decimal places.

`#,###.00,,`

Another variation follows. This adds the letter M to the end of the value.

`#,###,,M`

The following format string is a bit more complex. It adds the letter M to the end of the value — and also displays negative values in parentheses as well as displaying zeros.

`#,###.0,,"M"_);(#,###.0,,"M)";0.0"M"_)`

The following table shows examples of these format strings:

Value	Number Format	Display
123456789	#,###,,	123
1.23457E+11	#,###,,	123,457
1000000	#,###,,	1
5000000	#,###,,	5
-5000000	#,###,,	-5
0	#,###,,	(blank)
123456789	#,###.00,,	123.46
1.23457E+11	#,###.00,,	123,456.79
1000000	#,###.00,,	1.00
5000000	#,###.00,,	5.00
-5000000	#,###.00,,	-5.00
0	#,###.00,,	.00
123456789	#,###,,"M"	123M
1.23457E+11	#,###,,"M"	123,457M
1000000	#,###,,"M"	1M
5000000	#,###,,"M"	5M
-5000000	#,###,,"M"	-5M
0	#,###,,"M"	M
123456789	#,###.0,,"M"_);(#,###.0,,"M)";0.0"M"_)	123.5M
1.23457E+11	#,###.0,,"M"_);(#,###.0,,"M)";0.0"M"_)	123,456.8M
1000000	#,###.0,,"M"_);(#,###.0,,"M)";0.0"M"_)	1.0M
5000000	#,###.0,,"M"_);(#,###.0,,"M)";0.0"M"_)	5.0M
-5000000	#,###.0,,"M"_);(#,###.0,,"M)";0.0"M"_)	(5.0M)
0	#,###.0,,"M"_);(#,###.0,,"M)";0.0"M"_)	0.0M

ADDING ZEROS TO A VALUE

The following format string displays a value with three additional zeros and no decimal places. A value with this number format appears as if it's rounded to no decimal places and then multiplied by 1,000.

```
#",000,"
```

Examples of this format string, plus a variation that adds six zeros, are shown in the following table:

Value	Number Format	Display
1	#",000"	1,000
1.5	#",000"	2,000
43	#",000"	43,000
-54	#",000"	-54,000
5.5	#",000"	6,000
0.5	#",000,000"	1,000,000
0	#",000,000"	,000,000
1	#",000,000"	1,000,000
1.5	#",000,000"	2,000,000
43	#",000,000"	43,000,000
-54	#",000,000"	-54,000,000
5.5	#",000,000"	6,000,000
0.5	#",000,000"	1,000,000

Hiding zeros

In the following format string, the third element of the string is empty, which causes zero value cells to display as blank.

```
General;General;;@
```

This format string uses the General format for positive and negative values. You can, of course, substitute any other format codes.

Displaying leading zeros

To display leading zeros, create a custom number format that uses the 0 character. For example, if you want all numbers to display with 10 digits, use the number format string that follows. Values with fewer than 10 digits will display with leading zeros.

```
0000000000
```

You also can force all numbers to display with a fixed number of leading zeros. The format string that follows, for instance, appends three zeros to the beginning of each number.

```
"000"#
```

In the following example, the format string uses the repeat character code (an asterisk) to apply leading zero to fill the entire width of the cell.

```
*00
```

Formatting percentages

Using a percent symbol (%) in a format string causes the cell to display in percentage format. Note that the percent sign also appears in the formula bar.

The following format string formats values less than or equal to 1 in Percentage format. Values greater than 1 and text are formatted using the General format.

```
[<=1]0.0%;General
```

When you mix cells with percent and normal formatting in a column, you may prefer to see the non-percent values indented from the right so the values line up properly. To do so, apply the following number format to non-percent cells. This format string uses an underscore followed by the percent symbol. The result is a space equal to the width of the percent symbol.

```
#.00_%
```

Figure C-3 shows a worksheet that uses this number format for the non-percent cells (the range C6:C12).

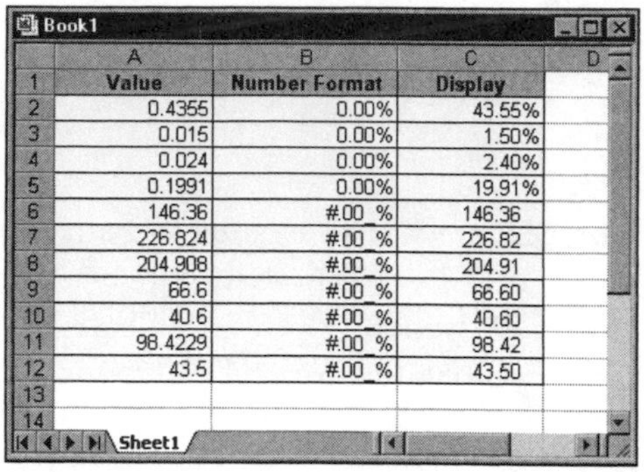

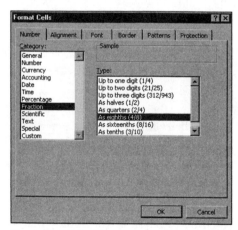

Figure C-3: Use a custom number format to align numbers.

Displaying fractions

Excel supports quite a few built-in fraction number formats (select the Fraction category). For example, to display the value .125 as a fraction with 8 as the denominator, select As eighths (4/8) from the Type list (see Figure C-4).

Figure C-4: Selecting a number format to display a value as a fraction

You can use a custom format string to create other fractional formats. For example, the following format string displays a value in 50ths.

```
# ??/50
```

The following format string displays a value in terms of fractional dollars. For example, the value 154.87 is displayed as *154 and 87/100 Dollars*.

```
0 "and "??/100 "Dollars"
```

The following example displays the value in sixteenths, with a quotation mark appended to the right. This format string is useful when you deal with inches (for example, 2/16").

```
# ??/16\"
```

Displaying N/A for text

The following number format string uses General formatting for all cell entries except text. Text entries appear as N/A.

```
General;General;General;N\/A
```

You can, of course, modify the format string to display specific formats for values. The following variation displays values with one decimal place.

```
0.0;0.0;0.0;N\/A
```

Displaying text in quotes

The following format string displays numbers normally, but surrounds text with quotation marks.

```
General;General;General;"@"
```

Repeating text

The number format string displays the contents of the cell three times. For example, if the cell contains the text *Budget*, the cell displays *Budget Budget Budget*.

```
;;;@ @ @
```

Testing Custom Number Formats

When you create a custom number format, don't overlook the Sample box in the Number tab of the Format Cells dialog box. This box displays the value in the active cell using the format string in the Type box.

It's a good idea to test your custom number formats using the following data: a positive value, a negative value, a zero value, and text. Often, creating a custom number format takes several tries. Each time you edit a format string, it is added to the list. When you finally get the correct format string, access the Format Cells dialog box one more time and delete your previous attempts.

Displaying a negative sign on the right

The following format string displays negative values with the negative sign to the right of the number. Positive values have an additional space on the right, so both positive and negative numbers align properly on the right.

```
0.00_-;0.00-
```

Figure C-5 shows this format string in use.

	A	B	C	
1	Value	Number Format	Display	
2	1.5	0.00_-;0.00-	1.50	
3	0	0.00_-;0.00-	0.00	
4	-1.25	0.00_-;0.00-	1.25-	
5	-3.26	0.00_-;0.00-	3.26-	
6	1	0.00_-;0.00-	1.00	
7	2	0.00_-;0.00-	2.00	
8	1.5	0.00_-;0.00-	1.50	
9	0	0.00_-;0.00-	0.00	
10	-0.05	0.00_-;0.00-	0.05-	
11	0.22	0.00_-;0.00-	0.22	
12	-0.22	0.00_-;0.00-	0.22-	
13				

Figure C-5: Using a custom number format that displays the negative sign on the right

Conditional number formatting

Conditional formatting refers to formatting that is applied based on the contents of a cell. Excel's Conditional Formatting feature provides the most efficient way to perform conditional formatting, but you also can use custom number formats.

Conditional formatting is limited to three conditions — two of them explicit, and the third one implied (that is, everything else). The conditions are enclosed in square brackets and must be simple numeric comparisons.

The following format string uses a different format, depending on the value in the cell. This format string essentially separates the numbers into three groups: less than or equal to 4, greater than or equal to 8, and other. Figure C-6 shows an example of this format string in use.

```
[<=4]"Low"* 0;[>=8]"High"* 0;"Medium"* 0
```

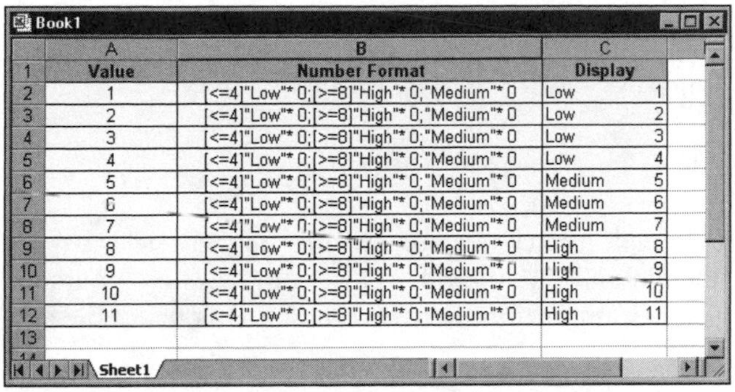

Value	Number Format	Display
1	[<=4]"Low"* 0;[>=8]"High"* 0;"Medium"* 0	Low 1
2	[<=4]"Low"* 0;[>=8]"High"* 0;"Medium"* 0	Low 2
3	[<=4]"Low"* 0;[>=8]"High"* 0;"Medium"* 0	Low 3
4	[<=4]"Low"* 0;[>=8]"High"* 0;"Medium"* 0	Low 4
5	[<=4]"Low"* 0;[>=8]"High"* 0;"Medium"* 0	Medium 5
6	[<=4]"Low"* 0;[>=8]"High"* 0;"Medium"* 0	Medium 6
7	[<=4]"Low"* 0;[>=8]"High"* 0;"Medium"* 0	Medium 7
8	[<=4]"Low"* 0;[>=8]"High"* 0;"Medium"* 0	High 8
9	[<=4]"Low"* 0;[>=8]"High"* 0;"Medium"* 0	High 9
10	[<=4]"Low"* 0;[>=8]"High"* 0;"Medium"* 0	High 10
11	[<=4]"Low"* 0;[>=8]"High"* 0;"Medium"* 0	High 11

Figure C-6: Cells in column C use a conditional number format.

The following number format string displays values less than 1 with a cent symbol on the right (for example, .54¢). Otherwise, values display with a dollar sign (for example, $3.54).

```
[<1].00¢;$0.00_¢
```

The following number format is useful for telephone numbers. Values greater than 9999999 (that is, numbers with area codes) are displayed as (xxx) xxx-xxxx. Other values (numbers without area codes) are displayed as xxx-xxxx.

```
[>9999999](000) 000-0000;000-0000
```

For zip codes, you might want to use the format string that follows. This displays zip codes using five digits. But if the number is greater than 99999, it uses the "zip plus four" format (xxxxx-xxxx).

```
[>99999]00000-0000;00000
```

Coloring values

Custom number format strings can display the cell contents in various colors. The following format string, for example, displays positive numbers in red, negative numbers in green, zero values in black, and text in blue.

```
[Red]General;[Green]-General;[Black]General;[Blue]General
```

Following is another example of a format string that uses colors. Positive values are displayed normally; negative numbers and text display the text ERROR! in red.

```
General;[Red]"Error!";0;[Red]"Error!"
```

Using the following format string, values that are less than 2 are displayed in red. Values greater than 4 are displayed in green. Everything else (text, or values between 2 and 4) displays in black.

```
[Red][<2]General;[Green][>4]General;[Black]General
```

As seen in the preceding examples, Excel recognizes color names such as [Red] and [Blue]. It also can use other colors from the color palette, indexed by a number. The following format string, for example, displays the cell contents using the six-teenth color in the color palette.

```
[Color16]General
```

You cannot change cells that are colored using a number format string by using normal cell formatting commands.

Formatting dates and times

When you enter a date into a cell, Excel formats the date using the system short date format. You can change this format using the Windows Control Panel (Regional Settings).

Excel provides many useful built-in date and time formats. The following table shows some other date and time formats that you may find useful. The first column of the table shows the date/time serial number.

Value	Number Format	Display
36676	Mmmm d, yyyy (dddd)	May 30, 2000 (Tuesday)
36676	"It's" dddd!	It's Tuesday!
36676	Dddd, mm/dd/yyyy	Tuesday, 05/30/2000
36676	"Month: "mmm	Month: May
36676	General (m/d/yyyy)	36676 (5/30/2000)
0.345	hh:mm:ss	8 Hours
0.345	h:mm o'clock	8:16 o'clock
0.345	h:mm a/p"m"	8:16 am
0.78	h:mm a/p".m."	6:43 p.m.

See Chapter 6 for more information about Excel's date and time serial number system.

Displaying text with numbers

The ability to display text with a value is one of the most useful benefits of using a custom number format. To add text, just create the number format string as usual and put the text within quotation marks. The following number format string, for example, displays a value with the text *(US Dollars)* added to the end.

```
#,##0.00 "(US Dollars)"
```

Here's another example that displays text before the number.

```
"Average: "0.00
```

If you use the preceding number format, you'll find that the negative sign appears before the text for negative values. To display number signs properly, use this variation:

```
"Average: "0.00;"Average: "-0.00
```

The following format string displays a value with the words *Dollars and Cents*. For example, the number 123.45 displays as *123 Dollars and .45 Cents*.

```
0 "Dollars and" .00 "Cents"
```

Displaying a zero with dashes

The following number format string displays zero values as a series of dashes.

```
#,##0.0;-#,##0.0;------
```

You can, of course, create lots of variations. For example, you can replace the six hyphens with any of the following:

```
<0>
-0-
~~
<NULL>
"[NULL]"
```

Note that, when using square brackets, you must place them within quotation marks.

Formatting Numbers Using the TEXT Function

Excel's TEXT function accepts a number format string as its second argument. For example the following formula displays the contents of cell A1 using a custom number format that displays a fraction.

```
=TEXT(A1,"# ??/50")
```

Not all formatting codes function, however. For example, colors and repeating characters are ignored. The following formula does not display the contents of cell A1 in red.

```
=TEXT(A1,"[Red]General")
```

Using special symbols

Your number format strings can use special symbols, such as the copyright symbol, degrees symbol, and so on. Figure C-7 shows some special symbols used in number format strings.

	A	B	C	D
1	Value	Number Format	Display	
2	1999	©General	©1999	
3	Microsoft Excel	;;;General®	Microsoft Excel®	
4	32	#°F	32°F	
5	32.45	0.00 ‰	32.45 ‰	
6	5.43	0.00 £	5.43 £	
7	0	General;General;Ø	Ø	
8	0.54	[h]° mm' ss\"	12° 57' 36"	

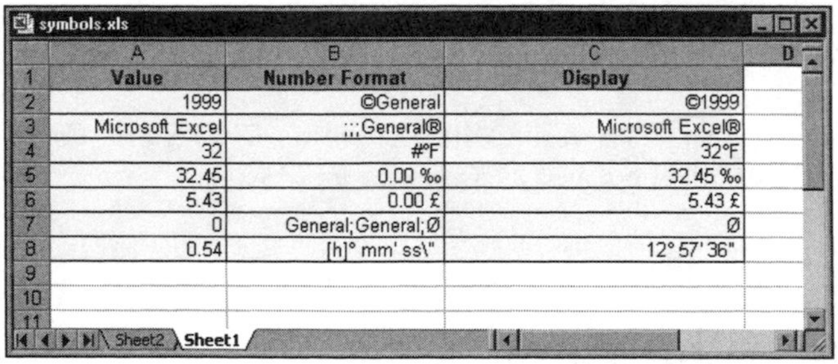

Figure C–7: Using special symbols in number format strings

To enter a symbol, you need to know the Alt+ keyboard sequence required to create the symbol. Use the Windows Character Map program to determine these codes (see Figure C-8). For example, you can produce the copyright symbol by pressing Alt+0169 (make sure you use the numeric keypad to enter the digits).

You can use these special characters to display currency symbols. For example, you might want to display the symbol for the Japanese yen (Alt+0165) or the British pound (Alt+0162).

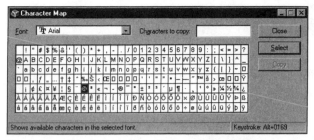

Figure C-8: Use the Windows Character Map program to determine the codes for special symbols.

Suppressing certain types of entries

You can use number formatting to hide certain types of entries. For example, the following format string displays text, but not values.

```
";;;@
```

This format string displays values, but not text.

```
0.0;-0.0;;
```

This format string displays everything except zeros.

```
0.0;-0.0;;@
```

You can use the following format string to completely hide the contents of a cell.

```
;;;
```

Note that when the cell is activated, however, the cell's contents are visible on the formula bar. A better way to hide a cell's contents is to select the Hidden option on the Protection tab of the Format Cells dialog box and protect the sheet.

If the cell contains more than 1,024 characters, the ;;; format string does not hide the contents.

Displaying a Number Format String in a Cell

Excel doesn't have a worksheet function that displays the number format for a specified cell. You can, however, create your own function using VBA. Insert the following Function procedure into a VBA module:

```
Function NumberFormat(cell) As String
'    Returns the number format string for a cell
     Application.Volatile True
     NumberFormat = cell.Range("A1").NumberFormat
End Function
```

Then, you can create a formula such as the following:

```
=NumberFormat(C4)
```

This formula returns the number format for cell C4.

This function can be useful in formulas that calculate a conditional sum. For example, you can create a formula that sums only the cells that use a particular number format. See Chapter 7 for information about computing conditional sums.

Refer to Part V for more information about creating custom worksheet functions using VBA.

Filling a cell with a repeating character

The asterisk (*) symbol specifies a repeating character in a number format string. The repeating character completely fills the cell and adjusts if the column width changes. The following format string, for example, displays the contents of a cell padded on the right with dashes.

```
General*-;General*-;General*-;General*-
```

Figure C-9 shows several examples of number format strings that use an asterisk to repeat a character.

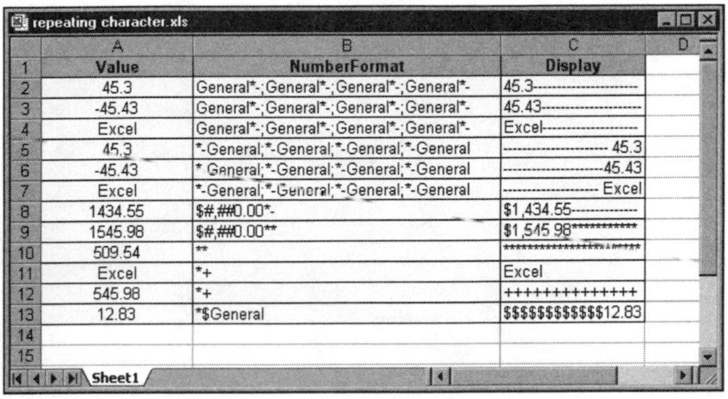
repeating character.xls

	Value	NumberFormat	Display
2	45.3	General*-;General*-;General*-;General*-	45.3--------------------
3	-45.43	General*-;General*-;General*-;General*-	45.43-------------------
4	Excel	General*-;General*-;General*-;General*-	Excel-------------------
5	45.3	*-General;*-General;*-General;*-General	-------------------- 45.3
6	-45.43	*-General;*-General;*-General;*-General	-------------------45.43
7	Excel	*-General;*-General;*-General;*-General	------------------- Excel
8	1434.55	$#,##0.00*-	$1,434.55-------------
9	1545.98	$#,##0.00**	$1,545.98***********
10	509.54	**	************************
11	Excel	*+	Excel
12	545.98	*+	++++++++++++++
13	12.83	*$General	$$$$$$$$$$$$12.83

Figure C-9: Examples of number formats that use a repeating character

Displaying leading dots

The following custom number format is a variation on the accounting format. Using this number format displays the dollar sign on the left and the value on the right. The space in between is filled with dots.

```
_($*.#,##0.00_);_($*.(#,##0.00);_($* "-"??_);_(@_)
```

Appendix D

Additional Excel Resources

IF I'VE DONE MY JOB, the information provided in this book will be very useful to you. The book, however, cannot cover every conceivable topic. Therefore, I've compiled a list of additional resources that you may find helpful. I classify these resources into three categories: Microsoft technical support, Internet newsgroups, and Internet Web sites.

Microsoft Technical Support

Technical support is the common term for assistance provided by a software vendor. In this case, I'm talking about assistance that comes directly from Microsoft. Microsoft's technical support is available in several different forms.

Support options

To find out your support options, choose the Help → About Microsoft Excel command, and then click the Tech Support button. This opens a help file that lists all the support options offered by Microsoft, including both free and fee-based support.

Through my experience, I suggest you use vendor *standard telephone* support only as a last resort. Chances are, you'll run up a big phone bill (assuming you can even get through) and spend lots of time on hold, but you may or may not find an answer to your question.

The truth is, the people who answer the phone are equipped to answer only the most basic questions. And the answers to these basic questions are usually readily available elsewhere.

Microsoft knowledge base

Your best bet for solving a problem may be the Microsoft Knowledge Base. This is the primary Microsoft product information source — an extensive, searchable database that consists of tens of thousands of detailed articles containing technical information, bug lists, fix lists, and more. You have free and unlimited access to the Knowledge Base via the Internet. The URL is

```
http://support.microsoft.com/support/search
```

Microsoft Excel home page

The official home page of Excel is at

```
http://www.microsoft.com/excel
```

Microsoft Office update

For information about Office 2000 (including Excel), try this site:

```
http://officeupdate.microsoft.com
```

 As you know, the Internet is a dynamic entity that changes rapidly. Web sites are often reorganized, so a particular URL listed in this appendix may not be available when you try to access it. Currently, each URL is accurate; but it's possible that an URL may change by the time you read this.

Internet Newsgroups

Usenet is an Internet service that provides access to several thousand special interest groups that enable you to communicate with people who share common interests. A newsgroup works like a public bulletin board. You can post a message or questions, and (usually) others reply to your message.

There are thousands of newsgroups covering virtually every topic you can think of (and many that you haven't thought of). Typically, questions posed on a newsgroup are answered within 24 hours – assuming, of course, that you ask the questions in a manner that makes others want to reply.

 Besides an Internet connection, you need special newsreader software to access newsgroups. Microsoft Outlook Express (free) is a good choice. This product is available on your Office 2000 CD-ROM.

Spreadsheet newsgroups

The primary Usenet newsgroup for general spreadsheet users is:

```
comp.apps.spreadsheets
```

This newsgroup is intended for users of any spreadsheet brand, but about 90 percent of the postings deal with Excel.

Microsoft newsgroups

Microsoft has an extensive list of newsgroups, including quite a few devoted to Excel. If your Internet service provider doesn't carry the Microsoft newsgroups, you can access them directly from Microsoft's news server. You need to configure your newsreader software or Web browser to access Microsoft's news server at this address:

`msnews.microsoft.com`

Table D-1 lists the key newsgroups found on Microsoft's news server.

TABLE D-1 MICROSOFT.COM'S EXCEL-RELATED NEWSGROUPS

Newsgroup	Topic
`microsoft.public.excel.programming`	Programming Excel with VBA or XLM macros
`microsoft.public.excel.123quattro`	Converting 1-2-3 or Quattro Pro sheets into Excel sheets
`microsoft.public.excel.worksheet.functions`	Worksheet functions
`microsoft.public.excel.charting`	Building charts with Excel
`microsoft.public.excel.printing`	Printing with Excel
`microsoft.public.excel.queryDAO`	Using Microsoft Query and Data Access Objects (DAO) in Excel
`microsoft.public.excel.datamap`	Using the Data Map feature in Excel
`microsoft.public.excel.crashesGPFs`	Help with General Protection Faults or system failures
`microsoft.public.excel.misc`	General topics that do not fit one of the other categories
`microsoft.public.excel.links`	Using links in Excel
`microsoft.public.excel.macintosh`	Excel issues on the Macintosh operating system
`microsoft.public.excel.interopoledde`	OLE, DDE, and other cross-application issues

Continued

TABLE **D-1** MICROSOFT.COM'S EXCEL–RELATED NEWSGROUPS *(Continued)*

Newsgroup	Topic
microsoft.public.excel.setup	Setting up and installing Excel
microsoft.public.excel.templates	Spreadsheet Solutions templates and other XLT files
microsoft.public.excel.sdk	Issues regarding the Excel Software Development Kit

Searching newsgroups

Many people don't realize that you can perform a keyword search on past newsgroup postings. Often, this is an excellent alternative to posting a question to the newsgroup because you can get the answer immediately. The best source for searching newsgroup postings is Deja.com, at the following Web address:

http://www.deja.com

For example, suppose you have a problem with the ListBox control on a UserForm. You can perform a search using the following keywords: **Excel, ListBox,** and **UserForm.** The Deja search engine probably will find dozens of newsgroup postings that deal with these topics. It may take a while to sift through the messages, but you have an excellent chance of finding an answer to your question.

Internet Web Sites

If you have access to the World Wide Web (WWW), you can find some very useful Web sites devoted to Excel. I list a few of my favorites here.

The Spreadsheet Page

This is my own Web site, which contains files to download, developer tips, instructions for accessing Excel Easter Eggs, spreadsheet jokes, an extensive list of links to other Excel sites, and information about my books. The URL is:

http://www.j-walk.com/ss

Tips for Posting to a Newsgroup

1. Make sure that your question has not already been answered. Check the FAQ (if one exists) and also perform a Deja.com search (see "Searching Newsgroups" in this appendix).

2. Make the subject line descriptive. Postings with a subject line, such as "Help me!" and "Excel Question," are less likely to be answered than postings with a more specific subject such as, "Need Help With Custom Worksheet Function."

3. Specify the spreadsheet product and version that you use. In many cases, the answer to your question depends on your version of Excel.

4. Make your question as specific as possible.

5. Keep your question brief and to the point, but provide enough information so someone can answer it adequately.

6. Indicate what you've done to try to answer your own question.

7. Post in the appropriate newsgroup, and don't cross-post to other groups unless the question applies to multiple groups.

8. Don't type in all uppercase or all lowercase, and check your grammar and spelling.

9. Don't include a file attachment.

10. Avoid posting in HTML format.

11. If you request an e-mail reply in addition to a newsgroup reply, don't use an "anti-spam" e-mail address that requires the responder to modify your address. Why cause extra work for someone doing *you* a favor?

 This site also contains a list of errors that I've found in each of my books, including the book you're reading now. (Yes, a few errors have been known to creep into these pages.)

Chip Pearson's Excel Pages

This site contains dozens of useful examples of VBA and clever formula techniques. The URL is:

```
http://home.gvi.net/~cpearson/excel.htm
```

Stephen Bullen's Excel Page

Stephen is an Excel developer based in the United Kingdom. His Web site contains some fascinating examples of Excel code, including a section titled "They Said it Couldn't be Done." The URL is:

```
http://www.bmsltd.co.uk/excel
```

Spreadsheet FAQ

Many newsgroups have a *FAQ* — a list of frequently asked questions. The purpose of providing a list of FAQs is to prevent the same questions from being asked over and over. The FAQ for the `comp.apps.spreadsheets` newsgroup is available at:

```
http://www.faqs.org/faqs/spreadsheets/faq
```

Appendix E

What's on the CD-ROM?

THIS APPENDIX DESCRIBES the contents of the companion CD-ROM.

CD-ROM Overview

The CD-ROM consists of three components:

◆ **Chapter Examples:** Excel workbooks that were discussed in the chapters of this book.

◆ **Power Utility Pak 2000:** A 30-day trial version of the author's popular Excel add-in (works with Excel 97 or Excel 2000). Use the coupon in this book to order the full version at a significant discount. The complete VBA source code also is available for a small fee.

◆ **Sound-Proof:** The demo version of the author's audio proofreader add-in.

 All CD-ROM files are read-only. Therefore, if you open a file from the CD-ROM and make any changes to it, you need to save it to your hard drive. Also, if you copy a file from the CD-ROM to your hard drive, the file retains its read-only attribute. To change this attribute after copying a file, right-click the file name or icon and select Properties from the shortcut menu. In the Properties dialog box, click the General tab and remove the checkmark from the Read-only checkbox.

Chapter Examples

Most of the chapters in this book refer to workbooks that are available on the CD-ROM. Each chapter has its own subdirectory on the CD-ROM. For example, the files for Chapter 5 are found in the following directory:

```
chapters\chap05\
```

Following is a list of the chapter examples, with a brief description of each. Note that not all chapters have example files.

Chapter 5	Example	Description
	identifying text in cells.xls	Examples of three functions (ISTEXT, CELL, and TYPE) that are supposed to identify the type of data in a cell
	character set.xls	Displays all characters for a selected font. Requires Excel 97 or later
	text histogram.xls	Displays a histogram using text characters rather than a chat
	text formula examples.xls	Contains the example formulas described in the chapter

Chapter 6	Example	Description
	day of the week count.xls	Counts the number of each day of the week for a particular year.
	ordinal dates.xls	Formulas that express a date as an ordinal number (e.g., June 13th, 1999).
	holidays.xls	Formulas that calculate the dates of various holidays.
	calendar array.xls	A single array formula that displays a monthly calendar.
	jogging log.xls	Formulas to keep track of jogging data.
	time sheet.xls	A workbook (with VBA macros) to keep track of hours worked in a week. This example is not discussed in Chapter 6.

Chapter 7	Example	Description
	basic counting.xls	Formulas that demonstrate basic counting techniques
	counting text in a range.xls	Formulas that demonstrate various ways to count text in a range
	count unique.xls	Formulas to count the number of unique entries in a range
	frequency distribution.xls	Creating a frequency distribution using the FREQUENCY function, the Analysis ToolPak, and formulas
	adjustable bins.xls	Demonstrates a histogram with adjustable bins
	conditional summing.xls	Formulas that demonstrate various ways to calculate conditional sums

Chapter 8	Example	Description
	basic lookup examples.xls	Demonstrates four basic lookup techniques
	lookup to the left.xls	Demonstrates how to perform a lookup when the index column is not the leftmost column in the lookup table
	multiple lookup tables.xls	Demonstrates how to use the IF function to work with multiple lookup tables
	grade lookup.xls	Using a lookup table to determine letter grades
	gpa.xls	Calculating a grade point average with multiple formulas or a single array formula
	two-way lookup.xls	Demonstrates how to perform a two-way lookup (by columns and by rows)

Continued

(Continued)

Chapter 8	Example	Description
	two-column lookup.xls	Demonstrates how to perform a lookup using two columns from the lookup table
	lookup address.xls	Demonstrates how to determine the cell address of a lookup item
	closest match.xls	Demonstrates how to perform a lookup using the closest matching value
	interpolated lookup.xls	Demonstrates how to perform a lookup using linear interpolation

Chapter 9	Example	Description
	real estate database.xls	A workbook that contains real estate listing information. Used to demonstrate advanced filtering.
	data table summary.xls	Demonstrates how to use a one-way and two-way data table to summarize information in a list.
	nested subtotals.xls	Demonstrates the use of the SUBTOTAL function.

Chapter 10	Example	Description
	loan payment.xls	Calculates a loan payment amount
	credit card payments.xls	Formulas to calculate the payoff period for a credit card balance
	irregular payments.xls	Calculates loan information with irregular payments

Chapter 10	**Example**	**Description**
	loan amortization schedule.xls	Computes a loan amortization schedule
	loan amortization wizard.xla	An add-in that creates loan amortization schedules
	loan data tables.xls	Demonstrates one-way and two-way data tables
	investment calculations.xls	Demonstrates calculation of simple and compound interest
	annuity calculator.xls	Demonstrates annuity calculations
	depreciation.xls	Demonstrates Excel's depreciation functions
	xe0962.doc	A Word document from Microsoft that contains the formulas used for financial functions

Chapter 11	**Example**	**Description**
	unit conversion tables.xls	Contains conversion tables for a variety of measurement units
	solve right triangle.xls	Formulas to calculate various parts of a right triangle, given two known parts
	simultaneous equations.xls	Formulas to solve simultaneous equations with two or three variables

Chapter 13	Example	Description
	single-cell array formulas.xls	Examples of array formulas that occupy a single cell
	logical functions.xls	Demonstrates how to use logical functions in an array formula
	sum every nth.xls	Two techniques to sum every nth value
	multi-cell array formulas.xls	Examples of array formulas that occupy multiple cells
	calendar array.xls	An array formula that displays a calendar
	SORTED function.xls	A custom VBA function that returns a sorted range

Chapter 14	Example	Description
	circular reference.xls	The introductory circular reference example file
	time stamp.xls	Demonstrates how to time-stamp a cell using a circular reference
	all-time high.xls	Demonstrates how to keep track of the highest value ever entered into a range
	unique random integers.xls	Demonstrates how to generate unique random integers by using circular references
	recursive equations.xls	Demonstrates how to use a circular reference to solve recursive equations
	simultaneous equations.xls	Demonstrates how to use a circular reference to solve simultaneous equations

Chapter 15	Example	Description
	thermometer chart.xls	Demonstrates a chart that displays progress towards a goal
	gantt chart.xls	Demonstrates a simple Gantt (timeline) chart
	comparative histogram.xls	Demonstrates a comparative histogram (population pyramid)
	box plot.xls	Demonstrates a box plot to summarize data across groups
	plot every nth data point.xls	Demonstrates a technique to plot every nth data point
	autoupdate chart.xls	Demonstrates a technique to plot new data as it's added to the worksheet
	plot last n data points.xls	Demonstrates a technique to plot only the most recent data
	chart data in active row.xls	Demonstrates a charting technique that uses the data in the row of the active cell
	chart from combo box.xls	Uses a combo box to select data to be plotted
	bullen function plotter.xls	Demonstrates a technique developed by Stephen Bullen that plots a function automatically
	surface chart.xls	Demonstrates the use of a surface chart to plot a function with two variables
	hypocycloid.xls	A chart that generates interesting geometric designs
	linear trendline.xls	Demonstrates linear trendlines
	nonlinear trendline.xls	Demonstrates nonlinear trendlines
	animated shapes.xls	Demonstrates animated objects (including charts)
	clock chart.xls	Displays an analog clock in a chart

Continued

(Continued)

Chapter 15	Example	Description
	clock chart vba.xls	An alternate version of the analog clock that uses VBA instead of formulas
	circle.xls	Demonstrates how to plot a circle in a chart
	xy sketch.xls	Interactive drawing on a chart

Chapter 16	Example	Description
	bank accounts.xls	A worksheet database used in several examples
	sales by date.xls	Demonstrates grouping pivot table items by date
	calculated field and item.xls	Demonstrates creating calculated fields and items in a pivot table

Chapter 17	Example	Description
	conditional formatting.xls	Contains the conditional formatting examples
	data validation.xls	Contains the data validation examples

Chapter 18	Example	Description
	no middle name.xls	Demonstrates three ways to remove the middle name from a full name (formulas, a megaformula, and a custom VBA function)
	position of last space.xls	Demonstrates a megaformula to return the character position of the last space character in a string
	credit card validation.xls	Demonstrates a megaformula to determine if a credit card number is valid

Chapter 23	Example	Description
	simple functions.xls	A workbook that demonstrates simple VBA functions
	cell type function.xls	Demonstrates the CELLTYPE function
	statfunction function.xls	Demonstrates the STATFUNCTION function
	commission function.xls	Demonstrates the COMMISSION function
	text manipulation functions.xls	Demonstrates the text manipulation functions
	spelldollars function.xls	Demonstrates the SPELLDOLLARS function
	counting and summing functions.xls	Demonstrates the counting and summing functions
	date functions.xls	Demonstrates the date functions
	\xdate directory	A directory that holds the files for the Extended Date Functions add-in
	last nonempty cell.xls	Demonstrates the LASTINCOLUMN and LASTINROW functions

Continued

(Continued)

Chapter 23	Example	Description
	multisheet functions.xls	Demonstrates the MAXALLSHEETS and SHEETOFFSET functions
	random integers function.xls	Demonstrates the RANDOMINTEGERS function
	range randomize function.xls	Demonstrates the RANGERANDOMIZE function
	mysum fuction.xls	Demonstrates the MYSUM function
	video function.xls	Demonstrates the VIDEO function
	disk information functions.xls	Demonstrates the DRIVEEXISTS and DRIVETYPE functions

Power Utility Pak 2000

Power Utility Pak 2000 (PUP 2000) is a comprehensive collection of Excel add-ins that I developed. It includes 50 general-purpose utilities, 40 custom worksheet functions, and enhanced shortcut menus. When the PUP 2000 add-in is installed, Excel displays a new menu. The companion CD-ROM contains a 30-day trial version of this product.

Registering Power Utility Pak

The normal registration fee for Power Utility Pak is $39.95. However, you can use the coupon in this book to get a copy of PUP 2000 for only $9.95, plus shipping and handling. Also, you can purchase the complete VBA source code for an additional $20.00.

Installing the trial version

To install the trial version of Power Utility Pak

1. Make sure Excel is not running.

2. Locate the PUP2000.EXE file on the CD-ROM. This file is located in the \Power Utility Pak directory.

3. Double-click PUP2000.EXE. This expands the files to a directory you specify on your hard drive. For best results, use the proposed directory.

4. Start Excel.

5. Select Tools → Add-Ins, and click the Browse button. Locate the PUP2000.XLA file in the directory you specified in Step 3.

6. In the Add-Ins dialog box, make sure Power Utility Pak 2000 is checked in the add-ins list.

7. Click OK to close the Add-Ins dialog box.

This procedure installs Power Utility Pak, and it will be available whenever you start Excel. When the product is installed, you'll have a new menu: PUP 2000. Access the Power Utility Pak features from the PUP 2000 menu.

Power Utility Pak includes extensive online help. Select Utilities@-->Help to view the Help file.

Uninstalling Power Utility Pak

If you decide that you don't want Power Utility Pak, follow these instructions to remove it from Excel's list of add-ins:

1. In Excel, select Tools → Add-Ins.

2. In the Add-Ins dialog box, remove the checkmark from Power Utility Pak 2000.

3. Click OK to close the Add-Ins dialog box.

After performing these steps, you can reinstall Power Utility Pak at any time during the 30-day trial period by placing a checkmark next to the Power Utility Pak 2000 item in the Add-Ins dialog box.

To permanently remove Power Utility Pak from your system, after you've uninstalled it from Excel using the previous steps, delete the directory into which you originally installed it.

Sound-Proof

Sound-Proof is an Excel add-in I developed. It uses a synthesized voice to read the contents of selected cells. It's the perfect proofreading tool for anyone who does data entry in Excel.

Cells are read back using natural language format. For example, 154.78 is read as "One hundred fifty-four point seven eight." Date values are read as actual dates (for example, "June fourteen, nineteen ninety-eight") and time values are read as actual times (for example, "Six forty-five AM").

The companion CD-ROM contains a demo version of Sound-Proof. The full version is available for $19.95. Ordering instructions are provided in the online Help file.

 The only limitation in the demo version is that it reads no more than 12 cells at a time.

Installing the demo version

To install the demo version of Sound-Proof

1. Make sure Excel is not running.

2. Locate the SPDEMO.EXE file on the CD-ROM. This file is located in the Sound Proof\ directory.

3. Double-click SPDEMO.EXE. This expands the files to a directory you specify on your hard drive.

4. Start Excel.

5. Select Tools → Add-Ins, and click the Browse button. Locate the SOUNDPRF.XLA file in the directory you specified in Step 3.

6. In the Add-Ins dialog box, make sure Sound-Proof is checked in the add-ins list.

7. Click OK to close the Add-Ins dialog box.

This process enables you to install Sound-Proof so that it will be available whenever you start Excel. Once the product is installed, you'll have a new menu command: Tools → >Sound-Proof. This command displays the Sound-Proof toolbar.

Uninstalling Sound-Proof

If you decide that you don't want Sound-Proof, follow these instructions to remove it from Excel's list of add-ins:

1. In Excel, select Tools → >Add-Ins.

2. In the Add-Ins dialog box, remove the checkmark from Sound-Proof.

3. Click OK to close the Add-Ins dialog box.

After performing these steps, you can reinstall Sound-Proof at any time by placing a checkmark next to the Sound-Proof item in the Add-Ins dialog box.

 To permanently remove Sound-Proof from your system, after you have performed the previous steps to uninstall the add-in, delete the directory into which you originally installed it.

Index

A

continued

continued

continued

continued

IDG Books Worldwide, Inc. End-User License Agreement

READ THIS. You should carefully read these terms and conditions before opening the software packet(s) included with this book ("Book"). This is a license agreement ("Agreement") between you and IDG Books Worldwide, Inc. ("IDGB"). By opening the accompanying software packet(s), you acknowledge that you have read and accept the following terms and conditions. If you do not agree and do not want to be bound by such terms and conditions, promptly return the Book and the unopened software packet(s) to the place you obtained them for a full refund.

1. **License Grant.** IDGB grants to you (either an individual or entity) a nonexclusive license to use one copy of the enclosed software program(s) (collectively, the "Software") solely for your own personal or business purposes on a single computer (whether a standard computer or a workstation component of a multiuser network). The Software is in use on a computer when it is loaded into temporary memory (RAM) or installed into permanent memory (hard disk, CD-ROM, or other storage device). IDGB reserves all rights not expressly granted herein.

2. **Ownership.** IDGB is the owner of all right, title, and interest, including copyright, in and to the compilation of the Software recorded on the disk(s) or CD-ROM ("Software Media"). Copyright to the individual programs recorded on the Software Media is owned by the author or other authorized copyright owner of each program. Ownership of the Software and all proprietary rights relating thereto remain with IDGB and its licensers.

3. **Restrictions On Use and Transfer.**

   (a) You may only (i) make one copy of the Software for backup or archival purposes, or (ii) transfer the Software to a single hard disk, provided that you keep the original for backup or archival purposes. You may not (i) rent or lease the Software, (ii) copy or reproduce the Software through a LAN or other network system or through any computer subscriber system or bulletin-board system, or (iii) modify, adapt, or create derivative works based on the Software.

   (b) You may not reverse engineer, decompile, or disassemble the Software. You may transfer the Software and user documentation on a permanent basis, provided that the transferee agrees to accept the terms and conditions of this Agreement and you retain no copies. If the Software is an update or has been updated, any transfer must include the most recent update and all prior versions.

4. **Restrictions on Use of Individual Programs.** You must follow the individual requirements and restrictions detailed for each individual program in Appendix E of this Book. These limitations are also contained in the individual license agreements recorded on the Software Media. These limitations may include a requirement that after using the program for a specified period of time, the user must pay a registration fee or discontinue use. By opening the Software packet(s), you will be agreeing to abide by the licenses and restrictions for these individual programs that are detailed in Appendix E and on the Software Media. None of the material on this Software Media or listed in this Book may ever be redistributed, in original or modified form, for commercial purposes.

5. **Limited Warranty.**

   (a) IDGB warrants that the Software and Software Media are free from defects in materials and workmanship under normal use for a period of sixty (60) days from the date of purchase of this Book. If IDGB receives notification within the warranty period of defects in materials or workmanship, IDGB will replace the defective Software Media.

   (b) IDGB AND THE AUTHOR OF THE BOOK DISCLAIM ALL OTHER WARRANTIES, EXPRESS OR IMPLIED, INCLUDING WITHOUT LIMITATION IMPLIED WARRANTIES OF MERCHANTABILITY AND FITNESS FOR A PARTICULAR PURPOSE, WITH RESPECT TO THE SOFTWARE, THE PROGRAMS, THE SOURCE CODE CONTAINED THEREIN, AND/OR THE TECHNIQUES DESCRIBED IN THIS BOOK. IDGB DOES NOT WARRANT THAT THE FUNCTIONS CONTAINED IN THE SOFTWARE WILL MEET YOUR REQUIREMENTS OR THAT THE OPERATION OF THE SOFTWARE WILL BE ERROR FREE.

   (c) This limited warranty gives you specific legal rights, and you may have other rights that vary from jurisdiction to jurisdiction.

6. **Remedies.**

   (a) IDGB's entire liability and your exclusive remedy for defects in materials and workmanship shall be limited to replacement of the Software Media, which may be returned to IDGB with a copy of your receipt at the following address: Software Media Fulfillment Department, Attn.: *Microsoft(r) Excel 2000 Formulas*, IDG Books Worldwide, Inc., 7260 Shadeland Station, Ste. 100, Indianapolis, IN 46256, or call 1-800-762-2974. Please allow three to four weeks for delivery. This Limited Warranty is void if failure of the Software Media has resulted from accident, abuse, or misapplication. Any replacement Software Media will be warranted for the remainder of the original warranty period or thirty (30) days, whichever is longer.

(b) In no event shall IDGB or the author be liable for any damages whatsoever (including without limitation damages for loss of business profits, business interruption, loss of business information, or any other pecuniary loss) arising from the use of or inability to use the Book or the Software, even if IDGB has been advised of the possibility of such damages.

(c) Because some jurisdictions do not allow the exclusion or limitation of liability for consequential or incidental damages, the above limitation or exclusion may not apply to you.

7. **U.S. Government Restricted Rights.** Use, duplication, or disclosure of the Software by the U.S. Government is subject to restrictions stated in paragraph (c)(1)(ii) of the Rights in Technical Data and Computer Software clause of DFARS 252.227-7013, and in subparagraphs (a) through (d) of the Commercial Computer – Restricted Rights clause at FAR 52.227-19, and in similar clauses in the NASA FAR supplement, when applicable.

8. **General.** This Agreement constitutes the entire understanding of the parties and revokes and supersedes all prior agreements, oral or written, between them and may not be modified or amended except in a writing signed by both parties hereto that specifically refers to this Agreement. This Agreement shall take precedence over any other documents that may be in conflict herewith. If any one or more provisions contained in this Agreement are held by any court or tribunal to be invalid, illegal, or otherwise unenforceable, each and every other provision shall remain in full force and effect.

my2cents.idgbooks.com

CD-ROM Installation Instructions

The *Microsoft Excel 2000 Formulas* CD-ROM contains:

◆ **Chapter Examples:** Contains the files described in the book. The files for each chapter are contained in a subdirectory. For example, the files for Chapter 13 are in the Chapters\Chap13 directory. Installation is not required. You can open the files directly from the CD-ROM.

◆ **Power Utility Pak 2000:** A 30-day trial version of the author's popular Excel add-in (works with Excel 97 or Excel 2000). To install this product, execute the PUP2000.EXE file in the \Power Utility Pak directory. Use the coupon in this book to order the full version at a significant discount. The complete VBA source code also is available for a small fee.

◆ **Sound-Proof:** The demo version of the author's audio proofreader add-in. To install Sound-Proof, execute the SPDEMO.EXE file in the Sound Proof\ directory.

See Appendix E for additional information regarding the contents of the CD-ROM and installation instructions for each item.